WHO

SAID

WHAT

WHO
SAID
WHAT

**Over 7,000 quotations from earliest
times to the present day.**

CHANCELLOR
PRESS

First British edition published in 1988 by Bloomsbury Publishing Limited
under the title Who Said What When

This 1993 edition published by Chancellor Press an imprint of
Reed Consumer Books Limited, Michelin House, 81 Fulham Road, London SW3 6RB
and Auckland, Melbourne, Singapore and Toronto

Copyright © 1988 by Bloomsbury Publishing Limited

ISBN 1-85152-419-3

A CIP catalogue record for this book is available at the British Library.

Printed in the UK by the Bath Press

contents

acknowledgments

Editors

John Daintith
Alan Isaacs
Elizabeth Martin
David Pickering
Anne Stibbs
Deborah Chapman
Hazel Egerton
Ruth Salomon
Kate Smith
Edmund Wright

Contributors

Elizabeth Bonham
Sue Cope
Eve Daintith
Rosalind Fergusson
Joanna Gosling
Jock Graham
Lawrence Holden
Amanda Isaacs
Valerie Illingworth
Stephen Jones
Jennifer Monk
Jessica Scholes
Gwynneth Shaw
Mary Shields
Jean Wright

introduction

This is a unique collection of quotations arranged chronologically from earliest times to the present day. Many of these have been selected for their historical interest—that is for the light they throw on some important event or figure, or on some attitude current at the time. Quotations like these will not appear in more conventional dictionaries of quotations. But we have also included many well-known, and not so well-known, literary quotations, witty remarks, etc. Each chapter of the book is a historical period:

1 The Old Testament
2 The Ancient World (before 50 BC)
3 The New Testament
4 The Roman World (50 BC–399 AD)
5 The Early Middle Ages (400–1099)
6 The Later Middle Ages (1100–1517)
7 The Reformation and Counter-Reformation (1518–1659)
8 The Age of Enlightenment (1660–1788)
9 The French Revolution (1789–1815)
10 Liberalism, Nationalism, and Reaction (1816–69)
11 The Age of Imperialism (1870–1913)
12 The World Wars (1914–45)
13 The Post-War World (1946–   )

History is a continuous process not necessarily designed for chopping into book chapters. However, we feel that this division is a useful and convenient way of presenting the information. The chapter titles are not, of course, exclusive. For example, the period from 1789 to 1815 has to be called *The French Revolution* because the revolution in France dominated European history in that time. But other things were happening during these years and quotations about these have been included. Similarly, the chapter on *The World Wars* includes quotations from 1914 before the outbreak of World War I, quotations from between the Wars, and quotations that are not connected with the Wars.

Each chapter begins with a short introductory article on the period, its importance, and the main events. There is also a list of contents in each chapter. Within each chapter the material is organized into four main sections:

Politics, Government, and World Events is the main historical section of the chapter. It includes quotations about specific events, politics, political figures, law and government, society, etc. Throughout the historical sections we have tried to include as much additional information as possible to place the quotations in context. This has been done by linking text for significant events (the Spanish Armada, the American Revolution, the Russian Revolution), or by explanatory notes attached to individual quotations (as in the Vicar of Bray or many nursery rhymes).

Attitudes contains a collection of quotations designed to show the attitudes of the time to various topics through quotations about them. The full list of topics used is:

Art, Literature, and Music
Daily Life
Death
Education, Knowledge, and Learning
History
Human Nature
Humour
Life
Love and Sex
Marriage and the Family
Men and Women
Morality, Vices, and Virtues
Other People
Religion
Wealth and Poverty
Work and Occupations

Sayings of the Time includes a few quotations that date from the period but do not fall into the two previous categories. These are usually well-known sayings, for example, 'Imitation is the sincerest form of flattery' (1820) or 'Tinker, Tailor, Soldier, Sailor' (1829).

With Hindsight gives a few later sayings about the period or about events or personalities in that period. Some of these are serious commentaries, but we have also included more light-hearted remarks. For instance, Alfonso the Wise commented on the complicated Ptolemaic model of the universe that had he been present at the Creation he would have recommended something simpler.

The quotations in the chapter are numbered sequentially throughout. Within each section, or sub-section, the quotations are arranged in date order. Note that most of the quotations were said or written in the year given, but we have also included quotations that are about the period—for example, Shakespeare on Elizabethan England.

Finally, in explaining the organization of the book, we have to say something about the difficulties in assigning dates to many of the quotations. There are two problems:

1. The quotation may be dateable, but we have been unable to find a reliable date reference.

2. The date of the quotation is unknown. Many quotations are 'Attributed' and nobody knows the exact year in which they were said (if they were said at all).

We have, generally, dated attributed quotations at the death date of the person involved, unless there is a logical reason for doing otherwise. For the others, we have made an arbitrary judgment about the year in order to put the quotation in some sort of historical context.

All quotations for which the date is uncertain, for whatever reason, are marked with an asterisk (*) after the quotation number. **These dates should be treated with caution.** If an asterisked quotation appears under the year 1805, it was not necessarily said in 1805. The asterisk means that it was probably said within a few years of 1805, and that 1805 is a convenient place to put it in the sequence. We feel that this is the best way of treating these 'problem' quotations. We would welcome any information from readers that would allow us to date these quotations more accurately.

We hope that the reader will find the book useful in a number of ways:

- To find quotations about a specific event, or things said in a certain year.
- To follow a period of history from what was said at the time.
- To look at the attitudes of people at a given time in the past to some subject.
- To compare the way that attitudes have changed to certain issues (or, perhaps more interestingly, how they have not changed).
- To trace the source of a known quotation, or the exact wording of a half-remembered one. We have included an extensive keyword-key phrase index in which the references are to chapter and quotation number (e.g. 6:230 is quotation number 230 in chapter 6).
- To find quotations by particular people. The name index has the same reference system as the keyword index.

But above all, we hope that the reader will find the book stimulating, sometimes amusing, and always interesting.

The Editors

1

The Old Testament

Attempting to date the events described in the Old Testament has led to the downfall of many theologians. It is now accepted by all but the most fundamental of fundamentalists that some biblical accounts, such as those of the creation of the world and of Eve from the rib of Adam, are no more than allegorical fables. Other incidents, such as the Flood, may or may not have been based on historical events – indeed, Noah may or may not have been a historical person. On the other hand, Kings Saul, David, and Solomon were undoubtedly historical iron-age monarchs; likewise the building and destruction of the first Temple can be fairly confidently dated. Nevertheless, it was felt that quotations from the Old Testament do not fit comfortably in a chronological sequence with quotations from less auspicious sources. For this reason, the following section lists the quotations taken from the Old Testament in book, chapter, and verse order, with no attempt to date the events described. It therefore follows that there will be some temporal overlap between the real biblical events and the events described in the quotations from the Ancient World, which appear in the next section.

1   In the beginning God created the heaven and
    the earth.
    And the earth was without form, and void; and
    darkness was upon the face of the deep.
    And the Spirit of God moved upon the face of
    the waters.
    And God said, Let there be light: and there
    was light.
    And God saw the light, that it was good: and
    God divided the light from the darkness.
    And God called the light Day, and the dark-
    ness he called Night. And the evening and
    the morning were the first day.
    Bible: Genesis
    1:1-5

2   And God called the dry land Earth; and the
    gathering together of the waters called he
    Seas: and God saw that it was good.
    And God said, Let the earth bring forth grass,
    the herb yielding seed, and the fruit tree
    yielding fruit after his kind, whose seed is in
    itself, upon the earth: and it was so.
    Bible: Genesis
    1:10-11

3   And God made two great lights: the greater
    light to rule the day, and the lesser light to rule
    the night: he made the stars also.
    Bible: Genesis
    1:16

4   And God said, Let the earth bring forth the liv-
    ing creature after his kind, cattle, and creep-
    ing thing, and beast of the earth after his kind:
    and it was so.
    Bible: Genesis
    1:24

5   And God said, Let us make man in our image,
    after our likeness: and let them have dominion
    over the fish of the sea, and over the fowl of
    the air, and over the cattle, and over all the
    earth, and over every creeping thing that
    creepeth upon the earth.
    So God created man in his own image, in the
    image of God created he him; male and fe-
    male created he them.
    And God blessed them, and God said unto
    them, Be fruitful, and multiply, and replenish
    the earth, and subdue it: and have domin-
    ion over the fish of the sea, and over the
    fowl of the air, and over every living thing that
    moveth upon the earth.
    Bible: Genesis
    1:26-28

6   And on the seventh day God ended his work
    which he had made; and he rested on the sev-
    enth day from all his work which he had
    made.
    Bible: Genesis
    2:2

7   But there went up a mist from the earth, and
    watered the whole face of the ground.
    And the Lord God formed man of the dust of
    the ground, and breathed into his nostrils
    the breath of life; and man became a living
    soul.
    And the Lord God planted a garden eastward

in Eden; and there he put the man whom he
had formed.
And out of the ground made the Lord God to
grow every tree that is pleasant to the sight,
and good for food; the tree of life also in
the midst of the garden, and the tree of
knowledge of good and evil.
And a river went out of Eden to water the
garden.
Bible: Genesis
2:6-10

8   And the Lord God took the man, and put him
    into the garden of Eden to dress it and to keep
    it.
    And the Lord God commanded the man, say-
    ing, Of every tree of the garden thou mayest
    freely eat:
    But of the tree of the knowledge of good and
    evil, thou shalt not eat of it: for in the day
    that thou eatest thereof thou shalt surely die.
    Bible: Genesis
    2:15-17

9   And the Lord God said, It is not good that the
    man should be alone; I will make him an help
    meet for him.
    And out of the ground the Lord God formed
    every beast of the field, and every fowl of
    the air; and brought them unto Adam to see
    what he would call them: and whatsoever
    Adam called every living creature, that was
    the name thereof.
    Bible: Genesis
    2:18-19

10 And the Lord God caused a deep sleep to fall
    upon Adam, and he slept: and he took one of
    his ribs, and closed up the flesh instead
    thereof;
    And the rib, which the Lord God had taken
    from man, made he a woman, and brought her
    unto the man.
    And Adam said, This is now bone of my
    bones, and flesh of my flesh: she shall be
    called Woman, because she was taken out of
    Man.
    Therefore shall a man leave his father and his
    mother, and shall cleave unto his wife: and
    they shall be one flesh.
    And they were both naked, the man and his
    wife, and were not ashamed.
    Bible: Genesis
    2:21-25

11 Now the serpent was more subtil than any
    beast of the field which the Lord God had
    made.
    Bible: Genesis
    3:1

12 God doth know that in the day ye eat thereof,
    then your eyes shall be opened, and ye shall
    be as gods, knowing good and evil.
    And when the woman saw that the tree was
    good for food, and that it was pleasant to
    the eyes, and a tree to be desired to make
    one wise, she took of the fruit thereof, and
    did eat, and gave also unto her husband
    with her; and he did eat.
    And the eyes of them both were opened, and

they knew that they were naked; and they
sewed fig leaves together; and made themselves aprons.
And they heard the voice of the Lord God
walking in the garden in the cool of the day:
and Adam and his wife hid themselves from
the presence of the Lord God amongst the
trees of the garden.
Bible: Genesis
3:5—8

13 And the man said, The woman whom thou
gavest to be with me, she gave me of the tree,
and I did eat.
And the Lord God said unto the woman, What
is this that thou hast done? And the woman
said, The serpent beguiled me, and I did
eat.
And the Lord God said unto the serpent, Because thou hast done this, thou art cursed
above all cattle, and above every beast of the
field; upon thy belly shalt thou go, and
dust shalt thou eat all the days of thy life:
And I will put enmity between thee and the
woman, and between thy seed and her seed;
it shall bruise thy head, and thou shalt
bruise his heel.
Unto the woman he said, I will greatly multiply thy sorrow and thy conception; in sorrow
thou shalt bring forth children; and thy desire shall be to thy husband, and he shall rule
over thee.
And unto Adam he said, Because thou hast
hearkened unto the voice of thy wife, and has
eaten of the tree, of which I commanded thee,
saying, Thou shalt not eat of it: cursed is the
ground for thy sake; in sorrow shalt thou eat
of it all the days of thy life.
Bible: Genesis
3:12—17

14 In the sweat of thy face shalt thou eat bread, till
thou return unto the ground; for out of it wast
thou taken: for dust thou art and unto dust
shalt thou return.
And Adam called his wife's name Eve; because she was the mother of all living.
Bible: Genesis
3:19—20

15 Abel was a keeper of sheep, but Cain was a
tiller of the ground.
Bible: Genesis
4:2

16 And the Lord said unto Cain, Where is Abel thy
brother? And he said, I know not: Am I my
brother's keeper?
And he said, What hast thou done? the voice
of thy brother's blood crieth unto me from
the ground.
Bible: Genesis
4:9—10

17 When thou tillest the ground, it shall not henceforth yield unto thee her strength; a fugitive
and a vagabond shalt thou be in the earth.
And Cain said unto the Lord, My punishment
is greater than I can bear.
Bible: Genesis
4:12—13

18 And the Lord said unto him, Therefore whosoever slayeth Cain, vengeance shall be taken
on him sevenfold. And the Lord set a mark
upon Cain, lest any finding him should kill him
And Cain went out from the presence of the
Lord, and dwelt in the land of Nod, on the
east of Eden.
Bible: Genesis
4:15—16

19 And they went in unto Noah into the ark, two
and two of all flesh, wherein is the breath of
life.
And they that went in, went in male and female of all flesh, as God had commanded
him: and the Lord shut him in.
And the flood was forty days upon the earth
and the waters increased, and bare up the
ark, and it was lift up above the earth.
Bible: Genesis
7:15—17

20 And the dove came in to him in the evening;
and, lo, in her mouth was an olive leaf pluckt
off: so Noah knew that the waters were abate
from off the earth.
Bible: Genesis
8:11

21 And surely your blood of your lives will I require; at the hand of every beast will I require
it, and at the hand of man; at the hand of
every man's brother will I require the life of
man.
Whoso sheddeth man's blood, by man shall
his blood be shed: for in the image of God
made he man.
Bible: Genesis
9:5—6

22 He was a mighty hunter before the Lord:
wherefore it is said, Even as Nimrod the mighty
hunter before the Lord.
Bible: Genesis
10:9

23 Therefore is the name of it called Babel; because the Lord did there confound the language of all the earth: and from thence did the
Lord scatter them abroad upon the face of all
the earth.
Bible: Genesis
11:9

24 Now the Lord had said unto Abram, Get thee
out of thy country, and from thy kindred, an
from thy father's house, unto a land that I will
shew thee:
And I will make of thee a great nation, and
will bless thee, and make thy name great;
and thou shalt be a blessing:
And I will bless them that bless thee, and
curse him that curseth thee: and in thee shal
all families of the earth be blessed.
Bible: Genesis
12:1—3

25 But his wife looked back from behind him, an
she became a pillar of salt.
Bible: Genesis
19:26

26 And Abraham lifted up his eyes, and looked,

and behold behind him a ram caught in a thicket by his horns: and Abraham went and took the ram, and offered him up for a burnt offering in the stead of his son.
Bible: Genesis
22:13

27 And Jacob said to Rebekah his mother, Behold, Esau my brother a hairy man, and I am a smooth man.
Bible: Genesis
27:11

28 Now Israel loved Joseph more than all his children, because he was the son of his old age: and he made him a coat of many colours.
Bible: Genesis
37:3

29 And they said one to another, Behold, this dreamer cometh.
Come now therefore, and let us slay him, and cast him into some pit, and we will say, Some evil beast hath devoured him: and we shall see what will become of his dreams.
Bible: Genesis
37:19-20

30 And the seven thin ears devoured the seven rank and full ears. And Pharaoh awoke, and, behold, it was a dream.
Bible: Genesis
41:7

31 And when she could not longer hide him, she took for him an ark of bulrushes, and daubed it with slime and with pitch, and put the child therein; and she laid it in the flags by the river's brink.
Bible: Exodus
2:3

32 He called his name Gershom: for he said, I have been a stranger in a strange land.
Bible: Exodus
2:22

33 And the angel of the Lord appeared unto him in a flame of fire out of the midst of a bush: and he looked, and, behold, the bush burned with fire, and the bush was not consumed.
Bible: Exodus
3:2

34 And I am come down to deliver them out of the hand of the Egyptians, and to bring them up out of that land unto a good land and a large, unto a land flowing with milk and honey; unto the place of the Canaanites, and the Hittites, and the Amorites, and the Perizzites, and the Hivites, and the Jebusites.
Bible: Exodus
3:8

35 And God said unto Moses, I AM THAT I AM: and he said, Thus shalt thou say unto the children of Israel, I AM hath sent me unto you.
Bible: Exodus
3:14

36 And thus shall ye eat it; with your loins girded, your shoes on your feet, and your staff in your hand; and ye shall eat it in haste: it is the Lord's passover.

For I will pass through the land of Egypt this night, and will smite all the firstborn in the land of Egypt, both man and beast; and against all the gods of Egypt I will execute judgment: I am the Lord.
Bible: Exodus
12:11-12

37 And the Lord went before them by day in a pillar of a cloud, to lead them the way; and by night in a pillar of fire, to give them light; to go by day and night.
Bible: Exodus
13:21

38 And the children of Israel went into the midst of the sea upon the dry ground: and the waters were a wall unto them on their right hand, and on their left.
Bible: Exodus
14:22

39 And when the children of Israel saw it, they said one to another, It is manna: for they wist not what it was. And Moses said unto them, This is the bread which the Lord hath given you to eat.
Bible: Exodus
16:15

40 I am the Lord thy God, which have brought thee out of the land of Egypt, out of the house of bondage.
Thou shalt have no other gods before me.
Thou shalt not make unto thee any graven image, or any likeness of any thing that is in heaven above, or that is in the earth beneath, or that is in the water under the earth:
Thou shalt not bow down thyself to them, nor serve them: for I the Lord thy God am a jealous God, visiting the iniquity of the fathers upon the children unto the third and fourth generation of them that hate me;
And shewing mercy unto thousands of them that love me, and keep my commandments.
Thou shalt not take the name of the Lord thy God in vain; for the Lord will not hold him guiltless that taketh his name in vain.
Remember the sabbath day, to keep it holy.
Six days shalt thou labour, and do all thy work:
But the seventh day is the sabbath of the Lord thy God: in it thou shalt not do any work, thou, nor thy son, nor thy daughter, thy manservant, nor thy maidservant, nor thy cattle, nor thy stranger that is within thy gates:
For in six days the Lord made heaven and earth, the sea, and all that in them is, and rested the seventh day: wherefore the Lord blessed the sabbath day, and hallowed it.
Honour thy father and thy mother: that thy days may be long upon the land which the Lord thy God giveth thee.
Thou shalt not kill.
Thou shalt not commit adultery.
Thou shalt not steal.
Thou shalt not bear false witness against thy neighbour.
Thou shalt not covet thy neighbour's house, thou shalt not covet thy neighbour's wife,

nor his manservant, nor his maidservant, nor
his ox, nor his ass, nor any thing that is thy
neighbour's.
Bible: Exodus
20:2–17

41 And if any mischief follow, then thou shalt give
life for life,
Eye for eye, tooth for tooth, hand for hand,
foot for foot,
Burning for burning, wound for wound, stripe
for stripe.
Bible: Exodus
21:23–25

42 Thou shalt not suffer a witch to live.
Bible: Exodus
22:18

43 And the Lord said unto Moses, Come up to me
into the mount, and be there: and I will give
thee tables of stone, and a law, and commandments which I have written; that thou may-
est teach them.
Bible: Exodus
24:12

44 Take heed to yourselves, that your heart be not
deceived, and ye turn aside, and serve other
gods, and worship them.
Bible: Deuteronomy
11:16

45 Be strong and of a good courage, fear not, nor
be afraid of them: for the Lord thy God, he it
is that doth go with thee; he will not fail
thee, nor forsake thee.
Bible: Deuteronomy
31:6

46 So the people shouted when the priests blew
with the trumpets: and it came to pass, when
the people heard the sound of the trumpet, and
the people shouted with a great shout, that
the wall fell down flat, so that the people went
up into the city, every man straight before
him, and they took the city.
Bible: Joshua
6:20

47 And the women answered one another as they
played, and said, Saul hath slain his
thousands, and David his ten thousands.
Bible: I Samuel
18:7

48 So David slept with his fathers, and was buried
in the city of David.
Bible: I Kings
2:10

49 Then the king answered and said, Give her the
living child, and in no wise slay it: she is the
mother thereof.
And all Israel heard of the judgment which the
king had judged; and they feared the king:
for they saw that the wisdom of God was in
him, to do judgment.
Bible: I Kings
The 'Judgment of Solomon'
3:27–28

50 And when the queen of Sheba heard of the
fame of Solomon concerning the name of the

Lord, she came to prove him with hard
questions.
Bible: I Kings
10:1

51 And he said, Go forth, and stand upon the
mount before the Lord. And, behold, the Lord
passed by, and a great and strong wind rent
the mountains, and brake in pieces the rocks
before the Lord; but the Lord was not in the
wind: and after the wind an earthquake; but
the Lord was not in the earthquake:
And after the earthquake a fire; but the Lord
was not in the fire: and after the fire a still
small voice.
Bible: I Kings
19:11–12

52 And it came to pass, as they still went on, and
talked, that, behold, there appeared a chariot
of fire, and horses of fire, and parted them
both asunder; and Elijah went up by a whirlwind into heaven.
And Elisha saw it, and he cried, My father, my
father, the chariot of Israel, and the horse-
men thereof. And he saw him no more: and
he took hold of his own clothes, and rent
them in two pieces.
Bible: II Kings
2:11–12

53 And he shall judge among the nations, and
shall rebuke many people: and they shall beat
their swords into plowshares, and their
spears into pruning-hooks: nation shall not lift
up sword against nation, neither shall they
learn war any more.
Bible: Isaiah
2:4

54 Comfort ye, comfort ye my people, saith your
God.
Speak ye comfortably to Jerusalem, and cry
unto her, that her warfare is accomplished,
that her iniquity is pardoned: for she hath received of the Lord's hand double for all her
sins.
The voice of him that crieth in the wilderness
Prepare ye the way of the Lord, make
straight in the desert a highway for our God.
Every valley shall be exalted, and every mountain and hill shall be made low: and the
crooked shall be made straight, and the
rough places plain:
And the glory of the Lord shall be revealed,
and all flesh shall see it together: for the
mouth of the Lord hath spoken it.
Bible: Isaiah
40:1–5

55 There is no peace, saith the Lord, unto the
wicked.
Bible: Isaiah
48:22

56 Then the king commanded, and they brought
Daniel, and cast him into the den of lions. Now
the king spake and said unto Daniel, Thy God
whom thou servest continually, he will deliver thee.
Bible: Daniel
6:16

57 For they have sown the wind, and they shall reap the whirlwind: it hath no stalk: the bud shall yield no meal: if so be it yield, the strangers shall swallow it up.
Bible: Hosea
8:7

58 Now the Lord had prepared a great fish to swallow up Jonah. And Jonah was in the belly of the fish three days and three nights.
Bible: Jonah
1:17

59 Behold, I will send my messenger, and he shall prepare the way before me: and the Lord, whom ye seek, shall suddenly come to his temple, even the messenger of the covenant, whom ye delight in: behold, he shall come, saith the Lord of hosts. But who may abide the day of his coming? and who shall stand when he appeareth? for he is like a refiner's fire, and like fullers' soap.
Bible: Malachi
3:2

Attitudes

Death

60 Whatsoever thy hand findeth to do, do it with thy might; for there is no work, nor device, nor knowledge, nor wisdom, in the grave, whither thou goest.
Bible: Ecclesiastes
9:10

Education, Knowledge, and Learning

61 With the ancient is wisdom; and in length of days understanding.
Bible: Job
12:12

62 No mention shall be made of coral, or of pearls: for the price of wisdom is above rubies.
Bible: Job
28:18

63 For in much wisdom is much grief: and he that increaseth knowledge increaseth sorrow.
Bible: Ecclesiastes
1:18

64 The words of wise men are heard in quiet more than the cry of him that ruleth among fools.
Bible: Ecclesiastes
9:17

65 Miss not the discourse of the elders: for they also learned of their fathers, and of them thou shalt learn understanding, and to give answer as need requireth.
Bible: Ecclesiasticus
8:9

66 The wisdom of a learned man cometh by opportunity of leisure: and he that hath little business shall become wise.
How can he get wisdom that holdeth the plough, and that glorieth in the goad, that driveth oxen, and is occupied in their labours, and whose talk is of bullocks?
Bible: Ecclesiasticus
38:24–25

67 For wisdom is more moving than any motion: she passeth and go through all things by reason of her pureness.
For she is the breath of the power of God, and a pure influence flowing from the glory of the Almighty: therefore can no defiled thing fall into her.
For she is the brightness of the everlasting light, the unspotted mirror of the power of God, and the image of his goodness.
And being but one, she can do all things: and remaining in herself, she maketh all things new: and in all ages entering into holy souls, she maketh them friends of God, and prophets.
For God loveth none but him that dwelleth with wisdom.
Bible: Wisdom
7:24–28

Human Nature

68 And I gave my heart to seek and search out by wisdom concerning all things that are done under heaven: this sore travail hath God given to the sons of man to be exercised therewith.
I have seen all the works that are done under the sun; and, behold, all is vanity and vexation of spirit.
Bible: Ecclesiastes
1:13–14

69 Two are better than one; because they have a good reward for their labour.
For if they fall, the one will lift up his fellow: but woe to him that is alone when he falleth; for he hath not another to help him up.
Bible: Ecclesiastes
4:9–10

70 Forsake not an old friend; for the new is not comparable to him: a new friend is as new wine; when it is old, thou shalt drink it with pleasure.
Bible: Ecclesiasticus
9:10

Humour

71 Then I commended mirth, because a man hath no better thing under the sun, than to eat, and to drink, and to be merry: for that shall abide with him of his labour the days of his life, which God giveth him under the sun.
Bible: Ecclesiastes
8:15

Life

72 For the world hath lost his youth, and the times begin to wax old.
Bible: II Esdras
14:10

73 Man that is born of a woman is of few days, and full of trouble.
Bible: Job
14:1

74 The thing that hath been, it is that which shall be; and that which is done is that which shall be done: and there is no new thing under the sun.
Bible: Ecclesiastes
1:7–9

75 To every thing there is a season, and a time to every purpose under the heaven:
A time to be born, and a time to die; a time to plant, and a time to pluck up that which is planted;
A time to kill, and a time to heal; a time to break down, and a time to build up;
A time to weep, and a time to laugh; a time to mourn, and a time to dance;
A time to cast away stones, and a time to gather stones together; a time to embrace, and a time to refrain from embracing;
A time to get, and a time to lose; a time to keep, and a time to cast away;
A time to rend, and a time to sew; a time to keep silence, and a time to speak;
A time to love, and a time to hate; a time of war, and a time of peace.
Bible: Ecclesiastes
3:1–8

76 I returned, and saw under the sun, that the race is not to the swift, nor the battle to the strong, neither yet bread to the wise, nor yet riches to men of understanding, nor yet favour to men of skill; but time and chance happeneth to them all.
For man also knoweth not his time: as the fishes that are taken in an evil net, and as the birds that are caught in the snare; so are the sons of men snared in an evil time, when it falleth suddenly upon them.
Bible: Ecclesiastes
9:11–12

77 If thou hast gathered nothing in thy youth, how canst thou find any thing in thine age?
Bible: Ecclesiasticus
25:3

78 And behold joy and gladness, slaying oxen, and killing sheep, eating flesh, and drinking wine: let us eat and drink; for tomorrow we shall die.
Bible: Isaiah
22:13
A similar sentiment is expressed in Corinthians 15:32–33

Marriage and the Family

79 He that spareth his rod hateth his son: but he that loveth him chasteneth him betimes.
Bible: Proverbs
13:24

80 Desire not a multitude of unprofitable children, neither delight in ungodly sons.
Bible: Ecclesiasticus
16:1

Men and Women

81 Who can find a virtuous woman? for her price is far above rubies
The heart of her husband doth safely trust in her, so that he shall have no need of spoil.
She will do him good and not evil all the days of her life.
Bible: Proverbs
31:10–12

Morality, Vices, and Virtues

82 Pride goeth before destruction, and an haughty spirit before a fall.
Bible: Proverbs
16:18

83 He that is slow to anger is better than the mighty; and he that ruleth his spirit than he that taketh a city.
Bible: Proverbs
16:32

84 Wine is a mocker, strong drink is raging: and whosoever is deceived thereby is not wise.
Bible: Proverbs
20:1

85 Let thy speech be short, comprehending much in few words; be as one that knoweth and yet holdeth his tongue.
Bible: Ecclesiasticus
32:8

86 Be not made a beggar by banqueting upon borrowing, when thou hast nothing in thy purse: for thou shalt lie in wait for thine own life, and be talked on.
Bible: Ecclesiasticus
18:33

87 Woe unto them that rise up early in the morning, that they may follow strong drink; that continue until night, till wine inflame them!
Bible: Isaiah
5:11

88 There is no peace, saith the Lord, unto the wicked.
Bible: Isaiah
48:22

89 Blessed is the man that endureth temptation: for when he is tried, he shall receive the crown of life, which the Lord hath promised to them that love him.
Bible: James
1:12

90 Can the Ethiopian change his skin, or the leopard his spots? then may ye also do good, that are accustomed to do evil.
Bible: Jeremiah
13:23

91 For the ear of jealousy heareth all things: and the noise of murmurings is not hid.
Bible: Wisdom
1:10

Other People

92 One of themselves, even a prophet of their own, said, The Cretians are alway liars, evil beasts, slow bellies.
Bible: Titus
1:12

Religion

93 The Lord is a man of war: the Lord is his name.
Bible: Exodus
15:3

94 For I know that my redeemer liveth, and that he shall stand at the latter day upon the earth: And though after my skin worms destroy this body, yet in my flesh shall I see God.
Bible: Job
19:25−26

95 Let us hear the conclusion of the whole matter: Fear God, and keep his commandments: for this is the whole duty of man.
Bible: Ecclesiastes
12:13

96 In the year that king Uzziah died I saw also the Lord sitting upon a throne, high and lifted up, and his train filled the temple.
Above it stood the seraphims: each one had six wings; with twain he covered his face, and with twain he covered his feet, and with twain he did fly.
And one cried unto another, and said, Holy, holy, holy, is the Lord of hosts: the whole earth is full of his glory.
And the posts of the door moved at the voice of him that cried, and the house was filled with smoke.
Then said I, Woe is me! for I am undone; because I am a man of unclean lips, and I dwell in the midst of a people of unclean lips: for mine eyes have seen the King, the Lord of hosts.
Then flew one of the seraphims unto me, having a live coal in his hand, which he had taken with the tongs from off the altar:
And he laid it upon my mouth, and said, Lo, this hath touched thy lips; and thine iniquity is taken away, and thy sin purged.
Also I heard the voice of the Lord, saying, Whom shall I send, and who will go for us? Then said I, Here am I; send me.
Bible: Isaiah
6:1−8

97 Therefore the Lord himself shall give you a sign; Behold, a virgin shall conceive, and bear a son, and shall call his name Immanuel.
Butter and honey shall he eat, that he may know to refuse the evil, and choose the good.
Bible: Isaiah
7:14−15

98 The people that walked in darkness have seen a great light: they that dwell in the land of the shadow of death, upon them hath the light shined.
Bible: Isaiah
9:2

99 For unto us a child is born, unto us a son is given: and the government shall be upon his shoulder: and his name shall be called Wonderful, Counsellor, The mighty God, The everlasting Father, The Prince of Peace.
Of the increase of his government and peace there shall be no end, upon the throne of David, and upon his kingdom, to order it, and to establish it with judgment and with justice from henceforth even for ever. The zeal of the Lord of hosts will perform this.
Bible: Isaiah
9:6−7

100 And there shall come forth a rod out of the stem of Jesse, and a Branch shall grow out of his roots:
And the spirit of the Lord shall rest upon him, the spirit of wisdom and understanding, the spirit of counsel and might, the spirit of knowledge and of the fear of the Lord.
Bible: Isaiah
11:1−2

Wealth and Poverty

101 A feast is made for laughter, and wine maketh merry: but money answereth all things.
Bible: Ecclesiastes
10:19

Sayings of the Time

102 Then Job answered and said, I have heard many such things: miserable comforters are ye all.
Bible: Job
16:1

103 Canst thou draw out leviathan with an hook? or his tongue with a cord which thou lettest down?
Bible: Job
41:1

104 Let us now praise famous men, and our fathers that begat us.
Bible: Ecclesiasticus
44:1

105 He calleth to me out of Seir, Watchman, what of the night? Watchman, what of the night?
The watchman said, The morning cometh, and

also the night: if ye will enquire, enquire ye: return, come.
Bible: Isaiah
21:11–12

106 Then the eyes of the blind shall be opened, and the ears of the deaf shall be unstopped.
Bible: Isaiah
35:5

107 And he said unto me, Son of man, can these bones live? And I answered, O Lord God, thou knowest.
Again he said unto me, Prophesy upon these bones, and say unto them, O ye dry bones, hear the word of the Lord.
Bible: Ezekiel
37:3–4

With Hindsight

13th century

108 Had I been present at the Creation, I would have given some useful hints for the better ordering of the universe.

Alfonso the Wise (c. 1221–84) King of Castile and Léon.
Referring to the complicated Ptolemaic model of the universe; often quoted as, 'Had I been consulted I would have recommended something simpler'.
Attrib.

14th century

109 Whan that the month in which the world bigan, That highte March, whan God first maked man.
Geoffrey Chaucer (c. 1342–1400) English poet.
The Canterbury Tales, 'The Nun's Priest's Tale'

17th century

110 Of Man's first disobedience, and the fruit Of that forbidden tree, whose mortal taste Brought death into the World, and all our woe . . .
John Milton (1608–74) English poet.
Paradise Lost, Bk. I

2

The Ancient World (before 50 BC)

While history goes back some 4000 years BC and the Hindu Vedas were being written in Sanskrit over 3500 years ago, the earliest quotable sources to have had a continuous and lasting influence on the western world are the Old Testament (see previous section) and the works of the ancient Greeks. Between the 6th and 4th centuries BC an astounding burst of creativity flourished throughout the ancient world. In China Lao Tse and Confucius, in India Guatama Buddha, and in Persia Zoroaster were roughly contemporary with the Jewish prophets and Pericles of Athens. But it was primarily the Greek city states that provided the starting points of western culture in history, philosophy, drama, and literature; it is, therefore, from this quarter that most of the quotations from the ancient world come.

When the rising Roman Republic absorbed Greece in the 2nd century BC, it also absorbed Greek culture and learning. Politically, Rome was a new phenomenon: a city-state that not only acquired an empire but eventually conquered most of the known world. Its political institutions were still those of a city-state, unsuited to controlling its vast territories. By 50 BC, when Julius Caesar completed his conquest of Gaul, they were ready to break.

Politics, Government, and World Events

6th century BC

1 Laws are like spider's webs: if some poor weak creature come up against them, it is caught; but a bigger one can break through and get away.
Solon (6th century BC) Athenian statesman.
Lives of the Eminent Philosophers (Diogenes Laertius), I

2 Recompense injury with justice, and recompense kindness with kindness.
Confucius (K'ung Fu-tzu; 551–479 BC) Chinese philosopher.
Analects

3 The people may be made to follow a course of action, but they may not be made to understand it.
Confucius
Analects

480 BC

4 Go, stranger, and tell the Lacedaemonians that here we lie, obedient to their commands.
Leonidas (died 480 BC) King of Sparta.
Epitaph over the tomb in which he and his followers were buried after their defeat at Thermopylae

430 BC

5 Our love of what is beautiful does not lead to extravagance; our love of the things of the mind does not make us soft.
Pericles (c. 495–429 BC) Greek statesman.
Part of the funeral oration, 430 BC, for the dead of the first year of the Peloponnesian War
Attrib. in *Histories* (Thucydides), Bk. II, Ch. 40

399 BC

6 Crito, we owe a cock to Aesculapius; please pay it and don't let it pass.
Socrates (469–399 BC) Athenian philosopher.
Before his execution by drinking hemlock
Phaedo (Plato), 118

4th century BC

7 Our object in the construction of the state is the greatest happiness of the whole, and not that of any one class.
Plato (429–347 BC) Greek philosopher.
Republic, Bk. IV

8 There will be no end to the troubles of states, or indeed, my dear Glaucon, of humanity itself, till philosophers become kings in this world, or till those we now call kings and rulers really and truly become philosophers.
Plato
Republic, Bk. V

9 I wonder if we could contrive . . . some magnificent myth that would in itself carry conviction to our whole community.
Plato
Republic, Bk. V

10 Democracy passes into despotism.
Plato
Republic, Bk. VIII

11 The difference between us is that my family begins with me, whereas yours ends with you.
Iphicrates (d. 353 BC) Athenian general.
Reply to a descendant of Harmodius (an Athenian hero), who had derided Iphicrates for being the son of a cobbler
Attrib.

12 If I were not Alexander, I would be Diogenes.
Alexander the Great (356–323 BC) King of Macedon.
Plutarch, *Life of Alexander*, Bk. XIV

13 Stand a little less between me and the sun.
Diogenes (412–322 BC) Greek philosopher.
When Alexander the Great asked if there was anything he wanted
Life of Alexander (Plutarch)

14 Man is by nature a political animal.
Aristotle (384–322 BC) Greek philosopher.
Politics, Bk. I

15 Where some people are very wealthy and others have nothing, the result will be either extreme democracy or absolute oligarchy, or despotism will come from either of those excesses.
Aristotle
Politics, Bk. IV

16 Inferiors revolt in order that they may be equal and equals that they may be superior. Such is the state of mind which creates revolutions.
Aristotle
Politics, Bk. V

279 BC

17 Such another victory and we are ruined.
Pyrrhus (319–272 BC) King of Epirus.
Commenting upon the costliness of his victory at the Battle of Asculum, 279 BC
Life of Pyrrhus (Plutarch)

2nd century BC

18 Carthage must be destroyed.
Cato the Elder (Marcius Porcius C.; 234–149 BC) Roman statesman.
Repeated on almost every possible occasion; war was declared on Carthage in 149 BC, and the city was destroyed in 146 BC.
Life of Cato (Plutarch)

19 Let them hate, so long as they fear.
Lucius Accius (170–c. 85 BC) Roman tragic playwright.
Atreus, 'Seneca'

63 BC

20 *O tempora! O mores!*
    What times! What customs!
    Cicero (106–43 BC) Roman orator and
    statesman.
    In Catilinam, I

62 BC

21* **Caesar's wife must be above suspicion.**
    Julius Caesar (100–44 BC) Roman general
    and statesman.
    Said in justification of his divorce from Pompeia,
    after she was unwittingly involved in a scandal
    Lives, 'Julius Caesar' (Plutarch)

51 BC

22* **All Gaul is divided into three parts.**
    Julius Caesar
    De Bello Gallico, Vol. I, Ch. 1

Attitudes

Art, Literature, and Music

5th century BC

23 **I depict men as they ought to be, but Euripides
    portrays them as they are.**
    Sophocles (c. 496–406 BC) Greek dramatist.
    Poetics (Aristotle)

4th century BC

24 **Now a whole is that which has a beginning, a
    middle, and an end.**
    Aristotle (384–322 BC) Greek philosopher.
    Referring specifically to the dramatic form of
    tragedy.
    Poetics, Ch. 7

1st century BC

25 **For the godly poet must be chaste himself, but
    there is no need for his verses to be so.**
    Catullus (c. 84–c. 54 BC) Roman poet.
    Carmina, XVI

Death

4th century BC

26 **Whom the gods love dies young.**
    Menander (c. 341–c. 290 BC) Greek dramatist.
    Dis Exapaton

Education, Knowledge, and Learning

6th century BC

27 **Learning without thought is labour lost; thought
    without learning is perilous.**
    Confucius (K'ung Fu-tzu; 551–479 BC) Chi-
    nese philosopher.
    Analects

4th century BC

28 **What we have to learn to do, we learn by doing.**
    Aristotle (384–322 BC) Greek philosopher.
    Nicomachean Ethics, Bk. II

History

6th century BC

29 **Study the past, if you would divine the future.**
    Confucius (K'ung Fu-tzu; 551–479 BC) Chi-
    nese philosopher.
    Analects

5th century BC

30 **Even God cannot change the past.**
    Agathon (c. 446–401 BC) Athenian poet and
    playwright.
    Nicomachean Ethics (Aristotle), VI

4th century BC

31 **For this reason poetry is something more philo-
    sophical and more worthy of serious attention
    than history.**
    Aristotle (384–322 BC) Greek philosopher.
    Poetics, Ch. 9

Human Nature

6th century BC

32 **Don't count your chickens before they are
    hatched.**
    Aesop (6th century BC) Reputed Greek writer of
    fables.
    Fables, 'The Milkmaid and her Pail'

33 **The lamb that belonged to the sheep whose
    skin the wolf was wearing began to follow the
    wolf in the sheep's clothing.**
    Aesop
    Fables, 'The Wolf in Sheep's Clothing'

34 **It is not only fine feathers that make fine birds.**
    Aesop
    Fables, 'The Jay and the Peacock'

35 **I am sure the grapes are sour.**
    Aesop
    Fables, 'The Fox and the Grapes'

36 **The boy cried 'Wolf, wolf!' and the villagers came out to help him.**
Aesop
Fables, 'The Shepherd's Boy'

37 **Have no friends not equal to yourself.**
Confucius (K'ung Fu-tzu; 551–479 BC) Chinese philosopher.
Analects

38 **Men's natures are alike; it is their habits that carry them far apart.**
Confucius
Analects

39 **When you have faults, do not fear to abandon them.**
Confucius
Analects

40 **The superior man is satisfied and composed; the mean man is always full of distress.**
Confucius
Analects

41 **The superior man is distressed by his want of ability.**
Confucius
Analects

42 **When you meet someone better than yourself, turn your thoughts to becoming his equal. When you meet someone not as good as you are, look within and examine your own self.**
Confucius
Analects

4th century BC

43 **Either a beast or a god.**
Aristotle (384–322 BC) Greek philosopher.
Politics, Bk. I

44 **Obstinate people can be divided into the opinionated, the ignorant, and the boorish.**
Aristotle
Nicomachean Ethics, Bk. VII

3rd century BC

45 **It is not so much our friends' help that helps us as the confident knowledge that they will help us.**
Epicurus (341–270 BC) Greek philosopher.

Life

6th century BC

46 **The gods help them that help themselves.**
Aesop (6th century BC) Reputed Greek writer of fables.
Fables, 'Hercules and the Waggoner'

47 **Because there is no difference.**
Thales (c. 624–547 BC) Greek philosopher and astronomer.
His reply when asked why he chose to carry on

living after saying there was no difference between life and death
The Story of Civilization (W. Durant), Vol. 2

5th century BC

48 **Everything flows and nothing stays.**
Heraclitus (c. 535–c. 475 BC) Greek philosopher.
Cratylus (Plato), 402a

49 **I am moved to pity, when I think of the brevity of human life, seeing that of all this host of men not one will still be alive in a hundred years' time.**
Xerxes (d. 465 BC) King of Persia.
On surveying his army

50 **To famous men all the earth is a sepulchre.**
Thucydides (c. 460–c. 400 BC) Greek historian and general.
History of the Peloponnesian War, Bk. II, Ch. 43

51 **I am not an Athenian or a Greek, but a citizen of the world.**
Socrates (469–399 BC) Athenian philosopher.
Of Banishment (Plutarch)

52 **The unexamined life is not worth living.**
Socrates
Apology (Plato)

3rd century BC

53 **I do not know whether I was then a man dreaming I was a butterfly, or whether I am now a butterfly dreaming I am a man.**
Chuang Tse (or Zhuangzi; c. 369–286 BC) Chinese philosopher.
Chuang Tse (H. A. Giles), Ch. 2

Love and Sex

5th century BC

54 **Someone asked Sophocles, 'How do you feel now about sex? Are you still able to have a woman?' He replied, 'Hush, man; most gladly indeed am I rid of it all, as though I had escaped from a mad and savage master.'**
Sophocles (c. 496–406 BC) Greek dramatist.
Republic (Plato), Bk. I

Men and Women

5th century BC

55 **It is a great glory in a woman to show no more weakness than is natural to her sex, and not be talked of, either for good or evil by men.**
Thucydides (c. 460–c. 400 BC) Greek historian and general.
History of the Peloponnesian War, Bk. II, Ch. 45

Morality, Vices, and Virtues

6th century BC

56 Beware that you do not lose the substance by grasping at the shadow.
Aesop (6th century BC) Reputed Greek writer of fables.
Fables, 'The Dog and the Shadow'

57 Thinking to get at once all the gold that the goose could give, he killed it, and opened it only to find — nothing.
Aesop
Fables, 'The Goose with the Golden Eggs'

58 Wrongdoing can only be avoided if those who are not wronged feel the same indignation at it as those who are.
Solon (6th century BC) Athenian statesman.
Greek Wit (F. Paley)

59 Fine words and an insinuating appearance are seldom associated with true virtue.
Confucius (K'ung Fu-tzu; 551–479 BC) Chinese philosopher.
Analects

60 To be able to practise five things everywhere under heaven constitutes perfect virtue... gravity, generosity of soul, sincerity, earnestness, and kindness.
Confucius
Analects

61 What you do not want done to yourself, do not do to others.
Confucius
Analects

62 This Ariyan Eightfold Path, that is to say: Right view, right aim, right speech, right action, right living, right effort, right mindfulness, right contemplation.
Buddha (Gautama Siddhartha; c. 563–c. 483 BC) Indian religious teacher.
Some Sayings of the Buddha (F. L. Woodward)

5th century BC

63 Nothing can harm a good man, either in life or after death.
Socrates (469–399 BC) Athenian philosopher.
Apology (Plato)

4th century BC

64 The good is the beautiful.
Plato (429–347 BC) Greek philosopher.
Lysis

65 The man who gets angry at the right things and with the right people, and in the right way and at the right time and for the right length of time, is commended.
Aristotle (384–322 BC) Greek philosopher.
Nicomachean Ethics, Bk. IV

66 Plato is dear to me, but dearer still is truth.
Aristotle
Attrib.

Other People

1st century BC

67 To the Greeks the Muse gave native wit, to the Greeks the gift of graceful eloquence.
Horace
Ars Poetica

Religion

6th century BC

68 All things, oh priests, are on fire... The eye is on fire; forms are on fire; eye-consciousness is on fire; impressions received by the eye are on fire.
Buddha (Gautama Siddhartha; c. 563–c. 483 BC) Indian religious teacher.
The Fire Sermon

69 Ye must leave righteous ways behind, not to speak of unrighteous ways.
Buddha
Some Sayings of the Buddha (F. L. Woodward)

70 The Ethiopians say that their gods are snub-nosed and black, the Thracians that theirs have light blue eyes and red hair.
Xenophanes (c. 560–c. 478 BC) Greek poet and philosopher.
Fragment 15

5th century BC

71 Those whom God wishes to destroy, he first makes mad.
Euripides (c. 480–406 BC) Greek dramatist.
Fragment

Science, Medicine, and Technology

5th century BC

72 The life so short, the craft so long to learn.
Hippocrates (c. 460–c. 377 BC) Greek physician.
Describing medicine. It is often quoted in Latin as *Ars longa, vita brevis*, and interpreted as 'Art lasts, life is short'
Aphorisms, I

73 Extreme remedies are most appropriate for extreme diseases.
Hippocrates
Aphorisms, I

4th century BC

74 Let no one ignorant of mathematics enter here.
Plato (429–347 BC) Greek philosopher.
Inscription written over the entrance to the Academy
Biographical Encyclopedia (I. Asimov)

323 BC

75 I am dying with the help of too many
physicians.
Alexander the Great (356–323 BC) King of
Macedon.
Attrib.

3rd century BC

76 There is no 'royal road' to geometry.
Euclid (c. 300 BC) Greek mathematician.
Said to Ptolemy I Soter, King of Egypt, when
asked if there were an easier way to solve
theorems
Comment on Euclid (Proclus)

77 *Quod erat demonstrandum.*
Which was to be proved.
Euclid
Hence, of course, Q.E.D.
Elements, I:5

78 *Eureka!*
I have found it!
Archimedes (c. 287–212 BC) Greek
mathematician.
An exclamation of joy supposedly uttered as,
stepping into a bath and noticing the water over-
flowing, he saw the answer to a problem and
began the train of thought that led to his principle of buoyancy
Attrib.

79 Give me a firm place to stand, and I will move
the earth.
Archimedes
On the Lever

Wealth and Poverty

4th century BC

80 If only it were as easy to banish hunger by rub-
bing the belly as it is to masturbate.
Diogenes (412–322 BC) Greek philosopher.
Lives and Opinions of Eminent Philosophers
(Diogenes Laertius)

Sayings of the Time

7th century BC

81 The fox knows many things – the hedgehog
one *big* one.
Archilochus (c. 680–c. 640 BC) Greek poet.
Attrib.

With Hindsight

1st century BC

82 Many brave men lived before Agamemnon's
time; but they are all, unmourned and unknown,
covered by the long night, because they lack
their sacred poet.
Horace (Quintus Horatius Flaccus; 65–8 BC)
Roman poet.
Odes, IV

1st century AD

83 Now there are fields where Troy once was.
Ovid (Publius Ovidius Naso; 43 BC–17 AD) Ro-
man poet.
Heroides, Bk. I

17th century

84 Which beginning of time according to our Chro-
nologie, fell upon the entrance of the night
preceding the twenty third day of *Octob.* in the
year of the Julian Calendar, 710.
James Ussher (1581–1656) Irish churchman.
Referring to the Creation, as described in Genesis, which, he had calculated, took place on
22 Oct 4004 BC
The Annals of the World

20th century

85 The Romans and Greeks found everything
human. Everything had a face, and a human
voice. Men spoke, and their fountains piped an
answer.
D. H. Lawrence (1885–1930) British novelist.
Fantasia of the Unconscious, Ch. 4

86 I'm surprised that a government organization
could do it that quickly.
Jimmy Carter (1924–) US statesman.
Visiting Egypt, when told that it took twenty
years to build the Great Pyramid
Presidential Anecdotes (P. Boller)

3

The New Testament

The Romans first conquered Judaea in 63 BC. In 4 BC, following the death of their puppet king, Herod the Great, it became a Roman province.

Jesus of Nazareth, who had been born in Bethlehem during the reign of Herod, began his preaching in Galilee. In approximately 30 AD he was crucified by the Roman procurator Pontius Pilate.

Jesus was one of several religious and political agitators to cause the Romans concern in the period following Herod's death. He was, however, the only one to have profoundly changed, indeed shaped, western culture for the next 2000 years. Some 35 years after his crucifixion, St Mark's Gospel established the beginnings of the New Testament. In the ensuing section, quotations from this part of the Bible, derived from the Gospels and the other sources of the New Testament, are given in book, chapter, and verse order, without dates. However, as with the Old Testament, there is considerable temporal overlap with other events occurring in the Roman world, which appear in the following section.

1 And the angel came in unto her, and said, Hail,
thou that art highly favoured, the Lord is with
thee: blessed art thou among women.
And when she saw him, she was troubled at
his saying, and cast in her mind what manner of salutation this should be.
Bible: Luke
1:28–29

2 And Mary said, My soul doth magnify the Lord,
And my spirit hath rejoiced in God my
Saviour.
For he hath regarded the low estate of his
handmaiden: for, behold, from henceforth all
generations shall call me blessed.
Bible: Luke
1:46–48

3 And it came to pass in those days, that there
went out a decree from Caesar Augustus,
that all the world should be taxed.
Bible: Luke
2:1

4 And she brought forth her firstborn son, and
wrapped him in swaddling clothes, and laid him
in a manger; because there was no room for
them in the inn.
Bible: Luke
2:7

5 And there were in the same country shepherds
abiding in the field, keeping watch over their
flock by night.
And, lo, the angel of the Lord came upon
them, and the glory of the Lord shone round
about them: and they were sore afraid.
And the angel said unto them, Fear not: for,
behold, I bring you good tidings of great
joy, which shall be to all people.
Bible: Luke
2:8–10

6 Glory to God in the highest, and on earth
peace, good will toward men.
Bible: Luke
2:14

7 But Mary kept all these things, and pondered
them in her heart.
Bible: Luke
2:19

8 Lord, now lettest thou thy servant depart in
peace, according to thy word:
For mine eyes have seen thy salvation,
Which thou hast prepared before the face of
all people;
A light to lighten the Gentiles, and the glory
of thy people Israel.
Bible: Luke
2:29–32

9 Now when Jesus was born in Bethlehem of Judaea in the days of Herod the king, behold,
there came wise men from the east to Jerusalem,
Saying, Where is he that is born King of the
Jews? for we have seen his star in the east,
and are come to worship him.

When Herod the king had heard these things,
he was troubled, and all Jerusalem with him.
Bible: Matthew
2:1–3

10 And when they were come into the house, they
saw the young child with Mary his mother,
and fell down, and worshipped him: and when
they had opened their treasures, they presented unto him gifts; gold, and frankincense,
and myrrh.
And being warned of God in a dream that they
should not return to Herod, they departed
into their own country another way.
Bible: Matthew
2:11–12

11 He it is, who coming after me is preferred
before me, whose shoe's latchet I am not worthy to unloose.
Bible: John
1:27

12 The next day John seeth Jesus coming unto
him, and saith, Behold the Lamb of God, which
taketh away the sin of the world.
Bible: John
1:29

13 There is a lad here, which hath five barley
loaves, and two small fishes: but what are they
among so many?
And Jesus said, Make the men sit down. Now
there was much grass in the place. So the
men sat down, in number about five
thousand.
Bible: John
6:9–10

14 Your fathers did eat manna in the wilderness,
and are dead.
This is the bread which cometh down from
heaven, that a man may eat thereof, and not
die.
I am the living bread which came down from
heaven: if any man eat of this bread, he
shall live for ever: and the bread that I will
give is my flesh, which I will give for the life
of the world.
Bible: John
6:49–51

15 And the devil, taking him up into an high mountain, shewed unto him all the kingdoms of the
world in a moment of time.
Bible: Luke
4:5

16 And Jesus answering said, A certain man went
down from Jerusalem to Jericho, and fell
among thieves, which stripped him of his raiment, and wounded him, and departed, leaving him half dead.
And by chance there came down a certain
priest that way: and when he saw him, he
passed by on the other side.
Bible: Luke
10:30–31

17 And there came a certain poor widow, and she
threw in two mites, which make a farthing.
And he called unto him his disciples, and saith
unto them, Verily I say unto you, That this

poor widow hath cast more in, than all they
which have cast into the treasury: For all they
did cast in of their abundance; but she of her
want did cast in all that she had, even all her
living.
Bible: Mark
12:42—44

18 From that time Jesus began to preach, and to
say, Repent: for the kingdom of heaven is at
hand.
Bible: Matthew
4:17

19 And he saith unto them, Follow me, and I will
make you fishers of men.
Bible: Matthew
4:19

20 And his disciples came to him, and awoke him,
saying, Lord, save us: we perish.
And he saith unto them, Why are ye fearful, O
ye of little faith? Then he arose, and rebuked
the winds and the sea; and there was a
great calm.
But the men marvelled, saying, What manner
of man is this, that even the winds and the
sea obey him!
Bible: Matthew
8:25—27

21 But when Herod's birthday was kept, the
daughter of Herodias danced before them, and
pleased Herod.
Whereupon he promised with an oath to give
her whatsoever she would ask.
And she, being before instructed of her mother,
said, Give me John Baptist's head in a
charger.
Bible: Matthew
14:6—8

22 And in the fourth watch of the night Jesus went
unto them, walking on the sea.
And when the disciples saw him walking on
the sea, they were troubled, saying, It is a
spirit; and they cried out for fear.
But straightway Jesus spake unto them, saying, Be of good cheer; it is I; be not afraid.
Bible: Matthew
14:25—27

23 And I say also unto thee, That thou art Peter,
and upon this rock I will build my church;
and the gates of hell shall not prevail against it.
And I will give unto thee the keys of the kingdom of heaven: and whatsoever thou shalt
bind on earth shall be bound in heaven: and
whatsoever thou shalt loose on earth shall
be loosed in heaven.
Bible: Matthew
16:18—19

24 Then said Jesus unto his disciples, If any man
will come after me, let him deny himself, and
take up his cross, and follow me.
Bible: Matthew
16:24

25 And a very great multitude spread their garments in the way; others cut down branches
from the trees, and strawed them in the way.
And the multitudes that went before, and that
followed, cried, saying, Hosanna to the Son
of David: Blessed is he that cometh in the
name of the Lord; Hosanna in the highest.
Bible: Matthew
21:8—9

26 And he answered and said, He that dippeth his
hand with me in the dish, the same shall betray me.
The Son of man goeth as it is written of him
but woe unto that man by whom the Son of
man is betrayed! it had been good for that
man if he had not been born.
Then Judas, which betrayed him, answered
and said, Master, is it I? He said unto him,
Thou hast said.
Bible: Matthew
26:23—25

27 And as they were eating, Jesus took bread, and
blessed it, and brake it, and gave it to the disciples, and said, Take, eat; this is my body.
And he took the cup, and gave thanks, and
gave it to them, saying, Drink ye all of it;
For this is my blood of the new testament,
which is shed for many for the remission of
sins.
Bible: Matthew
26:26—28

28 Jesus said unto him, Verily I say unto thee,
That this night, before the cock crow, thou shal
deny me thrice.
Peter said unto him, Though I should die with
thee, yet will I not deny thee. Likewise also
said all the disciples.
Bible: Matthew
26:34—35

29 And forthwith he came to Jesus, and said, Hail
master; and kissed him.
And Jesus said unto him, Friend, wherefore
art thou come? Then came they, and laid
hands on Jesus, and took him.
Bible: Matthew
26:49—50

30 Then cried they all again, saying, Not this man
but Barabbas. Now Barabbas was a robber.
Bible: John
18:40

31 Then came Jesus forth, wearing the crown of
thorns, and the purple robe. And Pilate saith
unto them, Behold the man!
Bible: John
19:5

32 Pilate answered, What I have written I have
written.
Bible: John
19:22

33 When Pilate saw that he could prevail nothing
but that rather a tumult was made, he took
water, and washed his hands before the multitude, saying, I am innocent of the blood of
this just person: see ye to it.
Then answered all the people, and said, His
blood be on us, and on our children.
Bible: Matthew
27:24—25

34 And when they were come to the place, which is called Calvary, there they crucified him, and the malefactors, one on the right hand, and the other on the left.
Bible: Luke
23:33

35 Then said Jesus, Father, forgive them; for they know not what they do. And they parted his raiment, and cast lots.
Bible: Luke
23:34

36 When Jesus therefore saw his mother, and the disciple standing by, whom he loved, he saith unto his mother, Woman, behold thy son! Then saith he to the disciple, Behold thy mother! And from that hour that disciple took her unto his own home.
Bible: John
19:26−27

37 And about the ninth hour Jesus cried.with a loud voice, saying, Eli, Eli, lama sabachthani? that is to say, My God, my God, why hast thou forsaken me?
Bible: Matthew
27:46

38 When Jesus therefore had received the vinegar, he said, It is finished: and he bowed his head, and gave up the ghost.
Bible: John
19:30

39 Jesus, when he had cried again with a loud voice, yielded up the ghost.
And, behold, the veil of the temple was rent in twain from the top to the bottom; and the earth did quake, and the rocks rent;
And the graves were opened; and many bodies of the saints which slept arose.
Bible: Matthew
27:50−52

40 And when Jesus had cried with a loud voice, he said, Father, into thy hands I commend my spirit: and having said thus, he gave up the ghost.
Bible: Luke
23:46

41 *Consummatum est.*
It is finished.
Bible: John
Vulgate 19:30

42 Then saith he to Thomas, Reach hither thy finger, and behold my hands; and reach hither thy hand, and thrust it into my side: and be not faithless, but believing.
And Thomas answered and said unto him, My Lord and my God.
Bible: John
20:27−28

43 And when he had spoken these things, while they beheld, he was taken up; and a cloud received him out of their sight.
Bible: Acts
1:9

44 And when the day of Pentecost was fully come, they were all with one accord in one place.
And suddenly there came a sound from heaven as of a rushing mighty wind, and it filled all the house where they were sitting.
And there appeared unto them cloven tongues like as of fire, and it sat upon each of them.
And they were all filled with the Holy Ghost, and began to speak with other tongues, as the Spirit gave them utterance.
Bible: Acts
2:1−4

45 And as he journeyed, he came near Damascus: and suddenly there shined round about him a light from heaven:
And he fell to the earth, and heard a voice saying unto him, Saul, Saul, why persecutest thou me?
And he said, Who art thou, Lord? And the Lord said, I am Jesus whom thou persecutest: it is hard for thee to kick against the pricks.
Bible: Acts
9:3−5

46 But Peter took him up, saying, Stand up; I myself also am a man.
Bible: Acts
10:26

47 (For all the Athenians and strangers which were there spent their time in nothing else, but either to tell, or to hear some new thing.)
Then Paul stood in the midst of Mars' hill, and said, Ye men of Athens, I perceive that in all things ye are too superstitious.
For as I passed by, and beheld your devotions, I found an altar with this inscription, TO THE UNKNOWN GOD. Whom therefore ye ignorantly worship, him declare I unto you.
God that made the world and all things therein, seeing that he is Lord of heaven and earth, dwelleth not in temples made with hands.
Bible: Acts
17:21−24

48 And when they heard these sayings, they were full of wrath, and cried out, saying, Great is Diana of the Ephesians.
Bible: Acts
19:28

49 Then Festus, when he had conferred with the council, answered, Hast thou appealed unto Caesar? Unto Caesar shalt thou go.
Bible: Acts
25:12

50 Honour all men. Love the brotherhood. Fear God. Honour the king.
Bible: I Peter
2:17

51 And almost all things are by the law purged with blood; and without shedding of blood is no remission.
Bible: Hebrews
9:22

Attitudes

Daily Life

52 Drink no longer water, but use a little wine for thy stomach's sake and thine often infirmities.
Bible: I Timothy
5:23

Death

53 Behold, I shew you a mystery; We shall not all sleep, but we shall all be changed,
In a moment, in the twinkling of an eye, at the last trump: for the trumpet shall sound, and the dead shall be raised incorruptible, and we shall be changed.
For this corruptible must put on incorruption, and this mortal must put on immortality.
So when this corruptible shall have put on incorruption, and this mortal shall have put on immortality, then shall be brought to pass the saying that is written, Death is swallowed up in victory.
O death, where is thy sting? O grave, where is thy victory?
Bible: I Corinthians
15:51–55

54 And I looked, and behold a pale horse: and his name that sat on him was Death, and Hell followed with him. And power was given unto them over the fourth part of the earth, to kill with sword, and with hunger, and with death, and with the beasts of the earth.
Bible: Revelations
6:8

55 And I saw a great white throne, and him that sat on it, from whose face the earth and the heaven fled away; and there was found no place for them.
And I saw the dead, small and great, stand before God; and the books were opened: and another book was opened, which is the book of life: and the dead were judged out of those things which were written in the books, according to their works.
And the sea gave up the dead which were in it; and death and hell delivered up the dead which were in them: and they were judged every man according to their works.
Bible: Revelations
20:11–13

Education, Knowledge, and Learning

56 Now as touching things offered unto idols, we know that we all have knowledge. Knowledge puffeth up, but charity edifieth.
Bible: I Corinthians
8:1

Human Nature

57 Judge not, that ye be not judged.
Bible: Matthew
7:1

58 Neither do men put new wine into old bottles: else the bottles break, and the wine runneth out, and the bottles perish: but they put new wine into new bottles, and both are preserved.
Bible: Matthew
9:17

59 Watch and pray, that ye enter not into temptation: the spirit indeed is willing, but the flesh is weak.
Bible: Matthew
26:41

60 Greater love hath no man than this, that a man lay down his life for his friends.
Bible: John
15:13

61 For ye suffer fools gladly, seeing ye yourselves are wise.
Bible: II Corinthians
11:19

62 Beware lest any man spoil you through philosophy and vain deceit, after the tradition of men, after the rudiments of the world, and not after Christ.
Bible: Colossians
2:8

63 If we say that we have no sin, we deceive ourselves, and the truth is not in us.
If we confess our sins, he is faithful and just to forgive us our sins, and to cleanse us from all unrighteousness.
Bible: I John
1:8–9

64 Grudge not one against another, brethren, lest ye be condemned: behold, the judge standeth before the door.
Bible: James
5:9

Life

65 But many that are first shall be last; and the last shall be first.
Bible: Matthew
19:30

66 What? know ye not that your body is the temple of the Holy Ghost which is in you, which ye have of God, and ye are not your own?
Bible: I Corinthians
6:19

67 And they that use this world, as not abusing it: for the fashion of this world passeth away.
Bible: I Corinthians
7:31

68 For the earth is the Lord's, and the fulness thereof.
Bible: I Corinthians
10:26

69 For we walk by faith, not by sight.
Bible: II Corinthians
5:7

70 Be not deceived: God is not mocked: for whatsoever a man soweth, that shall he also reap.
For he that soweth to his flesh shall of the
flesh reap corruption; but he that soweth to
the Spirit shall of the Spirit reap life
everlasting.
And let us not be weary in well doing: for in
due season we shall reap, if we faint not.
Bible: Galatians
6:7−9

71 For we brought nothing into this world, and it is
certain we carry nothing out.
Bible: I Timothy
6:7

Love and Sex

72 Beloved, let us love one another: for love is of
God; and every one that loveth is born of God,
and knoweth God.
He that loveth not knoweth not God; for God
is love.
Bible: I John
4:7−8

Marriage and the Family

73 Wherefore they are no more twain, but one
flesh. What therefore God hath joined together,
let not man put asunder.
Bible: Matthew
19:6

74 But if they cannot contain, let them marry: for it
is better to marry than to burn.
Bible: I Corinthians
7:9

75 Children, obey your parents in the Lord: for this
is right.
Bible: Ephesians
6:1

Men and Women

76 A woman when she is in travail hath sorrow,
because her hour is come: but as soon as she
is delivered of the child, she remembereth no
more the anguish, for joy that a man is born
into the world.
Bible: John
16:21

77 Even as Sara obeyed Abraham, calling him lord:
whose daughters ye are, as long as ye do
well, and are not afraid with any amazement.
Likewise, ye husbands, dwell with them according to knowledge, giving honour unto the
wife, as unto the weaker vessel, and as being heirs together of the grace of life; that
your prayers be not hindered.
Bible: I Peter
3:6−7

Morality, Vices, and Virtues

78 Then was Jesus led up of the Spirit into the wilderness to be tempted of the devil.
And when he had fasted forty days and forty
nights, he was afterward an hungred.
And when the tempter came to him, he said, If
thou be the Son of God, command that these
stones be made bread.
But he answered and said, It is written, Man
shall not live by bread alone, but by every
word that proceedeth out of the mouth of
God.
Bible: Matthew
4:1−4

79 Blessed are the poor in spirit: for theirs is the
kingdom of heaven.
Blessed are they that mourn: for they shall be
comforted.
Blessed are the meek: for they shall inherit
the earth.
Blessed are they which do hunger and thirst
after righteousness: for they shall be filled.
Blessed are the merciful: for they shall obtain
mercy.
Blessed are the pure in heart: for they shall
see God.
Blessed are the peacemakers: for they shall
be called the children of God.
Blessed are they which are persecuted for
righteousness' sake: for theirs is the kingdom
of heaven.
Bible: Matthew
5:3−10

80 Blessed are the meek: for they shall inherit the
earth.
Bible: Matthew
5:5

81 Ye are the salt of the earth: but if the salt have
lost his savour, wherewith shall it be salted? it
is thenceforth good for nothing, but to be
cast out, and to be trodden under foot of men.
Ye are the light of the world. A city that is set
on an hill cannot be hid.
Neither do men light a candle, and put it
under a bushel, but on a candlestick; and it
giveth light unto all that are in the house.
Let your light so shine before men, that they
may see your good works, and glorify your
Father which is in heaven.
Bible: Matthew
5:13−16

82 And if thy right eye offend thee, pluck it out,
and cast it from thee: for it is profitable for thee
that one of thy members should perish, and
not that thy whole body should be cast into
hell.
Bible: Matthew
5:29

83 But I say unto you, That ye resist not evil: but
whosoever shall smite thee on thy right
cheek, turn to him the other also.
And if any man will sue thee at the law, and
take away thy coat, let him have thy cloke
also.

And whosoever shall compel thee to go a mile, go with him twain.
Bible: Matthew
5:39—41

84   But I say unto you, Love your enemies, bless them that curse you, do good to them that hate you, and pray for them which despitefully use you, and persecute you;
That ye may be the children of your Father which is in heaven: for he maketh his sun to rise on the evil and on the good, and sendeth rain on the just and on the unjust.
For if ye love them which love you, what reward have ye? do not even the publicans the same?
Bible: Matthew
5:44—46

85   Lay not up for yourselves treasures upon earth, where moth and rust doth corrupt, and where thieves break through and steal:
But lay up for yourselves treasures in heaven, where neither moth nor rust doth corrupt, and where thieves do not break through nor steal:
For where your treasure is, there will your heart be also.
Bible: Matthew
6:19—21

86   Behold the fowls of the air: for they sow not, neither do they reap, nor gather into barns; yet your heavenly Father feedeth them. Are ye not much better than they?
Which of you by taking thought can add one cubit unto his stature?
And why take ye thought for raiment? Consider the lilies of the field, how they grow; they toil not, neither do they spin:
And yet I say unto you, That even Solomon in all his glory was not arrayed like one of these.
Wherefore, if God so clothe the grass of the field, which today is, and tomorrow is cast into the oven, shall he not much more clothe you, O ye of little faith?
Therefore take no thought, saying, What shall we eat? or, What shall we drink? or, Wherewithal shall we be clothed?
Bible: Matthew
6:26—31

87   But seek ye first the kingdom of God, and his righteousness; and all these things shall be added unto you.
Take therefore no thought for the morrow: for the morrow shall take thought for the things of itself. Sufficient unto the day is the evil thereof.
Bible: Matthew
6:33—34

88   And why beholdest thou the mote that is in thy brother's eye, but considerest not the beam that is in thine own eye?
Bible: Matthew
7:3

89   Give not that which is holy unto the dogs, neither cast ye your pearls before swine, lest

they trample them under their feet, and turn again and rend you.
Bible: Matthew
7:6

90   Then came Peter to him, and said, Lord, how oft shall my brother sin against me, and I forgive him? till seven times?
Jesus saith unto him, I say not unto thee, Until seven times: but, Until seventy times seven.
Bible: Matthew
18:21—22

91   Then said Jesus unto his disciples, Verily I say unto you, That a rich man shall hardly enter into the kingdom of heaven.
And again I say unto you, It is easier for a camel to go through the eye of a needle, than for a rich man to enter into the kingdom of God.
Bible: Matthew
19:23—24

92   Woe unto you, scribes and Pharisees, hypocrites! for ye are like unto whited sepulchres, which indeed appear beautiful outward, but are within full of dead men's bones, and of all uncleanness.
Bible: Matthew
23:27

93   For what shall it profit a man, if he shall gain the whole world, and lose his own soul? Or what shall a man give in exchange for his soul?
Bible: Mark
8:36—37

94   So when they continued asking him, he lifted up himself, and said unto them, He that is without sin among you, let him first cast a stone at her.
Bible: John
8:7

95   Though I speak with the tongues of men and of angels, and have not charity, I am become as sounding brass, or a tinkling cymbal.
And though I have the gift of prophecy, and understand all mysteries, and all knowledge; and though I have all faith, so that I could remove mountains, and have not charity, I am nothing.
And though I bestow all my goods to feed the poor, and though I give my body to be burned, and have not charity, it profiteth me nothing.
Charity suffereth long, and is kind; charity envieth not; charity vaunteth not itself, is not puffed up,
Doth not behave itself unseemly, seeketh not her own, is not easily provoked, thinketh no evil;
Rejoiceth not in iniquity, but rejoiceth in the truth;
Beareth all things, believeth all things, hopeth all things, endureth all things.
Charity never faileth: but whether there be prophecies, they shall fail; whether there be tongues, they shall cease; whether there be knowledge, it shall vanish away.
For we know in part, and we prophesy in part.

But when that which is perfect is come, then that which is in part shall be done away.

When I was a child, I spake as a child, I understood as a child, I thought as a child: but when I became a man, I put away childish things.

For now we see through a glass, darkly; but then face to face: now I know in part; but then shall I know even as also I am known.

And now abideth faith, hope, charity, these three; but the greatest of these is charity.

Bible: I Corinthians
13:1—13

96   Wherefore putting away lying, speak every man truth with his neighbour: for we are members one of another.

Be ye angry, and sin not: let not the sun go down upon your wrath:

Neither give place to the devil.

Let him that stole steal no more: but rather let him labour, working with his hands the thing which is good, that he may have to give to him that needeth.

Bible: Ephesians
4:25—28

97   For the love of money is the root of all evil: which while some coveted after, they have erred from the faith, and pierced themselves through with many sorrows.

Bible: I Timothy
6:10

98   Let brotherly love continue.

Be not forgetful to entertain strangers: for thereby some have entertained angels unawares.

Bible: Hebrews
13:1—2

99   Submit yourselves therefore to God. Resist the devil, and he will flee from you.

Draw nigh to God, and he will draw nigh to you. Cleanse your hands, ye sinners; and purify your hearts, ye double minded.

Bible: James
4:7—8

00   And the woman was arrayed in purple and scarlet colour, and decked with gold and precious stones and pearls, having a golden cup in her hand full of abominations and filthiness of her fornication:

And upon her forehead was a name written, MYSTERY, BABYLON THE GREAT, THE MOTHER OF HARLOTS AND ABOMINATIONS OF THE EARTH.

And I saw the woman drunken with the blood of the saints, and with the blood of the martyrs of Jesus: and when I saw her, I wondered with great admiration.

Bible: Revelations
17:4—6

Religion

01   For I say unto you, That except your righteousness shall exceed the righteousness of the

scribes and Pharisees, ye shall in no case enter into the kingdom of heaven.

Bible: Matthew
5:20

102   But when ye pray, use not vain repetitions, as the heathen do: for they think that they shall be heard for their much speaking.

Be not ye therefore like unto them: for your Father knoweth what things ye have need of, before ye ask him.

After this manner therefore pray ye: Our Father which art in heaven, Hallowed be thy name.

Thy kingdom come. Thy will be done in earth, as it is in heaven.

Give us this day our daily bread.

And forgive us our debts, as we forgive our debtors.

And lead us not into temptation, but deliver us from evil: For thine is the kingdom, and the power, and the glory, for ever. Amen.

Bible: Matthew
6:7—13

103   Jesus said unto him, Thou shalt love the Lord thy God with all thy heart, and with all thy soul, and with all thy mind.

This is the first and great commandment.

And the second is like unto it, Thou shalt love thy neighbour as thyself.

On these two commandments hang all the law and the prophets.

Bible: Matthew
22:37—40

104   Verily I say unto you, Except ye be converted, and become as little children, ye shall not enter into the kingdom of heaven.

Bible: Matthew
18:3

105   Heaven and earth shall pass away, but my words shall not pass away.

Bible: Matthew
24:35

106   He hath shewed strength with his arm; he hath scattered the proud in the imagination of their hearts.

He hath put down the mighty from their seats, and exalted them of low degree.

He hath filled the hungry with good things; and the rich he hath sent empty away.

Bible: Luke
1:51—53

107   For God so loved the world, that he gave his only begotten Son, that whosoever believeth in him should not perish, but have everlasting life.

Bible: John
3:16

108   And this is the condemnation, that light is come into the world, and men loved darkness rather than light, because their deeds were evil.

Bible: John
3:19

109   And Jesus said unto them, I am the bread of life: he that cometh to me shall never hunger;

and he that believeth on me shall never thirst.
Bible: John
6:35

110 Then spake Jesus again unto them, saying, I am the light of the world: he that followeth me shall not walk in darkness, but shall have the light of life.
Bible: John
8:12

111 I am the door: by me if any man enter in, he shall be saved, and shall go in and out, and find pasture.
Bible: John
10:9

112 I am the good shepherd: the good shepherd giveth his life for the sheep.
Bible: John
10:11

113 Jesus said unto her, I am the resurrection, and the life: he that believeth in me, though he were dead, yet shall he live.
Bible: John
11:25

114 In my Father's house are many mansions: if it were not so, I would have told you. I go to prepare a place for you.
Bible: John
14:2

115 Jesus saith unto him, I am the way, the truth, and the life: no man cometh unto the Father, but by me.
Bible: John
14:6

116 And said unto them, It is written, My house shall be called the house of prayer; but ye have made it a den of thieves.
Bible: Matthew
21:13

117 And he saith unto them, Whose is this image and superscription?
They say unto him, Caesar's. Then saith he unto them, Render therefore unto Caesar the things which are Caesar's; and unto God the things that are God's.
Bible: Matthew
22:20—21

118 For the kingdom of God is not in word, but in power.
Bible: I Corinthians
4:20

119 Now faith is the substance of things hoped for, the evidence of things not seen.
Bible: Hebrews
11:1

120 Behold, he cometh with clouds; and every eye shall see him, and they also which pierced him: and all kindreds of the earth shall wail because of him. Even so, Amen.
I am Alpha and Omega, the beginning and the ending, saith the Lord, which is, and which was, and which is to come, the Almighty.
I John, who also am your brother, and com-

panion in tribulation, and in the kingdom and patience of Jesus Christ, was in the isle that is called Patmos, for the word of God, and for the testimony of Jesus Christ.
Bible: Revelations
1:7—9

121 And I saw in the right hand of him that sat on the throne a book written within and on the backside, sealed with seven seals.
And I saw a strong angel proclaiming with a loud voice, Who is worthy to open the book, and to loose the seals thereof?
Bible: Revelations
5:1—2

122 And I beheld, and, lo, in the midst of the throne and of the four beasts, and in the midst of the elders, stood a Lamb as it had been slain, having seven horns and seven eyes, which are the seven Spirits of God sent forth into all the earth.
Bible: Revelations
5:6

123 And he hath on his vesture and on his thigh a name written, KING OF KINGS, AND LORD OF LORDS.
Bible: Revelations
19:16

124 And I saw a new heaven and a new earth: for the first heaven and the first earth were passed away; and there was no more sea.
And I John saw the holy city, new Jerusalem coming down from God out of heaven, prepared as a bride adorned for her husband.
And I heard a great voice out of heaven saying, Behold, the tabernacle of God is with men, and he will dwell with them, and they shall be his people, and God himself shall be with them, and be their God.
And God shall wipe away all tears from their eyes; and there shall be no more death, neither sorrow, nor crying, neither shall there be any more pain: for the former things are passed away.
And he that sat upon the throne said, Behold I make all things new. And he said unto me, Write: for these words are true and faithful.
Bible: Revelations
21:1—5

Work and Occupations

125 Woe unto you, lawyers! for ye have taken away the key of knowledge: ye entered not in yourselves, and them that were entering in ye hindered.
Bible: Luke
11:52

126 For even when we were with you, this we commanded you, that if any would not work, neither should he eat.
Bible: II Thessalonians
3:10

127 This is a true saying, If a man desire the office of a bishop, he desireth a good work.
A bishop then must be blameless, the hus-

band of one wife, vigilant, sober, of good behaviour, given to hospitality, apt to teach;
Not given to wine, no striker, not greedy of
filthy lucre; but patient, not a brawler, not
covetous.
Bible: I Timothy
3:1–3

Sayings of the Time

128 *Quo vadis?*
Whither goest thou?
Bible: John
Vulgate 16:5

129 Ask, and it shall be given you; seek, and ye
shall find; knock, and it shall be opened unto
you:
For every one that asketh receiveth; and he
that seeketh findeth; and to him that knocketh
it shall be opened.
Bible: Matthew
7:7–8

130 Enter ye in at the strait gate: for wide is the
gate, and broad is the way, that leadeth to destruction, and many there be which go in
thereat:
Because strait is the gate, and narrow is the
way, which leadeth unto life, and few there
be that find it.
Bible: Matthew
7:13–14

131 He that hath ears to hear, let him hear.
Bible: Matthew
11:15

132 And immediately Jesus stretched forth his
hand, and caught him, and said unto him, O
thou of little faith, wherefore didst thou doubt?
Bible: Matthew
14:31

133 Then said Jesus unto him, Put up again thy
sword into his place: for all they that take the
sword shall perish with the sword.
Bible: Matthew
26:52

134 And he asked him, What is thy name? And he
answered, saying. My name is Legion: for we
are many.
Bible: Mark
5:9

135 And that no man might buy or sell, save he that
had the mark, or the name of the beast, or the
number of his name.
Here is wisdom. Let him that hath understanding count the number of the beast: for it
is the number of a man; and his number is
Six hundred threescore and six.
Bible: Revelations
13:17–18

With Hindsight

136 It was just one of those parties which got out of
hand.
Lenny Bruce (1925–66) US comedian.
Referring to the Crucifixion
The Guardian, 10 May 1979

4

The Roman World (50 BC–399 AD)

Julius Caesar completed his conquest of Gaul in 50 BC; a year later, refusing to resign his command, he initiated the Roman Civil War. The conflicts of the following years ended with the decisive victory of Caesar's great-nephew Augustus over Mark Antony at the battle of Actium (31 BC). Augustus nominally restored the republic, but, by ensuring that he held enough key positions for his authority to be unquestioned, he came to be regarded as the first emperor of Rome.

This empire – within roughly the boundaries Augustus had established – endured for 400 years. During its evolution the image of the empire changed: from a city-state on the Tiber that had subjugated the peoples of the Mediterranean, it became a state that encompassed the known world. Distinctions between Roman citizens and subject peoples were removed, so that by 330 AD, the capital itself was able to move from Rome to Constantinople. The office of emperor itself changed over the years. Initially, Augustus was merely the first citizen of the state; by the time of Diocletian (reigned 284–305), who restored the empire after anarchy in the 3rd century, the emperor had acquired not only monarchical but also divine attributes. With the adoption of Christianity – personally by Constantine (reigned 312–337) and as the sole religion of the empire by Theodosius (in 391) – the emperor became God's representative on earth. Rome bequeathed to the Middle Ages the concept of a universal empire coterminous with Christendom, ruled by an emperor whose power derived directly from God.

In fact, the empire had passed its prime by 200 AD. Wealth declined and pressure on its frontiers from tribal peoples increased. As it evolved into a world state, it was found to be too large to administer effectively. Diocletian and his successors experimented with dividing it into two parts, each with its own emperor. After the death of Theodosius (395), this division became permanent. The Eastern Empire continued, with varying degrees of success, for another thousand years; but the Western – poorer and with longer frontiers – soon succumbed to barbarian invasions.

Politics, Government, and World Events

1st century BC

1 The good of the people is the chief law.
Cicero (106–43 BC) Roman orator and statesman.
De Legibus, III

2 Necessity knows no law.
Publilius Syrus (1st century BC) Roman dramatist.
Attrib.

49 BC

3 *Alea jacta est.*
The die is cast.
Julius Caesar (100–44 BC) Roman general and statesman.
Said on crossing the River Rubicon, N Italy (49 BC), at the start of the civil war against Pompey
Attrib.

47 BC

4 *Veni, vidi, vici.*
I came, I saw, I conquered.
Julius Caesar
Referring to his campaign against Pharnaces, King of the Cimmerian Bosporus
The Twelve Caesars (Suetonius)

44 BC

5 Beware the ides of March.
William Shakespeare (1564–1616) English dramatist.
Julius Caesar, I:2 (1599)

6 *Et tu, Brute?*
You too, Brutus?
William Shakespeare
Said by Julius Caesar
Julius Caesar, III:1 (1599)

7 Friends, Romans, countrymen, lend me your ears
I come to bury Caesar, not to praise him.
The evil that men do lives after them;
The good is oft interred with their bones.
William Shakespeare
Said by Mark Antony
Julius Caesar, III:2 (1599)

8 His life was gentle; and the elements
So mix'd in him that Nature might stand up
And say to all the world 'This was a man!'
William Shakespeare
Referring to Brutus
Julius Caesar, V:5 (1599)

9 This was the noblest Roman of them all.
All the conspirators save only he
Did that they did in envy of great Caesar.
William Shakespeare
Julius Caesar, V:5 (1599)

30 BC

10 Dost thou not see my baby at my breast
That sucks the nurse asleep?
William Shakespeare
Said by Cleopatra, holding the asp to her breast
Antony and Cleopatra, V:2 (1607)

23 BC

11 Force, if unassisted by judgement, collapses through its own mass.
Horace (Quintus Horatius Flaccus; 65–8 BC) Roman poet.
Odes, III

12 What do the ravages of time not injure? Our parents' age (worse than our grandparents') has produced us, more worthless still, who will soon give rise to a yet more vicious generation.
Horace
Odes, III

13 *Dulce et decorum est pro patria mori.*
It is a sweet and seemly thing to die for one's country.
Horace
Odes, III

14 Undeservedly you will atone for the sins of your fathers.
Horace (Quintus Horatius Flaccus; 65–8 BC) Roman poet.
Odes, III

20 BC

15 *Nullius addictus iurare in verba magistri,*
Quo me cumque rapit tempestas, deferor hospes.
Not bound to swear allegiance to any master, wherever the wind takes me I travel as a visitor.
Horace
Nullius in verba is the motto of the Royal Society
Epistles, I

19 BC

16 Maybe one day we shall be glad to remember even these hardships.
Virgil (Publius Vergilius Maro; 70–19 BC) Roman poet.
Aeneid, Bk. I

2 BC

17 He sometimes forgets that he is Caesar, but I always remember that I am Caesar's daughter.
Julia (39 BC–AD 14) Daughter of Augustus.
Replying to suggestions that she should live in the simple style of her father, which contrasted with her own extravagance
Saturnalia (Macrobius)

1st century AD

18 *Ave Caesar, morituri te salutant.*
Hail Caesar; those who are about to die sa-
lute you.
Anonymous
Greeting to the Roman Emperor by gladiators

40 AD

19* **Would that the Roman people had but one
neck!**
Caligula (Gaius Caesar; 12–41 AD) Roman
emperor.
Life of Caligula (Suetonius), Ch. 30

79 AD

20 **Dear me, I believe I am becoming a god. An
emperor ought at least to die on his feet.**
Vespasian (9–79 AD) Roman emperor.
Lives of the Caesars (Suetonius)

84 AD

21 **They make a wilderness and call it peace.**
Tacitus (c. 55–c. 120 AD) Roman historian.
Agricola, 30

100 AD

22 **I will have this done, so I order it done; let my
will replace reasoned judgement.**
Juvenal (Decimus Junius Juvenalis; 60–130
AD) Roman satirist.
Satires, VI

23 *Quis custodiet ipsos
custodes?*
Who is to guard the guards themselves?
Juvenal
Satires, VI

24 **The people long eagerly for just two things –
bread and circuses.**
Juvenal
Satires, X

2nd century AD

25 **Remember that to change your mind and follow
him who sets you right is to be none the less
free than you were before.**
Marcus Aurelius (121–180 AD) Roman
emperor.
Meditations, Bk. VIII, Ch. 16

4th century AD

26 **Let him who desires peace, prepare for war.**
Vegetius (Flavius Vegetius Renatus; 4th cen-
tury AD) Roman writer.
Epitoma Rei Militaris, 3, 'Prologue'

Attitudes

Art, Literature, and Music

23 BC

27 **And if you include me among the lyric poets, I'll
hold my head so high it'll strike the stars.**
Horace (Quintus Horatius Flaccus; 65–8 BC)
Roman poet.
Odes, I

8 BC

28 **If you believe Cratinus from days of old, Mae-
cenas, (as you must know) no verse can give
pleasure for long, nor last, that is written by
drinkers of water.**
Horace
Epistles, I

29 **I'm aggrieved when sometimes even excellent
Homer nods.**
Horace
Ars Poetica

30 **Not gods, nor men, nor even booksellers have
put up with poets' being second-rate.**
Horace
Ars Poetica

31 **Many terms which have now dropped out of favour, will be revived, and those that are at present respectable will drop out, if usage so
choose, with whom resides the decision and
the judgement and the code of speech.**
Horace
Ars Poetica

32 **You will have written exceptionally well if, by
skilful arrangement of your words, you have
made an ordinary one seem original.**
Horace
Ars Poetica

33 **'Painters and poets alike have always had licence to dare anything.' We know that, and we
both claim and allow to others in their turn
this indulgence.**
Horace
Ars Poetica

2nd century AD

34 **Many suffer from the incurable disease of writ-
ing, and it becomes chronic in their sick
minds.**
Juvenal (Decimus Junius Juvenalis; 60–130
AD) Roman satirist.
Satires, VII

270 AD

35 **It is bad enough to be condemned to drag
around this image in which nature has impris-**

oned me. Why should I consent to the perpet-
uation of the image of this image?
Plotinus (205–270 AD) Egyptian-born Greek
philosopher.
Refusing to have his portrait painted
Attrib.

Daily Life

36 *In vino veritas.*
Truth comes out in wine.
Pliny the Elder (Gaius Plinius Secundus; 23–
79 AD) Roman scholar.
Natural History, XIV

Death

23 BC

37 Pale Death kicks his way equally into the cot-
tages of the poor and the castles of kings.
Horace (Quintus Horatius Flaccus; 65–8 BC)
Roman poet.
Odes, I

1st century AD

38 He's gone to join the majority.
Petronius Arbiter (1st century AD) Roman
satirist.
Referring to a dead man
Satyricon: Cena Trimalchionis, 42

Education, Knowledge, and Learning

161 BC

39 Nothing has yet been said that's not been said
before.
Terence (Publius Terentius Afer; c. 190–159
BC) Roman poet.
Eunuchus, Prologue

20 BC

40 And seek for truth in the groves of Academe.
Horace (Quintus Horatius Flaccus; 65–8 BC)
Roman poet.
Epistles, II

History

1st century BC

41 History is philosophy teaching by examples.
Dionysius of Halicarnassus (40–8 BC)
Greek historian.
Ars rhetorica, XI:2

150 AD

42 All things from eternity are of like forms and
come round in a circle.
Marcus Aurelius (121–180 AD) Roman
emperor.
Meditations, Bk. II, Ch. 14

Human Nature

2nd century BC

43 I am a man, I count nothing human foreign to
me.
Terence (Publius Terentius Afer; c. 190–159
BC) Roman poet.
Heauton Timorumenos

44 So many men, so many opinions.
Terence
Phormio

1st century BC

45 What is food to one man is bitter poison to
others.
Lucretius (Titus Lucretius Carus; c. 99–55 BC)
Roman philosopher.
On the Nature of the Universe, IV

43 BC

46 To like and dislike the same things, that is in-
deed true friendship.
Sallust (Gaius Sallustius Crispus; c. 86–c. 34
BC) Roman historian and politician.
Bellum Catilinae

37 BC

47 Everyone is dragged on by their favourite
pleasure.
Virgil (Publius Vergilius Maro; 70–19 BC) Roman poet.
Eclogue, Bk. II

20 BC

48 To marvel at nothing is just about the one and
only thing, Numicius, that can make a man
happy and keep him that way.
Horace (Quintus Horatius Flaccus; 65–8 BC)
Roman poet.
Epistles, I

49 You may drive out nature with a pitchfork, yet
she'll be constantly running back.
Horace
Epistles, I

13 BC

50 Not the owner of many possessions will you be
right to call happy: he more rightly deserves
the name of happy who knows how to use the
gods' gifts wisely and to put up with rough

poverty, and who fears dishonour more than
death.
Horace
Odes, IV

1st century AD
---

51 Love of fame is the last thing even learned men
can bear to be parted from.
Tacitus (c. 55–c. 120 AD) Roman historian.
Histories, IV, 6

---
98 AD
---

52 It is part of human nature to hate the man you
have hurt.
Tacitus (c. 55–c. 120 AD) Roman historian.
Agricola, 42

2nd century AD
---

53 If you hear that someone is speaking ill of you,
instead of trying to defend yourself you should
say: 'He obviously does not know me very
well, since there are so many other faults he
could have mentioned'.
Epictetus (c. 60–110 AD) Stoic philosopher.
Enchiridion

54 Whatever this is that I am, it is a little flesh and
breath, and the ruling part.
Marcus Aurelius (121–180 AD) Roman
emperor.
Meditations, Bk. II, Ch. 2

Humour

1st century AD
---

55 It's hard not to write satire.
Juvenal (Decimus Junius Juvenalis; 60–130
AD) Roman satirist.
Satires, I

Life

3rd century BC
---

56 Each man the architect of his own fate.
Appius Caecus (4th–3rd century BC) Roman
statesman.
De Civitate (Sallust), Bk. I

1st century BC
---

57 Constant dripping hollows out a stone.
Lucretius (Titus Lucretius Carus; c. 99–55 BC)
Roman philosopher.
On the Nature of the Universe, I.

58 *Inque brevi spatio mutantur saecla animantum*

Et quasi cursores vitai lampada tradunt.
The generations of living things pass in a
short time, and like runners hand on the torch
of life.
Lucretius
On the Nature of the Universe, II

---
29 BC
---

59 But meanwhile it is flying, irretrievable time is
flying.
Virgil (Publius Vergilius Maro; 70–19 BC) Roman poet.
Georgics, Bk. III

---
23 BC
---

60 Believe each day that has dawned is your last.
Horace (Quintus Horatius Flaccus; 65–8 BC)
Roman poet.
Epistles, I

61 We are just statistics, born to consume
resources.
Horace
Epistles, I

62 Drop the question what tomorrow may bring,
and count as profit every day that Fate allows
you.
Horace
Odes, I

63 *Carpe diem.*
Seize the day.
Horace
Odes, I

64 Life's short span forbids us to enter on far-
reaching hopes.
Horace
Odes, I

1st century AD
---

65 Woe to the vanquished.
Livy (Titus Livius; 59 BC–17 AD) Roman
historian.
History, V:48

---
77 AD
---

66 There is always something new out of Africa.
Pliny the Elder (Gaius Plinius Secundus; 23–
79 AD) Roman scholar.
Natural History, VIII

---
100 AD
---

67 *Orandum est ut sit mens sana in corpore sano*
Your prayer must be for a sound mind in a
sound body.
Juvenal (Decimus Junius Juvenalis; 60–130
AD) Roman satirist.
Satires, X

2nd century AD

68 And thou wilt give thyself relief, if thou doest every act of thy life as if it were the last.
Marcus Aurelius (121–180 AD) Roman emperor.
Meditations, Bk. II. Ch. 5

69 The universe is transformation; our life is what our thoughts make it.
Marcus Aurelius
Meditations, Bk. IV, Ch. 3

70 Everything that happens happens as it should, and if you observe carefully, you will find this to be so.
Marcus Aurelius
Meditations, Bk. IV, Ch. 10

71 Time is like a river made up of the events which happen, and its current is strong; no sooner does anything appear than it is swept away, and another comes in its place, and will be swept away too.
Marcus Aurelius
Meditations, Bk. IV, Ch. 43

72 Nothing happens to any man that he is not formed by nature to bear.
Marcus Aurelius
Meditations, Bk. V, Ch. 18

73 Whatever may happen to you was prepared for you from all eternity; and the implication of causes was from eternity spinning the thread of your being.
Marcus Aurelius
Meditations, Bk. X, Ch. 5

Love and Sex

37 BC

74 Love conquers all things: let us too give in to Love.
Virgil (Publius Vergilius Maro; 70–19 BC) Roman poet.
Eclogue, Bk. X

23 BC

75 My life with girls has ended, though till lately I was up to it and soldiered on not ingloriously; now on this wall will hang my weapons and my lyre, discharged from the war.
Horace (Quintus Horatius Flaccus; 65–8 BC) Roman poet.
Odes, III

Marriage and the Family

65 AD

76 I have a wife, I have sons: all of them hostages given to fate.
Lucan (Marcus Annaeus Lucanus; 39–65 AD) Roman poet.
Works, VII

Men and Women

19 BC

77 Woman is always fickle and changing.
Virgil (Publius Vergilius Maro; 70–19 BC) Roman poet.
Aeneid, Bk. IV

1st century AD

78 No one delights more in vengeance than a woman.
Juvenal (Decimus Junius Juvenalis; 60–130 AD) Roman satirist.
Satires, XIII

8 AD

79 Whether a pretty woman grants or withholds her favours, she always likes to be asked for them.
Ovid (Publius Ovidius Naso; 43 BC–17 AD) Roman poet.
Ars Amatoria

Morality, Vices, and Virtues

1st century BC

80 He gives twice who gives promptly.
Publilius Syrus (1st century BC) Roman dramatist.
Attrib.

19 BC

81 What do you not drive human hearts into, cursed craving for gold!
Virgil (Publius Vergilius Maro; 70–19 BC) Roman poet.
Aeneid, Bk. III

8 BC

82 To save a man's life against his will is the same as killing him.
Horace (Quintus Horatius Flaccus; 65–8 BC) Roman poet.
Ars Poetica

1st century AD

83 Live among men as if God beheld you; speak to God as if men were listening.
Seneca (c. 4 BC–65 AD) Roman author.
Epistles

3rd century AD

84 Give me chastity and continence, but not yet.
St Augustine of Hippo (354–430) Bishop of Hippo.
Confessions, Bk. VIII, Ch. 7

85 We make ourselves a ladder out of our vices if
    we trample the vices themselves underfoot.
    St Augustine of Hippo
    Sermons, Bk. III, 'De Ascensione'

Religion

23 BC

86 Do not try to find out — we're forbidden to
    know — what end the gods have in store for
    me, or for you.
    Horace (Quintus Horatius Flaccus; 65–8 BC)
    Roman poet.
    Odes, I

2nd century AD

87 I believe because it is impossible.
    Tertullian (c. 160–225 AD) Carthaginian father
    of the church.
    The usual misquotation of 'It is certain because it
    is impossible.'
    De Carne Christi, V

88 See how these Christians love one another.
    Tertullian
    Apologeticum, XXXIX

89 The blood of the martyrs is the seed of the
    Church.
    Tertullian
    Traditional misquotation: more accurately, 'Our
    numbers increase as often as you cut us down:
    the blood of Christians is the seed.'
    Apologeticum, L

5th century AD

90 There is no salvation outside the church.
    St Augustine of Hippo (354–430) Bishop
    of Hippo.
    De Bapt., IV

Wealth and Poverty

1st century BC

91 If possible honestly, if not, somehow, make
    money.
    Horace (Quintus Horatius Flaccus; 65–8 BC)
    Roman poet.
    Epistles, I

23 BC

92 Hard to train to accept being poor.
    Horace
    Odes, I

1st century AD

93 The misfortunes of poverty carry with them

nothing harder to bear than that it exposes me
to ridicule.
Juvenal (Decimus Junius Juvenalis; 60–130
AD) Roman satirist.
Satires, III

94 It's not easy for people to rise out of obscurit
    when they have to face straitened circum-
    stances at home.
    Juvenal
    Satires, III

Work and Occupations

1st century BC

95 There is nothing so absurd but some philoso-
    pher has said it.
    Cicero (106–43 BC) Roman orator and
    statesman.
    De Divinatione, II

Sayings of the Time

1st century BC

96 *Atque in perpetuum, frater, ave atque vale.*
    And for ever, brother, hail and farewell!
    Catullus (c. 84–c. 54 BC) Roman poet.
    Carmina, CI

With Hindsight

17th century

97 Had Cleopatra's nose been shorter, the whol
    face of the world would have changed.
    Blaise Pascal (1623–62) French philosophe
    and mathematician.
    Pensées, II

18th century

98 When the British warrior queen,
    Bleeding from the Roman rods,
    Sought, with an indignant mien,
    Counsel of her country's gods.
    William Cowper (1731–1800) British poet.
    Boadicea

99 The various modes of worship, which prevaile
    in the Roman world, were all considered by
    the people as equally true; by the philosopher
    as equally false; and by the magistrate, as
    equally useful. And thus toleration produced
    not only mutual indulgence, but even religious
    concord.
    Edward Gibbon (1737–94) British historian.
    Decline and Fall of the Roman Empire, Ch. 2

19th century

100 'How different, how very different from the home life of our own dear Queen!'
Anonymous
Remark by Victorian lady about the character of Cleopatra as performed by Sarah Bernhardt

101 A man of great common sense and good taste, − meaning thereby a man without originality or moral courage.
George Bernard Shaw (1856−1950) Irish dramatist and critic.
Referring to Julius Caesar
Caesar and Cleopatra, Notes

20th century

102 The Roman Conquest was, however, a *Good Thing*, since the Britons were only natives at the time.
W. C. Sellar (1898−1951) British humorous writer.
1066 And All That

5

The Earlier Middle Ages (400–1099)

The division of the Roman Empire in 395 effectively sounded the death knell for the Western Empire. Soon Germanic tribes were settling freely in imperial territory, and Rome itself was sacked in 410; in 476 the last emperor was deposed. However, the idea of the empire persisted. The Germans had not wanted to destroy it; rather, they had wished to settle in it and participate in its superior civilization. Christianity, the religion of the empire, was adopted by successive waves of invaders; and the universal, if conveniently remote, sovereignty of the Eastern Emperor in Constantinople was acknowledged. In 800, after Charlemagne had built up the greatest of the Germanic kingdoms, the pope crowned him as emperor – the beginning of what later became known as the Holy Roman Empire.

In a wider perspective, these successor states in the west were crude barbarian kingdoms. Always there was the threat not only of further invasions from outside, but also of political anarchy. Not until the 11th century were the beginnings of permanent stability achieved. Most ancient knowledge was lost and learning of any kind was scarce. Charlemagne's capital, Aachen, was a mere village when compared to Constantinople or the cities of the Arabic world, such as Baghdad. Indeed, after the great Moslem expansion of the 7th century, the Arabic Caliphate that stretched from Spain to Persia was more civilized and cultured than any Christian kingdom.

Politics, Government, and World Events

5th century

1 They came from three very powerful nations of the Germans; that is, from the *Saxones, Angli,* and *Iutae.*
St Bede (The Venerable Bede; c. 673–735 AD)
English churchman and historian.
Referring to the Anglo-Saxon invaders of Britain
Historia Ecclesiastica, Bk. I

533

2 Justice is the constant and perpetual wish to render to every one his due.
Justinian I (482–565 AD) Byzantine emperor.
Institutes, I

596

3* *Non Angli sed Angeli*
Not Angles, but angels.
Gregory I (540–604) Pope and saint.
On seeing child slaves in Rome and being told that they were Angles
Attrib.

7th century

4 ... of middle stature, neither tall nor short. His complexion was rosy white; his eyes black; his hair, thick, brilliant, and beautiful, fell to his shoulders. His profuse beard fell to his breast ... There was such sweetness in his visage that no one, once in his presence, could leave him. If I hungered, a single look at the Prophet's face dispelled the hunger. Before him all forgot their griefs and pains.
Ali (c. 600–661) Son-in-law of Mohammed and fourth caliph
Describing Mohammed (570–632)
Chronique (Abu Jafar Mohammed al-Tabari), Pt. III, Ch. 46

770

5* *Vox populi, vox dei.*
The voice of the people is the voice of God.
Alcuin (c. 735–804) Anglo-Saxon scholar.
Letter to Charlemagne

796

6* But above all things I strive to train them to be useful to the Holy Church of God and for the glory of your kingdom.
Alcuin
Referring to his school at Tours
Letter to Charlemagne, c. 796

799

7 If many people follow your enthusiastic en-

deavours, perhaps a new Athens might be created in the land of the Franks, or rather a much better one.
Alcuin
Letter to Charlemagne, Mar 799

800

8 I should never have entered the church on that day, though it was an important feast, could I have known the Pope's intention in advance.
Charlemagne (742–814) Holy Roman Emperor.
Referring to his coronation as emperor, 25 Dec 800
Attrib.

962

9 Nevertheless, this measure is to be common to all the nation, whether Englishmen, Danes or Britons, and every province of my dominion to the end that poor men and rich may possess what they rightly acquire and that a thief may not find a place to bring what he has stolen.
Edgar (944–75) King of England.
Law, 96263

1061

10 As these two, the kingdom and the priesthood, are brought together by divine mystery, so are their two heads, by the force of mutual loves; the King may be found in the Roman pontiff, and the Roman pontiff be found in the King.
St Peter Damian (1007–72) Bishop of Ostia.
Written just after the enthronement of Pope Alexander II (1061)
Disceptatio synodalis

1066

11 He will give him seven feet of English ground, or as much more as he may be taller than other men.
Harold II (1022–1066) King of England (1066).
Offer to Harald, King of Norway, who invaded England immediately before William the Conqueror (1066)
Heimskringla (Snorri Sturluson)

12 By the splendour of God I have taken possession of my realm; the earth of England is in my two hands.
William the Conqueror (1027–87) King of England.
Said after falling over when coming ashore at Pevensey with his army of invasion
Attrib.

1077

13 There for three days, before the castle gate, he laid aside all his royal gear; barefoot and wearing coarse wool, he stood pitifully, and did not stop begging for our apostolic help and compassion, until he had moved everyone

there, or who heard tell of this, to great rever-
ence and pity.
Gregory VII (c. 1020–85) Pope and saint.
Referring to the excommunicate Emperor Henry
IV's submission at Canossa, N Italy; he re-
ceived absolution on 28 Jan 1077
Letter

1087

14 He caused castles to be built
Which were a sore burden to the poor,
A hard man was the king
And took from his subjects many marks
In gold and many more hundreds of pounds in
silver.
These sums he took by weight from his peo-
ple,
Most unjustly and for little need.
He was sunk in greed
And utterly given up to avarice.
He set apart a vast deer preserve and im-
posed laws concerning it.
Whoever slew a hart or a hind
Was to be blinded.
He forbade the killing of boars
Even as the killing of harts.
For he loved the stags as dearly
As though he had been their father.
Hares, also, he decreed should go
unmolested.
The rich complained and the poor lamented,
But he was too relentless to care though all
might hate him,
And they were compelled, if they wanted
To keep their lives and their lands
And their goods and the favour of the king,
To submit themselves wholly to his will.
Alas! that any man should bear himself so
proudly
And deem himself exalted above all other
men!
May Almighty God shew mercy to his soul
And pardon him his sins.
Written on the death of William the Conqueror
The Peterborough Chronicle (part of *The An-
glo-Saxon Chronicle*)

1089

15 . . . belching from daily excess he came hiccup-
ping to the war.
William of Malmesbury (c. 1080–c. 1143)
English cleric and historian.
Referring to Philip I of France
Gesta Regum, Bk. II

1093 .

16 . . . no one before Anselm became a bishop or
abbot who did not first become the king's man
and from his hand receive investiture by the
gift of the pastoral staff.
Eadmer (c. 1055–c. 1124) English cleric and
historian.
Historia Novorum in Anglia

1097

17 The mounted knight is irresistable; he would
bore his way through the walls of Babylon.
Anna Comnena
Describing the French knights of the First Crusade, who passed through Constantinople in
1097
The Alexiad

1098

18 Since it is neither right nor natural for
Frenchmen to be subject to Englishmen, but
rather for Englishmen to be subject to
Frenchmen, the outcome of the event mocked
his vile expectation.
Suger, Abbot of St Denis (1081–1152)
French monk and diplomat.
Referring to William II of England's campaigns i
Normandy
Life of Louis VI

Attitudes

Daily Life

839

19 . . . the illustrious place, built by the skill of th
ancient Romans, called throughout the world
the great city of London.
Bishop Helmstan of Winchester
Cartularium Saxonicum

926

20 We declare . . . that there shall be one coinag
throughout the king's dominions and that
there shall be no minting except in a *port*. And
if a minter be convicted of striking bad
money, the hand with which he was guilty sha
be cut off and set up on the mint-smithy.
Athelstan (d. 939) King of Wessex and Merci
and later of England.
The Laws of Athelstan

1020

21 We give warning that a festival must be observed on Sunday and honoured with full inter
from noon on Saturday until dawn on Monday,
and that no person shall presume either to
practise trade or attend any meeting on this
Holy Day; and all men, poor and rich, shall g
to their church and offer supplication for their
sins and observe zealously every appointed
fast and honour readily those saints whose
feasts shall be commended by the priests.
Canute (995–1035) King of England, Denmar
and Norway.
Letter to the Archbishops and people of Englan

Education, Knowledge, and Learning

894

22 ...all the youth now in England of free men, who are rich enough to be able to devote themselves to it, be set to learn as long as they are not fit for any other occupation, until they are able to read English writing well.
Alfred the Great (849–901) King of Wessex
Cura Pastoralis, Preface

Human Nature

524

23* In every adversity of fortune, to have been happy is the most unhappy kind of misfortune.
Boethius (c. 480–524) Roman statesman, philosopher, and scholar.
The Consolation of Philosophy

Life

731

24 The present life of men on earth, O king, as compared with the whole length of time which is unknowable to us, seems to me to be like this: as if, when you are sitting at dinner with your chiefs and ministers in wintertime, ... one of the sparrows from outside flew very quickly through the hall; as if it came in one door and soon went out through another. In that actual time it is indoors it is not touched by the winter's storm; but yet the tiny period of calm is over in a moment, and having come out of the winter it soon returns to the winter and slips out of your sight. Man's life appears to be more or less like this; and of what may follow it, or what preceded it, we are absolutely ignorant.
St Bede (The Venerable Bede; c. 673–735 AD) English churchman and historian.
Ecclesiastical History of the English People, Bk. II, Ch. 13

Marriage and the Family

7th century

25 Marry those who are single among you, and such as are honest of your men-servants and your maid-servants: if they be poor, God will enrich them of his abundance; for God is bounteous and wise.
Koran
Ch. XXIV

26 Suffer the women whom ye divorce to dwell in some part of the houses wherein ye dwell; according to the room and conveniences of the habitations which ye possess; and make them

not uneasy, that ye may reduce them to straits.
Koran
Ch. LXV

Morality, Vices, and Virtues

7th century

27 The whore, and the whoremonger, shall ye scourge with a hundred stripes.
Koran
Ch. XXIV

Religion

5th century

28 *Roma locuta est; causa finita est.*
Rome has spoken; the case is concluded.
St Augustine of Hippo (354–430) Bishop of Hippo.
Sermons, Bk. I

29 *Da mihi castitatem et continentiam, sed noli modo.*
Give me chastity and continence, but not yet.
St Augustine of Hippo
Confessions

30 If this man is not faithful to his God, how can he be faithful to me, a mere man?
Theodoric (c. 445–526) King of the Ostrogoths.
Explaining why he had had a trusted minister, who had said he would adopt his master's religion, beheaded
Dictionnaire Encyclopédique (E. Guérard)

7th century

31 The month of Ramadan shall ye fast, in which the Koran was sent down from heaven, a direction unto men, and declarations of direction, and the distinction between good and evil.
Koran
Ch. II

11th century

32 Hail Mary, full of grace, the Lord is with thee: Blessed art thou among women, and blessed is the fruit of thy womb, Jesus.
Anonymous
Ave Maria, 11th century

1078

33 It is the custom of the Roman Church which I unworthily serve with the help of God, to tolerate some things, to turn a blind eye to some, following the spirit of discretion rather than the rigid letter of the law.
Gregory VII (c. 1020–85) Pope and saint.
Letter, 9 Mar 1078

Science, Medicine, and Technology

10th century

34 The sciences were transmitted into the Arabic language from different parts of the world; by it they were embellished and penetrated the hearts of men, while the beauties of the language flowed in their veins and arteries.
Al-Biruni (973–1048) Arabic scholar.
Kitab as-Saidana

With Hindsight

20th century

35 Unlike Christianity, which preached a peace that it never achieved, Islam unashamedly came with a sword.
Steven Runciman (1903–   ) British academic and diplomat.
A History of the Crusades, 'The First Crusade'

6

The Later Middle Ages (1100–1517)

Late in the 11th century, learning in western Europe began to revive; the clouds that caused the period known as the Dark Ages began to lift as the knowledge of the ancient world was rediscovered. This quickly flowered into the twelfth-century Renaissance. Aristotle's philosophy and science, when reconciled with Christianity, were held in great esteem; indeed, Aristotelian logic was seized upon as the essential tool with which to rationalize a thousand years of Christian canon law and theology. This 12th-century enthusiasm for knowledge did not last, however. As knowledge and correct doctrine were defined ever more clearly and closely, so previously acceptable beliefs came to be regarded as unacceptable and even, in some cases, heretical. There was, moreover, an influx of heretical ideas, such as those adopted by the Cathars, from outside western Europe. Such extremes of ideology made the Church nervous; its reaction was to set up the Inquisition (in 1231). Even St Thomas Aquinas, whose *Summa Theologica* was regarded as the high point of medieval scholastic theology, had some of his doctrines posthumously condemned. As the Church became more defensive, intellectual emphasis moved to secular learning. The Renaissance proper, which began in Italy in the 14th century, was a secular movement based on a reappraisal, uninfluenced by the theological preconceptions, of all forms of classical art and learning. Mankind's potential for positive achievement was emphasized. In painting, religious subjects were treated with an emphasis on human feelings. Renaissance architecture, with its domed structures and classical pediments, brought to Europe a revitalized form of the best building techniques of the ancient world.

Politics, Government, and World Events

12th century

1 Were the world all mine
From the sea to the Rhine
I'd give it all
If so be the Queen of England
Lay in may arms.
Anonymous
Referring to Eleanor of Aquitaine
Wandering Scholars (Helen Waddell); a free
translation of *Carmina Burana* (ed. Schmeller),
108a

1100

2 By intermarriage and by every means in his
power he bound the two peoples into a firm
union
Walter Map (c. 1140–c. 1209) Welsh cleric
and writer.
Referring to Henry I of England, and specifically
to his marriage (1100) to Matilda, a descendant of the Anglo-Saxon royal family
De Nugis Curialium, Pt. V, Ch. 5

3 Who killed Cock Robin?
I, said the Sparrow,
With my bow and arrow,
I killed Cock Robin.
Who saw him die?
I, said the Fly,
With my little eye,
I saw him die.
Thought to refer to William II, who was killed by
a stray arrow while hunting in the New Forest
Tommy Thumb's Pretty Song Book

1135

4* He who was strongest got most, and everyone
held on to what he had seized as if by right.
Referring to the anarchy of King Stephen's reign,
1135–1154
Chronicon Monasterii de Bello

5 In this king's time there was nothing but dis-
turbance and wickedness and robbery, for
forthwith the powerful men who were traitors
rose against him
Referring to the reign of Stephen, 1135–54
Anglo-Saxon Chronicle

1147

6* The Christian glories in the death of a pagan
because thereby Christ himself is glorified.
St Bernard (1090–1153) French monk and
theologian.
Richard the Lionheart (J. Gillingham), Ch. 9

7* Oh mighty soldier, O man of war, at last you
have a cause for which you can fight without
endangering your soul; a cause in which to win
is glorious and for which to die is but gain.
Are you a shrewd businessman, quick to see

the profits of this world? If you are, I can offer you a bargain which you cannot afford to
miss. Take the sign of the cross. At once you
will have an indulgence for all the sins
which you confess with a contrite heart. The
cross is cheap and if you wear it with
humility you will find that you have obtained the
Kingdom of Heaven.
St Bernard
Referring in particular to the second Crusade
Richard the Lionheart (J. Gillingham), Ch. 6

1157

8 Our kingdom and whatever anywhere is subject
to our rule we place at your disposal and commit to your power, that everything may be arranged at your nod, and that the will of your
empire may be carried out in all respects. Let
there be between us and our peoples an undivided unity of love and peace and safety of
commerce, in such a way that to you, who
are pre-eminent in dignity, be given the authority of command, and to us the will to obey
shall not be lacking.
Henry II (1133–89) King of England.
Letter to the Emperor Frederick Barbarossa,
1157

1160

9* Your lord the King of England, who lacks nothing, has men, horses, gold, silk, jewels, fruits,
game and everything else. We in France
have nothing but bread and wine and gaiety.
Louis VII (c. 1120–80) King of France.
By 'France' Louis meant the comparatively small
area around Paris that he ruled directly
Remark to Walter Map; cited in *Richard the
Lionheart* (J. Gillingham), Ch. 4

1162

10 . . . a patron of play-actors and a follower of
hounds to become a shepherd of souls.
Herbert of Bosham (fl. 1162–86) Chaplain
and biographer of Thomas Becket.
Referring to Becket
Vita Sancti Thomae

1170

11 Will no one rid me of this turbulent priest?
Henry II (1133–89) King of England.
Referring to Thomas Becket, Archbishop of Canterbury; four of Henry's household knights took
these words literally, hurried to Canterbury,
and killed Becket in the cathedral (Dec 1170)
Attrib.

12 I am ready to die for my Lord, that in my blood
the Church may obtain liberty and peace.
Thomas Becket (c. 1118–70) English
churchman.
One version of his last words
*Vita S. Thomae, Cantuariensis Archiepiscopi et
Martyris* (Edward Grim)

1173

13 This is how war is begun: such is my advice.
First destroy the land, deal after with the foe.
Philip, Count of Flanders
Advice to William, King of Scotland
*Chronique de la guerre entre les Anglois et les
Ecossois en 1173 et 1174* (Jordan Fantosme)

14 I order you to hold a free election, but forbid
you to elect anyone but Richard my clerk.
Henry II (1133–89) King of England.
Writ to the electors of the See of Winchester regarding the election of a new bishop; Richard
d'Ilchester was one of the king's trusted
servants
*Recueil des Historiens des Gaules et de la
France,* XIV

15 St. Thomas, guard for me my kingdom! To you I
declare myself guilty of that for which others
bear the blame.
Henry II
Said at the outbreak of the Great Rebellion,
1173–74; one of Henry's first actions was to
perform a public penance for Thomas Becket's
murder
*Chronique de la guerre entre les Anglois et les
Ecossais en 1173 et 1174* (Jordan Fantosme)

16* . . . now in Ireland, now in England, now in Nor-
mandy, he must fly rather than travel by horse
or ship.
Louis VII (c. 1120–80) King of France.
Referring to Henry II of England
Imagines Historiarum (Ralph de Diceto)

1181

17 . . . the rustics vie with each other in bringing
up their ignoble and degenerate offspring to
the liberal arts.
Walter Map (c. 1140–c. 1209) Welsh cleric
and writer.
Drawing a comparison with the aristocracy, who
were 'too poud or too lazy to put their children
to learning'
De Nugis Curialium, Pt. I, Ch. 10

1183

18 Rich, noble, lovable, eloquent, handsome, gallant, every way attractive, a little lower than
the angels – all these gifts he turned to the
wrong side.
Walter Map
Referring to Henry, 'The Young King', eldest son
of Henry II
De Nugis Curialium, Pt. I, Ch. 1

1189

19* I would sell London, if I could find a suitable
purchaser.
Richard I (1157–1199) King of England.
Comment while raising money for the third
Crusade.
Historia Rerum Anglicarum (William of New-
burgh), Bk. IV, Ch. 5

20* The four eaglets are my four sons who cease
not to persecute me even unto death. The
youngest of them, whom I now embrace with so
much affection, will sometime in the end insult me more grievously and more dangerously
than any of the others.
Henry II (1133–89) King of England.
Describing a painting of four eaglets preying on
their parent. 'The youngest' refers to the future
King John
De Principis Instructione (Gerald of Wales)

1190

21* The laity found him more than a king, the clergy
more than a pope, and both an intolerable
tyrant.
William of Newburgh (1136–c. 1198) English monk and historian.
Referring to William Longchamp, Justiciar and
Chancellor of England during Richard I's absence
on Crusade
Historia Rerum Anglicarum, Bk. IV, Ch. 14

1192

22 I have long since been aware that your king is a
man of the greatest honour and bravery, but
he is imprudent.
Saladin (1137–93) Sultan of Egypt and Syria.
Referring to Richard I
Remark to the Bishop of Salisbury, 1192

1193

23* My brother John is not the man to conquer a
country if there is anyone to offer even the
feeblest resistance.
Richard I (1157–99) King of England.
From Domesday Book to Magna Carta (A. L.
Poole)

1194

24 Think no more of it, John; you are only a child
who has had evil counsellors.
Richard I
Said at his reconciliation, at Lisieux in May 1294,
with his brother John, who had attempted to
overthrow him while he was held prisoner in
Germany (1193–94)
Histoire de Guillaume le Maréchal

1198

25 Just as the moon receives its light from the
sun, . . . so the royal power takes all its reputation and prestige from the pontifical power.
Innocent III (1160–1216) Pope.
Letter to recteurs of Tuscany, 1198

26 Thus we have defeated the king of France at
Gisors but it is not we who have done it, but
God and our right through us.
Richard I (1157–99) King of England.
Letter to the Bishop of Durham, 1198

27 *Dieu et mon droit.*

God and my right.
Richard I
Motto on the royal arms of Great Britain; originally used as a war-cry, Sept 1198

13th century

28 **So passes the glory of the world.**
Anonymous
Referring to the large number of ruined castles in England, Normandy, and Anjou, which had been demolished after the rebellion (1173–74) against Henry II
Histoire de Guillaume le Maréchal

29 **...hanged privily by night or in the luncheon hour.**
Anonymous
Referring to abuses of the procedure for trying clerics
From Domesday Book to Magna Carta (A. L. Poole)

1207

30 **Any service rendered to the temporal king to the prejudice of the eternal king is, without doubt, an act of treachery.**
Stephen Langton (c. 1150–1228) Archbishop of Canterbury.
Letter to the barons of England, 1207

1209

31 **I have two huge lions tearing at my flanks, the so-called Emperor Otto and John, King of England. Both try with all their might to upset the Kingdom of France. I cannot leave the country myself or do without my son here.**
Philip II (1165–1223) King of France.
Explaining, to Pope Innocent III, his refusal to crusade against the Albigensian heretics

1215

32 **This charter has been forced from the king. It constitutes an insult to the Holy See, a serious weakening of the royal power, a disgrace to the English nation, a danger to all Christendom, since this civil war obstructs the crusade.**
Innocent III (1160–1216) Pope.
Referring to Magna Carta
Papal Bull, 24 Aug 1215

1216

33 **A certain versifier, a false one, said, 'Just as England has been filthy with the defiler John, so now the filth of Hell is fouled by his foul presence'; but it is dangerous to write against a man who can easily do you wrong.**
Matthew Paris (fl. 1235–50) Chronicler.
Referring to King John of England (r. 1199–1216); this quotation is better known in the form used by J. R. Green in his *Short History of the English People* (1875): "Foul as it is, Hell itself is defiled by the fouler presence of King John."
Chronica Majora, 1216

1238

34 **They illuminate our whole country with the bright light of their preaching and teaching.**
Robert Grosseteste (c. 1175–1253) Bishop of Lincoln.
Referring to the Franciscans
Letter to Pope Gregory IX, 1238

1260

35* **Human law is law only by virtue of its accordance with right reason, and by this means it is clear that it flows from Eternal law. In so far as it deviates from right reason it is called an Unjust law; and in such a case, it is no law at all, but rather an assertion of violence.**
St Thomas Aquinas (1225–74) Italian theologian.
Summa Theologiae

1264

36 **So whether it is that the King, misled**
By flattering talk to giving his consent,
And truly ignorant of their designs
Unknowingly approves such wrongs as these
Whose only end can be destruction, and
The ruin of his land; or whether he,
With malice in his heart, and ill-intent,
Commits these shameful crimes by raising up
His royal state and power far beyond
The reach of all his country's laws, so that
His whim is satisfied by the abuse
Of royal privilege and strength; if thus
Or otherwise this land of ours is brought
To total rack and ruin, and at last
The kingdom is left destitute, it is
The duty of the great and noble men
To rescue it, to purge the land of all
Corruption and all false authority.
Roger de Berksted
Referring to Henry III
The Song of Lewes

1297

37 **By God, O King, I will neither go nor hang!**
Roger Bigod, Earl of Norfolk (1245–1306) Marshal of England.
Reply to Edward I's 'By God, Earl, you shall either go or hang!'; Edward had ordered Norfolk and other barons to invade France from Gascony
Hemingburgh's Chronicle, Bk. II

1298

38* **The whole city is arrayed in squares just like a chess-board, and disposed in a manner so**

perfect and masterly that it is impossible to
give a description that should do it justice.
Marco Polo (c. 1254–1324) Venetian traveller.
Referring to Kublai Khan's capital, Cambaluc
(later Peking)
The Book of Marco Polo

14th century

39   ...whenever kingship approaches tyranny it is
near its end, for by this it becomes ripe for
division, change of dynasty, or total destruction, especially in a temperate climate...
where men are habitually, morally and naturally
free.
Nicholas of Oresme (c. 1320–82) Chaplain
to Charles V of France.
De Moneta

1301

40   In this year King Edward of England made Lord
Edward, his son and heir, Prince of Wales and
Earl of Chester. When the Welsh heard this,
they were overjoyed, thinking him their lawful
master, as he was born in their lands.
Thomas of Walsingham (d. 1419) English
monk and chronicler.
Edward of Caernarfon, later Edward II, began the
tradition that male heirs to the English throne
were invested with these titles
Historia Anglicana

1327

41   The king is incompetent to govern in person.
Throughout his reign he has been controlled
and governed by others who have given him
evil counsel.
John de Stratford (d. 1348) Archbishop of
Canterbury.
Referring to Edward II
Historiae Anglicanae Scriptores (Twysden)

1337

42   ...the king of France, hardened in his malice,
would assent to no peace or treaty, but called
together his strong host to take into his hand
the duchy of Aquitaine, declaring against all
truth that it was forfeit to him.
Edward III (1312–77) King of England.
Proclamation on the outbreak of the Hundred
Years War
Foedera (ed. T. Rymer), Vol. IV

1344

43   *Honi soit qui mal y pense*
Evil be to him who evil thinks.
Edward III
Reputedly said on retrieving the Countess of Sal-
isbury's garter, which had fallen off
Attrib. in later tradition; associated with the foun-
dation of the Order of the Garter (1344)

1346

44   Let the boy win his spurs.
Edward III
Replying to a suggestion that he should send
reinforcements to his son, the Black Prince, du
ing the Battle of Crécy, 1346
Attrib.

1348

45   In scarcely any house did only one die, but a
together, man and wife with their children and
household, traversed the same road, the
road of death...I leave the parchment for th
work to be continued in case in the future any
human survivor should remain, or someone
of the race of Adam should be able to escap
this plague and continue what I have begun.
John of Clyn Irish friar.
Recording the effects of the Black Death in
Kilkenny
Annals of Ireland

1363

46   ...his lieges who from their hearts entirely
thank God who has given them such a lord an
governor, who has delivered them from servitude to other lands and from the charges
sustained by them in times past.
A tribute by the Commons to Edward III
Rotuli Parliamentorum, Vol. II

1376

47   It is neither fitting nor safe that all the keys
should hang from the belt of one woman.
Thomas Brinton (c. 1320–89) Bishop of
Rochester.
Criticizing the influence of Alice Perrers over th
ageing Edward III
Sermon, Westminister Abbey, 18 May 1376

1377

48   For, he said, albeit unworthy, he was a king's
son and one of the greatest lords in the kingdom after the king: and what had been so evil
spoken of him could rightly be called plain
treason...And if any man were so bold as t
charge him with treason or other disloyalty or
with anything prejudicial to the realm, he wa
ready to defend himself with his body as
though he were the poorest bachelor in the
land.
John of Gaunt (1340–99) Duke of Lancaste
Report of a speech to Richard II's first parliamer
Rotuli Parliamentorum, Vol. III

1381

49* When Adam delved and Eve span,
Who was then the gentleman?
John Ball (d. 1381) English priest.
Text of sermon

50   From the beginning all were created equal by

nature, slavery was introduced through the
injust oppression of worthless men, against the
will of God; for, if God had wanted to create
slaves, he would surely have decided at the
beginning of the world who was to be slave
and who master.
John Ball
Sermon, Blackheath, 1381

51   No man should be a serf, nor do homage or any
manner of service to any lord, but should give
fourpence rent for an acre of land, and that
no one should work for any man but as his own
will, and on terms of a regular covenant.
Wat Tyler (d. 1381) English rebel.
Anonimalle Chronicle

52   I believe that in the end the truth will conquer.
John Wycliffe (1329–84) English religious
reformer.
Said to John of Gaunt, Duke of Lancaster, 1381
Short History of the English People (J. R.
Green)

1399

53   My God! this is a wonderful land and a faithless
one; for she has exiled, slain, destroyed and
ruined so many Kings, so many rulers, so
many great men, and she is always diseased
and suffering from differences, quarrels and hatred between her people.
Richard II (1365–99) King of England.
Attrib. remark, Tower of London, 21 Sept 1399

54   I did not usurp the crown, but was duly elected.
Henry IV (1367–1413) King of England.
Reply when accused by Richard Frisby, a Fran-
ciscan on trial for plotting (1402) to overthrow
him
Eulogium Historiarum

55   For God's sake let us sit upon the ground
And tell sad stories of the death of kings:
How some have been depos'd, some slain in
war,
Some haunted by the ghosts they have de-
pos'd,
Some poison'd by their wives, some sleeping
kill'd,
All murder'd – for within the hollow crown
That rounds the mortal temples of a king
Keeps Death his court.
William Shakespeare (1564–1616) English
dramatist.
Said by Richard II
Richard II, III:2 (1597)

15th century

56   Baa, baa, black sheep,
Have you any wool?
Yes, sir, yes, sir,
Three bags full;
One for the master,
And one for the dame,
And one for the little boy
Who lives down the lane.
Possibly a reference to the perceived iniquities
of the medieval wool trade in England: the

king (the 'master') and a small group of wool
merchants (the 'dame') made large profits,
from which the rest of the kingdom (the 'little
boy') was excluded
Tommy Thumb's Pretty Song Book

57   A great ship which sailed for many a day in the
sea of prosperity is that plenteous realm, the
realm of England. The forecastle of this ship
is the clergy, prelates, religious, and priests;
the hindcastle is the barony, the king with
his nobles; the body of the ship is the commons, merchants, craftsmen and labourers.
From a sermon preached in the reign of Henry V
(1413–22)
Literature and Pulpit in Medieval England (G. R.
Owst)

1402

58   It was not, as our enemies say, our intention to
kill the king and his sons, but to make him the
duke of Lancaster, which is what he ought to
be.
Referring to Henry IV; said by one of the Franciscans condemned for plotting (1402) to overthrow him
Eulogium Historiarum

1403

59   The whole of the Welsh nation in these parts
are concerned in this rebellion.
John Fairfield Receiver of Brecon.
Referring to the rebellion of Owen Glendower
Letter to Henry IV

1407

60   You have gold and I want gold; where is it?
Henry IV (1367–1413) King of England.
Said to merchants at a Great Council (Apr–June
1407) when trying to borrow money to pay the
garrison at Calais, which had mutinied because of arrears in its wages
Attrib. in *Eulogium Historiarum*

1415

61   Once more unto the breach, dear friends, once
more;
Or close the wall up with our English dead.
William Shakespeare (1564–1616) English
dramatist.
Henry V exhorting his troops at the siege of
Harfleur
Henry V, III:1 (1600)

62   Fair stood the wind for France
When we our sails advance.
Michael Drayton (1563–1631) English poet.
Agincourt

1418

63   Everyone knows that I act in everything with
kindness and mercy, for I am forcing Rouen

into submission by starvation, not by fire, sword or bloodshed.
Henry V (1387–1422) King of England.
Remark to an envoy from Rouen, 1418

1429

64*   ...a disciple and limb of the fiend, called the Pucelle, that used false enchantments and sorcery.
John of Lancaster, Duke of Bedford (1389–1435) Brother of Henry V.
Referring to Joan of Arc
Proceeding and Ordinances of the Privy Council (ed. N. H. Nicolas), Vol. IV

1430

65*   It is much safer to obey than to rule.
Thomas à Kempis (Thomas Hemmerken; c. 1380–1471) German monk.
The Imitation of Christ, I

1431

66   If I said that God did not send me, I should condemn myself; truly God did send me.
St Joan of Arc (c. 1412–31) French patriotic leader.
Said at her trial

1433

67   Daily many warantis come to me of paiementz ... of much more than all youre revenuz wold come to, thowe they were not assigned afore ... the which warrantes yf I shuld paye hem, youre Household, chambre and warderope and youre werkes, shuld be unservid and unpaide and yf I paye hem not, I renne in grete indignation of my lordes and grete sclandre, noyse and maugre of all youre peple.
Lord Cromwell (c. 1394–1456) Treasurer of England.
Rotuli Parliamentorum, Vol. IV

1440s

68   Myn hert ys set and all myn hole entent,
To serve this flour in my most humble wyse
As faythfully as can be thought or ment,
Wythout feynyng or slouthe in my servyse;
For wytt the wele, yt ys a paradyse
To se this floure when yt begyn to sprede,
Wyth colours fressh ennewyd, white and rede.
Duke of Suffolk (1396–1450) English nobleman.
Poem dedicated to Margaret of Anjou, Queen of England
Secular Lyrics of XIVth and XVth Centuries (ed. R. H. Robbins)

1452

69   It would be better to see the royal turban of the Turks in the midst of the city than the Latin mitre.
Michael Ducas (?1400–?70) Byzantine historian.
Referring to Emperor Constantine XI's reunification of the Orthodox and Roman Churches (1452), in an attempt to save the Byzantine Empire from the Turks
Attrib.

1453

70   Of the two lights of Christendom, one has been extinguished.
Aeneas Silvius (1405–64) Bishop of Trieste.
Remark on hearing of the fall of Constantinople to the Turks (29 May 1453)

1460

71   I know of no one in the realm who would not more fitly to come to me than I to him.
Richard, Duke of York (1411–60) Father of Edward IV.
Reply when asked, in parliament, whether he wished to go and see the king; York formally claimed the throne six days later
Remark, 10 Oct 1460

1461

72   And in that journey was Owen Tudor taken and brought unto Haverfordwest, and he was beheaded at the market place, and his head set upon the highest grice of the market cross, and a mad woman combed his hair and washed away the blood of his face, and she got candles and set about him burning more than a hundred.
William Gregory (d. 1467) Chronicler.
Owen Tudor was the grandfather of Henry VII
Gregory's Chronicle

1468

73   Hence it comes about that there is scarcely a man learned in the laws to be found in the realm who is not noble or sprung of noble lineage.
Sir John Fortescue (c. 1394–c. 1476) Chief justice of the King's Bench.
The Governance of England

74   The greatest harm that cometh of a king's poverty is, that he shall by necessity be forced to find exquisite means of getting goods, as to put in default some of his subjects that be innocent, and upon the rich men more than the poor, because they may the better pay.
Sir John Fortescue
The Governance of England

75   The king's council was wont to be chosen of the great princes, and of the greatest lords of the land, both spiritual and temporal ... Wherethrough, when they came together they were so occupied with their own matters that

they attended but little, and other whiles noth-
ing, to the king's matters.
Sir John Fortescue
The Governance of England

1469

6* And much more am I sorrier for my good
knights' loss than for the loss of my fair queen;
for queens I might have enough, but such a
fellowship of good knights shall never be together in no company.
Thomas Malory (1400–71) English writer.
Morte d'Arthur, Bk. XX, Ch. 9

1478

77 This year, that is to mean ye 18 day of February, the Duke of Clarence and second brother
to the king, then being prisoner in ye Tower,
was secretly put to death and drowned in a barrel of malvesye within the said Tower.
Robert Fabyan (d. 1513) English chronicler.
This account is apocryphal and reflects popular
rumour
Chronicle

1482

78 I'll bell the cat.
Archibald Douglas (1449–1514) Scottish
nobleman.
Of his proposed capture of Robert Cochrane (executed 1482); the phrase 'bell the cat' was earlier used by Eustache Deschamps in his
Ballade: Le Chat et les souris

1483

79 He used towardes every men of highe and low
degree more than mete famylyarytie which
trade of life he never changed.
Polydore Vergil (c. 1470–c. 1555) Italian
historian.
Referring to Edward IV
Anglica Historia

80 Of hearte couragious, politique in counsaile in
adversitie nothynge abashed, in peace juste
and mercifull, in warre sharpe and fyerce, in
the fielde bolde and hardye and natheless no
farther than wysedome woulde adventurouse.
Whose warres whoso will consyder, hee shall
no lesse commende hys wysedome where
he voyded than hys mannehode where he vanquished. He was of visage louelye, of body
myghtie, strong and cleane made.
Thomas More (1478–1535) English lawyer
and scholar.
Referring to Edward IV
The Historie of Kyng Rycharde the Thirde

81 Now is the winter of our discontent
Made glorious summer by this sun of York.
William Shakespeare (1564–1616) English
dramatist.
Said by Richard III
Richard III, I:1 (1597)

1484

82* The Cat, the Rat, and Lovell our dog
Rule all England under a hog.
William Collingbourne (d. 1484) English
landowner.
The cat was Sir William Catesby; the rat Sir Richard Ratcliffe; the dog Lord Lovell, who had a
dog on his crest. The wild boar refers to the emblem of Richard III.
Chronicles (R. Holinshed), III

83 He contents the people where he goes best
that ever did Prince, for many a poor man that
hath suffered wrong many days has been re-
lieved and helped by him.
Thomas Langton (c. 1440–1501) Bishop of
St David's.
Referring to Richard III
Remark

1485

84 A horse! a horse! my kingdom for a horse.
William Shakespeare (1564–1616) English
dramatist.
Said by Richard III at the Battle of Bosworth (22
Aug 1485)
Richard III, V:4 (1597)

1499

85 He was my crowned King, and if the Parliamentary authority of England set the Crown upon
a stock, I will fight for that stock: And as I
fought then for him, I will fight for you, when
you are established by the said authority.
Earl of Surrey
Reply when asked by Henry VII why he had
fought for Richard III at the Battle of Bosworth
(22 Aug 1485)
Remains Concerning Britain (W. Camden)

86 In the midst stood Prince Henry, who showed
already something of royalty in his demeanour, in which there was a certain dignity combined with singular courtesy.
Erasmus (1466–1536) Dutch humanist,
scholar, and writer.
Remark on first meeting the future Henry VIII

16th century

87 . . . the state of things and the dispositions of
men were then such, that a man could not
well tell whom he might trust or whom he might
fear.
Thomas More (1478–1535) English lawyer
and scholar.
Refering to England
The English Works of Sir Thomas More, Vol. I

1500

88 I believe that the earthly Paradise lies here,
which no one can enter except by God's leave.
I believe that this land which your Highnesses
have commanded me to discover is very
great, and that there are many other lands in

the south of which there have never been reports.
Christopher Columbus (1451–1506) Italian navigator.
From the narrative of his third voyage, on which he discovered South America

---

1509

89 Oh, my Erasmus, if you could see how all the world here is rejoicing in the possession of so great a prince, how his life is all their desire, you could not contain your tears for joy. The heavens laugh, the earth exults, all things are full of milk, of honey and of nectar! Avarice is expelled the country. Liberality scatters wealth with bounteous hand. Our king does not desire gold or gems or precious metals, but virtue, glory, immortality . . . The other day he wished he was more learned. I said, that is not what we expect of your Grace, but that you will foster and encourage learned men. Yea, surely, said he, for indeed without them we should scarcely exist at all.
Lord Mountjoy
Referring to Henry VIII
Letter to Erasmus, 27 May 1509

1513

90* Since God has given us the papacy, let us enjoy it.
Leo X (Giovanni de' Medici; 1475–1521) Pope (1513–21).
Men of Art (T. Craven)

91 We Italians then owe to the Church of Rome and to her priests our having become irreligious and bad, but we owe her a still greater debt, and one that will be the cause of our ruin, namely that the Church has kept and still keeps our country divided.
Machiavelli (1469–1527) Italian statesman.
Discourses on First Ten Books of Livy

Attitudes

Art, Literature, and Music

12th century

92 The wanton and effeminate sound produced by caressing, chiming and intertwining melodies, a veritable harmony of sirens.
John of Salisbury (c. 1115–80) English churchman and scholar.
Referring to polyphony in music, contrasted with unison of Gregorian chant
Richard the Lionheart (J. Gillingham), Ch. 3

1385

93* And for ther is so greet diversitee in English and in wryting of our tonge

So preye I God that noon miswryte thee
Ne thee mismetre for defaute of tonge.
And red wherso thou be, or elles songe,
That thou be understonde, I God beseche.
Geoffrey Chaucer (c. 1343–1400) English poet.
Troilus and Criseyde

Daily Life

1176

94 . . . the sanctuary and special delight of kings, where, laying aside their cares, they withdraw to refresh themselves with a little hunting; there, away from the turmoils inherent in a court, they breathe the pleasure of natural freedom.
Richard FitzNigel Treasurer of England and Bishop of London.
Referring to the royal forests
Dialogus de Scaccario, Bk. I, Ch. 11

1182

95* If die I must, let me die drinking in an inn.
Walter Map (c. 1140–c. 1209) Welsh clergyman and writer.
De Nugis Curialium

13th century

96 I love the gay Eastertide, which brings forth leaves and flowers; and I love the joyous song of the birds, re-echoing through the copse. But I also love to see, admist the meadows, tents and pavilions spread; it gives me great joy to see, drawn up on the field, knights and horses in battle array.
Bertrand le Born French troubadour.

1250

97* Sumer is icumen in,
Lhude sing cuccu!
Groweth sed, and bloweth med,
And springth the wude nu.
Anonymous
Cuckoo Song

1390

98 So was hir joly whistle wel y-wet.
Geoffrey Chaucer (c. 1342–1400) English poet.
The Canterbury Tales, 'The Reve's Tale'

1501

99 Strong be thy wallis that about thee standis;
Wise be the people that within thee dwellis;
Fresh be thy ryver with his lusty strandis;
Blithe by thy chirches, wele swonyng be thy bellis;
Riche by they merchauntis in substaunce that excellis;

Fair be their wives, right lovesom, white and
small;
Clere by thy virgyns, lusty under kellis:
London, thou art the flour of Cities all.
William Dunbar (1460–1530)
Referring to London
The Earlier Tudors (J. D. Mackie)

Education, Knowledge, and Learning

13th century

100 This dumb ox will fill the whole world with his
bellowing.
Albertus Magnus (c. 1200–80) German
bishop.
Referring to his pupil Thomas Aquinas, whose
nickname was "The Dumb Ox"
Aquinas (A. Kenny)

1224

101 We keep the students within view of their parents; we save them many toils and long foreign journeys; we protect them from robbers.
They used to be pillaged while travelling
abroad; now, they may study at small cost and
short wayfaring, thanks to our liberality.
Frederick II (1194–1250) Holy Roman
Emperor.
Foundation charter of Naples University

14th century

102 Entities should not be multiplied unnecessarily.
No more things should be presumed to exist
than are absolutely necessary.
William of Okham (c. 1280–1349) English
philosopher.
'Okham's Razor'. Despite its attribution to William of Okham, it was in fact a repetition of an
ancient philosophical maxim

1323

103* There are as many miracles as there are arti-
cles of the *Summa.*
John XXII (Jacques d'Euse; c. 1249–1334)
Pope.
Referring to the *Summa Theologiae* of Thomas
Aquinas, who was in the process of being
canonized
Attrib.

1390

104 A Clerk ther was of Oxenford also,
That un-to logik hadde longe y-go.
Geoffrey Chaucer (c. 1342–1400) English
poet.
The Canterbury Tales, Prologue

105 This is to seyn, to syngen and to rede,
As smale children doon in hire childhede.
Geoffrey Chaucer
The Canterbury Tales, 'The Prioress's Tale'

Human Nature

14th century

106 Manners maketh man.
William of Wykeham (1324–1404) English
churchman.
Motto of Winchester College and New College,
Oxford

107 Only do always in health what you have often
promised to do when you are sick.
Sigismund (1368–1437) Holy Roman Emperor
(1411–37).
His advice on achieving happiness
Biographiana, Vol. I

1307

108 There is no greater sorrow than to recall a time
of happiness when in misery.
Dante Alighieri (1265–1321) Italian poet.
Divine Comedy, Inferno, V

15th century

109 If you cannot mould yourself as you would
wish, how can you expect other people to be
entirely to your liking?
Thomas à Kempis (Thomas Hemmerken;
c. 1380–1471) German monk.
The Imitation of Christ, I

1513

110 It is the nature of men to be bound by the benefits they confer as much as by those they
receive.
Machiavelli (1469–1527) Italian statesman.
The Prince

Life

1145

111 . . . how, not many years before, one John,
King and Priest, who dwells in the extreme Orient beyond Persia and Armenia . . . is said to
be of the ancient race of those Magi who are
mentioned in the Gospel.
Otto, Bishop of Freising (c. 1111–58) German chronicler.
The first mention of Prester John; the legend of a
great Christian Priest-King in Asia persisted
throughout the Middle Ages
Chronicle, 1145

1390

112 This world nis but a thurghfare ful of wo,
And we ben pilgrimes, passinge to and fro;
Deeth is an ende of every worldly sore.
Geoffrey Chaucer (c. 1342–1400) English
poet.
The Canterbury Tales, 'The Knight's Tale'

15th century

113 *O quam cito transit gloria mundi.*
Oh how quickly the glory of the world passes away.
Thomas à Kempis (Thomas Hemmerken;
c. 1380–1471) German monk.
Generally misquoted as 'Sic transit gloria mundi
(Thus passes the glory of the world)' — a
formula spoken during papal coronations from
1409
The Imitation of Christ, I

1508

114 **While I thought that I was learning how to live, I have been learning how to die.**
Leonardo da Vinci (1452–1519) Italian artist.
Notebooks

1516

115 **Nature made him, and then broke the mould.**
Ludovico Ariosto (1474–1533) Italian poet.
Referring to Charlemagne's paladin, Roland
Orlando furioso

Love and Sex

1469

116* **For love that time was not as love is nowadays.**
Thomas Malory (1400–71) English writer.
Morte d'Arthur, Bk. XX, Ch. 3

16th century

117 **Love of honour and honour of love.**
Philip Sidney (1554–86) English poet and
courtier.
Referring to the ideal of chivalry
English Literature: Mediaeval (W. P. Ker)

Marriage and the Family

1390

118 **She was a worthy womman al hir lyve, Housbondes at chirche-dore she hadde fyve, Withouten other companye in youthe.**
Geoffrey Chaucer (c. 1342–1400) English
poet.
Referring to the wife of Bath
The Canterbury Tales, Prologue

Morality, Vices, and Virtues

1367

119 **Dowel, Dobet and Dobest.**
William Langland (c. 1330–c. 1400) English
poet.
Do well, Do better, and Do Best: three concepts

central to the search for Truth in *Piers Plowman,* in which they appear as allegorical
characters
The Vision of Piers Plowman

1370

120 **A Knyght ther was and that a worthy man, That fro the tyme that he first bigan To riden out, he loved chivalrie, Trouthe and honour, fredom and curteisie.**
...
He was a verray parfit, gentil knyght.
Geoffrey Chaucer (c. 1342–1400) English
poet.
The Canterbury Tales, Prologue

1390

121 **Mordre wol out, that see we day by day.**
Geoffrey Chaucer
The Canterbury Tales, 'The Nun's Priest's Tale'

Religion

12th century

122 **...kept a hearth-girl in his house who kindled his fire but extinguished his virtue.**
Gerald of Wales (c. 1146–c. 1220) Welsh to-
pographer, archdeacon, and writer.
Referring to the parish priest
Gemma Ecclesiastica

1307

123 **Abandon hope, all ye who enter here.**
Dante Alighieri (1265–1321) Italian poet.
The inscription at the entrance to Hell
Divine Comedy, Inferno, III

1390

124 **Ful wel she song the service divyne, Entuned in hir nose ful semely.**
Geoffrey Chaucer (c. 1342–1400) English
poet.
Referring to the prioress
The Canterbury Tales, Prologue

15th century

125 **Man proposes but God disposes.**
Thomas à Kempis (Thomas Hemmerken;
c. 1380–1471) German monk.
The Imitation of Christ, I

16th century

126 **I believe firmly what I read in the holy Scriptures, and the Creed, called the Apostles', and I don't trouble my head any farther: I leave the rest to be disputed and defined by the clergy, if they please; and if any Thing is in common use with Christians that is not repugnant to the**

holy Scriptures, I observe it for this Reason, that I may not offend other people.
Erasmus (c. 1467–1536) Dutch humanist.
Commenting on the teachings of John Colet
The Colloquies of Erasmus, Vol. I

Science, Medicine, and Technology

1267

127   All science requires mathematics
Roger Bacon (c. 1214–c. 1292) English monk, scholar, and scientist.
Opus Maius, Pt. IV

1380

128*   That lyf so short, the craft so long to lerne,
Th' assay so hard, so sharp the conquerynge.
Geoffrey Chaucer (c. 1342–1400) English poet.
Referring to medicine
The Parliament of Fowls

1505

129   A man with wings large enough and duly attached might learn to overcome the resistance of the air, and conquering it succeed in subjugating it and raise himself upon it.
Leonardo da Vinci (1452–1519) Italian artist.
Flight of Birds

Wealth and Poverty

1380

130*   For of fortunes sharp adversitee
The worst kinde of infortune is this,
A man to have ben in prosperitee,
And it remembren, what is passed is.
Geoffrey Chaucer (c. 1342–1400) English poet.
Troilus and Criseyde, 3

Work and Occupations

1390

131   No-wher so bisy a man as he ther nas,
And yet he semed bisier than he was.
Geoffrey Chaucer
Referring to the man of law
The Canterbury Tales, Prologue

132   For gold in phisik is a cordial,
Therfore he lovede gold in special.
Geoffrey Chaucer
Referring to the doctor
The Canterbury Tales, Prologue

Sayings of the Time

12th century

133   *Rex illiteratus, asinus coronatus.*
An unlettered king is a crowned ass.
A saying common in the 12th century; also said, by William of Malmesbury, to have been used by Henry I of England in his youth

With Hindsight

17th century

134   . . . it was ordained that the winding ivy of a Plantagenet should kill the true tree itself.
Francis Bacon (1561–1626) English philosopher.
Referring to the execution (1499) of Perkin Warbeck, who claimed to be Edward V's brother, and the Earl of Warwick, the true heir of the house of York
The Life of Henry VII

135   Being a king that loved wealth and treasure, he could not endure to have trade sick.
Francis Bacon
Referring to Henry VII
The Life of Henry VII

19th century

136   There may have been disillusionments in the lives of the medieval saints, but they would scarcely have been better pleased if they could have foreseen that their names would be associated nowadays chiefly with racehorses and the cheaper clarets.
Saki (Hector Hugh Munro; 1870–1916) British writer.
Reginald at the Carlton

20th century

137   . . . the pulpit was the cradle of English prose.
A. G. Little (1863–1945) British historian.
English Historical Review, xlix (1934)

138   In essence the Renaissance was simply the green end of one of civilization's hardest winters.
John Fowles (1926–) British novelist.
The French Lieutenant's Woman, Ch. 10

139   Compared with this revolution the Renaissance is a mere ripple on the surface of literature.
C. S. Lewis (1898–1963) British academic and writer.
Referring to the appearance of the concept of courtly love in the 12th century
The Allegory of Love

7

The Reformation and Counter-Reformation (1518–1659)

On 31 October, 1517, Martin Luther nailed to the door of the castle church at Wittenburg, 95 theses attacking abuses in the Roman Catholic Church. These complaints were not new, but because the time was ripe they set off the Reformation of the Catholic Church. Within a few years Protestant ideas had spread widely and several rulers had renounced the authority of the Pope. Notably, Henry VIII of England defied the Pope to divorce his first queen; thereafter he assumed full religious authority within his kingdom. For the next century and more, religious conflicts played a central role in politics and diplomacy, and most disputes acquired a religious dimension. In this period the Catholic Church attempted, notably at the Council of Trent (1545–63), to put its own house in order. This became known as the Counter-Reformation. Only in the later stages of the Thirty Years War (1618–48) did religion's political importance decline; and by 1661, when Louis XIV began his personal government of France, dynastic and national ambitions were again paramount.

Politics, Government, and World Events

1518

1 The King has a way of making every man feel that he is enjoying his special favour, just as the London wives pray before the image of Our Lady by the Tower till each of them believes it is smiling upon her.
Thomas More (1478–1535) English lawyer and scholar.
Referring to Henry VIII
Letter to Bishop John Fisher, 1518

2 I shall never be a heretic, I may err in dispute; but I do not wish to decide anything finally; on the other hand, I am not bound by the opinions of men.
Martin Luther (1483–1546) German Protestant.
Letter to the chaplain to the Elector of Saxony, 28 Aug 1518

1519

3 This cardinal is the person who rules both the king and the entire kingdom.
Sebastian Giustiniani Venetian ambassador to England.
Referring to Cardinal Wolsey
Wolsey (A. F. Pollard)

4 Nothing pleased him more than to be styled the arbitrator of the affairs of Christendom.
Sebastian Giustiniani
Referring to Cardinal Wolsey
Letters and Papers of Henry VIII, Vol. III

1520

5* My cousin Francis and I are in perfect accord – he wants Milan, and so do I.
Charles V (1500–58) Holy Roman Emperor.
Referring to his dispute with Francis I of France over Italian territory
The Story of Civilization (W. Durant), Vol. 5

6 Arise, O Lord, plead Thine own cause; remember how the foolish man reproacheth Thee daily; the foxes are wasting Thy vineyard, which Thou hast given to Thy Vicar Peter, the boar out of the wood doth waste it, and the wild beast of the field doth devour it.
Leo X (Giovanni de' Medici; 1475–1521) Pope (1513–21).
Papal Bull, Exsurge, Domine, Preface

1521

7 Here stand I. I can do no other. God help me. Amen.
Martin Luther (1483–1546) German Protestant.
Speech, Diet of Worms, 18 Apr 1521

8 A single friar who goes counter to all Christianity for a thousand years must be wrong.
Charles V (1500–58) Holy Roman Emperor.
Referring to Martin Luther
Remark, Diet of Worms, 19 Apr 1521

9 If I had heard that as many devils would set on me in Worms as there are tiles on the roofs, I should none the less have ridden there.
Martin Luther (1483–1546) German Protestant.
Referring to the Diet of Worms
Luthers Sämmtliche Schriften

10 We are so much bounden to the See of Rome that we cannot do too much honour to it . . . for we received from that See our Crown Imperial.
Henry VIII (1491–1547) King of England.
Remark to Thomas More

11 As time requireth, a man of marvellous mirth and pastimes, and sometimes of as sad gravity, as who say: a man for all seasons.
Robert Whittington (16th century) English writer.
Referring to Sir Thomas More; after Erasmus
Vulgaria, Pt. II, 'De constructione nominum'

1525

12 Of all I had, only honour and life have been spared.
Francis I (1494–1547) King of France.
Referring to his defeat and capture by the forces of the Emperor Charles V at the Battle of Pavia, 24 Feb 1525; usually misquoted as 'All is lost save honour'
Letter to Louise of Savoy (his mother), 1525

13 Anyone who can be proved to be a seditious person is an outlaw before God and the emperor; and whoever is the first to put him to death does right and well.
Martin Luther (1483–1546) German Protestant.
Referring to the 'Peasants' War', an uprising (1524–25) of peasants in Germany partly inspired by Luther's teachings
Against the Robbing and Murdering Hordes of Peasants (Broadsheet, May 1525)

14 In my opinion it is better that all of these peasants should be killed rather than that the sovereigns and magistrates should be destroyed, because the peasants take up the sword without God's authorization.
Martin Luther
Letter to Nicholas von Ansdorf, 30 May 1525

1529

15 I perceive that that man hath the sow by the right ear.
Henry VIII (1491–1547) King of England.
Referring to Cranmer
Letter to Edward Foxe and Stephen Gardiner, 3 Aug 1529

1530

16 I speak Spanish to God, Italian to women,
French to men, and German to my horse.
Charles V (1500–58) Holy Roman Emperor.
Attrib.

17 Had I but served God as diligently as I have
served the king, he would not have given me
over in my gray hairs.
Cardinal Wolsey (1475–1530) English
churchman.
Remark to Sir William Kingston; Wolsey, Henry
VIII's chief minister from 1515 to 1529, had
been discarded following his failure to secure
Henry's divorce from Catherine of Aragon
Negotiations of Thomas Wolsey (Cavendish)

18 He is a prince of royal courage and hath a
princely heart; and rather than he will miss or
want part of his appetite, he will hazard the
loss of one-half of his kingdom.
Cardinal Wolsey
Referring to Henry VIII
Remark, Nov 1530

1534

19 Is not this house as nigh heaven as my own?
Thomas More (1478–1535) English lawyer
and scholar.
Referring to the Tower of London; More was imprisoned here, and in 1535 executed, for treason arising from his defiance of Henry VIII's
religious policies
Life of Sir Thomas More (Roper)

1535

20 I cumber you goode Margaret muche, but I
woulde be sorye, if it shoulde be any lenger
than to morrowe, for it is S. Thomas evin and
the vtas of Sainte Peter and therefore I to
morowe longe I to goe to God, it were a daye
very meete and conveniente for me. I neuer
liked your maner towarde me better then when
you kissed me laste for I loue when dought-
erly loue and deere charitie hathe no laisor to
looke to worldely curtesye. Fare well my
deere childe and praye for me, and I shall for
you and all your friendes that we maie merily
meete in heaven.
Thomas More
Last letter to Margaret Roper, his daughter, on
the eve of his execution on 6 July 1535

21 I pray you, Master Lieutenant, see me safe up,
and for coming down let me shift for myself.
Thomas More
On climbing onto the scaffold prior to his
execution
Life of Sir Thomas More (William Roper)

22 Pluck up thy spirits, man, and be not afraid to
do thine office; my neck is very short; take
heed therefore thou strike not awry, for saving
of thine honesty.
Thomas More
Said to the headsman
Life of Sir Thomas More (Roper)

23 This hath not offended the king.
Thomas More
Said as he drew his beard aside before putting
his head on the block

1536

24 The king has been very good to me. He promoted me from a simple maid to be a marchion-
ess. Then he raised me to be a queen. Now he
will raise me to be a martyr.
Anne Boleyn (1507–36) Second wife of Henry
VIII.
Notable Women in History (W. Abbot)

1537

25* Little Jack Horner
Sat in the corner,
Eating a Christmas pie;
He put in his thumb,
And pulled out a plum,
And said, What a good boy am I!
Thought to relate to an incident when the Ab-
bot of Glastonbury, in an attempt to pacify
Henry VIII, sent his steward, John Horner, to
the king with a pie containing the title deeds to
12 Somerset manors. John Horner is be-
lieved to have discovered these deeds in the
pie and kept them himself
Namby Pamby (Henry Carey)

26 We should easily convert even the Turks to the
obedience of our gospel, if only we would
agree among ourselves and unite in some holy
confederacy.
Thomas Cranmer (1489–1556) English
churchman.
Letter to the Swiss scholar, Joachim Vadian,
1537

27 Pity it is that the folly of one brainsick Pole —
or, to say better, of one witless fool — should
be the ruin of so great a family.
Thomas Cromwell (c. 1485–1540) English
statesman.
Referring to the denunciation of Reginald Pole
(the King's cousin) for siding with the Pope in the
disputes of the English Reformation
Letter to Michael Throgmorton (Pole's confidant),
Sept 1537

1539

28 You have sent me a Flanders mare.
Henry VIII (1491–1547) King of England.
Remark on meeting his fourth wife, Anne of
Cleves, for the first time; generally assumed to
have been said to Thomas Cromwell
Attrib.

1540

29 It much grieves me that I should be noted a
traitor when I always had your laws on my
breast, and that I should be a sacramentary.

God he knoweth the truth, and that I am of the one and the other guiltless.
Thomas Cromwell (c. 1485–1540) English statesman.
On being condemned to death for treason and heresy
Letter to Henry VIII, 30 June 1540

30* Junker Henry means to be God and do as he pleases.
Martin Luther (1483–1546) German Protestant.
Referring to Henry VIII's religious policy
The Earlier Tudors (J. D. Mackie)

1543

31 We at no time stand so highly in our estate royal as in the time of Parliament, wherein we as head and you as members are conjoined and knit together into one body politic.
Henry VIII (1491–1547) King of England.
Speech to a deputation from the House of Commons, 31 Mar 1543

1545

32 I am very sorry to know and hear how unreverently that most precious jewel, the Word of God, is disputed, rhymed, sung and jangled in every ale-house and tavern, contrary to the true meaning and doctrine of the same.
Henry VIII
Commenting on the translation of the Bible into English
Speech, Parliament, 24 Dec 1545

1546

33 I make war on the living, not on the dead.
Charles V (1500–58) Holy Roman Emperor.
After the death of Martin Luther, when it was suggested that he hang the corpse on a gallows
Attrib.

1547

34 I came, I saw, God conquered.
Charles V
Remark after the Battle of Mühlberg, 23 Apr 1547

1550

35* My father made the most part of you almost out of nothing.
Mary I (1516–58) Queen of England.
Reply when threatened, during the reign of Edward VI, because of her Catholicism
The Earlier Tudors (J. D. Mackie)

1555

36 England's chief defence depends upon the navy

being always ready to defend the realm against invasion.
Philip II (1527–98) King of Spain.
Philip, as husband of Mary I, was King-Consort of England (1554–58)
Submission to the Privy Council

1556

37 Three blind mice, see how they run!
They all run after the farmer's wife,
Who cut off their tails with a carving knife,
Did you ever see such a thing in your life,
As three blind mice?
The 'three blind mice' are thought to be Archbishop Cranmer, Bishop Ridley, and Bishop Latimer, who were executed in the reign of Mary I (the 'farmer's wife') for heresy
Deuteromelia (Thomas Ravenscroft)

38 Be of good comfort, Master Ridley, and play the man; we shall this day light such a candle, by God's grace, in England as I trust shall never be put out.
Hugh Latimer (1485–1555) English churchman.
Said to Nicholas Ridley as they were about to be burnt at the stake for heresy
Famous Last Words (B. Conrad)

1558

39 When I am dead and opened, you shall find 'Calais' lying in my heart.
Mary I (1516–58) Queen of England.
Chronicles (Holinshed), III

40 After all the stormy, tempestuous, and blustering windy weather of Queen Mary was overblown, the darksome clouds of discomfort dispersed, the palpable fogs and mist of the most intolerable misery consumed, and the dashing showers of persecution overpast: it pleased God to send England calm and quiet season, a clear and lovely sunshine, a quietsest from former broils of a turbulent estate, and a world of blessings by good Queen Elizabeth.
Raphael Holinshed (d. 1580) English chronicler.
Chronicles

41 The First Blast of the Trumpet Against the Monstrous Regiment of Women.
John Knox (c. 1514–72) Scottish religious reformer.
Title of pamphlet, 1558

42 This judgment I have of you, that you will not be corrupted with any manner of gift and that you will be faithful to the state, and that, without respect of my private will, you will give me that counsel that you think best.
Elizabeth I (1533–1603) Queen of England.
To William Cecil, 1558

1559

43 To me it shall be a full satisfaction both for the memorial of my name, and for the glory also, if

when I shall let my last breath, it be engraven upon my marble tomb, 'Here lieth Elizabeth, who reigned a virgin and died a virgin'.
Elizabeth I
Reply to a petition from the House of Commons, 6 Feb 1559

1564

44 Let justice be done, though the world perish.
Ferdinand I (1503–64) Holy Roman Emperor.
Attrib.

1565

45* In old time we had treen chalices and golden priests, but now we have treen priests and golden chalices.
John Jewel (1522–71) English bishop.
Certain Sermons Preached Before the Queen's Majesty

1566

46 The queen of Scots is this day leichter of a fair son, and I am but a barren stock.
Elizabeth I (1533–1603) Queen of England.
Memoirs of Sir James Melville (1549–93)

47 No more tears now; I will think upon revenge.
Mary Stuart (1542–87) Queen of Scots.
Remark on hearing of the murder (9 March 1566) of her secretary, David Riccio, by her husband, Lord Darnley

48 I muse how men of wit can so hardly use that gift they hold.
Elizabeth I (1533–1603) Queen of England.
Speech to a delegation from parliament, 5 Nov 1566

49 Most excellent Royall Majesty, of our *Elizabeth* (sitting at the *Helm* of this Imperial Monarchy: or rather, at the Helm of the Imperiall Ship).
John Dee (1527–1608) English mathematician and astrologer.
General and Rare Memorials pertaining to the Perfect Arte of Navigation

50 Those who follow their conscience directly are of my religion; and, for my part, I am of the same religion as all those who are brave and true.
Henri IV (1533–1610) King of France.
Henri had become a Roman Catholic, as a political move, in 1576
Letter to M. de Batz, 1577

1579

51 Be assured on the faith of a monkey that your frog lives in hope.
Jean de Simier
The 'monkey' was Elizabeth I's pet name for Simier, who tried unsuccessfully to arrange a marriage between Elizabeth and his master, the Duke of Anjou (the 'frog')

1580s

52* Hey diddle diddle,
The cat and the fiddle,
The cow jumped over the moon;
The little dog laughed
To see such sport,
And the dish ran away with the spoon.
Believed to depict the Elizabethan court; the characters represented are Elizabeth I (the cat) Sir Francis Walsingham (the moon), and Earl of Leicester (the dog)
Mother Goose's Melody

1580

53* I am your anointed Queen. I will never be by violence constrained to do anything. I thank God that I am endued with such qualities that I were turned out of the Realm in my petticoat I were able to live in any place in Christome.
Elizabeth I (1533–1603) Queen of England.
Sayings of Queen Elizabeth (Chamberlin)

1584

54 My question is not whether there be witches or nay; but whether they can do such marvellous works as are imputed to them. Good Master Dean, is it possible for a man to break his fast with you at Rochester, and to dine that day at Durham with Master Doctor Matthew; or can your enemy maim you, when the Ocean sea is betwixt you? May a spiritual body become temporal at his pleasure? Or may a carnal body become invisible? . . . Alas, I am sorry and ashamed to see how many die, that being said to be bewitched, only seek for magical cures, whom wholesome diet and good medicines would have recovered.
Reginald Scot
The Discoverie of Witchcraft

1586

55 As for me, I see no such great cause why I should either be fond to live or fear to die. I have had good experience of this world, and I know what it is to be a subject and what to be a sovereign. Good neighbours I have had, and I have met with bad: and in trust I have found treason.
Elizabeth I (1533–1603) Queen of England.
Speech to Parliament, 1586

56* A dead woman bites not.
Lord Gray (d. 1612) Scottish nobleman.
Advocating the execution of Mary, Queen of Scots
Attrib.

57 The daughter of debate, that eke discord doth sow.
Elizabeth I (1533–1603) Queen of England.
Referring to Mary Queen of Scots
Sayings of Queen Elizabeth (Chamberlin)

1587

8* God may pardon you, but I never can.
Elizabeth I
To the Countess of Nottingham
History of England under the House of Tudor
(Hume), Vol. II, Ch. 7

59 I have singed the Spanish king's beard.
Francis Drake (1540–96) British navigator.
Referring to the raid on Cadiz harbour, 1587
Attrib.

1588

60 Here lies a valiant warrior
Who never drew a sword;
Here lies a noble courtier
Who never kept his word;
Here lies the Earl of Leicester
Who governed the estates
Whom the earth could never living love,
And the just heaven now hates.
Ben Jonson (1573–1637) English dramatist.
Attrib. in *Collection of Epitaphs* (Tissington)

The Spanish Armada (1588)

Philip II of Spain sent a fleet of 130 ships to transport his army across the Channel to invade England and overthrow the 'heretical' Queen Elizabeth I. Disrupted by English fireships and defeated off Gravelines, it suffered further losses from Atlantic storms and returned to Spain with only 86 ships.

61 The advantage of time and place in all practical actions is half a victory; which being lost is irrecoverable.
Francis Drake (1540–96) British navigator.
Letter to Elizabeth I, 1588

62 There is plenty of time to win this game, and to thrash the Spaniards too.
Francis Drake
Referring to the sighting of the Armada during a game of bowls, 20 July 1588
Attrib.

63 Drake he's in his hammock till the great Armadas come.
(Capten, art tha sleepin' there below?)
Slung atween the round shot, listenin' for the drum,
An dreamin' arl the time o' Plymouth Hoe.
Henry John Newbolt (1862–1938) British poet.
Drake's Drum

64 'Take my drum to England, hang et by the shore,
Strike et when your powder's runnin' low;
If the Dons sight Devon, I'll quit the port o' Heaven,
An' drum them up the Channel as we drummed them long ago.'
Henry John Newbolt
Drake's Drum

65 I know I have the body of a weak and feeble woman, but I have the heart and stomach of a King, and of a King of England too.
Elizabeth I (1533–1603) Queen of England.
Speech at Tilbury on the approach of the Spanish Armada

66 *Flavit deus et dissipati sunt.*
God blew and they were scattered.
Inscription on the medallion minted to commemorate the defeat of the Spanish Armada

67 They did not, in all their sailing round about England, so much as sink or take one ship, bark, pinnace, or cockboat of ours, or even burn so much as one sheepcote in this land.
Anonymous
Referring to the Spanish Armada
The Reign of Elizabeth (J. D. Black), Ch. 10

1594

68 Paris is worth a mass.
Henri IV (1553–1610) King of France.
Said on entering Paris (March 1594), having secured its submission to his authority by becoming a Roman Catholic
Attrib.

1596

69 This royal throne of kings, this sceptred isle,
This earth of majesty, this seat of Mars,
This other Eden, demi-paradise,
This fortress built by Nature for herself
Against infection and the hand of war,
This happy breed of men, this little world,
This precious stone set in the silver sea,
Which serves it in the office of a wall,
Or as a moat defensive to a house,
Against the envy of less happier lands;
This blessed plot, this earth, this realm, this England,
This nurse, this teeming womb of royal kings,
Fear'd by their breed, and famous by their birth.
William Shakespeare (1564–1616) English dramatist.
Richard II, II:1

70 Not all the water in the rough rude sea
Can wash the balm from an anointed king;
The breath of worldly men cannot depose
The deputy elected by the Lord.
William Shakespeare
Richard II, III:2

1598

71 ...her face oblong, fair but wrinkled; her eyes small, yet black and pleasant; her nose a little hooked, her lips narrow and her teeth black (a defect the English seem subject to from their too great use of sugar)...She wore false hair and that red.
Paul Hentzner (fl. 1590s) German tutor.
Referring to Elizabeth I
Journey into England

72 Uneasy lies the head that wears a crown.
William Shakespeare (1564–1616) English
dramatist.
Henry IV, Part Two, III:1

73 The sun does not set in my dominions.
Friedrich von Schiller (1759–1805) German
dramatist.
Said by Philip II of Spain
Don Carlos, I:6

1599

74* That realm cannot be rich whose coin is poor or
base.
William Cecil, Lord Burghley (1520–98)
English statesman
Referring to Elizabeth I's reform of coinage
Attrib.

75 Every subject's duty is the King's; but every
subject's soul is his own.
William Shakespeare (1564–1616) English
dramatist.
Henry V, IV:1

1600
---

76 Perhaps your fear in passing judgement is
greater than mine in receiving it.
Giordano Bruno (1548–1600) Italian
philosopher.
Said on being sentenced to death for heresy, 8
Feb 1600
Attrib.

77 Cry 'Havoc!' and let slip the dogs of war.
William Shakespeare (1564–1616) English
dramatist.
Julius Caesar, III:1

78 I want there to be no peasant in my kingdom so
poor that he is unable to have a chicken in his
pot every Sunday.
Henri IV (1553–1610) King of France.
Hist. de Henry le Grand (Hardouin de Péréfixe)

1601
---

79 I have been, though unworthy, a member of this
House in six or seven Parliaments, yet never
did I see the House in so great confusion. This
is more fit for a grammar school than a Court
of Parliament.
Robert Cecil, 1st Earl of Salisbury (1563–
1612) English statesman.
Speech, House of Commons, 24 Nov 1601

80 Though God hath raised me high, yet this I
count the glory of my crown: that I have
reigned with your loves.
Elizabeth I (1533–1603) Queen of England.
Speech to a deputation from the House of Commons (the Golden Speech), 30 Nov 1601

81 Of myself I must say this, I never was any
greedy, scraping grasper, nor a strait fast-hold-
ing prince, nor yet a waster; my heart was

never set on wordly goods, but only for my
subjects' good.
Elizabeth I
Speech to a deputation from the House of Commons (the Golden Speech), 30 Nov 1601

82 There's such divinity doth hedge a king
That treason can but peep to what it would.
William Shakespeare (1564–1616) English
dramatist.
Hamlet, IV:5

1603
---

83 Must! Is *must* a word to be addressed to
princes? Little man, little man! thy father, if h
had been alive, durst not have used that word.
Elizabeth I (1533–1603) Queen of England.
Said to Robert Cecil, on her death bed
A Short History of the English People (J. R.
Green), Ch. 7

84 I will that a king succeed me, and who but m
kinsman the king of Scots.
Elizabeth I
Said shortly before she died, when pressed con
cerning the succession
The Reign of Elizabeth (J. D. Black), Ch. 13

85 . . . by putting her hand to her head, when th
King of Scots was named to succeed her, they
all knew he was the man she desired should
reign after her.
Sir Robert Carey (c. 1560–1639) English
courtier.
Referring to the death of Elizabeth I
Memoirs

1604
---

86 No Bishop, no King.
James I (1566–1625) King of England.
An expression, at a conference on doctrinal reform, of his belief that a non-episcopal form of
church government was incompatible with
monarchy
Remark, Hampton Court, 14 Jan 1604; reporte
by William Barlow

1605
---

87 Please to remember the Fifth of November,
Gunpowder Treason and Plot.
We know no reason why gunpowder treason
Should ever be forgot.
Anonymous
Traditional

88 A desperate disease requires a dangerous
remedy.
Guy Fawkes (1570–1606) English conspirato
In justification of the Gunpowder Plot; said whe
questioned by the King and council immediately
after his arrest (5 Nov 1605)
Dictionary of National Biography

89 . . . to blow the Scots back again into Scotland
Guy Fawkes
One of his professed objectives for the Gunpow
der Plot, referring to the Scottish-born King
James I; said when questioned by the King and

council immediately after his arrest, 5 Nov 1605
Dictionary of National Biography

90 On the 5th of November we began our Parliament, to which the King should have come in person, but refrained, through a practice but that morning discovered. The plot was to have blown up the King.
Sir Edward Hoby (1560–1617) English politician.
Letter to Sir Thomas Edmondes, 19 Nov 1605

91 . . . in general sorrow that so monstrous a wickedness should have been harboured with in the breast of any of their religion.
Charles Cornwallis (c. 1580–1629) British ambassador in Madrid.
Describing Spanish reaction to the Gunpowder Plot
Letter to Lord Salisbury, Nov 1605

92 The law of the realm cannot be changed but by Parliament.
Edward Coke (1552–1634) English lawyer and politician.
Dictum, in the case *Articuli Cleri*, 1605

93 The king reigns, but does not govern.
Jan Zamoyski (1541–1605) Grand chancellor of Poland.
Speech, Polish Parliament, 1605

94 That in the captain's but a choleric word
Which in the soldier is flat blasphemy.
William Shakespeare (1564–1616) English dramatist.
Measure for Measure, II:2

95 Farewell the neighing steed and the shrill trump,
The spirit-stirring drum, th'ear piercing fife,
The royal banner, and all quality,
Pride, pomp, and circumstance, of glorious war!
William Shakespeare
Othello, III:3

1609
---

96 The state of monarchy is the supremest thing upon earth; for kings are not only God's Lieutenants upon earth, and sit upon God's throne, but even by God himself they are called Gods.
James I (1566–1625) King of England.
Speech, Parliament, 21 Mar 1609

97 Kings are earth's gods; in vice their law's their will.
William Shakespeare (1564–1616) English dramatist.
Pericles, I:1

1610

98* Mahomet made the people believe that he would call a hill to him . . . when the hill stood still, he was never a whit abashed, but said,

'If the hill will not come to Mahomet, Mahomet will go to the hill.'
Francis Bacon (1561–1626) English philosopher.
Often misquoted as 'If the mountain will not come to Mohammed'
Essays, 'Of Boldness'

99* Nothing destroyeth authority so much as the unequal and untimely interchange of power pressed too far, and relaxed too much.
Francis Bacon
Essays, 'Of Empire'

100 The wisest fool in Christendom.
Henri IV (1553–1610) King of France.
Referring to James I of England
Attrib.

1611
---

101 Who but my father would keep such a bird in a cage?
Henry, Prince of Wales (1594–1612) First-born son of James I.
Referring to Sir Walter Raleigh, who was imprisoned in the Tower of London for treason from 1603
Remark

102 Though authority be a stubborn bear, yet he is oft led by the nose with gold.
William Shakespeare (1564–1616) English dramatist.
The Winter's Tale, IV:3

1615
---

103 There are only two families in the world, my old grandmother used to say, The *Haves* and the *Have-Nots*.
Miguel de Cervantes (1547–1616) Spanish novelist.
Don Quixote, Pt. II, Ch. 20

1618
---

104 Treason doth never prosper: what's the reason? For if it prosper, none dare call it treason.
John Harington (1561–1612) English writer.
Epigrams, 'Of Treason'

105 So the heart be right, it is no matter which way the head lies.
Walter Raleigh
On laying his head on the executioner's block
Attrib.

106 Tis a sharp remedy, but a sure one for all ills.
Walter Raleigh (1554–1618) English explorer.
Referring to the executioner's axe just before he was beheaded
Attrib.

1620
---

107 May not and ought not the children of these fathers rightly say: 'Our fathers were English-

men which came over this great ocean, and were ready to perish in this wilderness.'
William Bradford (1590–1657) Pilgrim Father.
Referring to the Pilgrim Fathers, after their arrival at Cape Cod
Of Plymouth Plantation, Ch. 10

1621

108 I will govern according to the common weal, but not according to the common will.
James I (1566–1625) King of England.
History of the English People (J. R. Green)

1623

109* He that makes a good war makes a good peace.
George Herbert (1593–1633) English poet.
Outlandish Proverbs, 420

1624

110 One of the Seven was wont to say: 'That laws were like cobwebs; where the small flies were caught, and the great brake through.'
Francis Bacon (1561–1626) English philosopher.
Apothegms

1628

111 Magna Charta is such a fellow, that he will have no sovereign.
Edward Coke (1552–1634) English lawyer and politician.
Speaking on the Lords' Amendment to the Petition of Right, 17 May 1628
Hist. Coll. (Rushworth), I

1635

112 That pig of a Henry VIII committed such sacrilege by profaning so many ecclesiastical benefices in order to give their goods to those who being so rewarded might stand firmly for the King in the Lower House; and now the King's greatest enemies are those who are enriched by these benefices.
Sir Francis Windebank (1582–1646) English politician.
Remark to the Papal envoy, Apr 1635

1636

113 Never make a defence or apology before you be accused.
Charles I (1600–49) King of England.
Letter to Lord Wentworth, 3 Sept 1636

1640

114 They say princes learn no art truly, but the art of horsemanship. The reason is, the brave

beast is no flatterer. He will throw a prince as soon as his groom.
Ben Jonson (1573–1637) English dramatist.
Timber, or Discoveries made upon Men and Matter

1641

115 To know how to dissimulate is the knowledge of kings.
Cardinal Richelieu (1585–1642) French statesman.
Testament Politique, Maxims

116 Not least among the qualities in a great King is a capacity to permit his ministers to serve him.
Cardinal Richelieu
Testament Politique, Maxims

117 Secrecy is the first essential in affairs of the State.
Cardinal Richelieu
Testament Politique, Maxims

1642

118 Richelieu leaned to the good whenever his interests did not draw him towards evil.
Cardinal de Retz (1614–79) French churchman.
Mémoires

119 Stone walls do not a prison make,
Nor iron bars a cage.
Richard Lovelace (1618–58) English poet.
To Althea, from Prison

The English Civil War, the Commonwealth, and the Protectorate (1642–59)

The English Civil War was the conflict between royalists (Cavaliers) and parliamentarians (Roundheads) which began on 22 August 1642 when King Charles raised his standard at Nottingham. At first finely balanced, it tilted decisively against the king from c 1645. He was captured in 1646, but escaped in 1647 he was recaptured and, in 1649, executed. Oliver Cromwell formed the Commonwealth and overcame residual resistance to end the warfare in 1651. In 1653, he dismissed Parliament, set up the Protectorate, and assumed power himself. He ruled until his death (1658), and was briefly succeeded by his son until the Restoration of King Charles II (1660).

120 Well, since I see all the birds are flown, I do expect from you that you shall send them unto me as soon as they return hither.
Charles I (1600–49) King of England.
On entering the House of Commons to arrest five MPs
Remark, 4 Jan 1642

121 I have neither eye to see, nor tongue to speak

here, but as the House is pleased to direct
me.
William Lenthall (1591–1662) English
parliamentarian.
A succinct restatement of the Speaker's traditional role; said on 4 Jan 1642 in the House of
Commons, when asked by Charles I if he had
seen five MPs whom the King wished to arrest
Historical Collections (Rushworth)

122   O Lord! thou knowest how busy I must be this
day: if I forget thee, do not thou forget me.
Lord Astley (1579–1652) English Royalist
general.
Prayer before taking part in the Battle of Edgehill
Memoires (Sir Philip Warwick)

1643

123   Tell me not, Sweet, I am unkind,
That from the nunnery
Of thy chaste breast and quiet mind
To war and arms I fly.

True, a new mistress now I chase,
The first foe in the field;
And with a stronger faith embrace
A sword, a horse, a shield.

Yet this inconstancy is such
As thou too shalt adore;
I could not love thee, Dear, so much,
Loved I not Honour more.
Richard Lovelace
To Lucasta, Going to the Wars

124*   Humpty Dumpty sat on a wall,
Humpty Dumpty had a great fall.
All the king's horses,
And all the king's men,
Couldn't put Humpty together again.
Believed to be based on an incident in the Civil
War; Charles I attempted to bridge the river
Severn at Gloucester using a huge machine,
nicknamed 'Humpty Dumpty' by the troops. The
machine collapsed in the middle of the river
Gammer Gurton's Garland

1644

125   I laboured nothing more than that the external
public worship of God, too much slighted in
most parts of this kingdom, might be
preserved.
William Laud (1573–1645) Archbishop of
Canterbury.
Remark at his trial, 12 Mar 1644

126   The State, in choosing men to serve it, takes no
notice of their opinions. If they be willing faithfully to serve it, that satisfies.
Oliver Cromwell (1599–1658) English soldier
and statesman.
Said before the Battle of Marston Moor, 2 July
1644

127   If we beat the King ninety and nine times yet he
is King still, and so will his posterity be after

him; but if the King beat us once we shall all
be hanged, and our posterity made slaves.
Earl of Manchester
Remark

128   My lord, if this be so, why did we take up arms
at first? This is against fighting ever hereafter.
Oliver Cromwell (1599–1658) English soldier
and statesman.
Reply to the Earl of Manchester (above)
Remark

1645

129*   New Presbyter is but old Priest writ large.
John Milton (1608–74) English poet.
Sonnet: 'On the New Forcers of Conscience
under the Long Parliament'

130*   The parliament intended to have hanged him;
and he expected no less, but resolved to be
hanged with the Bible under one arm and
Magna Carta under the other.
John Aubrey (1626–1697) English antiquary.
David Jenkins (1582–1663), a Welsh judge and
royalist, was imprisoned by parliament (1645–
60)
Brief Lives, 'David Jenkins'

1646

131   Every old woman with a wrinkled face, a furr'd
brow, a hairy lip, a gobber tooth, a squint eye,
a squeaking voice, or a scolding tongue . . . a
dog or cat by her side, is not only suspected
but pronounced for a witch.
John Gaule (fl. 1660) Vicar of Great Stoughton
(Huntingdonshire).
Sermons on Witchcraft

1647

132   The poorest he that is in England hath a life to
live as the greatest he.
Thomas Rainborowe (d. 1648) English soldier and vice-admiral.
Life of Rainborowe (Peacock)

1648

133   'Twixt kings and tyrants there's this difference
known;
Kings seek their subjects' good: tyrants their
own.
Robert Herrick (1591–1674) English poet.
Hesperides, 'Kings and Tyrants'

134   Do you not know, my son, with how little wisdom the world is governed?
Axel Oxenstierna (1583–1654) Swedish
statesman.
Letter to his son, 1648

1649

135   A Subject and a Sovereign are clean different
things.
Charles I (1600–49) King of England.
Speech on the scaffold, 30 Jan 1649

136 I die a Christian, according to the Profession of
     the Church of England, as I found it left me by
     my Father.
     Charles I
     Speech on the scaffold, 30 Jan 1649

137 He nothing common did or mean
     Upon that memorable scene,
     But with his keener eye
     The axe's edge did try.
     Andrew Marvell (1621–78) English poet.
     Referring to the execution of Charles I
     *An Horatian Ode upon Cromwell's Return from
     Ireland*

138 Oh let that day from time be blotted quite,
     And let belief of't in next age be waived.
     In deepest silence th'act concealed might,
     So that the Kingdom's credit might be saved.

     But if the Power Divine permitted this,
     His Will's the law and ours must acquiesce.
     Lord Thomas Fairfax (1612–71) General.
     Referring to the execution of Charles I
     The Faber Book of English History in Verse
     (Kenneth Baker)

139 I paid a visit of condolence to the Queen of
     England. Her husband had been beheaded by
     order of the British parliament. The court did
     not go into general mourning on this occasion,
     for want of funds. I found her not so deeply
     affected as she should have been.
     Duchess of Montpensier (1627–93) Niece
     of Louis XIII.
     Referring to the French court
     Mémoires, Feb 1649

140 You noble Diggers all, stand up now,
     The waste land to maintain, seeing Cavaliers
     by name
     Your digging do disdain and persons all
     defame.
     Gerrard Winstanley (c. 1609–c. 1660)
     Leader of the Diggers.
     The Diggers were a radical group that believed in
     land reform and practised a primitive agrarian
     communism. Important in 1649, they were dis-
     persed by the Commonwealth government in
     1650
     The Diggers' Song

141 Seeing the common people of England by joint
     consent of person and purse have cast out
     Charles our Norman oppressor, we have by
     this victory recovered ourselves from under his
     Norman yoke.
     Gerrard Winstanley
     Remark to Lord Fairfax, 8 Dec 1649

142 None ought to be lords or landlords over an-
     other, but the earth is free for every son and
     daughter of mankind to live free upon.
     Gerrard Winstanley
     Letter to Lord Fairfax, 1649

143 None can love freedom heartily, but good men;
     the rest love not freedom, but licence.
     John Milton (1608–74) English poet.
     Tenure of Kings and Magistrates

144 The power of kings and magistrates is nothing
     else, but what only is derivative, transformed
     and committed to them in trust from the
     people to the common good of them all, in
     whom the power yet remains fundamentally,
     and cannot be taken from them, without a viola-
     tion of their natural birthright.
     John Milton
     The Tenure of Kings and Magistrates

1650

145 I beseech you, in the bowels of Christ, think it
     possible you may be mistaken.
     Oliver Cromwell (1599–1658) English soldier
     and statesman.
     Letter to the General Assembly of the Church of
     Scotland, 3 Aug 1650

146 So restless Cromwell could not cease
     In the inglorious arts of peace.
     Andrew Marvell (1621–78) English poet.
     *An Horatian Ode upon Cromwell's Return from
     Ireland*

1651

147 The condition of man . . . is a condition of war
     of everyone against everyone.
     Thomas Hobbes (1588–1679) English
     philosopher.
     Leviathan, Pt. I, Ch. 4

148 They that approve a private opinion, call it opin-
     ion; but they that mislike it, heresy: and yet
     heresy signifies no more than private opinion.
     Thomas Hobbes
     Leviathan, Pt. I, Ch. 11

149 No arts; no letters; no society; and which is
     worst of all, continual fear and danger of violent
     death; and the life of man, solitary, poor,
     nasty, brutish, and short.
     Thomas Hobbes
     Leviathan, Pt. I, Ch. 13

150 The only way to erect such a common power,
     as may be able to defend them from the inva-
     sion of foreigners, and the injuries of one an-
     other . . . is, to confer all their power and
     strength upon one man, or upon one assembly
     of men, that may reduce all their wills, by plu-
     rality of voices, unto one will . . . This is the
     generation of that great Leviathan, or rather (to
     speak more reverently) of that *Mortal God*, to
     which we owe under the *Immortal God*, our
     peace and defence.
     Thomas Hobbes
     Leviathan, Pt. II, Ch. 17

151 Covenants without the sword are but words
     and of no strength to secure a man at all.
     Thomas Hobbes
     Leviathan, Pt. II, Ch. 17

152 They that are discontented under *monarchy*,
     call it *tyranny* ; and they that are displeased
     with *aristocracy*, call it *oligarchy*: so also, they
     which find themselves grieved under a *democ-
     racy*, call it *anarchy*, which signifies the want
     of government; and yet I think no man believes,

that want of government, is any new kind of government.
Thomas Hobbes
Leviathan, Pt. II, Ch. 19

153 The Papacy is not other than the Ghost of the deceased Roman Empire, sitting crowned upon the grave thereof.
Thomas Hobbes
Leviathan, Pt. IV, Ch. 37

1652

154 It is upon the navy under the Providence of God that the safety, honour, and welfare of this realm do chiefly attend.
Charles II (1630–1685) King of England.
Articles of War

155 Peace hath her victories
No less renowned than war.
John Milton (1608–74) English poet.
Sonnet: 'To the Lord General Cromwell, May 1652'

1653

156 Take away that fool's bauble, the mace.
Oliver Cromwell (1599–1658) English soldier and statesman.
Speech dismissing the Rump Parliament, 20 Apr 1653

157 It is not fit that you should sit here any longer! ... you shall now give place to better men.
Oliver Cromwell
Speech dismissing the Rump Parliament, 20 Apr 1653

1654

158 The people would be just as noisy if they were going to see me hanged.
Oliver Cromwell
Referring to a cheering crowd

159 Necessity hath no law.
Oliver Cromwell
Speech, Parliament, 12 Sept 1654

1655

160* Mr Lely, I desire you would use all your skill to paint my picture truly like me, and not flatter me at all; but remark all these roughnesses, pimples, warts, and everything as you see me, otherwise I will never pay a farthing for it.
Oliver Cromwell
The origin of the expression 'warts and all'
Anecdotes of Painting (Horace Walpole), Ch. 12

1656

161 For the Colonies in the Indies, they are yet babes that cannot live without sucking the breasts of their mother-Cities, but such as, I

mistake, if when they come of age they do not wean themselves.
James Harrington (1611–77) English political writer.
The Commonwealth of Oceana

1660

162* Christianity is part of the Common Law of England.
Matthew Hale (1609–76) English judge.
Historia Placitorum Coronae (ed. Sollom Emlyn)

163 He will be looked upon by posterity as a brave bad man.
Edward Hyde, Earl of Clarendon (1609–74) English statesman and historian.
Referring to Cromwell
History of the Great Rebellion

164 Here out of the window it was a most pleasant sight to see the City from one end to the other with a glory about it, and so high was the light of the bonfires, and so thick round the City, and the bells rang everywhere.
Samuel Pepys (1633–1703) English diarist.
Describing the celebrations in London at the end of the Commonwealth
Diary, 21 Feb 1660

165 Of this you may be assured, that you shall none of you suffer for your opinions or religion, so long as you live peaceably, and you have the word of a king for it.
Charles II (1630–85)
Said to a deputation of quakers
Works (R. Hubberthorn)

Attitudes

Art, Literature, and Music

1595

166 There have been many most excellent poets that have never versified, and now swarm many versifiers that need never answer to the name of poets.
Philip Sidney (1554–86) English poet and courtier.
The Defence of Poesy

1597

167 The man that hath no music in himself,
Nor is not mov'd with concord of sweet sounds,
Is fit for treasons, stratagems, and spoils.
William Shakespeare (1564–1616) English dramatist.
The Merchant of Venice, V:1

1600

168* Good painters imitate nature, bad ones spew it up.
Miguel de Cervantes (1547–1616) Spanish novelist.
El Licenciado Vidriera

169 O that Ocean did not bound our style
Within these strict and narrow limits so:
But that the melody of our sweet isle
Might now be heard to Tiber, Arne, and Po:
That they might know how far Thames doth outgo
The music of declined Italy.
Michael Drayton
Referring to the English Language
The Reign of Elizabeth (J. B. Black), Ch. 8

170 The truest poetry is the most feigning.
William Shakespeare (1564–1616) English dramatist.
As You Like It, III:3

1601

171 The play, I remember, pleas'd not the million; 'twas caviare to the general.
William Shakespeare
Hamlet, II:2

1602

172 If music be the food of love, play on,
Give me excess of it, that, surfeiting,
The appetite may sicken and so die.
William Shakespeare
Twelfth Night, I:1

1609

173 Not marble, nor the gilded monuments
Of princes, shall outlive this powerful rhyme.
William Shakespeare
Sonnet 55

1612

174 Our revels now are ended. These our actors,
As I foretold you, were all spirits, and
Are melted into air, into thin air;
And, like the baseless fabric of this vision,
The cloud-capp'd towers, the gorgeous palaces,
The solemn temples, the great globe itself,
Yea, all which it inherit, shall dissolve,
And, like this insubstantial pageant faded,
Leave not a rack behind. We are such stuff
As dreams are made on; and our little life
Is rounded with a sleep.
William Shakespeare
The Tempest, IV:1

1616

175 Sweet Swan of Avon!
Ben Jonson (1573–1637) English dramatist.
To the Memory of William Shakespeare

176 He was not of an age, but for all time!
Ben Jonson
To the Memory of William Shakespeare

1621

177 From this it is clear how much more cruel the pen is than the sword.
Robert Burton (1577–1640) English scholar and explorer.
Anatomy of Melancholy, Pt. I

1624

178 In *Architecture* as in all other *Operative Arts,* the *end* must direct the *Operation.* The *end* is to build well. Well building hath three Conditions. *Commodity, Firmness,* and *Delight.*
Henry Wotton (1568–1639) English poet and diplomat.
Elements of Architecture, Pt. I

1630

179 My soul; sit thou a patient looker-on;
Judge not the play before the play is done:
Her plot hath many changes, every day
Speaks a new scene; the last act crowns the play.
Francis Quarles (1592–1644) English poet.
Epigram, Respice Finem

1632

180 Or sweetest Shakespeare, Fancy's child,
Warble his native wood-notes wild.
John Milton (1608–74) English poet.
L'Allegro

1637

181 The reading of all good books is like a conversation with the finest men of past centuries.
René Descartes (1596–1650) French philosopher.
Le Discours de la méthode

1644

182 Who kills a man kills a reasonable creature, God's image; but he who destroys a good book kills reason itself, kills the image of God, as it were in the eye.
John Milton (1608–74) English poet.
Areopagitica

183 A good book is the precious life-blood of a master spirit, embalmed and treasured up on purpose to a life beyond life.
John Milton
Areopagitica

Daily Life

1530

184 Who loves not wine, woman and song,
Remains a fool his whole life long.
Martin Luther (1483–1546) German
Protestant.
Attrib.

1531

185 ... wherein is nothing but beastly fury and extreme violence, whereof proceedeth hurt; and
consequently rancour and malice do remain
with them that be wounded.
Sir Thomas Elyot (?1450–1522) English
diplomat.
Referring to football
Boke called the Governour

1534

186 I drink for the thirst to come.
François Rabelais (1483–1553) French
satirist.
Gargantua, Bk. I, Ch. 5

1550

187* For when the wine is in, the wit is out.
Thomas Becon (1512–67) English Protestant
churchman.
Catechism, 375

1557

188 At Christmas play and make good cheer,
For Christmas comes but once a year.
Thomas Tusser (1524–80) English farmer.
Five Hundred Points of Good Husbandry, 'The
Farmer's Daily Diet'

189 Seek home for rest,
For home is best.
Thomas Tusser
Five Hundred Points of Good Husbandry, 'In-
structions to Housewifery'

1583

190 Football ... causeth fighting, brawling, conten-
tion, quarrel picking, murder, homicide and
great effusion of bloode, as daily experience
teacheth.
Philip Stubbes (fl. 1583–91) English puritan
pamphleteer.
Anatomie of Abuses

1584

191 ... many thousands of idle persons are within
this realm which, being no way to be set on
work, be either mutinous and seek alteration in
the state or at least very burdensome to the
common wealth and often fall to pilfering and
thieving and other lewdness, whereby all the
prisons of the land are daily pestered and
stuffed full of them.
Richard Hakluyt (c. 1552–1616) Geographer.
Particular Discourse of Western Planting

1598

192 Ods me, I marvel what pleasure or felicity they
have in taking their roguish tobacco. It is good
for nothing but to choke a man, and fill him
full of smoke and embers.
Ben Jonson (1573–1637) English dramatist.
Every Man in His Humour, III:5

1604

193 A branch of the sin of drunkenness, which is
the root of all sins.
James I (1566–1625) King of England.
A Counterblast to Tobacco

194 A custom loathsome to the eye, hateful to the
nose, harmful to the brain, dangerous to the
lungs, and in the black, stinking fume
thereof, nearest resembling the horrible Stygian
smoke of the pit that is bottomless.
James I
A Counterblast to Tobacco

1610

195* Houses are built to live in and not to look on;
therefore let use be preferred before uniform-
ity, except where both may be had.
Francis Bacon (1561–1626) English
philosopher.
Essays, 'Of Building'

1611

196 I would there were no age between ten and
three and twenty, or that youth would sleep out
the rest; for there is nothing in the between
but getting wenches with child, wronging the
ancientry, stealing, fighting.
William Shakespeare (1564–1616) English
dramatist and critic.
The Winter's Tale, III:3

1614

197 Neither do thou lust after that tawney weed
tobacco.
Ben Jonson (1573–1637) English dramatist.
Bartholomew Fair, II:6

1616

198 And he that will go to bed sober,
Falls with the leaf still in October.
John Fletcher (1579–1625) English dramatist.
The Bloody Brother, II:2

1622

199* The house of every one is to him as his castle
and fortress.
Edward Coke (1552–1634) English lawyer
and politician.
Semayne's Case

1632
---

200 Popular stage-plays are sinful, heathenish,
lewd, ungodly Spectacles and most pernicious
Corruptions, condemned in all ages as intolerable Mischiefs to Churches, to Republics,
to the manners, minds and souls of men.
William Prynne (1600–69) English Puritan.
Histriomastix

Death

1589
---

201 Sleep after toil, port after stormy seas,
Ease after war, death after life does greatly
please.
Edmund Spenser (1552–99) English poet.
The Faerie Queene, I:9

1598
---

202 I care not; a man can die but once; we owe
God a death.
William Shakespeare (1564–1616) English
dramatist.
Henry IV, Part Two, III:2

1600
---

203 I have often thought upon death, and I find it
the least of all evils.
Francis Bacon (1561–1626) English
philosopher.
An Essay on Death

204 I do not believe that any man fears to be dead,
but only the stroke of death.
Francis Bacon
An Essay on Death

205 Men fear death, as children fear to go in the
dark; and as that natural fear in children is increased with tales, so is the other.
Francis Bacon
An Essay on Death

206 It is natural to die as to be born; and to a little
infant, perhaps, the one is as painful as the
other.
Francis Bacon
An Essay on Death

207 Why, he that cuts off twenty years of life
Cuts off so many years of fearing death.
William Shakespeare (1564–1616) English
dramatist.
Julius Caesar, III:1

1601
---

208 The dread of something after death –
The undiscover'd country, from whose bourn
No traveller returns.
William Shakespeare
Hamlet, III:1

209 To be, or not to be – that is the question;
Whether 'tis nobler in the mind to suffer
The slings and arrows of outrageous fortune,
Or to take arms against a sea of troubles,
And by opposing end them? To die, to
sleep –
No more; and by a sleep to say we end
The heart-ache and the thousand natural
shocks
That flesh is heir to, 'tis a consummation
Devoutly to be wish'd. To die, to sleep;
To sleep, perchance to dream. Ay, there's the
rub;
For in that sleep of death what dreams may
come,
When we have shuffled off this mortal coil,
Must give us pause.
William Shakespeare
Hamlet, III:1

1606
---

210 As flies to wanton boys are we to th' gods –
They kill us for their sport.
William Shakespeare
King Lear, IV:1

1609
---

211 Like as the waves make towards the pebbled
shore,
So do our minutes hasten to their end.
William Shakespeare
Sonnet 60

1610
---

212 Fear no more the heat o' th' sun
Nor the furious winter's rages;
Thou thy worldly task hast done,
Home art gone, and ta'en thy wages.
Golden lads and girls all must,
As chimney-sweepers, come to dust.
William Shakespeare
Cymbeline, IV:2

1615
---

213 Well, now, there's a remedy for everything except death.
Miguel de Cervantes (1547–1616) Spanish
novelist.
Don Quixote, Pt. II, Ch. 10

1623
---

214 Any man's death diminishes me, because I am
involved in Mankind; And therefore never

send to know for whom the bell tolls; it tolls
for thee.
John Donne (1573–1631) English poet.
Devotions, 17

Education, Knowledge, and Learning

1570

15 I remember when I was young, in the north,
they went to the grammar school little children:
they came from thence great lubbers: always
learning, and little profiting: learning without
book everything, understanding within the book
little or nothing.
Roger Ascham (1515–68)
The Scholemaster

1595

16 Wisely and slow; they stumble that run fast.
William Shakespeare (1564–1616) English
dramatist.
Romeo and Juliet, II:3

1605

17 If a man will begin with certainties, he shall end
in doubts, but if he will be content to begin
with doubts, he shall end in certainties.
Francis Bacon (1561–1626) English
philosopher.
The Advancement of Learning, Bk. I, Ch. 5

18 For all knowledge and wonder (which is the
seed of knowledge) is an impression of pleasure in itself.
Francis Bacon
The Advancement of Learning, Bk. I, Ch. 1

1610

19* A wise man will make more opportunities than
he finds.
Francis Bacon
Essays, 'Of Ceremonies and Respects'

20* *Nam et ipsa scientia potestas est.*
Knowledge itself is power.
Francis Bacon
Religious Meditations, 'Of Heresies'

21* Reading maketh a full man; conference a ready
man; and writing an exact man.
Francis Bacon
Essays, 'Of Studies'

1642

22 Learning hath gained most by those books by
which the printers have lost.
Thomas Fuller (1608–61) English historian.
The Holy State and the Profane State

23 Many have been the wise speeches of fools,

though not so many as the foolish speeches of
wise men.
Thomas Fuller
The Holy State and the Profane State

Human Nature

1579

224 And he that strives to touch the stars,
Oft stumbles at a straw.
Edmund Spenser (1552–99) English poet.
The Shepherd's Calendar, 'July'

1580

225 Unless a man feels he has a good enough
memory, he should never venture to lie.
Michel de Montaigne (1533–92) French
essayist.
Also quoted in *Le Menteur*, IV:5 by Pierre Corneille (1606–84)
Essais, I

226 A man who fears suffering is already suffering
from what he fears.
Michel de Montaigne
Essais, III

227 The dark night of the soul.
St John of the Cross (Juan de Yepes y Alvarez; 1542–91) Spanish churchman and poet.
English translation of *Noche obscura del alma*,
the title of a poem

1583

228 We are as near to heaven by sea as by land.
Humphrey Gilbert (c. 1539–83) English
navigator.
Remark made shortly before he went down with
his ship *Squirrel*
A Book of Anecdotes (D. George)

1595

229 What's in a name? That which we call a rose
By any other name would smell as sweet.
William Shakespeare (1564–1616) English
dramatist.
Romeo and Juliet, II:2

1597

230 The devil can cite Scripture for his purpose.
William Shakespeare
The Merchant of Venice, I:3

231 Hath not a Jew eyes? Hath not a Jew hands,
organs, dimensions, senses, affections, passions, fed with the same food, hurt with the
same weapons, subject to the same diseases,
healed by the same means, warmed and
cooled by the same winter and summer, as a
Christian is? If you prick us, do we not bleed?
If you tickle us, do we not laugh? If you

poison us, do we not die? And if you wrong us,
shall we not revenge?
William Shakespeare
The Merchant of Venice, III:1

1598

232 Care I for the limb, the thews, the stature, bulk,
and big assemblance of a man! Give me the
spirit.
William Shakespeare
Henry IV, Part Two, III:2

1599

233 Friendship is constant in all other things
Save in the office and affairs of love.
William Shakespeare
Much Ado About Nothing, II:1

234 Men of few words are the best men.
William Shakespeare
Henry V, III:2

235 To be a well-favoured man is the gift of fortune;
but to write and read comes by nature.
William Shakespeare
Much Ado About Nothing, III:3

1600

236 A friend should bear his friend's infirmities,
But Brutus makes mine greater than they are.
William Shakespeare
Julius Caesar, IV:3

237 Most friendship is feigning, most loving mere
folly.
William Shakespeare
As You Like It, II:7

1601

238 Costly thy habit as thy purse can buy,
But not express'd in fancy; rich, not gaudy;
For the apparel oft proclaims the man.
William Shakespeare
Hamlet, I:3

239 To be honest, as this world goes, is to be one
man pick'd out of ten thousand.
William Shakespeare
Hamlet, II:2

240 What a piece of work is a man! How noble in
reason! how infinite in faculties! in form and
moving, how express and admirable! in action,
how like an angel! in apprehension, how like a
god! the beauty of the world! the paragon of
animals! And yet, to me, what is this quintes-
sence of dust? Man delights not me — no,
nor woman neither.
William Shakespeare
Hamlet, II:2

1603

241 Our remedies oft in ourselves do lie,

Which we ascribe to heaven.
William Shakespeare
All's Well that Ends Well, I:1

1605

242 The miserable have no other medicine
But only hope.
William Shakespeare
Measure for Measure, III:1

1606

243 This is the excellent foppery of the world, that
when we are sick in fortune, often the surfeits
of our own behaviour, we make guilty of our
disasters the sun, the moon, and stars.
William Shakespeare
King Lear, I:2

244 Yet do I fear thy nature;
It is too full o' th' milk of human kindness
To catch the nearest way.
William Shakespeare
Macbeth, I:5

1609

245 3RD FISHERMAN. Master, I marvel how the fishes
live in the sea.
1ST FISHERMAN. Why, as men do a-land — the
great ones eat up the little ones.
William Shakespeare
Pericles, II:1

1610

246 There is in human nature generally more of the
fool than of the wise.
Francis Bacon (1561–1626) English
philosopher.
Essays, 'Of Boldness'

247* A man's nature runs either to herbs, or to
weeds; therefore let him seasonably water the
one, and destroy the other.
Francis Bacon
Essays, 'Of Nature in Men'

248 Nature is often hidden, sometimes overcome,
seldom extinguished.
Francis Bacon
Essays, 'Of Nature in Men'

249 You are no better than you should be.
Francis Beaumont (1584–1616) English
dramatist.
The Coxcomb, IV:3

1611

250 It is the wisdom of the crocodiles, that shed
tears when they would devour.
Francis Bacon (1561–1626) English
philosopher.
Essays, 'Of Wisdom for a Man's Self'

1612

51   When they will not give a doit to relieve a lame beggar, they will lay out ten to see a dead Indian.
William Shakespeare (1564–1616) English dramatist.
The Tempest, II:2

1615

52   Every man is as Heaven made him, and sometimes a great deal worse.
Miguel de Cervantes (1547–1616) Spanish novelist.
Don Quixote, Pt. II, Ch. 4

1623

53   He that would govern others, first should be
The master of himself.
Philip Massinger (1583–1640) English dramatist.
The Bondman, I

1632

54   Hence, vain deluding Joys,
The brood of Folly without father bred!
John Milton (1608–74) English poet.
Il Penseroso

1637

55   We triumph without glory when we conquer without danger.
Pierre Corneille (1606–84) French dramatist.
Le Cid, II:2

1641

56   Talking and eloquence are not the same: to speak, and to speak well, are two things.
Ben Jonson (1573–1637) English dramatist.
Timber, or Discoveries made upon Men and Matter

57   One often calms one's grief by recounting it.
Pierre Corneille (1606–84) French dramatist.
Polyeucte, I:3

1642

58   If you give me six lines written by the most honest man, I will find something in them to hang him.
Cardinal Richelieu (1585–1642) French statesman.
Exact wording uncertain
Attrib.

59   Anger is one of the sinews of the soul.
Thomas Fuller (1608–61) English historian.
The Holy State and the Profane State

Humour

1595

260   A jest's prosperity lies in the ear
Of him that hears it, never in the tongue
Of him that makes it.
William Shakespeare (1564–1616) English dramatist.
Love's Labour's Lost, V:2

Life

1530

261   Nature abhors a vacuum.
François Rabelais (1483–1553) French satirist.
Attrib.

1549

262   The drop of rain maketh a hole in the stone, not by violence, but by oft falling.
Hugh Latimer (1485–1555) English churchman.
Sermon preached before Edward VI

1580

263   Change is not made without inconvenience, even from worse to better.
Richard Hooker (c. 1554–1600) English theologian.
English Dictionary (Johnson), Preface

264   The world is but a school of inquiry.
Michel de Montaigne (1533–92) French essayist.
Essais, III

265   A man must keep a little back shop where he can be himself without reserve. In solitude alone can he know true freedom.
Michel de Montaigne
Essais, I

1592

266   When all the world dissolves,
And every creature shall be purified,
All place shall be hell that is not heaven.
Christopher Marlowe (1564–93) English dramatist.
Doctor Faustus, II:1

1596

267   The purest treasure mortal times afford
Is spotless reputation; that away,
Men are but gilded loam or painted clay.
William Shakespeare (1564–1616) English dramatist.
Richard II, I:1

268   How sour sweet music is
When time is broke and no proportion kept!

So is it in the music of men's lives.
William Shakespeare
Richard II, V:5

269 Things sweet to taste prove in digestion sour.
William Shakespeare
Richard II, I:3

270 Teach thy necessity to reason thus:
There is no virtue like necessity.
William Shakespeare
Richard II, I:3

1597

271 Life is as tedious as a twice-told tale
Vexing the dull ear of a drowsy man.
William Shakespeare
King John, III:4

1599

272 I think the King is but a man as I am: the violet
smells to him as it doth to me.
William Shakespeare
Henry V, IV:1

273 Crabbed age and youth cannot live together:
Youth is full of pleasure, age is full of care;
Youth like summer morn, age like winter
weather;
Youth like summer brave, age like winter
bare.
William Shakespeare (1564–1616) English
dramatist.
The Passionate Pilgrim, XII

1600

274 All the world's a stage,
And all the men and women merely players;
They have their exits and their entrances;
And one man in his time plays many parts,
His acts being seven ages.
William Shakespeare
As You Like It, II:7

275 Last scene of all,
That ends this strange eventful history,
Is second childishness and mere oblivion;
Sans teeth, sans eyes, sans taste, sans every
thing.
William Shakespeare
As You Like It, II:7

276 And so, from hour to hour, we ripe and ripe,
And then, from hour to hour, we rot and rot;
And thereby hangs a tale.
William Shakespeare
As You Like It, II:7

277 There is a tide in the affairs of men
Which, taken at the flood, leads on to fortune;
Omitted, all the voyage of their life
Is bound in shallows and in miseries.
On such a full sea are we now afloat,
And we must take the current when it serves,
Or lose our ventures.
William Shakespeare
Julius Caesar, IV:3

1601

278 When sorrows come, they come not single
spies,
But in battalions!
William Shakespeare
Hamlet, IV:5

279 Why, then the world's mine oyster,
Which I with sword will open.
William Shakespeare
The Merry Wives of Windsor, II:2

280 There are more things in heaven and earth, Ho
ratio,
Than are dreamt of in your philosophy.
William Shakespeare
Hamlet, I:5

281 How weary, stale, flat, and unprofitable,
Seem to me all the uses of this world!
William Shakespeare
Hamlet, I:2

1602

282 Some are born great, some achieve greatness
and some have greatness thrust upon 'em.
William Shakespeare
Twelfth Night, II:5

1603

283 The world itself is but a large prison, out of
which some are daily led to execution.
Walter Raleigh (1554–1618) English explorer
Said after his trial for treason, 1603
Attrib.

284 The web of our life is of a mingled yarn, good
and ill together.
William Shakespeare (1564–1616) English
dramatist.
All's Well that Ends Well, IV:3

1605

285 Reputation, reputation, reputation! O, I have
lost my reputation! I have lost the immortal par
of myself, and what remains is bestial.
William Shakespeare
Othello, II:3

286 To mourn a mischief that is past and gone
Is the next way to draw new mischief on.
William Shakespeare
Othello, I:3

1606

287 Tomorrow, and tomorrow, and tomorrow,
Creeps in this petty pace from day to day
To the last syllable of recorded time,
And all our yesterdays have lighted fools
The way to dusty death. Out, out, brief
candle!
Life's but a walking shadow, a poor player,
That struts and frets his hour upon the stage
And then is heard no more; it is a tale
Told by an idiot, full of sound and fury,

Signifying nothing.
William Shakespeare
Macbeth, V:5

288 When we are born, we cry that we are come
To this great stage of fools.
William Shakespeare
King Lear, IV:6

289 The worst is not
So long as we can say 'This is the worst'.
William Shakespeare
King Lear, IV:1

290 Come what come may,
Time and the hour runs through the roughest
day.
William Shakespeare
Macbeth, I:3

1607
---

291 My salad days,
When I was green in judgment, cold in blood,
To say as I said then!
William Shakespeare
Antony and Cleopatra, I:5

1610

292* There is no excellent beauty that hath not some
strangeness in the proportion.
Francis Bacon (1561–1626) English
philosopher.
Essays, 'Of Beauty'

293* He that will not apply new remedies must expect new evils: for time is the greatest
innovator.
Francis Bacon
Essays, 'Of Innovations'

294 Dreams and predictions ought to serve but for
winter talk by the fireside.
Francis Bacon (1561–1626) English
philosopher.
Essays, 'Of Prophecies'

1612
---

295 Misery acquaints a man with strange
bedfellows.
William Shakespeare (1564–1616) English
dramatist.
The Tempest, II:2

1613
---

296 Farewell, a long farewell, to all my greatness!
This is the state of man: to-day he puts forth
The tender leaves of hopes: to-morrow
blossoms
And bears his blushing honours thick upon
him;
The third day comes a frost, a killing frost,
And when he thinks, good easy man, full
surely
His greatness is a-ripening, nips his root,

And then he falls, as I do.
William Shakespeare
Henry VIII, III:2

1620

297* A man that is young in years may be old in
hours, if he have lost no time.
Francis Bacon (1561–1626) English
philosopher.
Essays, 'Of Youth and Age'

1621
---

298 If there is a hell upon earth, it is to be found in
a melancholy man's heart.
Robert Burton (1577–1640) English scholar
and explorer.
Anatomy of Melancholy, Pt. I

1623
---

299 No man is an Island, entire of itself; every man
is a piece of the Continent, a part of the main.
John Donne (1573–1631) English poet.
Devotions, 17

1625
---

300 For my name and memory, I leave it to men's
charitable speeches, and to foreign nations,
and the next ages.
Francis Bacon (1561–1626) English
philosopher.
Will, 19 Dec 1625

1630
---

301 Tempt not the stars, young man, thou canst not
play
With the severity of fate.
John Ford (c. 1586–c. 1640) English
dramatist.
The Broken Heart, I:3

1635
---

302 For man's greatest crime is to have been born.
Pedro Calderón de la Barca (1600–81)
Spanish dramatist.
La Vida es Sueño, I

303 For I see now that I am asleep that I dream
when I am awake.
Pedro Calderón de la Barca
La Vida es Sueño, II

1637
---

304 *Cogito, ergo sum.*
I think, therefore I am.
René Descartes (1596–1650) French
philosopher.
Le Discours de la méthode

305 Travelling is almost like talking with men of
other centuries.
René Descartes
Le Discours de la méthode

306 Fame is the spur that the clear spirit doth raise
(That last infirmity of noble mind)
To scorn delights, and live laborious days.
John Milton (1608–74) English poet.
Lycidas

1642
-----

307 All things are artificial, for nature is the art of
God.
Thomas Browne (1605–82) English physician
and writer.
Religio Medici, Pt. I

308 There is surely a piece of divinity in us, something that was before the elements, and owes
no homage unto the sun.
Thomas Browne
Religio Medici, Pt. II

309 For the world, I count it not an inn, but an hos-
pital, and a place, not to live, but to die in.
Thomas Browne
Religio Medici, Pt. II

310 Fame is sometimes like unto a kind of mushroom, which Pliny recounts to be the greatest
miracle in nature, because growing and having no root.
Thomas Fuller (1608–61) English historian.
The Holy State and the Profane State

Love and Sex

1580
-----

311 The daughter-in-law of Pythagoras said that a
woman who goes to bed with a man ought to
lay aside her modesty with her skirt, and put it
on again with her petticoat.
Michel de Montaigne (1533–92) French
essayist.
Essais, I

1590

312* Love built on beauty, soon as beauty, dies.
John Donne (1573–1631) English poet.
Elegies, 2, 'The Anagram'

1595
-----

313 Therefore love moderately: long love doth so;
Too swift arrives as tardy as too slow.
William Shakespeare (1564–1616) English
dramatist.
Romeo and Juliet, II:6

1596
-----

314 For aught that I could ever read,
Could ever hear by tale or history,

The course of true love never did run smooth.
William Shakespeare
A Midsummer Night's Dream, I:1

315 Love looks not with the eyes, but with the
mind;
And therefore is wing'd Cupid painted blind.
William Shakespeare
A Midsummer Night's Dream, I:1

1597
-----

316 But love is blind, and lovers cannot see
The pretty follies that themselves commit.
William Shakespeare
The Merchant of Venice, II:6

1598
-----

317 Who ever loved, that loved not at first sight?
Christopher Marlowe (1564–93) English
dramatist.
Hero and Leander, I

1600
-----

318 If thou rememb'rest not the slightest folly
That ever love did make thee run into,
Thou hast not lov'd.
William Shakespeare (1564–1616) English
dramatist.
As You Like It, II:4

319 Men have died from time to time, and worms
have eaten them, but not for love.
William Shakespeare
As You Like It, IV:1

1602
-----

320 What is love? 'Tis not hereafter;
Present mirth hath present laughter;
What's to come is still unsure.
In delay there lies no plenty,
Then come kiss me, sweet and twenty;
Youth's a stuff will not endure.
William Shakespeare
Twelfth Night, II:3

321 Love sought is good, but given unsought is
better.
William Shakespeare
Twelfth Night, III:1

322 To be wise and love
Exceeds man's might.
William Shakespeare
Troilus and Cressida, III:2

323 Lechery, lechery! Still wars and lechery! Noth-
ing else holds fashion.
William Shakespeare
Troilus and Cressida, V:2

1609
-----

324 Let me not to the marriage of true minds
Admit impediments. Love is not love
Which alters when it alteration finds,
Or bends with the remover to remove.

O, no! it is an ever-fixed mark,
That looks on tempests and is never shaken.
William Shakespeare
Sonnet 116

25 Th' expense of spirit in a waste of shame
Is lust in action; and till action, lust
Is perjur'd, murd'rous, bloody, full of blame,
Savage, extreme, rude, cruel, not to trust;
Enjoy'd no sooner but despised straight.
William Shakespeare
Sonnet 129

1610

26* Nuptial love maketh mankind; friendly love
perfecteth it; but wanton love corrupteth and
embaseth it.
Francis Bacon (1561–1626) English
philosopher.
Essays, 'Of Love'

1611

27 Those have most power to hurt us that we love.
Francis Beaumont (1584–1616) English
dramatist.
The Maid's Tragedy, V:6

1614

28 Love is a sickness full of woes,
All remedies refusing;
A plant that with most cutting grows,
Most barren with best using.
Why so?
More we enjoy it, more it dies;
If not enjoyed, it sighing cries,
Hey ho.
Samuel Daniel (c. 1562–1619) English poet
and dramatist.
Hymen's Triumph, I

1616

29 Drink to me only with thine eyes,
And I will pledge with mine;
Or leave a kiss but in the cup,
And I'll not look for wine.
The thirst that from the soul doth rise
Doth ask a drink divine;
But might I of Jove's nectar sup,
I would not change for thine.

I sent thee late a rosy wreath,
Not so much honouring thee,
As giving it a hope that there
It could not wither'd be.
Ben Jonson (1573–1637) English dramatist.
The Forest, IX, 'To Celia'

1648

30 Gather ye rosebuds while ye may,
Old time is still a-flying:
And this same flower that smiles today

Tomorrow will be dying.
Robert Herrick (1591–1674) English poet.
Hesperides, 'To the Virgins, to Make Much of
Time'

Marriage and the Family

1580

331 Marriage is like a cage; one sees the birds
outside desperate to get in, and those inside
equally desperate to get out.
Michel de Montaigne (1533–92) French
essayist.
Essais, III

1597

332 It is a wise father that knows his own child.
William Shakespeare (1564–1616) English
dramatist.
The Merchant of Venice, II:2

1606

333 Ingratitude, thou marble-hearted fiend,
More hideous when thou show'st thee in a
child
Than the sea-monster!
William Shakespeare
King Lear I:4

1610

334* Wives are young men's mistresses, companions for middle age, and old men's nurses.
Francis Bacon (1561–1626) English
philosopher.
Essays, 'Of Marriage and Single Life'

335* Children sweeten labours, but they make mis-
fortunes more bitter.
Francis Bacon
Essays, 'Of Parents and Children'

336* He that hath wife and children hath given hostages to fortune; for they are impediments to
great enterprises, either of virtue or
mischief.
Francis Bacon
Essays, 'Of Marriage and Single Life'

337* He was reputed one of the wise men, that made
answer to the question, when a man should
marry? A young man not yet, an elder man not
at all.
Francis Bacon
Essays, 'Of Marriage and Single Life'

1650

338* He that loves not his wife and children, feeds a
lioness at home and broods a nest of sorrows.
Jeremy Taylor (1613–67) English Anglican
theologian.
Sermons, 'Married Love'

1662

339 To have and to hold from this day forward, for better for worse, for richer for poorer, in sickness and in health, to love and to cherish, till death us do part.
The Book of Common Prayer
Solemnization of Matrimony

Men and Women

1558

340 To promote a Woman to bear rule, superiority, dominion or empire, above any Realm, Nation, or City, is repugnant to Nature; contumely to God, a thing most contrarious to his revealed will and approved ordinance, and finally it is the subversion of good Order, of all equity and justice.
John Knox (c. 1514–72) Scottish religious reformer.
Opening words
First Blast of the Trumpet against the Monstrous Regiment of Women

1583

341 A ship is sooner rigged than a gentlewoman made ready.
Philip Stubbes
The Anatomie of Abuses

1595

342 I have no other but a woman's reason:
I think him so, because I think him so.
William Shakespeare (1564–1616) English dramatist.
The Two Gentlemen of Verona, I:2

1600

343 Do you not know I am a woman? When I think, I must speak.
William Shakespeare
As You Like It, III:2

1601

344 Frailty, thy name is woman!
William Shakespeare
Hamlet, I:2

1607

345 Were't not for gold and women, there would be no damnation.
Cyril Tourneur (1575–1626) English dramatist.
The Revenger's Tragedy, II:1

1610

346* These are rare attainments for a damsel, but pray tell me, can she spin?
James I (1566–1625) King of England.
On being introduced to a young girl proficient i
Latin, Greek, and Hebrew
Attrib.

1632

347 . . . it being natural and comely to women to nourish their hair, which even God and nature have given them for a covering, a token of subjection, and a natural badge to distinguish them from men.
William Prynne (1600–69) English Puritan.
Histriomastix

Morality, Vices, and Virtues

1534

348 In their rules there was only one clause: Do what you will.
François Rabelais (1483–1553) French satirist.
Referring to the fictional Abbey of Thélème
Gargantua, Bk. I, Ch. 57

1550

349* To give and not to count the cost;
To fight and not to heed the wounds;
To toil and not to seek for rest;
To labour and not ask for any reward
Save that of knowing that we do Thy will.
St Ignatius Loyola (1491–1556) Spanish priest.
Prayer for Generosity

1594

350 Our purses shall be proud, our garments poor
For 'tis the mind that makes the body rich;
And as the sun breaks through the darkest clouds,
So honour peereth in the meanest habit.
William Shakespeare (1564–1616) English dramatist.
The Taming of the Shrew, IV:3

1597

351 Bell, book, and candle, shall not drive me back
When gold and silver becks me to come on
William Shakespeare
King John, III:3

352 How far that little candle throws his beams!
So shines a good deed in a naughty world.
William Shakespeare
The Merchant of Venice, V:1

1598

353 Honour pricks me on. Yea, but how if honour prick me off when I come on? How then? Can honour set to a leg? No. Or an arm? No. Or take away the grief of a wound? No. Honour hath no skill in surgery, then? No. What is honour? A word. What is in that word? Honour. What is that honour? Air.
William Shakespeare
Henry IV, Part One, V:1

354 The better part of valour is discretion; in the which better part I have saved my life.
William Shakespeare
Henry IV, Part One, V:4

355 Anger makes dull men witty, but it keeps them poor.
Elizabeth I (1533–1603) Queen of England.
Apophthegms (Bacon)

1599

356 Though patience be a tired mare, yet she will plod.
William Shakespeare (1564–1616) English dramatist.
Henry V, II:1

1600

357 Blow, blow, thou winter wind,
Thou art not so unkind
As man's ingratitude.
William Shakespeare
As You Like It, II:7

358 Ambition should be made of sterner stuff.
William Shakespeare
Julius Caesar, III:2

1601

359 There is nothing either good or bad, but thinking makes it so.
William Shakespeare
Hamlet, II:2

360 Neither a borrower nor a lender be;
For loan oft loses both itself and friend,
And borrowing dulls the edge of husbandry.
This above all: to thine own self be true,
And it must follow, as the night the day,
Thou canst not then be false to any man.
William Shakespeare
Hamlet, I:3

361 Murder most foul, as in the best it is;
But this most foul, strange, and unnatural.
William Shakespeare
Hamlet, I:5

1602

362 Dost thou think, because thou art virtuous, there shall be no more cakes and ale?
William Shakespeare
Twelfth Night, II:3

363 I hate ingratitude more in a man

Than lying, vainness, babbling drunkenness,
Or any taint of vice whose strong corruption
Inhabits our frail blood.
William Shakespeare
Twelfth Night, III:4

1605

364 Just as it is always said of slander that something always sticks when people boldly slander, so it might be said of self-praise (if it is not entirely shameful and ridiculous) that if we praise ourselves fearlessly, something will always stick.
Francis Bacon (1561–1626) English philosopher.
The Advancement of Learning

365 I have always heard, Sancho, that doing good to base fellows is like throwing water into the sea.
Miguel de Cervantes (1547–1616) Spanish novelist.
Don Quixote, Pt. I, Ch. 23

366 O, beware, my lord, of jealousy;
It is the green-ey'd monster which doth mock
The meat it feeds on.
William Shakespeare (1564–1616) English dramatist.
Othello, III:3

1607

367 Celerity is never more admir'd
Than by the negligent.
William Shakespeare
Antony and Cleopatra, III:7

1610

368* Be so true to thyself, as thou be not false to others.
Francis Bacon (1561–1626) English philosopher.
Essays, 'Of Wisdom for a Man's Self'

369* A man that studieth revenge keeps his own wounds green.
Francis Bacon
Essays, 'Of Revenge'

370* As in nature things move violently to their place and calmly in their place, so virtue in ambition is violent, in authority settled and calm.
Francis Bacon
Essays, 'Of Great Place'

371* Revenge is a kind of wild justice; which the more man's nature runs to, the more ought law to weed it out.
Francis Bacon
Essays, 'Of Revenge'

372* Suspicions amongst thoughts are like bats amongst birds, they ever fly by twilight.
Francis Bacon
Essays, 'Of Suspicion'

373* It is always good

When a man has two irons in the fire.
Francis Beaumont (1584–1616) English dramatist.
The Faithful Friends, I:2

1611
---

374 Though I am not naturally honest, I am so sometimes by chance.
William Shakespeare (1564–1616) English dramatist.
The Winter's Tale, IV:3

1613
---

375 Men's evil manners live in brass: their virtues We write in water.
William Shakespeare
Henry VIII, IV:2

1614

376* Good thoughts his only friends,
His wealth a well-spent age,
The earth his sober inn
And quiet pilgrimage.
Thomas Campion (1567–1620) English poet.
The Man of Life Upright

1615
---

377 A private sin is not so prejudicial in the world as a public indecency.
Miguel de Cervantes (1547–1616) Spanish novelist.
Don Quixote, Pt. II, Ch. 22

1623
---

378 Other sins only speak; murder shrieks out.
John Webster (1580–1625) English dramatist.
The Duchess of Malfi, IV:2

1633
---

379 Only a sweet and virtuous soul,
Like season'd timber, never gives;
But though the whole world turn to coal,
Then chiefly lives.
George Herbert (1593–1633) English poet.
Virtue

1642
---

380 No man can justly censure or condemn another, because indeed no man truly knows another.
Thomas Browne (1605–82) English physician and writer.
Religio Medici, Pt. II

1644
---

381 Let her and Falsehood grapple; who ever knew

Truth put to the worse, in a free and open encounter?
John Milton (1608–74) English poet.
Areopagitica

Other People

1591
---

382 England is the paradise of women, the purgatory of men, and the hell of horses.
John Florio (c. 1553–1625) English lexicographer.
Second Fruits

1598
---

383 Well, I cannot last ever; but it was always ye the trick of our English nation, if they have a good thing, to make it too common.
William Shakespeare (1564–1616) English dramatist.
Henry IV, Part Two, I:2

1606
---

384 The Englishman's dress is like a traitor's body that hath been hanged, drawn, and quartered, and is set up in various places; his codpiece is in Denmark, the collar of his doublet and the belly in France; the wing and narrow sleeve in Italy; the short waist hangs over a Dutch butcher's stall in Utrecht; his huge slop speak Spanishly . . . And thus we that mock every nation for keeping of one fashion, yet steal patches from every one of them to piec out our pride.
Thomas Dekker (c. 1570–1632) English writer.
Seven Deadly Sins of London

1615
---

385 The French are wiser than they seem, and th Spaniards seem wiser than they are.
Francis Bacon (1561–1626) English philosopher.
Essays, 'Of Seeming Wise'

1621
---

386 England is a paradise for women, and hell for horses: Italy a paradise for horses, hell for women.
Robert Burton (1577–1640) English scholar and explorer.
Anatomy of Melancholy, Pt. III

1630

387* The English take their pleasures sadly after th fashion of their country.
Duc de Sully (1560–1641) French statesma
Memoirs

1638

388 For howbeit the Irish might do very good Service, being a People removed from the Scottish, as well in Affections as Religion; yet is not safe to train them up more than needs must in the military Way.
Thomas Wentworth (1593–1641) English statesman.
Letter to King Charles I, from Ireland, 28 July 1638

Religion

1522

389 To arrive at the truth in all things, we ought always to be ready to believe that what seems to us white is black if the hierarchical Church so defines it.
St Ignatius Loyola (1491–1556) Spanish priest.
Spiritual Exercises

1530

390* I have a Catholic soul, but a Lutheran stomach.
Erasmus (1466–1536) Dutch humanist, scholar, and writer.
Replying to criticism of his failure to fast during Lent
Dictionnaire Encyclopédique

391* Be a sinner and sin strongly, but more strongly have faith and rejoice in Christ.
Martin Luther (1483–1546) German Protestant.
Letter to Melanchthon

1532

392 Man never found the deities so kindly
As to assure him that he'd live tomorrow.
François Rabelais (1483–1553) French satirist.
Pantagruel, Bk. III, Ch. 2

1572

393 A man with God is always in the majority.
John Knox (c. 1514–72) Scottish religious reformer.
Inscription, Reformation Monument, Geneva, Switzerland

1577

394 Alas, O Lord, to what a state dost Thou bring those who love Thee!
St Teresa of Avila (1515–82) Spanish mystic.
The Interior Castle, VI

1580

395 I die because I do not die.
St John of the Cross (Juan de Yepes y Alvarez; 1542–91) Spanish churchman and poet.
Coplas del alma que pena por ver a dios

396 Man is quite insane. He wouldn't know how to create a maggot and he creates Gods by the dozen.
Michel de Montaigne (1533–92) French essayist.
Essais, II

1592

397* I count religion but a childish toy,
And hold there is no sin but ignorance.
Christopher Marlowe (1564–93) English dramatist.
The Jew of Malta, Prologue

1601

398 Do not, as some ungracious pastors do,
Show me the steep and thorny way to heaven,
Whiles, like a puff'd and reckless libertine,
Himself the primrose path of dalliance treads
And recks not his own rede.
William Shakespeare (1564–1616) English dramatist.
Hamlet, I:3

399 There's a divinity that shapes our ends,
Rough-hew them how we will.
William Shakespeare
Hamlet, V:2

1610

400* God never wrought miracle to convince atheism, because his ordinary works convince it.
Francis Bacon (1561–1626) English philosopher.
Essays, 'Of Atheism'

401* For none deny there is a God, but those for whom it maketh that there were no God.
Francis Bacon
Essays, 'Of Atheism'

402* Take heed of thinking. *The farther you go from the church of Rome, the nearer you are to God.*
Henry Wotton (1568–1639) English poet and diplomat.
Reliquiae Wottonianae (Izaak Walton)

403* It were better to have no opinion of God at all, than such an opinion as is unworthy of him.
Francis Bacon (1561–1626) English philosopher.
Essays, 'Of Superstition'

1621

404 One religion is as true as another.
Robert Burton (1577–1640) English scholar and explorer.
Anatomy of Melancholy, Pt. III

Science, Medicine, and Technology

1610

405* Books must follow sciences, and not sciences
books.
Francis Bacon (1561–1626) English
philosopher.
Proposition touching Amendment of Laws

406* Cure the disease and kill the patient.
Francis Bacon
Essays, 'Of Friendship'

407* And new Philosophy calls all in doubt,
The Element of fire is quite put out;
The Sun is lost, and th' earth, and no man's
wit
Can well direct him where to look for it.
John Donne (1573–1631) English poet.
An Anatomy of the World, 205

1615

408   . . . in my studies of astronomy and philosophy
I hold this opinion about the universe, that the
Sun remains fixed in the centre of the circle
of heavenly bodies, without changing its place;
and the Earth, turning upon itself, moves
round the Sun.
Galileo Galilei (1564–1642) Italian scientist.
Letter to Cristina di Lorena, 1615

1632

409   *Eppur si muove.*
Yet it moves.
Galileo Galilei
Referring to the Earth. Remark supposedly made
after his recantation (1632) of belief in the Co-
pernican system
Attrib.

Wealth and Poverty

1530

410   So our Lord God commonly gives riches to
those gross asses to whom he vouchsafes
nothing else.
Martin Luther (1483–1546) German
Protestant.
Colloquia (J. Aurifaber), Ch. XX

1597

411   Well, whiles I am a beggar, I will rail
And say there is no sin but to be rich;
And being rich, my virtue then shall be
To say there is no vice but beggary.
William Shakespeare (1564–1616) English
dramatist.
King John, II:1

1610

412* Riches are for spending.
Francis Bacon (1561–1626) English
philosopher.
Essays, 'Of Expense'

413* Money is like muck, not good except it be
spread.
Francis Bacon
Essays, 'Of Seditions and Troubles'

Work and Occupations

1604

414   An ambassador is an honest man sent to lie
abroad for the good of his country.
Henry Wotton (1568–1639) English poet and
diplomat.
Life (Izaak Walton)

Sayings of the Time

1570

415   Thirty days hath September,
April, June, and November;
All the rest have thirty-one,
Excepting February alone
And that has twenty-eight days clear
And twenty-nine in each leap year.
Abridgement of the Chronicles of England
(Richard Grafton)

1611

416   A frog he would a-wooing go,
Heigh ho! says Rowley,
A frog he would a-wooing go,
Whether his mother would let him or no.
With a rowley, powley, gammon and spinach
Heigh ho! says Anthony Rowley.
Melismata (Thomas Ravenscroft)

1616

417   I'll put a spoke among your wheels.
Francis Beaumont (1584–1616) English
dramatist.
The Mad Lover, III:6

With Hindsight

19th century

418   Persecution produced its natural effect on

them. It found them a sect; it made them a faction.
Lord Macaulay (1800–59) British historian.
Referring to the early Puritans
History of England

20th century

19 Burnings of people and (what was more valuable) works of art.
A. L. Rowse (1903–   ) British historian and critic.
Historical Essays (H. R. Trevor-Roper)

420 If Galileo had said in verse that the world moved, the Inquisition might have let him alone.
Thomas Hardy (1840–1928) British novelist.
The Later Years of Thomas Hardy (F. E. Hardy)

421 The Cavaliers (wrong but Wromantic) and the Roundheads (Right but Repulsive).
W. C. Sellar (1898–1951) British humorous writer.
1066 And All That

8

The Age of Enlightenment (1660–1788)

With Louis XIV of France, absolute monarchy reached its zenith. Regarding the monarchy as a status ordained by God, he permitted no challenge to his authority; he was, moreover, imitated throughout western Europe. Even in England, where the king had been beheaded not many years before and parliament was strong, there lingered a fear – or in some quarters a hope – that the king would assert himself and dispense with parliament. When James II showed real signs of doing so, the Glorious Revolution (1688) deposed him.

At the same time scientific progress, led by such men as Newton, Pascal, and Descartes, was beginning to suggest that at least some events in the world could be predicted. The view that everything that happened was the result of God's capricious will became less acceptable; instead, the belief grew that the world was governed by natural laws, amenable to rational inquiry. During the 18th century this spirit of Enlightenment spread into other fields, notably political thought. Philosophers such as Locke and Voltaire criticized both society and established authority on the grounds of reason, establishing what was later called the Age of Reason. The response of rulers was mixed. Some Enlightened Despots, such as Frederick the Great of Prussia and Joseph II of Austria, claimed to follow rational principles in the formulation of their policies, without actually lessening the absolute and arbitrary authority they exercised over their subjects; others, notably the kings of France, were more conservative. However, all monarchs continued to draw a fine line between permissible speculation and seditious thinking.

The period ended with the revolt of Britain's American colonies (1775–83), Europe's first experience from the New World of aspirations aimed at substituting nationhood for a colonial status. The ideas of liberty, fostered by the Enlightenment in Europe, had a profound influence on the revolutionaries, whose case was now based on emerging notions of human rights as well as the traditionally English view of liberty.

Politics, Government, and World Events

1661

1 I owe you everything, Sire, but I believe I can pay some of my debt with this gift – Colbert.
Cardinal Mazarin (1602–61) Italian-born French statesman.
Remark to Louis XIV, shortly before Mazarin's death; referring to Jean-Baptiste Colbert

1664

2 You will have heard of our taking of New Amsterdam . . . It did belong to England heretofore, but the Dutch by degrees drove our people out and built a very good town, but we have got the better of it, and 'tis now called New York.
Charles II (1630–85) King of England.
Letter, 24 Oct 1664

1665

3 Pretty witty Nell.
Samuel Pepys (1633–1703) English diarist.
Referring to Nell Gwynne
Diary, 3 Apr 1665

4 Thence I walked to the Tower; but Lord! how empty the streets are and how melancholy, so many poor sick people in the streets full of sores . . . in Westminster, there is never a physician and but one apothecary left, all being dead.
Samuel Pepys
Written during the Great Plague – the last major outbreak of bubonic plague in England, and the worst since the Black Death of 1348
Diary, 16 Sept 1665

5 Ring-a-ring o'roses,
A pocket full of posies,
A-tishoo! A-tishoo!
We all fall down.
Thought to refer to plague: 'ring o'roses' was the skin-marking indicating a victim of the disease; 'posies' were the herbs carried in an attempt to ward off the disease
Mother Goose (Kate Greenway)

6 Oh what a pity were the greatest and most virtuous of kings, of that real virtue which makes the greatest of princes, to be measured by the yardstick of Versailles!
Jean-Baptiste Colbert (1619–83) French statesman.
Letter to Louis XIV, 28 Sept 1665

7 The love of justice in most men is simply the fear of suffering injustice.
Duc de la Rochefoucauld (1613–80) French writer.
Maximes, 78

1666

8 This fatal night about ten, began that deplorable fire near Fish Street in London . . . all the sky were of a fiery aspect, like the top of a burning Oven, and the light seen above 40 miles round about for many nights.
John Evelyn (1620–1706) English diarist.
The Fire of London (2–5 Sept 1666) began in a bakehouse in Pudding Lane and spread to two-thirds of the city
Diary, 23 Sept 1666

9 The fire, mean time, walks in a broader gross,
To either hand his wings he opens wide:
He wades the streets, and straight he reaches cross,
And plays his longing flames on th'other side.

At first they warm, then scorch, and then they take:
Now with long necks from side to side they feed:
At length, grown strong, their Mother fire forsake,
And a new collony of flames succeed.
John Dryden (1631–1700) British poet and dramatist.
Annus Mirabilis

1667

10 Who overcomes
By force, hath overcome but half his foe.
John Milton (1608–74) English poet.
Paradise Lost, Bk. I

11 To reign is worth ambition, though in Hell:
Better to reign in Hell than serve in Heaven.
John Milton
Paradise Lost, Bk. I

12 . . . always with right reason dwells
Twinn'd, and from her hath no dividual being.
John Milton
Referring to liberty
Paradise Lost, Bk. XII

1670

13* Not a religion for gentlemen.
Charles II (1630–85) King of England.
Referring to Presbyterianism
History of My Own Time (Burnet), Vol. I, Bk. II, Ch. 2

14 Better than a play.
Charles II
Referring to House of Lords debate on the Divorce Bill
Attrib.

1672

15* Our business is to break with them and yet to lay the breache at their door.
Earl of Arlington (1618–85)
Referring to the diplomacy that preceded the third Dutch War (1672–74)
Arlington (Violet Barbour)

16   I will drive a coach and six horses through the
     Act of Settlement.
     Stephen Rice (1637–1715) English politician.
     State of the Protestants of Ireland (W. King),
     Ch. 3

1675

17   God is always on the side of the big battalions.
     Vicomte de Turenne (1611–75) French
     marshal.
     Attrib.

1676

18* A merry monarch, scandalous and poor.
     Earl of Rochester (1647–80) English poet.
     Referring to Charles II
     A Satire on King Charles II

1678

The Exclusion Crisis (1678–81)

In 1678, a 'Jesuit conspiracy' to kill Charles II and replace him with his Catholic brother James was 'revealed' by Titus Oates and Israel Tonge. Although
quickly exposed as a fabrication, the anti-Catholic fer-
vour aroused by this 'Popish Plot' led to the execution
of 35 people and persistent demands in parliament that
James be excluded from the succession to the throne
in favour of the Duke of Monmouth, an illegitimate but
Protestant son of Charles. Charles resisted these demands, which were encouraged by men such as the
Earl of Shaftesbury for their own political purposes.
The crisis abated in 1681, when an annual subsidy
from Louis XIV of France enabled Charles to rule without parliament; but the issues it raised resurfaced in
Monmouth's rebellion (1685) and the Glorious Revolution (1688).

19* I am sure no man in England will take away my
     life to make you King.
     Charles II (1630–85) King of England.
     To his brother James following the revelation of
     the Popish Plot
     Attrib.

20   Pray, good people, be civil. I am the Protestant
     whore.
     Nell Gwyn (1650–87) English actress.
     On being surrounded in her coach by an angry
     mob in Oxford at the time of the Popish Plot. The
     mob, thinking that the coach contained the
     King's Catholic mistress, Louise de Kérouoille,
     shouted 'It is the Catholic whore!'
     Nell Gwyn (Bevan), Ch. 13

1679

21   If His Majesty shall come by any violent death,

it shall be revenged to the utmost upon all
Papists.
Resolution of the House of Commons, 1679

1680

22* Here lies our sovereign lord the King
     Whose word no man relies on;
     He never said a foolish thing,
     Nor ever did a wise one.
     Lord Rochester (1647–80) English courtier
     and poet.
     Suggested epitaph for Charles II

23* This is very true: for my words are my own, an
     my actions are my ministers'.
     Charles II (1630–85) King of Great Britain ar
     Ireland.
     Replying to Lord Rochester
     King Charles II (A. Bryant)

24* Brother, I am too old to go again to my travel
     Charles II
     Referring to his exile, 1651–60
     History of Great Britain (Hume), Vol. II, Ch. 7

25   Whatever he may promise me he will break
     everything to get a regular income from his
     parliament.
     Louis XIV (1638–1715) King of France.
     Referring to Charles II of England
     Letter to Barillon, 1680

26   He only treats with me to derive an advantag
     in his future negotiations with his subjects.
     Louis XIV
     Referring to Charles II of England
     Letter to Barillon, 1680

27* I have forgotten more law than you ever knev
     but allow me to say, I have not forgotten
     much.
     John Maynard (1602–90) English judge.
     Replying to Judge Jeffreys' suggestion that he
     was so old he had forgotten the law

1681

28   No Popery, No Slavery.
     Slogan of the London MPs at the Oxford Parli
     ment (Mar 1681)

29   You had better have one King than five
     hundred.
     Charles II (1630–85) King of England.
     Remark after dissolving the Oxford Parliament,
     28 Mar 1681; he did not summon parliament
     again

30   Then, my lord, be his blood on your own con
     science. You might have saved him if you
     would. I cannot pardon him because I dare no
     Charles II
     Reply to the Earl of Essex, who had protested
     Oliver Plunket's innocence of the treason for
     which he had been sentenced to death
     The Later Stuarts (Sir George Clark)

31 Government has no other end but the preservation of property.
    John Locke (1632–1704) English philosopher.
    Second Treatise on Civil Government

1681
---

32 The people's prayer, the glad diviner's theme,
    The young men's vision, and the old men's dream!
    John Dryden (1631–1700) British poet and dramatist.
    John Dryden's poem, written at the request of Charles II, is a satire of the Exclusion Crisis: 'Absolom' is the Duke of Monmouth, and 'Achitophel' is the Earl of Shaftesbury.
    Absalom and Achitophel, I

33 Nor is the Peoples Judgment always true:
    The Most may err as grossly as the Few.
    John Dryden
    Absalom and Achitophel, I

34 In pious times, e'r Priest-craft did begin,
    Before Polygamy was made a Sin.
    John Dryden
    Absalom and Achitophel, I

35 During his Office, Treason was no Crime.
    The Sons of Belial had a Glorious Time.
    John Dryden
    Absalom and Achitophel, I

36 To die for faction is a common evil,
    But to be hanged for nonsense is the Devil.
    John Dryden
    Absalom and Achitophel, II

1683
---

37 I came; I saw; God conquered.
    John III Sobieski (1624–96) King of Poland.
    Announcing his victory over the Turks at Vienna to the pope (paraphrasing Caesar's 'veni, vidi, vici')
    Attrib.

38 'Tis not necessary to light a candle to the sun.
    Algernon Sidney (1622–83) English statesman.
    Discourses concerning Government, Ch. 2

1684
---

39 The multitude is always in the wrong.
    Earl of Roscommon (1633–85) Irish-born English poet.
    Essay on Translated Verse

1685
---

40 He had been, he said, a most unconscionable time dying; but he hoped that they would excuse it.
    Charles II (1630–85) King of England.
    History of England (Macaulay), Vol. I, Ch. 4

41 Let not poor Nelly starve.
    Charles II
    Referring to Nell Gwynne
    Said on his death bed

42 He said once to myself that he was no atheist but he could not think God would make a man miserable only for taking a little pleasure out of the way.
    Gilbert Burnet (1643–1715) English bishop and historian.
    Referring to Charles II
    History of My Own Times

43 I have often heretofore ventured my life in defence of this nation; and I shall go as far as any man in preserving it in all its just rights and liberties.
    James II (1633–1701)
    Address to the Privy Council on becoming King (1685)

44 Do not hack me as you did my Lord Russell.
    Duke of Monmouth (1649–85) An illegitimate son of Charles II.
    Said to the headsman before his execution
    History of England (Macaulay), Vol. I, Ch. 5

45 I was not half bloody enough for him who sent me thither.
    Judge Jeffreys (George, Baron J.; 1648–89) English Chief Justice and Lord Chancellor.
    Referring to his 'Bloody Assizes' following Monmouth's rebellion (1685)
    Remark made later (Apr 1689) to the chaplain of the Tower of London

46 When the People contend for their Liberty, they seldom get anything by their Victory but new masters.
    George Saville Halifax (1633–95) English statesman.
    Political, Moral, and Miscellaneous Thoughts and Reflections

47 Power is so apt to be insolent and Liberty to be saucy, that they are seldom upon good Terms.
    George Saville Halifax
    Political, Moral, and Miscellaneous Thoughts and Reflections

48 Men are not hanged for stealing horses, but that horses may not be stolen.
    George Saville Halifax
    Political, Moral and Miscellaneous Thoughts and Reflections

---
1687
---

49 ... establish such a politie of civil and military power and create and secure such a large revenue ... as may be the foundation of a large, well-grounded sure English dominion in India for all time to come.
    Dispatch from the East India Company to its chief executive in Surat

---
1688
---

50 The Duke of Buckingham gave me once a short but severe character of the two brothers. It was the more severe, because it was true: the

King (he said) could see things if he would, and the Duke would see things if he could.
Gilbert Burnet (1643–1715) English bishop and historian.
Referring to Charles II and James II
History of My Own Times

51 One of the strangest catastrophes that is in any history. A great king, with strong armies and mighty fleets, a great treasure and powerful allies, fell all at once, and his whole strength, like a spider's web, was . . . irrecoverably broken at a touch.
Gilbert Burnet
Referring to the Glorious Revolution, 1688
History of My Own Times

52 This is a standard of rebellion.
James II (1633–1701) King of England.
Referring to a petition from seven bishops against his Declaration of Indulgence (1687; re-issued 7 May 1688); the bishops were prosecuted for sedititious libel, but acquitted
Remark, 2 June 1688

53 . . . to long for and desire the landing of that Prince, whom they looked on as their deliverer from Popish tyranny, praying incessantly for an Easterly wind . . .
John Evelyn (1620–1706) English diarist.
Referring to William III
Diary, 6 Oct 1688

54 If the circumstances stand so with your Highness, that you believe you can get here time enough, in a condition to give assistance this year sufficient for a relief under these circumstances which have been now represented, we, who subscribe this, will not fail to attend your Highness upon your landing.
Letter from seven English notables to William of Orange, 10 July 1688

55 Party loyalty lowers the greatest of men to the petty level of the masses.
Jean de La Bruyère (1645–96) French satirist.
Les Caractères

56 If by the people you understand the multitude, the *hoi polloi*, 'tis no matter what they think; they are sometimes in the right, sometimes in the wrong; their judgement is a mere lottery.
John Dryden (1631–1700) British poet and dramatist.
Essay of Dramatic Poesy

1689

57 She came into Whitehall laughing and jolly, as to a wedding, so as to seem quite transported.
John Evelyn (1620–1706) English diarist.
Referring to Mary II's arrival in London
Diary, 21 Feb 1689

58 In Hide Park he rides like a hog in armour,
In Whitehall he creeps like a country farmer,
Old England may boast of a godly reformer;

A dainty fine king indeed.
Anonymous
Referring to William III
The Faber Book of English History in Verse
(Kenneth Baker)

59 Good People come buy
The Fruit that I cry,
That now is in Season, tho' Winter is nigh;
'Twill do you all good
And sweeten your Blood,
I'm sure it will please when you've once understood
'Tis an *Orange*.
Anonymous
Referring to William III
The Faber Book of English History in Verse
(Kenneth Baker)

60 Ignorance of the law excuses no man; not that all men know the law, but because 'tis an excuse every man will plead, and no man can tell how to confute him.
John Selden (1584–1654) English historian.
Table Talk

61 Every law is a contract between the king and the people and therefore to be kept.
John Selden
Table Talk

1690

62 Most men were in fear that the French would invade, but I was always of another opinion, for I always said that, whilst we had a fleet in being, they would not dare to make an attempt.
Earl of Torrington English admiral.
Justifying his refusal to give battle to a numerically superior French fleet; when subsequently ordered to do so, he was defeated off Beachy Head (10 July 1690)
The Later Stuarts (Sir George Clark)

63 When a King has Dethron'd himself and put himself in a state of War with his People, what shall hinder them from prosecuting him who is no King?
John Locke (1632–1704) English philosopher
Second Treatise on Civil Government

1692

64* . . . was apt to suffer things to run on till there was a great heap of papers laid before him, so then he signed them a little too precipitately.
Gilbert Burnet (1643–1715) Scottish-born English bishop.
Referring to William III; his authorization of the Glencoe Massacre (1692) may have been one consequence of this habit
History of My Own Times

65 Our dear King James is good and honest, but the most incompetent man I have ever seen

in my life. A child of seven years would not
make such silly mistakes as he does.
Duchess of Orleans (1652–1722) Sister-in-
law to Louis XIV.
Referring to James II, who was in exile in France
Letter to the Electress Sophia, 6 June 1692

1693

66 Let the people think they govern and they will
be governed.
William Penn 1644–1718
Some Fruits of Solitude, 337

1694

67 Your peoples die of hunger. Agriculture is almost stationary, industry languishes every-
wherè, all commerce is destroyed.... You
relate everything to yourself as though you
were God on earth.
François Fénelon (1651–1715) French writer
and prelate.
Letter to Louis XIV

1698

68 The rights of parliament should be preserved
sacred and inviolable, wherever they are found.
This kind of government, once so universal
all over Europe, is now almost vanished from
amongst the nations thereof. Our king's dominions are the only supporters of this noble
Gothic constitution, save only what little remains may be found thereof in Poland.
William Molyneux
*The Case of Ireland's being Bound by Acts of
Parliament in England stated* (Pamphlet, 1698)

18th century

69 In good King Charles's golden days,
When loyalty no harm meant,
A zealous High Churchman was I,
And so I got preferment.

And this is law, that I'll maintain,
Unto my dying day, Sir,
That whatsoever King shall reign,
I'll be the Vicar of Bray, Sir.
Anonymous
Thought to refer to Symon Symonds, who was
vicar of Bray in the reigns of Henry VIII, Ed-
ward VI, Mary, and Elizabeth I. He was twice a
Papist and twice a Protestant, but when accused
of time-serving replied, 'Not so, neither, for if I
changed my religion, I am sure that I kept true to
my principle, which is to live and die the vicar
of Bray.'
The Vicar of Bray

70 Certainty is the Mother of Repose, and therefore the Law aims at Certainty.
A maxim used by Lord Hardwicke (Lord Chancellor, 1737–1756)

71 The King over the Water.
Anonymous
Jacobite toast

1700

72* Every time I make an appointment, I make one
ungrateful person and a hundred with a
grievance.
Louis XIV (1638–1715) French king.
Siècle de Louis XIV (Voltaire), Ch. 26

73* Let us consider the reason of the case. For
nothing is law that is not reason.
John Powell (1645–1713) English judge.
Coggs v. Bernard, 2 Lord Raymond, 911

74 Il n'y a plus de Pyrénées.
There are no more Pyrenees.
Louis XIV (1638–1715) French king.
On the accession of his grandson to the Spanish
throne (1700); attributed by Voltaire

1701

75 And of all plagues with which mankind are
curst,
Ecclesiastic tyranny's the worst.
Daniel Defoe (1660–1731) British journalist
and writer.
The True-Born Englishman, Pt. II

1702

76 I know my own heart to be entirely English.
Anne (1665–1714)
Drawing a contrast with her predecessor, the
Dutch William III
Speech on opening parliament, 1702

1704

77 I have not time to say more, but to beg you will
give my duty to the Queen, and let her know
her army has had a glorious victory. Monsieur Tallard and two other generals are in my
coach, and I am following the rest...
Duke of Marlborough (1650–1722) British
military commander.
Referring to the Battle of Blenheim, 13 Aug 1704
Note to his wife, written on a tavern bill

78 How could God do this to me after all I have
done for him?
Louis XIV (1638–1715) French king.
On receiving news of the French army's defeat at
the Battle of Blenheim
Saint-Simon at Versailles (L. Norton)

1705

79 Neither is money the sinews of war (as it is triv-
ially said).
John Aubrey (1626–1697) English antiquary.
Essays, 'Of the True Greatness of Kingdoms'

80 Neither will it be, that a people overlaid with
taxes should ever become valiant and martial.
John Aubrey
Essays, 'Of the True Greatness of Kingdoms'

1707

81 Justice is such a fine thing that we cannot pay
    too dearly for it.
    Alain-René Lesage (1668–1747) French
    writer.
    Crispin rival de son maître, IX

1709

82 Now indeed with God's help the final stone has
    been laid in the foundation of St Petersburg.
    Peter the Great (1672–1725) Tsar of Russia.
    Referring to his victory over Charles XII of Swe-
    den at the Battle of Poltava (28 June 1709)
    Letter to Admiral Apraksin, 27 June 1709

83 Laws are like cobwebs, which may catch small
    flies, but let wasps and hornets break through.
    Jonathan Swift (1667–1745) Irish-born
    Anglican priest and writer.
    A Tritical Essay upon the Faculties of the Mind

1710

84 In the first place, I have only five guineas in my
    pocket; and in the second, they are very much
    at your service.
    Lord Peterborough (1658–1735) English mil-
    itary and naval commander.
    Persuading an angry mob that he was not the
    Duke of Marlborough, notorious for his
    meanness
    Dictionary of National Biography

1711

85 I have changed my ministers, but I have not
    changed my measures; I am still for moderation
    and will govern by it.
    Anne (1665–1714) Queen of Great Britain
    To members of the new Tory ministry, Jan 1711

86 It is folly of too many to mistake the echo of
    a London coffee-house for the voice of the
    kingdom.
    Jonathan Swift (1667–1745) Irish-born
    Anglican priest and writer.
    The Conduct of the Allies

1712

87 He warns the heads of parties against believing
    their own lies.
    John Arbuthnot (1667–1735) Scottish writer
    and physician.
    The Art of Political Lying

88 The hungry judges soon the sentence sign,
    And wretches hang that jury-men may dine.
    Alexander Pope (1688–1744) British poet.
    The Rape of the Lock, III

1713

89 What pity is it

That we can die but once to serve our
country!
Joseph Addison (1672–1719) British
essayist.
Cato, IV:4

1715

90 L'État c'est moi.
    I am the State.
    Louis XIV (1638–1715) French king.
    Attrib.

91 I almost had to wait.
    Louis XIV
    Attrib.

92* Try to keep peace with your neighbours. I hav
    loved war too much; do not copy me in that
    nor in my extravagance.
    Louis XIV
    Remark to his great-grandson, the future Louis
    XV

93 Why are you weeping? Did you imagine that
    was immortal?
    Louis XIV
    Noticing as he lay on his deathbed that his at-
    tendants were crying
    Louis XIV (V. Cronin)

94* ...for the most part the worst instructed, an
    the least knowing of any of their rank, I ever
    went amongst.
    Gilbert Burnet (1643–1715) Scottish-born
    English bishop.
    Referring to the English gentry
    History of My Own Times, Conclusion

1722

95 Let pride be taught by this rebuke,
    How very mean a thing's a Duke;
    From all his ill-got honours flung,
    Turn'd to that dirt from whence he sprung.
    Jonathan Swift (1667–1745) Irish-born
    Anglican priest and writer.
    Referring to the Duke of Marlborough
    *A Satirical Elegy on the Death of a Late Fa-
    mous General*

1723

96 Si monumentum requiris, circumspice.
    If you seek my monument, look around you.
    Sir Christopher Wren (1632–1723) English
    architect.
    Inscription in St Paul's Cathedral, London

1726

97 I cannot but conclude the bulk of your native
    to be the most pernicious race of little odious
    vermin that nature ever suffered to crawl
    upon the surface of the earth.
    Jonathan Swift (1667–1745) Irish-born
    Anglican priest and writer.
    Gulliver's Travels, 'Voyage to Brobdingnag',
    Ch. 6

8 Whoever could make two ears of corn or two blades of grass to grow upon a spot of ground where only one grew before would deserve better of mankind and do more essential service to his country than the whole race of politicians put together.
Jonathan Swift
Gulliver's Travels, 'Voyage to Brobdingnag', Ch. 7

1728
---

9 The right divine of kings to govern wrong.
Alexander Pope (1688–1744) British poet.
The Dunciad, IV

1730

0* For God's sake, madam, don't say that in England for if you do, they will surely tax it.
Jonathan Swift (1667–1745) Irish-born Anglican priest and writer.
Responding to Lady Carteret's admiration for the quality of the air in Ireland
Lives of the Wits (H. Pearson)

1731

•1 With favour and fortune fastidiously blest,
He's loud in his laugh and he's coarse in his jest;
. . .
Though I name not the wretch you know who I mean –
'Tis the cur dog of Britain and spaniel of Spain.
Jonathan Swift
Referring to Sir Robert Walpole
Two Character Studies

1733
---

02 Order is heaven's first law.
Alexander Pope (1688–1744) British poet.
An Essay on Man, IV

1734
---

03 An empire founded by war has to maintain itself by war.
Baron de Montesquieu (1688–1755) French writer.
Considérations sur les causes de la grandeur et de la décadence des romains, Ch. 8

04 Madam, there are fifty thousand men slain this year in Europe, and not one Englishman.
Robert Walpole (1676–1745) British statesman.
Referring to his determination not to involve Britain in the War of Polish Succession (1733–35), despite considerable political pressure
Remark to Queen Caroline, 1734

05* I took the right sow by the ear.
Robert Walpole
Commenting on his perception that, to influence George II, the correct woman to cultivate was

Queen Caroline, not any of the King's mistresses – a mistake made by his political opponents
Remark to a friend, c. 1734

1736
---

106 Lost or strayed out of this house, a man who left a wife and six children on the parish; whoever will give any tidings of him to the churchwardens of St. James's Parish, so he may be got again, shall receive four shillings and sixpence. N.B. This reward will not be increased, nobody judging him to deserve a Crown.
Anonymous
Referring to George II, whose frequent absences in Hanover made him unpopular
Notice posted on the gate of St. James's Palace

1737
---

107 No, I shall have mistresses.
George II (1683–1760) King of Great Britain and Ireland.
Reply to Queen Caroline's suggestion, as she lay on her deathbed, that he should marry again after her death
Memoirs of George the Second (Hervey), Vol. II

1738
---

108 Faction is to party what the superlative is to the positive: party is a political evil and faction is the worst of all parties.
Bolingbroke, Henry St John, Viscount (1678–1751) British politician and writer.
The Patriot King

1739
---

109 I have lived long enough in the world, Sir, . . . to know that the safety of a minister lies in his having the approbation of this House. Former ministers, Sir, neglected this, and therefore they fell; I have always made it my first study to obtain it, and therefore I hope to stand.
Robert Walpole (1717–97) British statesman.
Speech, House of Commons, 21 Nov 1739

110 All those men have their price.
Robert Walpole
Memoirs of Sir Robert Walpole (W. Coxe)

111 They now *ring* the bells, but they will soon *wring* their hands.
Robert Walpole
Said when war was declared with Spain, against Walpole's wishes
Memoirs of Sir Robert Walpole (W. Coxe)

1740

112* Great lords have their pleasures, but the people have fun.
Baron de Montesquieu (1688–1755) French writer.
Pensées diverses

113* A crown is merely a hat that lets the rain in.
Frederick the Great (1712–86) King of
Prussia.
Remark

114 God save our Gracious King,
Long live our noble King,
God save the King.
Send him victorious,
Happy and glorious.
Henry Carey (c. 1690–1743) English poet and
musician.
God Save the King

115 When Britain first, at heaven's command,
Arose from out the azure main,
This was the charter of the land,
And guardian angels sung this strain:
'Rule, Britannia, rule the waves;
Britons never will be slaves.'
James Thomson (1700–48) British poet.
Alfred: a Masque, Act II

1741

116 The balance of power.
Robert Walpole (1676–1745) British
statesman.
Speech, House of Commons, 13 Feb 1741

1742

117 It is now apparent that this great, this powerful,
this formidable Kingdom is considered only as
a province of a despicable Electorate.
William Pitt the Elder (1708–78) British
statesman.
Referring to Hanover, which Pitt accused George
II of favouring over England
Speech, House of Commons, 10 Dec 1742

118 My Lord Bath, you and I are now two as insignificant men as any in England.
Robert Walpole (1676–1745) British
statesman.
Said to William Pulteney, Earl of Bath, when they
were promoted to the peerage (1742)
Political & Literary Anecdotes (W. King)

1743

119 Our supreme governors, the mob.
Horace Walpole (1717–97) British writer.
Letter to Sir Horace Mann, 7 Sept 1743

1745

120 Gentlemen of the French Guard, fire first!
Lord Charles Hay (d. 1760) British soldier.
Said at the Battle of Fontenoy, 1745
Attrib.

121 I'll be at your Board, when at leisure from
cricket.
John Montagu, Earl of Sandwich (1718–
92) British politician.
Message on being appointed a lord commissioner of the Admiralty, June 1745

1748

122 It must be owned, that the Graces do not see
to be natives of Great Britain; and I doubt, th
best of us here have more of rough than polished diamond.
Earl of Chesterfield (1694–1773) English
statesman.
Letter to his son, 18 Nov 1748

123 Liberty is the right to do everything which th
laws allow.
Baron de Montesquieu (1688–1755) Fren
writer.
L'Esprit des lois

124 See, the conquering hero comes!
Sound the trumpets, beat the drums!
Thomas Morell (1703–84) British classicist
The libretto for Handel's oratorio
Joshua, Pt. III

1750

125 It is impossible that a man who is false to h
friends and neighbours should be true to the
public.
Bishop Berkeley (1685–1753) Irish church
man and philosopher.
Maxims Concerning Patriotism

1751

126 Here lies Fred,
Who was alive and is dead:
Had it been his father,
I had much rather;
Had it been his brother,
Still better than another;
Had it been his sister,
No one would have missed her;
Had it been the whole generation,
Still better for the nation:
But since 'tis only Fred,
Who was alive and is dead, –
There's no more to be said.
Referring to Frederick, Prince of Wales (d.
1751), eldest son of George II and father of
George III.
Memoirs of George II (Horace Walpole)

1755

127 There are kings enough in England. I am not
ing there, I am old and want rest and should
only go to be plagued and teased there
about that D—d House of Commons.
George II (1683–1760) King of Great Britai
and Ireland.
George II's reply when urged to leave Hanove
and return to England
Letter from the Earl of Holderness to the Duke
Newcastle, 3 Aug 1755

1756

8 I know that I can save this country and that no one else can.
William Pitt the Elder (1708–78) British statesman.
Remark, Nov 1756, during the political crisis at the start of the Seven Years War; Pitt became secretary of state for the southern department, and effective head of the government, on 4 Dec 1756

1757

9 Rascals, would you live for ever?
Frederick the Great (1712–86) King of Prussia.
Addressed to reluctant soldiers at the Battle of Kolin, 18 June 1757

30 *Après nous le déluge.*
After us the deluge.
Madame de Pompadour (1721–64) The mistress of Louis XV of France.
After the Battle of Rossbach, 5 Nov 1757

1758

31 *Laissez faire, laissez passer.*
Liberty of action, liberty of movement.
Jean Claude Vincent de Gournay (1712–59) French economist.
Speech, Sept 1758

1759

32 Come cheer up, my lads! 'tis to glory we steer,
To add something more to this wonderful year;
To honour we call you, not press you like slaves,
For who are so free as the sons of the waves?
Heart of oak are our ships,
Heart of oak are our men:
We always are ready;
Steady, boys, steady;
We'll fight and we'll conquer again and again.
David Garrick (1717–79) British actor and manager.
Heart of Oak

33* Oh! he is mad, is he? Then I wish he would bite some other of my generals.
George II (1683–1760) King of Great Britain and Ireland.
Replying to advisors who told him that General James Wolfe (1727–59) was mad
Attrib.

34 I would rather have written those lines than take Quebec.
James Wolfe (1727–59) British general.
Referring to Gray's Elegy, on the eve of the Battle of Quebec (13 Sept 1759)
Attrib.

135 Now God be praised, I will die in peace.
James Wolfe
After being mortally wounded at the Battle of Quebec, 1759
Historical Journal of Campaigns, 1757–60 (J. Knox), Vol. II

136 *Dans ce pays-ci, il est bon de tuer de temps en temps un amiral pour encourager les autres.*
In this country it is good to kill an admiral from time to time, to encourage the others.
Voltaire (François-Marie Arouet; 1694–1778) French writer.
Referring to England: Admiral Byng was executed for failing to engage the French at Minorca (1757)
Candide, Ch. 23

1760s

137 Taxation without representation is tyranny.
James Otis (1725–83) US political activist.
As 'No taxation without representation' this became the principal slogan of the American Revolution
Attrib.

1760

138* A cow is a very good animal in the field; but we turn her out of a garden.
Samuel Johnson (1709–84) British lexicographer.
Responding to Boswell's objections to the expulsion of six Methodists from Oxford University
The Personal History of Samuel Johnson (C. Hibbert)

139 Born and educated in this country I glory in the name of Briton.
George III (1738–1820) King of Great Britain and Ireland.
Speech on opening parliament, 18 Nov 1760

140 I think for my part one half of the nation is mad
– and the other not very sound.
Tobias Smollett (1721–71) British novelist.
The Adventures of Sir Launcelot Greaves

141 True patriotism is of no party.
Tobias Smollett
The Adventures of Sir Launcelote Greaves

1761

142 George, be a King.
Augusta of Saxe-Gotha, Princess of Wales (1719–72) Mother of King George III.
Attrib.

1762

143* I shall be an autocrat: that's my trade. And the good Lord will forgive me: that's his.
Catherine the Great (1729–96) Empress of Russia (1762–96).
Attrib.

144 Man was born free and everywhere he is in
     chains.
     Jean Jacques Rousseau (1712–78) French
     philosopher.
     Du contrat social, Ch. 1

1763

145 In vain will such a minister, or the foul dregs of
     his power, the tools of despotism and corrup-
     tion, preach up 'the spirit of concord . . .'
     They have sent the spirit of discord through the
     land and I will prophesy it will never be dist-
     ingushed but by the extinction of their
     power.
     John Wilkes (1725–97) British politician.
     Part of a libellous article on George III's speech
     (which was drafted by George Grenville, the
     'minister') at the opening of parliament. This arti-
     cle led to a celebrated legal battle, and
     launched his career as a champion of the com-
     mon man against overbearing government
     North Briton, 45 (23 Apr 1763)

146* Wilkes and Liberty.
     Slogan of the London mob

147 Your levellers wish to level *down* as far as
     themselves; but they cannot bear levelling *up*
     to themselves.
     Samuel Johnson (1709–84) British
     lexicographer.
     Life of Johnson (J. Boswell), Vol. I

1764

148* The poorest man may in his cottage bid defi-
     ance to all the forces of the Crown. It may be
     frail – its roof may shake – the wind may
     blow through it – the storm may enter – the
     rain may enter – but the King of England
     cannot enter! – all his force dares not cross
     the threshold of the ruined tenement!
     William Pitt the Elder (1708–78) British
     statesman.
     Statesmen in the Time of George III (Lord
     Brougham), Vol. I

149 Be England what she will,
     With all her faults, she is my country still.
     Charles Churchill (1731–64) British poet.
     The Farewell

150 Where wealth and freedom reign, contentment
     fails,
     And honour sinks where commerce long
     prevails.
     Oliver Goldsmith (1728–74) Irish-born British
     writer.
     The Traveller

151 Laws grind the poor, and rich men rule the law.
     Oliver Goldsmith
     The Traveller

152 Parliaments are the great lie of our time.
     Konstantin Pobedonostsev (1827–1907)
     Russian jurist and Procurator of the Holy Synod.
     Moskovskii Sbornik

153 Laws are generally found to be nets of such a

texture, as the little creep through, the great
break through, and the middle-sized are alone
entangled in.
William Shenstone
Essays on Men, Manners, and Things, 'On
Politics'

1765

154 Caesar had his Brutus – Charles the First, h
     Cromwell – and George the Third – ('Trea-
     son,' cried the Speaker) . . . *may profit by the*
     example. If this be treason, make the most of
     it.
     Patrick Henry (1736–99) US statesman.
     Speech, Virginia Convention, May 1765

155 Man was formed for society.
     William Blackstone (1723–80) British juris
     Commentaries on the Laws of England, Intro-
     duction

156 The king never dies.
     William Blackstone
     Commentaries on the Laws of England, Bk. I
     Ch. 7

157 The Royal Navy of England has ever been its
     greatest defence and ornament; it is its ancie
     and natural strength, the floating bulwark of
     the island.
     Willian Blackstone
     Commentaries on the Laws of England, Bk. I
     Ch. 13

158 Time whereof the memory of man runneth no
     to the contrary.
     William Blackstone
     Commentaries on the Laws of England, Bk. I,
     Ch. 18

159 That the king can do no wrong, is a necessa
     and fundamental principle of the English
     constitution.
     William Blackstone
     Commentaries on the Laws of England, Bk. I
     Ch. 17

160 It is better that ten guilty persons escape tha
     one innocent suffer.
     William Blackstone
     Commentaries on the Laws of England, Bk. I
     Ch. 27

161 The British parliament has no right to tax the
     Americans . . . Taxation and representation ar
     inseparably united.
     Charles Pratt (1714–94) Lord Chancellor.
     Speech, House of Lords, Dec 1765

1766

162 I rejoice that America has resisted. Three mil
     lions of people, so dead to all the feelings of
     liberty, as voluntarily to submit to be slaves,
     would have been fit instruments to make slave
     of the rest.
     William Pitt the Elder (1708–78) British
     statesman.
     Speech, House of Commons, 14 Jan 1766

163   Once the people begin to reason, all is lost.
Voltaire (François-Marie Arouet: 1694–1778)
French writer.
Letter to Damilaville, 1 Apr 1766

1767

164   The sovereign is absolute; for, in a state whose
expanse is so vast, there can be no other appropriate authority except that which is concentrated in him.
Catherine II (1729–96) Empress of Russia
(1762–96).
Nakaz

165   I am not like a lady at the court of Versailles,
who said: 'What a dreadful pity that the
bother at the tower of Babel should have got
language all mixed up, but for that, everyone
would always have spoken French.
Voltaire (François-Marie Arouet: 1694–1778)
French writer.
Letter to Catherine the Great, Empress of Russia, 26 May 1767

1768

166   The best sun we have is made of Newcastle
coal.
Horace Walpole (1717–97) British writer.
Letter to Montagu, 15 June 1768

1769

167*   The Liberty of the press is the *Palladium* of all
the civil, political and religious rights of an
Englishman.
Junius An unidentified writer of letters (1769–
72) to the *London Public Advertiser.*
Letters, 'Dedication'

168   There is a holy, mistaken zeal in politics, as
well as religion. By persuading others we convince ourselves.
Junius
Letter, 19 Dec 1769

169   This agglomeration which was called and which
still calls itself the Holy Roman Empire was
neither holy, nor Roman, nor an empire.
Voltaire (François-Marie Arouet: 1694–1778)
French writer.
Essai sur les moeurs et l'esprit des nations,
LXX

170   Why, Sir, most schemes of political improvement are very laughable things.
Samuel Johnson (1709–84) British
lexicographer.
Life of Johnson (J. Boswell), Vol. II

1770

171*   Consider what you think justice requires, and
decide accordingly. But never give your rea-

sons; for your judgement will probably be right,
but your reasons will certainly be wrong.
Lord Mansfield (1705–93) British judge and
politician.
Advice given to a new colonial governor
Lives of the Chief Justices (Campbell), Ch. 40

172   Unlimited power is apt to corrupt the minds of
those who possess it.
William Pitt the Elder (1708–78) British
statesman.
Speech, House of Lords, 9 Jan 1770

173   Where laws end, tyranny begins.
William Pitt the Elder
Referring to the case of John Wilkes, who had
been elected to parliament four times but, because of government opposition, not allowed to
take his seat
Speech, House of Lords, 9 Jan 1770

174   There is something behind the throne greater
than the King himself.
William Pitt the Elder
Speech, House of Lords, 2 Mar 1770

175   At daylight in the morning we discovered a bay,
which appeared to be tolerably well sheltered
from all winds, into which I resolved to go
with the ship.
James Cook (1728–79) British navigator and
cartographer.
On the discovery of Botany Bay
Journal, 28 Apr 1770

176   Upon the whole New Holland, tho' in every respect the most barren country I have seen, is
not so bad that between the products of sea
and land, a company of people who should
have the misfortune of being shipwrecked upon
it might support themselves.
Sir Joseph Banks (1744–1820) British
scientist.
Note, as a participant in Captain Cook's circumnavigation of the world (1768–71), on leaving
New South Wales.
Journal, Aug 1770

177   When bad men combine, the good must associate; else they will fall one by one, an unpitied
sacrifice in a contemptible struggle.
Edmund Burke (1729–97) British politician.
Thoughts on the Cause of the Present Discontents

178   My people and I have come to an agreement
which satisfies us both. They are to say what
they please, and I am to do what I please.
Frederick the Great (1712–86) King of
Prussia.
Attrib.

179   Everybody talks of the constitution, but all sides
forget that the constitution is extremely well,
and would do very well, if they would but let it
alone.
Horace Walpole (1717–97) British writer.
Letter to Sir Horace Mann, 1770

180   Ill fares the land, to hast'ning ills a prey,
Where wealth accumulates, and men decay;
Princes and lords may flourish, or may fade;

A breath can make them, as a breath has
made;
But a bold peasantry, their country's pride,
When once destroy'd, can never be supplied.
Oliver Goldsmith (1728–74) Irish-born British
writer.
The Deserted Village

1771

181 The greater the power, the more dangerous the
abuse.
Edmund Burke (1729–97) British politician.
Speech, House of Commons, 7 Feb 1771

1772

182 Walpole was a minister given by the King to the
people: — Pitt was a minister given by the people to the King.
Samuel Johnson (1709–84) British
lexicographer.
Life of Johnson (J. Boswell)

183 It was easier to conquer it than to know what to
do with it.
Horace Walpole (1717–97) British writer.
Referring to the East
Letter to Sir Horace Mann, 27 Mar 1772

184 Every man who comes to England is entitled to
the protection of the English law, whatever oppression he may heretofore have suffered,
and whatever may be the colour of his skin,
whether it is black or whether it is white.
Lord Mansfield (1705–93) British judge and
politician.
From the judgment in the case of James Somer-
sett, a fugitive negro slave (May 1772); it established the principle that slaves enjoyed the
benefits of freedom while in England

185 I would not give half a guinea to live under one
form of government rather than another. It is
of no moment to the happiness of an
individual.
Samuel Johnson (1709–84) British
lexicographer.
Life of Johnson (J. Boswell), Vol. II

186 Much may be made of a Scotchman, if he be
caught young.
Samuel Johnson
Referring to Lord Mansfield
Life of Johnson (J. Boswell), Vol. II

1773

187 By God, Mr Chairman, at this moment I stand
astonished at my own moderation!
Clive of India (1725–74) British soldier and
governor of Bengal.
Referring to allegations of corruption and extor-
tion in India for personal gain
Reply to House of Commons select committee,
Mar 1773

188 No, Sir; there were people who died of drop-

sies, which they contracted in trying to get
drunk.
Samuel Johnson (1709–84) British
lexicographer.
Scornfully criticizing the strength of the wine in
Scotland before the Act of Union in response
to Boswell's claim that there had been a lot of
drunkenness
Tour to the Hebrides (J. Boswell)

1774

189 Your representative owes you, not his industry
only, but his judgement; and he betrays instead of serving you if he sacrifices it to your
opinion.
Edmund Burke (1729–97) British politician.
Speech to the electors of Bristol, 3 Nov 1774

190 A savage old Nabob, with an immense fortune,
a tawny complexion, a bad liver and a worse
heart.
Lord Macaulay (1800–59) British historian.
Referring to Clive of India (1725–74)
Historical Essays, 'Lord Clive'

191 I am not a Virginian, but an American.
Patrick Henry (1736–99) US statesman.
Speech, Continental Congress, 5 Sept 1774

1775

192 *Excise.* A hateful tax levied upon commodities.
Samuel Johnson (1709–84) British
lexicographer.
Dictionary of the English Language

193 Politics are now nothing more than a means of
rising in the world.
Samuel Johnson
Life of Johnson (J. Boswell), Vol. II

194 I think the full tide of human existence is at
Charing-Cross.
Samuel Johnson
Life of Johnson (J. Boswell), Vol. II

195 Patriotism is the last refuge of a scoundrel.
Samuel Johnson
Life of Johnson (J. Boswell), Vol. II

The American Revolution
(1775–83)

Claiming equality with their British kinsmen, they jeal-
ously guarded their way of life, resenting any interfer-
ence with their large measure of *de facto*
independence. In the 1760s their discontent focused
on attempts by the British government to tax them effectively – primarily to pay for their defence. Various
ill-considered acts culminated in armed revolution
breaking out in 1775, and a formal Declaration of Independence was issued on 4 July 1776. In the war that
followed, the British had some successes; but disasters at Saratoga (1777) and Yorktown (1781), and the
entry of France (1788) and other European countries
into the conflict on the American side, led to disheart-

enment in Britain. The war ended in 1783, with the recognition of American independence.

196 I do not know the method of drawing up an indictment against an whole people.
Edmund Burke (1729–97) British politician.
Speech on Conciliation with America (House of Commons, 22 Mar 1775)

197 All government, indeed every human benefit and enjoyment, every virtue, and every prudent act, is founded on compromise and barter.
Edmund Burke
Speech on Conciliation with America (House of Commons, 22 Mar 1775)

198 The use of force alone is but *temporary*. It may subdue for a moment; but it does not remove the necessity of subduing again: and a nation is not governed, which is perpetually to be conquered.
Edmund Burke
Speech on Conciliation with America (House of Commons, 22 Mar 1775)

199 The concessions of the weak are the concessions of fear.
Edmund Burke
Speech on Conciliation with America (House of Commons, 22 Mar 1775)

200 I know not what course others may take; but as for me, give me liberty or give me death.
Patrick Henry (1736–99) US statesman.
Speech, Virginia Convention, 23 Mar 1775

201 Stand your ground. Don't fire unless fired upon, but if they mean to have a war, let it begin here!
John Parker (1729–75) US general.
Command given at the start of the Battle of Lexington (19 Apr 1775)
Familiar Quotations (J. Bartlett)

202 By the waters of Babylon we sit down and weep, when we think of thee, O America!
Horace Walpole (1717–97) British writer.
On the eve of the American Revolution
Letter to Mason, 12 June 1775

203 Don't fire until you see the whites of their eyes.
William Prescott (1726–95) US revolutionary soldier.
Command given at the Battle of Bunker Hill (17 June 1775)

1776

204 That these United Colonies are, and of right ought to be, free and independent states.
Richard Henry Lee (1732–94) US Revolutionary patriot and Senator.
Motion, Continental Congress, Philadelphia, 7 June 1776

205 The second day of July 1776 will be the most memorable epoch in the history of America
. . . It ought to be solemnized with pomp and parade, with shows, games, sports, guns, bells, bonfires and illuminations from one end of this continent to the other, from this time forward, for ever more.
John Adams (1735–1826) Second president of the USA.
The Continental Congress voted for independence from Britain on 2 July
Letter to his wife, 3 July 1776

206 When in the course of human events, it becomes necessary for one people to dissolve the political bonds which have connected them with another, and to assume among the powers of the earth the separate and equal station to which the laws of nature and of Nature's God entitle them, a decent respect to the opinions of mankind requires that they should declare the causes which impel them to the separation.
Thomas Jefferson (1743–1826) US statesman.
Declaration of Independence, Preamble

207 We hold these truths to be self-evident: that all men are created equal; that they are endowed by their Creator with certain unalienable rights; that among these are life, liberty, and the pursuit of happiness.
Thomas Jefferson
Declaration of American Independence, 4 July 1776

208 We must indeed all hang together, or most assuredly, we shall all hang separately.
Benjamin Franklin (1706–90) US scientist and statesman.
Remark on signing the Declaration of Independence, 4 July 1776

209 There, I guess King George will be able to read that.
John Hancock (1737–93) US revolutionary.
Referring to his signature, written in a bold hand, on the US Declaration of Independence
The American Treasury (C. Fadiman)

210 A nation of shop-keepers are very seldom so disinterested.
Samuel Adams (1722–1803) US revolutionary leader.
Referring to Britain, following the Declaration of Independence, 4 July 1776
Speech, Philadelphia, 1 Aug 1776

211 I only regret that I have but one life to lose for my country.
Nathan Hale (1755–76) US revolutionary hero.
Speech before his execution, 22 Sept 1776

212* Yankee Doodle came to town,
Riding on a pony;
He stuck a feather in his cap
And called it macaroni.
Believed to have been sung by British troops ridiculing the Americans in the American Revolution. The Americans adopted the song and added new verses telling of their victories in the war
Gammer Gurton's Garland

213 There is no art which one government sooner

learns of another than that of draining money from the pockets of the people.
Adam Smith (1723–90) Scottish economist.
The Wealth of Nations

214 People of the same trade seldom meet together but the conversation ends in a conspiracy against the public, or in some diversion to raise prices.
Adam Smith
The Wealth of Nations

215 Government, even in its best state, is but a necessary evil; in its worst state, an intolerable one.
Thomas Paine (1737–1809) British writer.
Common Sense, Ch. 1

216 As to religion, I hold it to be the indispensable duty of government to protect all conscientious professors thereof, and I know of no other business which government hath to do therewith.
Thomas Paine
Common Sense, Ch. 4

217 A man who has not been in Italy, is always conscious of an inferiority, from his not having seen what it is expected a man should see. The grand object of travelling is to see the shores of the Mediterranean.
Samuel Johnson (1709–84) British lexicographer.
Life of Johnson (J. Boswell), Vol. III

218 Sir, it is not so much to be lamented that Old England is lost, as that the Scotch have found it.
Samuel Johnson
Life of Johnson (J. Boswell), Vol. III

219 The principles of a free constitution are irrecoverably lost, when the legislative power is nominated by the executive.
Edward Gibbon (1737–94) British historian.
Decline and Fall of the Roman Empire, Ch. 3

1777

220 Yonder are the Hessians. They were bought for seven pounds and tenpence a man. Are you worth more? Prove it. Tonight the American flag floats from yonder hill or Molly Stark sleeps a widow!
John Stark (1728–1822) US general.
Urging on his troops at the Battle of Bennington in 1777
The American Treasury (C. Fadiman)

221 You cannot conquer America.
William Pitt the Elder (1708–78) British statesman.
Speech, House of Lords, 18 Nov 1777

222 I invoke the genius of the Constitution.
William Pitt the Elder
Referring to the American Revolution
Speech, House of Lords, 18 Nov 1777

223 If I were an American, as I am an Englishman, while a foreign troop was landed in my coun-

try, I never would lay down my arms, – never – never – never!
William Pitt the Elder
Speech, House of Lords, 18 Nov 1777

224 Liberty, too, must be limited in order to be possessed.
Edmund Burke (1729–97) British politician.
Letter to the Sheriffs of Bristol, 1777

225 Among a people generally corrupt, liberty cannot long exist.
Edmund Burke
Letter to the Sheriffs of Bristol, 1777

226 When a man is tired of London, he is tired of life; for there is in London all that life can afford.
Samuel Johnson (1709–84) British lexicographer.
Life of Johnson (J. Boswell), Vol. III

1778

227 I will rather risk my Crown than do what I think personally disgraceful, and whilst I have no wish but for the good and prosperity of my country, it is impossible that the nation shall not stand by me; if they will not, they shall have another King.
George III (1738–1820) King of Great Britain and Ireland.
Letter to Lord North, 17 Mar 1778

228 I am willing to love all mankind, *except an American*.
Samuel Johnson (1709–84) British lexicographer.
Life of Johnson (J. Boswell), Vol. III

229 A country governed by a despot is an inverted cone.
Samuel Johnson
Life of Johnson (J. Boswell), Vol. III

230 When I forget my sovereign, may God forget me!
Lord Thurlow (1731–1806) British lawyer.
Speech, House of Lords, 15 Dec 1778

231 I disapprove of what you say, but I will defend to the death your right to say it.
Voltaire (François-Marie Arouet; 1694–1778) French writer.
Attrib.

232 Governments needs to have both shepherds and butchers.
Voltaire
Notebooks

1779

233 I have not yet begun to fight.
John Paul Jones (1747–92) Scottish-born US naval commander.
Retort when informed his ship was sinking
Life and Letters of J. P. Jones (De Koven), Vol. I

234   Worth seeing? yes; but not worth going to see.
Samuel Johnson (1709–84) British lexicographer.
Referring to the Giant's Causeway
Life of Johnson (J. Boswell), Vol. III

1780

235   I can never suppose this country so far lost to all ideas of self-importance as to be willing to grant America independence; if that could ever be adopted I shall despair of this country being ever preserved from a state of inferiority and consequently falling into a very low class among the European States.
George III (1738–1820) King of Great Britain and Ireland.
Letter to Lord North, 7 Mar 1780

236   The influence of the Crown has increased, is increasing, and ought to be diminished.
John Dunning (1731–83) British lawyer and politician.
Motion passed by the House of Commons, 1780

237   The people are the masters.
Edmund Burke (1729–97) British politician.
Speech on the Economical Reform (House of Commons, 11 Feb 1780)

238   Kings are naturally lovers of low company.
Edmund Burke
Speech on the Economical Reform (House of Commons, 11 Feb 1780)

239   One man shall have one vote.
John Cartwright (1740–1824) British writer.
People's Barrier Against Undue Influence

240*   Dublin, though a place much worse than London, is not so bad as Iceland.
Samuel Johnson (1709–84) British lexicographer.
Letter to Mrs Christopher Smart
Life of Johnson (J. Boswell), Vol. IV

241*   I have got no further than this: Every man has a right to utter what he thinks truth, and every other man has a right to knock him down for it. Martyrdom is the test.
Samuel Johnson
Life of Johnson (J. Boswell), Vol. IV

242   No man could be so wise as Thurlow looked.
Charles James Fox (1749–1806) British Whig politician.
Lives of the Lord Chancellors (Campbell), Vol. V

243   When security and equality are in conflict, it will not do to hesitate a moment. Equality must yield.
Jeremy Bentham (1748–1832) British philosopher.
Principles of Legislation

1781

44   The whole commerce between master and slave is a perpetual exercise of the most bois-

terous passions, the most unremitting despotism on the one part, and degrading submissions on the other.
Thomas Jefferson (1743–1826) US statesman.
Notes on the State of Virginia

245*   He snatched the lightning shaft from heaven, and the sceptre from tyrants.
Anne-Robert-Jacques Turgot (1727–81) French economist.
An inscription for a bust of Benjamin Franklin, alluding both to Franklin's invention of the lightning conductor and to his role in the American Revolution
Vie de Turgot (A. N. de Condorcet)

246   ...we are moved to grant the right of private worship to the Lutheran, Calvinist and non-Uniat Greek religions everywhere.
Joseph II (1741–90) Holy Roman Emperor.
Edict of Toleration, 13 Oct 1781

247   He was not merely a chip of the old block, but the old block itself.
Edmund Burke (1729–97) British politician.
Referring to William Pitt the Younger's first speech in the House of Commons, 26 Feb 1781
Attrib.

1782

248   My opinion is, that power should always be distrusted, in whatever hands it is placed.
Sir William Jones (1746–1794) British jurist, linguist and orientalist.
Letter to Lord Althorpe, 5 Oct 1782

1783

249   There never was a good war or a bad peace.
Benjamin Franklin (1706–90) US scientist and statesman.
Letter to Josiah Quincy, 11 Sept 1783

250   Necessity is the plea for every infringement of human freedom. It is the argument of tyrants; it is the creed of slaves.
William Pitt the Younger (1759–1806) British statesman.
Speech, House of Commons, 18 Nov 1783

251   The King of England changes his ministers as often as he changes his shirts.
Frederick the Great (1712–86) King of Prussia.
Referring to George III
Attrib.

1784

252   If a man were to go by chance at the same time with Burke under a shed, to shun a shower, he would say – 'this is an extraordinary man.'
Samuel Johnson (1709–84) British lexicographer.
Referring to Edmund Burke
Life of Johnson (J. Boswell), Vol. IV

1785

253 The summer soldier and the sunshine patriot will, in this crisis, shrink from the service of their country.
Thomas Paine (1737–1809) British writer.
Pennsylvania Journal, 'The American Crisis'

254* He was uniformly of an opinion which, though not a popular one, he was ready to aver, that the right of governing was not property but a trust.
Charles James Fox (1749–1806) British Whig politician.
Referring to William Pitt's plans for parliamentary reform
C.J. Fox (J. L. Hammond)

255 Mountains interposed
Make enemies of nations, who had else,
Like kindred drops, been mingled into one.
William Cowper (1731–1800) British poet.
The Task

256 Slaves cannot breathe in England; if their lungs
Receive our air, that moment they are free;
They touch our country, and their shackles fall.
William Cowper
A situation resulting from a judicial decision in 1772
The Task

1787

257 Let Americans disdain to be the instruments of European greatness. Let the Thirteen States, bound together in a strict and indissoluble union, concur in erecting one great American system.
Alexander Hamilton (1755–1804) American statesman.
Federalist Papers, XI

258 A little rebellion now and then is a good thing.
Thomas Jefferson (1743–1826) US statesman.
Letter to James Madison, 30 Jan 1787

259 The tree of liberty must be refreshed from time to time with the blood of patriots and tyrants. It is its natural manure.
Thomas Jefferson
Letter to W. S. Smith, 13 Nov 1787

260 A bill of rights is what the people are entitled to against every government on earth, general or particular and what no just government should refuse to rest on inference.
Thomas Jefferson
Letter to James Madison, 20 Dec 1787

1788

261 There is not a single crowned head in Europe whose talents or merits would entitle him to be elected a vestryman by the people of any parish in America.
Thomas Jefferson
Written from Paris
Letter to George Washington, 2 May 1788

262 A thing may look specious in theory, and yet be ruinous in practice; a thing may look evil in theory, and yet be in practice excellent.
Edmund Burke (1729–97) British politician.
Impeachment of Warren Hastings, 19 Feb 1788

1789

263 The King bathes, and with great success; a machine follows the Royal one into the sea, filled with fiddlers, who play *God Save the King* as his Majesty takes his plunge.
Fanny Burney (Frances Burney D'Arblay; 1752–1840) British novelist.
Referring to George III at Weymouth
Diary, 8 July 1789

1790

264 Here lies Joseph, who failed in everything he undertook.
Joseph II (1741–90) Holy Roman Emperor.
Suggesting his own epitaph when reflecting upon the disappointment of his hopes for reform
Attrib.

265 The condition upon which God hath given liberty to man is eternal vigilance.
John Philpot Curran (1750–1817) Irish judge.
Speech on the Right of Election of Lord Mayor of Dublin, 10 July 1790

1793

266 Let them eat cake.
Marie-Antoinette (1755–93) Queen of France.
On being told that the people had no bread to eat; in fact she was repeating a much older saying
Attrib.

Attitudes

Art, Literature, and Music

17th century

267 Blest pair of Sirens, pledges of Heaven's joy,
Sphere-born harmonious sisters, Voice and Verse.
John Milton (1608–74) English poet.
At a Solemn Music

1666

268 I could also have stepped into a style much higher than this in which I have here discoursed, and could have adorned all things more than here I have seemed to do, but I dare not. God did not play in convincing of me, the devil did not play in tempting of me neither did I play when I sunk into a bottomless pit,

when the pangs of hell caught hold upon me;
wherefore I may not play in my relating of
them, but be plain and simple, and lay down the
thing as it was.
John Bunyan (1628–88)
Referring to literary style
Grace Abounding to the Chief of Sinners,
Preface

1667

269 Rhyme being no necessary adjunct or true ornament of poem or good verse, in longer
works especially, but the invention of a barbarous age, to set off wretched matter and lame
metre.
John Milton (1608–74) English poet.
Paradise Lost, The Verse. Preface to 1668 ed.

1668

270 He was the man who of all modern, and perhaps ancient poets had the largest and most
comprehensive soul.
John Dryden (1631–1700) British poet and
dramatist.
Referring to Shakespeare
Essay of Dramatic Poesy

1675

271 Words may be false and full of art,
Sighs are the natural language of the heart.
Thomas Shadwell (1642–92) English
dramatist.
Psyche, III

1683

272 . . . just imitation of the most fam'd Italian masters: principally, to bring the seriousness and
gravity of that sort of musick into vogue and
reputation among our countrymen, whose hu-
mor, 'tis time now, should begin to loath the
levity, and balladry of our neighbours.
Henry Purcell (1659–95) English composer.
Preface to a volume of sonatas

1693

273 When he killed a calf he would do it in a high
style, and make a speech.
John Aubrey (1626–1697) English antiquary.
Brief Lives, 'William Shakespeare'

274 He was so fair that they called him *the lady of*
Christ's College.
John Aubrey
Brief Lives, 'John Milton'

1697

275 Music has charms to soothe a savage breast.
William Congreve (1670–1729) British Res-
toration dramatist.
The Mourning Bride, I

18th century

276 The secret of the arts is to correct nature.
Voltaire (François-Marie Arouet; 1694–1778)
French writer.
Épîtres, 'À M. de Verrière'

1711

277 A reader seldom peruses a book with pleasure
until he knows whether the writer of it be a
black man or a fair man, of a mild or choleric
disposition, married or a bachelor.
Joseph Addison (1672–1719) British
essayist.
The Spectator, 1

278 Nothing is capable of being well set to music
that is not nonsense.
Joseph Addison
The Spectator, 18

279 True ease in writing comes from art, not
chance,
As those move easiest who have learn'd to
dance.
'Tis not enough no harshness gives offence,
The sound must seem an echo to the sense.
Alexander Pope (1688–1744) British poet.
An Essay on Criticism

1723

280* Architecture has its political use; publick buildings being the ornament of a country; it estab-
lishes a nation, draws people and commerce;
makes the people love their native country,
which passion is the original of all great actions
in a commonwealth.
Sir Christopher Wren (1632–1723) English
architect and scientist.
Parentalia

1734

281 For painters, poets and builders have very high
flights, but they must be kept down.
Sarah, Duchess of Marlborough (1660–
1744) Wife of John Churchill, 1st Duke of
Marlborough.
Letter to the Duchess of Bedford, 21 June 1734

1736

282 There's sure no passion in the human soul,
But finds its food in music.
George Lillo (1693–1739) English dramatist.
Fatal Curiosity, I:2

1745

283 Ah, a German and a genius! a prodigy, admit
him!
Jonathan Swift (1667–1745) Irish-born
Anglican priest and writer.
Learning of the arrival of Handel: Swift's last
words
Attrib.

284 Words are men's daughters, but God's sons
are things.
Samuel Madden (1686–1765) Irish writer.
Boulter's Monument

1750

285 Was there ever yet anything written by mere
man that was wished longer by its readers, excepting *Don Quixote, Robinson Crusoe,* and
the *Pilgrim's Progress*?
Samuel Johnson (1709–84) British
lexicographer.
Johnsonian Miscellanies (ed. G. B. Hill), Vol. I

1752

286 I have laboured to refine our language to gram-
matical purity, and to clear it from colloquial
barbarisms, licentious idioms, and irregular
combinations.
Samuel Johnson
The Rambler

1755

287* I suffer from the disease of writing books and
being ashamed of them when they are
finished.
Baron de Montesquieu (1688–1755) French
writer.
Pensées diverses

1756

288 The reciprocal civility of authors is one of the
most risible scenes in the farce of life.
Samuel Johnson (1709–84) British
lexicographer.
Life of Sir Thomas Browne

1759

289 That great Cham of literature, Samuel Johnson.
Tobias Smollett (1721–71) British novelist.
Letter to John Wilkes, 16 Mar 1759

290 Writing, when properly managed, (as you may
be sure I think mine is) is but a different
name for conversation.
Laurence Sterne (1713–68) Irish-born British
writer.
Tristram Shandy

1763

291 It is burning a farthing candle at Dover, to shew
light at Calais.
Samuel Johnson (1709–84) British
lexicographer.
Referring to the impact of Sheridan's works upon
the English language
Life of Johnson (J. Boswell), Vol. I

1764

292 There can hardly be a stranger commodity in
the world than books. Printed by people who
don't understand them; sold by people who
don't understand them; bound, criticized and
read by people who don't understand them; and
now even written by people who don't understand them.
Georg Christoph Lichtenberg (1742–99)
German physicist and writer.
Aphorisms

293 One of the greatest geniuses that ever existed,
Shakespeare, undoubtedly wanted taste.
Horace Walpole (1717–97) British writer.
Letter to Wren, 9 Aug 1764

1769

294 There is no arguing with Johnson; for when his
pistol misses fire, he knocks you down with
the butt end of it.
Oliver Goldsmith (1728–74) Irish-born British
writer.
Life of Johnson (J. Boswell)

1769

295 Shakespeare never had six lines together without a fault. Perhaps you may find seven, but
this does not refute my general assertion.
Samuel Johnson (1709–84) British
lexicographer.
Life of Johnson (J. Boswell), Vol. II

1770

296 A mere copier of nature can never produce any-
thing great.
Joshua Reynolds (1723–92) British portrait
painter.
Discourse to Students of the Royal Academy, 1
Dec 1770

1772

297 For instrumental music there is a certain
Haydn, who has some peculiar ideas, but he is
only just beginning.
Maria Theresa (1717–80) Empress and ruler
of the Habsburg dominions.
Letter to Archduchess Marie Beatrix, 1772

1773

298 Read over your compositions, and where ever
you meet with a passage which you think is
particularly fine, strike it out.
Samuel Johnson (1709–84) British
lexicographer.
Recalling the advice of a college tutor
Life of Johnson (J. Boswell), Vol. II

1775

299 He was dull in a new way, and that made many
people think him *great.*
Samuel Johnson
Referring to the poet Thomas Gray
Life of Johnson (J. Boswell), Vol. II

1776

00 No man but a blockhead ever wrote, except for money.
Samuel Johnson
Life of Johnson (J. Boswell), Vol. III

01 *Sturm und Drang.*
Storm and stress.
Friedrich Maximilian von Klinger (1752–1831) German dramatist and novelist.
Used to designate a late 18th-century literary movement in Germany
Play title

1778

'02 I do not think this poem will reach its destination.
Voltaire (François-Marie Arouet; 1694–1778) French writer.
Reviewing Rousseau's poem 'Ode to Posterity'
Attrib.

1780

03 They are forced plants, raised in a hot-bed; and they are poor plants; they are but cucumbers after all.
Samuel Johnson (1709–84) British lexicographer.
Referring to Gray's *Odes*
Life of Johnson (J. Boswell), Vol. IV

1781

04 Classical quotation is the *parole* of literary men all over the world.
Samuel Johnson
Life of Johnson (J. Boswell), Vol. IV

1784

05* The only sensual pleasure without vice.
Samuel Johnson
Referring to music
Johnsonian Miscellanies (ed. G. B. Hill), Vol. II

06* What is written without effort is in general read without pleasure.
Samuel Johnson
Johnsonian Miscellanies (ed. G. B. Hill), Vol. II

07* Now that the old lion is dead, every ass thinks he may kick at him.
Samuel Parr (1747–1825) British writer and scholar.
Referring to Dr Johnson.
Life of Johnson (J. Boswell)

1786

308 All his own geese are swans, as the swans of others are geese.
Horace Walpole (1717–97) British writer.
Referring to Sir Joshua Reynolds
Letter to the Countess of Upper Ossory, 1 Dec 1786

1788

309 Another damned, thick, square book! Always scribble, scribble, scribble! Eh! Mr Gibbon?
William, Duke of Gloucester (1743–1805)
The brother of George III.
Addressing Edward Gibbon, author of *The History of the Decline and Fall of the Roman Empire*; also attributed to George III
Literary Memorials (Best)

Daily Life

1674

310 'Tis to be wondered at our ancestors who were given so much to eat spices. Wee now, since the pox came up, eat none and will suffer none to be in meat.
Anthony Wood
Life and Times, Vol. II

1682

311* I have often seen the King consume four plates of different soups, a whole pheasant, a partridge, a large plate of salad, two big slices of ham, a dish of mutton in garlic sauce, a plateful of pastries followed by fruit and hard-boiled eggs. The King and Monsieur greatly like hard-boiled eggs.
Duchess of Orleans (1652–1722) Sister-in-law to Louis XIV.
Letter, ?1682

1689

312 'Tis not the drinking that is to be blamed, but the excess.
John Selden (1584–1654) English historian.
Table Talk

1729

313 Where's Troy, and where's the Maypole in the Strand?
Pease, cabbages and turnips once grew where
Now stands New Bond Street and a newer Square;
Such piles of buildings now rise up and down,
London itself seems going out of Town.
Our Fathers crossed from Fulham in a Wherry,
Their sons enjoy a Bridge at Putney Ferry.
James Bramston (c. 1694–1744) British poet.
The Whig Supremacy (Basil Williams), Ch. 15

1774

314 The way to ensure summer in England is to have it framed and glazed in a comfortable room.
Horace Walpole (1717–97) British writer.
Letter to Cole, 28 May 1774

1776

315 There is nothing which has yet been contrived
by man, by which so much happiness is produced as by a good tavern or inn.
Samuel Johnson (1709–84) British
lexicographer.
Life of Johnson (J. Boswell), Vol. II

Death

1668

316 Rather suffer than die is man's motto.
Jean de La Fontaine (1621–95) French poet.
Fables, I, 'La Mort et le Bûcheron'

1732

317 How often are we to die before we go quite off
this stage? In every friend we lose a part of
ourselves, and the best part.
Alexander Pope (1688–1744) British poet.
Letter to Jonathan Swift, 5 Dec 1732

1751

318 It hath been often said, that it is not death, but
dying, which is terrible.
Henry Fielding (1707–54) British novelist.
Amelia, Bk. III, Ch. 4

319 Can storied urn or animated bust
Back to its mansion call the fleeting breath?
Can honour's voice provoke the silent dust,
Or flatt'ry soothe the dull cold ear of death?
Thomas Gray (1716–71) British poet.
Elegy Written in a Country Churchyard

320 The boast of heraldry, the pomp of pow'r,
And all that beauty, all that wealth e'er gave,
Awaits alike th' inevitable hour,
The paths of glory lead but to the grave.
Thomas Gray
Elegy Written in a Country Churchyard

1769

321 It matters not how a man dies, but how he
lives. The act of dying is not of importance, it
lasts so short a time.
Samuel Johnson (1709–84) British
lexicographer.
Life of Johnson (J. Boswell), Vol. II

1785

322* What argufies pride and ambition?
Soon or late death will take us in tow:
Each bullet has got its commission,
And when our time's come we must go.
Charles Dibdin (1745–1814) British actor and
dramatist.
Each Bullet has its Commission

Education, Knowledge, and Learning

1662

323 A proverb is much matter decorated into few
words.
Thomas Fuller (1608–61) English historian.
The History of the Worthies of England, Ch. 2

1665

324 The intellect is always fooled by the heart.
Duc de la Rochefoucauld (1613–80) French
writer.
Maximes, 102

1667

325 Vain wisdom all, and false philosophy.
John Milton (1608–74) English poet.
Paradise Lost, Bk. II

1685

326 Most men make little use of their speech than
to give evidence against their own
understanding.
Lord Halifax (1633–95) English statesman.
*Political, Moral, and Miscellaneous Thoughts
and Reflections*

1688

327 There are some who speak one moment before
they think.
Jean de La Bruyère (1645–96) French
satirist.
Les Caractères

1690

328 New opinions are always suspected, and usually opposed, without any other reason but
because they are not already common.
John Locke (1632–1704) English philosopher
An Essay Concerning Human Understanding,
dedicatory epistle

329 It is one thing to show a man that he is in an
error, and another to put him in possession of
truth.
John Locke (1632–1704) English philosopher
An Essay Concerning Human Understanding,
Bk. IV, Ch. 7

18th century

330 From ignorance our comfort flows,
The only wretched are the wise.
Matthew Prior (1664–1721) British poet.
To the Hon. Charles Montague

331 . . . it a great error to waste young gentlemen'
years so long in learning Latin by so tedious a
grammar.
Gilbert Burnet (1643–1715) Scottish-born
English bishop
The Later Stuarts (Sir George Clark)

332 Reading is to the mind what exercise is to the body.
Richard Steele (1672–1729) Dublin-born British essayist.
The Tatler, 147

333 Some for renown, on scraps of learning dote,
And think they grow immortal as they quote.
Edward Young (1683–1765) British poet.
Love of Fame, I

334 The King, observing with judicious eyes
The state of both his universities,
To Oxford sent a troop of horse, and why?
That learned body wanted loyalty;
To Cambridge books, as very well discerning
How much that loyal body wanted learning.
Joseph Trapp (1679–1747) English churchman and academic.
Written after George I donated the Bishop of Ely's library to Cambridge
Literary Anecdotes (Nichols), Vol. III

335 The King to Oxford sent a troop of horse,
For Tories own no argument but force:
With equal skill to Cambridge books he sent,
For Whigs admit no force but argument.
William Browne (1692–1774) English physician.
Literary Anecdotes (Nichols), Vol. III

336 Beware you be not swallowed up in books! An ounce of love is worth a pound of knowledge.
John Wesley (1703–91) British religious leader.
Life of Wesley (R. Southey), Ch. 16

1711

337 For fools rush in where angels fear to tread.
Alexander Pope (1688–1744) British poet.
An Essay on Criticism

338 Words are like leaves; and where they most abound,
Much fruit of sense beneath is rarely found.
Alexander Pope
An Essay on Criticism

1731

339 'Tis education forms the common mind,
Just as the twig is bent, the tree's inclined.
Alexander Pope
Moral Essays, I

1742

340 Public schools are the nurseries of all vice and immorality.
Henry Fielding (1707–54) British novelist.
Joseph Andrews, Bk. III, Ch. 5

1745

341 Be wiser than other people if you can, but do not tell them so.
Earl of Chesterfield (1694–1773) English statesman.
Letter to his son, 19 Nov 1745

1748

342 If we take in our hand any volume; of divinity or school metaphysics, for instance; let us ask, *Does it contain any abstract reasoning concerning quantity or number?* No. *Does it contain any experimental reasoning, concerning matter of fact and existence?* No. commit it then to the flames: for it can contain nothing but sophistry and illusion.
David Hume (1711–76) Scottish philosopher.
An Enquiry Concerning Human Understanding

343 Some folk are wise, and some are otherwise.
Tobias Smollett (1721–71) British novelist.
Roderick Random, Ch. 6

1749

344 Due attention to the inside of books, and due contempt for the outside, is the proper relation between a man of sense and his books.
Earl of Chesterfield (1694–1773) English statesman.
Letter to his son, 10 Jan 1749

345 There mark what ills the scholar's life assail
Toil, envy, want, the patron, and the jail.
Samuel Johnson (1709–84) British lexicographer.
Vanity of Human Wishes

1759

346 The true system of the World has been recognized, developed and perfected . . . Everything has been discussed and analysed, or at least mentioned.
Jean d'Alembert (1717–83) French philosopher and mathematician.
Referring to the *Encyclopédie* (1751–80), which he helped to edit
Elements of Philosophy

347 Integrity without knowledge is weak and useless, and knowledge without integrity is dangerous and dreadful.
Samuel Johnson (1709–84) British lexicographer.
Rasselas, Ch. 41

1764

348 Superstition sets the whole world in flames; philosophy quenches them.
Voltaire (François-Marie Arouet; 1694–1778) French writer.
Dictionnaire philosophique, 'Superstition'

349 I never approved either the errors of his book, or the trivial truths he so vigorously laid down. I have, however, stoutly taken his side when absurd men have condemned him for these same truths.
Voltaire
Referring to Helvetius's *De L'Esprit*, which was publicly burnt in 1758; usually misquoted as 'I disapprove of what you say, but I will defend to the death your right to say it'
Dictionnaire Philosophique Portaif, 'Homme'

1771

350* Education made us what we are.
Claude-Adrien Helvétius (1715–71) French
philosopher.
Discours XXX, Ch. 30

1773

351 Let schoolmasters puzzle their brain,
With grammar, and nonsense, and learning,
Good liquor, I stoutly maintain,
Gives genius a better discerning.
Oliver Goldsmith (1728–74) Irish-born British
writer.
She Stoops to Conquer, I

1774

352 He who resolves never to ransack any mind but
his own, will be soon reduced, from mere barrenness, to the poorest of all imitations; he
will be obliged to imitate himself, and to repeat
what he has before often repeated.
Joshua Reynolds (1723–92) British portrait
painter.
Discourse to Students of the Royal Academy, 10
Dec 1774

1775

353 All knowledge is of itself of some value. There
is nothing so minute or inconsiderable, that I
would not rather know it than not.
Samuel Johnson (1709–84) British
lexicographer.
Life of Johnson (J. Boswell)

354 I am not yet so lost in lexicography, as to forget
that words are the daughters of earth, and that
things are the sons of heaven. Language is
only the instrument of science, and words are
but the signs of ideas: I wish, however, that
the instrument might be less apt to decay, and
that signs might be permanent, like the things
which they denote.
Samuel Johnson
Dictionary of the English Language

1779

355 The true genius is a mind of large general powers, accidentally determined to some particular direction.
Samuel Johnson
Lives of the English Poets, 'Cowley'

1783

356 My dear friend, clear your *mind* of cant ... You
may *talk* in this manner; it is a mode of talking
in Society: but don't *think* foolishly.
Samuel Johnson (1709–84) British
lexicographer.
Life of Johnson (J. Boswell), Vol. IV

1785

357 Knowledge dwells
In heads replete with thoughts of other men;
Wisdom in minds attentive to their own.
William Cowper (1731–1800) British poet.
The Task

1788

358* To the University of Oxford I acknowledge no
obligation; and she will as cheerfully renounce
me for a son, as I am willing to disclaim her
for a mother. I spent fourteen months at Mag-
dalen College: they proved the fourteen
months the most idle and unprofitable of my
whole life.
Edward Gibbon (1737–94) British historian.
Autobiography

History

18th century

359 A good historian is timeless; although he is a
patriot, he will never flatter his country in any
respect.
François Fénelon (1651–1715) French writer
and prelate.
Letter to M. Dacier

1745

360* Anything but history, for history must be false.
Robert Walpole (1676–1745) British
statesman.
Walpoliana

1763

361 Great abilities are not requisite for an Historian
... Imagination is not required in any high
degree.
Samuel Johnson (1709–84) British
lexicographer.
Life of Johnson (J. Boswell), Vol. I

1764

362 All our ancient history, as one of our wits re-
marked, is no more than accepted fiction.
Voltaire (François-Marie Arouet; 1694–1778)
French writer.
Jeannot et Colin

1767

363 Indeed, history is nothing more than a tableau
of crimes and misfortunes.
Voltaire
L'Ingénu, Ch. 10

1776

364 His reign is marked by the rare advantage of
furnishing very few materials for history; which

is, indeed, little more than the register of the crimes, follies, and misfortunes of mankind.
Edward Gibbon (1737–94) British historian.
Referring to the reign of Antoninus Pius
Decline and Fall of the Roman Empire, Ch. 3

1778

65* We owe respect to the living; to the dead we owe only truth.
Voltaire (François-Marie Arouet; 1694–1778) French writer.
Oeuvres, 'Première lettre sur Oedipe'

Human Nature

1656

66 I have made this letter longer than usual, only because I have not had the time to make it shorter.
Blaise Pascal (1623–62) French philosopher and mathematician.
Lettres provinciales, XVI

1662

67 We have erred, and strayed from thy ways like lost sheep.
The Book of Common Prayer
Morning Prayer, General Confession

68 We have left undone those things which we ought to have done; and we have done those things we ought not to have done.
The Book of Common Prayer
Morning Prayer, General Confession

1663

69 When civil fury first grew high,
And men fell out they knew not why.
Samuel Butler (1612–80) English satirist.
Hudibras, Pt. I

1665

70 He who lives without tobacco is not worthy to live.
Molière (Jean Baptiste Poquelin; 1622–73) French dramatist.
Don Juan, I:1

71 We are never so happy nor so unhappy as we imagine.
Duc de la Rochefoucauld (1613–80) French writer.
Maximes, 49

72 It is more shameful to distrust one's friends than to be deceived by them.
Duc de la Rochefoucauld
Maximes, 84

73 Silence is the best tactic for him who distrusts himself.
Duc de la Rochefoucauld
Maximes, 79

374 In the misfortune of our best friends, we always find something which is not displeasing to us.
Duc de la Rochefoucauld
Maximes, 99

375 There is scarcely a single man sufficiently aware to know all the evil he does.
Duc de la Rochefoucauld
Maximes, 269

376 The accent of one's birthplace lingers in the mind and in the heart as it does in one's speech.
Duc de la Rochefoucauld
Maximes, 342

377 Nothing prevents us from being natural so much as the desire to appear so.
Duc de la Rochefoucauld
Maximes, 431

1667

378 Accuse not Nature, she hath done her part;
Do thou but thine.
John Milton (1608–74) English poet.
Paradise Lost, Bk. VIII

379 In solitude
What happiness? who can enjoy alone,
Or, all enjoying, what contentment find?
John Milton
Paradise Lost, Bk. VIII

1668

380 One should oblige everyone to the extent of one's ability. One often needs someone smaller than oneself.
Jean de La Fontaine (1621–95) French poet.
Fables, II, 'Le Lion et le Rat'

381 Patience and passage of time do more than strength and fury.
Jean de La Fontaine
Fables, II, 'Le Lion et le Rat'

382 He told me never to sell the bear's skin before one has killed the beast.
Jean de La Fontaine
Fables, V, 'L'Ours et les deux Compagnons'

1669

383 The more intelligence one has the more people one finds original. Commonplace people see no difference between men.
Blaise Pascal (1623–62) French philosopher and mathematician.
Pensées, I

384 The heart has its reasons which reason does not know.
Blaise Pascal
Pensées, IV

1670

385 I have striven not to laugh at human actions,

not to weep at them, nor to hate them, but to understand them.
Benedict Spinoza (Baruch de Spinoza; 1632–77) Dutch philosopher.
Tractatus Theologico-Politicus, Ch. 1

1677

386 Desire is the very essence of man.
Benedict Spinoza
Ethics

387 Man is a social animal.
Benedict Spinoza
Ethics

1678

388 Men are but children of a larger growth;
Our appetites as apt to change as theirs,
And full as craving too, and full as vain.
John Dryden (1631–1700) British poet and dramatist.
All for Love, IV

389 People must help one another; it is nature's law.
Jean de La Fontaine (1621–95) French poet.
Fables, VIII, 'L'Âne et le Chien'

1680

390 But words once spoke can never be recall'd.
Earl of Roscommon (1633–85) Irish-born English poet.
Art of Poetry

1681

391 Beware the Fury of a Patient Man.
John Dryden (1631–1700) British poet and dramatist.
Absalom and Achitophel, I

1685

392 It is a general mistake to think the men we like are good for everything, and those we do not, good for nothing.
Lord Halifax (1633–95) English statesman.
Political, Moral and Miscellaneous Thoughts and Reflections

393 It is flattering some men to endure them.
Lord Halifax
Political, Moral and Miscellaneous Thoughts and Reflections

1687

394 For present joys are more to flesh and blood
Than a dull prospect of a distant good.
John Dryden (1631–1700) British poet and dramatist.
The Hind and the Panther, III

1688

395 One must laugh before one is happy, or one may die without ever laughing at all.
Jean de La Bruyère (1645–96) French satirist.
Les Caractères

1689

396 Pleasures are all alike simply considered in themselves . . . He that takes pleasure to hear sermons enjoys himself as much as he that hears plays.
John Selden (1584–1654) English historian.
Table Talk

397 Pleasure is nothing else but the intermission of pain.
John Selden
Table Talk

1701

398 Nature has left this tincture in the blood,
That all men would be tyrants if they could.
Daniel Defoe (1660–1731) British journalist and writer.
The Kentish Petition, Addenda

1706

399 A man should never be ashamed to own he has been in the wrong, which is but saying, in other words, that he is wiser to-day than he was yesterday.
Alexander Pope (1688–1744) British poet.
Thoughts on Various Subjects

400 I never wonder to see men wicked, but I often wonder to see them not ashamed.
Jonathan Swift (1667–1745) Irish-born Anglican priest and writer.
Thoughts on Various Subjects

1711

401 To err is human, to forgive, divine.
Alexander Pope (1688–1744) British poet.
An Essay on Criticism

402 Most sorts of diversion in men, children, and other animals, are an imitation of fighting.
Jonathan Swift (1667–1745) Irish-born Anglican priest and writer.
Thoughts on Various Subjects

1716

403 They do most by Books, who could do much without them, and he that chiefly owes himself unto himself, is the substantial Man.
Thomas Browne (1605–82) English physician and writer.
Christian Morals, Pt. II

1718

04 For hope is but the dream of those that wake.
Matthew Prior (1664–1721) British poet.
Solomon, II

1728

05 A moment of time may make us unhappy for
ever.
John Gay (1685–1732) English poet and
dramatist.
The Beggar's Opera

1733

06 And hence one master-passion in the breast,
Like Aaron's serpent, swallows up the rest.
Alexander Pope (1688–1744) British poet.
An Essay on Man, II

07 Know then thyself, presume not God to scan,
The proper study of Mankind is Man.
Alexander Pope
An Essay on Man, II

08 The ruling passion, be it what it will
The ruling passion conquers reason still.
Alexander Pope
Moral Essays, III

1735

09 Three may keep a secret, if two of them are
dead.
Benjamin Franklin (1706–90) US scientist
and statesman.
Poor Richard's Almanack

1736

10 A really intelligent man feels what other men
only know.
Baron de Montesquieu (1688–1755) French
writer.
*Essai sur les causes qui peuvent affecter les
esprits et les caractères*

1739

11 We never remark any passion or principle in
others, of which, in some degree or other, we
may not find a parallel in ourselves.
David Hume (1711–76) Scottish philosopher.
A Treatise of Human Nature

12 Everyone has observed how much more dogs
are animated when they hunt in a pack, than
when they pursue their game apart. We might,
perhaps, be at a loss to explain this phenomenon, if we had not experience of a similar in
ourselves.
David Hume
A Treatise of Human Nature

13 There are two things for which animals are to

be envied: they know nothing of future evils,
or of what people say about them.
Voltaire (François-Marie Arouet; 1694–1778)
French writer.
Letter, 1739

1741

414 Beauty in things exists in the mind which con-
templates them.
David Hume (1711–76) Scottish philosopher.
Essays, 'Of Tragedy'

1743

415* Whoever would lie usefully should lie seldom.
Lord Hervey (1696–1743) English writer and
pamphleteer.
Memoirs of the Reign of George II, Vol. I

1751

416 These are called the pious frauds of friendship.
Henry Fielding (1707–54) British novelist.
Amelia, Bk. III, Ch. 4

1755

417 If a man does not make new acquaintance as
he advances through life, he will soon find
himself left alone. A man, Sir, should keep his
friendship in constant repair.
Samuel Johnson (1709–84) British
lexicographer.
Life of Johnson (J. Boswell), Vol. I

1757

418 I am convinced that we have a degree of delight, and that no small one, in the real misfortunes and pains of others.
Edmund Burke (1729–97) British politician.
On the Sublime and Beautiful, Pt. I

1758

419 Pleasure is very seldom found where it is
sought; our brightest blazes of gladness are
commonly kindled by unexpected sparks.
Samuel Johnson (1709–84) British
lexicographer.
The Idler

420 We are inclined to believe those whom we do
not know because they have never deceived
us.
Samuel Johnson
The Idler

1762

421 The true use of speech is not so much to express our wants as to conceal them.
Oliver Goldsmith (1728–74) Irish-born British
writer.
Essays, 'The Use of Language'

1766

422 That all who are happy, are equally happy, is
     not true. A peasant and a philosopher may be
     equally *satisfied*, but not equally *happy*. Hap-
     piness consists in the multiplicity of agree-
     able consciousness.
     Samuel Johnson (1709–84) British
     lexicographer.
     Life of Johnson (J. Boswell), Vol. II

1772

423 A man who does not lose his reason over cer-
     tain things has none to lose.
     Gotthold Ephraim Lessing (1729–81) Ger-
     man dramatist.
     Emilia Galotti, IV:7

1776

424 All that is human must retrograde if it does not
     advance.
     Edward Gibbon (1737–94) British historian.
     Decline and Fall of the Roman Empire, Ch. 71

1778

425 Drinking when we are not thirsty and making
     love all year round, madam; that is all there is
     to distinguish us from other animals.
     Beaumarchais (1732–99) French dramatist.
     Le Mariage de Figaro, II:21

426 All censure of a man's self is oblique praise. It
     is in order to shew how much he can spare.
     Samuel Johnson (1709–84) British
     lexicographer.
     Life of Johnson (J. Boswell), Vol. III

1779

427 If it is abuse — why one is always sure to hear
     of it from one damned good-natured friend or
     other!
     Richard Brinsley Sheridan (1751–1816)
     British dramatist.
     The Critic, I

1781

428 Always, Sir, set a high value on spontaneous
     kindness. He whose inclination prompts him to
     cultivate your friendship of his own accord,
     will love you more than one whom you have
     been at pains to attach to you.
     Samuel Johnson (1709–84) British
     lexicographer.
     Life of Johnson (J. Boswell), Vol. IV

1782

429 Society, friendship, and love,
     Divinely bestowed upon man,
     Oh, had I the wings of a dove,

How soon would I taste you again!
William Cowper (1731–1800) British poet.
*Verses supposed to be written by Alexander
Selkirk*

1783

430 As I know more of mankind I expect less of
     them, and am ready now to call a man *a good
     man*, upon easier terms than I was formerly.
     Samuel Johnson (1709–84) British
     lexicographer.
     Life of Johnson (J. Boswell), Vol. IV

431 There is a wicked inclination in most people to
     suppose an old man decayed in his intellects.
     If a young or middle-aged man, when leaving
     a company, does not recollect where he laid
     his hat, it is nothing; but if the same inatten-
     tion is discovered in an old man, people will
     shrug up their shoulders and say, 'His memory
     is going.'
     Samuel Johnson
     Life of Johnson (J. Boswell), Vol. IV

1784

432 Sir, I look upon every day to be lost, in which I
     do not make a new acquaintance.
     Samuel Johnson
     Life of Johnson (J. Boswell), Vol. IV

433 No man is a hypocrite in his pleasures.
     Samuel Johnson
     Life of Johnson (J. Boswell), Vol. IV

1785

434* Out of the crooked timber of humanity no
      straight thing can ever be made.
      Immanuel Kant (1724–1804) German
      philosopher.
      *Idee zu einer allgemeinen Geschichte in
      weltbürgerlicher Absicht*

435 Happiness is not an ideal of reason but of
     imagination.
     Immanuel Kant
     Grundlegung zur Metaphysik der Sitten, II

Humour

1704

436 Satire is a sort of glass, wherein beholders do
     generally discover everybody's face but their
     own.
     Jonathan Swift (1667–1745) Irish-born
     Anglican priest and writer.
     The Battle of the Books, 'Preface'

1711

437 True wit is nature to advantage dress'd;
     What oft was thought, but ne'er so well
     express'd.
     Alexander Pope (1688–1744) British poet.
     An Essay on Criticism

1733

8 Satire should, like a polished razor keen,
Wound with a touch that's scarcely felt or
seen.
Lady Mary Wortley Montagu (1689–1762)
English writer.
To the Imitator of the First Satire of Horace,
Bk. II

1759

9 An ounce of a man's own wit is worth a ton of
other people's.
Laurence Sterne (1713–68) Irish-born British
writer.
Tristram Shandy

1763

0 A joke's a very serious thing.
Charles Churchill (1731–64) British poet.
The Ghost, Bk. IV

1778

1* God is on the side not of the heavy battalions,
but of the best shots.
Voltaire (François-Marie Arouet; 1694–1778)
French writer.
Notebooks

1784

2* Every man has, some time in his life, an ambition to be a wag.
Samuel Johnson (1709–84) British
lexicographer.
Diary and Letters (Mme D'Arblay), Vol. III, Ch.
46

Life

1651

3 As our life is very short, so it is very miserable,
and therefore it is well it is short.
Jeremy Taylor (1613–67) English Anglican
theologian.
The Rule and Exercise of Holy Dying, Ch. 1

1656

4 Life is an incurable disease.
Abraham Cowley (1618–67) English poet.
To Dr Scarborough

1665

5 To succeed in the world, we do everything we
can to appear successful.
Duc de la Rochefoucauld (1613–80) French
writer.
Maximes, 50

1666

446 It is a stupidity second to none, to busy oneself
with the correction of the world.
Molière (Jean Baptiste Poquelin; 1622–73)
French dramatist.
Le Misanthrope, I:1

1681

447 Great Wits are sure to Madness near alli'd
And thin Partitions do their Bounds divide.
John Dryden (1631–1700) British poet and
dramatist.
Absalom and Achitophel, I

1684

448 He that is down needs fear no fall;
He that is low, no pride.
John Bunyan (1628–88) English writer.
The Pilgrim's Progress, 'Shepherd Boy's Song'

449 As I walked through the wilderness of this
world.
John Bunyan
The Pilgrim's Progress, Pt. I

1688

450 There are only three events in a man's life;
birth, life, and death; he is not conscious of being born, he dies in pain, and he forgets to
live.
Jean de La Bruyère (1645–96) French
satirist.
Les Caractères

451 If poverty is the mother of crime, stupidity is its
father.
Jean de La Bruyère
Les Caractères

1706

452 The vanity of human life is like a river, constantly passing away, and yet constantly coming on.
Alexander Pope (1688–1744) British poet.
Thoughts on Various Subjects

453 When men grow virtuous in their old age, they
only make a sacrifice to God of the devil's
leavings.
Alexander Pope
Thoughts on Various Subjects

454 When a true genius appears in the world, you
may know him by this sign, that the dunces
are all in confederacy against him.
Jonathan Swift (1667–1745) Irish-born
Anglican priest and writer.
Thoughts on Various Subjects

1711

455 Thus I live in the world rather as a Spectator of
mankind, than as one of the species, by which
means I have made myself a speculative
statesman, soldier, merchant, and artisan, with-

out ever meddling with any practical part of
life.
Joseph Addison (1672–1719) British
essayist.
The Spectator, 1

1712

456 We are always doing something for posterity,
but I would fain see posterity do something
for us.
Joseph Addison
The Spectator, 583

1713

457 'Tis not in mortals to command success,
But we'll do more, Sempronius; we'll deserve
it.
Joseph Addison
Cato, I:2

1715

458 Lord, I ascribe it to Thy grace,
And not to chance, as others do,
That I was born of Christian race,
And not a Heathen, or a Jew.
Isaac Watts (1674–1748) English theologian
and hymn writer.
Divine Songs for Children, 'Praise for the
Gospel'

1726

459 A little rule, a little sway,
A sunbeam in a winter's day,
Is all the proud and mighty have
Between the cradle and the grave.
John Dyer (1700–58) British poet.
Grongar Hill

1732

460 Life is a jest; and all things show it.
I thought so once; but now I know it.
John Gay (1685–1732) English poet and
dramatist.
My Own Epitaph

1741

461 The atrocious crime of being a young man . . . I
shall neither attempt to palliate nor deny.
William Pitt the Elder (1708–78) British
statesman.
Speech, House of Commons, 27 Jan 1741

1742

462 Time flies, death urges, knells call, heaven in-
vites,
Hell threatens.
Edward Young (1683–1765) British poet.
Night Thoughts

1746

463 To achieve great things we must live as thou
we were never going to die.
Marquis de Vauvenargues (1715–47)
French soldier and writer.
Réflexions et maximes

1747

464 I recommend you to take care of the minute
for hours will take care of themselves.
Earl of Chesterfield (1694–1773) English
statesman.
Letter to his son, 6 Nov 1747

465 Not all that tempts your wand'ring eyes
And heedless hearts, is lawful prize;
Nor all, that glisters, gold.
Thomas Gray (1716–71) British poet.
Ode on the Death of a Favourite Cat

1748

466 Custom, then, is the great guide of human li
David Hume (1711–76) Scottish philosophe
An Enquiry Concerning Human Understandin

1757

467 Beauty in distress is much the most affectin
beauty.
Edmund Burke (1729–97) British politician
On the Sublime and Beautiful, Pt. III

1759

468 True genius walks along a line, and, perhaps
our greatest pleasure is in seeing it so often
near falling, without being ever actually dow
Oliver Goldsmith (1728–74) Irish-born Briti
writer.
The Bee, 'The Characteristics of Greatness'

469 A man should know something of his own
country, too, before he goes abroad.
Laurence Sterne (1713–68) Irish-born Briti
writer.
Tristram Shandy

470 All is for the best in the best of possible worl
Voltaire (François-Marie Arouet; 1694–1778
French writer.
Candide, Ch. 30

471 What a fine comedy this world would be if o
did not play a part in it!
Denis Diderot (1713–84) French writer.
Letters to Sophie Volland

1764

472 Just as the meanest and most vicious deeds
quire spirit and talent, so even the greatest
deeds require a certain insensitiveness whic
on other occasions is called stupidity.
Georg Christoph Lichtenberg (1742–99
German physicist and writer.
Aphorisms

1766

473 Man wants but little here below,
Nor wants that little long.
Oliver Goldsmith (1728–74) Irish-born British writer.
Edwin and Angelina, or the Hermit

1769

474 If you have great talents, industry will improve them: if you have but moderate abilities, industry will supply their deficiency.
Joshua Reynolds (1723–92) British portrait painter.
Discourse to Students of the Royal Academy, 11 Dec 1769

475 The world is a comedy to those who think, a tragedy to those who feel.
Horace Walpole (1717–97) British writer.
Letter to Sir Horace Mann, 1769

1776

476 It is better that some should be unhappy than that none should be happy, which would be the case in a general state of equality.
Samuel Johnson (1709–84) British lexicographer.
Life of Johnson (J. Boswell), Vol. III

1778

477 All argument is against it; but all belief is for it.
Samuel Johnson
Referring to the ghost of a dead person
Life of Johnson (J. Boswell), Vol. III

1785

478 God made the country, and man made the town.
William Cowper (1731–1800) British poet.
The Task

479 Oh for a lodge in some vast wilderness,
Some boundless contiguity of shade,
Where rumour of oppression and deceit,
Of unsuccessful or successful war,
Might never reach me more!
William Cowper
The Task

1787

480 A useless life is an early death.
Goethe (1749–1832) German poet and dramatist.
Iphegenie, I:2

1788

481 Two things fill the mind with ever new and increasing wonder and awe, the more often and the more seriously reflection concentrates

upon them: the starry heaven above me and the moral law within me.
Immanuel Kant (1724–1804) German philosopher.
Critique of Practical Reason, Conclusion

Love and Sex

1665

482 There are very few people who are not ashamed of having been in love when they no longer love each other.
Duc de la Rochefoucauld (1613–80) French writer.
Maximes, 71

483 If one judges love by its visible effects, it looks more like hatred than like friendship.
Duc de la Rochefoucauld
Maximes, 72

1666

484 Age will bring all things, and everyone knows, Madame, that twenty is no age to be a prude.
Molière (Jean Baptiste Poquelin; 1622–73) French dramatist.
Le Misanthrope, III:4

1667

485 Oh, I have loved him too much to feel no hate for him.
Jean Racine (1639–99) French dramatist.
Andromaque, II:1

1680

486* For, Heaven be thanked, we live in such an age, When no man dies for love, but on the stage.
John Dryden (1631–1700) British poet and dramatist.
Mithridates, Epilogue

1692

487 It is with our passions as it is with fire and water, they are good servants, but bad masters.
Roger L'Estrange (1616–1704) English journalist and writer.
Aesop's Fables, 38

1700

488 Say what you will, 'tis better to be left than never to have been loved.
William Congreve (1670–1729) British Restoration dramatist.
The Way of the World, II:1

1712

489 What dire offence from am'rous causes springs,

What mighty contests rise from trivial things.
Alexander Pope (1688–1744) British poet.
The Rape of the Lock, I

1743

490   He in a few minutes ravished this fair creature,
or at least would have ravished her, if she had
not, by a timely compliance, prevented him.
Henry Fielding (1707–54) British novelist.
Jonathan Wild, Bk. III, Ch. 7

1749

491   What is commonly called love, namely the desire of satisfying a voracious appetite with a
certain quantity of delicate white human flesh.
Henry Fielding
Tom Jones, Bk. VI, Ch. 1

1768

492   Friendship is a disinterested commerce between equals; love, an abject intercourse between tyrants and slaves.
Oliver Goldsmith (1728–74) Irish-born British
writer.
The Good-Natured Man, I

1778

493* It is one of the superstitions of the human mind
to have imagined that virginity could be a
virtue.
Voltaire (François-Marie Arouet; 1694–1778)
French writer.
Notebooks

1785

494* *Plaisir d'amour ne dure qu'un moment,
Chagrin d'amour dure toute la vie.*
Love's pleasure lasts but a moment; love's
sorrow lasts all through life.
Jean-Pierre Claris de Florian (1755–94)
French writer of fables.
Celestine

Marriage and the Family

1662

495   If any of you know cause, or just impediment.
The Book of Common Prayer
Solemnization of Matrimony

1665

496   Strange to say what delight we married people
have to see these poor fools decoyed into our
condition.
Samuel Pepys (1633–1703) English diarist.
Diary, 25 Dec 1665

1672

497   A mistress should be like a little country retrea
near the town, not to dwell in constantly, but
only for a night and away.
William Wycherley (1640–1716) English
dramatist.
The Country Wife, I:1

1678

498   Love is a boy, by poets styl'd,
Then spare the rod, and spoil the child.
Samuel Butler (1612–80) English satirist.
Hudibras, Pt. II

1689

499   Marriage is nothing but a civil contract.
John Selden (1584–1654) English historian.
Table Talk

1693

500   SHARPER. Thus grief still treads upon the heels
pleasure:
Marry'd in haste, we may repent at leisure.
SETTER. Some by experience find those words
mis-plac'd:
At leisure marry'd, they repent in haste.
William Congreve (1670–1729) British Res
toration dramatist.
The Old Bachelor, V:8

501   Men are generally more careful of the breed
their horses and dogs than of their children.
William Penn (1644–1718) English preacher
*Some Fruits of Solitude, in Reflections and
Maxims relating to the conduct of Humane Lif*
Pt. I, No 52

1696

502   No man worth having is true to his wife, or ca
be true to his wife, or ever was, or ever will be
so.
John Vanbrugh (1664–1726) English architect and dramatist.
The Relapse, III:2

1706

503   What they do in heaven we are ignorant of;
what they do *not* we are told expressly, that
they neither marry, nor are given in marriage.
Jonathan Swift (1667–1745) Irish-born
Anglican priest and writer.
Thoughts on Various Subjects

1749

504   His designs were strictly honourable, as the
phrase is; that is, to rob a lady of her fortune b
way of marriage.
Henry Fielding (1707–54) British novelist.
Tom Jones, Bk. XI, Ch. 4

1759

05 Marriage has many pains, but celibacy has no
pleasures.
Samuel Johnson (1709–84) British
lexicographer.
Rasselas, Ch. 26

1770

06 The triumph of hope over experience.
Samuel Johnson (1709–84) British
lexicographer.
Referring to the hasty remarriage of an acquaintance following the death of his first wife, with
whom he had been most unhappy
Life of Johnson (J. Boswell), Vol. II

Men and Women

1660

07 The souls of women are so small,
That some believe they've none at all.
Samuel Butler (1612–80) English satirist.
Miscellaneous Thoughts

1662

08 My wife, who, poor wretch, is troubled with her
lonely life.
Samuel Pepys (1633–1703) English diarist.
Diary, 19 Dec 1662

09 One tongue is sufficient for a woman.
John Milton (1608–74) English poet.
On being asked whether he would allow his
daughters to learn foreign languages
Attrib.

1675

10 Vain man is apt to think we were meerly intended for the world's propagation and to keep
its humane inhabitants sweet and clean; but,
by their leaves, had we the same literature
he would find our brains as fruitful as our
bodies.
Hanna Woolley
Gentlewoman's Companion, 1675

1676

11 Well, a widow, I see, is a kind of sinecure.
William Wycherley (1640–1716) English
dramatist.
The Plain Dealer, V:3

1688

12 Women run to extremes; they are either better
or worse than men.
Jean de La Bruyère (1645–96) French
satirist.
Les Caractères

1696

513 Once a woman has given you her heart you can
never get rid of the rest of her.
John Vanbrugh (1664–1726) English architect and dramatist.
The Relapse, II:1

1697

514 Heaven has no rage like love to hatred turned,
Nor hell a fury like a woman scorned.
William Congreve (1670–1729) British Res-
toration dramatist.
The Mourning Bride, III

1712

515 A woman seldom asks advice until she has
bought her wedding clothes.
Joseph Addison (1672–1719) British
essayist.
The Spectator, 475

1728

516 How, like a moth, the simple maid
Still plays about the flame!
John Gay (1685–1732) English poet and
dramatist.
The Beggar's Opera

1732

517 Most women have no characters at all.
Alexander Pope (1688–1744) British poet.
Moral Essays, II

518 Men, some to business, some to pleasure take;
But every woman is at heart a rake.
Alexander Pope
Moral Essays, II

1749

519 Women are much more like each other than
men: they have, in truth, but two passions, vanity and love; these are their universal
characteristics.
Earl of Chesterfield (1694–1773) English
statesman.
Letter to his son, 19 Dec 1749

1752

520 Every woman is infallibly to be gained by every
sort of flattery, and every man by one sort or
other.
Earl of Chesterfield
Letter to his son, 16 Mar 1752

1763

521 A woman's preaching is like a dog's walking on

his hinder legs. It is not done well; but you are surprised to find it done at all.
Samuel Johnson (1709–84) British lexicographer.
Life of Johnson (J. Boswell), Vol. I

1784
---

522 A man is in general better pleased when he has a good dinner upon his table, than when his wife talks Greek.
Samuel Johnson
Johnsonian Miscellanies (ed. G. B. Hill), Vol. II

Morality, Vices, and Virtues

1664
---

523 The manner of giving is worth more than the gift.
Pierre Corneille (1606–84) French dramatist.
Le Menteur, I:1

524 It is a public scandal that gives offence, and it is no sin to sin in secret.
Molière (Jean Baptiste Poquelin; 1622–73) French dramatist.
Tartuffe, IV:5

1665
---

525 We need greater virtues to sustain good fortune than bad.
Duc de la Rochefoucauld (1613–80) French writer.
Maximes, 25

526 If we had no faults of our own, we would not take so much pleasure in noticing those of others.
Duc de la Rochefoucauld
Maximes, 31

527 Self-interest speaks all sorts of tongues, and plays all sorts of roles, even that of disinterestedness.
Duc de la Rochefoucauld
Maximes, 39

528 To refuse praise reveals a desire to be praised twice over.
Duc de la Rochefoucauld
Maximes, 149

529 Hypocrisy is the homage paid by vice to virtue.
Duc de la Rochefoucauld
Maximes, 218

530 Most usually our virtues are only vices in disguise.
Duc de la Rochefoucauld
Maximes, added to the 4th edition

1666
---

531 One should examine oneself for a very long time before thinking of condemning others.
Molière (Jean Baptiste Poquelin; 1622–73) French dramatist.
Le Misanthrope, III:4

1667
---

532 For neither man nor angel can discern Hypocrisy, the only evil that walks Invisible, except to God alone.
John Milton (1608–74) English poet.
Paradise Lost, Bk. III

533 Revenge, at first though sweet, Bitter ere long back on itself recoils.
John Milton
Paradise Lost, Bk. IX

1669
---

534 If you want people to think well of you, do not speak well of yourself.
Blaise Pascal (1623–62) French philosopher and mathematician.
Pensées, I

1671
---

535 Most men admire Virtue, who follow not her lore.
John Milton (1608–74) English poet.
Paradise Regained, Bk. I

1674
---

536 Often the fear of one evil leads us into a worse.
Nicolas Boileau (1636–1711) French writer.
L'Art poétique, I

1677
---

537 Crime, like virtue, has its degrees.
Jean Racine (1639–99) French dramatist.
Phèdre, IV:2

1678
---

538 Errors, like Straws, upon the surface flow; He who would search for Pearls must dive below.
John Dryden (1631–1700) British poet and dramatist.
All for Love, Prologue

1684
---

539 It beareth the name of Vanity Fair, because the town where 'tis kept is lighter than vanity.
John Bunyan (1628–88) English writer.
The Pilgrim's Progress, Pt. I

1685
---

540 Popularity is a crime from the moment it is sought; it is only a virtue where men have it whether they will or no.
Lord Halifax (1633–95) English statesman.
Political, Moral and Miscellaneous Thoughts and Reflections

541 Our virtues and vices couple with one another

and get children that resemble both their parents.
Lord Halifax
Political, Moral and Miscellaneous Thoughts and Reflections

1688

42 Liberality lies less in giving liberally than in the timeliness of the gift.
Jean de La Bruyère (1645–96) French satirist.
Les Caractères

1693

43 The dreadful burden of having nothing to do.
Nicolas Boileau (1636–1711) French writer.
Épitres, XI

1694

44 See how love and murder will out.
William Congreve (1670–1729) British Restoration dramatist.
The Double Dealer, IV:6

1711

45 Fondly we think we honour merit then,
When we but praise ourselves in other men.
Alexander Pope (1688–1744) British poet.
An Essay on Criticism

46 Of all the causes which conspire to blind
Man's erring judgment, and misguide the mind,
What the weak head with strongest bias rules,
Is Pride, the never-failing vice of fools.
Alexander Pope
An Essay on Criticism

47 To err is human, to forgive, divine.
Alexander Pope
An Essay on Criticism

1715

48 For Satan finds some mischief still
For idle hands to do.
Isaac Watts (1674–1748) English theologian and hymn writer.
Divine Songs for Children, 'Against Idleness and Mischief'

1725

49 That action is best, which procures the greatest happiness for the greatest numbers.
Francis Hutcheson (1694–1746) Scottish philosopher.
Inquiry into the Original of our Ideas of Beauty and Virtue, Treatise II, 'Concerning Moral Good and Evil'

1739

550 Grief and disappointment give rise to anger, anger to envy, envy to malice, and malice to grief again, till the whole circle be completed.
David Hume (1711–76) Scottish philosopher.
A Treatise of Human Nature

1742

551 Procrastination is the thief of time.
Edward Young (1683–1765) British poet.
Night Thoughts

1746

552 Whatever is worth doing at all is worth doing well.
Earl of Chesterfield (1694–1773) English statesman.
Letter to his son, 10 Mar 1746

1747

553 Do as you would be done by is the surest method that I know of pleasing.
Earl of Chesterfield
Letter to his son, 16 Oct 1747

1749

554 Idleness is only the refuge of weak minds.
Earl of Chesterfield
Letter to his son, 20 July 1749

1759

555 Integrity without knowledge is weak and useless, and knowledge without integrity is dangerous and dreadful.
Samuel Johnson (1709–84) British lexicographer.
Rasselas, Ch. 41

556 'Tis known by the name of perseverance in a good cause, – and of obstinacy in a bad one.
Laurence Sterne (1713–68) Irish-born British writer.
Tristram Shandy

1763

557 The danger chiefly lies in acting well,
No crime's so great as daring to excel.
Charles Churchill (1731–64) British poet.
Epistle to William Hogarth

558 But if he does really think that there is no distinction between virtue and vice, why, Sir, when he leaves our houses let us count our spoons.
Samuel Johnson (1709–84) British lexicographer.
Life of Johnson (J. Boswell), Vol. I

1764

559 The best is the enemy of the good.
Voltaire (François-Marie Arouet; 1694–1778)
French writer.
Dictionnaire philosophique, 'Art dramatique'

1768

560 We must touch his weaknesses with a delicate
hand. There are some faults so nearly allied to
excellence, that we can scarce weed out the
fault without eradicating the virtue.
Oliver Goldsmith (1728–74) Irish-born British
writer.
The Good-Natured Man, I

1769

561 There is, however, a limit at which forbearance
ceases to be a virtue.
Edmund Burke (1729–97) British politician.
Observations on a Publication, 'The Present
State of the Nation'

1776

562 Corruption, the most infallible symptom of con-
stitutional liberty.
Edward Gibbon (1737–94) British historian.
Decline and Fall of the Roman Empire, Ch. 21

1777

563 He who praises everybody praises nobody.
Samuel Johnson (1709–84) British
lexicographer.
Life of Johnson (J. Boswell), Vol. III

1779

564 The bud may have a bitter taste,
But sweet will be the flower.
William Cowper (1731–1800) British poet.
Olney Hymns, 35

1782

565 I am not over-fond of resisting temptation.
William Beckford (1759–1844) British writer.
Vathek

1785

566 Finally, there is an imperative which commands
a certain conduct immediately . . . This imperative is Categorical . . . This imperative may be
called that of Morality.
Immanuel Kant (1724–1804) German
philosopher.
Grundlegung zur Metaphysik der Sitten, II

567 All universal moral principles are idle fancies.
Marquis de Sade (1740–1814) French
novelist.
The 120 Days of Sodom

Other People

1662

568 But Lord! to see the absurd nature of Englishmen, that cannot forbear laughing and jeering
at everything that looks strange.
Samuel Pepys (1633–1703) English diarist.
Diary, 27 Nov 1662

1688

569 If we heard it said of Orientals that they habitually drank a liquor which went to their heads,
deprived them of reason and made them
vomit, we should say: 'How very barbarous!'
Jean de La Bruyère (1645–96) French
satirist.
Les Caractères

1734

570 The English nation is the only one on earth
which has successfully regulated the power of
its kings by resisting them; and which, after
repeated efforts, has established that beneficial government under which the Prince, all
powerful for good, is restrained from doing ill.
Voltaire (François Marie Arouet; 1694–1778)
French writer.
Lettres philosophiques

1755

571 The Englishman . . . always has in his hands an
accurate pair of scales in which he scrupu-
lously weighs up the birth, the rank, and above
all, the wealth of the people he meets, in order to adjust his behaviour towards them
accordingly.
Jean Rouquet
The Reign of George III (J. Steven Watson),
Ch. 3

1758

572 When two Englishmen meet, their first talk is of
the weather.
Samuel Johnson (1709–84) British
lexicographer.
The Idler

1763

573 Norway, too, has noble wild prospects; and
Lapland is remarkable for prodigious noble wild
prospects. But, Sir, let me tell you, the noblest
prospect which a Scotchman ever sees, is
the high road that leads him to England!
Samuel Johnson
Life of Johnson (J. Boswell), Vol. I

1768

574 They are a loyal, a gallant, a generous, an ingenious, and good-temper'd people as is under

heaven – if they have a fault, they are too
serious.
Laurence Sterne (1713–68) Irish-born British
writer.
A Sentimental Journey, 'The Character.
Versailles'

1773

575 **Come, let me know what it is that makes a
Scotchman happy!**
Samuel Johnson
Ordering for himself a glass of whisky
Tour to the Hebrides (J. Boswell)

1774

576* **I hate the French because they are all slaves,
and wear wooden shoes.**
Oliver Goldsmith (1728–74) Irish-born British
writer.
Essays, 'Distresses of a Common Soldier'

1775

577 **The Irish are a fair people; – they never speak
well of one another.**
Samuel Johnson
Life of Johnson (J. Boswell), Vol. II

1780

578 **A Frenchman must be always talking, whether
he knows anything of the matter or not; an
Englishman is content to say nothing, when he
has nothing to say.**
Samuel Johnson (1709–84) British
lexicographer.
Life of Johnson (J. Boswell), Vol. IV

1782

579 **When you see how in this happy country the
lowest and poorest member of society takes an
interest in all public affairs; when you see
how high and low, rich and poor, are all willing
to declare their feelings and convictions;
when you see how a carter, a common sailor, a
beggar is still a man, nay, even more, an Englishman – then, believe me, you find yourself very differently affected from the
experience you feel when staring at our
soldiers drilling in Berlin.**
Karl Philipp Moritz (1756–93) German Lutheran pastor.
Reaction to a by-election at Westminster
Letter to a friend, 1782

1787

580 **I do not dislike the French from the vulgar antipathy between neighbouring nations, but for
their insolent and unfounded airs of
superiority.**
Horace Walpole (1717–97) British writer.
Letter to Hannah More, 14 Oct 1787

Religion

1651

581 **The Papacy is no other than the ghost of the
deceased Roman empire, sitting crowned upon
the grave thereof.**
Thomas Hobbes (1588–1679) English
philosopher.
Leviathan, Pt. IV, Ch. 47

1652

582 **God doth not need
Either man's work or his own gifts. Who best
Bear his mild yoke, they serve him best: his
state
Is kingly; thousands at his bidding speed,
And post o'er land and ocean without rest;
They also serve who only stand and wait.**
John Milton (1608–74) English poet.
Sonnet: 'On his Blindness'

1653

583 **Though the mills of God grind slowly, yet they
grind exceeding small;
Though with patience He stands waiting, with
exactness grinds He all.**
Friedrich von Logau (1604–55) German
poet and writer.
Sinngedichte, III

1662

584 **Renounce the devil and all his works.**
The Book of Common Prayer
Publick Baptism of Infants

1667

585 **What in me is dark
Illumine, what is low raise and support;
That, to the height of this great argument,
I may assert Eternal Providence,
And justify the ways of God to men.**
John Milton (1608–74) English poet.
Paradise Lost, Bk. I

586 **Long is the way
And hard, that out of hell leads up to light.**
John Milton
Paradise Lost, Bk. II

587 **Which way I fly is Hell; myself am Hell;
And, in the lowest deep, a lower deep
Still threat'ning to devour me opens wide,
To which the Hell I suffer seems a Heaven.**
John Milton
Paradise Lost, Bk. IV

1669

588 **I cannot forgive Descartes; in all his philosophy
he did his best to dispense with God. But he
could not avoid making Him set the world in**

motion with a flip of His thumb; after that he had no more use for God.
Blaise Pascal (1623–62) French philosopher and mathematician.
Pensées, II

1677

589   We feel and know that we are eternal.
Benedict Spinoza (Baruch de Spinoza; 1632–77) Dutch philosopher.
Ethics

1688

590   A pious man is one who would be an atheist if the king were.
Jean de La Bruyère (1645–96) French satirist.
Les Caractères

591   The Puritan hated bear-baiting, not because it gave pain to the bear, but because it gave pleasure to the spectators.
Lord Macaulay (1800–59) British historian.
History of England, Vol. I, Ch. 2

1689

592   For a priest to turn a man when he lies a-dying, is just like one that has a long time solicited a woman, and cannot obtain his end; at length makes her drunk, and so lies with her.
John Selden (1584–1654) English historian.
Table Talk

1700

593   While shepherds watch'd their flocks by night,
All seated on the ground,
The Angel of the Lord came down,
And Glory shone around.
Nahum Tate (1652–1715) Irish-born English poet.
Supplement to the New Version of the Psalms, 'While Shepherds Watched'

1701

594   Wherever God erects a house of prayer,
The Devil always builds a chapel there;
And 'twill be found, upon examination,
The latter has the largest congregation.
Daniel Defoe (1660–1731) British journalist and writer.
The True-Born Englishman, Pt. I

1721

595   No kingdom has ever had as many civil wars as the kingdom of Christ.
Baron de Montesquieu (1688–1755) French writer.
Lettres persanes

596   There is a very good saying that if triangles in-

vented a god, they would make him three-sided.
Baron de Montesquieu (1688–1755) French writer.
Lettres persanes

1739

597   I look upon all the world as my parish.
John Wesley (1703–91) British religious leader.
Journal, 11 June 1739

1741

598   The Christian religion not only was at first attended with miracles, but even at this day cannot be believed by any reasonable person without one. Mere reason is insufficient to convince us of its veracity: and whoever is moved by faith to assent to it, is conscious of a continued miracle in his own person, which subverts all the principles of his understanding, and gives him a determination to believe what is most contrary to custom and experience.
David Hume (1711–76) Scottish philosopher.
Essays, 'Of Miracles'

1743

599   Many a long dispute among divines may be thus abridged: It is so. It is not so. It is so. It is not so.
Benjamin Franklin (1706–90) US scientist and statesman.
Poor Richard's Almanack

1750

600   Religion is by no means a proper subject of conversation in a mixed company.
Earl of Chesterfield (1694–1773) English statesman.
Letter to his godson

1759

601   Whenever a man talks loudly against religion, always suspect that it is not his reason, but his passions which have got the better of his creed.
Laurence Sterne (1713–68) Irish-born British writer.
Tristram Shandy

1762

602* Wandering in a vast forest at night, I have only a faint light to guide me. A stranger appears and says to me: 'My friend, you should blow out your candle in order to find your way more clearly.' This stranger is a theologian.
Denis Diderot (1713–84) French writer.
Addition aux Pensées philosophiques

1763
---

603 Truth, Sir, is a cow, which will yield such people no more milk, and so they are gone to milk
the bull.
Samuel Johnson (1709–84) British
lexicographer.
Referring to sceptics
Life of Johnson (J. Boswell), Vol. I

1764

604* Probably no invention came more easily to man
than Heaven.
Georg Christoph Lichtenberg (1742–99)
German physicist and writer.
Aphorisms

1768
---

605 I never saw, heard, nor read, that the clergy
were beloved in any nation where Christianity
was the religion of the country. Nothing can
render them popular, but some degree of
persecution.
Jonathan Swift (1667–1745) Irish-born
Anglican priest and writer.
Thoughts on Religion

606 I am positive I have a soul; nor can all the
books with which materialists have pestered
the world ever convince me of the contrary.
Laurence Sterne (1713–68) Irish-born British
writer.
A Sentimental Journey, 'Maria, Moulines'

1769
---

607 There is no idolatry in the Mass. They believe
God to be there, and they adore him.
Samuel Johnson (1709–84) British
lexicographer.
Life of Johnson (J. Boswell), Vol. II

1773
---

608 As I take my shoes from the shoemaker, and
my coat from the tailor, so I take my religion
from the priest.
Oliver Goldsmith (1728–74) Irish-born British
writer.
Life of Johnson (J. Boswell)

1778

609* Faith consists in believing when it is beyond
the power of reason to believe. It is not enough
that a thing be possible for it to be believed.
Voltaire (François-Marie Arouet; 1694–1778)
French writer.
Questions sur l'encyclopédie

610* If God made us in His image, we have certainly
returned the compliment.
Voltaire
Le Sottisier

611 Everything is good when it leaves the Creator's
hands; everything degenerates in the hands of
man.
Jean Jacques Rousseau (1712–78) French
philosopher.
Attrib.

1788

612* If God did not exist, it would be necessary to
invent Him.
Voltaire
Épîtres, 'À l'auteur du livre des trois Imposteurs'

Science, Medicine, and Technology

1661
---

613 It is my intent to beget a good understanding
between the chymists and the mechanical
philosophers who have hitherto been too little
acquainted with one another's learning.
Robert Boyle (1627–91) British scientist.
The Sceptical Chymist

1675
---

614 If I have seen further it is by standing on the
shoulders of giants.
Isaac Newton (1642–1727) British scientist.
Letter to Robert Hooke, 5 Feb 1675

1704
---

615 Nature is very consonant and conformable with
herself.
Isaac Newton
Opticks, Bk. III

1727
---

616 I do not know what I may appear to the world,
but to myself I seem to have been only like a
boy playing on the sea-shore, and diverting
myself in now and then finding a smoother
pebble or a prettier shell than ordinary, whilst
the great ocean of truth lay all undiscovered
before me.
Isaac Newton
Isaac Newton (L. T. More)

617* O Diamond! Diamond! thou little knowest the
mischief done!
Isaac Newton
Said to a dog that set fire to some papers, repre-
senting several years' work, by knocking over a
candle
Wensley-Dale . . . a Poem (Thomas Maude)

618* Nature, and Nature's laws lay hid in night:
God said, *Let Newton be!* and all was light.
Alexander Pope (1688–1744) British poet.
Epitaphs, 'Intended for Sir Isaac Newton'

1762

619 Men will always be mad and those who think they can cure them are the maddest of all.
Voltaire (François-Marie Arouet; 1694–1778) French writer.
Letter, 1762

1778

620 Man is a tool-making animal.
Benjamin Franklin (1706–90) US scientist and statesman.
Life of Johnson (J. Boswell), 7 Apr 1778

1779

621 We are perpetually moralists, but we are geometricians only by chance. Our intercourse with intellectual nature is necessary; our speculations upon matter are voluntary, and at leisure.
Samuel Johnson (1709–84) British lexicographer.
Lives of the English Poets, 'Milton'

1788

622 The art of medicine consists of amusing the patient while Nature cures the disease.
Voltaire (1694–1788) French writer.
Attrib.

Wealth and Poverty

1673

623 He must have killed a lot of men to have made so much money.
Molière (Jean Baptiste Poquelin; 1622–73) French dramatist.
Le Malade imaginaire, I:5

1688

624 The shortest and best way to make your fortune is to let people see clearly that it is in their interests to promote yours.
Jean de La Bruyère (1645–96) French satirist.
Les Caractères

1707

625 There's no scandal like rags, nor any crime so shameful as poverty.
George Farquhar (1678–1707) Irish dramatist.
The Beaux' Strategem, I:1

1747

626 I knew once a very covetous, sordid fellow, who

used to say, 'Take care of the pence, for the pounds will take care of themselves.'
Earl of Chesterfield (1694–1773) English statesman.
Possibly referring to William Lowndes
Letter to his son, 6 Nov 1747

1751

627 Let not Ambition mock their useful toil,
Their homely joys, and destiny obscure;
Nor Grandeur hear with a disdainful smile,
The short and simple annals of the poor.
Thomas Gray (1716–71) British poet.
Elegy Written in a Country Churchyard

1753

628 I am rich beyond the dreams of avarice.
Edward Moore (1712–57) British dramatist.
The Gamester, II

1775

629 There are few ways in which a man can be more innocently employed than in getting money.
Samuel Johnson (1709–84) British lexicographer.
Life of Johnson (J. Boswell), Vol. II

1776

630 With the great part of rich people, the chief employment of riches consists in the parade of riches.
Adam Smith (1723–90) Scottish economist.
The Wealth of Nations

1778

631 Sir, the insolence of wealth will creep out.
Samuel Johnson (1709–84) British lexicographer.
Life of Johnson (J. Boswell), Vol. III

1782

632 Resolve not to be poor: whatever you have, spend less. Poverty is a great enemy to human happiness; it certainly destroys liberty, and it makes some virtues impracticable and others extremely difficult.
Samuel Johnson
Life of Johnson (J. Boswell), Vol. IV

1785

633 Riches have wings, and grandeur is a dream.
William Cowper (1731–1800) British poet.
The Task

Work and Occupations

1660

634 A client is fain to hire a lawyer to keep from the injury of other lawyers – as Christians that travel in Turkey are forced to hire Janissaries, to protect them from the insolencies of other Turks.
Samuel Butler (1835–1902) British writer.
Prose Observations

1669

635 Not to care for philosophy is to be a true philosopher.
Blaise Pascal (1623–62) French philosopher and mathematician.
Pensées, I

1681

636 For Politicians neither love nor hate.
John Dryden (1631–1700) British poet and dramatist.
Absalom and Achitophel, I

1715

637 How doth the little busy bee
Improve each shining hour,
And gather honey all the day
From every opening flower!
Isaac Watts (1674–1748) English theologian and hymn writer.
Divine Songs for Children, 'Against Idleness and Mischief'

1734

638 I am as sober as a Judge.
Henry Fielding (1707–54) British novelist.
Don Quixote in England, III:14

1742

639 For clergy are men as well as other folks.
Henry Fielding (1707–54) British novelist.
Joseph Andrews, Bk II, Ch. 6

1756

640 The booksellers are generous liberal-minded men.
Samuel Johnson (1709–84) British lexicographer.
Life of Johnson (J. Boswell), Vol. I

1759

641 Work banishes those three great evils, boredom, vice, and poverty.
Voltaire (François-Marie Arouet; 1694–1778) French writer.
Candide, Ch. 30

1762

642 To a philosopher no circumstance, however trifling, is too minute.
Oliver Goldsmith (1728–74) Irish-born British writer.
The Citizen of the World

1770

643 I do not care to speak ill of any man behind his back, but I believe the gentleman is an *attorney*.
Samuel Johnson (1709–84) British lexicographer.
Life of Johnson (J. Boswell), Vol. II

1772

644 A man who is good enough to go to heaven, is good enough to be a clergyman.
Samuel Johnson
Life of Johnson (J. Boswell), Vol. II

1773

645 A lawyer has no business with the justice or injustice of the cause which he undertakes, unless his client asks his opinion, and then he is bound to give it honestly. The justice or injustice of the cause is to be decided by the judge.
Samuel Johnson
Tour to the Hebrides (J. Boswell)

1776

646 We would all be idle if we could.
Samuel Johnson
Life of Johnson (J. Boswell), Vol. III

1780

647 Remember that time is money.
Benjamin Franklin (1706–90) US scientist and statesman.
Advice to a Young Tradesman

Sayings of the Time

1660

648 And so to bed.
Samuel Pepys (1633–1703) English diarist.
Diary, 6 May 1660 and *passim*

1684

649 The gentleman's name that met him was Mr Worldly Wiseman.
John Bunyan (1628–88) English writer.
The Pilgrim's Progress, Pt. I

1707

650 Spare all I have, and take my life.
George Farquhar (1678–1707) Irish dramatist.
The Beaux' Strategem, V:2

651 Lady Bountiful.
Bernard de Fontenelle (1657–1757) French philosopher.
The Beaux' Strategem, I:1

1708

652 Boys and girls come out to play,
The moon doth shine as bright as day.
Useful Transactions in Philosophy (William King)

1719

653 I takes my man Friday with me.
Daniel Defoe (1660–1731) British journalist and writer.
Robinson Crusoe, Pt. I

1725

654 London Bridge is broken down,
My fair lady.
Namby Pamby (Henry Carey)

1735

655 Some are weather-wise, some are otherwise.
Benjamin Franklin (1706–90) US scientist and statesman.
Poor Richard's Almanack

656 Damn with faint praise, assent with civil leer,
And, without sneering, teach the rest to sneer.
Alexander Pope (1688–1744) British poet.
Epistle to Dr. Arbuthnot

1742

657 Far from the madding crowd's ignoble strife,
Their sober wishes never learn'd to stray;
Along the cool sequester'd vale of life
They kept the noiseless tenor of their way.
Thomas Gray (1716–71) British poet.
Elegy Written in a Country Churchyard

1763

658 The distance doesn't matter; it is only the first step that is difficult.
Marquise du Deffand (Marie de Vichy-Chamrond; 1697–1780) French noblewoman.
Referring to the legend of St Denis, who is traditionally believed to have carried his severed head for six miles after his execution
Letter to d'Alembert, 7 July 1763

With Hindsight

18th century

659 'And everybody praised the Duke,
Who this great fight did win.'
'But what good came of it at last?'
Quoth little Peterkin.
'Why that I cannot tell,' said he,
'But 'twas a famous victory.'
Robert Southey (1774–1843) British poet.
The Battle of Blenheim

660 His views and affections were singly confined to the narrow compass of the Electorate;
England was too big for him.
Earl of Chesterfield (1694–1773) English statesman.
Referring to George I
Letters

661 George the First knew nothing, and desired to know nothing; did nothing, and desired to do nothing; and the only good thing that is told of him is, that he wished to restore the crown to its hereditary successor.
Samuel Johnson (1709–84) British lexicographer.
Life of Johnson (J. Boswell)

19th century

662 Better lo'ed ye canna be,
Will ye no come back again?
Carolina Nairne (1766–1845) Scottish songwriter.
Referring to Bonnie Prince Charlie
Bonnie Charlie's now awa!

663 Charlie is my darling, my darling, my darling,
Charlie is my darling, the young Chevalier.
Carolina Nairne
Referring to Bonnie Prince Charlie
Charlie is my Darling

664 Wi' a hundred pipers an' a', an' a'.
Carolina Nairne
A romantic glorification of the 1745 Jacobite Rebellion
The Hundred Pipers

665 ... this haughty, vigilant, resolute, sagacious blue-stocking, half Mithridates and half Trissotin, bearing up against a world in arms
Lord Macaulay (1800–59) British historian.
Referring to Frederick the Great
Historical Essays, 'Frederick the Great'

666 Dr Johnson's morality was as English an articl as a beefsteak.
Nathaniel Hawthorne (1804–64) US novelist and writer.
Our Old Home, 'Lichfield and Uttoxeter'

667 Throughout the greater part of his life George III was a kind of 'consecrated obstruction'.
Walter Bagehot (1826–1877) British economist and journalist.
The English Constitution, 'The Monarchy'

20th century

668 I'm glad you like my Catherine. I like her too.
She ruled thirty million people and had three
thousand lovers. I do the best I can in two
hours.
Mae West (1892–1980) US actress.
After her performance in *Catherine the Great*
Speech from the stage

669 Too much counterpoint; what is worse, Protes-
tant counterpoint.
Thomas Beecham (1879–1961) British
conductor.
Said of J. S. Bach
The Guardian, 8 Mar 1971

670 It is sobering to consider that when Mozart was
my age he had already been dead for a year.
Tom Lehrer (1928–   ) US university teacher
and songwriter.
An Encyclopedia of Quotations about Music
(N. Shapiro)

671 The sonatas of Mozart are unique; they are too
easy for children, and too difficult for artists.
Artur Schnabel (1882–1951) Austrian con-
cert pianist.
An Encyclopedia of Quotations about Music
(N. Shapiro)

9

The French Revolution (1789–1815)

In the 18th century, the French monarchy represented the *ancien régime*. Vast, intricate, and archaic, its power and authority rested on a web of expedients woven over the centuries. By 1788, it was financially and politically bankrupt; yet it dared not initiate any far-reaching reforms for fear of undermining its whole structure. In desperation Louis XVI summoned the States General, the medieval assembly of the realm, which had not met since 1614. However, his shaky control of the political process combined with an increasing radicalism throughout the country to destroy the monarchy. By 1793, when Louis XVI was executed, France had taken an unprecedented step: the basic continuity of political and social institutions, together with the legitimacy offered by the past, had been explicitly rejected. In their place the revolutionaries sought to construct a state based on the rational principles of the Enlightenment, epitomized by the slogan 'Liberty, Equality, Fraternity'.

War with the rest of Europe began in 1792. The revolutionaries were keen to export their ideas, which, not unnaturally, were anathema to the remaining traditional monarchies of Europe. From late 1792, the French were everywhere victorious. The emergence of a soldier of genius, Napoleon Bonaparte, added a new dimension to this situation. In 1799 he seized control of France and in 1804 declared himself emperor. France now became an exporter of Bonapartist imperialism rather than revolution. Invincible in battle, Napoleon was the arbiter of Europe until his disastrous attack on Russia in 1812. When France was finally defeated in 1815, Napoleon was exiled; nevertheless the ideas of the French Revolution lived on to terrify the traditional monarchies for another half century.

In Britain during this period, a quite separate, but equally profound, change was beginning – the Industrial Revolution. The exploitation of technological discoveries, especially the steam engine, encouraged the concentration of production in factories. This revolution made industry more efficient, enabling larger volumes of goods to be produced at low prices. By 1815 Britain had acquired a decisive industrial advantage over the rest of the world. Although this continued to increase, it brought with it a number of new social problems, particularly the large-scale movement of the population from the countryside to the towns and the appalling working conditions in the new factories. The industrial methods of production pioneered in Britain were not made use of in the rest of Europe and in America until the middle of the 19th century.

Politics, Government, and World Events

1788

1 No National Assembly ever threatened to be so stormy as that which will decide the fate of the monarchy, and which is gathering in such haste, and with so much distrust on both sides.
Comte de Mirabeau (1749–91) French statesman.
Letter, 6 Dec 1788

1789

2 *Liberté! Égalité! Fraternité!*
Freedom! Equality! Brotherhood!
Anonymous
Motto for French Revolutionaries

3 Let us take as our emblem green cockades, green the colour of hope!
Camille Desmoulins (1760–94) French Revolutionary leader.
Le Vieux Cordelier

4 Who will dare deny that the Third Estate contains within itself all that is needed to constitute a nation?
Abbé de Sieyès (1748–1836) French churchman.
The 'Third Estate' comprised all the French people except the nobility (the First Estate) and the clergy (the Second Estate)
Qu'est-ce que le Tiers État? (pamphlet, Jan 1789)

5 *Rien*
Nothing.
Louis XVI (1754–93) King of France.
Diary, 14 July 1789 – the day the Bastille fell

6 How much the greatest event it is that ever happened in the world! and how much the best!
Charles James Fox (1749–1806) British Whig politician.
Referring to the fall of the Bastille, 14 July 1789
Letter to Fitzpatrick, 30 July 1789

7 Every law is an evil, for every law is an infraction of liberty.
Jeremy Bentham (1748–1832) British philosopher.
An Introduction to the Principles of Morals and Legislation

1790s

8 Oh! the grand old Duke of York
He had ten thousand men;
He marched them up to the top of the hill,
And he marched them down again.
And when they were up they were up,
And when they were down they were down,
And when they were only half way up,
They were neither up nor down.
Anonymous
Referring to Frederick Augustus, son of George

III and Duke of York, who commanded two unsuccessful campaigns against the French (1793 and 1799)
Traditional

1790

9 To tell the truth, Napoleone is a dangerous man in a free country. He seems to me to have the makings of a tyrant.
Lucien Bonaparte (1775–1840) Brother of Napoleon I.
Letter to Joseph Bonaparte, 1790

10 But the age of chivalry is gone. That of sophisters, economists, and calculators, has succeeded; and the glory of Europe is extinguished for ever.
Edmund Burke (1729–97) British politician.
Reflections on the Revolution in France

11 Vice itself lost half its evil, by losing all its grossness.
Edmund Burke
Reflections on the Revolution in France

12 Kings will be tyrants from policy when subjects are rebels from principle.
Edmund Burke
Reflections on the Revolution in France

1791

13 The Commons, faithful to their system, remained in a wise and masterly inactivity.
James Mackintosh (1765–1832) Scottish lawyer, philosopher, and historian.
Vindiciae Gallicae

1792

14 Unquestionably there never was a time in the history of this country when, from the situation of Europe, we might more reasonably expect fifteen years of peace, than we may at this present moment.
William Pitt the Younger (1759–1806) British statesman.
Revolutionary France declared war on Britain on 1 Feb 1793
Speech, House of Commons, 17 Feb 1792

15 Dangers by being despised grow great.
Edmund Burke (1729–97) British politician.
Speech, House of Commons, 11 May 1792

16 *Allons, enfants, de la patrie,
Le jour de gloire est arrivé.*
Come, children of our native land,
The day of glory has arrived.
Rouget de Lisle (Claude Joseph Rouget de Lisle; 1760–1836) French military engineer and composer.
La Marseillaise (French national anthem)

17 The tocsin you hear today is not an alarm but an alert: it sounds the charge against our enemies. To conquer them we must dare, and

dare again, and dare for ever; and thus will
France be saved
Georges Jacques Danton (1759–94)
French political activist.
Speech, Paris, 2 Sept 1792

18 From today and from this place there begins a
new epoch in the history of the world.
Goethe (1749–1832) German poet and
dramatist.
On witnessing revolutionary France's first military
victory, at the battle of Valmy (20 Sept 1792)
The Story of Civilization (W. Durant), Vol. II

19 How, indeed, may we judge a king as a citizen?
For judging means applying the law. But law
implies a common foundation of justice. And
what common foundation of justice is there
between humanity and kings?
Louis de Saint-Just (1767–94) French
politician.
Speech, Convention, 18 Nov 1792

20 Citizens, we are talking of a republic, and yet
Louis lives! We are talking of a republic, and
the person of the King still stands between us
and liberty.
Robespierre (1758–94) French lawyer and
revolutionary.
Speech, Convention, 3 Dec 1792

1793

21 Any institution which does not suppose the
people good, and the magistrate corruptible is
evil.
Robespierre
Déclaration des Droits de l'homme, 24 Apr
1793

22 Son of Saint Louis, ascend to heaven.
Abbé Edgeworth de Firmont (1745–1807)
Irish-born confessor to Louis XVI.
Said to Louis XVI as he climbed up to the guillo-
tine; Saint Louis was Louis IX of France (1226–
79)
Attrib.

23 *'O liberté! O liberté! Que de crimes on commet
en ton nom!'*
Oh liberty! Oh liberty! What crimes are com-
mitted in thy name!
Madame Roland (1754–93) French
revolutionary.
Said as she mounted the steps of the guillotine
Attrib.

24 There has been reason to fear that the Revolution may, like Saturn, devour each of her children one by one.
Pierre Vergniaud (1753–93) French
revolutionary.
Said at his trial, Nov 1793
Attrib.

25 Prisons are built with stones of Law, brothels
with bricks of Religion.
William Blake (1757–1827) British poet.
The Marriage of Heaven and Hell, 'Proverbs of
Hell'

1794

26 Thou wilt show my head to the people: it is
worth showing.
Georges Jacques Danton (1759–94)
French political activist.
Said as he mounted the scaffold, 5 Apr 1794
French Revolution (Carlyle), Bk. VI, Ch. 2

27* *J'ai vécu.*
I survived.
Abbé de Sieyès (1748–1836) French
churchman.
Replying to an enquiry concerning what he had
done during the Terror
Dictionnaire Encyclopédique (E. Guérard)

1795

28 Somebody has said, that a king may make a no
bleman, but he cannot make a gentleman.
Edmund Burke (1729–97) British politician.
Letter to William Smith, 29 Jan 1795

29 Harris, I am not well; pray get me a glass of
brandy.
George IV (1762–1830) King of the United
Kingdom.
On seeing Caroline of Brunswick (his future wife)
for the first time
Diaries (Earl of Malmesbury)

30 In *this* country, my Lords, . . . the individual
subject . . . 'has nothing to do with the laws but
to obey them.'
Samuel Horsley (1733–1806) British bishop.
House of Lords, 13 Nov 1795

31 The courtiers who surrounded him have forgot-
ten nothing and learnt nothing.
Charles-François Dumouriez (1739–1823)
French general.
Referring to Louis XVIII. This remark is also at-
tributed to Talleyrand
Attrib.

32* A whiff of grapeshot.
Thomas Carlyle (1795–1881) Scottish
historian.
Describing how Napoleon, early in his career,
quelled a minor riot in Paris
History of the French Revolution, Pt. I, Bk. V,
Ch. 3

1796

33 The French Revolution is merely the herald of a
far greater and much more solemn revolution,
which will be the last . . . The hour has come
for founding the Republic of Equals, that great
refuge open to every man.
François-Noël Babeuf (1760–97) French
revolutionary.
Conjuration des Egaux

1797

34 In Scotland there is no shadow even of representation. There is neither a representation of

property for the counties, nor of population
for the towns.
Charles James Fox (1749–1806) British
politician.
Parliamentary History of England (W. Cobbett),
Vol. XXXIII

1798
---

35 Think of it, soldiers; from the summit of these
pyramids, forty centuries look down upon
you.
Napoleon I (Napoleon Bonaparte; 1769–
1821) French emperor.
Speech before the Battle of the Pyramids, 21
July 1798

36 The perpetual struggle for room and food.
Thomas Robert Malthus (1766–1834) Brit-
ish clergyman and economist.
Essays on the Principle of Population

1799
---

37 His taxes now prove
His great love for the people,
So wisely they're managed
To starve the poor souls.
Charles Morris (1745–1838) Song-writer.
Referring to William Pitt the Younger
The Faber Book of English History in Verse
(Kenneth Baker)

1800

38* You must hate a Frenchman as you hate the
devil.
Lord Nelson (1758–1805) British admiral.
Life of Nelson (Southey), Ch. 3

39 Providence has given to the French the empire
of the land, to the English that of the sea, and
to the Germans that of the air.
Jean Paul Richter (Johann Paul Friedrich
Richter; 1763–1825) German novelist.
Quoted by Thomas Carlyle

1801
---

40 I have only one eye: I have a right to be blind
sometimes: I really do not see the signal.
Lord Nelson (1758–1805) British admiral.
Remark, Battle of Copenhagen, 2 Apr 1801; Nelson ignored Admiral Parker's order to disen-
gage by placing his telescope to his blind eye;
an hour later, he was victorious

41 He clapped the glass to his sightless eye,
And 'I'm damned if I see it', he said.
Henry John Newbolt (1862–1938) British
poet.
Referring to Lord Nelson at the Battle of
Copenhagen
Admirals All

42 Ye Mariners of England
That guard our native seas,

Whose flag has braved, a thousand years,
The battle and the breeze –
Your glorious standard launch again
To match another foe!
And sweep through the deep,
While the stormy winds do blow, –
While the battle rages loud and long,
And the stormy winds do blow.
Thomas Campbell (1777–1844) British poet.
Ye Mariners of England

1802
---

43 Think of your forefathers! Think of your
posterity!
John Quincy Adams (1767–1848) Sixth
president of the USA.
Speech, Plymouth, Massachusetts, 22 Dec 1802

44 We must be free or die, who speak the tongue
That Shakspeare spake; the faith and morals
hold
Which Milton held.
William Wordsworth (1770–1850) British
poet.
Sonnets, 'It is not to be thought of'

1803

45* Pitt is to Addington
As London is to Paddington.
George Canning (1770–1827) British
statesman.
Henry Addington had become Prime Minister
when Pitt resigned (1801) over George III's refusal to accept Catholic emancipation; Pitt returned as Prime Minister in 1804
The Oracle

46 I do not say the French cannot come, I only say
they cannot come by sea.
John Jervis, Earl St Vincent (1735–1823)
British admiral.
Remark to the Cabinet, 1803

47 The strongest poison ever known
Came from Caesar's laurel crown.
William Blake (1757–1827) British poet.
Auguries of Innocence

1804
---

48 He is an ordinary human being after all! . . . now
he will put himself above everyone else and
become a tyrant.
Ludwig van Beethoven (1770–1827) German composer.
Referring to Napoleon, on hearing that he had
declared himself emperor
Remark to Ferdinand Ries, a pupil

49 It is worse than a crime, it is a blunder.
Antoine Boulay de la Meurthe (1761–
1840) French politician.
Referring to the summary execution of the Duc
d'Enghien by Napoleon, 1804
Attrib.

1805

Battle of Trafalgar (1805)

The naval battle (21 October 1805), during the Napoleonic wars, in which the British, led by Nelson in the *Victory*, defeated the French and ended the threat of an invasion of Britain. The success was marred by the death of Nelson.

50 The Nelson touch.
Lord Nelson (1758–1805) British admiral.
Diary, 9 Oct 1805

51 Now, gentlemen, let us do something today which the world may talk of hereafter.
Lord Collingwood (1750–1810) British admiral.
Said before Trafalgar, 21 Oct 1805
Correspondence and Memoir of Lord Collingwood (G. L. Newnham; ed. Collingwood)

52 In case signals can neither be seen nor perfectly understood, no captain can do very wrong if he places his ship alongside that of an enemy.
Lord Nelson (1758–1805) British admiral.
Memorandum before Trafalgar, 9 Oct 1805

53 England expects every man will do his duty.
Lord Nelson
Signal hoisted prior to the Battle of Trafalgar, 1805

54 Kiss me, Hardy.
Lord Nelson
Spoken to Sir Thomas Hardy, captain of the *Victory*, during the Battle of Trafalgar, 1805

55 The death of Nelson was felt in England as something more than a public calamity; men started at the intelligence and turned pale, as if they had heard of the loss of a dear friend.
Robert Southey (1774–1843) British poet.
The Life of Nelson

56 England has saved herself by her exertions, and will, as I trust, save Europe by her example.
William Pitt the Younger (1759–1806) British statesman.
Speech, Guildhall, 1805

57 Roll up that map: it will not be wanted these ten years.
William Pitt the Younger
On learning that Napoleon had won the Battle of Austerlitz (2 Dec 1805)
Attrib.

58 Venice, the eldest Child of Liberty.
She was a maiden City, bright and free.
William Wordsworth (1770–1850) British poet.
Venice, a republic since the Middle Ages, was conquered by Napoleon in 1797 and absorbed into his Kingdom of Italy in 1805
Sonnets, 'Once did she hold'

59 O Caledonia! stern and wild,
Meet nurse for a poetic child!
Land of brown heath and shaggy wood,
Land of the mountain and the flood,
Land of my sires! what mortal hand
Can e'er untie the filial band
That knits me to thy rugged strand!
Walter Scott (1771–1832) Scottish novelist
The Lay of the Last Minstrel, VI

1806

60 I think I could eat one of Bellamy's veal pies
William Pitt the Younger (1759–1806) British statesman.
Last words
Attrib.

61 Oh, my country! How I leave my country!
William Pitt the Younger

62 With death doomed to grapple,
Beneath this cold slab, he
Who lied in the chapel
Now lies in the Abbey.
Byron, George Gordon, 6th Baron (1788–1824) British poet.
Epitaph for William Pitt

63* England is a nation of shopkeepers.
Napoleon I (Napoleon Bonaparte; 1769–182
French emperor.
Attrib.

64 Another year! – another deadly blow!
Another mighty empire overthrown!
And we are left, or shall be left, alone.
William Wordsworth (1770–1850) British poet.
Napoleon defeated Prussia at the Battles of Jen and Anerstädt, 14 Oct 1806
Sonnets, 'Another year!'

1807

65 The wealth of our island may be diminished, b the strength of mind of the people cannot easily pass away ... We cannot lose our liberty, because we cannot cease to think.
Humphry Davy (1778–1829) British chemis
Letter to Thomas Poole, 28 Aug 1807

66 A more virtuous man, I believe, does not exis nor one who is more enthusiastically devoted to better the condition of mankind.
Thomas Jefferson (1743–1826) US statesman.
Referring to Tsar Alexander I
Letter to William Duane, 20 July 1807

67 A power is passing from the earth
To breathless Nature's dark abyss;
But when the great and good depart,
What is it more than this –

That Man who is from God sent forth,
Doth yet again to God return? –
Such ebb and flow must ever be,

Then wherefore should we mourn?
William Wordsworth (1770–1850) British poet.
Referring to Charles James Fox, the hero of the liberal Whigs, who died in 1806
Lines on the Expected Dissolution of Mr. Fox

68 The moment the very name of Ireland is mentioned, the English seem to bid adieu to common feeling, common prudence, and common sense, and to act with the barbarity of tyrants, and the fatuity of idiots.
Sydney Smith (1771–1845) British clergyman and essayist.
The Letters of Peter Plymley

69 The harp that once through Tara's halls
The soul of music shed,
Now hangs as mute on Tara's walls
As if that soul were fled. –
So sleeps the pride of former days,
So glory's thrill is o'er;
And hearts, that once beat high for praise,
Now feel that pulse no more.
Thomas Moore (1779–1852) Irish poet.
Irish Melodies, 'The Harp that Once'

70 Me this uncharter'd freedom tires;
I feel the weight of chance-desires:
My hopes no more must change their name,
I long for a repose that ever is the same.
William Wordsworth (1770–1850) British poet.
Ode to Duty

71 Milton! thou shouldst be living at this hour:
England hath need of thee; she is a fen
Of stagnant waters: altar, sword, and pen,
Fireside, the heroic wealth of hall and bower,
Have forfeited their ancient English dower
Of inward happiness.
William Wordsworth
Sonnets, 'Milton! thou shouldst'

72 I travelled among unknown men
In lands beyond the sea;
Nor, England! did I know till then
What love I bore to thee.
William Wordsworth
I Travelled among Unknown Men

1808

73 And did those feet in ancient time
Walk upon England's mountains green?
And was the holy lamb of God
On England's pleasant pastures seen?
. . .
I will not cease from mental fight,
Nor shall my sword sleep in my hand,
Till we have built Jerusalem
In England's green and pleasant land.
William Blake (1757–1827) British poet.
Better known as the hymn 'Jerusalem', with music by Sir Hubert Parry; not to be confused with Blake's longer poem *Jerusalem*
Milton, Preface

74 *Noblesse oblige.*

Nobility has its own obligations.
Duc de Lévis (1764–1830) French writer and soldier.
Maximes et Réflexions

1809

75 I still love you, but in politics there is no heart, only head.
Napoleon I (Napoleon Bonaparte; 1769–1821) French emperor.
Referring to his divorce, for reasons of state, from the Empress Josephine (1809)
Bonaparte (C. Barnett)

76 Not a drum was heard, not a funeral note,
As his corse to the rampart we hurried,
Charles Wolfe (1791–1823) Irish poet.
The Burial of Sir John Moore at Corunna, I

77 We carved not a line, and we raised not a stone –
But we left him alone with his glory.
Charles Wolfe
The Burial of Sir John Moore at Corunna, VIII

1810

78 My principle is: France before everything.
Napoleon I (Napoleon Bonaparte; 1769–1821) French emperor.
Letter to Eugène Beauharnais, 23 Aug 1810

79* Every French soldier carries in his cartridge-pouch the baton of a marshal of France.
Napoleon I
La Vie Militaire sous l'Empire (E. Blaze)

80* Maybe it would have been better if neither of us had been born.
Napoleon I
Said while looking at the tomb of the philosopher Jean-Jacques Rousseau, whose theories had influenced the French Revolution
The Story of Civilization (W. Durant), Vol. II

81 I don't know what effect these men will have on the enemy, but, by God, they frighten me.
Duke of Wellington (1769–1852) British general and statesman.
Referring to his soldiers
Attrib.

82* What His Royal Highness most particularly prides himself upon, is the excellent harvest.
Richard Brinsley Sheridan (1751–1816) British dramatist.
Lampooning George IV's habit of taking credit for everything good in England
The Fine Art of Political Wit (L. Harris)

83* Who's your fat friend?
'Beau' Brummell (George Bryan Brummell; 1778–1840) British dandy.
Referring to George, Prince of Wales
Reminiscences (Gronow)

84* Shut the door, Wales.
'Beau' Brummell
Said to the Prince of Wales
Attrib.

1811

85 If I were asked at this moment for a summary opinion of what I have seen in England, I might probably say that its political institutions present a detail of corrupt practices, of profusion, and of personal ambition, under the mask of public spirit very carelessly put on, more disgusting than I should have expected. ...On the other hand, I should admit very readily that I have found the great mass of the people richer, happier, and more respectable than any other with which I am acquainted.
L. Simond French traveller and diarist.
Journal of a Tour and Residence in Great Britain during 1810 and 1811 by a French Traveller

86 Every country has the government it deserves.
Joseph de Maistre (1753–1821) French monarchist.
Lettres et Opuscules Inédits, 15 Aug 1811

87 As it will be the right of all, so it will be the duty of some, definitely to prepare for a separation, amicably if they can, violently if they must.
Josiah Quincy (1772–1864) US statesman.
Abridgement of Debates of Congress, Vol. IV, 14 Jan 1811

1812

88 It's the most beautiful battlefield I've ever seen.
Napoleon I (Napoleon Bonaparte; 1769–1821) French emperor.
Referring to carnage on the field of Borodino, near Moscow, after the battle (7 Sept 1812)
Attrib.

89 There rises the sun of Austerlitz.
Napoleon I
Said at the Battle of Borodino (7 Sept 1812), near Moscow; the Battle of Austerlitz (2 Dec 1805) was Napoleon's great victory over the Russians and Austrians

90 It is only a step from the sublime to the ridiculous.
Napoleon I
Remark following the retreat from Moscow, 1812
Attrib.

91 Napoleon is a torrent which as yet we are unable to stem. Moscow will be the sponge that will suck him dry.
Mikhail Kutuzov (1745–1813) Russian marshal.
Address to the commanders of the Russian army, 13 Sept 1812

92* Then was seen with what a strength and majesty the British soldier fights.
Sir William Napier (1785–1860) British general and historian.
History of the War in the Peninsula Bk. XII, Ch. 6

93 Never under the most despotic of infidel governments did I behold such squalid wretch-
edness as I have seen since my return in the very heart of a Christian country.
Lord Byron (1788–1824) British poet.
Speaking against the death penalty for machine wrecking
Speech, House of Lords, 27 Feb 1812

94 Hereditary bondsmen! know ye not
Who would be free themselves must strike the blow?
Lord Byron
Childe Harold's Pilgrimage, I

95 This delightful, blissful, wise, pleasurable, honourable, virtuous, true and immortal Prince was a violator of his word, a libertine over head and ears in debt and disgrace, and despiser of domestic ties, the companion of gamblers and demireps, a man who has just closed half a century without one single claim on the gratitude of his country or the respect of posterity.
Leigh Hunt (1784–1859) British poet.
Referring to the Prince Regent. Hunt was imprisoned for two years for this libellous attack
The Examiner, 22 Mar 1812

1813

96 It is the beginning of the end.
Talleyrand (Charles Maurice de Talleyrand-Périgord; 1754–1838) French politician.
Referring to Napoleon's defeat at Borodino, 1813
Attrib.

97 France has more need of me than I have need of France.
Napoleon I (Napoleon Bonaparte; 1769–1821) French emperor.
Speech, 31 Dec 1813

98 We have met the enemy, and they are ours.
Oliver Hazard Perry (1785–1819) US naval officer.
Message sent reporting his victory in a naval battle on Lake Erie
Familiar Quotations (J. Bartlett)

99 I am my own ancestor.
Duc d'Abrantès (1771–1813) French general.
Said on being made a duke
Attrib.

1814

100 One could forgive the fiend for becoming a torrent, but to become an earthquake was really too much.
Charles-Joseph, Prince de Ligne (1735–1814) Austrian diplomat.
Referring to Napoleon I
Attrib.

101 The bullet that is to kill me has not yet been moulded.
Napoleon I (Napoleon Bonaparte; 1769–1821) French emperor.
In reply to his brother Joseph, King of Spain,

who had asked whether he had ever been hit by a cannonball
Attrib.

02 **The Congress is getting nowhere, it dances.**
Le Congrès ne marche pas, il danse.
Charles-Joseph, Prince de Ligne (1735–1814) Austrian diplomat.
Referring to the Congress of Vienna
Remark, Nov 1814

03 **'Tis the star-spangled banner; O long may it wave**
O'er the land of the free, and the home of the brave!
Francis Scott Key (1779–1843) US lawyer.
The Star-Spangled Banner

1815

04 **Metternich and Talleyrand held forth in their usual way, while I sensed as never before the futility of human endeavour, the failings of men who hold the fate of the world in their hands.**
Friedrich von Gentz (1764–1832) Austrian bureaucrat.
Referring to a dinner at the Congress of Vienna
Diary, 12 Jan 1815

Battle of Waterloo (1815)

he battle (18 June 1815) in which the Duke of Wellington and the Prussian marshal von Blücher defeated Napoleon Bonaparte, leading to his second, and final, bdication and exile.

05 **An army marches on its stomach.**
Napoleon I (Napoleon Bonaparte; 1769–1821) French emperor.
Attrib.

06 **I have got an infamous army, very weak and ill-equipped, and a very inexperienced staff.**
Duke of Wellington (1769–1852) British general and statesman.
Written at the beginning of the Waterloo campaign
Letter to Lord Stewart, 8 May 1815

07 **Our troops are all moving from this place at present. Lord Wellington was at the ball tonight as composed as ever.**
Thomas Creevey (1768–1838) British politician and diarist.
Written at Brussels
Journal, 16 June 1815

08 **It all depends upon that article there.**
Duke of Wellington (1769–1852) British general and statesman.
Indicating a passing infantryman when asked if he would be able to defeat Napoleon
The Age of Elegance (A. Bryant)

109 **Not upon a man from the colonel to the private in a regiment –both inclusive. We may pick up a marshal or two perhaps; but not worth a damn.**
Duke of Wellington
Said during the Waterloo campaign, when asked whether he anticipated any desertions from Napoleon's army
Creevey Papers, Ch. X

110 **It is not the business of generals to shoot one another.**
Duke of Wellington
Refusing an artillery officer permission to fire upon Napoleon himself during the Battle of Waterloo, 1815
Attrib.

111 **Up, Guards, and at 'em.**
Duke of Wellington
Order given at the battle of Waterloo, 18 June 1815
Attrib.

112 **It has been a damned serious business – Blücher and I have lost 30,000 men. It has been a damned nice thing – the nearest run thing you ever saw in your life . . . By God! I don't think it would have done if I had not been there.**
Duke of Wellington
Referring to the Battle of Waterloo
Creevey Papers, Ch. X

113 **Yes, and they went down very well too.**
Duke of Wellington
Replying to the observation that the French cavalry had come up very well during the Battle of Waterloo
The Age of Elegance (A. Bryant)

114 **Oh well, no matter what happens, there's always death.**
Napoleon I (Napoleon Bonaparte; 1769–1821) French emperor.
Attrib.

115 **I used to say of him that his presence on the field made the difference of forty thousand men.**
Duke of Wellington (1769–1852) British general and statesman.
Referring to Napoleon
Notes of Conversations with the Duke of Wellington (Stanhope), 2 Nov 1831

116* **A battle of giants.**
Duke of Wellington
Referring to the Battle of Waterloo; said to Samuel Rogers
Attrib.

Attitudes

Art, Literature, and Music

1790

117 I should desire that the last words which I should pronounce in this Academy, and from this place, might be the name of — Michael Angelo.
Joshua Reynolds (1723–92) British portrait painter.
Discourse to Students of the Royal Academy, 10 Dec 1790

1791

118 One of Edward's Mistresses was Jane Shore, who has had a play written about her, but it is a tragedy and therefore not worth reading.
Jane Austen (1775–1817) British novelist.
The History of England

1798

119 Poetry is the spontaneous overflow of powerful feelings: it takes its origin from emotion recollected in tranquillity.
William Wordsworth (1770–1850) British poet.
Lyrical Ballads, Preface

1800

120 There neither is, nor can be, any *essential* difference between the language of prose and metrical composition.
William Wordsworth
Lyrical Ballads, Preface

121 Every great and original writer, in proportion as he is great and original, must himself create the taste by which he is to be relished.
William Wordsworth
Lyrical Ballads, Preface

1802

122 An original writer is not one who imitates nobody, but one whom nobody can imitate.
Vicomte de Chateaubriand (1768–1848) French diplomat and writer.
Génie du Christianisme

123 But as we went along there were more and yet more and there at last under the boughs of the trees, we saw that there was a long belt of them along the shore, about the breadth of a country turnpike road. I never saw daffodils so beautiful they grew among the mossy stones about and about them, some rested their heads upon these stones as on pillow for weariness and the rest tossed and reeled and danced and seemed as if they verily laughed with the wind that blew upon them over the lake.
Dorothy Wordsworth (1771–1855) British diarist and sister of William Wordsworth.
The Grasmere Journals, 15 Apr 1802

1805

124 For ne'er
Was flattery lost on poet's ear:
A simple race! they waste their toil
For the vain tribute of a smile.
Walter Scott (1771–1832) Scottish novelist.
The Lay of the Last Minstrel, IV

1809

125 A man may surely be allowed to take a glass of wine by his own fireside.
Richard Brinsley Sheridan (1751–1816) British dramatist.
As he sat in a coffeehouse watching his Drury Lane Theatre burn down
Memoirs of the Life of the Rt. Hon. Richard Brinsley Sheridan (T. Moore)

1810

126* The faults of great authors are generally excellences carried to an excess.
Samuel Taylor Coleridge (1772–1834) British poet.
Miscellanies, 149

1812

127 Mad, bad, and dangerous to know.
Lady Caroline Lamb (1785–1828) The wife of William Lamb (later Lord Melbourne).
Said of Byron in her journal
Journal, March 1812

128 I awoke one morning and found myself famous.
Lord Byron (1788–1824) British poet.
Remark made after the publication of *Childe Harold's Pilgrimage* (1812)
Entry in Memoranda

Daily Life

1796

129 What dreadful hot weather we have! It keeps me in a continual state of inelegance.
Jane Austen (1775–1817) British novelist.
Letter, 18 Sept 1796

1802

130 Earth has not anything to show more fair:
Dull would he be of soul who could pass by
A sight so touching in its majesty:
The City now doth, like a garment, wear
The beauty of the morning; silent, bare,
Ships, towers, domes, theatres, and temples lie
Open unto the fields, and to the sky;

All bright and glittering in the smokeless air.
William Wordsworth (1770–1850) British poet.
Sonnets, 'Composed upon Westminster Bridge'

1810

131* No perfumes, but very fine linen, plenty of it, and country washing.
'Beau' Brummell (George Bryan Brummell; 1778–1840) British dandy.
Memoirs (Harriette Wilson), Ch. 2

132* They hated everybody, and abused everybody, and would sit together in White's bay window, or the pit boxes at the Opera, weaving tremendous crammers. They swore a good deal, never laughed, looked hazy after dinner, and had most of them been patronized at one time or other by Brummell and the Prince Regent.
Rees Howell Gronow (1795–1865) MP and social observer.
Referring to Regency 'dandies'
Reminiscences, Vol. I

1814

133* There is nothing good to be had in the country, or, if there is, they will not let you have it.
William Hazlitt (1778–1830) British essayist.
Observations on Wordsworth's 'Excursion'

Death

1798

134 We are laid asleep
In body, and become a living soul:
While with an eye made quiet by the power
Of harmony, and the deep power of joy,
We see into the life of things.
William Wordsworth (1770–1850) British poet.
Lines composed a few miles above Tintern Abbey

1814

135 The good die first,
And they whose hearts are dry as summer dust
Burn to the socket.
William Wordsworth
The Excursion

Education, Knowledge, and Learning

1793

136 What is now proved was once only imagined.
William Blake (1757–1827) British poet.
The Marriage of Heaven and Hell, 'Proverbs of Hell'

137 A fool sees not the same tree that a wise man sees.
William Blake
The Marriage of Heaven and Hell, 'Proverbs of Hell'

1801

138 Against stupidity the gods themselves struggle in vain.
Friedrich von Schiller (1759–1805) German dramatist.
Die Jungfrau von Orleans, III:6

1804

139 I care not whether a man is Good or Evil; all that I care
Is whether he is a Wise Man or a Fool. Go! put off Holiness,
And put on Intellect.
William Blake (1757–1827) British poet.
Jerusalem

1808

140 Dear friend, theory is all grey,
And the golden tree of life is green.
Goethe (1749–1832) German poet and dramatist.
Faust, Pt. I

1815

141* The battle of Waterloo was won on the playing fields of Eton.
Duke of Wellington (1769–1852) British general.
Attrib.

History

1789

142 The history of the World is the World's court of justice.
Friedrich von Schiller (1759–1805) German dramatist.
Lecture, Jena, 26 May 1789

1798

143 A historian is a prophet in reverse.
Friedrich von Schlegel (1772–1829) German diplomat, writer, and critic.
Das Athenäum

1799

144 What millions died — that Caesar might be great!
Thomas Campbell (1777–1844) British poet.
Pleasures of Hope, II

Human Nature

1790

145 Talent develops in quiet places, character in the full current of human life.
Goethe (1749–1832) German poet and dramatist.
Torquato Tasso, I

1798

146 I do not want people to be very agreeable, as it saves me the trouble of liking them a great deal.
Jane Austen (1775–1817) British novelist.
Letter, 24 Dec 1798

147 If this belief from heaven be sent,
If such be Nature's holy plan,
Have I not reason to lament
What man has made of man?
William Wordsworth (1770–1850) British poet.
Lines written in Early Spring

1800

148* Pleasures newly found are sweet
When they lie about our feet.
William Wordsworth
To the Small Celandine

1803

149 Every tear from every eye
Becomes a babe in Eternity.
William Blake (1757–1827) British poet.
Auguries of Innocence

1806

150 Mankind are always happy for having been happy, so that if you make them happy now, you make them happy twenty years hence by the memory of it.
Sydney Smith (1771–1845) British clergyman and essayist.
Elementary Sketches of Moral Philosophy

1807

151 I wandered lonely as a cloud
That floats on high o'er vales and hills,
When all at once I saw a crowd,
A host, of golden daffodils;
Beside the lake, beneath the trees,
Fluttering and dancing in the breeze.
William Wordsworth (1770–1850) British poet.
I Wandered Lonely as a Cloud

1810

152* There is not a more mean, stupid, dastardly, pitiful, selfish, spiteful, envious, ungrateful

animal than the public. It is the greatest of cowards, for it is afraid of itself.
William Hazlitt (1778–1830) British essayist.
On Living to Oneself

153* The art of pleasing consists in being pleased.
William Hazlitt
On Manner

154* Men are we, and must grieve when even the shade
Of that which once was great is passed away.
William Wordsworth (1770–1850) British poet.
Sonnets, 'Once did she hold'

1813

155 For what do we live, but to make sport for our neighbours, and laugh at them in our turn?
Jane Austen (1775–1817) British novelist.
Pride and Prejudice, Ch. 57

156 I have been a selfish being all my life, in practice, though not in principle.
Jane Austen
Pride and Prejudice, Ch. 58

Life

1790

157 Superstition is the religion of feeble minds.
Edmund Burke (1729–97) British politician.
Reflections on the Revolution in France

1793

158 Without Contraries is no progression. Attraction and Repulsion, Reason and Energy, Love and Hate, are necessary to Human existence.
William Blake (1757–1827) British poet.
The Marriage of Heaven and Hell, 'The Argument'

159 For everything that lives is holy, life delights in life.
William Blake
America

1794

160 The sublime and the ridiculous are often so nearly related that it is difficult to class them separately. One step above the sublime makes the ridiculous; and one step above the ridiculous makes the sublime again.
Thomas Paine (1737–1809) British writer.
The Age of Reason, Pt. 2

1796

161 Example is the school of mankind, and they will learn at no other.
Edmund Burke
Letters on a Regicide Peace, letter 1

1798

162 I have learned
To look on nature, not as in the hour
Of thoughtless youth; but hearing often-times
The still, sad music of humanity.
William Wordsworth (1770–1850) British
poet. ·
Lines composed a few miles above Tintern Abbey

163 Nor greetings where no kindness is, nor all
The dreary intercourse of daily life,
Shall e'er prevail against us, or disturb
Our cheerful faith, that all which we behold
Is full of blessings.
William Wordsworth
Lines composed a few miles above Tintern Abbey

1799

164 'Tis distance lends enchantment to the view,
And robes the mountain in its azure hue.
Thomas Campbell (1777–1844) British poet.
Pleasures of Hope, I

1800

165* The good old rule
Sufficeth them, the simple plan,
That they should take, who have the power,
And they should keep who can.
William Wordsworth (1770–1850) British
poet.
Rob Roy's Grave

166* No young man believes he shall ever die.
William Hazlitt (1778–1830) British essayist.
On the Feeling of Immortality in Youth

167 The wiser mind
Mourns less for what age takes away
Than what it leaves behind.
William Wordsworth (1770–1850) British
poet.
The Fountain

1803

168 To see a World in a grain of sand,
And a Heaven in a wild flower,
Hold Infinity in the palm of your hand,
And Eternity in an hour.
William Blake (1757–1827) British poet.
Auguries of Innocence

1805

169 Breathes there the man, with soul so dead,
Who never to himself hath said,
This is my own, my native land!
Whose heart hath ne'er within him burn'd,
As home his footsteps he hath turn'd
From wandering on a foreign strand!
Walter Scott (1771–1832) Scottish novelist.
The Lay of the Last Minstrel, VI

1806

170 The sight of it gave me infinite pleasure, as it
proved that I was in a civilized society.
Mungo Park (1771–1806) Scottish explorer.
Remark on finding a gibbet in an unexplored part
of Africa
Attrib.

1807

171 Though nothing can bring back the hour
Of splendour in the grass, of glory in the
flower;
We will grieve not, rather find
Strength in what remains behind . . .
William Wordsworth (1770–1850) British
poet.
Ode. Intimations of Immortality, IX

172 The world is too much with us; late and soon,
Getting and spending, we lay waste our
powers:
Little we see in Nature that is ours.
William Wordsworth
Sonnets, 'The world is too much with us'

1808

173 Dear friend, theory is all grey,
And the golden tree of life is green.
Goethe (1749–1832) German poet and
dramatist.
Faust, Pt. I

1812

174 Live as long as you may, the first twenty years
are the longest half of your life.
Robert Southey (1774–1843) British poet.
The Doctor, Ch. 130

1814

175* Lift not the painted veil which those who live
Call life.
Percy Bysshe Shelley (1792–1822) British
poet.
Lift not the Painted Veil

1816

176 One does not love a place the less for having
suffered in it unless it has all been suffering,
nothing but suffering.
Jane Austen (1775–1817) British novelist.
Persuasion, Ch. 20

Marriage and the Family

1790

177 What is your fortune, my pretty maid?
My face is my fortune, sir, she said.
Then I can't marry you, my pretty maid.

Nobody asked you, sir, she said.
Archaeologia Cornu-Britannica (William Pryce)

1800

178* It doesn't much signify whom one marries, for one is sure to find next morning that it was someone else.
Samuel Rogers (1763–1855) British poet.
Recollections of the Table Talk of Samuel Rogers (ed. Alexander Dyce)

1813

179 It is a truth universally acknowledged, that a single man in possession of a good fortune must be in want of a wife.
Jane Austen (1775–1817) British novelist.
The opening words of the book
Pride and Prejudice, Ch. 1

180 Happiness in marriage is entirely a matter of chance.
Jane Austen
Pride and Prejudice, Ch. 6

Men and Women

1792

181 I do not wish them to have power over men; but over themselves.
Mary Wollstonecraft (1759–97) British writer.
Referring to women
A Vindication of the Rights of Woman, Ch. 4

182 The *divine right* of husbands, like the divine right of kings, may, it is hoped, in this enlightened age, be contested without danger.
Mary Wollstonecraft
A Vindication of the Rights of Woman, Ch. 3

183 A king is always a king – and a woman always a woman: his authority and her sex ever stand between them and rational converse.
Mary Wollstonecraft
A Vindication of the Rights of Woman, Ch. 4

1800

184* Can anything be more absurd than keeping women in a state of ignorance, and yet so vehemently to insist on their resisting temptation?
Vicesimus Knox (1752–1821) British essayist.
Liberal Education, Vol. I, 'On the Literary Education of Women'

1813

185 One cannot be always laughing at a man without now and then stumbling on something witty.
Jane Austen (1775–1817) British novelist.
Pride and Prejudice, Ch. 40

186 Next to being married, a girl likes to be crossed in love a little now and then.
Jane Austen (1775–1817) British novelist.
Pride and Prejudice, Ch. 24

Morality, Vices, and Virtues

1798

187 That best portion of a good man's life,
His little, nameless, unremembered acts
Of kindness and of love.
William Wordsworth (1770–1850) British poet.
Lines composed a few miles above Tintern Abbey

1803

188 A truth that's told with bad intent
Beats all the lies you can invent.
William Blake (1757–1827) British poet.
Auguries of Innocence

1804

189 He who would do good to another must do it in Minute Particulars.
General Good is the plea of the scoundrel, hypocrite, and flatterer.
William Blake
Jerusalem

1810

190* One impulse from a vernal wood
May teach you more of man,
Of moral evil and of good,
Than all the sages can.
William Wordsworth (1770–1850) British poet.
The Tables Turned

191* We can scarcely hate any one that we know.
William Hazlitt (1778–1830) British essayist.
On Criticism

Other People

1806

192* England is a nation of shopkeepers.
Napoleon I (Napoleon Bonaparte; 1769–1821) French emperor.
Attrib.

1810

193* Scratch the Russian and you will find the Tartar.
Joseph de Maistre (1753–1821) French monarchist.
Attributed also to Napoleon and Prince de Ligne

1814

194 What a place to plunder!
Gebhard Blücher (1742−1819) Prussian general.
Referring to London
Attrib.

1815

195 I look upon Switzerland as an inferior sort of Scotland.
Sydney Smith (1771−1845) British clergyman and essayist.
Letter to Lord Holland, 1815

Religion

1790

196 Man is by his constitution a religious animal.
Edmund Burke (1729−97) British politician.
Reflections on the Revolution in France

1793

197 Man has no Body distinct from his Soul; for that called Body is a portion of Soul discerned by the five Senses, the chief inlets of Soul in this age.
William Blake (1757−1827) British poet.
The Marriage of Heaven and Hell, 'The Voice of the Devil'

1795

198 Nothing is so fatal to religion as indifference, which is, at least, half infidelity.
Edmund Burke (1729−97) British politician.
Letter to William Smith, 29 Jan 1795

1807

199 Whither is fled the visionary gleam?
Where is it now, the glory and the dream?

Our birth is but a sleep and a forgetting:
The Soul that rises with us, our life's Star,
Hath had elsewhere its setting,
And cometh from afar;
Not in entire forgetfulness,
And not in utter nakedness,
But trailing clouds of glory do we come
From God, who is our home:
Heaven lies about us in our infancy!
Shades of the prison-house begin to close
Upon the growing boy.
William Wordsworth (1770−1850) British poet.
Ode. Intimations of Immortality, IV

Science, Medicine, and Technology

1801

200 I believe the souls of five hundred Sir Isaac Newtons would go to the making up of a Shakespeare or a Milton.
Samuel Taylor Coleridge (1772−1834) British poet.
Letter to Thomas Poole, 23 Mar 1801

1810

201* I have no need of that hypothesis.
Marquis de Laplace (1749−1827) French mathematician and astronomer.
On being asked by Napoleon why he had made no mention of God in his book about the universe, *Mécanique céleste*.
Men of Mathematics (E. Bell)

Wealth and Poverty

1795

202* The only infallible criterion of wisdom to vulgar minds − success.
Edmund Burke (1729−97) British politician.
Letter to a Member of the National Assembly

Work and Occupations

1810

203* Now Barabbas was a publisher.
Thomas Campbell (1777−1844) British poet.
Attrib.

Sayings of the Time

1800

204 I came home ... hungry as a hunter.
Charles Lamb (1775−1834) British essayist.
Letter to Coleridge, Apr 1800

1806

205 Twinkle, twinkle, little star,
How I wonder what you are!
Up above the world so high,
Like a diamond in the sky!
Jane Taylor (1783−1824) British writer.
Rhymes for the Nursery (with Ann Taylor), 'The Star'

Who Said What

With Hindsight

19th century

206 France was a long despotism tempered by epigrams.
Thomas Carlyle (1795–1881) Scottish historian and essayist.
History of the French Revolution, Pt. I, Bk. I, Ch. 1

207 The seagreen Incorruptible.
Thomas Carlyle
Referring to Robespierre
History of the French Revolution, Pt. II, Bk. IV, Ch. 4

208 Bliss was it in that dawn to be alive,
But to be young was very heaven!
William Wordsworth (1770–1850) British poet.
The Prelude, XI

209 The three-o'-clock in the morning courage, which Bonaparte thought was the rarest.
Henry David Thoreau (1817–62) US writer.
Walden, 'Sounds'

210 It was the best of times, it was the worst of times, it was the age of wisdom, it was the age of foolishness, it was the epoch of belief, it was the epoch of incredulity, it was the season of Light, it was the season of Darkness, it was the spring of hope, it was the winter of despair, we had everything before us, we had nothing before us, we were all going direct to Heaven, we were all going direct the other way.

Charles Dickens (1812–70) British novelist.
The opening words of the book
A Tale of Two Cities, Bk. I, Ch. 1

211 It has been said, not truly, but with a possible approximation to truth, 'that in 1802 every hereditary monarch was insane'.
Walter Bagehot (1826–1877) British economist and journalist.
The English Constitution, 'The House of Lords'

20th century

212 Napoleon's armies used to march on their stomachs, shouting: 'Vive l'intérieur!'
W. C. Sellar (1898–1951) British humorous writer.
1066 And All That

213 If the French noblesse had been capable of playing cricket with their peasants, their chateaux would never have been burnt.
George Macaulay Trevelyan (1876–1962) British historian.
English Social History, Ch. XIII

214 It is still too early to form a final judgement on the French Revolution.
George Macaulay Trevelyan
Speech, National Book League, 30 May 1945

215 No visit to Dove Cottage, Grasmere, is complete without examining the outhouse where Hazlitt's father, a Unitarian minister of strong liberal views, attempted to put his hand up Dorothy Wordsworth's skirt.
Alan Coren (1938–   ) British humorist and writer.
All Except the Bastard, 'Bohemia'

10

Liberalism, Nationalism, and Reaction (1816—69)

Even after Napoleonic France had been finally defeated, the two dominant themes of the revolutionary period continued to loom over European politics and diplomacy: Liberalism, the idea that a king's power should not be so absolute that his subjects have no say in how they are governed; and Nationalism, the desire of each nationality to govern itself, which had been encouraged to undermine Napoleon's empire. From 1815, the Great Powers, led by Austria and Russia, pursued a policy of reaction in which the first sign of popular discontent was sharply and instantly repressed. Even in Britain, reform of any kind was resisted until well into the 1820s. In 1848 a series of revolutions broke out in Europe (France, Italy, Prussia, Austria); although all were eventually repressed, they nevertheless marked the end of reaction. As the dread of revolution faded, rulers felt able to accommodate at least some of their subjects' aspirations. Exploiting the tide of nationalism, Victor Emmanuel created the kingdom of Italy (1861) and Bismarck achieved his ambition for a German Empire (1871).

The USA was unaffected by these European concerns, but tensions, epitomized by the issue of slavery, grew between the very different Northern and Southern states. This culminated in the American Civil War (1861—65). In this period Britain continued to forge ahead in industrial production, becoming the 'workshop of the world'. The Great Exhibition of 1851 celebrated her supremacy.

Politics, Government, and World Events

1816

1 Our country! In her intercourse with foreign nations, may she always be in the right; but our country, right or wrong.
Stephen Decatur (1779–1820) US naval officer.
Speech, Norfolk, Virginia, Apr 1816

1817

2 The interest of the landlord is always opposed to the interests of every other class in the community.
David Ricardo (1772–1823) English political economist.
Principles of Political Economy and Taxation

3 The natural price of labour is that price which is necessary to enable the labourers, one with another, to subsist and perpetuate their race, without either increase or diminution.
David Ricardo
Principles of Political Economy and Taxation

1819

4 An old, mad, blind, despised and dying king, –
Princes, the dregs of their dull race, who flow
Through public scorn.
Percy Bysshe Shelley (1792–1822) British poet.
Referring to George III and his sons
England in 1819

5 The fault of our younger politicians – who have never seen the Indian States in the days of their power – is a contempt for the natives, and an inclination to carry everything with a high hand.
Mountstuart Elphinstone (1779–1859) Governor of Bombay.
Letter to Sir John Malcolm

6 The mountains look on Marathon –
And Marathon looks on the sea:
And musing there an hour alone,
I dream'd that Greece might still be free.
Lord Byron (1788–1824) British poet.
Byron later died, of fever, while fighting in the war for Greek independence from Turkey (1821–32) – a cause that caught the imagination of cultured circles in Britain
Don Juan, III

1820

7* Don't quote Latin; say what you have to say, and then sit down.
Duke of Wellington (1769–1852) British general and statesman.
Advice to a new Member of Parliament
Attrib.

8* The greatest happiness of the greatest number is the foundation of morals and legislation.
Jeremy Bentham (1748–1832) British philosopher.
The Commonplace Book

9 This is THE MAN – all shaven and shorn,
All cover'd with Orders – and all forlorn;
THE DANDY OF SIXTY, who bows with a grace,
And has *taste* in wigs, collars, cuirasses and lace;
Who, to tricksters, and fools, leaves the State and its treasure,
And, when Britain's in tears, sails about at his pleasure;
Who spurn'd from his presence the Friends of his youth,
And now has not one who will tell him the truth;
Who took to his counsels, in evil hour,
The Friends to the Reasons of lawless Power;
That back the Public Informer, who
Would put down the *Thing*, that, in spite of new Acts,
And attempts to restrain it, by Soldiers of Tax,
Will *poison* the Vermin,
That plunder the Wealth,
That lay in the House,
That Jack built.
William Hone (1780–1842) Author and bookseller.
Referring to George IV
The Political House that Jack Built

10 A better farmer ne'er brushed dew from lawn,
A worse king never left a realm undone!
Lord Byron (1788–1824) British poet.
Referring to George III
The Vision of Judgment, VIII

11 I take it for granted that the present question is a mere preamble – a title-page to a great tragic volume.
John Quincy Adams (1767–1848) Sixth president of the USA.
Referring to the Missouri Compromise – a measure in the US Congress allowing Missouri to be admitted as the 24th state of the Union. At the time Congress was equally divided between 'slave states' and 'free states'. Missouri applied for admission as a slave state, and the North feared that this would upset the balance of power. The compromise involved the admission of Maine as a free state
Diary, Mar 1820

12 This momentous question, like a firebell in the night, awakened and filled me with terror. I considered it at once as the knell of the Union.
Thomas Jefferson (1743–1826) US statesman.
Referring to the Missouri Compromise
Letter to John Adams, Apr 1820

1821

13 The prison inspector would have a good salary; that, in England, is never omitted. It is equally a matter of course that he would be taken

from among Treasury retainers, and that he would never look at a prison.
Sydney Smith (1771–1845) British clergyman and essayist.
English Prisons under Local Government (S. and B. Webb)

14   I wish . . . that the Greeks were put in possession of their whole patrimony and that the Sultan were driven, bag and baggage, into the heart of Asia.
Stratford Canning (1786–1880) British diplomat.
Letter to George Canning, 29 Sept 1821

15   Whenever books are burned men also in the end are burned.
Heinrich Heine (1797–1856) German poet and writer.
Almansor

1822

16   Let there be light! said Liberty,
And like sunrise from the sea,
Athens arose!
Percy Bysshe Shelley (1792–1822) British poet.
Hellas, I

17* I met Murder on the way –
He had a mask like Castlereagh.
Percy Bysshe Shelley
Viscount Castlereagh (1769–1822) was British foreign secretary (1812–22); he was highly unpopular and became identified with such controversial events as the Peterloo massacre (16 Aug 1819) – an incident at a rally at St Peter's Field, Manchester, when hussars killed 11 people and wounded hundreds. The name 'Peterloo' is a reference to Waterloo
The Mask of Anarchy, 5

1823

18   The land self-interest groans from shore to shore,
For fear that plenty should attain the poor.
Lord Byron (1788–1824) British poet.
The Age of Bronze, XIV

19   Our first and fundamental maxim should be never to entangle ourselves in the broils of Europe. Our second, never to suffer Europe to intermeddle with cis-Atlantic affairs.
Thomas Jefferson (1743–1826) US president.
Letter to James Monroe, 24 Oct 1823

20   The American continents, by the free and independent condition which they have assumed and maintain, are henceforth not to be considered as subjects for future colonization by any European powers . . . In the wars of the European powers in matters relating to themselves we have never taken any part, nor does it comport with our policy to do so.
James Monroe (1758–1831) US president.
A statement of principle that, as the 'Monroe

Doctrine', became a cornerstone of US foreign policy
Message to Congress, 2 Dec 1823

1824

21   States, like men, have their growth, their manhood, their decrepitude, their decay.
Walter Savage Landor (1775–1864) British poet and writer.
Imaginary Conversations, 'Pollio and Calvus'

1825

22   Many politicians of our time are in the habit of laying it down as a self-evident proposition, that no people ought to be free till they are fit to use their freedom. The maxim is worthy of the fool in the old story, who resolved not to go into the water till he had learnt to swim. If men are to wait for liberty till they become wise and good in slavery, they may indeed wait for ever.
Lord Macaulay (1800–59) British historian.
Literary Essays Contributed to the 'Edinburgh Review', 'Milton'.

1826

23   I called the New World into existence to redress the balance of the Old.
George Canning (1770–1827) British statesman.
Speech, 12 Dec 1826

24   It is said to be hard on His Majesty's Ministers to raise objections to this proposition. For my part, I think it no more hard on His Majesty's Opposition to compel them to take this course.
John Cam Hobhouse (1786–1869) British radical politician.
First recorded use of the phrase 'His Majesty's Opposition'
Speech, House of Commons, 27 Apr 1826

1828

25* That prig Peel seems as deeply bitten by "liberality" . . . as any of his fellows.
Thomas Creevey (1768–1838) British politician.
Referring to the question of the corn laws
The Creevey Papers (ed. Sir H. Maxwell)

26   The reluctant obedience of distant provinces generally costs more than it is worth.
Lord Macaulay (1800–59) British historian.
Historical Essays Contributed to the 'Edinburgh Review', 'Lord Mahon's War of the Succession'

27   There never was such a humbug as the Greek affair altogether. However, thank God it never cost us a shilling, and never shall.
Duke of Wellington (1769–1852) British general and statesman.
Referring to the Greek War of Independence
Remark, Feb 1828

The gallery in which the reporters sit has become a fourth estate of the realm.
Lord Macaulay (1800–59) British historian.
Referring to the press gallery in the House of Commons
Historical Essays Contributed to the 'Edinburgh Review', 'Hallam's 'Constitutional History''

?9 As for rioting, the old Roman way of dealing with that is always the right one; flog the rank and file, and fling the ringleaders from the Tarpeian rock.
Thomas Arnold (1795–1842) British educator.
Cornhill Magazine, Aug 1868

1829

?0 His Majesty's dominions, on which the sun never sets.
Christopher North (John Wilson; 1785–1854) Scottish writer.
Noctes Ambrosianae, 20 Apr 1829

?1 What all the wise men promised has not happened, and what all the d—d fools said would happen has come to pass.
Lord Melbourne (1779–1848) British statesman.
Referring to Catholic Emancipation
Lord Melbourne (H. Dunckley)

?2 There is no middle course between the throne and the scaffold.
Charles X (1757–1836) King of France.
Remark to Talleyrand, Dec 1829; Talleyrand is said to have replied, 'You are forgetting the post-chaise'

?3 I am very far from being prepared to admit that the improvement of the situation of a common police constable by the giving him more money would increase the efficiency of the establishment
Robert Peel (1788–1850) British Conservative prime minister.
Letter to John Croker, 10 Oct 1829

1830

?4 We now are, as we always have been, decidedly and conscientiously attached to what is called the Tory, and which might with more propriety be called the Conservative, party.
John Wilson Croker (1780–1857) British Tory politician.
The first use of the term 'Conservative Party'
In *Quarterly Review*, Jan 1830

?5 I will be good.
Victoria (1819–1901) Queen of the United Kingdom.
On learning that she would succeed to the throne
Remark to her governess, Louise (afterwards Baroness) Lehzen, 11 Mar 1830

?6 Beginning reform is beginning revolution.
Duke of Wellington (1769–1852) British general and statesman.
Remark to Mrs Arbuthnot, 7 Nov 1830

37 But what is to be the fate of the great wen of all?
William Cobbett (1763–1835) British journalist and writer.
Referring to London; a wen is a sebaceous cyst
Rural Rides

38 The king reigns, and the people govern themselves.
Louis Adolphe Thiers (1797–1877) French statesman and historian.
In an unsigned article attributed to Thiers
Le National, 20 Jan 1830

39 We are dancing on a volcano.
Comte de Salvandy (1795–1856) French nobleman.
A remark made before the July Revolution in 1830

40 When Paris sneezes, Europe catches cold.
Clement Metternich (1773–1859) Austrian diplomat and Chancellor.
Remark, reflecting European anxiety at the July Revolution in France (1830)
Liberalism

41 The people's government, made for the people, made by the people, and answerable to the people.
Daniel Webster (1782–1852) US statesman.
Second speech on Foote's resolution, 26 Jan 1830

42* Absolutism tempered by assassination.
Ernst Friedrich Herbert Münster (1766–1839) Hanoverian statesman.
Referring to the Russian Constitution
Letter

43 The spirit of revolution, the spirit of insurrection is a spirit radically opposed to liberty.
François Guizot (1787–1874) French statesman and historian.
Speech, Paris, 29 Dec 1830

1831

44 It is impossible that the whisper of a faction should prevail against the voice of a nation.
Lord John Russell (1792–1878)
Following the rejection in the House of Lords of the Reform Bill
Letter to T. Attwood, Oct 1831

45 So here is a pretty fly out of the King of the Netherlands! Who has bit him I cannot guess; we have some suspicion of France.
Lord Palmerston (1784–1865) British statesman.
Comment on the French invasion of Belgium, 1831
Life of Viscount Palmerston (H. W. Bulwer), Vol. II

46 I always say that, next to a battle lost, the greatest misery is a battle gained.
Duke of Wellington (1769–1852) British general and statesman.
Diary (Frances, Lady Shelley)

1832
---

47 War is the continuation of politics by other means.
Karl von Clausewitz (1780–1831) Prussian general.
The usual misquotation of 'War is nothing but a continuation of politics with the admixture of other means'
Vom Kriege

48 From a very early age, I had imbibed the opinion, that it was every man's duty to do all that lay in his power to leave his country as good as he had found it.
William Cobbett (1763–1835) British journalist and writer.
Political Register, 22 Dec 1832

49 A nation is the universality of citizens speaking the same tongue.
Giuseppe Mazzini (1805–72) Italian republican leader and political theorist.
La Giovine Italia

1833
---

50 And if it be true anywhere that such enactments are forced on the legislature by public opinion is Apostasy too hard a word to describe the temper of the nation?
John Keble (1792–1866) British poet and clergyman.
Assize Sermon, Oxford, 14 July 1833

51 We were meeting together to preserve ourselves, our wives, and our children, from utter degradation and starvation.
George Loveless (b. 1805) Dorset farm-labourer and Trade Unionist.
Defending the activities of the 'Tolpuddle Martyrs', six members of an agricultural labourers' union. Convicted of administering unlawful oaths and transported to Australia, they were pardoned in 1836
Statement, Dorchester Assizes, Mar 1833

52 God is our guide! from field, from wave,
From plough, from anvil, and from loom;
We come, our country's rights to save,
And speak a tyrant faction's doom:
We raise the watchword liberty;
We will, we will, we will be free!

God is our guide! no swords we draw,
We kindle not war's battle fires;
By reason, union, justice, law,
We claim the birthright of our sires:
We raise the watchword liberty;
We will, we will, we will be free!!!
George Loveless
Referring to the Tolpuddle Martyrs
The Faber Book of English History in Verse
(Kenneth Baker)

53 A broken head in Cold Bath Fields produces a greater sensation among us than three pitched battles in India.
Lord Macaulay (1800–59) British historian.
Speech, 10 July 1833

54 Every time I come near him, I pray God to preserve me from the Devil.
Nicholas I (1796–1855) Tsar of Russia.
Referring to Metternich
Letter to his wife, Sept 1833

55 But what is Freedom? Rightly understood,
A universal licence to be good.
Hartley Coleridge (1796–1849) British poet
Liberty

1834

56* It is as difficult to elevate the poor as it is easy to depress the rich. In human affairs . . . it is much easier to do harm than good.
Nassau Senior (1790–1864) British economist.
Nassau Senior (M. Bowley)

57 By the workhouse system is meant having all relief through the workhouse, making this workhouse an uninviting place of wholesome restraint.
Edwin Chadwick (1800–90) British social reformer.
Report of the Royal Commission on the Poor Laws

58 Unfortunately almost all trades unions hitherto formed have relied for success upon extorted oaths and physical force. The fault and destruction of all trades unions has hitherto been that they have copied the vices which they professed to condemn . . . Hence their failure was inevitable.
Committee of the London Compositors' Society
History of Trade Unionism (S. and B. Webb)

59 I have always thought complaints of ill-usage contemptible, whether from a seduced disappointed girl or a turned out Prime Minister.
Lord Melbourne (1779–1848) British statesman.
Following his dismissal by William IV
Miss Eden's Letters (ed. V. Dickinson)

60* You must build your House of Parliament upon the river: so . . . that the populace cannot exact their demands by sitting down round you.
Duke of Wellington (1769–1852) British general and statesman.
Words on Wellington (Sir William Fraser)

61 Equality may perhaps be a right, but no power on earth can ever turn it into a fact.
Honoré de Balzac (1799–1850) French novelist.
La Duchesse de Langeais

1835
---

62 The Public is an old woman. Let her maunder and mumble.
Thomas Carlyle (1795–1881) Scottish historian and essayist.
Journal, 1835

63 The worst of the present day is that men hat

one another so damnably. For my part I love them all.
Lord Melbourne (1779–1848) British statesman.
Attrib.

64 **Peel's smile: like the silver plate on a coffin.**
Daniel O'Connell (1775–1847) Irish politician.
Referring to Sir Robert Peel; quoting J. P. Curran (1750–1817)
Hansard, 26 Feb 1835

65 **An army is a nation within a nation; it is one of the vices of our age.**
Alfred de Vigny (1797–1863) French writer.
Servitude et grandeur militaire, 1

1836
---

66 **I know you do not make the laws but I also know that you are the wives and mothers, the sisters and daughters of those who do . . .**
Angelina Grimké (1805–79) US writer.
The Anti-Slavery Examiner (Sep 1836), 'Appeal to the Christian Women of the South'

1837
---

67 **. . . nothing could be more amiable and agreeable than she was. Can you wish for a better account of a little tit of 18 made all at once into a Queen?**
Thomas Creevey (1768–1838) British politician and diarist.
Letter to Elizabeth Ord, 5 Aug 1837

68 **I will sit down now, but the time will come when you will hear me.**
Benjamin Disraeli (1804–81) British statesman.
Maiden Speech, House of Commons, 7 Dec 1837

69 **In no country, I believe, are the marriage laws so iniquitous as in England, and the conjugal relation, in consequence, so impaired.**
Harriet Martineau (1802–76) British writer.
Society in America, Vol. III, 'Marriage'

70 **Our country is the world – our countrymen are all mankind.**
William Lloyd Garrison (1805–79) US abolitionist.
The Liberator, 15 Dec 1837

1838
---

71 **All reform except a moral one will prove unavailing.**
Thomas Carlyle (1795–1881) Scottish historian and essayist.
Critical and Miscellaneous Essays, 'Corn Law Rhymes'

72 **Oliver Twist has asked for more.**
Charles Dickens (1812–70) British novelist.
Oliver Twist, Ch. 2

73 **'If the law supposes that,' said Mr Bumble . . . , 'the law is a ass – a idiot.'**
Charles Dickens
In reply to Mr Brounlow's statement that 'the law supposes that your wife acts under your direction'
Oliver Twist, Ch. 51

74 **The Continent will not suffer England to be the workshop of the world.**
Benjamin Disraeli (1804–81) British statesman.
Speech, House of Commons, 15 Mar 1838

75 **Property has its duties as well as its rights.**
Thomas Drummond (1797–1840) British engineer and statesman.
Letter to the Earl of Donoughmore, 22 May 1838

1839
---

76 **The rising hope of those stern and unbending Tories.**
Lord Macaulay (1800–59) British historian.
Referring to Gladstone
Historical Essays, 'Gladstone on Church and State'

77 **Dear Uncle is given to believe that he must rule the roast everywhere. However that is not a necessity.**
Victoria (1819–1901) Queen of the United Kingdom.
Referring to Leopold of Belgium

1840

78* **Now, is it to lower the price of corn, or isn't it? It is not much matter which we say, but mind, we must all say *the same*.**
Lord Melbourne (1779–1848) British statesman.
Said at a cabinet meeting
The English Constitution (Bagehot), Ch. 1

79* **While I cannot be regarded as a pillar, I must be regarded as a buttress of the church, because I support it from the outside.**
Lord Melbourne
Attrib.

80* **If a traveller were informed that such a man was leader of the House of Commons, he may well begin to comprehend how the Egyptians worshipped an insect.**
Benjamin Disraeli (1804–81) British statesman.
Referring to Lord John Russell
Attrib.

81* **For God's sake, ma'am, let's have no more of that. If you get the English people into the way of making kings, you'll get them into the way of *unmaking* them.**
Lord Melbourne (1779–1848) British statesman.
Advising Queen Victoria against granting Prince Albert the title of King Consort
Lord M. (Lord David Cecil)

82 **I am a cousin to the Queen,
And our mothers they are cronies,**

My father lives at home,
And deals in nice polonies.
Anonymous
Referring to Prince Albert
The Faber Book of English History in Verse
(Kenneth Baker)

83* Accidentally.
Talleyrand (Charles Maurice de Talleyrand-Périgord; 1754–1838) French politician.
Replying, during the reign of Louis Philippe, to the query 'How do you think this government will end?'
The Wheat and the Chaff (F. Mitterand)

84 The truth is that Louis Philippe is the prime mover of the foreign relations of France, and one must admit in one's own mind that if he had been a very straightforward, scrupulous and high-minded man, he would not now have been sitting on the French throne.
Lord Palmerston (1784–1865) British statesman.
Life of Viscount Palmerston (H. L. Bulwer), Vol. II

85 All Frenchmen want to encroach and extend their territorial possessions at the expense of other nations. Their rarity prompts them to be the first nation in the world.
Lord Palmerston
Life of Viscount Palmerston (H. L. Bulmer), Vol. II

86 Property is theft.
Pierre Joseph Proudhon (1809–65) French socialist.
Qu'est-ce que la Propriété?, Ch. 1

1841

87 When I first came into Parliament, Mr Tierney, a great Whig authority, used always to say that the duty of an Opposition was very simple – it was, to oppose everything, and propose nothing.
Edward Stanley, Earl of Derby (1799–1869) British Conservative prime minister.
Speech, House of Commons, 4 June 1841

88 I was totally ignorant both of political economy and of the commerce of the country . . . In a spirit of ignorant mortification I said to myself at the moment: the science of politics deals with the government of men, but I am set to govern packages.
William Ewart Gladstone (1809–98) British statesman.
Referring to his appointment as vice-president of the board of trade
Life of Gladstone (Morley), Vol. I

89 *Deutschland, Deutschland über alles.*
Germany, Germany before all else.
Heinrich Hoffmann von Fallersleben (1798–1876) German poet.
German national anthem

90 Let wealth and commerce, laws and learning die,

But leave us still our old nobility
Lord John Manners (1818–1906) British politician.
England's Trust, Pt. III, Ch. 1

91 Such grace had kings when the world begun!
Robert Browning (1812–89) British poet.
Pippa Passes, Pt. I

1842

92 Not in vain is Ireland pouring itself all over the earth . . . The Irish, with their glowing hearts and reverent credulity, are needed in this cold age of intellect and skepticism.
Lydia M. Child (1802–80) US abolitionist campaigner.
Letters from New York, Vol. I, No. 33, 8 Dec 1842

1843

93 The compact which exists between the North and the South is a covenant with death and a agreement with hell.
William Lloyd Garrison (1805–79) US abolitionist.
Resolution, Massachusetts Anti-Slavery Society 27 Jan 1843

94 *La cordiale entente qui existe entre mon gouvernement et le sien.*
The friendly understanding that exists between my government and hers.
Louis Philippe (1773–1850) King of France.
Referring to an informal understanding reached between Britain and France in 1843. The more familiar phrase, 'entente cordiale', was first used in 1844
Speech, 27 Dec 1843

95 Oh! God! that bread should be so dear,
And flesh and blood so cheap!
Thomas Hood (1799–1845) British poet.
The Song of the Shirt

1844

96 Thus you have a starving population, an absentee aristocracy, and an alien Church, and in addition the weakest executive in the world. That is the Irish Question.
Benjamin Disraeli (1804–81) British statesman.
Speech, House of Commons, 16 Feb 1844

97 Trial by jury itself, instead of being a security to persons who are accused, will be a delusion, a mockery, and a snare.
Thomas Denman (1779–1854) British judge
Judgment in O'Connell v The Queen, 4 Sept 1844

98 Fifty-four forty or fight!
William Allen US Senator.
Slogan widely used in the 1844 US presidential election campaign, referring to the northern boundary of Oregon, which was disputed with Britain; the 49th parallel was agreed as the frontier in 1846

1845

99 The right honourable gentleman caught the Whigs bathing, and walked away with their clothes.
Benjamin Disraeli (1804–81) British statesman.
Referring to Sir Robert Peel
Speech, House of Commons, 28 Feb 1845

100 A Conservative government is an organized hypocrisy.
Benjamin Disraeli
Speech, 17 Mar 1845

1 O let us love our occupations,
Bless the squire and his relations,
Live upon our daily rations,
And always know our proper stations.
Charles Dickens (1812–70) British novelist.
The Chimes, '2nd Quarter'

2 'Two nations; between whom there is no inter-course and no sympathy; who are as ignorant of each other's habits, thoughts, and feel-ings, as if they were dwellers in different zones, or inhabitants of different planets; who are formed by a different breeding, are fed by a different food, are ordered by different man-ners, and are not governed by the same laws.'
'You speak of –' said Egremont, hesitatingly 'THE RICH AND THE POOR.'
Benjamin Disraeli (1804–81) British statesman.
Sybil, Bk. II, Ch. 5

1846

3 Deprive me of power tomorrow, you can never deprive me of the consciousness that I have exercised the powers committed to me from no corrupt or interested motives, from no desire to gratify ambition, or attain any personal object.
Robert Peel (1788–1850) British Conservative prime minister.
Referring to the proposed repeal of the Corn Laws, which split the Conservative party; Peel resigned on 29 June, four days after the repeal was passed
Speech, House of Commons, 15 May 1846

4* I know he is, and he adores his maker.
Benjamin Disraeli (1804–81) British statesman.
Replying to a remark made in defence of John Bright that he was a self-made man; often also attributed to Bright referring to Disraeli
The Fine Art of Political Wit (L. Harris)

5 He is so vain that he wants to figure in history as the settler of all the great questions; but a Parliamentary constitution is not favourable to such ambitions: things must be done by par-ties, not by persons using parties as tools.
Benjamin Disraeli
Referring to Sir Robert Peel
Letter to Lord John Manners, 17 Dec 1846

1847

106 A majority is always the best repartee.
Benjamin Disraeli
Tancred, Bk. II, Ch. 14

107 It is enough. That is the right place.
Brigham Young (1801–77) US Mormon leader.
Referring to the Great Salt Lake Valley, Utah; the Mormons settled there after a fifteen-week jour-ney westwards to escape persecution
Remark, 24 July 1847

108 Whenever he met a great man he grovelled before him, and my-lorded him as only a free-born Briton can do.
William Makepeace Thackeray (1811–63) British novelist.
Vanity Fair, Ch. 13

1848

109 I think that your being the leader of the Tory party is the greatest triumph that Liberalism has ever achieved.
François Guizot (1787–1874) French histo-rian and statesman.
Letter to Disraeli upon his appointment as leader of the Tory party in the House of Commons
Life of Disraeli (W. F. Monypenny and G. E. Buckle), Vol. III

110* We have used the Bible as if it was a consta-ble's handbook – an opium-dose for keeping beasts of burden patient while they are be-ing overloaded.
Charles Kingsley (1819–75) British writer.
Letters to the Chartists, 2

111 Italia farà da se.
Italy will do it alone.
Charles Albert (1798–1849) King of Piedmont.
Referring to the movement to liberate and unify Italy
Proclamation, Mar 1848

112* Anyone who wants to carry on the war against the outsiders, come with me. I can't offer you either honours or wages; I offer you hunger, thirst, forced marches, battles and death. Any-one who loves his country, follow me.
Giuseppe Garibaldi (1807–82) Italian general and political leader.
Garibaldi (Guerzoni)

113 Let me pass, I have to follow them, I am their leader.
Alexandre Auguste Ledru-Rollin (1807–74) French lawyer and politician.
Trying to force his way through a mob during the Revolution of 1848, of which he was one of the chief instigators. A similar remark is attributed to Bonar Law
The Fine Art of Political Wit (L. Harris)

114 Henceforth Prussia merges into Germany.
Frederick William IV (1795–1861) King of Prussia.
Proclamation, 21 Mar 1848

115 I am the emperor, and I want dumplings.
     Ferdinand I (1793–1875) Emperor of Austria.
     The Fall of the House of Habsburg (E. Crank-
     shaw)

116 A spectre is haunting Europe — the spectre of
     communism.
     Karl Marx (1818–83) German philosopher and
     revolutionary.
     Opening words
     Communist Manifesto

117 The history of all hitherto existing society is the
     history of class struggles.
     Karl Marx
     The Communist Manifesto, 1

118 The workers have nothing to lose but their
     chains. They have a world to gain. Workers of
     the world, unite.
     Karl Marx
     The Communist Manifesto, 4

1849

119 Misery generates hate; these sufferers hated
     the machines which they believed took their
     bread from them; they hated the buildings
     which contained these machines; they hated
     the manufacturers who owned those buildings.
     Charlotte Brontë (1816–55) British novelist.
     Referring to the effect of the introduction of knit-
     ting frames into the mills of northern England
     Shirley, Ch. 2

120 In every age the vilest specimens of human na-
     ture are to be found among demagogues.
     Lord Macaulay (1800–59) British historian.
     History of England, Vol. I, Ch. 5

121 Under a government which imprisons any un-
     justly, the true place for a just man is also a
     prison.
     Henry David Thoreau (1817–62) US writer.
     Civil Disobedience

1850

122 No man has come so near our definition of a
     constitutional statesman — the powers of a
     first-rate man and the creed of a second-rate
     man.
     Walter Bagehot (1826–77) British economist
     and journalist.
     Historical Essays, 'The Character of Sir Robert
     Peel'

123 As the Roman, in days of old, held himself free
     from indignity when he could say *Civis
     Romanus sum*, so also a British subject in
     whatever land he may be, shall feel confident
     that the watchful eye and the strong arm of
     England will protect him against injustice and
     wrong.
     Lord Palmerston (1784–1865) British
     statesman.
     Speech, House of Commons, 26 June 1850

124 The object of oratory alone is not truth, but
     persuasion.
     Lord Macaulay (1800–59) British historian.
     Works (1898), Vol. XI, 'Essay on Athenian Ora-
     tors'

125* Conquering kings their titles take.
     John Chandler (1806–76) British clergyman
     and writer.
     Poem title

126* Austria will astound the world with the magni-
     tude of her ingratitude.
     Prince Schwarzenberg (1800–52) Austrian
     statesman.
     On being asked whether Austria was under an
     obligation to Russia for help received
     previously
     The Fall of the House of Habsburg (E. Crank-
     shaw)

127 From each according to his abilities, to each
     according to his needs.
     Karl Marx (1818–83) German philosopher and
     revolutionary.
     Criticism of the Gotha Programme

128 The dictatorship of the proletariat.
     Karl Marx
     Attrib.

1851

129 This is the negation of God erected into a sys-
     tem of Government.
     William Ewart Gladstone (1809–98) British
     statesman.
     First *Letter to Earl of Aberdeen on State Per-
     secutions of Neapolitan Government*

130 The cause of which my name is the symbol
     that is to say, France regenerated by the Rev-
     olution and organised by the Emperor.
     Napoleon III (1808–73) French emperor.
     Proclamation to the French people and army,
     Dec 1851; issued during his *coup d'état*

131 The works of art, by being publicly exhibited
     and offered for sale, are becoming articles of
     trade, following as such the unreasoning
     laws of markets and fashion; and public and
     even private patronage is swayed by their ty-
     rannical influence.
     Prince Albert (1819–61) The consort of
     Queen Victoria.
     Referring to the Great Exhibition, a display of the
     industrial products of Britain and Europe that he
     had organized
     Speech, Royal Academy Dinner, 3 May 1851

132 An enchanted pile, which the sagacious taste
     and prescient philanthropy of an accomplished
     and enlightened Prince have raised for the
     glory of England and the instruction of two
     hemispheres.
     Benjamin Disraeli (1804–81) British
     statesman.
     Referring to the Crystal Palace, built in Hyde
     Park to house the Great Exhibition
     The Faber Book of English History in Verse
     (Kenneth Baker)

3   Sparrowhawks, Ma'am.
    Duke of Wellington (1769–1852) British general and statesman.
    Advice when asked by Queen Victoria how to remove sparrows from the Crystal Palace
    Attrib.

1852

4   The Duke of Wellington had exhausted nature and exhausted glory. His career was one unclouded longest day.
    Written on Wellington's death
    The Times, 16 Sept 1852

5   For too long Society has resembled a pyramid which has been turned upside down and made to rest on its summit. I have replaced it on its base.
    Napoleon III (1808–73) French emperor.
    Speech, 29 Mar 1852

6   In a mood of defiance certain people are saying, 'The Empire means War'. Personally I say, 'The Empire means Peace'
    Napoleon III
    Speech, Bordeaux, 15 Oct 1852; the Second Empire was established on 2 Dec 1852

7   Hegel says somewhere that all great events and personalities in world history reappear in one fashion or another. He forgot to add: the first time as tragedy, the second as farce.
    Karl Marx (1818–83) German philosopher and revolutionary.
    The Eighteenth Brumaire of Louis Napoleon

8   Whipping and abuse are like laudanum: You have to double the dose as the sensibilities decline.
    Harriet Beecher Stowe (1811–96) US novelist.
    Uncle Tom's Cabin, Ch. 20

9* I did not write it. God wrote it. I merely did his dictation.
    Harriet Beecher Stowe
    Referring to *Uncle Tom's Cabin*
    Attrib.

The Crimean War (1853–56)

aused by Russian expansionist ambitions in the Turkh-ruled Balkans, the main activity of the war was an nglo-French-Turkish punitive expedition to capture evastopol in the Crimea. The British contribution was aracterized by incompetence in almost every field. e famous charge of the Light Brigade, for example, as the result of a misunderstanding; and Florence ghtingale made her name by reforming the appalling onditions in the military hospitals. Eventually the war ded out without resolving its causes.

1853

140 We have on our hands a sick man — a very sick man.
    Nicholas I (1796–1855) Tsar of Russia.
    Referring to Turkey, the 'sick man of Europe'; said to Sir G. H. Seymour, British envoy to St Petersburg, Jan 1853
    Attrib.

141 Russia has two generals in whom she can confide — Generals Janvier and Février.
    Nicholas I
    Referring to the Russian winter. Nicholas himself succumbed to a February cold in 1855 — the subject of the famous *Punch* Cartoon, 'General Février turned traitor', 10 Mar 1855
    Attrib.

142 If peace cannot be maintained with honour, it is no longer peace.
    Lord John Russell (1792–1878) British statesman.
    Speech, Greenock, 19 Sep 1853

1854

143* I think there is a certain basis of truth in the fear which the Russian government is beginning to have of communism: for communism is Tsarist autocracy turned upside down.
    Alexander Herzen (1812–70) Russian writer.
    My Past and Thoughts

144 Lads, war is declared with a numerous and bold enemy. Should they meet and offer battle, you know how to dispose of them. Should they remain in port, we must try and get at them. Success depends upon the quickness and precision of your firing. Also, lads, sharpen your cutlasses, and the day is your own.
    Sir Charles Napier (1786–1860) British admiral.
    Referring to the declaration of war against Russia, 1854
    Signal to his command

145 Is it that war is a luxury? Is it that we are fighting — to use a cant phrase of Mr Pitt's time — to secure indemnity for the past and security for the future? Are we to be the Don Quixotes of Europe, to go about fighting for every cause where we find that someone has been wronged?
    Richard Cobden (1804–65) British politician.
    Referring to the Crimean War
    Speech, House of Commons, 22 Dec 1854

146 Lord Raglan wishes the cavalry to advance rapidly to the front and try to prevent enemy carrying away the guns. Troop of Horse Artillery may accompany. French cavalry is on your left. Immediate.
    Lord Raglan (1788–1855) British field marshal.
    Order to Lord Lucan, Battle of Balaclava, 25 Oct 1854; the result was the charge of the Light Brigade.

147 Half a league, half a league,
Half a league onward,
All in the valley of Death
Rode the six hundred.
Alfred, Lord Tennyson (1809–92) British
poet.
The Charge of the Light Brigade

148 Into the jaws of Death,
Into the mouth of Hell.
Alfred, Lord Tennyson
The Charge of the Light Brigade

149 'Forward the Light Brigade!'
Was there a man dismay'd?
Not tho' the soldier knew
Some one had blunder'd:
Their's not to make reply,
Their's not to reason why,
Their's but to do and die:
Into the valley of Death
Rode the six hundred.
Alfred, Lord Tennyson
The Charge of the Light Brigade

150 *C'est magnifique, mais ce n'est pas la guerre.*
It is magnificent, but it is not war.
Pierre Bosquet (1810–61) French marshal.
Referring to the Charge of the Light Brigade
Attrib.

151 They dashed on towards that *thin red line
tipped with steel.*
William Howard Russell (1820–1907) Brit-
ish journalist.
Description of the Russian charge against the
British at the Battle of Balaclava, 25 Oct 1854
The British Expedition to the Crimea

152 No man is good enough to govern another man
without that other's consent.
Abraham Lincoln (1809–65) US statesman.
Speech, 1854

1855

153 The Angel of Death has been abroad throughout the land: you may almost hear the beating
of his wings.
John Bright (1811–89) British radical
politician.
Referring to the Crimean War
Speech, House of Commons, 23 Feb 1855

154 The army is the true nobility of our country.
Napoleon III (1808–73) French emperor.
Speech, 20 Mar 1855

155 That knuckle-end of England – that land of Cal-
vin, oat-cakes, and sulphur.
Sydney Smith (1771–1845) British clergyman
and essayist.
Referring to Scotland
Memoir (Lady Holland)

156 When one has been threatened with a great in-
justice, one accepts a smaller as a favour.
Jane Welsh Carlyle (1801–66) The wife of
Thomas Carlyle.
Journal, 21 Nov 1855

157 His majesty, King Cotton, is forced to continue

the employment of his slaves; and, by their
toil, is riding on, conquering and to conquer.
David Christy (1802–c. 59) American writer.
*Cotton is King: or Slavery in the Light of Politi-
cal Economy*

158 The almighty dollar, that great object of universal devotion throughout our land, seems to
have no genuine devotees in these peculiar
villages.
Washington Irving (1783–1859) US writer.
Wolfert's Roost, 'The Creole Village'

1856

159 Knight of the Crimean Burial Grounds, I
suppose?
Florence Nightingale (1820–1910) British
nurse.
Referring to the KCB awarded to Dr John Hall
the British Chief of Medical Staff in the Crimea
Remark

160* Sir, it was said of Augustus that he found Rome
brick and left it marble. May it be said of you
that you found Paris stinking and left it
sweet.
Edwin Chadwick (1800–90) British social
reformer.
Remark to Napoleon III

161 It is better to begin to abolish serfdom from
above than to wait for it to abolish itself from
below.
Alexander II (1818–81) Tsar of Russia.
Speech, 30 Mar 1856

162 Those who deny freedom to others, deserve it
not for themselves.
Abraham Lincoln (1809–65) US statesman.
Speech, 19 May 1856

163 The ballot is stronger than the bullet.
Abraham Lincoln
Speech, 19 May 1856

164 Where the populace rise at once against the
never-ending audacity of elected persons.
Walt Whitman (1819–92) US poet.
Referring to revolution
Song of the Broad Axe, 5

1857

165* Had any Christian bishop visited that scene of
butchery when I saw it, I verily believe that he
would have buckled on his sword.
Sir G. Wolseley (1833–1913) British soldier
and writer.
Referring to the massacres at Delhi during the Indian Mutiny

166 Accidental and fortuitous concurrence of
atoms.
Lord Palmerston (1784–1865) British
statesman.
Referring to rumours of an impending coalition
with Disraeli
Speech, House of Commons, 1857

167 Whatever was required to be done, the Circum-
locution Office was beforehand with all the

public departments in the art of perceiving –
HOW NOT TO DO IT.
Charles Dickens (1812–70) British novelist.
Little Dorrit, Bk. I, Ch. 10

1858

I see no prospect of the formation of an efficient party, let alone Government, out of the chaos on the Opposition benches. No one reigns over or in it, but discord and antipathy.
Sidney Herbert (1810–61) British statesman.
Referring to the Whigs
Memoir of Sydney Herbert (Lord Stanmore), Vol. II

I believe this government cannot endure permanently, half slave and half free.
Abraham Lincoln (1809–65) US statesman.
Speech, Springfield, Illinois, 16 June 1858

... slavery cannot exist a day or an hour anywhere unless it is supported by local police regulations ...
Stephen A. Douglas (1813–61) US senator.
Speech, 27 Aug 1858

It is an irrepressible conflict between opposing and enduring forces, and it means that the United States must and will, sooner or later, become either entirely a slave-holding nation, or entirely a free-labour nation.
William Henry Seward (1801–72) US senator.
Speech, Rochester (New York), 25 Oct 1858

1859

I am as content to die for God's eternal truth on the scaffold as in any other way.
John Brown (1800–59) American slave abolitionist.
On the day before his execution
Letter to his children, 2 Dec 1859

That new saint, than whom nothing purer or more brave was ever led by love of men into conflict and death ... will make the gallows glorious like the cross.
Ralph Waldo Emerson (1803–82) US poet and essayist.
Referring to John Brown's execution (Dec 1859)

John Brown's body lies a-mouldering in the grave,
His soul is marching on!
Charles Sprague Hall (19th century) US songwriter.
The song commemorates the American hero who died in the cause of abolishing slavery
John Brown's Body

The best thing I know between France and England is – the sea.
Douglas William Jerrold (1803–57) British dramatist.
Wit and Opinions of Douglas Jerrold, 'The Anglo-French Alliance'

176 I don't care for war, there's far too much luck in it for my liking.
Napoleon III (1808–73) French emperor.
Said after the narrow but bloody French victory at Solferino (24 June 1859)
The Fall of the House of Habsburg (E. Crankshaw)

177 England is one of the greatest powers of the world, no event or series of events bearing on the balance of power, or on probabilities of peace or war can be matters of indifference to her, and her right to have and to express opinions on matters thus bearing on her interests is unquestionable.
Lord Palmerston (1784–1865) British statesman.
Letter to Queen Victoria, 23 Aug 1859

178 If all mankind minus one, were of one opinion, and only one person were of the contrary opinion, mankind would be no more justified in silencing that one person, than he, if he had the power, would be justified in silencing mankind.
John Stuart Mill (1806–73) British philosopher.
On Liberty, Ch. 2

179 A party of order or stability, and a party of progress or reform, are both necessary elements of a healthy state of political life.
John Stuart Mill
On Liberty, Ch. 2

180 The liberty of the individual must be thus far limited; he must not make himself a nuisance to other people.
John Stuart Mill
On Liberty, Ch. 3

181 The worth of a State in the long run is the worth of the individuals composing it.
John Stuart Mill
On Liberty, Ch. 5

182 Every man meets his Waterloo at last.
Wendell Phillips (1811–84) US reformer.
Speech, Brooklyn, 1 Nov 1859

183 Authority forgets a dying king.
Alfred, Lord Tennyson (1809–92) British poet.
Idylls of the King, 'The Passing of Arthur'

1860

184* He believes, with all his heart and soul and strength, that there *is* such a thing as truth; he has the soul of a martyr with the intellect of an advocate.
Walter Bagehot (1826–77) British economist and journalist.
Referring to Gladstone
Historical Essays, 'Mr Gladstone'

185* Your dexterity seems a happy compound of the smartness of an attorney's clerk and the intrigue of a Greek of the lower empire.
Benjamin Disraeli (1804–81) British statesman.
Speaking to Lord Palmerston
Attrib.

186* England, we love thee better than we know.
Richard Trench (1807–86) Archbishop of Dublin.
Gibraltar

187 If we were to do for ourselves what we have done for our country, we should indeed be very great rogues.
Camillo Cavour (1810–61) Italian statesman.
Remark, Sept 1860

188* You can fool some of the people all the time and all the people some of the time; but you can't fool all the people all the time.
Abraham Lincoln (1809–65) US statesman.
Attrib.

189* Die when I may, I want it said of me by those who know me best, that I have always plucked a thistle and planted a flower where I thought a flower would grow.
Abraham Lincoln
Presidential Anecdotes (P. Boller)

190 What is conservatism? Is it not adherence to the old and tried, against the new and untried?
Abraham Lincoln
Speech, 27 Feb 1860

191 Let us have faith that right makes might; and in that faith let us to the end, dare to do our duty as we understand it.
Abraham Lincoln
Speech, 27 Feb 1860

1861

The American Civil War (1861–65)

The result of deep-seated tensions between the Northern and Southern states, war broke out after 11 states seceded from the USA. Fought at first over the right of states to secede from the Union, the war's main theme, the emancipation of all slaves, was adopted as a Northern war aim by President Abraham Lincoln in 1862. Initially the war was an even contest, but the greater resources of the North eventually proved decisive.

192 All we ask is to be let alone.
Jefferson Davis (1808–89) President of the rebel Confederate States of America.
Inaugural address, 18 Feb 1861

193 This country, with its institutions, belongs to the people who inhabit it. Whenever they shall grow weary of the existing government, they can exercise their constitutional right of amending it, or their revolutionary right to dismember or overthrow it.
Abraham Lincoln (1809–65) US statesman.
First Inaugural Address, 4 Mar 1861

194 I think the necessity of being *ready* increase. Look to it.
Abraham Lincoln (1809–65) US statesman.
Letter to Andrew Curtin, Governor of Pennsylvania, 8 Apr 1861

195 Let us determine to die here, and we will conquer.
There is Jackson standing like a stone wa.
Rally behind the Virginians.
Barnard Elliot Bee (1824–61) US soldier
Said at the First Battle of Bull Run, 1861; he
Gen Thomas Jackson's nickname, 'Stonewal
Jackson'
Reminiscences of Metropolis (Poore), II

196* There they are cutting each other's throats, cause one half of them prefer hiring their se vants for life, and the other by the hour.
Thomas Carlyle (1795–1881) Scottish his rian and essayist.
Referring to the American Civil War
Attrib.

197 Rome must be the capital of Italy because w out Rome Italy cannot be constituted.
Camillo Cavour (1810–61) Italian statesm
Speech, Turin, 25 Mar 1861

1862

198* So you're the little woman who wrote the b that made this great war!
Abraham Lincoln (1809–65) US statesm
Said on meeting Harriet Beecher Stowe, the thor of *Uncle Tom's Cabin* (1852), which stim lated opposition to slavery before the US Civ War
Abraham Lincoln: The War Years (Carl Sandburg), Vol. II, Ch. 39

199* 'Shoot, if you must, this old gray head, But spare your country's flag,' she said.

A shade of sadness, a blush of shame, Over the face of the leader came.
John Greenleaf Whittier (1807–92) US poet.
Barbara Frietchie

200 No terms except unconditional and immedia surrender can be accepted. I propose to move immediately upon your works.
Ulysses Simpson Grant (1822–85) US general.
Message to opposing commander, Simon Bo Buckner, during siege of Fort Donelson, 16 F 1862

201 My paramount object in this struggle is to s the Union . . . If I could save the Union witho freeing any slave, I would do it; and if I coul save it by freeing all the slaves, I would do . . . I have here stated my purpose according to my views of official duty and I intend no

modification of my oft-expressed personal wish that all men everywhere could be free.
Abraham Lincoln (1809–65) US statesman.
Letter to Horace Greeley, 22 Aug 1862

»2 A Star for every State and a State for every Star.
Robert Charles Winthrop (1809–94)
Speech, Boston Common, 27 Aug 1862

»3 In giving freedom to the slave, we assure freedom to the free — honourable alike in what we give and what we preserve.
Abraham Lincoln (1809–65) US statesman.
Annual Message to Congress, 1 Dec 1862

»4 If you don't want to use the army, I should like to borrow it for a while. Yours respectfully, A. Lincoln.
Abraham Lincoln
Letter to General George B. McClellan, whose lack of activity during the US Civil War irritated Lincoln

)5 It is well that war is so terrible; else we would grow too fond of it.
Robert E. Lee (1807–70) US general.
Speaking to another general during the battle of Fredericksburg
The American Treasury (C. Fadiman)

)6 Mine eyes have seen the glory of the coming of the Lord:
He is trampling out the vintage where the grapes of wrath are stored.
Julia Ward Howe (1819–1910) US writer.
Battle Hymn of the American Republic

)7 The great questions of our day cannot be solved by speeches and majority votes . . . but by iron and blood.
Bismarck (1815–98) German statesman.
Usually misquoted as 'blood and iron' — a form Bismarck himself used in 1886
Speech, Prussian Chamber, 30 Sept 1862

»8 Whereas it has long been known and declared that the poor have no right to the property of the rich, I wish it also to be known and declared that the rich have no right to the property of the poor.
John Ruskin (1819–1900) British art critic and writer.
Unto this Last, Essay III

1863

)9 In a larger sense we cannot dedicate, we cannot consecrate, we cannot hallow this ground. The brave men, living and dead, who struggled here, have consecrated it far above our power to add or detract. The world will little note, nor long remember, what we say here, but it can never forget what they did here. It is for us, the living, rather to be dedicated here to the unfinished work which they who fought here have thus far so nobly advanced. It is rather for us to be here dedicated to the great task remaining before us . . . that we here highly resolve that the dead shall not have died in vain, that this nation, under God, shall

have a new birth of freedom; and that government of the people, by the people, and for the people, shall not perish from the earth.
Abraham Lincoln (1809–65) US statesman.
Report of Lincoln's address at the dedication (19 Nov 1863) of the national cemetery on the site of the Battle of Gettysburg

210 Give them the cold steel, boys!
Lewis Addison Arminstead (1817–63) US general.
Exhortation given to his troops during the US Civil War
Attrib.

211* I got there fustest with the mostest.
Nathan Bedford Forrest (1821–77) Confederate general.
Popular misquotation of his explanation of his success in capturing Murfreesboro; his actual words were, 'I just took the short cut and got there first with the most men'
A Civil War Treasury (B. Botkin)

212 There are only three men who have ever understood it: one was Prince Albert, who is dead; the second was a German professor, who became mad. I am the third — and I have forgotten all about it.
Lord Palmerston (1784–1865) British statesman.
Referring to the Schleswig-Holstein question
Attrib.

213 Politics is not an exact science.
Bismarck (1815–98) German statesman.
Speech, Prussian Chamber, 18 Dec 1863

1864

214 I claim not to have controlled events, but confess plainly that events have controlled me.
Abraham Lincoln (1809–65) US statesman.
Letter to A. G. Hodges, 4 Apr 1864

215 I purpose to fight it out on this line, if it takes all summer.
Ulysses Simpson Grant (1822–85) US general.
Dispatch to Washington, 11 May 1864

216 An old Dutch farmer, who remarked to a companion once that it was not best to swap horses in mid-stream.
Abraham Lincoln (1809–65) US statesman.
Speech, 9 June 1864

217* I can't spare this man; he fights.
Abraham Lincoln
Resisting demands for the dismissal of Ulysses Grant
Attrib.

218 Nonsense, they couldn't hit an elephant at this distance
John Sedgwick (1813–64) US general.
In response to a suggestion that he should not show himself over the parapet during the Battle of the Wilderness
Attrib.

219* 'Hurrah! hurrah! we bring the Jubilee!

Hurrah! hurrah! the flag that makes you free!'
So we sang the chorus from Atlanta to the
sea
As we were marching through Georgia.
Henry Clay Work (1832–84) US songwriter.
Commemorating the march (Nov–Dec 1864) by
a Union army under General Sherman through
Confederate Georgia
Marching Through Georgia

220 The foreign policy of the noble Earl . . . may be
summed up in two truly expressive words:
'meddle' and 'muddle'.
Edward Stanley, Earl of Derby (1799–
1869) British Conservative prime minister.
Referring to Lord Russell's policy towards the
American Civil War
Speech, House of Lords, Feb 1864

221 I venture to say that every man who is not presumably incapacitated by some consideration
of personal unfitness or of political danger,
is morally entitled to come within the pale of
the constitution.
William Ewart Gladstone (1809–98) British
statesman.
Referring to the reform of the franchise
Speech, House of Commons, 11 May 1864

1865

222* As President, I have no eyes but constitutional
eyes, I cannot see you.
Abraham Lincoln (1809–65)
Reply to the South Carolina Commissioners
Attrib.

223 I don't know who my grandfather was; I am
much more concerned to know what his grand-
son will be.
Abraham Lincoln
Taking part in a discussion on ancestry
Attrib.

224 The much talked of surrendering of Lee's sword
and my handing it back, this and much more
that has been said about it is the purest
romance.
Ulysses Simpson Grant (1822–85) US
general.
Personal Memoirs of Ulysses S. Grant

225* Go West, young man, and grow up with the
country.
Horace Greeley (1811–72) US politician and
journalist.
Also attributed to the US writer John Soule
(1815–91), *Terre Haute* (Indiana) *Express*, 1851
Hints toward Reform

226 With malice toward none; with charity for all;
with firmness in the right, as God gives us to
see the right, let us strive on to finish the work
we are in: to bind up the nation's wounds; to
care for him who shall have borne the battle,
and for his widow and his orphan, to do all
which may achieve and cherish a just and lasting peace among ourselves, and with all
nations.
Abraham Lincoln (1809–65) US
statesman.
Second Inaugural Address, 4 Mar 1865

227 England is the mother of parliaments.
John Bright (1811–89) British radical
politician.
Speech, Birmingham, 18 Jan 1865

228 I think . . . that it is the best club in London.
Charles Dickens (1812–70) British novelist
Mr Tremlow describing the House of Common
Our Mutual Friend, Bk. II, Ch. 3

229 When I invented the phrase 'His Majesty's O
position' he paid me a compliment on the fortunate hit.
John Cam Hobhouse (1786–1869) British
politician.
Speaking about Canning
Recollections of a Long Life, II, Ch. 12

230 Home of lost causes, and forsaken beliefs, a
unpopular names, and impossible loyalties!
Matthew Arnold (1822–88) British poet an
critic.
Referring to Oxford
Essays in Criticism, First Series, Preface

231 My fellow citizens, the President is dead, bu
the Government lives and God Omnipotent
reigns.
James A. Garfield (1831–81) US statesma
Speech following the assassination of Lincoln

232 Assassination has never changed the history
the world.
Benjamin Disraeli (1804–81) British
statesman.
Speech, House of Commons, 1 May 1865

1866

233 You cannot fight against the future. Time is
our side.
William Ewart Gladstone (1809–98) Britis
statesman.
Advocating parliamentary reform
Speech, 1866

234 The right hon. Gentleman . . . has retired into
what may be called his political Cave of
Adullam.
John Bright (1811–99) English radical
politician.
Referring to Robert Lowe, the leader of the L
erals who opposed Parliamentary Reform;
hence their name, the 'Adullamites'
Speech, House of Commons, 13 Mar 1866

1867

235 We have dished the Whigs.
Edward Stanley, Earl of Derby (1799–
1869) British Conservative prime minister.
Referring to the Parliamentary Reform Act, 18
Remark

236 A severe though not unfriendly critic of our
stitutions said that 'the cure for admiring the
House of Lords was to go and look at it.'
Walter Bagehot (1826–77) British economi
and journalist.
The English Constitution, 'The House of Lords

237 The Sovereign has, under a constitutional mo

archy such as ours, three rights – the right to be consulted, the right to encourage, the right to warn.
Walter Bagehot
The English Constitution, 'The Monarchy'

238 It has been said that England invented the phrase, 'Her Majesty's Opposition'.
Walter Bagehot
The English Constitution, 'The Monarchy'

239 The characteristic of the English Monarchy is that it retains the feelings by which the heroic kings governed their rude age, and has added the feeling by which the constitutions of later Greece ruled in more refined ages.
Walter Bagehot
The English Constitution, 'The Monarchy'

240 But of all nations in the world the English are perhaps the least a nation of pure philosophers.
Walter Bagehot
The English Constitution, 'The Monarchy'

241 The best reason why Monarchy is a strong government is that it is an intelligible government. The mass of mankind understand it, and they hardly anywhere in the world understand any other.
Walter Bagehot
The English Constitution, 'The Monarchy'

242 *The Times* has made many ministries.
Walter Bagehot
The English Constitution, 'The Cabinet'

243 Capitalist production begets, with the inexorability of a law of nature, its own negation.
Karl Marx (1818–83) German philosopher and revolutionary.
Das Kapital, Ch. 15

244 The centralization of the means of production and the socialization of labour reach a point where they prove incompatible with their capitalist husk. This bursts asunder. The knell of private property sounds. The expropriators are expropriated.
Karl Marx
Das Kapital

1868

245 Yes, I have climbed to the top of the greasy pole.
Benjamin Disraeli (1804–81) British statesman.
On being appointed prime minister
Remark, Feb 1868

246 The great Unwashed.
Henry Peter Brougham (1778–1868) Scottish lawyer and politician.
Attrib.

247 Let us have peace.
Ulysses Simpson Grant (1822–85) US general.
On accepting nomination
Letter, 29 May 1868

248 I do not have to forgive my enemies, I have had them all shot.
Ramón Maria Narváez (1800–68) Spanish general and political leader.
Said on his deathbed, when asked by a priest if he forgave his enemies
Famous Last Words (B. Conrad)

1869

249 The Common Law adapts itself by a perpetual process of growth to the perpetual roll of the tide of circumstances as society advances.
Sir William Erle (1793–1880) Judge.
Memorandum on Trade Union Law

250 Our society distributes itself into Barbarians, Philistines, and Populace; and America is just ourselves, with the Barbarians quite left out, and the Populace nearly.
Matthew Arnold (1822–88) British poet and critic.
Culture and Anarchy, Preface

251 One has often wondered whether upon the whole earth there is anything so unintelligent, so unapt to perceive how the world is really going, as an ordinary young Englishman of our upper class.
Matthew Arnold
Culture and Anarchy, Ch. 2

252 I often, therefore, when I want to distinguish clearly the aristocratic class from the Philistines proper, or middle class, name the former, in my own mind *the Barbarians*.
Matthew Arnold
Culture and Anarchy, Ch. 3

253 But that vast portion, lastly, of the working-class which, raw and half-developed, has long lain half-hidden amidst its poverty and squalor, and is now issuing from its hiding-place to assert an Englishman's heaven-born privilege of doing as he likes, and is beginning to perplex us by marching where it likes, meeting where it likes, bawling what it likes, breaking what it likes – to this vast residuum we may with great propriety give the name of Populace.
Matthew Arnold
Culture and Anarchy, Ch. 3

254 I know no method to secure the repeal of bad or obnoxious laws so effective as their stringent execution.
Ulysses Simpson Grant (1822–85) US president.
Inaugural address, 4 Mar 1869

255 The only good Indians I ever saw were dead.
Philip H. Sheridan (1831–88) US general.
The People's Almanac 2 (D. Wallechinsky)

256* I should be trading on the blood of my men.
Robert E. Lee (1807–70) US general.
Refusing to write his memoirs
Nobody Said It Better (M. Ringo)

Attitudes

Art, Literature, and Music

1816

257 Then felt I like some watcher of the skies
When a new planet swims into his ken;
Or like stout Cortez when with eagle eyes
He star'd at the Pacific — and all his men
Look'd at each other with a wild surmise —
Silent, upon a peak in Darien.
John Keats (1795–1821) British poet.
On first looking into Chapman's Homer

1817

258 Our myriad-minded Shakespeare.
Samuel Taylor Coleridge (1772–1834) British poet.
Biographia Literaria, Ch. 15

259 The excellence of every art is its intensity, capable of making all disagreeables evaporate, from their being in close relationship with beauty and truth.
John Keats (1795–1821) British poet.
Letter to G. and T. Keats, 21 Dec 1817

1818

260 Poetry is not the proper antithesis to prose, but to science. Poetry is opposed to science, and prose to metre.
Samuel Taylor Coleridge (1772–1834) British poet.
Lectures and Notes of 1818, I

261 We hate poetry that has a palpable design upon us — and if we do not agree, seems to put its hand in its breeches pocket. Poetry should be great and unobtrusive, a thing which enters into one's soul, and does not startle or amaze it with itself, but with its subject.
John Keats (1795–1821) British poet.
Letter to J. H. Reynolds, 3 Feb 1818

262 If poetry comes not as naturally as leaves to a tree it had better not come at all.
John Keats
Letter to John Taylor, 27 Feb 1818

263 I think I shall be among the English Poets after my death.
John Keats
Letter to George and Georgiana Keats, 14 Oct 1818

264 Art for art's sake.
Victor Cousin (1792–1867) French philosopher.
Lecture, Sorbonne, 1818

265 He talked on for ever; and you wished him to talk on for ever.
William Hazlitt (1778–1830) British essayist.
Referring to Coleridge
Lectures on the English Poets, Lecture VIII, 'On the Living Poets'

1820

266* With Donne, whose muse on dromedary trots,
Wreathe iron pokers into true-love knots.
Samuel Taylor Coleridge (1772–1834) British poet.
On Donne's Poetry

267* His worst is better than any other person's best.
William Hazlitt (1778–1830) British essayist.
English Literature, Ch. XIV, 'Sir Walter Scott'

1821

268 Poetry is the record of the best and happiest moments of the happiest and best minds.
Percy Bysshe Shelley (1792–1822) British poet.
A Defence of Poetry

269 I weep for Adonais — he is dead!
O, weep for Adonais! though our tears
Thaw not the frost which binds so dear a head!
Percy Bysshe Shelley
Prompted by the death of Keats
Adonais, I

1822

270 I love to lose myself in other men's minds. When I am not walking, I am reading; I cannot sit and think. Books think for me.
Charles Lamb (1775–1834) British essayist.
Last Essays of Elia, 'Detached Thoughts on Books and Reading'

1824

271 If they had said the sun and the moon was gone out of the heavens it could not have struck me with the idea of a more awful and dreary blank in the creation than the words: Byron is dead.
Jane Welsh Carlyle (1801–66) The wife of Thomas Carlyle.
Letter to Thomas Carlyle, 1824

272 Prose on certain occasions can bear a great deal of poetry: on the other hand, poetry sinks and swoons under a moderate weight of prose.
Walter Savage Landor (1775–1864) British poet and writer.
Imaginary Conversations, 'Archdeacon Hare and Walter Landor'

273 Clear writers, like clear fountains, do not seem so deep as they are; the turbid look the most profound.
Walter Savage Landor
Imaginary Conversations, 'Southey and Porson'

1825

274 We know no spectacle so ridiculous as the Brit-

ish public in one of its periodical fits of morality.
Lord Macaulay (1800–59) British historian.
Literary Essays Contributed to the 'Edinburgh Review', 'Moore's 'Life of Lord Byron''

275 As civilization advances, poetry almost necessarily declines.
Lord Macaulay
Literary Essays Contributed to the 'Edinburgh Review', 'Milton'

276 Perhaps no person can be a poet, or can even enjoy poetry, without a certain unsoundness of mind.
Lord Macaulay
Literary Essays Contributed to the 'Edinburgh Review', 'Milton'

277 Romanticism is the art of presenting people with the literary works which are capable of affording them the greatest possible pleasure, in the present state of their customs and beliefs.
Classicism, on the other hand, presents them with the literature that gave the greatest possible pleasure to their great-grandfathers.
Stendhal (Henri Beyle; 1783–1842) French novelist.
Racine et Shakespeare, Ch. 3

1826

278 The Big Bow-Wow strain I can do myself like any now going; but the exquisite touch, which renders ordinary commonplace things and characters interesting, from the truth of the description and the sentiment, is denied to me.
Walter Scott (1771–1832) Scottish novelist.
In praise of Jane Austen
Journal, 14 Mar 1826

1830

279 A novel is a mirror walking along a main road.
Stendhal (Henri Beyle; 1783–1842) French novelist.
Le Rouge et le noir, Ch. 49

1831

280 Ancient sculpture is the true school of modesty. But where the Greeks had modesty, we have cant; where they had poetry, we have cant; where they had patriotism, we have cant; where they had anything that exalts, delights, or adorns humanity, we have nothing but cant, cant, cant.
Thomas Love Peacock (1785–1866) British novelist.
Crotchet Castle, Ch. 7

281 A book that furnishes no quotations is, *me judice*, no book – it is a plaything.
Thomas Love Peacock
Crotchet Castle, Ch. 9

1833

282 I wish our clever young poets would remember

my homely definitions of prose and poetry; that is, prose = words in their best order; – poetry = the best words in the best order.
Samuel Taylor Coleridge (1772–1834) British poet.
Table Talk

283 The misfortune is, that he has begun to write verses without very well understanding what metre is.
Samuel Taylor Coleridge
Referring to Tennyson
Table Talk

284 I hate the whole race ... There is no believing a word they say – your professional poets, I mean – there never existed a more worthless set than Byron and his friends for example.
Duke of Wellington (1769–1852) British general and statesman.
Lady Salisbury's diary, 26 Oct 1833

1837

285 Poetry's unnat'ral; no man ever talked poetry 'cept a beadle on boxin' day.
Charles Dickens (1812–70) British novelist.
Pickwick Papers, Ch. 33

1838

286 A poet without love were a physical and metaphysical impossibility.
Thomas Carlyle (1795–1881) Scottish historian and essayist.
Critical and Miscellaneous Essays, 'Burns'

287 Literary men are ... a perpetual priesthood.
Thomas Carlyle
Critical and Miscellaneous Essays, 'The State of German Literature'

288 A good book is the best of friends, the same today and for ever.
Martin Farquhar Tupper (1810–89) British writer.
Proverbial Philosophy, 'Of Reading'

1839

289 Beneath the rule of men entirely great,
The pen is mightier than the sword.
Edward Bulwer-Lytton (1803–73) British novelist and politician.
Richelieu, II:2

290 Rules and models destroy genius and art.
William Hazlitt (1778–1830) British essayist.
On Taste

1840

291* In my situation as Chancellor of the University of Oxford, I have been much exposed to authors.
Duke of Wellington (1769–1852) British general and statesman.
Collections and Recollections (G. W. E. Russell)

292 A good book is the purest essence of a human
soul.
Thomas Carlyle (1795–1881) Scottish histo-
rian and essayist.
Speech made in support of the London Library
Carlyle and the London Library (F. Harrison)

1841

293 I shall not be satisfied unless I produce something that shall for a few days supersede the
last fashionable novel on the tables of young
ladies.
Lord Macaulay (1800–59) British historian.
Letter to Macvey Napier, 5 Nov 1841

1842

294 When once the itch of literature comes over a
man, nothing can cure it but the scratching of
a pen.
Samuel Lover (1797–1868) Irish novelist.
Handy Andy, Ch. 36

295 Whatever sentence will bear to be read twice,
we may be sure was thought twice.
Henry David Thoreau (1817–62) US writer.
Journal, 1842

1845

296* My business is to paint not what I know, but
what I see.
Joseph Turner (1775–1851) British painter.
Responding to a criticism of the fact that he had
painted no portholes on the ships in a view of
Plymouth
Proust: The Early Years (G. Painter)

1848

297 The *Pall Mall Gazette* is written by gentlemen
for gentlemen.
William Makepeace Thackeray (1811–63)
British novelist.
This fictional journal inspired a real counterpart,
founded in 1855
Pendennis, Ch. 32

1849

298 When we build let us think that we build for
ever.
John Ruskin (1819–1900) British art critic and
writer.
The Seven Lamps of Architecture, Ch. 6, 'The
Lamp of Memory'

1850

299* It always seems to me that the right sphere for
Shelley's genius was the sphere of music, not
of poetry.
Matthew Arnold (1822–88) British poet and
critic.
Maurice de Guérin, Footnote

300 . . . essentially a cold, hard, silent, practical

man . . . a man of an immense head, and great
jaws like a crocodile's, cast in a mould
designed for prodigious work.
Thomas Carlyle (1795–1881) Scottish historian and essayist.
Referring to William Wordsworth
Attrib.

301* If people only knew as much about painting as I
do, they would never buy my pictures.
Edwin Landseer (1802–73) British painter
and sculptor.
Said to W. P. Frith
Landseer the Victorian Paragon (Campbell Len-
nie), Ch. 12

302* Great artists have no country.
Alfred de Musset (1810–57) French drama-
tist and poet.
Lorenzaccio, I:5

303* A picture has been said to be something between a thing and a thought.
Samuel Palmer (1805–81) British landscape
painter.
Life of Blake (Arthur Symons)

1852

304 . . . a bottle of beautiful soda-water . . . very
pleasant company now and then.
Thomas Carlyle (1795–1881) Scottish histo-
rian and essayist.
Referring to Ruskin
Attrib.

1853

305* He spoke, and loos'd our heart in tears.
He laid us as we lay at birth
On the cool flowery lap of earth.
Matthew Arnold (1822–88) British poet and
critic.
Referring to Wordsworth
Memorial Verses

306 Time may restore us in his course
Goethe's sage mind and Byron's force:
But where will Europe's latter hour
Again find Wordsworth's healing power?
Matthew Arnold
Memorial Verses

307 All one's inventions are true, you can be sure of
that. Poetry is as exact a science as geometry.
Gustave Flaubert (1821–80) French novelist.
Letter to Louise Colet, 14 Aug 1853

308 No person who is not a great sculptor or
painter can be an architect. If he is not a sculptor or painter, he can only be a *builder*.
John Ruskin (1819–1900) British art critic and
writer.
Lectures on Architecture and Painting

309 I expect a judgment. Shortly.
Charles Dickens (1812–70) British novelist.
An overoptimistic hope: the case, *Jarndyce vs.
Jarndyce*, lasted for many years and formed a
satire on the abuses of the court of Chancery.
Bleak House, Ch. 3

1854

10 Books, we are told, propose to *instruct* or to *amuse*. Indeed! . . . The true antithesis to knowledge, in this case, is not *pleasure*, but *power*. All that is literature seeks to communicate power; all that is not literature, to communicate knowledge.
Thomas De Quincey (1785–1859) British writer.
Letters to a Young Man

1856

11 . . . the most honourable thing that man, as a gregarious animal, has ever produced.
John Ruskin (1819–1900) British art critic and writer.
Referring to a ship of the line
Attrib.

1858

12 Writers, like teeth, are divided into incisors and grinders.
Walter Bagehot (1826–77) British economist and journalist.
Estimates of some Englishmen and Scotchmen, 'The First Edinburgh Reviewers'

1859

13 Nobody cares much at heart about Titian, only there is a strange undercurrent of everlasting murmur about his name, which means the deep consent of all great men that he is greater than they.
John Ruskin (1819–1900) British art critic and writer.
The Two Paths, Lecture II

14 Fine art is that in which the hand, the head, and the heart of man go together.
John Ruskin
The Two Paths, Lecture II

1860

15* Talent alone cannot make a writer. There must be a man behind the book.
Ralph Waldo Emerson (1803–82) US poet and essayist.
Goethe

16* I have tried lately to read Shakespeare, and found it so intolerably dull that it nauseated me.
Charles Darwin (1809–82) British life scientist.
Autobiography

17* When I want to read a novel I write one.
Benjamin Disraeli (1804–81) British statesman.
Attrib.

1862

18 With the aid of a few columns stuck here and

there, or rich window dressings and rustications in another place, and aided by the fatal facility of stucco, they managed to get over an immense amount of space with a very slight expenditure of thought.
James Fergusson (1808–86) British writer on architecture.
Referring to contemporary architects, such as Nash
History of Architecture, Vol. III

1865

319 All books are divisible into two classes, the books of the hour, and the books of all time.
John Ruskin (1819–1900) British art critic and writer.
Sesame and Lilies, 'Of Kings' Treasuries'

1867

320 Wagner has lovely moments but awful quarters of an hour.
Gioacchino Rossini (1792–1868) Italian operatic composer.
Remark made to Emile Naumann, April 1867
Italienische Tondichter (Naumann)

321 Not that the story need be long, but it will take a long while to make it short.
Henry David Thoreau (1817–62) US writer.
Letter, 16 Nov 1867

1868

322 Give me a laundry-list and I'll set it to music.
Gioacchino Rossini (1792–1868) Italian operatic composer.
Attrib.

1869

323 Historians tell the story of the past, novelists the story of the present.
Edmond de Goncourt (1822–96) French novelist.
Journal

324 For this class we have a designation which now has become pretty well known, and which we may as well still keep for them, the designation of Philistines.
Matthew Arnold (1822–88) British poet and critic.
Referring to the middle class
Culture and Anarchy, Ch. 3

Daily Life

1816

325 Nobody is healthy in London, nobody can be.
Jane Austen (1775–1817) British novelist.
Emma, Ch. 12

326 One has no great hopes from Birmingham. I al-

ways say there is something direful in the
sound.
Jane Austen
Emma, Ch. 36

1818
---

327   Oh! who can ever be tired of Bath?
Jane Austen
Northanger Abbey, Ch. 10

328   I like the weather, when it is not rainy,
That is, I like two months of every year.
Lord Byron (1788–1824) British poet.
Beppo

1819
---

329   Man, being reasonable, must get drunk;
The best of life is but intoxication.
Lord Byron
Don Juan, II

330   Give me books, fruit, French wine and fine
weather and a little music out of doors, played
by somebody I do not know.
John Keats (1795–1821) British poet.
Letter to Fanny Keats, 29 Aug 1819

1820
---

331   London, that great sea, whose ebb and flow
At once is deaf and loud, and on the shore
Vomits its wrecks, and still howls on for
more.
Percy Bysshe Shelley (1792–1822) British
poet.
Letter to Maria Gisborne, I

1822
---

332   Newspapers always excite curiosity. No one
ever lays one down without a feeling of
disappointment.
Charles Lamb (1775–1834) British essayist.
Last Essays of Elia, 'Detached Thoughts on
Books and Reading'

1823
---

333   'Twas the night before Christmas, when all
through the house
Not a creature was stirring, not even a
mouse;
The stockings were hung by the chimney with
care,
In hopes that St Nicholas soon would be
there.
Clement Clarke Moore (1779–1863) US
writer.
In *Troy Sentinel*, 23 Dec 1823, 'A Visit from St.
Nicholas'

1826
---

334   Summer has set in with its usual severity.
Samuel Taylor Coleridge (1772–1834) Brit
ish poet.
Quoted in Lamb's letter to V. Novello, 9 May
1826

1827
---

335   The trivial round, the common task,
Would furnish all we ought to ask;
Room to deny ourselves; a road
To bring us, daily, nearer God.
John Keble (1792–1866) British poet and
clergyman.
The Christian Year, 'Morning'

1830

336* They will steal the very teeth out of your mouth
as you walk through the streets. I know it from
experience.
William Arabin (1773–1841) British judge.
Referring to the people of Uxbridge
Arabinesque at Law (Sir R. Megarry)

1834
---

337   He who drinks a tumbler of London water has
literally in his stomach more animated beings
than there are men, women and children on
the face of the globe.
Sydney Smith (1771–1845) British clergyman
and essayist.
Letter

1835
---

338   The loco-motive Monster, carrying *eighty* tons
of goods, and navigated by a tail of smoke
and sulphur, coming thro' every man's grounds
between Manchester and Liverpool.
Thomas Creevey (1768–1838) British
politician.
The Creevey Papers (ed. Sir H. Maxwell)

1836
---

339   . . . I *too* well know its truth, from experience,
that whenever any poor Gipsies are en-
camped anywhere and crimes and robberies
&c. occur, it is invariably laid to their account
which is shocking; and if they are always
looked upon as vagabonds, how *can* they become good people?
Victoria (1819–1901) Queen of the United
Kingdom.
Journal, 29 Dec 1836

1847
---

340   What a blessing this smoking is! perhaps the
greatest that we owe to the discovery of
America.
Arthur Helps (1813–75) British historian.
Friends in Council

1851

341 There are no countries in the world less known by the British than these selfsame British Islands.
George Henry Borrow (1803–81) British writer.
Lavengro, Preface

1853

342 This is a London particular . . . A fog, miss.
Charles Dickens (1812–70) British novelist.
Bleak House, Ch. 3

1854

343 The blue ribbon of the turf.
Benjamin Disraeli (1804–81) British statesman.
Describing the Derby
Life of Lord George Bentinck, Ch. 26

1857

344 It's more than a game. It's an institution.
Thomas Hughes (1822–96) British novelist.
Referring to cricket
Tom Brown's Schooldays, Pt. II, Ch. 7

1858

345 The comic almanacs give us dreadful pictures of January and February; but, in truth, the months which should be made to look gloomy in England are March and April. Let no man boast himself that he has got through the perils of winter till at least the seventh of May.
Anthony Trollope (1815–82) British novelist.
Doctor Thorne, Ch. 47

1859

346 . . . that old monkish place which I have a horror of.
Victoria (1819–1901) Queen of the United Kingdom
Referring to Oxford
Letter to Princess Victoria, 31 Oct 1859

1860

347* This vice brings in one hundred million francs in taxes every year. I will certainly forbid it at once – as soon as you can name a virtue that brings in as much revenue.
Napoleon III (1808–73) French emperor.
Reply when asked to ban smoking
Anekdotenschatz (H. Hoffmeister)

1865

348 Jolly boating weather,
And a hay harvest breeze,
Blade on the feather,
Shade off the trees
Swing, swing together

With your body between your knees.
William Johnson Cory (1823–92) British schoolmaster and poet.
Eton Boating Song

1867

349 That sweet City with her dreaming spires
She needs not June for beauty's heightening.
Matthew Arnold (1822–88) British poet and critic.
Referring to Oxford
Thyrsis

Death

1820

350 Darkling I listen; and, for many a time
I have been half in love with easeful Death,
Call'd him soft names in many a mused rhyme,
To take into the air my quiet breath;
Now more than ever seems it rich to die,
To cease upon the midnight with no pain,
While thou art pouring forth thy soul abroad
In such an ecstasy!
John Keats (1795–1821) British poet.
Ode to a Nightingale

351 Death is the veil which those who live call life:
They sleep, and it is lifted.
Percy Bysshe Shelley (1792–1822) British poet.
Prometheus Unbound, III

1821

352 I shall soon be laid in the quiet grave – thank God for the quiet grave – O! I can feel the cold earth upon me – the daisies growing over me – O for this quiet – it will be my first.
John Keats (1795–1821) British poet.
In a letter to John Taylor by Joseph Severn, 6 Mar 1821

1839

353 Grieve not that I die young. Is it not well
To pass away ere life hath lost its brightness?
Lady Flora Hastings (1806–39) British poet.
Swan Song

354 There is a Reaper whose name is Death,
And, with his sickle keen,
He reaps the bearded grain at a breath,
And the flowers that grow between.
Henry Wadsworth Longfellow (1807–82) US poet.
The Reaper and the Flowers

1844

355 He'd make a lovely corpse.
Charles Dickens (1812–70) British novelist.
Martin Chuzzlewit, Ch. 25

1859

356 It is a far, far, better thing that I do, than I have ever done; it is a far, far, better rest that I go to, than I have ever known.
Charles Dickens
Said by Sydney Carton
A Tale of Two Cities, Bk. II, Ch. 15

1862

357 Go and try to disprove death. Death will disprove you, and that's all!
Ivan Turgenev (1818–83) Russian novelist.
Fathers and Sons, Ch. 27

1865

358 The bitterest tears shed over graves are for words left unsaid and deeds left undone.
Harriet Beecher Stowe (1811–96) US novelist.
Little Foxes, Ch. 3

Education, Knowledge, and Learning

1817

359 The primary imagination I hold to be the living power and prime agent of all human perception, and as a repetition in the finite mind of the eternal act of creation in the infinite I AM.
Samuel Taylor Coleridge (1772–1834) British poet.
Biographia Literaria, Ch. 13

1818

360 Axioms in philosophy are not axioms until they are proved upon our pulses; we read fine things but never feel them to the full until we have gone the same steps as the author.
John Keats (1795–1821) British poet.
Letter to J. H. Reynolds, 3 May 1818

361 He was sent, as usual, to a public school, where a little learning was painfully beaten into him, and from thence to the university, where it was carefully taken out of him.
Thomas Love Peacock (1785–1866) British novelist.
Nightmare Abbey, Ch. 1

1820

362* You will hear more good things on the outside of a stagecoach from London to Oxford than if you were to pass a twelvemonth with the undergraduates, or heads of colleges, of that famous university.
William Hazlitt (1778–1830) British essayist.
The Ignorance of the Learned

1823

363 Man is an intellectual animal, and therefore an

everlasting contradiction to himself. His senses centre in himself, his ideas reach to the ends of the universe; so that he is torn in pieces between the two, without a possibility of its ever being otherwise.
William Hazlitt
Characteristics

1828

364 My object will be, if possible to form Christian men, for Christian boys I can scarcely hope to make.
Thomas Arnold (1795–1842) British educator.
Letter on appointment as Headmaster of Rugby, 1828

365 Knowledge advances by steps, and not by leaps.
Lord Macaulay (1800–59) British historian.
Essays and Biographies, 'History'. *Edinburgh Review*

1830

366* Intellect is invisible to the man who has none.
Arthur Schopenhauer (1788–1860) German philosopher.
Aphorismen zur Lebensweisheit

1832

367 He never knew prosperity and adversity, passion nor satiety; he never had even the experiences which sickness gives . . . He knew no dejection, no heaviness of heart . . . He was a boy to the last.
John Stuart Mill (1806–73) British philosopher.
Referring to Jeremy Bentham
Dissertations

1835

368 What we must look for here is, first, religious and moral principles; secondly, gentlemanly conduct; thirdly, intellectual ability.
Thomas Arnold (1795–1842) British educator.
Address to the Scholars at Rugby

369 The highest intellects, like the tops of mountains, are the first to catch and to reflect the dawn.
Lord Macaulay (1800–59) British historian.
Historical Essays Contributed to the 'Edinburgh Review', 'Sir James Mackintosh'

1836

370 Be not the slave of Words.
Thomas Carlyle (1795–1881) Scottish historian and essayist.
Sartor Resartus, Bk. I, Ch. 8

1837

371 The difference between Orthodoxy or My-doxy and Heterodoxy or Thy-doxy.
Thomas Carlyle
A similar remark is attributed to the British churchman William Warburton (1698–1779)
History of the French Revolution, Pt. II, Bk. IV, Ch. 2

1839

372 When he has learnt that bottinney means a knowledge of plants, he goes and knows 'em. That's our system, Nickleby; what do you think of it?
Charles Dickens (1812–70) British novelist.
Said by Mr Squeers
Nicholas Nickleby, Ch. 8

373 There is an unseemly exposure of the mind, as well as of the body.
William Hazlitt (1778–1830) British essayist.
On Disagreeable People

1841

374 The true University of these days is a collection of books.
Thomas Carlyle (1795–1881) Scottish historian and essayist.
Heroes and Hero-Worship, 'The Hero as Man of Letters'

375 A foolish consistency is the hobgoblin of little minds, adored by little statesmen and philosophers and divines. With consistency a great soul has simply nothing to do.
Ralph Waldo Emerson (1803–82) US poet and essayist.
Essays, 'Self-reliance'

1845

376 Little things affect little minds.
Benjamin Disraeli (1804–81) British statesman.
Sybil, Bk. III, Ch. 2

1847

377 Reading is sometimes an ingenious device for avoiding thought.
Arthur Helps (1813–75) British historian.
Friends in Council

1848

378 I don't know, Ma'am, why they make all this fuss about education; none of the Pagets can read or write, and they get on well enough.
Lord Melbourne (1779–1848) British statesman.
Said to Queen Victoria
Attrib.

1850

379* A stand can be made against invasion by an army; no stand can be made against invasion by an idea.
Victor Hugo (1802–85) French writer.
Histoire d'un Crime, 'La Chute'

1851

380 To expect a man to retain everything that he has ever read is like expecting him to carry about in his body everything that he has ever eaten.
Arthur Schopenhauer (1788–1860) German philosopher.
Parerga and Paralipomena

1857

381 A thought is often original, though you have uttered it a hundred times.
Oliver Wendell Holmes (1809–94) US writer.
The Autocrat of the Breakfast Table, Ch. 1

1859

382 On earth there is nothing great but man; in man there is nothing great but mind.
William Hamilton (1788–1856) Scottish philosopher.
Lectures on Metaphysics

383 All good things which exist are the fruits of originality.
John Stuart Mill (1806–73) British philosopher.
On Liberty, Ch. 3

1860

384 A moment's insight is sometimes worth a life's experience.
Oliver Wendell Holmes (1809–94) US writer.
The Professor at the Breakfast Table, Ch. 10

1864

385 The true God, the mighty God, is the God of ideas.
Alfred de Vigny (1797–1863) French writer.
La Bouteille à la mer

1867

386 To make your children *capable of honesty* is the beginning of education.
John Ruskin (1819–1900) British art critic and writer.
Time and Tide, Letter VIII

History

1820

387* If men could learn from history, what lessons it might teach us! But passion and party blind our eyes and the light which experience gives is a lantern on the stern, which shines only on the waves behind us!
Samuel Taylor Coleridge (1772–1834) British poet.
Recollections (Allsop)

1825

388* What experience and history teach is this – that people and governments never have learned anything from history, or acted on principles deduced from it.
Hegel (1770–1831) German philosopher.
Philosophy of History, Introduction

1830

389 The past, at least, is secure.
Daniel Webster (1782–1852) US statesman.
Speech, US Senate, 26 Jan 1830

1838

390 History is the essence of innumerable biographies.
Thomas Carlyle (1795–1881) Scottish historian and essayist.
Critical and Miscellaneous Essays, 'History'

1840

391 There is properly no history; only biography.
Ralph Waldo Emerson (1803–82) US poet and essayist.
Essays, 'History'

1841

392 No great man lives in vain. The history of the world is but the biography of great men.
Thomas Carlyle (1795–1881) Scottish historian and essayist.
Heroes and Hero-Worship, 'The Hero as Divinity'

1848

393 The history of England is emphatically the history of progress.
Lord Macaulay (1800–59) British historian.
History of England

Human Nature

1816

394 Human nature is so well disposed towards those who are in interesting situations, that a young person, who either marries or dies, is sure to be kindly spoken of.
Jane Austen (1775–1817) British novelist.
Emma, Ch. 22

1817

395 But with the morning cool repentance came.
Walter Scott (1771–1832) Scottish novelist.
Rob Roy, Ch. 12

1818

396 Scenery is fine – but human nature is finer.
John Keats (1795–1821) British poet.
Letter to Benjamin Bailey, 13 Mar 1818

1820

397* Speech was given to man to disguise his thoughts.
Talleyrand (Charles Maurice de Talleyrand-Périgord; 1754–1838) French politician.
Attrib.

398 Upon the whole I dislike mankind: whatever people on the other side of the question may advance, they cannot deny that they are always surprised at hearing of a good action and never of a bad one.
John Keats (1795–1821) British poet.
Letter, 1820

399* Nobody ever did anything very foolish except from some strong principle.
Lord Melbourne (1779–1848) British statesman.
The Young Melbourne (Lord David Cecil)

1822

400 To great evils we submit; we resent little provocations.
William Hazlitt (1778–1830) British essayist.
On Great and Little Things

401 The human species, according to the best theory I can form of it, is composed of two distinct races, the men who borrow, and the men who lend.
Charles Lamb (1775–1834) British essayist.
Essays of Elia, 'The Two Races of Men'

402 Credulity is the man's weakness, but the child's strength.
Charles Lamb
Essays of Elia, 'Witches and other Night Fears'

403 Man is a gaming animal. He must always be trying to get the better in something or other.
Charles Lamb
Essays of Elia, 'Mrs Battle's Opinions on Whist'

404 How sickness enlarges the dimensions of a man's self to himself.
Charles Lamb
Last Essays of Elia, 'The Convalescent'

1827

405 What though the spicy breezes

Blow soft o'er Ceylon's isle;
Though every prospect pleases,
And only man is vile...
Reginald Heber (1783–1826) British bishop
and hymn writer .
From Greenland's Icy Mountains

1829

406 I do not know myself, and God forbid that I
should.
Goethe (1749–1832) German poet and
dramatist.
Conversations with Eckermann, 10 Apr 1829

1830

407 Woodman, spare that tree!
Touch not a single bough!
In youth it sheltered me,
And I'll protect it now.
George Pope Morris (1802–64) US
journalist.
Woodman, Spare That Tree

1836

408 There are three things which the public will al-
ways clamour for, sooner or later: namely,
Novelty, novelty, novelty.
Thomas Hood (1799–1845) British poet.
Announcement of *Comic Annual*, 1836

1839

409 The most fluent talkers or most plausible rea-
soners are not always the justest thinkers.
William Hazlitt (1778–1830) British essayist.
On Prejudice

410 When men understand what each other mean,
they see, for the most part, that controversy
is either superfluous or hopeless.
Cardinal Newman (1801–90) British
theologian.
Sermon, Oxford, Epiphany 1839

1840

411* Happiness is no laughing matter.
Richard Whately (1787–1863) British
churchman.
Apophthegms

412* A Friend may well be reckoned the masterpiece
of Nature.
Ralph Waldo Emerson (1803–82) US poet
and essayist.
Essays, 'Friendship'

413 You must not think me necessarily foolish because I am facetious, nor will I consider you
necessarily wise because you are grave.
Sydney Smith (1771–1845) British clergyman
and essayist.
Letter to Bishop Blomfield

1841

414 To be great is to be misunderstood.
Ralph Waldo Emerson (1803–82) US poet
and essayist.
Essays, 'Self-Reliance'

1844

415 Here's the rule for bargains: 'Do other men, for
they would do you.' That's the true business
precept.
Charles Dickens (1812–70) British novelist.
Martin Chuzzlewit, Ch. 11

1847

416 It is impossible, in our condition of society, not
to be sometimes a Snob.
William Makepeace Thackeray (1811–63)
British novelist.
The Book of Snobs, Ch. 3

417 Tears, idle tears, I know not what they mean,
Tears from the depth of some divine despair.
Alfred, Lord Tennyson (1809–92) British
poet.
The Princess, IV

418 He who meanly admires mean things is a Snob.
William Makepeace Thackeray (1811–63)
British novelist.
The Book of Snobs, Ch. 2

1849

419 Job endured everything – until his friends
came to comfort him, then he grew impatient.
Søren Kierkegaard (1813–55) Danish
philosopher.
Journal

1850

420 For words, like Nature, half reveal
And half conceal the Soul within.
Alfred, Lord Tennyson (1809–92) British
poet.
In Memoriam A.H.H., V

421 'Tis held that sorrow makes us wise.
Alfred, Lord Tennyson
In Memoriam A.H.H., CXIII

422* Tyndall, I must remain plain Michael Faraday to
the last; and let me now tell you, that if I accepted the honour which the Royal Society
desires to confer upon me, I would not answer
for the integrity of my intellect for a single
year.
Michael Faraday (1791–1867) British
scientist.
Said when Faraday was offered the Presidency
of the Royal Society
Faraday as a Discoverer (J. Tyndall), 'Illustra-
tions of Character'

1852

423 It is almost a definition of a gentleman to say that he is one who never inflicts pain.
Cardinal Newman (1801–90) British theologian.
The Idea of a University, 'Knowledge and Religious Duty'

1854

424 I never found the companion that was so companionable as solitude.
Henry David Thoreau (1817–62) US writer.
Walden, 'Solitude'

1855

425 Best be yourself, imperial, plain and true!
Robert Browning (1812–89) British poet.
Bishop Blougram's Apology

426 You find people ready enough to do the Samaritan, without the oil and twopence.
Sydney Smith (1771–1845) British clergyman and essayist.
Memoir (Lady Holland)

1858

427 Errors look so very ugly in persons of small means — one feels they are taking quite a liberty in going astray; whereas people of fortune may naturally indulge in a few delinquencies.
George Eliot (Mary Ann Evans; 1819–80) British novelist.
Janet's Repentance, Ch. 25

1860

428* The earth does not argue,
Is not pathetic, has no arrangements,
Does not scream, haste, persuade, threaten, promise,
Makes no discriminations, has no conceivable failures,
Closes nothing, refuses nothing, shuts none out.
Walt Whitman (1819–92) US poet.
To the sayers of words

429* One is happy as a result of one's own efforts, once one knows the necessary ingredients of happiness — simple tastes, a certain degree of courage, self denial to a point, love of work, and, above all, a clear conscience. Happiness is no vague dream, of that I now feel certain.
George Sand (Aurore Dupin, Baronne Dudevant; 1804–76) French novelist.
Correspondence, Vol. V

430 A person seldom falls sick, but the bystanders are animated with a faint hope that he will die.
Ralph Waldo Emerson (1803–82) US poet and essayist.
Conduct of Life, 'Considerations by the Way'

431 The louder he talked of his honour, the faster we counted our spoons.
Ralph Waldo Emerson
Conduct of Life, 'Worship'

432* If a man make a better mouse-trap than his neighbour, though he build his house in the woods, the world will make a beaten path to his door.
Ralph Waldo Emerson
Attrib.

1862

433 I agree with no man's opinion. I have some of my own.
Ivan Turgenev (1818–83) Russian novelist.
Fathers and Sons, Ch. 13

1863

434 He did not know that a keeper is only a poacher turned outside in, and a poacher a keeper turned inside out.
Charles Kingsley (1819–75) British writer.
The Water Babies, Ch. 1

1865

435* Resolve to be thyself: and know, that he
Who finds himself, loses his misery.
Matthew Arnold (1822–88) British poet and critic.
Self-Dependence

436* The gentleman will please remember that when his half-civilized ancestors were hunting the wild boar in Silesia, mine were princes of the earth.
Judah Philip Benjamin (1811–84) US politician.
Replying to a senator of Germanic origin who had made an antisemitic remark
Attrib.

Humour

1833

437 No mind is thoroughly well organized that is deficient in a sense of humour.
Samuel Taylor Coleridge (1772–1834) British poet.
Table Talk

1836

438 Sarcasm I now see to be, in general, the language of the devil.
Thomas Carlyle (1795–1881) Scottish historian and essayist.
Sartor Resartus, Bk. II, Ch. 4

1843

439 *Peccavi!*

I have sinned!
Charles James Napier (1782-1853) British general.
Reporting his subjugation of Sind, N India (Feb 1843)
Attrib.

1857
---

440 Sir, you are like a pin, but without either its head or its point.
Douglas William Jerrold (1803-57) British dramatist.
Speaking to a small thin man who was boring him
Attrib.

Life

1816
---

441 One half of the world cannot understand the pleasures of the other.
Jane Austen (1775-1817) British novelist.
Emma, Ch. 9

442 Nothing can be more obvious than that all animals were created solely and exclusively for the use of man.
Thomas Love Peacock (1785-1866) British novelist.
Headlong Hall, Ch. 2

1817
---

443 O for a life of sensations rather than of thoughts!
John Keats (1795-1821) British poet.
Letter to Benjamin Bailey, 22 Nov 1817

1819
---

444 Society is now one polish'd horde,
Form'd of two mighty tribes, the *Bores* and *Bored*.
Lord Byron (1788-1824) British poet.
Don Juan, XIII

445 Superstition is the poetry of life.
Goethe (1749-1832) German poet and dramatist.
Sprüche in Prosa, III

446 'Beauty is truth, truth beauty,' — that is all
Ye know on earth, and all ye need to know.
John Keats (1795-1821) British poet.
Ode on a Grecian Urn

447 Nothing ever becomes real till it is experienced
— even a proverb is no proverb to you till your life has illustrated it.
John Keats
Letter to George and Georgiana Keats, 19 Mar 1819

448 There is a Southern proverb, — fine words butter no parsnips.
Walter Scott (1771-1832) Scottish novelist.
The Legend of Montrose, Ch. 3

1820
---

449 When you have nothing to say, say nothing.
Charles Caleb Colton (?1780-1832) British clergyman and writer.
Lacon, Vol. I

450 Is there another life? Shall I awake and find all this a dream? There must be, we cannot be created for this sort of suffering.
John Keats (1795-1821) British poet.
Letter, 1820

1821
---

451 He hath awakened from the dream of life —
'Tis we, who lost in stormy visions, keep
With phantoms an unprofitable strife,
And in mad trance, strike with our spirit's knife
Invulnerable nothings.
Percy Bysshe Shelley (1792-1822) British poet.
Adonais, XXXIX

1822
---

452 We are nothing; less than nothing, and dreams. We are only what might have been, and must wait upon the tedious shores of Lethe millions of ages before we have existence, and a name.
Charles Lamb (1775-1834) British essayist.
In Greek mythology, Lethe was a river in the underworld, whose waters were drunk by souls about to be reborn in order to forget their past lives
Essays of Elia, 'Dream Children'

1823
---

453 If the world were good for nothing else, it is a fine subject for speculation.
William Hazlitt (1778-1830) British essayist.
Characteristics

1824
---

454 Fleas know not whether they are upon the body of a giant or upon one of ordinary size.
Walter Savage Landor (1775-1864) British poet and writer.
Imaginary Conversations, 'Southey and Porson'

455 Punctuality is the politeness of kings.
Louis XVIII (1755-1824) French king.
Attrib.

1830

456* We might have been — These are but common words,
And yet they make the sum of life's bewailing.
Letitia Landon (1802-38) British poet and novelist.
Three Extracts from the Diary of a Week

457* Oh, Vanity of vanities!
How wayward the decrees of Fate are;

How very weak the very wise,
How very small the very great are!
William Makepeace Thackeray (1811–63)
British novelist.
Vanitas Vanitatum

1838

458 The three great elements of modern civilization,
Gunpowder, Printing, and the Protestant
Religion.
Thomas Carlyle (1795–1881) Scottish historian and essayist.
Critical and Miscellaneous Essays, 'The State
of German Literature'

459 Popularity? It's glory's small change.
Victor Hugo (1802–85) French writer.
Ruy Blas, III

1840

460 Nothing great was ever achieved without
enthusiasm.
Ralph Waldo Emerson (1803–82) US poet
and essayist.
Essays, 'Circles'

1841

461 Men talk of killing time, while time quietly kills
them.
Dion Boucicault (Dionysius Lardner Boursiquot; 1820–90) Irish-born US actor and
dramatist.
London Assurance, II:1

1844

462 As she frequently remarked when she made
any such mistake, it would be all the same a
hundred years hence.
Charles Dickens (1812–70) British novelist.
Said by Mrs Squeers
Martin Chuzzlewit, Ch. 9

463 Almost everything that is great has been done
by youth.
Benjamin Disraeli (1804–81) British
statesman.
Coningsby, Bk. III, Ch. 1

1847

464 Revolts, republics, revolutions, most
No graver than a schoolboy's barring out.
Alfred, Lord Tennyson (1809–92) British
poet.
The Princess, Conclusion

1849

465 *Plus ça change, plus c'est la même chose.*
The more things change, the more they stay
the same.
Alphonse Karr (1808–90) French writer.
Les Guêpes, Jan 1849

1850

466* Time is a great teacher, but unfortunately it ki
all its pupils.
Hector Berlioz (1803–69) French compose
Almanach des lettres françaises

467* Some say that the age of chivalry is past, th
the spirit of romance is dead. The age of chiv
alry is never past, so long as there is a
wrong left unredressed on earth.
Charles Kingsley (1819–75) British writer.
Life (Mrs C. Kingsley), Vol. II, Ch. 28

468* To be alone is the fate of all great minds —
fate deplored at times, but still always chosen as the less grievous of two evils.
Arthur Schopenhauer (1788–1860) Germ
philosopher.
Aphorismen zur Lebensweisheit

469* I don't pretend to understand the Universe
it's a great deal bigger than I am ... People
ought to be modester.
Thomas Carlyle (1795–1881) Scottish hist
rian and essayist.
Attrib.

470 At last awake
From life, that insane dream we take
For waking now.
Robert Browning (1812–89) British poet.
Easter-Day, XIV

471* 'Tis better to have fought and lost,
Than never to have fought at all.
Arthur Hugh Clough (1819–61) British po
Peschiera

472 One God, one law, one element,
And one far-off divine event,
To which the whole creation moves.
Alfred, Lord Tennyson (1809–92) British
poet.
In Memoriam A.H.H., CXXXI

473 But what am I?
An infant crying in the night:
An infant crying for the light:
And with no language but a cry.
Alfred, Lord Tennyson
In Memoriam A.H.H., LIV

1851

474 Now, what I want is Facts ... Facts alone a
wanted in life.
Charles Dickens (1812–70) British novelis
Hard Times, Bk. I, Ch. 1

475 Remember that the most beautiful things in
world are the most useless, peacocks and li
ies for instance.
John Ruskin (1819–1900) British art critic a
writer.
The Stones of Venice, Vol. I, Ch. 2

476 The thing-in-itself, the will-to-live, exists wh
and undivided in every being, even in the tin

est; it is present as completely as in all that ever were, are, and will be, taken together.
Arthur Schopenhauer (1788–1860) German philosopher.
Parerga and Paralipomena

1853

477 Before this strange disease of modern life,
With its sick hurry, its divided aims.
Matthew Arnold (1822–88) British poet and critic.
The Scholar Gipsy

1854

478 Our life is frittered away by detail . . . Simplify, simplify.
Henry David Thoreau (1817–62) US writer.
Walden, 'Where I Lived, and What I Lived For'

479 Time is but the stream I go a-fishing in.
Henry David Thoreau
Walden, 'Where I Lived, and What I Lived For'

1855

480 Ah, but a man's reach should exceed his grasp,
Or what's a heaven for?
Robert Browning (1812–89) British poet.
Andrea del Sarto

1856

481 Since when was genius found respectable?
Elizabeth Barrett Browning (1806–61) British poet.
Aurora Leigh, Bk. VI

482 A great city is that which has the greatest men and women.
Walt Whitman (1819–92) US poet.
Song of the Broad-Axe, 5

1857

483 The world's great men have not commonly been great scholars, nor great scholars great men.
Oliver Wendell Holmes (1809–94) US writer.
The Autocrat of the Breakfast Table, Ch. 6

484 Life isn't all beer and skittles.
Thomas Hughes (1822–96) British novelist.
Tom Brown's Schooldays, Pt. I, Ch. 2

1858

485 Genius (which means transcendent capacity of taking trouble, first of all).
Thomas Carlyle (1795–1881) Scottish historian and essayist.
Frederick the Great, Vol. IV, Ch. 3

486 In these days a man is nobody unless his biography is kept so far posted up that it may be

ready for the national breakfast-table on the morning after his demise.
Anthony Trollope (1815–82) British novelist.
Doctor Thorne, Ch. 25

1859

487 The Wine of Life keeps oozing drop by drop,
The Leaves of Life keep falling one by one.
Edward Fitzgerald (1809–83) British poet.
The Rubáiyát of Omar Khayyám (4th edn.), VIII

488 Ah, my Belovéd, fill the Cup that clears
TO-DAY of past Regrets and Future Fears:
To-morrow! – Why, To-morrow I may be
Myself with Yesterday's Sev'n thousand Years.
Edward Fitzgerald
The Rubáiyát of Omar Khayyám (1st edn.), XX

489 Ah, fill the Cup: – what boots it to repeat
How Time is slipping underneath our Feet:
Unborn TOMORROW, and dead YESTERDAY,
Why fret about them if TODAY be sweet!
Edward Fitzgerald
The Rubáiyát of Omar Khayyám (1st edn.), XXXVII

490 No human being, however great, or powerful, was ever so free as a fish.
John Ruskin (1819–1900) British art critic and writer.
The Two Paths, Lecture V

491 For man is man and master of his fate.
Alfred, Lord Tennyson (1809–92) British poet.
Idylls of the King, 'The Marriage of Geraint'

1860

492* A wanderer is man from his birth.
He was born in a ship
On the breast of the river of Time.
Matthew Arnold (1822–88) British poet and critic.
The Future

493* If God were suddenly condemned to live the life which he has inflicted on men, He would kill Himself.
Alexandre Dumas, fils (1824–95) French writer.
Pensées d'album

494* Life is mostly froth and bubble;
Two things stand like stone,
Kindness in another's trouble,
Courage in your own.
Adam Lindsay Gordon (1833–70) Australian poet.
Ye Wearie Wayfarer, Fytte 8

495* The chess-board is the world; the pieces are the phenomena of the universe; the rules of the game are what we call the laws of Nature. The player on the other side is hidden from us. We know that his play is always fair, just, and patient. But also we know, to our cost, that he

never overlooks a mistake, or makes the smallest allowance for ignorance.
T. H. Huxley (1825–95) British biologist.
Lay Sermons, 'A Liberal Education'

1862

496 The temerity to believe in nothing.
Ivan Turgenev (1818–83) Russian novelist.
Fathers and Sons, Ch. 14

1863

497 To know how to say what others only know how to think is what makes men poets or sages; and to dare to say what others only dare to think makes men martyrs or reformers — or both.
Elizabeth Charles (1828–96) British writer.
Chronicle of the Schönberg-Cotta Family

1865

498 'If everybody minded their own business,' the Duchess said in a hoarse growl, 'the world would go round a deal faster than it does.'
Lewis Carroll (Charles Lutwidge Dodgson; 1832–98) British writer.
Alice's Adventures in Wonderland, Ch. 6

1868

499 It takes people a long time to learn the difference between talent and genius, especially ambitious young men and women.
Louisa May Alcott (1832–88) US novelist.
Little Women, Pt. II

Love and Sex

1819

500 Man's love is of man's life a thing apart,
'Tis woman's whole existence.
Lord Byron (1788–1824) British poet.
Don Juan, I

501 Now hatred is by far the longest pleasure;
Men love in haste, but they detest at leisure.
Lord Byron
Don Juan, XIII

502 Love is my religion — I could die for that.
John Keats (1795–1821) British poet.
Letter to Fanny Brawne, 13 Oct 1819

1822

503 Life may change, but it may fly not;
Hope may vanish, but can die not;
Truth be veiled, but still it burneth;
Love repulsed, — but it returneth!
Percy Bysshe Shelley (1792–1822) British poet.
Hellas, I

1837

504 If there is any country on earth where the course of true love may be expected to run smooth, it is America.
Harriet Martineau (1802–76) British writer.
Society in America, Vol. III, 'Marriage'

1840

505 In the Spring a young man's fancy lightly turns to thoughts of love.
Alfred, Lord Tennyson (1809–92) British poet.
Locksley Hall

1841

506 'There are strings', said Mr Tappertit, 'in the human heart that had better not be wibrated.'
Charles Dickens (1812–70) British novelist.
Barnaby Rudge, Ch. 22

1847

507 O tell her, brief is life but love is long.
Alfred, Lord Tennyson (1809–92) British poet.
The Princess, IV

1855

508 Onaway! Awake, beloved!
Henry Wadsworth Longfellow (1807–82) US poet.
Opening of the song sung by Chibiabos at Hiawatha's wedding feast; best known in the setting by Coleridge-Taylor
The Song of Hiawatha, XI, 'Hiawatha's Wedding feast'

1859

509 Love's like the measles — all the worse when it comes late in life.
Douglas William Jerrold (1803–57) British dramatist.
Wit and Opinions of Douglas Jerrold, 'A Philanthropist'

1860

510* The way to a man's heart is through his stomach.
Fanny Fern (1811–72) US writer.
Willis Parton

1865

511 All, everything that I understand, I understand only because I love.
Leo Tolstoy (1828–1910) Russian writer.
War and Peace, Bk. VII, Ch. 16

Marriage and the Family

1822

12 A poor relation – is the most irrelevant thing in nature.
Charles Lamb (1775–1834) British essayist.
Last Essays of Elia, 'Poor Relations'

13 Boys are capital fellows in their own way, among their mates; but they are unwholesome companions for grown people.
Charles Lamb
Essays of Elia, 'The Old and the New Schoolmaster'

1823

14 Mid pleasures and palaces though we may roam,
Be it ever so humble, there's no place like home;
...
Home, home, sweet, sweet home!
There's no place like home! there's no place like home!
John Howard Payne (1791–1852) US actor and dramatist.
Clari, or the Maid of Milan

1828

15 The majority of husbands remind me of an orangutang trying to play the violin.
Honoré de Balzac (1799–1850) French novelist.
La Physiologie du mariage

1837

16 ...the early marriages of silly children... where... every woman is married before she well knows how serious a matter human life is.
Harriet Martineau (1802–76) British writer.
Society in America, Vol. III, 'Marriage'

1847

17 This I set down as a positive truth. A woman with fair opportunities and without a positive hump, may marry whom she likes.
William Makepeace Thackeray (1811–63) British novelist.
Vanity Fair, Ch. 4

1853

18 It is a melancholy truth that even great men have their poor relations.
Charles Dickens (1812–70) British novelist.
Bleak House, Ch. 28

1862

19 For there is no friend like a sister
In calm or stormy weather;
To cheer one on the tedious way,
To fetch one if one goes astray,

To lift one if one totters down,
To strengthen whilst one stands.
Christina Rossetti (1830–74) British poet.
Goblin Market

1870

520 Every woman should marry – and no man.
Benjamin Disraeli (1804–81) British statesman.
Lothair, Ch. 30

Men and Women

1808

521 The extension of women's rights is the basic principle of all social progress.
Fourier, Charles (1772–1837) French social reformer.
Théorie des Quatre Mouvements

1818

522 A woman, especially if she have the misfortune of knowing anything, should conceal it as well as she can.
Jane Austen (1775–1817) British novelist.
Northanger Abbey, Ch. 14

1840

523 There are some meannesses which are too mean even for man – woman, lovely woman alone, can venture to commit them.
William Makepeace Thackeray (1811–63) British novelist.
A Shabby-Genteel Story, Ch. 3

1842

524 How sweet are looks that ladies bend
On whom their favours fall!
Alfred, Lord Tennyson (1809–92) British poet.
Sir Galahad

1843

525 O! men with sisters dear,
O! men with mothers and wives!
It is not linen you're wearing out,
But human creatures' lives!
Thomas Hood (1799–1845) British poet.
The Song of the Shirt

1844

526 What are little boys made of?
Frogs and snails
And puppy-dogs' tails,
That's what little boys are made of.
What are little girls made of?
Sugar and spice
And all that's nice,

That's what little girls are made of.
Nursery Rhymes (J. O. Halliwell)

1847
---

527   Man is the hunter; woman is his game:
The sleek and shining creatures of the chase,
We hunt them for the beauty of their skins.
Alfred, Lord Tennyson (1809–92) British
poet.
The Princess, V

528   Man for the field and woman for the hearth:
Man for the sword and for the needle she:
Man with the head and woman with the heart:
Man to command and woman to obey;
All else confusion.
Alfred, Lord Tennyson
The Princess, V

1850

529*   The fundamental fault of the female character is
that it has no sense of justice.
Arthur Schopenhauer (1788–1860) German
philosopher.
Gedanken über vielerlei Gegenstände, XXVII

530*   God made the woman for the man,
And for the good and increase of the world.
Alfred, Lord Tennyson (1809–92) British
poet.
Edwin Morris

1852
---

531   'Tis strange what a man may do, and a woman
yet think him an angel.
William Makepeace Thackeray (1811–63)
British novelist.
Henry Esmond, Ch. 7

1853
---

532   I do not ask for my rights. I have no rights; I
have only wrongs.
Caroline Norton (1808–77) British poet and
campaigner for women's rights.
Said when a court upheld her husband's refusal
to maintain her
Remark, Aug 1853

1855
---

533   God be thanked, the meanest of his creatures
Boasts two soul-sides, one to face the world
with,
One to show a woman when he loves her!
Robert Browning (1812–89) British poet.
One Word More, XVII

1859
---

534   I expect that Woman will be the last thing civilized by Man.
George Meredith (1828–1909) British
novelist.
The Ordeal of Richard Feverel, Ch. 1

1860
---

535   I should like to know what is the proper function of women, if it is not to make reasons for
husbands to stay at home, and still stronger
reasons for bachelors to go out.
George Eliot (Mary Ann Evans; 1819–80) Br
ish novelist.
The Mill on the Floss, Ch. 6

536*   ... is it to be understood that the principles
the Declaration of Independence bear no rela
tion to half of the human race?
Harriet Martineau (1802–76) British writer
Society in America, Vol. III, 'Marriage'

1863
---

537   I am a source of satisfaction to him, a nurse,
piece of furniture, a *woman* – nothing more
Sophie Tolstoy (1844–1919) Russian write
A Diary of Tolstoy's Wife, 1860–1891

1865

538*   It is only rarely that one can see in a little b
the promise of a man, but one can almost al
ways see in a little girl the threat of a
woman.
Alexandre Dumas, fils (1824–95) French
writer.
Attrib.

539   With many women I doubt whether there be
any more effectual way of touching their hear
than ill-using them and then confessing it. If
you wish to get the sweetest fragrance from
the herb at your feet, tread on it and bruise
Anthony Trollope (1815–82) British noveli
Miss Mackenzie, Ch. 10

1867
---

540   To employ women and children unduly is sim
ply to run into debt with Nature.
The Times, 4 Mar 1867

541   Women – one half the human race at least
care fifty times more for a marriage than a
ministry.
Walter Bagehot (1826–77) British econom
and journalist.
The English Constitution, 'The Monarchy'

1868
---

542   Housekeeping ain't no joke.
Louisa May Alcott (1832–88) US novelist
Little Women, Pt. I

543   ... girls are so queer you never know what
they mean. They say No when they mean Ye
and drive a man out of his wits for the fun of
...
Louisa May Alcott
Little Women, Pt. II

1869

544 The most important thing women have to do is to stir up the zeal of women themselves.
John Stuart Mill (1806–73) British philosopher.
Letter to Alexander Bain, 14 July 1869

Morality, Vices, and Virtues

1817

545 Nothing can permanently please, which does not contain in itself the reason why it is so, and not otherwise.
Samuel Taylor Coleridge (1772–1834) British poet.
Biographia Literaria, Ch. 14

546 I am certain of nothing but the holiness of the heart's affections and the truth of imagination – what the imagination seizes as beauty must be truth – whether it existed before or not.
John Keats (1795–1821) British poet.
Letter to Benjamin Bailey, 22 Nov 1817

1819

547 Though sages may pour out their wisdom's treasure,
There is no sterner moralist than Pleasure.
Lord Byron (1788–1824) British poet.
Don Juan, III

548 Agree to a short armistice with truth.
Lord Byron
Don Juan, III

549 The love of liberty is the love of others; the love of power is the love of ourselves.
William Hazlitt (1778–1830) British essayist.
The Times, 1819

550 'Beauty is truth, truth beauty,' – that is all
Ye know on earth, and all ye need to know.
John Keats (1795–1821) British poet.
Ode on a Grecian Urn

1824

551 Goodness does not more certainly make men happy than happiness makes them good.
Walter Savage Landor (1775–1864) British poet and writer.
Imaginary Conversations, 'Lord Brooke and Sir Philip Sidney'

1827

552 Murder considered as one of the Fine Arts.
Thomas De Quincey (1785–1859) British writer.
Essay title

1837

553 To a shower of gold most things are penetrable.
Thomas Carlyle (1795–1881) Scottish historian and essayist.
History of the French Revolution, Pt. I, Bk. III, Ch. 7

1839

554 The greatest offence against virtue is to speak ill of it.
William Hazlitt (1778–1830) British essayist.
On Cant and Hypocrisy

1840

555 The reward of a thing well done is to have done it.
Ralph Waldo Emerson (1803–82) US poet and essayist.
Essays, 'New England Reformers'

1842

556 My strength is as the strength of ten,
Because my heart is pure.
Alfred, Lord Tennyson (1809–92) British poet.
Sir Galahad

1847

557 Sorrow and silence are strong, and patient endurance is godlike.
Henry Wadsworth Longfellow (1807–82) US poet.
Evangeline

558 That a lie which is all a lie may be met and fought with outright,
But a lie which is part a truth is a harder matter to fight.
Alfred, Lord Tennyson (1809–92) British poet.
The Grandmother

1850

559* There are three kinds of lies: lies, damned lies and statistics.
Benjamin Disraeli (1804–81) British statesman.
Autobiography (Mark Twain)

560* Know how sublime a thing it is
To suffer and be strong.
Henry Wadsworth Longfellow (1807–82) US poet.
The Light of Stars

561* Honesty is the best policy; but he who is governed by that maxim is not an honest man.
Richard Whately (1787–1863) British churchman.
Apophthegms

1851
---

562   Better sleep with a sober cannibal than a
drunken Christian.
Herman Melville (1819–91) US novelist.
Moby Dick, Ch. 3

1852
---

563   What men call social virtues, good fellowship,
is commonly but the virtue of pigs in a litter,
which lie close together to keep each other
warm. It brings men together in crowds and
mobs in bar-rooms and elsewhere, but it does
not deserve the name of virtue.
Henry David Thoreau (1817–62) US writer.
Journal, 1852

1860
---

564   If you would hit the mark, you must aim a little
above it;
Every arrow that flies feels the attraction of
earth.
Henry Wadsworth Longfellow (1807–82)
US poet.
Elegiac Verse

565   Let us all be happy, and live within our means,
even if we have to borrer the money to do it
with.
Artemus Ward (Charles Farrar Browne; 1834–
67) US humorous writer.
Science and Natural History

566* We cannot kindle when we will
The fire which in the heart resides,
The spirit bloweth and is still,
In mystery our soul abides.
Matthew Arnold (1822–88) British poet and
critic.
Morality

567* Years hence, perhaps, may dawn an age,
More fortunate, alas! than we,
Which without hardness will be sage,
And gay without frivolity.
Matthew Arnold
The Grande Chartreuse

1862
---

568   Thou shalt not kill; but needst not strive
Officiously to keep alive.
Arthur Hugh Clough (1819–61) British poet.
The Latest Decalogue, 11

569   As for conceit, what man will do any good who
is not conceited? Nobody holds a good opinion of a man who has a low opinion of himself.
Anthony Trollope (1815–82) British novelist.
Orley Farm, Ch. 22

1864
---

570   Those who offend us are generally punished for
the offence they give; but we so frequently

miss the satisfaction of knowing that we are
avenged!
Anthony Trollope
The Small House at Allington, Ch. 50

1865
---

571   But men never violate the laws of God witho
suffering the consequences, sooner or later.
Lydia M. Child (1802–80) US abolitionist
campaigner.
The Freedmen's Book, 'Toussaint L'Ouverture

572   Everything's got a moral, if only you can find
Lewis Carroll (Charles Lutwidge Dodgson;
1832–98) British writer.
Alice's Adventures in Wonderland, Ch. 9

1867
---

573   What's a man's first duty? The answer's brie
To be himself.
Henrik Ibsen (1828–1906) Norwegian
dramatist.
Peer Gynt, IV:1

574   To kill a human being is, after all, the least i
jury you can do him.
Henry James (1843–1916) US novelist.
My Friend Bingham

1869
---

575   The pursuit of perfection, then, is the pursuit
sweetness and light. . . . He who works for
sweetness and light united, works to make rea
son and the will of God prevail.
Matthew Arnold (1822–88) British poet an
critic.
Culture and Anarchy, Ch. 1

Other People

1820

576* The English (it must be owned) are rather a
foul-mouthed nation.
William Hazlitt (1778–1830) British essayis
On Criticism

577* I found there a country with thirty-two religio
and only one sauce.
Talleyrand (Charles Maurice de Talleyrand-Pe
igord; 1754–1838) French politician.
Referring to America
Autant en apportent les mots (Pedrazzini)

1821
---

578   While spewy sands and gravel near London a
enclosed and built on, good lands in other
parts are neglected. These enclosures are a
waste; they are means misapplied; they are
proof of national decline and not of
prosperity.
William Cobbett (1763–1835) British journa
ist and writer.
Rural Rides

1822

579   I have been trying all my life to like Scotchmen, and am obliged to desist from the experiment in despair.
Charles Lamb (1775–1834) British essayist.
Essays of Elia, 'Imperfect Sympathies'

1835

580   The French want no-one to be their *superior*. The English want *inferiors*. The Frenchman constantly raises his eyes above him with anxiety. The Englishman lowers his beneath him with satisfaction. On either side it is pride, but understood in a different way.
Alexis de Tocqueville (1805–59) French writer, historian, and politician.
Voyage en Angleterre et en Irlande de 1835, 18 May

1847

581   Italy is a geographical expression.
Clement Metternich (1773–1859) Austrian diplomat and Chancellor.
Letter, 6 Aug 1847

1850

582*   Thirty millions, mostly fools.
Thomas Carlyle (1795–1881) Scottish historian and essayist.
When asked what the population of England was
Attrib.

1862

583   We cannot bring ourselves to believe it possible that a foreigner should in any respect be wiser than ourselves. If any such point out to us our follies, we at once claim those follies as the special evidences of our wisdom.
Anthony Trollope (1815–82) British novelist.
Orley Farm, Ch. 18

Religion

1816

584   If a man could pass through Paradise in a dream, and have a flower presented to him as a pledge that his soul had really been there, and if he found that flower in his hand when he awoke – Aye, and what then?
Samuel Taylor Coleridge (1772–1834) British poet.
Anima Poetae

1820

585   Men will wrangle for religion; write for it; fight for it; anything but – live for it.
Charles Caleb Colton (?1780–1832) British clergyman and writer.
Lacon, Vol. I

1825

586   He who begins by loving Christianity better than Truth will proceed by loving his own sect or church better than Christianity, and end by loving himself better than all.
Samuel Taylor Coleridge (1772–1834) British poet.
Aids to Reflection: Moral and Religious Aphorisms,

1833

587   Lead, kindly Light, amid the encircling gloom,
Lead thou me on;
The night is dark, and I am far from home,
Lead thou me on.
Cardinal Newman (1801–90) British theologian.
Lead Kindly Light

1836

588   You will be damned if you do – And you will be damned if you don't.
Lorenzo Dow (1777–1834) British churchman.
Speaking of Calvinism
Reflections on the Love of God

1840

589*   It established a religion without a prelate, a government without a king.
George Bancroft (1800–91) US historian.
Referring to Calvinism
History of the United States (1834–40), Vol. III

590*   The sedate, sober, silent, serious, sad-coloured sect.
Thomas Hood (1799–1845) British poet.
Referring to the Quakers
The Doves and the Crows

1841

591   All service ranks the same with God –
With God, whose puppets, best and worst,
Are we: there is no last or first.
Robert Browning (1812–89) British poet.
Pippa Passes, Pt. I

592   O come all ye faithful,
Joyful and triumphant,
O come ye, O come ye to Bethlehem.
Frederick Oakeley (1802–80) British churchman.
Translated from the Latin hymn, *Adeste Fideles*
O Come All Ye Faithful

1844

593   The religions we call false were once true.
Ralph Waldo Emerson (1803–82) US poet and essayist.
Essays, 'Character'

1845

594   Vain are the thousand creeds
That move men's hearts: unutterably vain;
Worthless as wither'd weeds.
Emily Brontë (1818–48) British novelist.
Last Lines

1848

595   Once in royal David's city
Stood a lowly cattle shed,
Where a Mother laid her Baby
In a manger for His bed:
Mary was that Mother mild,
Jesus Christ her little Child.
C. F. Alexander (1818–95) British hymn
writer.
Once in Royal David's City

596   *We can believe what we choose.* We are answerable for what we choose to believe.
Cardinal Newman (1801–90) British
theologian.
Letter to Mrs Froude, 27 June 1848

1850

597* If Jesus Christ were to come to-day, people
would not even crucify him. They would ask
him to dinner, and hear what he had to say, and
make fun of it.
Thomas Carlyle (1795–1881) Scottish historian and essayist.
Carlyle at his Zenith (D. A. Wilson)

598* Ride on! ride on in majesty!
In lowly pomp ride on to die.
Henry Hart Milman (1791–1868) British poet
and historian.
Ride On

599   Fight the good fight with all thy might,
Christ is thy strength and Christ thy right,
Lay hold on life, and it shall be
Thy joy and crown eternally.
John Monsell (1811–75) British hymn writer.
Hymn

600* Jesus loves me – this I know,
For the Bible tells me so.
Susan Warner (1819–85) US novelist.
The Love of Jesus

601   Though Rome's gross yoke
Drops off, no more to be endured,
Her teaching is not so obscured
By errors and perversities,
That no truth shines athwart the lies.
Robert Browning (1812–89) British poet.
Christmas Eve, XI

602   Religion . . . is the opium of the people.
Karl Marx (1818–83) German philosopher and
revolutionary.
Criticism of the Hegelian Philosophy of Right,
Introduction

603   And so the Word had breath, and wrought
With human hands the creed of creeds
In loveliness of perfect deeds,

More strong than all poetic thought.
Alfred, Lord Tennyson (1809–92) British
poet.
In Memoriam A.H.H., XXXVI

1852

604   Yes, about ten minutes.
Duke of Wellington (1769–1852) British general and statesman.
Responding to a vicar's query as to whether
there was anything he would like his forthcoming
sermon to be about
Attrib.

1855

605   I embrace the purpose of God and the doom
assigned.
Alfred, Lord Tennyson (1809–92) British
poet.
Maud, III

606   But the churchmen fain would kill their church,
As the churches have kill'd their Christ.
Alfred, Lord Tennyson
Maud, V

1856

607   God will pardon me. It is His trade.
Heinrich Heine (1797–1856) German poet
and writer.
Journal (Edmond and Charles Goncourt), 23 Feb
1863

1859

608   If thou shouldst never see my face again,
Pray for my soul. More things are wrought by
prayer
Than this world dreams of.
Alfred, Lord Tennyson (1809–92) British
poet.
Idylls of the King, 'The Passing of Arthur'

1860

609* Whatever a man prays for, he prays for a mira-
cle. Every prayer reduces itself to this: 'Great
God grant that twice two be not four.'
Ivan Turgenev (1818–83) Russian novelist.
Prayer

Science, Medicine, and Technology

1816

610   By machines mankind are able to do that which
their own bodily powers would never effect to
the same extent. Machines are the produce
of the mind of man; and their existence distin-
guishes the civilized man from the savage.
William Cobbett (1763–1835) British journalist and writer.
Letter to the Luddites of Nottingham

1822

1 In everything that relates to science, I am a whole Encyclopaedia behind the rest of the world.
Charles Lamb (1775–1834) British essayist.
Essays of Elia, 'The Old and the New Schoolmaster'

1827

2 I see no reason to suppose that these machines will ever force themselves into general use.
Duke of Wellington (1769–1852) British general and statesman.
Referring to steam locomotives
Geoffrey Madan's Notebooks (J. Gere)

1836

3 Man is a tool-using animal.
Thomas Carlyle (1795–1881) Scottish historian and essayist.
Sartor Resartus, Bk. I, Ch. 5

1854

4 Where observation is concerned, chance favours only the prepared mind.
Louis Pasteur (1822–95) French scientist.
Said at the inauguration of the Faculty of Science
Address, University of Lille, 7 Dec 1854

1859

5 We will now discuss in a little more detail the struggle for existence.
Charles Darwin (1809–82) British life scientist.
Origin of Species, Ch. 3

6 I have called this principle, by which each slight variation, if useful, is preserved, by the term of Natural Selection.
Charles Darwin
Origin of Species, Ch. 3

7 The expression often used by Mr Herbert Spencer of the Survival of the Fittest is more accurate, and is sometimes equally convenient.
Charles Darwin
Origin of Species, Ch. 3

1860

8 And, in conclusion, I would like to ask the gentleman . . . whether the ape from which he is descended was on his grandmother's or his grandfather's side of the family.
Samuel Wilberforce (1805–73) British churchman.
Speech, 30 June 1860

9 I asserted – and I repeat – that a man has no reason to be ashamed of having an ape for his grandfather. If there were an ancestor whom I should feel shame in recalling it would rather be a *man* – a man of restless and versatile intellect – who, not content with an equivocal

success in his own sphere of activity, plunges into scientific questions with which he has no real acquaintance, only to obscure them by an aimless rhetoric, and distract the attention of his hearers from the real point at issue by eloquent digressions and skilled appeals to religious prejudice.
T. H. Huxley (1825–95) British biologist.
Replying to Bishop Wilberforce in the debate on Darwin's theory of evolution at the meeting of the British Association at Oxford. No transcript was taken at the time; the version above is commonly quoted. After hearing Wilberforce's speech, and before rising himself, Huxley is said to have remarked, 'The Lord has delivered him into my hands!'
Speech, 30 June 1860

1864

620 The question is this: Is man an ape or an angel? I, my lord, am on the side of the angels.
Benjamin Disraeli (1804–81) British statesman.
Speech, 25 Nov 1864

1869

621 The highest wisdom has but one science – the science of the whole – the science explaining the whole creation and man's place in it.
Leo Tolstoy (1828–1910) Russian writer.
War and Peace, Bk.V, Ch. 2

622 Our body is a machine for living. It is organized for that, it is its nature. Let life go on in it unhindered and let it defend itself, it will do more than if you paralyse it by encumbering it with remedies.
Leo Tolstoy
War and Peace, Bk. X, Ch. 29

Wealth and Poverty

1816

623 Business, you know, may bring money, but friendship hardly ever does.
Jane Austen (1775–1817) British novelist.
Emma, Ch. 34

1829

624 To be poor and independent is very nearly an impossibility.
William Cobbett (1763–1835) British journalist and writer.
Advice to Young Men

1831

625 Respectable means rich, and decent means poor. I should die if I heard my family called decent.
Thomas Love Peacock (1785–1866) British novelist.
Crotchet Castle, Ch. 3

1850

626 Annual income twenty pounds, annual expenditure nineteen nineteen six, result happiness. Annual income twenty pounds, annual expenditure twenty pounds ought and six, result misery.
Charles Dickens (1812–70) British novelist.
David Copperfield, Ch. 12

1851

627 Wealth is like sea-water; the more we drink, the thirstier we become; and the same is true of fame.
Arthur Schopenhauer (1788–1860) German philosopher.
Parerga and Paralipomena

Work and Occupations

1831

628 Ours is composed of the scum of the earth.
Duke of Wellington (1769–1852) British general.
Referring to the British army
Remark, 4 Nov 1831

1837

629 Medical men all over the world having merely entered into a tacit agreement to call all sorts of maladies people are liable to, in cold weather, by one name; so that one sort of treatment may serve for all, and their practice thereby be greatly simplified.
Jane Welsh Carlyle (1801–66) The wife of Thomas Carlyle.
Letter to John Welsh, 4 Mar 1837

1839

630 A man willing to work, and unable to find work, is perhaps the saddest sight that fortune's inequality exhibits under the sun.
Thomas Carlyle (1795–1881) Scottish historian and essayist.
Chartism

1840

631* There is no class of men whose rewards are so disproprotionate to their usefulness to the community.
Lord John Russell (1792–1878) British statesman.
Referring to schoolmasters
Attrib.

1854

632 There are now-a-days professors of philosophy but not philosophers.
Henry David Thoreau (1817–62) US writer.
Walden, 'Economy'

633 As for doing good, that is one of the professions which are full.
Henry David Thoreau
Walden, 'Economy'

1859

634 The ugliest of trades have their moments of pleasure. Now, if I were a grave-digger, or ev a hangman, there are some people I could work for with a great deal of enjoyment.
Douglas William Jerrold (1803–57) Britis dramatist.
Wit and Opinions of Douglas Jerrold, 'Ugly Trades'

635 No *man*, not even a doctor, ever gives any other definition of what a nurse should be th this – 'devoted and obedient.' This definitio would do just as well for a porter. It might even do for a horse. It would not do for a policeman.
Florence Nightingale (1820–1910) British nurse.
Notes on Nursing

Sayings of the Time

1820

636 Imitation is the sincerest form of flattery.
Charles Caleb Colton (?1780–1832) Brit clergyman and writer.
Lacon, Vol. I

637* Publish and be damned!
Duke of Wellington (1769–1852) British g eral and statesman.
On being offered the chance to avoid mentior the memoirs of Harriette Wilson by giving he money
Attrib.

1826

638 The Last of the Mohicans.
James Fenimore Cooper (1789–1851) L novelist.
Title of Novel

1831

639 Only one man ever understood me.... And didn't understand me.
Hegel (1770–1831) German philosopher.
Said on his deathbed
Famous Last Words (B. Conrad)

1838

640 Monday's child is fair of face,
Tuesday's child is full of grace,
Wednesday's child is full of woe,
Thursday's child has far to go,
Friday's child is loving and giving,
Saturday's child works hard for his living,

And the child that is born on the Sabbath day
Is bonny and blithe, and good and gay.
Traditions of Devonshire (A. E. Bray)

1843

641   'God bless us every one!' said Tiny Tim, the last of all.
Charles Dickens (1812–70) British novelist.
A Christmas Carol

1844

642   All for one, and one for all.
Alexandre Dumas, père (1802–70) French novelist and dramatist.
The Three Musketeers

1849

643   Tinker,
Tailor,
Soldier,
Sailor,
Rich man,
Poor man,
Beggarman,
Thief.
Popular Rhymes and Nursery Tales (J. O. Halliwell)

1850

644*   I have no pain, dear mother, now;
But oh! I am so dry:
Just moisten poor Jim's lips once more;
And, mother, do not cry!
Edward Farmer (1809–76) British writer.
The Collier's Dying Child

645*   'But the Emperor has nothing on at all!' cried a little child.
Hans Christian Andersen (1805–75) Danish writer.
The Emperor's New Clothes

646*   The Ugly Duckling.
Hans Christian Andersen
Story title

647   I am well aware that I am the 'umblest person going . . . .My mother is likewise a very 'umble person. We live in a numble-abode.
Charles Dickens (1812–70) British novelist.
Said by Uriah Heep
David Copperfield, Ch. 16

648   Some circumstantial evidence is very strong, as when you find a trout in the milk.
Henry David Thoreau (1817–62) US writer.
Journal, 1850

1854

649   Beware of all enterprises that require new clothes.
Henry David Thoreau (1817–62) US writer.
Walden, 'Economy'

1855

650   Come into the garden, Maud,
For the black bat, night, has flown,
Come into the garden, Maud,
I am here at the gate alone.
Alfred, Lord Tennyson (1809–92) British poet.
Maud, I

1856

651   If suffer we must, let's suffer on the heights.
Victor Hugo (1802–85) French writer.
Contemplations, 'Les Malheureux'

1860

652*   All generalizations are dangerous, even this one.
Alexandre Dumas, fils (1824–95) French writer.
Attrib.

653*   The shades of night were falling fast,
As through an Alpine village passed
A youth, who bore, 'mid snow and ice,
A banner with the strange device,
Excelsior!
Henry Wadsworth Longfellow (1807–82) US poet.
Opening of a poem best known as a Victorian drawing-room ballad, and the butt of many music-hall jokes. Excelsior means 'higher' (Latin)
Excelsior

1864

654   The formula 'Two and two make five' is not without its attractions.
Fedor Mikhailovich Dostoevsky (1821–81) Russian novelist.
Notes from the Underground

1865

655   The Owl and the Pussy-Cat went to sea
In a beautiful pea-green boat,
They took some honey, and plenty of money,
Wrapped up in a five-pound note.
Edward Lear (1812–88) British artist and writer.
The Owl and the Pussy-Cat

1870

656   I'm the king of the castle,
Get down you dirty rascal.
Brand's Popular Antiquities

With Hindsight

20th century

657   Albert was merely a young foreigner, who suf-

fered from having no vices, and whose only
claim to distinction was that he had happened
to marry the Queen of England.
Lytton Strachey (1880–1932) British writer.
Queen Victoria, Ch. 5

658   Yet her conception of God was certainly not
orthodox. She felt towards Him as she might
have felt towards a glorified sanitary engineer;
and in some of her speculations she seems
hardly to distinguish between the Deity and the
Drains.
Lytton Strachey
Eminent Victorians, 'Florence Nightingale'

659   He was what I often think is a dangerous thing
for a statesman to be – a student of history;
and like most of those who study history, he
learned from the mistakes of the past how to
make new ones.
A. J. P. Taylor (1906–   ) British historian.
Referring to Napoleon III
The Listener, 6 June 1963

660   No writer before the middle of the 19th century
wrote about the working classes other than as
grotesque or as pastoral decoration. Then
when they were given the vote certain writers
started to suck up to them.
Evelyn Waugh (1903–66) British novelist.
Interview
Paris Review, 1963

11

The Age of Imperialism (1870–1913)

Although not formally proclaimed until 1871, the Prussian-dominated German empire was forged by the military defeat of France in the Franco-Prussian War (1870). Brash and confident, the new German empire epitomized the imperialism that dominated European politics in this period. Most of the European powers, ambitious for prestige and new trading outlets for their rapidly developing industries, acquired colonies in other continents. From 1880 to 1912 most of Africa was partitioned; by 1913 the European powers ruled most of the world. The greatest of these European empires was British, although her lead in industrial production was now challenged – and, by 1913, surpassed – by Germany. This aggressive economic competition was reflected in the political relations between the powers and inevitably in preparations for the next war; indeed, the first of the alliances that operated in World War I was established as early as 1879.

This period was also remarkable for two other major developments – one technological and the other political. The internal-combustion engine brought the car and aeroplane into people's lives, while the radio made instant communication possible between the ends of the earth. The political consequence of this advance of technology in the imperialist framework was the emergence of socialism; an inevitable reaction against the exploitation of the masses by the industrial barons, it was confined at first to a few revolutionaries. However, before long socialist ideas took root in many countries to form the basis of the political party of the working classes.

Politics, Government, and World Events

1870

1 The Chancellor of the Exchequer is a man whose duties make him more or less of a taxing machine. He is intrusted with a certain amount of misery which it is his duty to distribute as fairly as he can.
Robert Lowe (1811–92) British lawyer and politician.
Speech, House of Commons, 11 Apr 1870

1872

2 We will not go to Canossa.
Bismarck (1815–98) German statesman.
A declaration of his anti-Roman Catholic policy; the Emperor Henry IV had submitted to Pope Gregory VII at Canossa, N. Italy, in 1077
Speech, Reichstag, 14 May 1872

3 The wish to spread those opinions that we hold conducive to our own welfare is so deeply rooted in the English character that few of us can escape its influence.
Samuel Butler (1835–1902) British writer.
Erewhon, Ch. 20

4 It would be better that England should be free than that England should be compulsorily sober.
William Connor Magee (1821–91) British clergyman.
Speech on the Intoxicating Liquor Bill, House of Lords, 2 May 1872

1874

5 . . . a great master of gibes and flouts and jeers.
Benjamin Disraeli (1804–81) British statesman.
Referring to Lord Salisbury
Speech, House of Commons, 5 Aug 1874

1876

6 Let the Turks now carry away their abuses in the only possible manner, namely by carrying off themselves. Their Zaptiehs and their Mudirs, their Bimbashis and their Yuzbachis, their Kaimakans and their Pashas, one and all, bag and baggage, shall, I hope, clear out from the province they have desolated and profaned.
William Ewart Gladstone (1809–98) British statesman.
Reaction to the massacres of Bulgarians committed by Turkish Bashi-Bazouks (irregular troops)
The Bulgarian Horrors and the Question of the East (pamphlet, 6 Sept 1876)

7 The healthy bones of a single Pomeranian grenadier.
Bismarck (1815–98) German statesman.
A price too high for Germany to pay regarding the Eastern Question
Speech, Reichstag, 5 Dec 1876

8 I am dead: dead, but in the Elysian fields.
Benjamin Disraeli (1804–81) British statesman.
Said on his move to the House of Lords
Attrib.

9 One good turn deserves another.
Caption to a cartoon after Disraeli had become Earl of Beaconsfield; Queen Victoria had been proclaimed Empress of India on 1 May 1876
Punch, 16 Aug 1876

1877

10 Gladstone, like Richelieu, can't write. Nothing can be more unmusical, more involved or more uncouth than all his scribblement.
Benjamin Disraeli (1804–81) British statesman.
Letter, 3 Oct 1877

11 Many, if not most, of our Indian wars have had their origin in broken promises and acts of injustice on our part.
Rutherford B. Hayes (1822–93) US president.
Message to Congress, 4 Dec 1877

12 Men are made by nature unequal. It is vain, therefore, to treat them as if they were equal.
J. A. Froude (1818–94) British historian.
Short Studies on Great Subjects, 'Party Politics'

1878

13 An honest broker.
Bismarck (1815–98) German statesman.
His professed role in the diplomacy of 1878, including the Congress of Berlin
Speech, Reichstag, 19 Feb 1878

14 Lord Salisbury and myself have brought you back peace – but a peace I hope with honour.
Benjamin Disraeli (1804–81) British statesman.
Speech, House of Commons, 16 July 1878

15 A sophistical rhetorician inebriated with the exuberance of his own verbosity.
Benjamin Disraeli
Referring to Gladstone
Speech, 27 July 1878

16 We don't want to fight, but, by jingo if we do,
We've got the ships, we've got the men, we've got the money too.
We've fought the Bear before, and while Britons shall be true,
The Russians shall not have Constantinople.
George William Hunt (c. 1829–1904) British writer.
We Don't Want to Fight

17 The state is not 'abolished', it withers away.
Friedrich Engels (1820–95) German communist.
Anti-Dühring

18 I always voted at my party's call,
And I never thought of thinking for myself at all.
W. S. Gilbert (1836–1911) British dramatist.
HMS Pinafore, I

19 Horny-handed sons of toil.
Denis Kearney (1847–1907) US trade-union leader.
Speech, San Francisco, c. 1878

1879
---

20 I am tired and sick of war. Its glory is all moonshine . . . War is hell.
General William Sherman (1820–91) US general.
Attrib. in address, Michigan Military Academy, 19 June 1879

1880
---

21 Force is not a remedy.
John Bright (1811–89) British radical politician.
Speech, Birmingham, 16 Nov 1880

22 When a man takes a farm from which another has been evicted, you must show him . . . by leaving him severely alone, by putting him into a moral Coventry, by isolating him from his kind as if he were a leper of old – you must show him your detestation of the crimes he has committed.
Charles Stewart Parnell (1846–91) Member of Parliament and champion of Irish Home Rule.
The first person to be so treated was a Captain Boycott – hence the verb, 'to boycott'
Speech, Ennis, 19 Sept 1880

23* He speaks to Me as if I was a public meeting.
Victoria (1819–1901) Queen of the United Kingdom.
Referring to Gladstone
Collections and Recollections (G. W. E. Russell), Ch. 14

24* Walk wide o' the Widow at Windsor,
For 'alf o' Creation she owns:
We have bought 'er the same with sword an' the flame,
An' we've salted it down with our bones.
Rudyard Kipling (1865–1936) Indian-born British writer.
Referring to Queen Victoria
The Widow at Windsor

1881
---

25 The danger is not that a particular class is unfit to govern. Every class is unfit to govern.
Lord Acton (1834–1902) British historian.
Letter to Mary Gladstone, 1881

26 No, it is better not. She will only ask me to take a message to Albert.
Benjamin Disraeli (1804–81) British statesman.
On his deathbed, declining an offer of a visit from Queen Victoria

27 . . . a man who, with all his great qualities, was unable to decide a general principle of action, or to ensure that when decided on it should be carried out by his subordinates.
Marquess of Salisbury (1830–1903) British statesman.
Referring to Benjamin Disraeli
Chapters of Autobiography (A. J. Balfour)

28* A balanced state of well-modulated dissatisfaction.
Eduard, Count von Taaffe (1833–95) Austrian Prime Minister (1868–70, 1879–93).
Referring to his policy towards nationalistic tensions within the Austro-Hungarian Empire
Remark

29* It was a brilliant affair; water flowed like champagne.
William M. Evarts (1818–1901) US lawyer and statesman.
Describing a dinner given by US President Rutherford B. Hayes (1877–81), an advocate of temperance
Attrib.

30 Log-cabin to White House.
W. M. Thayer (1820–98) US writer.
The title of his biography of James Garfield, 20th US president (1881), who was assassinated soon after taking office

---
1882
---

31 Argue as you please, you are nowhere, that grand old man, the Prime Minister, insists on the other thing.
Lord Northcote (1818–87) British statesman.
Referring to Gladstone; the phrase, and its acronym GOM, became his nickname – temporarily reversed to MOG ('Murderer of Gordon') in 1885, after the death of General Gordon at Khartoum
Speech, Liverpool, 12 Apr 1882

32 Bow, bow, ye lower middle classes!
Bow, bow, ye tradesmen, bow, ye masses!
W. S. Gilbert (1836–1911) British dramatist.
Iolanthe, I

33 The House of Peers, throughout the war,
Did nothing in particular,
And did it very well.
W. S. Gilbert
Iolanthe, II

34 I often think it's comical
How Nature always does contrive
That every boy and every gal
That's born into the world alive
Is either a little Liberal
Or else a little Conservative!
W. S. Gilbert
Iolanthe, II

35 The majority has the might – more's the pity

but it hasn't right . . . The minority is always right.
Henrik Ibsen (1828–1906) Norwegian dramatist.
An Enemy of the People, IV

6　The worst enemy of truth and freedom in our society is the compact majority. Yes, the damned, compact, liberal majority.
Henrik Ibsen
An Enemy of the People, IV

1883

7　Lord Salisbury constitutes himself the spokes-man of a class, of the class to which he him-self belongs, who 'toil not neither do they spin'.
Joseph Chamberlain (1836–1914) British politician.
Referring to the aristocracy
Speech, Birmingham, 30 Mar 1883

8　We the English seem, as it were, to have con-quered and peopled half the world in a fit of absence of mind.
John Robert Seeley (1834–95) British historian.
The Expansion of England, I

9　The philosophers have only interpreted the world in various ways; the point is to change it.
Karl Marx (1818–1883) German philosopher and revolutionary.
Theses on Feuerbach

10　All I know is that I am not a Marxist.
Karl Marx
Attrib.

11　Eena, meena, mina, mo,
Catch a nigger by his toe;
If he hollers, let him go,
Eena, meena, mina, mo.
Games and Songs of American Children
(Newell)

1884

2　The Empire is a Commonwealth of Nations.
Earl of Rosebery (1847–1929) British statesman.
Speech, Adelaide, 18 Jan 1884

3　For the purposes of recreation he has selected the felling of trees, and we may usefully re-mark that his amusements, like his politics, are essentially destructive . . . The forest laments in order that Mr Gladstone may perspire.
Randolph Churchill (1849–95) British Con-servative politician.
Speech, Blackpool, 24 Jan 1884

4　The liberty the citizen enjoys is to be measured not by the governmental machinery he lives under, whether representative or other, but by the paucity of restraints it imposes on him.
Herbert Spencer (1820–1903) British philospher.
Man versus the State

1885

45　The G.O.M., when his life ebbs out,
Will ride in a fiery chariot,
And sit in state
On a red-hot plate
Between Pilate and Judas Iscariot.
Anonymous
Gladstone, known as the Grand Old Man, was blamed for the death of General Gordon at Khartoum
The Faber Book of English History in Verse
(Kenneth Baker)

46　No man has a right to fix the boundary of the march of a nation; no man has a right to say to his country – thus far shalt thou go and no further.
Charles Stewart Parnell (1846–1891) Irish politician.
Speech at Cork, 21 Jan 1885

47　The public be damned. I am working for my stockholders.
William Henry Vanderbilt (1821–85) US railway chief.
Refusing to speak to a reporter, who was seek-ing to find out his views on behalf of the public

48　Three acres and a cow.
Jesse Collings (1831–1920) British politician.
Slogan used in his land-reform propaganda

1886

49　Ulster will fight; Ulster will be right.
Randolph Churchill (1849–95) British Con-servative politician.
Letter, 7 May 1886

50　All the world over, I will back the masses against the classes.
William Ewart Gladstone (1809–98) British statesman.
Speech, Liverpool, 28 June 1886

51　An old man in a hurry.
Randolph Churchill (1849–95) British Con-servative politician.
Referring to Gladstone
Speech, June 1886

52　Give me your tired, your poor,
Your huddled masses yearning to breathe free,
The wretched refuse of your teeming shore,
Send these, the homeless, tempest-tossed to me,
I lift my lamp beside the golden door!
Emma Lazarus (1849–87) US poet and philanthropist.
Used as an inscription on the Statue of Liberty
The New Colossus

53　Dialect words – those terrible marks of the beast to the truly genteel.
Thomas Hardy (1840–1928) British novelist.
The Mayor of Casterbridge, Ch. 20

1887

54　Power tends to corrupt, and absolute power

corrupts absolutely. Great men are almost al-
ways bad men . . . There is no worse heresy
than that the office sanctifies the holder of it.
Lord Acton (1834–1902) British historian.
Often misquoted as 'Power corrupts . . . '
Letter to Bishop Mandell Creighton, 5 Apr 1887

1888

55 We are part of the community of Europe and we
must do our duty as such.
Marquess of Salisbury (1830–1903) British
statesman.
Speech, Caernarvon, 11 Apr 1888

56 I haven't got time to be tired.
Wilhelm I (1797–1888) King of Prussia and
Emperor of Germany.
Said during his last illness

57 Eight little whores, with no hope of Heaven,
Gladstone may save one, then there'll be
seven.
Seven little whores begging for a shilling,
One stays in Heneage Court, then there's a
killing.

Six little whores, glad to be alive,
One sidles up to Jack, then there are five.
Four and whore rhyme aright, so do three and
me.
I'll set the town alight, ere there are two.

Two little whores, shivering with fright,
Seek a cosy doorway, in the middle of the
night.
Jack's knife flashes, then there's but one.
And the last one's ripest for Jack's idea of
fun.
Anonymous
Referring to the Whitechapel Murders (1888) –
a series of savage murders of about six prostitutes in the Whitechapel area of London. The
murderer, who was never caught, was
nicknamed 'Jack the Ripper' because of the extensive mutilation of most of the corpses
The Faber Book of English History in Verse
(Kenneth Baker)

58 I'm not a butcher,
I'm not a Yid,
Nor yet a foreign skipper,
But I'm your own light-hearted friend,
Yours truly, Jack the Ripper.
Anonymous
The Faber Book of English History in Verse
(Kenneth Baker)

59 Jack the Ripper's dead,
And lying in his bed.
He cut his throat
With Sunlight Soap.
Jack the Ripper's dead.
Anonymous
The Faber Book of English History in Verse
(Kenneth Baker)

1889

60 The Austrian Government . . . is a system of
despotism tempered by casualness.
Victor Adler (1852–1918) Austrian social
Speech, International Socialist Congress, Pa
17 July 1889

61 The people's flag is deepest red;
It shrouded oft our martyred dead,
And ere their limbs grew stiff and cold,
Their heart's blood dyed its every fold.
Then raise the scarlet standard high!
Within its shade we'll live or die.
Tho' cowards flinch and traitors sneer,
We'll keep the red flag flying here.
James Connell (1852–1929) British soci
Traditionally sung at the close of annual con
ences of the British Labour Party
The Red Flag, in *Songs that made History* (
Piggot), Ch. 6

1890

62 Dropping the pilot.
John Tenniel (1820–1914) British illustra
and cartoonist.
Caption of a cartoon; the cartoon refers to
marck's resignation portraying him as a ship
pilot walking down the gangway of the ship
while Wilhelm II watches from the deck
Punch, 29 Mar 1890

63 The white man knows how to make everyth
but he does not know how to distribute it.
Sitting Bull (c. 1834–90) US Sioux India
chief.
Attrib.

1891

64 I will not accept if nominated, and will not s
if elected.
General William Sherman (1820–91) U
politician and president.
Replying to a request that he accept the Rep
can presidential nomination
Attrib.

65 Democracy means simply the bludgeoning
the people by the people for the people.
Oscar Wilde (1854–1900) Irish-born Briti
dramatist.
The Soul of Man under Socialism

1892

66 The danger to the country, to Europe, to h
vast Empire, which is involved in having all
these great interests entrusted to the shak
hand of an old, wild, and incomprehensibl
man of 82½, is very great!
Victoria (1819–1901) Queen of the Unite
Kingdom.
Reaction to Gladstone's fourth and last app
ment as prime minister, 1892
Letter to Lord Lansdowne, 12 Aug 1892

67 Lizzie Borden took an axe
And gave her mother forty whacks;

When she saw what she had done
She gave her father forty-one!
Anonymous
On 4 Aug 1892 in Fall River, Massachusetts, Lizzie Borden was acquitted of the murder of her stepmother and her father

1893

68   It is only when you get to see and realize what India is — that she is the strength and the greatness of England — it is only then that you feel that every nerve a man may strain, every energy he may put forward, cannot be devoted to a nobler purpose than keeping tight the cords that hold India to ourselves.
George Curzon (1859–1925) British politician.
Speech, Southport, 15 Mar 1893

69   Between complete Socialism and Communism there is no difference whatever in my mind. Communism is in fact the completion of Socialism; when that ceases to be militant and becomes triumphant, it will be communism.
William Morris (1834–96) English Utopian socialist.
Lecture to the Hammersmith Socialist Society, 1893

70   O beautiful for spacious skies,
For amber waves of grain,
For purple mountain majesties
Above the fruited plain!
America! America!
God shed His grace on thee
And crown thy good with brotherhood
From sea to shining sea!
Katharine Lee Bates (1859–1929) US writer and poet.
America the Beautiful

1894

71   Before Irish Home Rule is conceded by the Imperial Parliament, England as the predominant member of the three kingdoms will have to be convinced of its justice and equity.
Lord Rosebery (1847–1929) British statesman.
Speech, House of Lords, 11 Mar 1894

72   The majestic egalitarianism of the law, which forbids rich and poor alike to sleep under bridges, to beg in the streets, and to steal bread.
Anatole France (Jacques Anatole François Thibault; 1844–1924) French writer.
The Red Lily, Ch. 7

1895

73*   I dreamt that I was making a speech in the House. I woke up, and by Jove I was!
Duke of Devonshire (1833–1908) Conservative politician.
Thought and Adventures (W. S. Churchill)

74   The duty of an opposition is to oppose.
Randolph Churchill (1849–95) British Conservative politician.
Lord Randolph Churchill (W. S. Churchill)

1896

75   I shall maintain the principle of autocracy just as firmly and unflinchingly as it was upheld by my own ever to be remembered dead father.
Nicholas II (1868–1918) Tsar of Russia.
Declaration to representatives of Tver, 17 Jan 1896

76   The German Empire has become a world empire.
Wilhelm II (1859–1941) King of Prussia and Emperor of Germany.
Speech, Berlin, 18 Jan 1896

77   We have stood alone in that which is called isolation — our splendid isolation, as one of our colonial friends was good enough to call it.
George Joachim Goschen (1831–1907) English Conservative politician.
Speech, Lewes, 26 Feb 1896

78   East and west on fields forgotten
Bleach the bones of comrades slain,
Lovely lads and dead and rotten;
None that go return again.
A. E. Housman (1859–1936) British scholar and poet.
A Shropshire Lad, 'The Welsh Marches'

79   Written by office boys for office boys.
Marquess of Salisbury (1830–1903) British statesman.
Reaction to the launch of the *Daily Mail*, 1896
Northcliffe, an Intimate Biography (Hamilton Fyfe), Ch. 4

1897

80   Move Queen Anne? Most certainly not! Why it might some day be suggested that *my* statue should be moved, which I should much dislike.
Victoria (1819–1901) Queen of the United Kingdom.
Said at the time of her Diamond Jubilee (1897), when it was suggested that the statue of Queen Anne should be moved from outside St. Paul's
Men, Women and Things (Duke of Portland), Ch. 5

81   The British soldier can stand up to anything except the British War Office.
George Bernard Shaw (1856–1950) Irish dramatist and critic.
The Devil's Disciple, II

82   It is by the goodness of God that in our country we have those three unspeakably precious things: freedom of speech, freedom of conscience, and the prudence never to practise either of them.
Mark Twain (Samuel Langhorne Clemens; 1835–1910) US writer.
Following the Equator, heading of Ch. 20

1898

83 If there is ever another war in Europe, it will come out of some damned silly thing in the Balkans.
Bismarck (1815–98) German statesman.
Remark to Ballen, shortly before Bismarck's death

84 Whatever happens, we have got
The Maxim Gun, and they have not.
Hilaire Belloc (1870–1953) French-born British poet.
Referring to African natives
The Modern Traveller

85 Don't cheer, boys; the poor devils are dying.
John Woodward Philip (1840–1900) US naval officer.
Restraining his victorious crew during the naval battle off Santiago in the Spanish-American War
Attrib.

86 *J'accuse.*
I accuse.
Emile Zola (1840–1902) French novelist.
Title of an open letter to the French President, denouncing the French army's conduct in the Dreyfus affair – a major political scandal in France that centred on the false conviction (1894) of Albert Dreyfus, a Jewish army officer, for betraying state secrets
L'Aurore, 13 Jan 1898

87 Truth is on the march; nothing can stop it now.
Emile Zola
Referring to the Dreyfus affair
Attrib.

88 I know not whether Laws be right,
Or whether Laws be wrong;
All that we know who lie in gaol
Is that the wall is strong;
And that each day is like a year,
A year whose days are long.
Oscar Wilde (1854–1900) Irish-born British dramatist.
The Ballad of Reading Gaol, V:1

1899

The Boer War (1899–1902)

The result of tensions between British and Boer (Afrikaner) settlers in southern Africa, the war was initially a success for the Boers. Large numbers of British reinforcements then forced them to adopt guerilla tactics. The British, under Lord Kitchener, responded by devastating the countryside and rounding up the population into concentration camps, where some 20 000 Boer women and children died. Finally brought to acknowledge defeat, the Boers' republics were annexed by Britain.

89 Please understand that there is no one depressed in *this* house; we are not interested in the possibilities of defeat; they do not exist.
Victoria (1819–1901) Queen of the United Kingdom.
Referring to the Boer War; said to Balfour
Life of Salisbury (Lady G. Cecil)

90 I thought he was a young man of promise; but it appears he was a young man of promises.
Arthur Balfour (1848–1930) British statesman.
Said of Winston Churchill on his entry into politics, 1899
Winston Churchill (Randolph Churchill), Vol. I

91 Conspicuous consumption of valuable goods is a means of reputability to the gentleman of leisure.
Thorstein Bunde Veblen (1857–1929) US social scientist.
The Theory of the Leisure Class

1900s

92 The Admiral of the Atlantic salutes the Admiral of the Pacific.
Wilhelm II (1859–1941) King of Prussia and Emperor of Germany.
Telegram sent to Czar Nicholas II during a naval exercise
The Shadow of the Winter Palace (E. Crankshaw)

93 And when we open our dykes, the waters are ten feet deep.
Wilhelmina (1880–1962) Queen of the Netherlands.
Replying to a boast by Wilhelm II of Germany that his guardsmen were all seven feet tall
Attrib.

1900

94 It is beginning to be hinted that we are a nation of amateurs.
Earl of Rosebery (1847–1929) British statesman.
Rectorial Address, Glasgow, 16 Nov 1900

95* Take up the White Man's burden –
And reap his old reward:
The blame of those ye better,
The hate of those ye guard.
Rudyard Kipling (1865–1936) Indian-born British writer.
The White Man's Burden

96* The radical invents the views. When he has worn them out, the conservative adopts them.
Mark Twain (Samuel Langhorne Clemens; 1835–1910) US writer.
Notebooks

1901

97 When was a war not a war? When it was carried on by methods of barbarism.
Henry Campbell-Bannerman (1836–1908) British statesman.
Referring to the Boer War
Speech, National Reform Union Dinner, 14 June 1901

98 There is a homely adage which runs 'Speak softly and carry a big stick, you will go far'.
Theodore Roosevelt (1858–1919) US Republican president.
Speech, Minnesota State Fair, 2 Sept 1901

99 You have to clean your plate.
Lord Rosebery (1847–1929) British statesman.
Said to the Liberal Party
Speech, Chesterfield, 16 Dec 1901

100 'My country, right or wrong' is a thing that no patriot would think of saying, except in a desperate case. It is like saying 'My mother, drunk or sober.'
G. K. Chesterton (1874–1936) British writer.
The Defendant

101 The time's come: there's a terrific thundercloud advancing upon us, a mighty storm is coming to freshen us up.... It's going to blow away all this idleness and indifference, and prejudice against work.... I'm going to work, and in twenty-five or thirty years' time every man and woman will be working.
Anton Chekhov (1860–1904) Russian dramatist.
Three Sisters, I

102 To disarm the strong and arm the weak would be to change the social order which it's my job to preserve. Justice is the means by which established injustices are sanctioned.
Anatole France (Jacques Anatole François Thibault; 1844–1924) French writer.
Crainquebille

1902

103 Perhaps it is God's will to lead the people of South Africa through defeat and humiliation to a better future and a brighter day.
Jan Smuts (1870–1950) South African statesman and general.
Speaking to Boer delegates at the peace conference that ended the Boer War
Speech, Vereeniging, 31 May 1902

104 Three words made peace and union in South Africa: 'methods of barbarism'.
Louis Botha (1862–1919) South African statesman.
Life of Campbell-Bannerman (J. A. Spender)

105 The rights and interests of the laboring man will be protected and cared for, not by the labor agitators, but by the Christian men to whom God in His infinite wisdom has given control of the property interests of the country.
George Baer (1842–1914) American railroad magnate.
Written during the Pennsylvania miners' strike
Letter to the press, Oct 1902

106 The first requisite of a good citizen in this Republic of ours is that he shall be able and willing to pull his weight.
Theodore Roosevelt (1858–1919) US Republican president.
Speech, New York, 11 Nov 1902

107 Remember that you are an Englishman, and have consequently won first prize in the lottery of life.
Cecil Rhodes (1853–1902) South African statesman.
Dear Me (Peter Ustinov), Ch. 4

108 So little done, so much to do.
Cecil Rhodes
Attrib.

109 ... militarism ... is one of the chief bulwarks of capitalism, and the day that militarism is undermined, capitalism will fail.
Helen Keller (1880–1968) US writer and lecturer.
The Story of My Life

1903

110 ... content to follow mechanically the lead given by their fathers. They worked shorter hours, and they exerted themselves less to obtain new practical ideas than their fathers had done, and thus a part of England's leadership was destroyed rapidly. In the 'nineties it became clear that in the future Englishmen must take business as seriously as their grandfathers had done, and as their American and German rivals were doing: that their training for business must be methodical, like that of their new rivals, and not merely practical, on lines that had sufficed for the simpler world of two generations ago: and lastly that the time had passed at which they could afford merely to teach foreigners and not learn from them in return.
Alfred Marshall (1842–1924) British economist.
Referring to British manufacturers
Memorandum; White Paper, 1908

111 In an English ship, they say, it is poor grub, poor pay, and easy work; in an American ship, good grub, good pay, and hard work. And this is applicable to the working populations of both countries.
Jack London (1876–1916) US novelist.
The People of the Abyss, Ch. 20

112 A man who is good enough to shed his blood for the country is good enough to be given a square deal afterwards. More than that no man

is entitled to, and less than that no man shall have.
Theodore Roosevelt (1858–1919) US Republican president.
Speech at the Lincoln Monument, Springfield, Illinois, 4 June 1903

113 Give women the vote, and in five years there will be a crushing tax on bachelors.
George Bernard Shaw (1856–1950) Irish dramatist.
Man and Superman, Preface

114 Titles distinguish the mediocre, embarrass the superior, and are disgraced by the inferior.
George Bernard Shaw
Man and Superman, 'Maxims for Revolutionists'

115* Democracy substitutes election by the incompetent many for appointment by the corrupt few.
George Bernard Shaw
Man and Superman, 'Maxims for Revolutionists'

116* Liberty means responsibility. That is why most men dread it.
George Bernard Shaw
Man and Superman, 'Maxims for Revolutionists'

117 I am a gentleman. I live by robbing the poor.
George Bernard Shaw
Man and Superman

118 Kings are not born, they are made by artificial hallucination.
George Bernard Shaw
Man and Superman

1904

119 Provided that the City of London remains as at present, the Clearing-house of the World.
Joseph Chamberlain (1836–1914) British politician.
Speech, Guildhall, London, 19 Jan 1904

120 The day of small nations has long passed away. The day of Empires has come.
Joseph Chamberlain
Speech, Birmingham, 12 May 1904

121 You cannot feed the hungry on statistics.
David Lloyd George (1863–1945) British Liberal statesman.
Advocating Tariff Reform
Speech, 1904

122 In the Western hemisphere the adherence of the United States to the Monroe Doctrine may force the United States, however reluctantly, in flagrant cases of wrongdoing or impotence, to the exercise of an international police power.
Theodore Roosevelt (1858–1919) US Republican president.
Message to Congress, 6 Dec 1904

123 We are all Socialists now.
William Harcourt (1827–1904) British statesman.
Attrib.

1905

124 'It is my duty to warn you that it will be used against you,' cried the Inspector, with the magnificent fair play of the British criminal law.
Arthur Conan Doyle (1856–1930) British writer.
The Dancing Men

1906

125 I am a Catholic. As far as possible I go to Mass every day. As far as possible I kneel down and tell these beads every day. If you reject me on account of my religion, I shall thank God that he has spared me the indignity of being your representative.
Hilaire Belloc (1870–1953) French-born British poet.
Said in his first election campaign
Speech, Salford, 1906

126 It cannot in the opinion of His Majesty's Government be classified as slavery in the extreme acceptance of the word without some risk of terminological inexactitude.
Winston Churchill (1874–1965) British statesman.
Speech, House of Commons, 22 Feb 1906

127 When a liberal is abused, he says: Thank God they didn't beat me. When he is beaten, he thanks God they didn't kill him. When he is killed, he will thank God that his immortal soul has been delivered from its mortal clay.
Lenin (Vladimir Ilich Ulyanov; 1870–1924) Russian revolutionary leader.
Lenin heard this characterization at a meeting, and repeated it with approval
The Government's Falsification of the Duma and the Tasks of the Social-Democrats, 'Proletary', Dec 1906

128 Lenin's method leads to this: the party organization at first substitutes itself for the party as a whole. Then the central committee substitutes itself for the party organization, and finally a single dictator substitutes himself for the central committee.
Leon Trotsky (Lev Davidovich Bronstein; 1879–1940) Russian revolutionary.
The Communist Parties of Western Europe (N. McInnes), Ch. 3

1907

129 The Tsar is not treacherous but he is weak. Weakness is not treachery, but it fulfils all its functions.
Wilhelm II (1859–1941) King of Prussia and Emperor of Germany.
Comment written on a despatch from the German ambassador to Russia, 16 Mar 1907
Referring to Nicholas II

130 Mr Balfour's Poodle.
David Lloyd George (1863–1945) British Liberal statesman.
Referring to the House of Lords and its in-built

Conservative majority; said in reply to a claim that it was 'the watchdog of the nation'
Remark, House of Commons, 26 June 1907

131 Property is organised robbery.
George Bernard Shaw (1856–1950) Irish dramatist and critic.
Major Barbara, Preface

132 Alcohol is a very necessary article . . . It enables Parliament to do things at eleven at night that no sane person would do at eleven in the morning.
George Bernard Shaw
Major Barbara, II

133 He knows nothing; and he thinks he knows everything. That points clearly to a political career.
George Bernard Shaw
Major Barbara, III

1908

134 In England, Justice is open to all, like the Ritz hotel.
James Mathew (1830–1908) British judge.
Also attrib. to Lord Darling
Miscellany-at-Law (R. E. Megarry)

135 America is God's Crucible, the great Melting-Pot where all the races of Europe are melting and re-forming!
Israel Zangwill (1864–1926) British writer.
The Melting Pot, I

The Suffragettes

The Women's Social and Political Union was founded in 1903 by Emmeline Pankhurst to campaign for female suffrage in parliamentary elections. Its protest activities steadily increased in militancy, but were called off on the outbreak of World War I. *See also* Attitudes: Men and Women.

136 Votes for Women.
Slogan

137 We are not ashamed of what we have done, because, when you have a great cause to fight for, the moment of greatest humiliation is the moment when the spirit is proudest.
Christabel Pankhurst (1880–1958) British suffragette.
Speech, Albert Hall, London, 19 Mar 1908

138 We have taken this action, because as women . . . we realize that the condition of our sex is so deplorable that it is our duty even to break the law in order to call attention to the reasons why we do so.
Emmeline Pankhurst (1858–1928) British suffragette.
Speech in court, 21 Oct 1908
Shoulder to Shoulder (ed. Midge Mackenzie)

39* . . . if civilisation is to advance at all in the future, it must be through the help of women,

women freed of their political shackles, women with full power to work their will in society. It was rapidly becoming clear to my mind that men regarded women as a servant class in the community, and that women were going to remain in the servant class until they lifted themselves out of it.
Emmeline Pankhurst
My Own Story

140* Women had always fought for men, and for their children. Now they were ready to fight for their own human rights. Our militant movement was established.
Emmeline Pankhurst
My Own Story

141* Here's to the lot of them, murderer, thief, Forger and lunatic too, Sir –
Infants, and those who get parish relief, And women, it's perfectly true, Sir –
Please to take note, they are in the same boat:
They have not a chance of recording the vote.
H. Crawford
Referring to the women's suffrage movement
In the Same Boat

142* I see some rats have got in; let them squeal, it doesn't matter.
David Lloyd George (1863–1945) British Liberal statesman.
Said when suffragettes interrupted a meeting
The Faber Book of English History in Verse (Kenneth Baker)

1909

143 There are no credentials They do not even need a medical certificate. They need not be sound either in body or mind. They only require a certificate of birth – just to prove that they are first of the litter. You would not choose a spaniel on these principles.
David Lloyd George
Referring to members of the House of Lords
Budget Speech, 1909

144 A fully equipped Duke costs as much to keep up as two Dreadnoughts, and Dukes are just as great a terror, and they last longer.
David Lloyd George
Speech, Limehouse, 30 July 1909

145 Assassination is the extreme form of censorship.
George Bernard Shaw (1856–1950) Irish dramatist and critic.
The Shewing-Up of Blanco Posnet, 'The Limits of Toleration'

1910

146 Wait and see.
Herbert Henry Asquith (1852–1928) British statesman.
In various speeches, 1910

147 Compromise used to mean that half a loaf was better than no bread. Among modern states-

men it really seems to mean that half a loaf is better than a whole loaf.
G. K. Chesterton (1874–1936) British writer.
What's Wrong with the World

148* **Have you heard? The Prime Minister has resigned and Northcliffe has sent for the King.**
Said by a member of Lord Northcliffe's staff; at the height of his career, Northcliffe owned, among other newspapers, *The Times*, *The Observer*, the *Daily Mail*, the *Daily Mirror*, and the *London Evening News*
Northcliffe, An Intimate Biography (Hamilton Fyfe)

149* **Land of Hope and Glory, Mother of the Free, How shall we extol thee, who are born of thee?**
Wider still and wider shall thy bounds be set; God who made thee mighty, make thee mightier yet.
A. C. Benson (1862–1925) British writer.
Land of Hope and Glory

150 **And this is good old Boston,
The home of the bean and the cod,
Where the Lowells talk only to Cabots,
And the Cabots talk only to God.**
John Collins Bossidy (1860–1928) US writer.
The Lowells and the Cabots were prominent families in Boston society
Toast at Holy Cross Alumni dinner, 1910

1911

151 **I would make great sacrifices to preserve peace. . . . But if a situation were to be forced upon us, in which peace could only be preserved by the surrender of the great and beneficent position Britain has won by centuries of heroism and achievement . . . I say emphatically that peace at that price would be a humiliation intolerable for a great country like ours to endure.**
David Lloyd George (1863–1945) British Liberal statesman.
British Documents (Gooch and Temperley), Vol. VII

152 **If, therefore, war should ever come between these two countries, which Heaven forbid! it will not, I think, be due to irresistible natural laws, it will be due to the want of human wisdom.**
Bonar Law (1858–1923) British statesman.
Referring to the UK and Germany
Speech, House of Commons, 27 Nov 1911

153 **We can now look forward with something like confidence to the time when war between civilized nations will be considered as antiquated as a duel.**
George Peabody Gooch (1873–1968) English historian and Liberal MP.
History of Our Time

154 **I hope to see the day when the American flag will float over every square foot of the British**

North American possessions clear to the North Pole.
James Beauchamp Clark (1850–1921)
Speaker of US House of Representatives.
Speech, House of Representatives, June 1911

1912

155 **In private conversation he tries on speeches like a man trying on ties in his bedroom to see how he would look in them.**
Lionel Curtis (1872–1955) British writer.
Referring to Winston Churchill
Letter to Nancy Astor, 1912

156 **The only tyrannies from which men, women and children are suffering in real life are the tyrannies of minorities.**
Theodore Roosevelt (1858–1919) US Republican president.
Speech, 22 Mar 1912

157 **Well, I have one consolation, No candidate was ever elected ex-president by such a large majority!**
William Howard Taft (1857–1930) US statesman.
Referring to his disastrous defeat in the 1912 presidential election
Attrib.

158 **Great God! this is an awful place.**
Captain Robert Falcon Scott (1868–1912)
British explorer.
Referring to the South Pole
Journal, 17 Jan 1912

159 **Had we lived, I should have had a tale to tell of the hardihood, endurance, and courage of my companions which would have stirred the heart of every Englishman. These rough notes and our dead bodies must tell the tale.**
Captain Robert Falcon Scott
Scott's second expedition (1910–12) to the Antarctic, which reached the South Pole, ended in disaster when all its members perished in blizzards, only a few miles from safety
Message to the Public

160 **I am just going outside and may be some time.**
Captain Lawrence Oates (1880–1912) British soldier and explorer.
Said before leaving the tent and vanishing into the blizzard on the ill-fated Antarctic expedition (1910–12); Oates was afraid that his lameness would slow down the others
Journal (R. F. Scott), 17 Mar 1912

161 **Hereabouts died a very gallant gentleman, Captain L. E. G. Oates of the Inniskilling Dragoons. In March 1912, returning from the Pole, he walked willingly to his death in a blizzard, to try and save his comrades, beset by hardships.**
E. L. Atkinson (1882–1929) British naval officer.
Epitaph on memorial in the Antarctic

162 **Well: while was fashioning
This creature of cleaving wing,
The Immanent Will that stirs and urges everything**

Prepared a sinister mate
For her – so gaily great –
A Shape of Ice, for the time far and
dissociate.

And as the smart ship grew
In stature, grace, and hue,
In shadowy silent distance grew the Iceberg
too.
Thomas Hardy (1840–1928) British novelist.
Referring to the 'Titanic', a luxury passenger
ship, thought to be unsinkable because of its
special design. It struck an iceberg on its maiden
voyage and sank, causing the loss of 1513 lives
The Convergence of the Twain

1913

3 I want to take this occasion to say that the
United States will never again seek one addi-
tional foot of territory by conquest.
Woodrow Wilson (1856–1924) US
statesman.
Speech, Mobile, 27 Oct 1913

4 Do not hit at all if it can be avoided, but never
hit softly.
Theodore Roosevelt (1858–1919) US Republican president.
Autobiography

5 So greatly did she care for freedom that she
died for it. So dearly did she love women that
she offered her life as their ransom. That is
the verdict given at the great Inquest of the
Nation on the death of Emily Wilding Davison.
Christabel Pankhurst (1880–1958) British
suffragette.
Emily Davison threw herself under the King's
horse in protest at the imprisoning of
suffragettes
The Suffragette, 13 June 1913

6 Booth died blind and still by faith he trod,
Eyes still dazzled by the ways of God.
Vachel Lindsay (1879–1931) US poet.
Referring to William Booth, the founder of the
Salvation Army, who died in 1912
General William Booth Enters Heaven

Attitudes

Art, Literature, and Music

1871

7 The Fleshly School of Poetry.
Robert Williams Buchanan (1841–1901)
British poet and writer.
Referring to Swinburne, William Morris, D. G.
Rossetti, etc.
Title of article in the *Contemporary Review*, Oct
1871

1873

168 Culture is the passion for sweetness and light,
and (what is more) the passion for making
them prevail.
Matthew Arnold (1822–88) British poet and
critic.
Literature and Dogma, Preface

1877

169 The song that we hear with our ears is only the
song that is sung in our hearts.
Ouida (Marie Louise de la Ramée; 1839–1908)
British novelist.
Wisdom, Wit and Pathos, 'Ariadne'

170 I have seen, and heard, much of Cockney impu-
dence before now; but never expected to hear
a coxcomb ask two hundred guineas for
flinging a pot of paint in the public's face.
John Ruskin (1819–1900) British art critic and
writer.
On Whistler's painting 'Nocturne in Black and
Gold'
Letter, 18 June 1877

1879

171 It takes a great deal of history to produce a lit-
tle literature.
Henry James (1843–1916) US novelist.
Life of Nathaniel Hawthorne, Ch. 1

172 He was unperfect, unfinished, inartistic; he was
worse than provincial – he was parochial.
Henry James
Referring to Thoreau
Life of Nathaniel Hawthorne, Ch. 4

1881

173 A sonnet is a moment's monument, –
Memorial from the Soul's eternity
To one dead deathless hour.
Dante Gabriel Rossetti (1828–82) British
painter and poet.
The House of Life, Introduction

174 Books are good enough in their own way, but
they are a mighty bloodless substitute for life.
Robert Louis Stevenson (1850–94) Scottish writer.
Virginibus Puerisque

1883

175 A master is dead. Today we sing no more.
Johannes Brahms (1833–97) German
composer.
Stopping a choral rehearsal on hearing of the
death of Wagner
Brahms (P. Latham)

176 Three hours a day will produce as much as a
man ought to write.
Anthony Trollope (1815–82) British novelist.
Autobiography, Ch. 15

1884

177* A good man fallen among Fabians.
Lenin (Vladimir Ilich Ulyanov; 1870–1924) Russian revolutionary leader.
Referring to Bernard Shaw
Attrib.

178 Make 'em laugh; make 'em cry; make 'em wait.
Charles Reade (1814–84) British novelist and dramatist.
Advice to an aspiring writer
Attrib.

1885

179 Listen! There never was an artistic period. There never was an Art-loving nation.
James Whistler (1834–1903) US painter.
Attrib.

1887

180 When all is said and done, no literature can outdo the cynicism of real life; you won't intoxicate with one glass someone who has already drunk up a whole barrel.
Anton Chekhov (1860–1904) Russian dramatist.
Letter, 1887

1888

181 A criticism of life under the conditions fixed for such a criticism by the laws of poetic truth and poetic beauty.
Matthew Arnold (1822–88) British poet and critic.
Essays in Criticism, Second Series, 'The Study of Poetry'

182* The difference between genuine poetry and the poetry of Dryden, Pope, and all their school, is briefly this: their poetry is conceived and composed in their wits, genuine poetry is conceived and composed in the soul.
Matthew Arnold
Thomas Gray

183 What is poetry? The suggestion, by the imagination, of noble grounds for the noble emotions.
John Ruskin (1819–1900) British art critic and writer.
Modern Painters, Vol. III

184 The only obligation to which in advance we may hold a novel, without incurring the accusation of being arbitrary, is that it be interesting.
Henry James (1843–1916) US novelist.
Partial Portraits, 'The Art of Fiction'

185 It is very simple. The artists retired. The British remained.
James Whistler (1834–1903) US painter.
Explaining his resignation as president of the Royal Society of British Artists
Whistler Stories (D. Seitz)

1890s

186 Our mistake, you see, was to write intermina large operas, which had to fill an entire eve ning . . . And now along comes someone with one- or two-act opera without all that pompous nonsense . . . that was a happy reform
Giuseppe Verdi (1813–1901) Italian composer.
Referring to Mascagni

1891

187 There is no such thing as a moral or an imme book. Books are well written, or badly writte
Oscar Wilde (1854–1900) Irish-born Britis dramatist.
The Picture of Dorian Gray, Preface

188 All Art is quite useless.
Oscar Wilde
The Picture of Dorian Gray, Preface

189 Art is the most intense mode of individualis that the world has known.
Oscar Wilde
The Soul of Man Under Socialism

190 Art never expresses anything but itself.
Oscar Wilde
The Decay of Lying

191* Genius does what it must, and Talent does what it can.
Owen Meredith (Robert Bulwer-Lytton, 1s Earl of Lytton; 1831–91) British statesman a poet.
Last Words of a Sensitive Second-rate Poe

1896

192 NINA. Your play's hard to act, there are no liv people in it.
TREPLEV. Living people! We should show lif neither as it is nor as it ought to be, but we see it in our dreams.
Anton Chekhov (1860–1904) Russian dramatist.
The Seagull, I

1897

193 A work that aspires, however humbly, to th condition of art should carry its justification every line.
Joseph Conrad (Teodor Josef Konrad Korzeniowski; 1857–1924) Polish-born Britis novelist.
The Nigger of the Narcissus, Preface

1898

194 Art is not a handicraft, it is the transmission feeling the artist has experienced.
Leo Tolstoy (1828–1910) Russian writer.
What is Art?, Ch. 19

1900s

195 I have already heard it. I had better not go

will start to get accustomed to it and finally like
it.
Nikolai Rimsky-Korsakov (1844–1908)
Russian composer.
Referring to music by Debussy
Conversations with Stravinsky (Robert Craft
and Igor Stravinsky)

96 To be played with both hands in the pocket.
Erik Satie (1866–1925) French composer.
Direction on one of his piano pieces
The Unimportance of Being Oscar (O. Levant)

97 *Hugo – hélas!*
André Gide (1869–1951) French novelist.
Replying to an inquiry as to whom he considered
the finest poet of the 19th century.
*André Gide–Paul Valéry Correspondence
1890–1942*

98 . . . poetry, 'The Cinderella of the Arts.'
Harriet Monroe (1860–1936) US poet and
editor.
Famous American Women (Hope Stoddard),
'Harriet Monroe'

99 Out of the quarrel with others we make rhetoric; out of the quarrel with ourselves we make
poetry.
W. B. Yeats (1865–1939) Irish poet.
Essay

1900

200 Something that everybody wants to have read
and nobody wants to read.
Mark Twain (Samuel Langhorne Clemens;
1835–1910) US writer.
Definition of a classic of literature
Speech at Nineteenth Century Club, New York,
20 Nov 1900

201 The play was a great success, but the audience
was a disaster.
Oscar Wilde (1854–1900) Irish-born British
dramatist.
Referring to a play that had recently failed
Attrib.

202 One would have to have a heart of stone to
read the death of Little Nell without laughing.
Oscar Wilde
Lecturing upon Dickens
Lives of the Wits (H. Pearson)

203 The last gentleman in Europe.
Ada Beddington Leverson (1862–1933)
British writer.
Said of Oscar Wilde
Letters to the Sphinx (Wilde), 'Reminiscences',
2

1901

204 It does not follow . . . that the right to criticize
Shakespeare involves the power of writing
better plays. And in fact . . . I do not profess to
write better plays.
George Bernard Shaw (1856–1950) Irish
dramatist and critic.
Three Plays for Puritans, Preface

1902

205 Art is ruled uniquely by the imagination.
Benedetto Croce (1866–1952) Italian
philospher.
Esthetic, Ch. 1

1903

206 Every man's work, whether it be literature or
music or pictures or architecture or anything
else, is always a portrait of himself.
Samuel Butler (1835–1902) British writer.
The Way of All Flesh, Ch. 14

207 Well, not bad, but there are decidedly too many
of them, and they are not very well arranged. I
would have done it differently.
James Whistler (1834–1903) US painter.
His reply when asked if he agreed that the stars
were especially beautiful one night
Attrib.

1905

208 A good novel tells us the truth about its hero;
but a bad novel tells us the truth about its
author.
G. K. Chesterton (1874–1936) British writer.
Heretics, Ch. 15

209 The artistic temperament is a disease that af-
flicts amateurs.
G. K. Chesterton
Heretics, Ch. 17

1906

210 The day is coming when a single carrot, freshly
observed, will set off a revolution.
Paul Cézanne (1839–1906) French postim-
pressionist painter.
Attrib.

211 The profession of letters is, after all, the only
one in which one can make no money without
being ridiculous.
Jules Renard (1894–1910) French writer.
Journal

212 Popular poets are the parish priests of the
Muse, retailing her ancient divinations to a long
since converted public.
George Santayana (1863–1952) US
philosopher.
The Life of Reason, 'Reason in Art'

1907

213 With the single exception of Homer, there is no
eminent writer, not even Sir Walter Scott,
whom I can despise so entirely as I despise
Shakespeare when I measure my mind against
his . . . It would positively be a relief to me to
dig him up and throw stones at him.
George Bernard Shaw (1856–1950) Irish
dramatist and critic.
Dramatic Opinions and Essays, Vol. 2

1909

214   Mr Shaw is (I suspect) the only man on earth
who has never written any poetry.
G. K. Chesterton (1874–1936) British writer.
Referring to George Bernard Shaw
Orthodoxy, Ch. 3

1911

215   "Music" she said dreamily, and such is the
force of habit that "I don't" she added, "know
anything about music really, but I know what I
like."
Max Beerbohm British writer.
Zuleika Dobson

216   Wonderful women! Have you ever thought how
much we all, and women especially, owe to
Shakespeare for his vindication of women in
these fearless, high-spirited, resolute and intel-
ligent heroines?
Ellen Terry (1847–1928) British actress.
Four Lectures on Shakespeare, 'The Triumphant
Women'

217   Words as is well known, are great foes of
reality.
Joseph Conrad (Teodor Josef Konrad
Korzeniowski; 1857–1924) Polish-born British
novelist.
Under Western Eyes

1912

218   When a man is in doubt about this or that in his
writing, it will often guide him if he asks himself how it will tell a hundred years hence.
Samuel Butler (1835–1902) British writer.
Notebooks

219   Sherard Blaw, the dramatist who had discovered himself, and who had given so ungrudg-
ingly of his discovery to the world.
Saki (Hector Hugh Munro; 1870–1916) British
writer.
The Unbearable Bassington, Ch. 13

1913

220   He could not think up to the height of his own
towering style.
G. K. Chesterton (1874–1936) British writer.
Speaking of Tennyson
The Victorian Age in Literature, Ch. 3

221   I like to write when I feel spiteful: it's like hav-
ing a good sneeze.
D. H. Lawrence (1885–1930) British novelist.
Letter to Lady Cynthia Asquith, Nov 1913

Daily Life

1870s

222   Father, dear father, come home with me now,

The clock in the steeple strikes one.
Henry Clay Work (1832–84) US songwrite
A temperance song
Come Home, Father

1870

223   Of all noxious animals, too, the most noxious
a tourist. And of all tourists the most vulgar,
ill-bred, offensive and loathsome is the Britis
tourist.
Francis Kilvert (1840–79) British diarist ar
clergyman.
Diary, 5 Apr 1870

1871

224   It is a fine thing to be out on the hills alone.
man can hardly be a beast or a fool alone on
great mountain.
Francis Kilvert
Diary, 29 May 1871

1880

225* The smoke of their foul dens
Broodeth on Thy Earth as a black pestilenc
Hiding the kind day's eye. No flower, no
grass there groweth,
Only their engines' dung which the fierce fu
nace throweth.
Wilfred Scawen Blunt (1840–1922) Britis
poet.
Describing a northern town
Satan Absolved: a Victorian Mystery

226   A population sodden with drink, steeped in
vice, eaten up by every social and physical
malady, these are the denizens of Darkest
England amidst whom my life has been spe
William Booth (1829–1912) British preache
and founder of the Salvation Army.
In Darkest England, and the Way Out

1887

227   London, that great cesspool into which all th
loungers of the Empire are irresistibly
drained.
Arthur Conan Doyle (1856–1930) British
writer.
A Study in Scarlet

1892

228   It is my belief, Watson, founded upon my experience, that the lowest and vilest alleys of
London do not present a more dreadful reco
of sin than does the smiling and beautiful
countryside.
Arthur Conan Doyle
Copper Beeches

1893

229   The English country gentleman galloping afte

fox — the unspeakable in full pursuit of the uneatable.
Oscar Wilde (1854–1900) Irish-born British dramatist.
A Woman of No Importance, I

1895

230 Really, if the lower orders don't set us a good example, what on earth is the use of them?
Oscar Wilde
The Importance of Being Earnest, I

1896

231 On Wenlock Edge the wood's in trouble;
His forest fleece the Wrekin heaves;
The gale, it plies the saplings double,
And thick on Severn snow the leaves.
A. E. Housman (1859–1936) British scholar and poet.
A Shropshire Lad, 'The Welsh Marches'

232 Loveliest of trees, the cherry now
Is hung with bloom along the bough,
And stands about the woodland ride
Wearing white for Eastertide.
A. E. Housman
A Shropshire Lad, '1887'

1900

233* This is the weather the cuckoo likes,
And so do I;
When showers betumble the chestnut spikes,
And nestlings fly:
And the little brown nightingale bills his best,
And they sit outside at 'The Travellers' Rest'.
Thomas Hardy (1840–1928) British novelist.
Weathers

1902

234 His Lordship may compel us to be equal upstairs, but there will never be equality in the servants' hall.
J. M. Barrie (1860–1937) British novelist and dramatist.
The Admirable Crichton, I

1910

235* They are only ten.
Lord Northcliffe (1865–1922) Irish-born British newspaper proprietor.
Rumoured to have been a notice to remind his staff of his opinion of the mental age of the general public
Attrib.

236 Common people do not pray; they only beg.
George Bernard Shaw (1856–1950) Irish dramatist and critic.
Misalliance

237* Come, Come, Come and have a drink with me

Down at the old 'Bull and Bush'.
Harry Tilzer (Albert von Tilzer; 1878–1956) British songwriter.
The Old Bull and Bush

238 Dirty British coaster with a salt-caked smoke stack,
Butting through the Channel in the mad March days,
With a cargo of Tyne coal,
Road-rail, pig-lead,
Firewood, iron-ware, and cheap tin trays.
John Masefield (1878–1967) British poet.
Cargoes

1911

239 Will anyone, a hundred years from now, consent to live in the houses the Victorians built, travel by their roads or railways, value the furnishings they made to live among or esteem, except for curious or historial reasons, their prevalent art and the clipped and limited literature that satisfied their souls?
H. G. Wells (1866–1946) British writer.
The New Machiavelli

1913

240 I have to live for others and not for myself; that's middle class morality.
George Bernard Shaw (1856–1950) Irish dramatist and critic.
Pygmalion

Death

1875

241 Sin brought death, and death will disappear with the disappearance of sin.
Mary Baker Eddy (1821–1910) US religious leader.
Science and Health, with Key to the Scriptures

1886

242 The thought of suicide is a great source of comfort: with it a calm passage is to be made across many a bad night.
Friedrich Wilhelm Nietzsche (1844–1900) German philosopher.
Jenseits von Gut und Böse (trans. *Beyond Good and Evil*)

1887

243 Under the wide and starry sky
Dig the grave and let me lie.
Glad did I live and gladly die,
– And I laid me down with a will.
This is the verse you grave for me:
'Here he lies where he longed to be;
Home is the sailor, home from sea,

And the hunter home from the hill.'
Robert Louis Stevenson (1850–94) Scottish writer.
Underwoods, Bk. I, 'Requiem'

1902

244 Our civilization is founded on the shambles, and every individual existence goes out in a lonely spasm of helpless agony.
William James (1842–1910) US psychologist and philosopher.
Varieties of Religious Experience

1910

245 Death destroys a man, the idea of Death saves him.
E. M. Forster (1879–1970) British novelist.
Howards End, Ch. 27

Education, Knowledge, and Learning

1872

246 Some who had received a liberal education at the Colleges of Unreason, and taken the highest degrees in hypothetics, which are their principal study.
Samuel Butler (1835–1902) British writer.
Erewhon, Ch. 9

247 It is the province of knowledge to speak and it is the privilege of wisdom to listen.
Oliver Wendell Holmes (1809–94) US writer.
The Poet at the Breakfast Table, Ch. 10

1879

248* It is the customary fate of new truths to begin as heresies and to end as superstitions.
T. H. Huxley (1825–95) British biologist.
The Coming of Age of the Origin of Species

1881

249 Give me the young man who has brains enough to make a fool of himself!
Robert Louis Stevenson (1850–94) Scottish writer.
Virginibus Puerisque

1886

250 I never heard tell of any clever man that came of entirely stupid people.
Thomas Carlyle (1795–1881) Scottish historian and essayist.
Speech, Edinburgh, 2 Apr 1886

251 I am too much of a sceptic to deny the possibility of anything.
T. H. Huxley (1825–95) British biologist.
Letter to Herbert Spencer, 22 Mar 1886

1891

252 There is no sin except stupidity.
Oscar Wilde (1854–1900) Irish-born British dramatist.
The Critic as Artist, Pt. 2

1892

253 Music-hall songs provide the dull with wit, just as proverbs provide them with wisdom.
W. Somerset Maugham (1874–1965) British novelist.
A Writer's Notebook

1893

254 Metaphysics is the finding of bad reasons for what we believe upon instinct; but to find these reasons is no less an instinct.
F. H. Bradley (1846–1924) British philosopher.
Appearance and Reality, Preface

255* Research! A mere excuse for idleness; it has never achieved, and will never achieve any results of the slightest value.
Benjamin Jowett (1817–93) British theologian.
Unforgotten Years (Logan Pearsall Smith)

1894

256 Oxford had not taught me, nor had any other place or person, the value of liberty as an essential condition of excellence in human things.
William Ewart Gladstone (1809–98) British statesman.
Gladstone graduated from Oxford in 1831
Note

257 A blind man in a dark room – looking for a black hat – which isn't there.
Lord Bowen (1835–94) British judge.
Characterization of a metaphysician
Attrib.

258 Language grows out of life, out of its needs and experiences . . . *Language* and *knowledge* are indissolubly connected; they are interdependent. Good work in language presupposes and depends on a real knowledge of things.
Annie Sullivan (1866–1936) US teacher of the handicapped.
Speech, American Association to Promote the Teaching of Speech to the Deaf, July 1894

1902

259 We are thinking beings, and we cannot exclude the intellect from participating in any of our functions.
William James (1842–1910) US psychologist and philosopher.
Varieties of Religious Experience

1904

260　LIBOV ANDREEVNA. Are you still a student?
TROFIMOV. I expect I shall be a student to the
end of my days.
Anton Chekhov (1860–1904) Russian
dramatist.
The Cherry Orchard, I

261　Paradoxes are useful to attract attention to
ideas.
Mandell Creighton (1843–1901) British
churchman.
Life and Letters

1905

262　There is no such thing on earth as an uninter-
esting subject; the only thing that can exist is
an uninterested person.
G. K. Chesterton (1874–1936) British writer.
Heretics, Ch. 1

263　The word 'orthodoxy' not only no longer means
being right; it practically means being wrong.
G. K. Chesterton
Heretics, Ch. 1

264　The philosopher is Nature's pilot. And there you
have our difference; to be in hell is to drift; to
be in heaven is to steer.
George Bernard Shaw (1856–1950) Irish
dramatist and critic.
Man and Superman

1906

265　They know enough who know how to learn.
Henry Brooks Adams (1838–1918) US
historian.
The Education of Henry Adams

266　*Logic, n.* The art of thinking and reasoning in
strict accordance with the limitations and inca-
pacities of the human understanding.
Ambrose Bierce (1842–?1914) US writer and
journalist.
The Devil's Dictionary

267　*Ignoramus, n.* A person unacquainted with certain kinds of knowledge familiar to yourself,
and having certain other kinds that you know
nothing about.
Ambrose Bierce
The Devil's Dictionary

1907

268　Nobody can say a word against Greek: it
stamps a man at once as an educated
gentleman.
George Bernard Shaw (1856–1950) Irish
dramatist and critic.
Major Barbara, I

1909

269　Nothing would more effectively further the development of education than for all flogging

pedagogues to learn to educate with the head
instead of with the hand.
Ellen Key (Karolina Sofia Key; 1849–1926)
Swedish writer.
The Century of the Child, Ch. 3

1911

270　We were taught as the chief subjects of in-
struction Latin and Greek. We were taught very
badly because the men who taught us did not
habitually use either of these languages.
H. G. Wells (1866–1946) British writer.
The New Machiavelli, Bk. I., Ch. 3

271　Americans have a perfect right to exist. But he
did often find himself wishing Mr. Rhodes had
not enabled them to excercise that right at
Oxford.
Max Beerbohm (1872–1936) British writer.
Zuleika Dobson

1913

272　An idea does not pass from one language to an-
other without change.
Miguel de Unamuno y Jugo (1864–1936)
Spanish writer.
The Tragic Sense of Life

History

1895

273　History is past politics, and politics present
history.
John Robert Seeley (1834–95) British
historian.
Quoting the historian E. A. Freeman
The Growth of British Policy

1903

274　My argument is that War makes rattling good
history; but Peace is poor reading.
Thomas Hardy (1840–1928) British novelist.
The Dynasts, II:5

1904

275　One step forward, two steps back . . . It happens in the lives of individuals, and it happens
in the history of nations and in the development of parties.
Lenin (Vladimir Ilich Ulyanov; 1870–1924) Russian revolutionary leader.
One Step Forward, Two Steps Back

1905

276　Progress, far from consisting in change, depends on retentiveness. Those who cannot remember the past are condemned to repeat it.
George Santayana (1863–1952) US
philosopher.
The Life of Reason

1909

277 It is impossible to write ancient history because
     we do not have enough sources, and impossi-
     ble to write modern history because we have
     far too many.
     Charles Pierre Péguy (1873–1914) French
     writer.
     Clio

1910

278* The past is the only dead thing that smells
     sweet.
     Edward Thomas (1878–1917) British poet.
     Early One Morning

279* Historians are like deaf people who go on an-
     swering questions that no one has asked
     them.
     Leo Tolstoy (1828–1910) Russian writer.
     A Discovery of Australia, 'Being an Historian'
     (Manning Clark)

280* There is always something rather absurd about
     the past.
     Max Beerbohm (1872–1956) British writer.
     1880

Human Nature

1873

281 Ask yourself whether you are happy, and you
     cease to be so.
     John Stuart Mill (1806–73) British
     philosopher.
     Autobiography, Ch. 5

1880

282 To show pity is felt as a sign of contempt be-
     cause one has clearly ceased to be an object
     of *fear* as soon as one is pitied.
     Friedrich Wilhelm Nietzsche (1844–1900)
     German philosopher.
     The Wanderer and His Shadow

1881

283 There is no duty we so much underrate as the
     duty of being happy.
     Robert Louis Stevenson (1850–94) Scot-
     tish writer.
     Virginibus Puerisque

1882

284 He who does not need to lie is proud of not be-
     ing a liar.
     Friedrich Wilhelm Nietzsche (1844–1900)
     German philosopher.
     Nachgelassene Fragmente

1883

285 I teach you the Superman. Man is somethin
     that is to be surpassed.
     Friedrich Wilhelm Nietzsche
     Thus Spake Zarathustra

1886

286 Wild animals never kill for sport. Man is the
     only one to whom the torture and death of
     fellow-creatures is amusing in itself.
     J. A. Froude (1818–94) British historian.
     Oceana, Ch. 5

1887

287 She likes stories that make her cry — I think
     all do, it's so nice to feel sad when you've
     nothing particular to be sad about.
     Annie Sullivan (1866–1936) US teacher o
     the handicapped.
     Referring to Helen Keller
     Letter, 12 Dec 1887

1889

288 It is impossible to enjoy idling thoroughly u
     less one has plenty of work to do.
     Jerome K. Jerome (1859–1927) British
     humorist.
     Idle Thoughts of an Idle Fellow

1891

289 There's a sucker born every minute.
     Phineas Barnum (1810–91) US showman
     Attrib.

290 It is only shallow people who do not judge
     appearances.
     Oscar Wilde (1854–1900) Irish-born British
     dramatist.
     The Picture of Dorian Gray, Ch. 2

291 A man who knows the price of everything a
     the value of nothing.
     Oscar Wilde
     Describing a cynic
     Lady Windermere's Fan, III

292 The man who sees both sides of a question i
     man who sees absolutely nothing at all.
     Oscar Wilde
     The Critic as Artist, Pt. 2

1893

293 From forty to fifty a man is at heart either a
     stoic or a satyr.
     Arthur Pinero (1855–1934) British dramat
     The Second Mrs Tanqueray, I

1894

294 Economy is going without something you do

want in case you should, some day, want something you probably won't want.
Anthony Hope (Sir Anthony Hope Hawkins; 1863–1933) British novelist.
The Dolly Dialogues

295　Adam was but human – this explains it all. He did not want the apple for the apple's sake, he wanted it only because it was forbidden.
Mark Twain (Samuel Langhorne Clemens; 1835–1910) US writer.
Pudd'nhead Wilson's Calendar, Ch. 2

1895

296　Other people are quite dreadful. The only possible society is oneself.
Oscar Wilde (1854–1900) Irish-born British dramatist.
An Ideal Husband, III

1896

297　Malt does more than Milton can
To justify God's ways to man.
A. E. Housman (1859–1936) British scholar and poet.
A Shropshire Lad, 'The Welsh Marches'

298　Two men look out through the same bars: One sees the mud, and one the stars.
Frederick Langbridge (1849–1923) British religious writer.
A Cluster of Quiet Thoughts

1897

299　Man is the only animal that blushes. Or needs to.
Mark Twain (Samuel Langhorne Clemens; 1835–1910) US writer.
Following the Equator, heading of Ch. 27

1899

300　Two may talk together under the same roof for many years, yet never really meet; and two others at first speech are old friends.
Mary Catherwood (1847–1901) US writer.
Mackinac and Lake Stories, 'Marianson'

1900

301　You shall judge of a man by his foes as well as by his friends.
Joseph Conrad (Teodor Josef Konrad Korzeniowski; 1857–1924) Polish-born British novelist.
Lord Jim, Ch. 34

1902

302*　Justice is being allowed to do whatever I like. Injustice is whatever prevents my doing it.
Samuel Butler (1835–1902) British writer.
Notebooks

1903

303　A good man can be stupid and still be good. But a bad man must have brains.
Maxim Gorky (Aleksei Maksimovich Peshkov; 1868–1936) Russian writer.
The Lower Depths

304　A lifetime of happiness: no man alive could bear it: it would be hell on earth.
George Bernard Shaw (1856–1950) Irish dramatist and critic.
Man and Superman, I

305　It was remarked to me by the late Mr Charles Roupell . . . that to play billiards well was a sign of an ill-spent youth.
Herbert Spencer (1820–1903) British philosopher.
Life and Letters of Spencer (Duncan), Ch. 20

1905

306　Happiness is a mystery like religion, and should never be rationalized.
G. K. Chesterton (1874–1936) British writer.
Heretics, Ch. 7

307　Happiness is the only sanction of life; where happiness fails, existence remains a mad and lamentable experiment.
George Santayana (1863–1952) US philosopher.
The Life of Reason

1906

308　I have always found that the man whose second thoughts are good is worth watching.
J. M. Barrie (1860–1937) British novelist and dramatist.
What Every Woman Knows, III

1909

309　The madman is not the man who has lost his reason. The madman is the man who has lost everything except his reason.
G. K. Chesterton (1874–1936) British writer.
Orthodoxy, Ch. 1

310*　The ignorant man always adores what he cannot understand.
Cesare Lombroso (1853–1909) Italian criminologist.
The Man of Genius, Pt. III, Ch. 3

1910

311*　When people do not respect us we are sharply offended; yet deep down in his heart no man much respects himself.
Mark Twain (Samuel Langhorne Clemens; 1835–1910) US writer.
Notebooks

1911

312　You cannot make a man by standing a sheep on its hind legs. But by standing a flock of sheep

in that position you can make a crowd of men.
Max Beerbohm (1872–1956) British writer.
Zuleika Dobson, Ch. 9

1912

313 Man is the only animal that can remain on friendly terms with the victims he intends to eat until he eats them.
Samuel Butler (1835–1902) British writer.
Notebooks

314 I wanted the experience of war. I thought there would be no more wars.
Joyce Cary (1888–1957) British novelist.
Reason for going to the Balkan War in 1912

1913

315 Conscience is the internal perception of the rejection of a particular wish operating within us.
Sigmund Freud (1856–1939) Austrian psychoanalyst.
Totem and Taboo

Humour

1876

316 A different taste in jokes is a great strain on the affections.
George Eliot (Mary Ann Evans; 1819–80) British novelist.
Daniel Deronda

1880

317 He played the King as though under momentary apprehension that someone else was about to play the ace.
Eugene Field (1850–95) US poet and journalist.
Referring to Creston Clarke's performance in the role of King Lear
Attrib.

1881

318 I will not go down to posterity talking bad grammar.
Benjamin Disraeli (1804–81) British statesman.
Remark made when correcting proofs of his last parliamentary speech, 31 Mar 1881
Disraeli (Blake), Ch. 32

1900s

319 I do love cricket — it's so very English.
Sarah Bernhardt (Sarah Henriette Rosine Bernard; 1844–1923) French actress.
On seeing a game of football
Nijinsky (R. Buckle)

320 Men will confess to treason, murder, arson,

false teeth, or a wig. How many of them will own up to a lack of humour?
Frank More Colby (1865–1925) US editor.
Essays, I

1904

321 My way of joking is to tell the truth. It's the funniest joke in the world.
George Bernard Shaw (1856–1950) Irish dramatist and critic.
John Bull's Other Island, II

1910

322 Candidates should not attempt more than six of these.
Hilaire Belloc (1870–1953) French-born British poet.
Suggested addition to the Ten Commandments
Attrib.

1912

323 He uses statistics as a drunken man uses lamp-posts — for support rather than illumination.
Andrew Lang (1844–1912) Scottish writer and poet.
Treasury of Humorous Quotations

Life

1870

324 When a man fell into his anecdotage it was a sign for him to retire from the world.
Benjamin Disraeli (1804–81) British statesman.
Lothair, Ch. 28

1873

325 Everything must be taken seriously, nothing tragically.
Louis Adolphe Thiers (1797–1877) French statesman and historian.
Speech, French National Assembly, 24 May 1873

1874

326 Our ingress into the world
Was naked and bare;
Our progress through the world
Is trouble and care.
Henry Wadsworth Longfellow (1807–82) US poet.
Tales of A Wayside Inn, 'The Student's Tale'

327 Ships that pass in the night, and speak each other in passing;
Only a signal shown and a distant voice in the darkness;
So on the ocean of life we pass and speak one another,

Only a look and a voice; then darkness again
and a silence.
Henry Wadsworth Longfellow
Tales of a Wayside Inn, 'The Theologian's Tale.
Elizabeth'

328 For life is but a dream whose shapes return,
Some frequently, some seldom, some by night
And some by day.
James Thomson (1834–82) British poet.
The City of Dreadful Night, I

1875
---

329 A place for everything, and everything in its
place.
Samuel Smiles (1812–1904) British writer.
Thrift, Ch. 5

1880
---

330 A day less or more
At sea or ashore,
We die – does it matter when?
Alfred, Lord Tennyson (1809–92) British
poet.
The Revenge, XI

1882
---

331 Fools are in a terrible, overwhelming majority,
all the wide world over.
Henrik Ibsen (1828–1906) Norwegian
dramatist.
An Enemy of the People, IV

1884
---

332 Take the saving lie away from the average man
and straight away you take away his
happiness.
Henrik Ibsen
The Wild Duck, V

333 I had never had a piece of toast
Particularly long and wide,
But fell upon the sanded floor,
And always on the buttered side.
James Payn (1830–98) British writer and
editor.
Chambers's Journal, 2 Feb 1884

1885
---

334 Not, I'll not, carrion comfort, Despair, not feast
on thee;
Not untwist – slack they may be – these last
strands of man
In me or, most weary, cry *I can no more*. I
can;
Can something, hope, wish day come, not
choose not to be.
Gerard Manley Hopkins (1844–99) British
Jesuit and poet.
Carrion Comfort

1888
---

335 It matters not how strait the gate,
How charged with punishments the scroll,
I am the master of my fate:
I am the captain of my soul.
William Ernest Henley (1849–1903) British
writer.
Echoes, IV, 'Invictus. In Mem. R.T.H.B.'

1889
---

336 The past was nothing to her; offered no lesson
which she was willing to heed. The future was
a mystery which she never attempted to pen-
etrate. The present alone was significant . . .
Kate Chopin (1851–1904) US writer.
The Awakening, Ch. 15

337 There are some people who leave impressions
not so lasting as the imprint of an oar upon
the water.
Kate Chopin
The Awakening, Ch. 34

1890
---

338 . . . we could never learn to be brave and patient, if there were only joy in the world.
Helen Keller (1880–1968) US writer and
lecturer.
Atlantic Monthly (May 1890)

339 Nature is usually wrong.
James Whistler (1834–1903) US painter.
The Gentle Art of Making Enemies

1891
---

340 There is only one thing in the world worse than
being talked about, and that is not being
talked about.
Oscar Wilde (1854–1900) Irish-born British
dramatist.
The Picture of Dorian Gray, Ch. 1

341 I can sympathize with everything, except
suffering.
Oscar Wilde
The Picture of Dorian Gray, Ch. 3

342 We are all in the gutter, but some of us are
looking at the stars.
Oscar Wilde
Lady Windermere's Fan, III

1892
---

343 They are not long, the days of wine and roses.
Ernest Dowson (1867–1900) British lyric
poet.
*Vitae Summa Brevis Spem Nos Vetat Incohare
Longam*

1895

344 In matters of grave importance, style, not sincerity, is the vital thing.
Oscar Wilde (1854–1900) Irish-born British dramatist.
The Importance of Being Earnest, III

1896

345 It's deadly commonplace, but, after all, the commonplaces are the great poetic truths.
Robert Louis Stevenson (1850–94) Scottish writer.
Weir of Hermiston, Ch. 6

346 Wealth I ask not; hope nor love,
Nor a friend to know me;
All I seek, the heaven above
And the road below me.
Robert Louis Stevenson
Songs of Travel, 'The Vagabond'

1897

347 Man has been endowed with reason, with the power to create, so that he can add to what he's been given. But up to now he hasn't been a creator, only a destroyer. Forests keep disappearing, rivers dry up, wild life's become extinct, the climate's ruined and the land grows poorer and uglier every day.
Anton Chekhov (1860–1904) Russian dramatist.
Uncle Vanya, I

1898

348 I remember my youth and the feeling that will never come back any more – the feeling that I could last for ever, outlast the sea, the earth, and all men; the deceitful feeling that lures us on to perils, to love, to vain effort – to death . . .
Joseph Conrad (Teodor Josef Konrad Korzeniowski; 1857–1924) Polish-born British novelist.
Youth

1902

349 Life is the art of drawing sufficient conclusions from insufficient premises.
Samuel Butler (1835–1902) British writer.
Notebooks

350 Life is one long process of getting tired.
Samuel Butler
Notebooks

351 All progress is based upon a universal innate desire on the part of every organism to live beyond its income.
Samuel Butler
Notebooks

1903

352 In heaven an angel is nobody in particular.
George Bernard Shaw (1856–1950) Irish dramatist and critic.
Man and Superman, 'Maxims for Revolutionists'

353 Live all you can; it's a mistake not to. It doesn't so much matter what you do in particular, so long as you have your life. If you haven't had that what *have* you had?
Henry James (1843–1916) US novelist.
The Ambassadors, Bk. V, Ch. 2

354 The follies which a man regrets most in his life are those which he didn't commit when he had the opportunity.
Helen Rowland (1876–1950) US writer.
Reflections of a Bachelor Girl

1904

355 We must be thoroughly democratic and patronise everybody without distinction of class.
George Bernard Shaw (1856–1950) Irish dramatist and critic.
John Bull's Other Island

1905

356 As enunciated today, 'progress' is simply a comparative of which we have not settled the superlative.
G. K. Chesterton (1874–1936) British writer.
Heretics, Ch. 2

357 A life of pleasure requires an aristocratic setting to make it interesting.
George Santayana (1863–1952) US philosopher.
Life of Reason, 'Reason in Society'

1906

358 Mankind is not a tribe of animals to which we owe compassion. Mankind is a club to which we owe our subscription.
G. K. Chesterton (1874–1936) British writer.
Daily News, 10 Apr 1906

359 Life is made up of sobs, sniffles and smiles, with sniffles predominating.
O. Henry (William Sydney Porter; 1862–1910) US short-story writer.
The Gifts of the Magi

360 The moral flabbiness born of the bitch-goddess Success.
William James (1842–1910) US psychologist and philosopher.
Letter to H. G. Wells, 11 Sept 1906

1908

361 The most important thing in the Olympic Games is not winning but taking part . . . The

essential thing in life is not conquering but fighting well.
Pierre de Coubertin (1863–1937) French educator and sportsman.
Speech, Banquet to Officials of Olympic Games, London, 24 July 1908

1909

362   Reason is itself a matter of faith. It is an act of faith to assert that our thoughts have any relation to reality at all.
G. K. Chesterton (1874–1936) British writer.
Orthodoxy, Ch. 3

363   All conservatism is based upon the idea that if you leave things alone you leave them as they are. But you do not. If you leave a thing alone you leave it to a torrent of change.
G. K. Chesterton
Orthodoxy, Ch. 7

1910

364   One sees great things from the valley; only small things from the peak.
G. K. Chesterton
The Hammer of God

365*   Everything great in the world is done by neurotics; they alone founded our religions and created our masterpieces.
Marcel Proust (1871–1922) French novelist.
The Perpetual Pessimist (Sagittarius and George)

1911

366   The dullard's envy of brilliant men is always assuaged by the suspicion that they will come to a bad end.
Max Beerbohm (1872–1956) British writer.
Zuleika Dobson

367   In the Country of the Blind the One-eyed Man is King.
H. G. Wells (1866–1946) British writer.
The Country of the Blind

1912

368   All that the young can do for the old is to shock them and keep them up to date.
George Bernard Shaw (1856–1950) Irish dramatist and critic.
Fannie's First Play

369   Business underlies everything in our national life, including our spiritual life. Witness the fact that in the Lord's Prayer the first petition is for daily bread. No one can worship God or love his neighbour on an empty stomach.
Woodrow Wilson (1856–1925) US statesman.
Speech, New York, 1912

1913

370   May God deny you peace but give you glory!
Miguel de Unamuno y Jugo (1864–1936) Spanish writer.
Closing words
The Tragic Sense of Life

1915

371*   Life is just one damned thing after another.
Elbert Hubbard (1856–1915) US writer.
A Thousand and One Epigrams

Love and Sex

1880s

372   Daisy, Daisy, give me your answer, do!
I'm half crazy, all for the love of you!
It won't be a stylish marriage,
I can't afford a carriage,
But you'll look sweet upon the seat
Of a bicycle made for two!
Harry Dacre (19th century) British songwriter.
Daisy Bell

1887

373   It seems to me that he has never loved, that he has only imagined that he has loved, that there has been no real love on his part. I even think that he is incapable of love; he is too much occupied with other thoughts and ideas to become strongly attached to anyone earthly.
Anna Dostoevsky (1846–1918) Russian diarist and writer.
Dostoevsky Portrayed by His Wife

1893

374   Young men make great mistakes in life; for one thing, they idealize love too much.
Benjamin Jowett (1817–93) British theologian.
Letters of B. Jowett (Abbott and Campbell)

1895

375   When a man is in love he endures more than at other times; he submits to everything.
Friedrich Wilhelm Nietzsche (1844–1900) German philosopher.
The Antichrist

1903

376   'Tis better to have loved and lost than never to have lost at all.
Samuel Butler (1835–1902) British writer.
The Way of All Flesh, Ch. 77

1905

377 We don't believe in rheumatism and true love until after the first attack.
Marie Ebner von Eschenbach (1830–1916) Austrian writer.
Aphorism

1910

378* But Love has pitched his mansion in
The place of excrement.
W. B. Yeats (1865–1939) Irish poet.
Crazy Jane Talks with the Bishop

379* A pity beyond all telling
Is hid in the heart of love.
W. B. Yeats
The Pity of Love

380* It doesn't matter what you do in the bedroom as long as you don't do it in the street and frighten the horses.
Mrs Patrick Campbell (Beatrice Stella Tanner; 1865–1940) British actress.
The Duchess of Jermyn Street (Daphne Fielding), Ch. 2

381 But oh, the farmyard world of sex!
Harley Granville-Barker (1877–1946) British actor and dramatist.
The Madras House, IV

1912

382 God is Love – I dare say. But what a mischievous devil Love is!
Samuel Butler (1835–1902) British writer.
Notebooks

Marriage and the Family

1881

383 Marriage is a step so grave and decisive that it attracts light-headed, variable men by its very awfulness.
Robert Louis Stevenson (1850–94) Scottish writer.
Virginibus Puerisque

1900

384 I married beneath me – all women do.
Nancy Astor (1879–1964) American-born British politician.
Dictionary of National Biography

1903

385 It takes a woman twenty years to make a man of her son, and another woman twenty minutes to make a fool of him.
Helen Rowland (1876–1950) US writer.
Reflections of a Bachelor Girl

386 If you strike a child, take care that you strike it in anger, even at the risk of maiming it for life.

A blow in cold blood neither can nor should be forgiven.
George Bernard Shaw (1856–1950) Irish dramatist and critic.
Man and Superman, 'Maxims for Revolutionists'

387 It is a woman's business to get married as soon as possible, and a man's to keep unmarried as long as he can.
George Bernard Shaw
Man and Superman

388 There is only one person an English girl hates more than she hates her elder sister; and that is her mother.
George Bernard Shaw
Man and Superman

1909

389 At every step the child should be allowed to meet the real experiences of life; the thorns should never be plucked from his roses.
Ellen Key (Karolina Sofia Key; 1849–1926) Swedish writer.
The Century of the Child, Ch. 3

390 Physically there is nothing to distinguish human society from the farm-yard except that children are more troublesome and costly than chickens and women are not so completely enslaved as farm stock.
George Bernard Shaw (1856–1950) Irish dramatist and critic.
Getting Married, Preface

1910

391 Many a man in love with a dimple makes the mistake of marrying the whole girl.
Stephen Leacock (1869–1944) English-born Canadian economist and humorist.
Literary Lapses

392 The Western custom of one wife and hardly any mistresses.
Saki (Hector Hugh Munro; 1870–1916) British writer.
Reginald in Russia

1911

393 Love is moral even without legal marriage, but marriage is immoral without love.
Ellen Key (Karolina Sofia Key; 1849–1926) Swedish writer.
The Morality of Woman and Other Essays, 'The Morality of Woman'

Men and Women

1870

394 The Queen is most anxious to enlist every one who can speak or write to join in checking this mad, wicked folly of 'Woman's Rights', with all its attendant horrors, on which her poor fee-

ble sex is bent, forgetting every sense of womanly feeling and propriety.
Victoria (1819–1901) Queen of England.
Letter to Sir Theodore Martin, 29 May 1870

1877

395   Taste is the feminine of genius.
Edward Fitzgerald (1809–83) British poet.
Letter to J. R. Lowell, Oct 1877

1881

396   *Declaration of Sentiments:* . . . We hold these truths to be self-evident: that all men and women are created equal . . .
Elizabeth Stanton (1815–1902) US suffragette.
History of Woman Suffrage (with Susan B. Anthony and Mathilda Gage), Vol. I

397   Womanhood is the great fact in her life; wifehood and motherhood are but incidental relations.
Elizabeth Stanton
History of Woman Suffrage (with Susan B. Anthony and Mathilda Gage), Vol. I

398   Man is a creature who lives not upon bread alone, but principally by catchwords; and the little rift between the sexes is astonishingly widened by simply teaching one set of catchwords to the girls and another to the boys.
Robert Louis Stevenson (1850–94) Scottish writer.
Virginibus Puerisque

1883

399   The really original woman is the one who first imitates a man.
Italo Svevo (Ettore Schmitz; 1861–1928) Italian writer.
A Life, Ch. 8

1887

400   She-who-must-be-obeyed.
H. Rider Haggard (1856–1925) British novelist.
She

1888

401   The silliest woman can manage a clever man; but it needs a very clever woman to manage a fool.
Rudyard Kipling (1865–1936) Indian-born British writer.
Plain Tales from the Hills, 'Three and – an Extra'

402   A woman despises a man for loving her, unless she returns his love.
Elizabeth Drew Stoddard (1823–1902) US novelist and poet.
Two Men, Ch. 32

1890s

403   Men their rights and nothing more; women their rights and nothing less.
Susan B. Anthony (1820–1906) US editor.
The Revolution, Motto

404   The prolonged slavery of women is the darkest page in human history.
Elizabeth Stanton (1815–1902) US suffragette.
History of Woman Suffrage (with Susan B. Anthony and Mathilda Gage), Vol. I

1890

405   The superiority of one man's opinion over another's is never so great as when the opinion is about a woman.
Henry James (1843–1916) US novelist.
The Tragic Muse, Ch. 9

1891

406   Women represent the triumph of matter over mind, just as men represent the triumph of mind over morals.
Oscar Wilde (1854–1900) Irish-born British dramatist.
The Picture of Dorian Gray, Ch. 4

1895

407   God created woman. And boredom did indeed cease from that moment – but many other things ceased as well! Woman was God's *second* mistake.
Friedrich Wilhelm Nietzsche (1844–1900) German philosopher.
The Antichrist

408   All women become like their mothers. That is their tragedy. No man does. That's his.
Oscar Wilde (1854–1900) Irish-born British dramatist.
The Importance of Being Earnest, I

1897

409   . . . there never will be complete equality until women themselves help to make laws and elect lawmakers.
Susan B. Anthony (1820–1906) US editor.
In *The Arena*, (May 1897) 'The Status of Women, Past, Present and Future'

410   A woman can become a man's friend only in the following stages – first an acquaintance, next a mistress, and only then a friend.
Anton Chekhov (1860–1904) Russian dramatist.
Uncle Vanya, II

1898

411   Where young boys plan for what they will

achieve and attain, young girls plan for whom they will achieve and attain.
Charlotte Perkins Gilman (1860–1935) US writer.
Women and Economics, Ch. 5

1900s

412   ...the emancipation of women is practically the greatest egoistic movement of the nineteenth century, and the most intense affirmation of the right of the self that history has yet seen...
Ellen Key (Karolina Sofia Key; 1849–1926) Swedish writer.
The Century of the Child, Ch. 2

1902

413   A homely face and no figure have aided many women heavenward.
Minna Antrim (1861–?) US writer.
Naked Truth and Veiled Allusions

1903

414   ...while there is more drinking, there is less drunkenness than formerly, and that the increase in drinking is to be laid mainly to the account of the female sex. This latter phase seems to be one of the unexpected results of the emancipation of women.
Charles Booth (1840–1916) British sociologist.
Life and Labour in London

1906

415   It's a sort of bloom on a woman. If you have it, you don't need to have anything else; and if you don't have it, it doesn't much matter what else you have.
J. M. Barrie (1860–1937) British novelist and dramatist.
Referring to 'charm'
What Every Woman Knows, I

416   If men knew how women pass their time when they are alone, they'd never marry.
O. Henry (William Sidney Porter; 1862–1910) US short-story writer.
The Four Million Memoirs of a Yellow Dog

1910s

417   When the Himalayan peasant meets the he-bear in his pride,
He shouts to scare the monster, who will often turn aside.
But the she-bear thus accosted rends the peasant tooth and nail
For the female of the species is more deadly than the male.
Rudyard Kipling (1865–1936) Indian-born British writer.
The Female of the Species

418   It's nothing to be born ugly. Sensibly, the ugly woman comes to terms with her ugliness and exploits it as a grace of nature.
Colette (Sidonie-Gabrielle C.; 1873–1954) French novelist.
Journey for Myself

1910

419   Scarce, sir. Mighty scarce.
Mark Twain (Samuel Langhorne Clemens; 1835–1910) US writer.
Responding to the question 'In a world without women what would men become?'
Attrib.

1911

420   You will find that the woman who is really kind to dogs is always one who has failed to inspire sympathy in men.
Max Beerbohm (1872–1956) British writer.
Zuleika Dobson, Ch. 6

Morality, Vices, and Virtues

1871

421   The highest possible stage in moral culture is when we recognize that we ought to control our thoughts.
Charles Darwin (1809–82) British life scientist.
Descent of Man, Ch. 4

1873

422   The eternal *not ourselves* that makes for righteousness.
Matthew Arnold (1822–88) British poet and critic.
Literature and Dogma, Ch. 8

1874

423   To be discontented with the divine discontent, and to be ashamed with the noble shame, is the very germ and first upgrowth of all virtue.
Charles Kingsley (1819–75) British writer.
Health and Education

1881

424   The cruellest lies are often told in silence.
Robert Louis Stevenson (1850–94) Scottish writer.
Virginibus Puerisque

425   To travel hopefully is a better thing than to arrive, and the true success is to labour.
Robert Louis Stevenson
Virginibus Puerisque

1886

426   Morality in Europe today is herd-morality.
Friedrich Wilhelm Nietzsche (1844–1900)
German philosopher.
*Jenseits von Gut und Böse (trans. Beyond
Good and Evil)*

1889

427   Much truth is spoken, that more may be
concealed.
Lord Darling (1849–1936) British judge.
Scintillae Juris

1891

428   As long as war is regarded as wicked, it will
always have its fascination. When it is looked
upon as vulgar, it will cease to be popular.
Oscar Wilde (1854–1900) Irish-born British
dramatist.
The Critic as Artist, Pt. 2

429   A little sincerity is a dangerous thing, and a
great deal of it is absolutely fatal.
Oscar Wilde
The Critic as Artist, Pt. 2

1892

430   If your morals make you dreary, depend upon it,
they are wrong.
Robert Louis Stevenson (1850–94) Scottish writer.
Across the Plains

1893

431   It is the restrictions placed on vice by our social. code which makes its pursuit so peculiarly agreeable.
Kenneth Grahame (1859–1932) Scottish
writer.
Pagan Papers

1895

432   Be modest! It is the kind of pride least likely to
offend.
Jules Renard (1894–1910) French writer.
Journal

1898

433   When a stupid man is doing something he is
ashamed of, he always declares that it is his
duty.
George Bernard Shaw (1856–1950) Irish
dramatist and critic.
Caesar and Cleopatra, III

1901

434   No people do so much harm as those who go
about doing good.
Mandell Creighton (1843–1901) British
churchman.
Life

1902

435   Some men love truth so much that they seem
to be in continual fear lest she should catch a
cold on overexposure.
Samuel Butler (1835–1902) British writer.
Notebooks

436   There is no worse lie than a truth misunderstood by those who hear it.
William James (1842–1910) US psychologist
and philosopher.
The Varieties of Religious Experience

437   It does not matter much what a man hates, provided he hates something.
Samuel Butler 1835–1902) British writer.
Notebooks

438   It is the function of vice to keep virtue within
reasonable bounds.
Samuel Butler
Notebooks

1903

439   Pleasure after all is a safer guide than either
right or duty.
Samuel Butler
The Way of All Flesh, Ch. 19

440   The advantage of doing one's praising for oneself is that one can lay it on so thick and exactly in the right places.
Samuel Butler
The Way of All Flesh, Ch. 34

441   Half the vices which the world condemns most
loudly have seeds of good in them and require
moderate use rather than total abstinence.
Samuel Butler
The Way of All Flesh

1905

442   Charity is the power of defending that which we
know to be indefensible. Hope is the power of
being cheerful in circumstances which we
know to be desperate.
G. K. Chesterton (1874–1936) British writer.
Heretics, Ch. 12

443   Self-denial is not a virtue; it is only the effect of
prudence on rascality.
George Bernard Shaw (1856–1950) Irish
dramatist and critic.
Man and Superman, 'Maxims for Revolutionists'

444   Vice is waste of life. Poverty, obedience and
celibacy are the canonical vices.
George Bernard Shaw
Man and Superman

445   Self-sacrifice enables us to sacrifice

Other people without blushing.
George Bernard Shaw
Man and Superman

446 It is dangerous to be sincere unless you are
also stupid.
George Bernard Shaw
Man and Superman

1906

447 *Saint, n.* a dead sinner revised and edited.
Ambrose Bierce (1842–?1914) US writer and
journalist.
The Devil's Dictionary

1907

448 Matilda told such Dreadful Lies
It made one Gasp and Stretch one's Eyes.
For every time she shouted "Fire"
They only answered "Little Liar"
And therefore when her Aunt returned
Matilda, and the House, were Burned.
Hilaire Belloc (1870–1953) French-born British poet.
Cautionary Tales

449 Morals are an acquirement — like music, like a
foreign language, like piety, poker, paralysis —
no man is born with them.
Mark Twain (Samuel Langhorne Clemens;
1835–1910) US writer.
Seventieth Birthday

1908

450 Not only is suicide a sin, it is the sin. It is the
ultimate and absolute evil, the refusal to take
the oath of loyalty to life. The man who kills
a man, kills a man. The man who kills himself
kills all men; as far as he is concerned he
wipes out the world.
G. K. Chesterton (1874–1936) British writer.
Orthodoxy

1909

451 There is false modesty, but there is no false
pride.
Jules Renard (1894–1910) French writer.
Journal

452 Corporal punishment is as humiliating for him
who gives it as for him who receives it; it is
ineffective besides. Neither shame nor physical
pain have any other effect than a hardening
one . . .
Ellen Key (Karolina Sofia Key; 1849–1926)
Swedish writer.
The Century of the Child, Ch. 8

1911

453 The belief in a supernatural source of evil is not

necessary; men alone are quite capable of every wickedness.
Joseph Conrad (Teodor Josef Konrad
Korzeniowski; 1857–1924) Polish-born British
novelist.
Under Western Eyes

454 All a man can betray is his conscience.
Joseph Conrad
Under Western Eyes

Other People

1870

455 America is a country of young men.
Ralph Waldo Emerson (1803–82) US poe
and essayist.
Society and Solitude, 'Old Age'

1891

456 Asia is not going to be civilized after the meods of the West. There is too much Asia an
she is too old.
Rudyard Kipling (1865–1936) Indian-born
British writer.
Life's Handicap, 'The Man Who Was'

1893

457 MRS ALLONBY. They say, Lady Hunstanton, tha
when good Americans die they go to Paris.
LADY HUNSTANTON. Indeed? And when bad
Americans die, where do they go to?
LORD ILLINGWORTH. Oh, they go to America.
Oscar Wilde (1854–1900) Irish-born British
dramatist.
A Woman of No Importance, I

1906

458 There are few more impressive sights in the
world than a Scotsman on the make.
J. M. Barrie (1860–1937) British novelist a
dramatist.
What Every Woman Knows, II

459 You've forgotten the grandest moral attribute
a Scotsman, Maggie, that he'll do nothing
which might damage his career.
J. M. Barrie
What Every Woman Knows, II

1907

460 Cusins is a very nice fellow, certainly; nobo
would ever guess that he was born in
Australia.
George Bernard Shaw (1856–1950) Irish
dramatist and critic.
Major Barbara, I

461* The law of dislike for the unlike will always p
vail. And whereas the unlike is normally sit
ated at a safe distance, the Jews bring the
unlike into the heart of *every milieu*, and m

there defend a frontier line as large as the
world.
Israel Zangwill (1864–1926) British writer.
Speeches, Articles and Letters, 'The Jewish
Race'

1912

2 The English have no respect for their language,
and will not teach their children to speak it . . .
It is impossible for an Englishman to open
his mouth, without making some other Englishman despise him.
George Bernard Shaw (1856–1950) Irish
dramatist and critic.
Pygmalion, Preface

Religion

1872

53 While to deny the existence of an unseen kingdom is bad, to pretend that we know more
about it than its bare existence is no better.
Samuel Butler (1835–1902) British writer.
Erewhon, Ch. 15

1875

64 The prayer that reforms the sinner and heals the
sick is an absolute faith that all things are
possible to God – a spiritual understanding of
Him, an unselfed love.
Mary Baker Eddy (1821–1910) US religious
leader.
Science and Health, with Key to the Scriptures

55 Christian Science explains all cause and effect
as mental, not physical.
Mary Baker Eddy
Science and Health, with Key to the Scriptures

66 Sickness, sin and death, being inharmonious,
do not originate in God, nor belong to His
government.
Mary Baker Eddy
Science and Health, with Key to the Scriptures

1876

67 An honest God is the noblest work of man.
Robert G. Ingersoll (1833–99) US lawyer
and agnostic.
Gods

1882

68 I have been into many of the ancient cathedrals
– grand, wonderful, mysterious. But I always
leave them with a feeling of indignation because of the generations of human beings who
have struggled in poverty to build these altars
to the unknown god.
Elizabeth Stanton (1815–1902) US
suffragette.
Diary

1890

469 God is dead: but considering the state the species Man is in, there will perhaps be caves,
for ages yet, in which his shadow will be
shown.
Friedrich Wilhelm Nietzsche (1844–1900)
German philosopher.
Die Fröhliche Wissenschaft, Bk. III

1892

470 No Jew was ever fool enough to turn Christian
unless he was a clever man.
Israel Zangwill (1864–1926) British writer.
Children of the Ghetto, Ch. 1

1893

471 I fled Him, down the nights and down the days;
I fled Him, down the arches of the years;
I fled Him, down the labyrinthine ways
Of my own mind; and in the mist of tears
I hid from Him, and under running laughter.
Francis Thompson (1859–1907) British poet.
The Hound of Heaven

472 If you don't find a God by five o'clock this afternoon you must leave the college.
Benjamin Jowett (1817–93) British
theologian.
Responding to a young student's assertion that
he could find no evidence for a God
Attrib.

1895

473 I call Christianity the one great curse, the one
enormous and innermost perversion, the one
great instinct of revenge, for which no
means are too venomous, too underhand, too
underground and too petty – I call it the one
immortal blemish of mankind.
Friedrich Wilhelm Nietzsche (1844–1900)
German philosopher.
The Antichrist

1900s

474 So many gods, so many creeds,
So many paths that wind and wind,
While just the art of being kind
Is all the sad world needs.
Ella Wheeler Wilcox (1850–1919) US poet.
The World's Need

1902

475 To be at all is to be religious more or less.
Samuel Butler (1835–1902) British writer.
Notebooks

1903

476 A local cult called Christianity.
Thomas Hardy (1840–1928) British novelist.
The Dynasts, I:6

1905

477 Carlyle said that men were mostly fools. Christianity, with a surer and more reverend realism, says that they are all fools.
G. K. Chesterton (1874–1936) British writer.
Heretics, Ch. 12

1906

478 *Pray, v.* To ask that the rules of the universe be annulled on behalf of a single petitioner, confessedly unworthy.
Ambrose Bierce (1842–?1914) US writer and journalist.
The Devil's Dictionary

1909

479 A Christian is a man who feels
Repentance on a Sunday
For what he did on Saturday
And is going to do on Monday.
Thomas Russell Ybarra (1880–   ) Venezuelan-born US writer.
The Christian

1910

480 Even in the valley of the shadow of death, two and two do not make six.
Leo Tolstoy (1828–1910) Russian writer.
Refusing to reconcile himself with the Russian Orthodox Church as he lay dying

1912

481 Whether you think Jesus was God or not, you must admit that he was a first-rate political economist.
George Bernard Shaw (1856–1950) Irish dramatist and critic.
Androcles and the Lion, Preface, 'Jesus as Economist'

1913

482 At bottom God is nothing more than an exalted father.
Sigmund Freud (1856–1939) Austrian psychoanalyst.
Totem and Taboo

483 For an idea ever to be fashionable is ominous, since it must afterwards be always old-fashioned.
George Santayana (1863–1952) US philosopher.
Winds of Doctrine, 'Modernism and Christianity'

Science, Medicine, and Technology

1871

484 We must, however, acknowledge, as it seems

to me, that man with all his noble qualities, still bears in his bodily frame the indelible stamp of his lowly origin.
Charles Darwin (1809–82) British life scientist.
Closing words
Descent of Man, Ch. 21

1872

485 There are no such things as applied scienc only applications of science.
Louis Pasteur (1822–95) French scientist
Address, 11 Sept 1872

1875

486 Mr. Darwin . . . has failed to hold definitely before his mind the principle that the differe of sex, whatever it may consist in, must its be subject to natural selection and to evolution.
Antoinette Brown Blackwell (1825–19 US feminist writer.
The Sexes Throughout Nature

1876

487 Mr Watson, come here; I want you.
Alexander Graham Bell (1847–1922) S tish scientist.
The first telephone conversation, 10 Mar 18 in Boston
Attrib.

1882

488 Do you really believe that the sciences wo ever have originated and grown if the way had not been prepared by magicians, alche mists, astrologers and witches whose prom and pretensions first had to create a thirst, hunger, a taste for *hidden* and *forbidden* powers? Indeed, infinitely more had to be *promised* than could ever be fulfilled in ord that anything at all might be fulfilled in the realms of knowledge.
Friedrich Wilhelm Nietzsche (1844–19 German philosopher.
The Gay Science

1885

489 Psychology has a long past, but only a sho history.
Hermann Ebbinghaus German psycholog
Summary of Psychology

1894

490 Science is nothing but trained and organize common sense, differing from the latter only a veteran may differ from a raw recruit: an its methods differ from those of common se only as far as the guardsman's cut and thru

differ from the manner in which a savage wields
his club.
T. H. Huxley (1825–95) British biologist.
Collected Essays, 'The Method of Zadig'

491   The great tragedy of Science – the slaying of a
beautiful hypothesis by an ugly fact.
T. H. Huxley
Collected Essays, 'Biogenesis and Abiogenesis'

1903

492*   The airplane stays up because it doesn't have
the time to fall.
Orville Wright (1871–1948) US aviator.
Explaining the principles of powered flight
Attrib.

1912

493   I like mathematics because it is *not* human and
has nothing particular to do with this planet or
with the whole accidental universe – because, like Spinoza's God, it won't love us in
return.
Bertrand Russell (1872–1970) British
philosopher.
Letter to Lady Ottoline Morrell, Mar 1912

1914

494*   The universe ought to be presumed too vast to
have any character.
C. S. Peirce (1839–1914) US physicist.
Collected Papers, VI

495   You cannot endow even the best machine with
initiative. The jolliest steam-roller will not
plant flowers.
Walter Lippmann (1889–1974) US editor and
author.
A Preface to Politics

Wealth and Poverty

1872

496   It has been said that the love of money is the
root of all evil. The want of money is so quite
as truly.
Samuel Butler (1835–1902) British writer.
Erewhon, Ch. 20

1879

497   Poverty is an anomaly to rich people. It is very
difficult to make out why people who want
dinner do not ring the bell.
Walter Bagehot (1826–77) British economist
and journalist.
Literary Studies, II

1880s

498   As I walk along the Bois Bou-long,

With an independent air,
You can hear the girls declare,
'He must be a millionaire',
You can hear them sigh and wish to die,
You can see them wink the other eye
At the man who broke the Bank at Monte
Carlo.
Fred Gilbert (1850–1903) British songwriter.
The Bois de Boulogne was a fashionable recrea-
tional area on the outskirts of Paris
The Man who Broke the Bank at Monte Carlo
(song)

1885

499   I have had no real gratification or enjoyment of
any sort more than my neighbor on the next
block who is worth only half a million.
William Henry Vanderbilt (1821–85) US
railway chief.
Famous Last Words (B. Conrad)

1889

500   It is easy enough to say that poverty is no
crime. No; if it were men wouldn't be ashamed
of it. It is a blunder, though, and is punished
as such. A poor man is despised the whole
world over.
Jerome K. Jerome (1859–1927) British
humorist.
Idle Thoughts of an Idle Fellow

1891

501   As for the virtuous poor, one can pity them, of
course, but one cannot possibly admire them.
Oscar Wilde (1854–1900) Irish-born British
dramatist.
The Soul of Man under Socialism

1905

502   Lack of money is the root of all evil.
George Bernard Shaw (1856–1950) Irish
dramatist and critic.
Man and Superman, 'Maxims for Revolutionists.'

503   The universal regard for money is the one hopeful fact in our civilization. Money is the most
important thing in the world. It represents
health, strength, honour, generosity and
beauty.
George Bernard Shaw
Major Barbara, Preface

504   I am a millionaire. That is my religion.
George Bernard Shaw
Major Barbara

505   CUSINS. Do you call poverty a crime?
UNDERSHAFT. The worst of all crimes. All the
other crimes are virtues beside it.
George Bernard Shaw
Major Barbara

1906

506 *Money, n.* A blessing that is of no advantage to us excepting when we part with it.
Ambrose Bierce (1842–?1914) US writer and journalist.
The Devil's Dictionary

1910s

507 I must say I hate money but it's the lack of it I hate most.
Katherine Mansfield (1888–1923) New-Zealand-born British writer.
Katherine Mansfield (Anthony Alpers)

1910

508 The very poor are unthinkable and only to be approached by the statistician and the poet.
E. M. Forster (1879–1970) British novelist.
Howards End

1911

509 To be clever enough to get all that money, one must be stupid enough to want it.
G. K. Chesterton (1874–1936) British writer.
The Innocence of Father Brown

1914

510 The rich are the scum of the earth in every country.
G. K. Chesterton
The Flying Inn

Work and Occupations

1872

511 Any officer who shall behave in a scandalous manner, unbecoming the character of an officer and a gentleman shall . . . be cashiered.
Anonymous
The words 'conduct unbecoming the character of an officer' are a direct quotation from the Naval Discipline Act (10 Aug 1860), Article 24
Articles of War (1872), *Disgraceful Conduct*, 79

1881

512 Man is so made that he can only find relaxation from one kind of labour by taking up another.
Anatole France (Jacques Anatole François Thibault; 1844–1924) French writer.
The Crime of Sylvestre Bonnard

1882

513 Politics is perhaps the only profession for which no preparation is thought necessary.
Robert Louis Stevenson (1850–94) Scottish writer.
Familiar Studies of Men and Books, 'Yoshida-Torajiro'

1886

514 In the philosopher there is nothing whatever impersonal; and, above all, his morality bears decided and decisive testimony to *who he is* – that is to say, to the order of rank in which the innermost drives of his nature stand in relation to one another.
Friedrich Wilhelm Nietzsche (1844–1900) German philosopher.
Jenseits von Gut und Böse

1890

515* It's Tommy this, an' Tommy that, an' 'Chuck him out, the brute!'
But it's 'Saviour of 'is country' when the guns begin to shoot.
Rudyard Kipling (1865–1936) Indian-born British writer.
Tommy

1891

516 There is much to be said in favour of modern journalism. By giving us the opinions of the uneducated, it keeps us in touch with the ignorance of the community.
Oscar Wilde (1854–1900) Irish-born British dramatist.
The Critic as Artist, Pt. 2

1893

517 I doubt if the philosopher lives, or ever has lived, who could know himself to be heartily despised by a street boy without some irritation.
T. H. Huxley (1825–95) British biologist.
Evolution and Ethics

1898

518 I hesitate to say what the functions of the modern journalist may be; but I imagine that they do not exclude the intelligent anticipation of facts even before they occur.
Lord Curzon (1859–1925) British politician.
Speech, House of Commons, 29 Mar 1898

1899

519 I wish to preach, not the doctrine of ignoble ease, but the doctrine of the strenuous life.
Theodore Roosevelt (1858–1919) US Republican president.
Speech, Chicago, 10 Apr 1899

1900

520 Work is the curse of the drinking classes.
Oscar Wilde (1854–1900) Irish-born British dramatist.
Attrib.

1903

521 When work is a pleasure, life is a joy! When work is a duty, life is slavery.
Maxim Gorky (Aleksei Maksimovich Peshkov; 1868–1936) Russian writer.
The Lower Depths

522 He who can, does. He who cannot, teaches.
George Bernard Shaw (1856–1950) Irish dramatist and critic.
Man and Superman, 'Maxims for Revolutionists'

1905

523 Everybody hates house-agents because they have everybody at a disadvantage. All other callings have a certain amount of give and take; the house-agent simply takes.
H. G. Wells (1866–1946) British writer.
Kipps, Bk. III, Ch. 1

1914

524 Optimistic lies have such immense therapeutic value that a doctor who cannot tell them convincingly has mistaken his profession.
George Bernard Shaw (1856–1950) Irish dramatist and critic.
Misalliance, Preface

Sayings of the Time

1871

525 Dr Livingstone, I presume?
Henry Morton Stanley (1841–1904) British explorer.
On finding David Livingstone at Ujiji on Lake Tanganyika, Nov 1871
How I found Livingstone, Ch. 11

1878

526 Beauty is altogether in the eye of the beholder.
Margaret Wolfe Hungerford (c. 1855–97) Irish novelist.
Also attributed to the US soldier and writer Lew Wallace (1827–1905)
Molly Bawn

1892

527 You know my method. It is founded upon the observance of trifles.
Arthur Conan Doyle (1856–1930) British writer.
The Boscombe Valley Mystery

528 It is an old maxim of mine that when you have excluded the impossible, whatever remains, however improbable, must be the truth.
Arthur Conan Doyle
The Beryl Coronet

529 Castles in the air – they're so easy to take refuge in. So easy to build, too.
Henrik Ibsen (1828–1906) Norwegian dramatist.
The Master Builder, III

530 Though I've belted you an' flayed you,
By the livin' Gawd that made you,
You're a better man than I am, Gunga Din!
Rudyard Kipling (1865–1936) Indian-born British writer.
Gunga Din

531 If you can keep your head when all about you
Are losing theirs and blaming it on you.
Rudyard Kipling
If

532 If you can talk with crowds and keep your virtue,
Or walk with Kings – nor lose the common touch,
If neither foes nor loving friends can hurt you,
If all men count with you, but none too much;
If you can fill the unforgiving minute
With sixty seconds' worth of distance run,
Yours is the Earth and everything that's in it,
And – which is more – you'll be a Man my son!
Rudyard Kipling
If

1893

533 'Excellent!' I cried. 'Elementary,' said he.
Arthur Conan Doyle (1856–1930) British writer.
Watson talking to Sherlock Holmes; Holmes's reply is often misquoted as 'Elementary my dear Watson'
The Crooked Man

1900s

534 She's only a bird in a gilded cage.
A. J. Lamb (1870–1928) British songwriter.
Song title

535 Once a jolly swagman camped by a billabong,
Under the shade of a coolibah tree,
And he sang as he sat and waited for his billy-boil,
'You'll come a-waltzing, Matilda, with me.'
Andrew Barton Paterson (1864–1941) Australian journalist and poet.
Waltzing Matilda

536 Where are the boys of the Old Brigade?
Frederic Edward Weatherly (1848–1929) British lawyer and songwriter.
The Old Brigade

537 Every day, in every way, I am getting better and better.
Emile Coué (1857–1920) French doctor.
Formula for a cure by autosuggestion

1900

538 I shall tell you a tale of four little rabbits whose

names were Flopsy, Mopsy, Cottontail and
Peter.
Beatrix Potter (1866–1943) British children's
writer.
The Tale of Peter Rabbit

1905

539 We seek him here, we seek him there,
Those Frenchies seek him everywhere.
Is he in heaven? – Is he in hell?
That damned elusive Pimpernel?
Baroness Orczy (1865–1947) British
novelist.
The Scarlet Pimpernel, Ch. 12

1908

540 The clever men at Oxford
Know all that there is to be knowed.
But none of them know one half as much
As intelligent Mr Toad.
Kenneth Grahame (1859–1932) Scottish
writer.
The Wind in the Willows, Ch. 10

1910

541* There's a breathless hush in the Close
tonight –
Ten to make and the match to win –
. . .
The sand of the desert is sodden red, –
Red with the wreck of a square that broke; –
The gatling's jammed and the colonel dead,
And the regiment blind with the dust and
smoke.
The river of death has brimmed its banks
And England's far and honour a name.
But the voice of a schoolboy rallies the ranks:
'Play up! play up! and play the game!'
Henry John Newbolt (1862–1938) British
poet.
Vitaï Lampada

542 It's 'Damn you, Jack – I'm all right!' with you
chaps.
David Bone (1874–1959) British sea captain
and writer.
The Brassbounder, Ch. 3

543* Oh, East is East, and West is West, and never
the twain shall meet.
Rudyard Kipling (1865–1936) Indian-born
British writer.
The Ballad of East and West

1911

544 There's a one-eyed yellow idol to the north of
Khatmandu,
There's a little marble cross below the town
There's a broken-hearted woman tends the
grave of Mad Carew
And the Yellow God forever gazes down.
J. Milton Hayes (1884–1940) British writer.
The Green Eye of the Yellow God

With Hindsight

20th century

545 So they told me how Mr Gladstone read Home
for fun, which I thought served him right.
Winston Churchill (1874–1965) British
statesman.
My Early Life, Ch. 2

546 They improvidentially piped growing volumes o
sewage into the sea, the healing virtues of
which were advertised on every railway
station.
Robert Cecil (1913–) British writer.
Referring to seaside resorts
Life in Edwardian England

547 Virtue consisted in avoiding scandal and vene
real disease.
Robert Cecil
Life in Edwardian England

548 Physics becomes in those years the greatest
collective work of science – no, more than
that, the great collective work of art of the
twentieth century.
Jacob Bronowski (1908–74) British scientis
and writer.
Referring to the period around the turn of the
century marked by the elucidation of atomic
structure and the development of the quantum
theory
The Ascent of Man, Ch. 10

549 To give an accurate and exhaustive account o
that period would need a far less brilliant pen
than mine.
Max Beerbohm (1872–1956) British writer.
1880

12

The World Wars (1914–45)

On 28 June 1914 the assassination of the heir to the Austro-Hungarian throne triggered a system of alliances that quickly plunged the whole of Europe into war. This was greeted with enthusiasm in many quarters: both sides expected it to be short and glorious, with everybody home by Christmas. The reality was very different. Such military developments as the machine gun, and the enormous power of the artillery, gave defensive warfare a decisive advantage. The war soon became a contest of attrition with enormous loss of life, especially in the trench warfare on the Western Front. It ended in 1918, after slaughter on a scale hitherto unknown. The strain of the war led to the collapse of the Austrian, German, and Russian monarchies, the last being replaced by the world's first communist state. Europe was now economically exhausted, with the old order totally shattered. Even the victorious British servicemen who had survived the war returned bitter and disillusioned to a country that was supposed to be 'fit for heroes'.

Economic recovery was slow and partial; what improvement there had been was destroyed in 1929 by the Wall Street Crash and the subsequent Great Depression. The USA retreated into isolationism and experimented with prohibition. In the USSR, Stalin, who succeeded Lenin in 1924, brutally imposed his vision of socialism on a reluctant nation. Other countries succumbed to the extreme right, with its cult of the militant dictator: Mussolini, Franco, Salazar, and Hitler. Hitler's combination of ethnic nationalism, antisemitism, and fascism was especially well-received in Germany, where the harshness of the Versailles peace settlement in 1919 accentuated economic hardship and stirred the martial aspirations of the failed Prussian imperialists. After gaining power in 1933, the Nazis attempted to turn their vision of world domination into reality. When appeasement had failed, Britain and France had no alternative but to deliver the ultimatum that led to World War II (1939–45).

Germany's initial successes led to the fall of France and the occupation of nearly the whole of Europe by the Nazis. Britain, expelled ignominiously from France at Dunkirk (June 1940), prepared to defend itself from an invasion that never came. Instead Hitler, his Luftwaffe badly damaged by the RAF in the Battle of Britain, launched an attack on the Soviet Union (June 1941). In December 1941 the Japanese attacked the Americans in Pearl Harbor, thereby joining the conflict on the side of the Axis Powers and forcing the USA to become one of the Allies. By June 1944 Anglo-American forces were ready to invade Europe; in May 1945, two days after Berlin had fallen to the Russians, Germany surrendered. The result of the conflict was the death of some 25 million combatants and civilians, the extermination of 6 million Jews by the Nazis, the ruin of Germany for the second time in a generation, and the devastation of most of Europe.

Politics, Government, and World Events

1914

1 Liberty does not consist in mere declarations of the rights of man. It consists in the translation of those declarations into definite action.
Woodrow Wilson (1856–1924) US statesman.
Speech, 4 July 1914

2 We sauntered through the crowd to Trafalgar Square where Labour, socialist, pacifist demonstrators — with a few trade union flags — were gesticulating from the steps of the monuments to a mixed crowd of admirers, hooligan warmongers and merely curious holidaymakers. It was an undignified and futile exhibition, this singing of the Red Flag and passing of well-worn radical resolutions in favour of universal peace.
Beatrice Webb (1858–1943) British economist and writer.
Referring to an anti-war demonstration, 2 Aug 1914
Diary, 4 Aug 1914; war was declared on Germany at 11 p.m.

3 The lamps are going out over all Europe; we shall not see them lit again in our lifetime.
Lord Grey (1862–1933) British statesman.
Remark made on 3 Aug 1914, the eve of World War I

4 We draw the sword with a clear conscience and with clean hands.
Wilhelm II (1859–1941) King of Prussia and Emperor of Germany.
Speech, Berlin, 4 Aug 1914

5 You will be home before the leaves have fallen from the trees.
Wilhelm II
Said to troops leaving for the Front, Aug 1914
August 1914 (Barbara Tuchman), Ch. 9

6 When you march into France, let the last man on the right brush the Channel with his sleeve.
Alfred Graf von Schlieffen (1833–1913) German general.
Referring to the Schlieffen plan – a German plan of attack
August 1914 (Barbara Tuchman), Ch. 2

7 When the war broke out she took down the signed photograph of the Kaiser and, with some solemnity, hung it in the menservants' lavatory; it was her one combative action.
Evelyn Waugh (1903–66) British novelist.
Vile Bodies, Ch. 3

8 The United States must be neutral in fact as well as in name during these days that are to try men's souls. We must be impartial in thought as well as in action.
Woodrow Wilson (1856–1924) US statesman.
Message to the Senate, 19 Aug 1914

9 It is my Royal and Imperial Command that you ... exterminate first the treacherous English, and ... walk over General French's contemptible little Army.
Wilhelm II (1859–1941) King of Prussia and Emperor of Germany.
Referring to the British Expeditionary Force; veterans of this force became known as 'Old Contemptibles'
The Times, 1 Oct 1914

10 We shall never sheathe the sword which we have not lightly drawn until Belgium receives in full measure all and more than all that she has sacrificed, until France is adequately secured against the menace of aggression, until the rights of the smaller nationalities of Europe are placed upon an unassailable foundation, and until the military domination of Prussia is wholly and finally destroyed.
Herbert Henry Asquith (1852–1928) British statesman.
Speech, Guildhall, 9 Nov 1914

11 The maxim of the British people is 'Business as usual'.
Winston Churchill (1874–1965) British statesman.
Speech, Guildhall, 9 Nov 1914

12 I don't mind your being killed, but I object to your being taken prisoner.
Lord Kitchener (1850–1916) British field marshal.
Said to the Prince of Wales (later Edward VIII) when he asked to go to the Front
Journal (Viscount Esher), 18 Dec 1914

13 Your country needs YOU.
British recruiting poster featuring Lord Kitchener

14 If Kitchener was not a great man he was, at least, a great poster.
Margot Asquith (1865–1945) The second wife of Herbert Asquith.
Kitchener: Portrait of an Imperialist (Sir Philip Magnus), Ch. 14

15* We Don't Want To Lose You But We Think You Ought To Go.
Paul Alfred Rubens (1875–1917) British dramatist and songwriter.
Title of patriotic music-hall song

16* Good-bye Piccadilly, Farewell Leicester Square; It's a long, long way to Tipperary, but my heart's right there!
Harry Williams (1874–1924) British songwriter.
Written with Jack Judge (1878–1938)
It's a Long Way to Tipperary

17 It's often safer to be in chains than to be free.
Franz Kafka (1883–1924) Czech novelist.
The Trial, Ch. 8

18* The old Lie: *Dulce et decorum est Pro patria mori.*
Wilfred Owen (1893–1918) British poet.
Dulce et decorum est

19 My pacifism is not based on any intellectual

theory but on a deep antipathy to every form of
cruelty and hatred.
Albert Einstein (1879–1955) German-born
US physicist.
Said on the outbreak of World War I
Attrib.

20* Above all I am not concerned with Poetry. My
subject is War, and the pity of War. The Poetry is in the pity.
Wilfred Owen (1893–1918) British poet.
Poems, Preface

21* The pallor of girls' brows shall be their pall;
Their flowers the tenderness of patient minds,
And each slow dusk a drawing-down of
blinds.
Wilfred Owen
Anthem for Doomed Youth

22* Red lips are not so red
As the stained stones kissed by the English
dead.
Wilfred Owen
Greater Love

23* Dead battles, like dead generals, hold the military mind in their dead grip.
Barbara W. Tuchman (1912–   ) US editor
and writer.
August 1914, Ch. 2

1915

24 No nation is fit to sit in judgement upon any
other nation.
Woodrow Wilson (1856–1925) US
statesman.
Address, Apr 1915

25* Once lead this people into war and they'll forget there ever was such a thing as tolerance.
Woodrow Wilson
Mr Wilson's War (John Dos Passos), Pt. III, Ch.
2

26 There is such a thing as a man being too proud
to fight.
Woodrow Wilson
Address to foreign-born citizens, 10 May 1915

27 LUDENDORFF. The English soldiers fight like lions.
HOFFMANN. True. But don't we know that they
are lions led by donkeys.
Max Hoffmann (1869–1927) German general.
The Donkeys (A. Clark)

28 In Flanders fields the poppies blow
Between the crosses, row on row,
That mark our place.
John McCrae (1872–1918) Canadian poet
and doctor.
In Flanders Fields, 'Ypres Salient', 3 May 1915

29 There is no room in this country for hyphenated
Americanism.
Theodore Roosevelt (1858–1919) US Re-
publican president.
Speech, New York, 12 Oct 1915

30* War knows no pause. Safe shall be my going,
Secretly armed against all death's endeavour,
Safe though all safety's lost; safe where men
fall;

And if these poor limbs die, safest of all.
Rupert Brooke (1887–1915) British poet.
Safety

31 If I should die, think only this of me:
That there's some corner of a foreign field
That is forever England.
Rupert Brooke
The Soldier

32 I realize that patriotism is not enough. I mus
have no hatred or bitterness towards anyone
Edith Cavell (1865–1915) British nurse.
Before her execution by the Germans in 1915

33 Smile at us, pay us, pass us; but do not quit
forget.
For we are the people of England, that nev
have spoken yet.
G. K. Chesterton (1874–1936) British write
The Secret People

34 Don't talk to me about naval tradition. It's not
ing but rum, sodomy, and the lash.
Winston Churchill (1874–1965) British
statesman.
Former Naval Person (Sir Peter Gretton), Ch.

1916

35 All dressed up, with nowhere to go.
William Allen White (1868–1944) US write
Referring to the Progressive Party, after Theo-
dore Roosevelt's withdrawal from the 1916 U
Presidential election

36 America cannot be an ostrich with its head i
the sand.
Woodrow Wilson (1856–1924) US
statesman.
Speech, Des Moines, 1 Feb 1916

37 Jellicoe was the only man on either side wh
could lose the war in an afternoon.
Winston Churchill (1874–1965) British
statesman.
Referring to Admiral Jellicoe, who commanded
the British fleet at the Battle of Jutland (31 M
1916)
The Observer, 'Sayings of the Week', 13 Feb
1927

38 He kept us out of war!
Martin H. Glynn (1891–1924) Governor of
New York State.
Referring to President Wilson
Speech, Democratic Convention, St Louis, 15
June 1916

39 What should I do? I think the best thing is t
order a new stamp to be made with my face
on it.
Charles (1887–1922) Emperor of Austria.
On hearing of his accession to·emperor
Anekdotenschatz (H. Hoffmeister)

40 Be the Emperor, be Peter the Great, John th
Terrible, the Emperor Paul – crush them all
under you – Now don't you laugh, naughty o
– but I long to see you so with those men

who try to govern *you* and it must be the contrary.
Alexandra (1872–1918) Empress-Consort of Russia
Letter (in English) to Nicholas II, 27 Dec 1916

41 Ireland is the old sow that eats her farrow.
James Joyce (1882–1941) Irish novelist.
A Portrait of the Artist as a Young Man, Ch. 5

42 This war, like the next war, is a war to end war.
David Lloyd George (1863–1945) British Liberal statesman.
Referring to the popular opinion that World War I would be the last major war

43* O Death, where is thy sting-a-ling-a-ling,
O Grave, thy victoree?
The bells of hell go ting-a-ling-a-ling
For you but not for me.
Anonymous
Song of World War I

44 What's the use of worrying?
It never was worth while,
So, pack up your troubles in your old kit-bag,
And smile, smile, smile.
George Asaf (George H. Powell; 1880–1951) US songwriter.
Pack up Your Troubles in Your Old Kit-bag

45 I have a rendezvous with Death
At some disputed barricade.
Alan Seeger (1888–1916) US poet.
I Have a Rendezvous with Death

46 *Ils ne passeront pas.*
They shall not pass.
Marshal Pétain (1856–1951) French marshal.
Attrib; probably derived from General R.-G. Nivelle's Order of the Day, *'Vous ne les laisserez pas passer'* (June 1916). It is also attributed to the Spanish politician Dolores Ibarruri in the Spanish Civil War.

47 I had always to remember that I could have lost the war in an afternoon.
Lord Jellicoe (1859–1935) British admiral.
Referring to the Battle of Jutland

48 Formerly, a nation that broke the peace did not trouble to try and prove to the world that it was done solely from higher motives . . . Now *war has a bad conscience*. Now every nation assures us that it is bleeding for a human cause, the fate of which hangs in the balance of its victory. . . . No nation dares to admit the guilt of blood before the world.
Ellen Key (Karolina Sofia Key; 1849–1926) Swedish writer.
War, Peace, and the Future, Preface

49 Everything, everything in war is barbaric . . . But the worst barbarity of war is that it forces men collectively to commit acts against which individually they would revolt with their whole being.
Ellen Key
War, Peace, and the Future, Ch. 6

1917

50 The first casualty when war comes is truth.
Hiram Warren Johnson (1866–1945) US politician.
Speech, US Senate, 1917

51 The world must be made safe for democracy.
Woodrow Wilson (1856–1925) US statesman.
Address to Congress, asking for a declaration of war 2 Apr 1917

52 Lafayette, we are here!
C. E. Stanton (1859–1933) US colonel.
The Marquis de Lafayette (1757–1834) aided the colonists in the US War of Independence
Address at Lafayette's grave, Paris, 4 July 1917

53* Deleted by French censor.
James Gordon Bennett (1841–1918) US newspaper owner and editor.
Used to fill empty spaces in his papers during World War I when news was lacking
Americans in Paris (B. Morton)

54 Now all roads lead to France
And heavy is the tread
Of the living; but the dead
Returning lightly dance.
Edward Thomas (1878–1917) British poet.
Roads

55 The Church should be no longer satisfied to represent only the Conservative Party at prayer.
Agnes Maude Royden (1887–1967) British Congregationalist minister.
Speech, London, 16 July 1917

56 America . . . is the prize amateur nation of the world. Germany is the prize professional nation.
Woodrow Wilson (1856–1925) US statesman.
Speech, Aug 1917
Mr Wilson's War (John Dos Passos), Pt. III, Ch. 13

57 His Majesty's Government views with favour the establishment in Palestine of a national home for the Jewish people . . .
Arthur Balfour (1848–1930) British statesman.
The so-called 'Balfour Declaration'
Letter to Lord Rothschild, 2 Nov 1917

58 The Germans turned upon Russia the most grisly of all weapons. They transported Lenin in a sealed truck like a plague bacillus from Switzerland to Russia.
Winston Churchill (1874–1965) British statesman.
The World Crisis

59 The proper memory for a politician is one that knows when to remember and when to forget.
John Morley (1838–1923) British statesman.
Recollections

The Russian Revolution (1917)

By 1900, Russia was almost alone among European powers in having a strong monarchy; there had been hardly any erosion of the Tsar's autocratic power or indeed any reform at all. Socially, economically, and politically Russia was far behind the rest of Europe. The revolutionary disturbances that had occurred throughout the 19th century culminated in Bloody Sunday (22 January, 1905). As a result of this uprising a parliament was established in 1906; thereafter the Tsar ruled by an ever-weakening mixture of autocratic repression and grudging social and political reform. In Feburary 1917, after the strain of two and a half years of war, the system collapsed. Strikes in the capital and mutinies in the army quickly escalated, forcing the Tsar to abdicate. Although a provisional government attempted to fill the political vacuum, the continuing instability played into the hands of the Bolsheviks, led by Lenin. In the revolution of October 1917 the Bolsheviks finally seized power. During the ensuing years they consolidated their power over the whole country, internal opposition and foreign-backed counter-revolutionaries being defeated by the Red Army in a civil war (1918–21). By 1922 the Soviet Union was firmly established as the world's first communist state.

60 **Peace, Bread and Land.**
Slogan of workers in Petrograd (St Petersburg) during the February Revolution

61 **Dear comrades, soldiers, sailors and workers! I am happy to greet in you the victorious Russian Revolution!**
Lenin (Vladimir Ilich Ulyanov; 1870–1924) Russian revolutionary leader.
Speech, Finland Station (Petrograd), 16 Apr 1917

62 **All Power to the Soviets!**
Slogan of workers in Petrograd (St Petersburg) during the October Revolution

63 **The substitution of the proletarian for the bourgeois state is impossible without a violent revolution.**
Lenin (Vladimir Ilich Ulyanov; 1870–1924)
State and Revolution, Ch. 1

64 **In a state worthy of the name there is no liberty. The people want to exercise power but what on earth would they do with it if it were given to them?**
Lenin
The State and Revolution

65 **If it were necessary to give the briefest possible definition of imperialism we should have to say that imperialism is the monopoly stage of capitalism.**
Lenin
Imperialism, the Highest Stage of Capitalism, Ch. 7

66 **We shall now proceed to construct the socialist order.**
Lenin
First words to the Congress of Soviets after the capture of the Winter Palace, 26 Oct 1917

67 **Ten Days that Shook the World.**
John Reed (1887–1920) American journalist.
Referring to the Bolshevik Revolution in Russia (Nov 1917)
Book title

68 **Neither can you expect a revolution, because there is no new baby in the womb of our society. Russia is a collapse, not a revolution.**
D. H. Lawrence (1885–1930) British novelist.
Phoenix, 'The Good Man'

69* **Patriotism to the Soviet State is a revolutionary duty, whereas patriotism to a bourgeois State is treachery.**
Leon Trotsky (Lev Davidovich Bronstein; 1879–1940) Russian revolutionary.
Disputed Barricade (Fitzroy Maclean)

70 **So long as the state exists there is no freedom. When there is freedom there will be no state.**
Lenin (Vladimir Ilich Ulyanov; 1870–1924) Russian revolutionary leader.
The State and Revolution, Ch. 5

71 **The 23rd of February was International Woman's Day . . . It had not occurred to anyone that it might become the first day of the revolution.**
Leon Trotsky (Lev Davidovich Bronstein; 1879–1940) Russian revolutionary.
History of the Russian Revolution, Pt. I, Ch. 7

72 **Under socialism *all* will govern in turn and will soon become accustomed to no one governing.**
Lenin (Vladimir Ilich Ulyanov; 1870–1924) Russian revolutionary leader.
The State and Revolution, Ch. 6

1918

73 *Per ardua ad astra.*
Through endeavour to the stars.
Anonymous
Motto of the Royal Air Force

74 **What we demand in this war is nothing peculiar to ourselves. It is that the world be made fit and safe to live in.**
Woodrow Wilson (1856–1924) US statesman.
Preamble to his 'Fourteen Points' for ensuring world peace
Speech to Congress, 8 Jan 1918

75 **Self-determination is not a mere phrase. It is an imperative principle which statesmen will henceforth ignore at their peril.**
Woodrow Wilson
Speech to Congress, 11 Feb 1918

76 **My home policy? I wage war. My foreign policy? I wage war. Always, everywhere, I wage war . . . And I shall continue to wage war until the last quarter of an hour.**
Georges Clemenceau (1841–1929) French statesman.
Speech, Chamber of Deputies, 8 Mar 1918

77 **A mademoiselle from Armenteers,
She hasn't been kissed for forty years,**

Hinky, dinky, par-lee-voo.
Edward Rowland (20th century) British songwriter.
Armentières was completely destroyed (1918) in World War I
Mademoiselle from Armentières (song)

8 Every position must be held to the last man: there must be no retirement. With our backs to the wall, and believing in the justice of our cause, each one of us must fight on to the end.
Earl Haig (1861–1928) British general.
Order to the British Army, 12 Apr 1918

9 Come on, you sons of bitches! Do you want to live for ever?
Dan Daly (20th century) Sergeant in the US Marines.
Exhorting his men at Belleau Wood, June 1918
Attrib.

0 My centre is giving way, my right is in retreat; situation excellent. I shall attack.
Marshal Foch (1851–1929) French soldier.
Message sent during the second battle of the Marne, 1918
Biography of Foch (Aston), Ch. 13

1 'Good morning; good morning!' the general said
When we met him last week on our way to the line.
Now the soldiers he smiled at are most of 'em dead,
And we're cursing his staff for incompetent swine.
Siegfried Sassoon (1886–1967) British poet.
The General

2 If I were fierce and bald and short of breath,
I'd live with scarlet Majors at the Base,
And speed glum heroes up the line to death.
Siegfried Sassoon
Base Details

3 Man, it seemed, had been created to jab the life out of Germans.
Siegfried Sassoon
Memoirs of an Infantry Officer, Pt. I, Ch. 1

4 Who will remember, passing through this gate
The unheroic dead who fed the guns?
Who shall absolve the foulness of their fate –
Those doomed, conscripted, unvictorious ones?
Siegfried Sassoon
On Passing the New Menin Gate

5 And when the war is done and youth stone dead
I'd toddle safely home and die – in bed.
Siegfried Sassoon
Base Details

6 I am making this statement as a wilful defiance of military authority because I believe that the War is being deliberately prolonged by those who have the power to end it.
Siegfried Sassoon
Memoirs of an Infantry Officer, Pt. X, Ch. 3

* I could not give my name to aid the slaughter in this war, fought on both sides for grossly material ends, which did not justify the sacrifice of a single mother's son. Clearly I must continue to oppose it, and expose it, to all whom I could reach with voice or pen.
Sylvia Pankhurst (1882–1960) British suffragette.
The Home Front, Ch. 25

88 Madam, I am the civilization they are fighting to defend.
Heathcote William Garrod (1878–1960) British classical scholar.
Replying to criticism that he was not fighting to defend civilization, during World War I
Oxford Now and Then (D. Balsdon)

89 They died to save their country and they only saved the world.
Hilaire Belloc (1870–1953) French-born British poet.
The English Graves

90* The shrill demented choirs of wailing shells
And buglers calling for them from sad shires.
Wilfred Owen (1893–1918) British poet.
Anthem for Doomed Youth

91 With proud thanksgiving, a mother for her children,
England mourns for her dead across the sea.
Laurence Binyon (1869–1943) British poet.
In response to the slaughter of World War I
Poems For the Fallen

92 They shall grow not old, as we that are left grow old:
Age shall not weary them, nor the years condemn.
At the going down of the sun and in the morning
We will remember them.
Laurence Binyon
Poems For the Fallen

93 Sire you no longer have an army.
Wilhelm Groener (1867–1939) German general.
Said to the Emperor Wilhelm II of Germany, 9 Nov 1918

94 As an English General has very truly said, 'The German army was stabbed in the back'.
Paul von Hindenburg (1847–1934) German Field Marshal and President.
Referring to Germany's defeat in World War I; it is not known whom Hindenburg was quoting
Statement to a Reichstag Committee, 18 Nov 1918

95 When the days of rejoicing are over,
When the flags are stowed safely away,
They will dream of another wild 'War to End Wars'
And another wild Armistice day.

But the boys who were killed in the trenches,
Who fought with no rage and no rant,
We left them stretched out on their pallets of mud
Low down with the worm and the ant.
Robert Graves (1895–1985) British poet and novelist.
Armistice Day, 1918

96* The war we have just been through, though it was shot through with terror, is not to be compared with the war we would have to face next time.
Woodrow Wilson (1856–1925) US statesman.
Mr Wilson's War (John Dos Passos), Pt. V, Ch. 22

97 The British flag has never flown over a more powerful or a more united empire . . . Never did our voice count for more in the councils of nations; or in determining the future destinies of mankind.
George Nathaniel Carson (1859–1925) British politician.
Speech, House of Lords, 18 Nov 1918

98 What is our task? To make Britain a fit country for heroes to live in.
David Lloyd George (1863–1945) British Liberal statesman.
Speech, 24 Nov 1918

99 The Germans, if this Government is returned, are going to pay every penny; they are going to be squeezed, as a lemon is squeezed — until the pips squeak. My only doubt is not whether we can squeeze hard enough, but whether there is enough juice.
Eric Campbell Geddes (1875–1937) British politician.
Speech, Cambridge, 10 Dec 1918

100 A lot of hard-faced men who look as if they had done very well out of the war.
Stanley Baldwin (1867–1947) British statesman.
Referring to the first House of Commons elected after World War I (1918)
Economic Consequences of the Peace (J. M. Keynes), Ch. 5

1919

101 There is nothing that war has ever achieved that we could not better achieve without it.
Havelock Ellis (1859–1939) British sexologist.
The Philosophy of Conflict

102 It is far easier to make war than to make peace.
Georges Clemenceau (1841–1929) French statesman.
Speech, 14 July 1919

103 We are all Home Rulers today.
The Times, 26 Mar 1919

104 I never met anyone in Ireland who understood the Irish question, except one Englishman who had only been there a week.
Keith Fraser (1867–1935) British politician.
Speech, House of Commons, May 1919

105 There is no right to strike against the public safety by anybody, anywhere, any time.
Calvin Coolidge (1872–1933) US President.
Referring to the Boston police strike
Remark, 14 Sept 1919

106 He was the Messiah of the new age, and his crucifixion was yet to come.
George Edward Slocombe (1894–1963) British journalist.
Referring to Woodrow Wilson and his visit to the Versailles conference
Mirror to Geneva

107 Of all tyrannies in history the Bolshevik tyranny is the worst, the most destructive, the most degrading
Winston Churchill (1874–1965) British statesman.
Speech, London, 11 Apr 1919

108 A democracy is a state which recognises the subjecting of the minority to the majority.
Lenin (Vladimir Ilich Ulyanov; 1870–1924) Russian revolutionary leader.
The State and The Revolution

109 I have seen the future and it works.
Lincoln Steffens (1866–1936) US journalist
Speaking to Bernard Baruch after visiting the Soviet Union, 1919
Autobiography, Ch. 18

1920

110 Russia will certainly inherit the future. What we already call the greatness of Russia is only her pre-natal struggling.
D. H. Lawrence (1885–1930) British novelist
Phoenix, Preface, 'All Things are Possible' by Leo Shostov

111 Communism is Soviet power plus the electrification of the whole country.
Lenin (Vladimir Ilich Ulyanov; 1870–1924) Russian revolutionary leader.
Political slogan of 1920, promoting the programme of electrification

112 Labour is not fit to govern.
Winston Churchill (1874–1965) British statesman.
Election speech, 1920

113 One to mislead the public, another to mislead the Cabinet, and the third to mislead itself.
Herbert Henry Asquith (1852–1928) British statesman.
Explaining why the War Office kept three sets of figures
The Price of Glory (Alastair Horne), Ch. 2

114 A man may build himself a throne of bayonets but he cannot sit on it.
Dean Inge (1860–1954) British churchman.
Wit and Wisdom of Dean Inge (ed. Marchant)

115 The enemies of Freedom do not argue; they shout and they shoot.
Dean Inge
The End of an Age, Ch. 4

116 Those only can care intelligently for the future of England to whom the past is dear.
Dean Inge
Assessments and Anticipations

117 There died a myriad,
And of the best, among them,
For an old bitch gone in the teeth,

For a botched civilization
Ezra Pound (1885-1972) US poet.
Hugh Selwyn Mauberley

18 Died some, pro patria,
non 'dulce' non 'et decor'
Ezra Pound
Hugh Selwyn Mauberley

19 The earth is still bursting with the dead bodies
of the victors.
George Bernard Shaw (1856-1950) Irish
dramatist and critic.
Heartbreak House, Preface

20 Peace is not only better than war, but infinitely
more arduous.
George Bernard Shaw
Heartbreak House (Preface)

21 Truth telling is not compatible with the defence
of the realm.
George Bernard Shaw
Heartbreak House

1921

22 They are the only people who like to be told
how bad things are – who like to be told the
worst.
Winston Churchill (1874-1965) British
statesman.
Speech, 1921

23 I have gone to war too ... I am going to fight
capitalism even if it kills me. It is wrong that
people like you should be comfortable and well
fed while all around you people are starving.
Sylvia Pankhurst (1882-1960) British
suffragette.
The Fighting Pankhursts (David Mitchell)

24 I am signing my death warrant.
Michael Collins (1890-1922) Irish nationalist.
Said on signing the agreement with Great Britain,
1921, that established the Irish Free State; he
was assassinated in an ambush some months
later
Peace by Ordeal (Longford), Pt. 6, Ch. 1

25 It is the government that should ask me for a
pardon.
Eugene Victor Debs (1855-1926) US trade
unionist, socialist, and pacifist.
When released from prison (1921) on the orders
of President Harding after being jailed for sedi-
tion (1918)
The People's Almanac (D. Wallechinsky)

1922

26 America has all that Russia has not. Russia has
things America has not. Why will America not
reach out a hand to Russia, as I have given
my hand?
Isadora Duncan (1878-1927) US dancer.
Speaking in support of Russia following the 1917
Revolution
Speech, Symphony Hall, Boston, 1922

127 The rogue elephant among British prime
ministers.
Dr Kenneth Morgan (1934-   ) British
historian.
Referring to Lloyd George
Life of David Lloyd George

128 Count not his broken pledges as a crime
He MEANT them, HOW he meant them – at
the time.
Kensal Green
Referring to David Lloyd George
The Faber Book of English History in Verse
(Kenneth Baker)

129 I have many times asked myself whether there
can be more potent advocates of peace upon
earth through the years to come than this
massed multitude of silent witnesses to the
desolation of war.
George V (1865-1936) King of the United
Kingdom.
Referring to the massed World War I graves in
Flanders, 1922
Silent Cities (ed. Gavin Stamp)

130 *Il Duce ha sempre ragione.*
The Duce is always right.
Fascist Slogan

131 I could have transformed this grey assembly
hall into an armed camp of Blackshirts, a
bivouac for corpses. I could have nailed up the
doors of Parliament.
Benito Mussolini (1883-1945) Italian
dictator.
Referring to the Fascist march on Rome, which
had resulted in Mussolini becoming prime minister (31 Oct 1922)
Speech, Chamber of Deputies, 16 Nov 1922

1923

132 "Liberty Mr Gumboil?" he said, "you don't
suppose any serious minded person imagines a
revolution is going to bring liberty do you?"
Aldous Huxley (1894-1964) British novelist.
Antic Hay

133 All those who are not racially pure are mere
chaff.
Adolf Hitler (1889-1945) German dictator.
Mein Kampf

134 The broad mass of a nation ... will more easily
fall victim to a big lie than to a small one.
Adolf Hitler
Mein Kampf

135 Only constant repetition will finally succeed in
imprinting an idea on the memory of the
crowd.
Adolf Hitler
Mein Kampf

136 The greater the lie, the greater the chance that
it will be believed.
Adolf Hitler
Mein Kampf

137 Germany will be either a world power or will
     not be at all.
     Adolf Hitler
     Mein Kampf

138 Look at that man's eyes. You will hear more of
     him later.
     Bonar Law (1858–1923) British statesman.
     Referring to Mussolini
     Attrib.

139 It is fitting that we should have buried the Un-
     known Prime Minister by the side of the Un-
     known Soldier.
     Herbert Henry Asquith (1852–1928) British
     statesman.
     Said at Bonar Law's funeral, 5 Nov 1923
     Attrib.

140 Of all the politicians I ever saw
     The least significant was Bonar Law.
     Unless it was MacDonald, by the way:
     Or Baldwin – it's impossible to say.
     Hilaire Belloc (1870–1953) French-born Brit-
     ish poet.
     The Faber Book of English History in Verse
     (Kenneth Baker)

141 Not even a public figure. A man of no experi-
     ence. And of the utmost insignificance.
     Lord Curzon (1859–1925) British politician.
     Referring to Stanley Baldwin on his appointment
     as Prime Minister
     Curzon: The Last Phase (Harold Nicolson)

142 You may be the most liberal Liberal English-
     man, and yet you cannot fail to see the categor-
     ical difference between the responsible and
     the irresponsible classes.
     D. H. Lawrence (1885–1930) British novelist.
     Kangaroo, Ch. 1

143 The inevitability of gradualness.
     Sydney Webb (1859–1947) British
     economist.
     Presidential Address to Labour Party Confer-
     ence, 1923

     ───────
       1924

144 Today 23 years ago dear Grandmama died. I
     wonder what she would have thought of a
     Labour Government.
     George V (1865–1936) King of the United
     Kingdom
     On the formation of the first Labour Government
     Diary, 22 Jan 1924

145 Well, what are you socialists going to do about
     me?
     George V
     To Ramsay MacDonald at his first meeting as
     prime minister
     Attrib.

146 Under capitalism we have a state in the proper
     sense of the word, that is, a special machine
     for the suppression of one class by another.
     Lenin (Vladimir Ilich Ulyanov; 1870–1924) Rus-
     sian revolutionary leader.
     The State and Revolution, Ch. 5

147 A Social-Democrat must never forget that the
     proletariat will inevitably have to wage a
     class struggle for Socialism even against the
     most democratic and republican bourgeoisie
     and petty bourgeoisie.
     Lenin
     The State and Revolution, Ch. 10

148 It is true that liberty is precious – so precious
     that it must be rationed.
     Lenin
     Attrib.

149 The state is an instrument in the hands of the
     ruling class for suppressing the resistance of
     its class enemies.
     Joseph Stalin (J. Dzhugashvili; 1879–1953)
     Soviet statesman.
     Stalin's Kampf (ed. M. R. Werner)

150 It was the supreme expression of the medioc-
     rity of the apparatus that Stalin himself rose
     to his position.
     Leon Trotsky (Lev Davidovich Bronstein;
     1879–1940) Russian revolutionary.
     My Life, Ch. 40

151 Their worst misfortune was his birth; their next
     worst – his death.
     Winston Churchill (1874–1965) British
     statesman.
     Referring to Lenin
     The World Crisis

152 The first time you meet Winston you see all his
     faults and the rest of your life you spend in
     discovering his virtues.
     Lady Constance Lytton (1869–1923) British
     suffragette.
     Referring to Winston Churchill
     Edward Marsh (Christopher Hassall), Ch. 7

153 The customer is always right.
     H. Gordon Selfridge (1857–1947) US-born
     businessman.
     Slogan adopted at his shops

154 The so-called white races are really pinko-gray.
     E. M. Forster (1879–1970) British novelist.
     A Passage to India, Ch. 7

155 The foundation of the government of a nation
     must be built upon the rights of the people, but
     the administration must be entrusted to
     experts.
     Sun Yat-sen (1867–1925) Chinese revolution-
     ary leader.
     The Three Principles of the People

156* This is virgin territory for whorehouses.
     Al Capone (1899–1947) Italian-born US
     gangster.
     Talking about suburban Chicago
     The Bootleggers (Kenneth Allsop), Ch. 16

     ───────
       1925

157* Is it possible that my people live in such awful
     conditions? . . . I tell you, Mr Wheatley, that if

I had to live in conditions like that I would be a revolutionary myself.
George V (1865–1936) King of the United Kingdom.
On being told Mr Wheatley's life story
The Tragedy of Ramsay MacDonald
(L. MacNeill Weir), Ch. 16

8 They hired the money, didn't they?
Calvin Coolidge (1872–1933) US president.
Referring to the war debts incurred by England and others

9 The business of America is business.
Calvin Coolidge
Speech, Washington, 17 Jan 1925

1926

0 Constitutional Government is being attacked ... The general strike is a challenge to Parliament, and is the road to anarchy and ruin.
Stanley Baldwin (1867–1947) British politician and prime minister.
The British Gazette, 6 May 1926

1 Not a penny off the pay; not a minute on the day.
A. J. Cook (1885–1931) British trade-union leader.
Slogan used in the miners' strike, 1926

2 That's what you are. That's what you all are. All of you young people who served in the war. You are a lost generation.
Gertrude Stein (1874–1946) US writer.
A Moveable Feast (E. Hemingway)

1927

3 Nation shall speak peace unto nation.
Montague John Rendall (1862–1950) British schoolmaster.
Motto of BBC, 1927

4 Every man has a House of Lords in his own head. Fears, prejudices, misconceptions — those are the peers, and they are hereditary.
David Lloyd George (1863–1945) British Liberal statesman.
Speech, Cambridge, 1927

5 A sad day this for Alexander
And many another dead commander.
Jealousy's rife in heroes' hall —
Winston Churchill has bluffed them all.
Kensal Green
The Faber Book of English History in Verse
(Kenneth Baker)

6 The most conservative man in the world is the British Trade Unionist when you want to change him.
Ernest Bevin (1881–1951) British trade-union leader and politician.
Speech, Trade Union Congress, 8 Sept 1927

7 I do not choose to run for President in 1928.
Calvin Coolidge (1872–1933) US president.
Announcement in 1927

8 Gentlemen, it was necessary to abolish the fez, which sat on the heads of our nation as an emblem of ignorance, negligence, fanaticism and hatred of progress and civilization, to accept in its place the hat, the headgear worn by the whole civilized world.
Kemal Ataturk (1880–1938) Founder of the Turkish Republic.
Speech, Turkish Assembly, Oct 1927

169 Communism is like prohibition, it's a good idea but it won't work.
Will Rogers (1879–1935) US actor and humorist.
Autobiography, Nov 1927

170 Nature has no cure for this sort of madness, though I have known a legacy from a rich relative work wonders.
F. E. Smith (1872–1930) British lawyer and politician.
Referring to Communism
Law, Life and Letters (1927), Vol. II

1928

171* Freedom of the press in Britain is freedom to print such of the proprietor's prejudices as the advertisers don't object to.
Hannen Swaffer (1879–1962) British journalist.
Attrib.

172 God forbid that any book should be banned. The practice is as indefensible as infanticide.
Rebecca West (Cicely Isabel Fairfield; 1892–1983) British novelist and journalist,
The Strange Necessity, 'The Tosh Horse'

173 Nonconformity and lust stalking hand in hand through the country, wasting and ravaging.
Evelyn Waugh (1903–66) British novelist.
Decline and Fall, Pt. I, Ch. 5

174 Our country has deliberately undertaken a great social and economic experiment, noble in motive and far-reaching in purpose.
Herbert Hoover (1874–1964) US president.
Referring to Prohibition
Letter to W.H. Borah, 28 Feb 1928

175 In a country economically backward, the proletariat can take power earlier than in countries where capitalism is advanced.
Leon Trotsky (Lev Davidovich Bronstein; 1879–1940) Russian revolutionary.
Permanent Revolution

1929

176 Moving through the silent crowd
Who stand behind dull cigarettes,
These men who idle in the road,
I have the sense of falling light.

They lounge at corners of the street
And greet friends with a shrug of the shoulder
And turn their empty pockets out,
The cynical gestures of the poor.
Stephen Spender (1909–   ) British poet.
Unemployed

177 There is in our hands as citizens an instrument to mould the minds of the young and to create

great and good and noble citizens for the future.
Edward Shortt (1862–1935) Home Secretary (1919–22); President of the British Board of Film Censors (1929–35).
Referring to the British Board of Film Censors
Remark, 1929

178 . . . I have no fears for the future of our country. It is bright with hope.
Herbert Hoover (1874–1964) US president.
Inaugural address, 4 Mar 1929

179 He is the apostle of class-hatred, the founder of a Satanic anti-religion, which resembles some religions in its cruelty, fanaticism and irrationality.
Dean Inge (1860–1954) British churchman.
Referring to Karl Marx
Assessments and Anticipations

1930

180 When a great many people are unable to find work, unemployment results.
Calvin Coolidge (1872–1933) US president.
City Editor

181 Democracy is only an experiment in government, and it has the obvious disadvantage of merely counting votes instead of weighing them.
Dean Inge (1860–1954) British churchman.
Possible Recovery?

182 The disastrous element in the Labour party is its intellectuals.
George Norman Clark (1890–1979) British historian.
A Man of the Thirties (A. L. Rowse)

183* He therefore was at strenuous pains
To atrophy his puny brains
And registered success in this
Beyond the dreams of avarice
Till when he had at last become
Blind, paralytic, deaf and dumb
Insensible and cretinous
He was admitted ONE OF US.
Hilaire Belloc (1870–1953) French-born British poet.
The Statesman

184 In a free society the state does not administer the affairs of men. It administers justice among men who conduct their own affairs.
Walter Lippman (1889–1974) US editor and writer.
An Enquiry into the Principles of a Good Society

185 The working of great institutions is mainly the result of a vast mass of routine, petty malice, self interest, carelessness, and sheer mistake. Only a residual fraction is thought.
George Santayana (1863–1952) US philosopher.
The Crime of Galileo

186 The hardest thing in the world to understand income tax.
Albert Einstein (1879–1955) German-born US physicist.
Attrib.

187 They can't collect legal taxes from illegal money.
Al Capone (1899–1947) Italian-born US gangster.
Objecting to the US Bureau of Internal Reven claiming large sums in unpaid back tax
Capone (J. Kobler)

188 For us, the tasks of education in socialism we closely integrated with those of fighting. Ideas that enter the mind under fire remain there securely and for ever.
Leon Trotsky (Lev Davidovich Bronstein; 1879–1940) Russian revolutionary.
My Life, Ch. 35

189 If we had more time for discussion we shoul probably have made a great many more mistakes.
Leon Trotsky
My Life

190* An ally has to be watched just like an enemy
Leon Trotsky
Expansion and Coexistence (A. Ulam)

191 Today violence is the rhetoric of the period.
José Ortega y Gasset (1883–1955) Spanis philosopher.
The Revolt of the Masses

192 Revolution is not the uprising against pre-existing order, but the setting-up of a new orde contradictory to the traditional one.
José Ortega y Gasset
The Revolt of the Masses, Ch. 6

193* Fascism means war.
John St Loe Strachey (1901–63) British politician.
Slogan, 1930s

194 All wars are planned by old men
In council rooms apart.
Grantland Rice (1880–1954) US sportswriter.
Two Sides of War

195 When we, the Workers, all demand: 'What are we fighting for? . . .
Then, then we'll end that stupid crime, that devil's madness — War.
Robert William Service (1874–1958) Canadian poet.
Michael

196 That all men are equal is a proposition to which, at ordinary times, no sane individual ha ever given his assent.
Aldous Huxley (1894–1964) British novelist
Proper Studies

197 A politician is a person with whose politics yo don't agree; if you agree with him he is a statesman.
David Lloyd George (1863–1945) British Liberal statesman.
Attrib.

198 Don't let's be beastly to the Germans.
Noël Coward (1899–1973) British dramatist.
Title of song

199 Let them especially put their demands in such a way that Great Britain could say that she supported both sides.
Ramsey MacDonald (1866–1937) British statesman and prime minister.
Referring to France and Germany
The Origins of the Second Word War (A. J. P. Taylor), Ch. 3

200 Those who can win a war well can rarely make a good peace and those who could make a good peace would never have won the war.
Winston Churchill (1874–1965) British statesman.
My Early Life, Ch. 26

201 Which brings me to my conclusion upon Free Will and Predestination, namely — let the reader mark it — that they are identical.
Winston Churchill
My Early Life, Ch. 3

202 Everyone threw the blame on me. I have noticed that they nearly always do. I suppose it is because they think I shall be able to bear it best.
Winston Churchill
My Early Life, Ch. 17

203 The loss of India would mark and consummate the downfall of the British Empire. That great organism would pass at a stroke out of life into history. From such a catastrophe there could be no recovery.
Winston Churchill
Speech to Indian Empire Society, London, 12 Dec 1930

204 When they circumcised Herbert Samuel they threw away the wrong bit.
David Lloyd George (1863–1945) British Liberal statesman.
Attrib. in *The Listener,* 7 Sept 1978

1931
------

205 Democracy means government by the uneducated, while aristocracy means government by the badly educated.
G. K. Chesterton (1874–1936) British writer.
New York Times, 1 Feb 1931

206 There is just one rule for politicians all over the world. Don't say in Power what you say in Opposition: if you do you only have to carry out what the other fellows have found impossible.
John Galsworthy (1867–1933) British novelist.
Maid in Waiting

207 What the proprietorship of these papers is aiming at is power, and power without responsibility — the prerogative of the harlot through the ages.
Stanley Baldwin (1867–1947) British statesman.
Attacking the press barons Lords Rothermere and Beaverbrook. It was first used by Kipling. When the Duke of Devonshire heard of the

speech he is said to have remarked 'Good God, that's done it. He's lost us the tarts' vote'.
Speech, election rally, 18 Mar 1931

208 India is a geographical term. It is no more a united nation than the Equator.
Winston Churchill (1874–1965) British statesman.
Speech, Royal Albert Hall, 18 Mar 1931

209 Liberty is the hardest test that one can inflict on a people. To know how to be free is not given equally to all men and all nations.
Paul Valéry (1871–1945) French poet and writer.
Reflections on the World Today, 'On the Subject of Dictatorship'

210 Insurrection is an art, and like all arts it has its laws.
Leon Trotsky (Lev Davidovich Bronstein; 1879–1940) Russian revolutionary.
History of the Russian Revolution, Pt. III, Ch. 6

211 Revolutions are always verbose.
Leon Trotsky
History of the Russian Revolution, Pt. II, Ch. 12

212 The fundamental premise of a revolution is that the existing social structure has become incapable of solving the urgent problems of development of the nation.
Leon Trotsky
History of the Russian Revolution, Pt. III, Ch. 6

213 The revolution does not choose its paths: it made its first steps towards victory under the belly of a Cossack's horse.
Leon Trotsky
History of the Russian Revolution, Pt. I, Ch. 7

214 From being a patriotic myth, the Russian people have become an awful reality.
Leon Trotsky
History of the Russian Revolution, Pt. III, Ch. 7

215 To slacken the tempo . . . would mean falling behind. And those who fall behind get beaten . . . We are fifty or a hundred years behind the advanced countries. We must make good this distance in ten years. Either we do it, or they crush us.
Joseph Stalin (J. Dzhugashvili; 1879–1953) Soviet statesman.

1932
------

216 Happy Days Are Here Again.
Jack Yellen (1892–) US lyricist.
Used by Roosevelt as a campaign song in 1932
Song title

217 The forgotten man at the bottom of the economic pyramid.
Franklin D. Roosevelt (1882–1945) US Democratic president.
Speech on radio, 7 Apr 1932

218 I pledge you, I pledge myself, to a new deal for the American people.
Franklin D. Roosevelt
Speech accepting nomination for presidency, Chicago, 2 July 1932

219   Let me assert my firm belief that the only thing
we have to fear is fear itself.
Franklin D. Roosevelt
Speech, 2 July 1932

220   If human beings could be propagated by cutting, like apple trees, aristocracy would be bio-
logically sound.
J. B. S. Haldane (1892–1964) British
geneticist.
The Inequality of Man, title essay

221   I think it is well also for the man in the street to
realise that there is no power on earth that
can protect him from being bombed. Whatever
people may tell him, the bomber will always
get through, and it is very easy to understand
that, if you realise the area of space.
Stanley Baldwin (1867–1947) British
statesman.
Speech, House of Commons, 10 Nov 1932

222   The essential thing is the formation of the political will of the nation: that is the starting point
for political action.
Adolf Hitler (1889–1945) German dictator.
Speech, Düsseldorf, 27 Jan 1932

223   War alone brings up to their highest tension all
human energies and imposes the stamp of nobility upon the peoples who have the courage to make it.
Benito Mussolini (1883–1945) Italian
dictator.
Encyclopedia Italiane

224   Fascism is not an article for export.
Benito Mussolini
Report in the German press, 1932

225   The only defence is in offence, which means
that you have to kill more women and children
more quickly than the enemy if you want to
save yourselves.
Stanley Baldwin (1867–1947) British
statesman.
Speech, Nov 1932

226   In England we have come to rely upon a comfortable time lag of fifty years or a century in-
tervening between the perception that
something ought to be done and a serious attempt to do it.
H. G. Wells (1866–1946) British writer.
The Work, Wealth and Happiness of Mankind

1933

227   Patriotism is easy to understand in America; it
means looking out for yourself while looking
out for your country.
Calvin Coolidge (1872–1933) US president.
Attrib.

228   Something must be done.
Duke of Windsor (1894–1972) King of the
United Kingdom; abdicated 1936.
Said while visiting areas of high unemployment in
South Wales during the 1930s
Attrib.

229   Fascism is a religion; the twentieth century will
be known in history as the century of Fascism.
Benito Mussolini (1883–1945) Italian
dictator.
On Hitler's seizing power
Sawdust Caesar (George Seldes), Ch. 24

230   That this house will in no circumstances fight
for its King and country.
Anonymous
Motion passed at the Oxford Union, 9 Feb 1933

231   Our movement took a grip on cowardly Marxism and from it extracted the meaning of socialism. It also took from the cowardly middle-
class parties their nationalism. Throwing both
into the cauldron of our way of life there
emerged, as clear as a crystal, the synthesis –
German National Socialism.
Hermann Goering (1893–1946) German
leader.
Speech, Berlin, 9 Apr 1933

232   What progress we are making. In the Middle
Ages they would have burned me. Now they are
content with burning my books.
Sigmund Freud (1856–1939) Austrian
psychoanalyst.
Referring to the public burning of his books in
Berlin
Letter to Ernest Jones, 1933

233   In the field of world policy; I would dedicate
this nation to the policy of the good neighbor.
Franklin D. Roosevelt (1882–1945) US
Democratic president.
First Inaugural Address, 4 Mar 1933

234   You can't adopt politics as a profession and remain honest.
Louis McHenry Howe (1871–1936) US
diplomat.
Speech, Columbia University, 17 Jan 1933

235   A nation is not in danger of financial disaster
merely because it owes itself money.
Andrew William Mellon (1855–1937) US
financier.
Attrib.

236   How could they tell?
Dorothy Parker (1893–1967) US writer.
Reaction to news of the death of Calvin Coo-
lidge, US President 1923–29; also attributed to
H. L. Mencken
You Might As Well Live (J. Keats)

237   This goat-footed bard, this half-human visitor to
our age from the hag-ridden magic and enchanted woods of Celtic antiquity.
John Maynard Keynes (1883–1946) British
economist.
Referring to Lloyd George
Essays and Sketches in Biography

238   As society is now constituted, a literal adherence to the moral precepts scattered
throughout the Gospels would mean sudden
death.
A. N. Whitehead (1861–1947) British
philosopher.
Adventures in Ideas

239 But not even Marx is more precious to us than the truth.
Simone Weil (1909–43) French philosopher.
Oppression and Liberty, 'Revolution Proletarienne'

1934
---

240 The trouble in modern democracy is that men do not approach to leadership until they have lost the desire to lead anyone.
Lord Beveridge (1879–1963) British economist.
The Observer, 'Sayings of the Week', 15 Apr 1934

241 When you think about the defence of England you no longer think of the chalk cliffs of Dover. You think of the Rhine. That is where our frontier lies to-day.
Stanley Baldwin (1867–1947) British statesman.
Speech, House of Commons, 30 July 1934

242 *Ein Reich, Ein Volk, Ein Führer.*
One Realm, One People, One Leader
Slogan of the Nazi Party; first used at Nuremberg, Sept 1934

243 He looks as if he had been weaned on a pickle.
Alice Roosevelt Longworth (1884–1980) US hostess.
Referring to Calvin Coolidge, US president 1923–29
Crowded Hours

1935
---

244 The government burns down whole cities while the people are forbidden to light lamps.
Mao Tse-Tung (1893–1976) Chinese communist leader.
Attrib.

245 I am not and never have been, a man of the right. My position was on the left and is now in the centre of politics.
Oswald Mosley (1896–1980) British politician.
The Times, 26 Apr 1968

246* *Kraft durch Freude.*
Strength through joy.
Robert Ley (1890–1945) German Nazi.
German Labour Front slogan

247 In starting and waging a war it is not right that matters, but victory.
Adolf Hitler (1889–1945) German dictator.
The Rise and Fall of the Third Reich (W. L. Shirer), Ch. 16

248 The keystone of the Fascist doctrine is its conception of the State, of its essence, its functions, and its aims. For Fascism the State is absolute, individuals and groups relative.
Benito Mussolini (1883–1945) Italian dictator.
Fascism, Doctrine and Institutions

I should be pleased, I suppose, that Hitler has carried out a revolution on our lines. But they are Germans. So they will end by ruining our idea.
Benito Mussolini
Benito Mussolini (C. Hibbert), Pt. II, Ch. 1

250 We cannot change our policy now. After all, we are not political whores.
Benito Mussolini
Hitler (Alan Bullock), Ch. 8

251 The former allies had blundered in the past by offering Germany too little, and offering even that too late, until finally Nazi Germany had become a menace to all mankind.
Allan Nevins (1890–1971) US historian.
Current History, May 1935

252 I have seldom spoken with greater regret, for my lips are not yet unsealed. Were these troubles over I would make a case, and I guarantee that not a man would go into the Lobby against us.
Stanley Baldwin (1867–1947) British statesman.
Referring to the Abyssinian crisis; usually misquoted as 'My lips are sealed'
Speech, House of Commons, 10 Dec 1935

253 . . . a bore, a bounder and a prig. He was intoxicated with his own youth and loathed any milieu which he couldn't dominate. Certainly he had none of a gentleman's instincts, strutting about Peace Conferences in Arab dress.
Henry Channon (1897–1958) British writer.
Referring to T. E. Lawrence
Diary, 25 May 1935

254 There are those who have tried to dismiss his story with a flourish of the Union Jack, a psycho-analytical catchword or a sneer; it should move our deepest admiration and pity. Like Shelley and like Baudelaire, it may be said of him that he suffered, in his own person, the neurotic ills of an entire generation.
Christopher Isherwood (1904–86) British novelist.
Referring to T. E. Lawrence
Exhumations

255 We believe in a League system in which the whole world should be ranged against an aggressor.
Clement Attlee (1883–1967) British statesman and Labour prime minister.
Speech, House of Commons, 11 Mar 1935

256* Sit down, man. You're a bloody tragedy.
James Maxton (1885–1946) Scottish Labour leader.
Said to Ramsay MacDonald when he made his last speech in Parliament
Attrib.

257 Politics and the fate of mankind are shaped by men without ideals and without greatness. Men who have greatness within them don't go in for politics.
Albert Camus (1913–60) French existentialist writer.
Notebooks, 1935–42

258 After I am dead the boy will ruin himself in twelve months.
George V (1865–1936) King of the United Kingdom
Referring to the Prince of Wales, later Edward VIII; said to Stanley Baldwin
Attrib.

259 Revolution by its very nature is sometimes compelled to take in more territory than it is capable of holding. Retreats are possible — when there is territory to retreat from.
Leon Trotsky (Lev Davidovich Bronstein; 1879–1940) Russian revolutionary.
Diary in Exile, 15 Feb 1935

260 The Pope! How many divisions has *he* got?
Joseph Stalin (J. Dzhugashvili; 1879–1953) Soviet statesman.
When urged by Pierre Laval to tolerate Catholicism in the USSR to appease the Pope, 13 May 1935
The Second World War (W. S. Churchill), Vol. I, Ch. 8

1936

261 How is the Empire?
George V (1865–1936) King of the United Kingdom.
Last words
The Times, 21 Jan 1936

262 Bugger Bognor.
George V
His alleged last words, when his doctor promised him he would soon be well enough to visit Bognor Regis

263 Spirits of well-shot woodcock, partridge, snipe
Flutter and bear him up the Norfolk sky.
John Betjeman (1906–84) British poet.
Death of King George V

264 A democracy must remain at home in all matters that affect the nature of her institutions . . . We do not want the racial antipathies or national antagonisms of the Old World translated to this continent, as they will should we become a part of European politics. The people of this country are overwhelmingly for a policy of neutrality.
William Edgar Borah (1865–1940) US senator.
Radio broadcast, 22 Feb 1936

265 To attempt to export revolution is nonsense.
Joseph Stalin (J. Dzhugashvili; 1879–1953) Soviet statesman.
Remark, 1 Mar 1936, to Roy Howard (US newspaper owner)

266 Peace is indivisible.
Maxim Litvinov (1876–1951) Russian statesman.
Speech to the League of Nations, 1 July 1936

267 Revolution is delightful in the preliminary stages. So long as it's a question of getting rid of the people at the top.
Aldous Huxley (1894–1964) British novelist.
Eyeless in Gaza

268 I go the way that Providence dictates with the assurance of a sleepwalker.
Adolf Hitler (1889–1945) German dictator.
Referring to his successful re-occupation of the Rhineland, despite advice against the attempt
Speech, Munich, 15 Mar 1936

269 They will conquer, but they will not convince
Miguel de Unamuno y Jugo (1864–1936) Spanish writer.
Referring to the Franco rebels
Attrib.

270 It is better to be the widow of a hero than the wife of a coward.
Dolores Ibarruri (1895–   ) Spanish politician.
Speech, Valencia, 1936

271 It is better to die on your feet than to live on your knees.
Dolores Ibarruri (1895–   ) Spanish politician.
Speech, Paris, 3 Sept 1936

272 Fire — without hatred.
Antonio Rivera (d. 1936) Spanish Nationalist hero.
Giving the order to open fire at the siege of the Alcázar
The Siege of the Alcázar (C. Eby)

273 This Berlin–Rome connection is not so much a diaphragm as an axis, around which can revolve all those states of Europe with a will towards collaboration and peace.
Benito Mussolini (1883–1945) Italian dictator.
Speech, Milan, 1 Nov 1936

274 Guns will make us powerful; butter will only make us fat.
Hermann Goering (1893–1946) German leader.
Radio broadcast, 1936

275 Before the organization of the Blackshirt movement free speech did not exist in this country
Oswald Mosley (1896–1980) British politician.
Selections from the *New Statesman, This England*, Pt. I

276 Practical men, who believe themselves to be quite exempt from any intellectual influences are usually the slaves of some defunct economist. Madmen in authority, who hear voices the air, are distilling their frenzy from some academic scribbler of a few years back.
John Maynard Keynes (1883–1946) British economist.
The General Theory of Employment, Interest and Money, Bk. VI, Ch. 24

277* If he became convinced tomorrow that coming out for cannibalism would get him the votes he so sorely needs, he would begin fattening a missionary on the White House backyard come Wednesday.
H. L. Mencken (1880–1956) US journalist.
Referring to Franklin Roosevelt
Franklin D. Roosevelt, A Profile (ed. W. E. Leuchtenburg)

278 One of the great attractions of patriotism — it fulfils our worst wishes. In the person of our nation we are able, vicariously, to bully and to cheat. Bully and cheat, what's more, with a feeling that we are profoundly virtuous.
Aldous Huxley (1894–1964) British novelist.
Eyeless in Gaza

279 Lloyd George could not see a belt without hitting below it.
Margot Asquith (1865–1945) The second wife of Herbert Asquith.
The Autiobiography of Margot Asquith

280 His modesty amounts to a deformity.
Margot Asquith
Referring to her husband
Autobiography

281 My Lord Archbishop, what a scold you are
And when a man is down, how bold you are,
Of Christian charity how scant you are
You auld Lang Swine, how full of cant you are!
Anonymous
Archbishop Lang was one of the chief opponents of Edward VIII's marriage to Mrs Wallis Simpson
The Faber Book of English History in Verse (Kenneth Baker)

282 Well, Mr Baldwin! *this* is a pretty kettle of fish!
Queen Mary (1867–1953) Consort of George V.
Referring to the abdication of Edward VIII
Life of Queen Mary (James Pope-Hennessy)

283 Our cock won't fight.
Lord Beaverbrook (1879–1964) Canadian-born British newspaper proprietor.
Said to Churchill during the abdication crisis, 1936
Edward VIII (Frances Donaldson), Ch. 22

284 I have found it impossible to carry the heavy burden of responsibility and to discharge my duties as King as I would wish to do without the help and support of the woman I love.
Duke of Windsor (1894–1972) King of the United Kingdom; abdicated 1936.
Radio broadcast, 11 Dec 1936

285 He will go from resort to resort getting more tanned and more tired.
Westbrook Pegler (1894–1969) US journalist.
On the abdication of Edward VIII
Six Men (Alistair Cooke), Pt. II

286 God grant him peace and happiness but never understanding of what he has lost.
Stanley Baldwin (1867–1947) British politician and prime minister.
Referring to Edward VIII

1937

287 I see one-third of a nation ill-housed, ill-clad, ill-nourished.
Franklin D. Roosevelt (1882–1945) US Democratic president.
Second Inaugural Address, 20 Jan 1937

288 His fame endures; we shall not quite forget
The name of Baldwin till we're out of debt.
Kensal Green
The Faber Book of English History in Verse (Kenneth Baker)

289* Then comes Winston with his hundred-horse-power mind and what can I do?
Stanley Baldwin (1867–1947) British statesman.
Stanley Baldwin (G. M. Young), Ch. 11

290 I often think how much easier the world would have been to manage if Herr Hitler and Signor Mussolini had been at Oxford.
Viscount Halifax (1881–1959) British politician.
Speech, York, 4 Nov 1937

291 *La quinta columna*
The Fifth Column
Emilio Mola (1887–1937) Spanish Nationalist General.
Reply when asked (Oct 1937) which of four Nationalist armies would capture Madrid; Mola was referring to Nationalist elements within the city

292 'Can't' will be the epitaph of the British Empire — unless we wake up in time.
Oswald Mosley (1896–1980) British politician.
Speech, Manchester, 9 Dec 1937

293 Sincerity is all that counts. It's a wide-spread modern heresy. Think again. Bolsheviks are sincere. Fascists are sincere. Lunatics are sincere. People who believe the earth is flat are sincere. They can't all be right. Better make certain first you've got something to be sincere about and with.
Tom Driberg (1905–76) British politician, journalist and author.
Daily Express, 1937

294 So long as men worship the Caesars and Napoleons, Caesars and Napoleons will arise to make them miserable.
Aldous Huxley (1894–1964) British novelist.
Ends and Means

295 The propagandist's purpose is to make one set of people forget that certain other sets of people are human.
Aldous Huxley
The Olive Tree

296 Freedom is the right to tell people what they do not want to hear.
George Orwell (Eric Blair; 1903–50) British novelist.
The Road to Wigan Pier

297 It is brought home to you . . . that it is only because miners sweat their guts out that superior persons can remain superior.
George Orwell
The Road to Wigan Pier, Ch. 2

298 I sometimes think that the price of liberty is not so much eternal vigilance as eternal dirt.
George Orwell
The Road to Wigan Pier, Ch. 4

299 As with the Christian religion, the worst advertisement for Socialism is its adherents.
George Orwell
The Road to Wigan Pier, Ch. 11

300 To the ordinary working man, the sort you would meet in any pub on Saturday night, Socialism does not mean much more than better wages and shorter hours and nobody bossing you about.
George Orwell
The Road to Wigan Pier, Ch. 11

1938

301 In war, whichever side may call itself the victor, there are no winners, but all are losers.
Neville Chamberlain (1869–1940) British statesman.
Speech, Kettering, 3 July 1938

302 Before us stands the last problem that must be solved and will be solved. It is the last territorial claim which I have to make in Europe, but it is the claim from which I will not recede.
Adolf Hitler (1889–1945) German dictator.
Referring to the Sudetenland (Czechoslovakia)
Speech, Berlin, 26 Sept 1938

303 How horrible, fantastic, incredible, it is that we should be digging trenches and trying on gas-masks here because of a quarrel in a far-away country between people of whom we know nothing.
Neville Chamberlain (1869–1940) British statesman.
Referring to Germany's annexation of the Sudetenland
Radio broadcast, 27 Sept 1938

304 I believe it is peace for our time . . . peace with honour.
Neville Chamberlain
Radio broadcast after Munich Agreement, 1 Oct 1938

305 We have sustained a defeat without a war.
Winston Churchill (1874–1965)
Speech, House of Commons, 5 Oct 1938

306 Dictators ride to and fro upon tigers which they dare not dismount. And the tigers are getting hungry.
Winston Churchill
While England Slept

307 Other nations use 'force'; we Britons alone use 'Might'.
Evelyn Waugh (1903–66) British novelist.
Scoop, Bk. II, Ch. 5

308 Every Communist must grasp the truth, 'Political power grows out of the barrel of a gun.'
Mao Tse-Tung (1893–1976) Chinese communist leader.
Selected Works, Vol. II, 'Problems of War and Strategy'

309 And here we are – just as before – safe in our skins;
Glory to God for Munich.
And stocks go up and wrecks
Are salved and politicians' reputations
Go up like Jack-on-the-Beanstalk; only the Czechs
Go down and without fighting.
Louis Macneice (1907–63) Irish-born British poet.
Autumn Journal

1939

310 If we are going in without the help of Russia we are walking into a trap.
David Lloyd George (1863–1945) British Liberal statesman.
Speech, House of Commons, 3 Apr 1939

311 That bastard of the Versailles treaty.
Vyacheslav Mikhailovich Molotov (1890–1986) Soviet statesman.
Referring to Poland

312 The machine is running away with *him* as it ran away with *me*.
Wilhelm II (1859–1941) King of Prussia and Emperor of Germany.
Referring to Hitler
Remark to Sir Robert Bruce-Lockhart and Sir John Wheeler-Bennett, 27 Aug 1939

313 Speak for England.
Leopold Amery (1873–1955) British statesman.
Shouted to Arthur Greenwood, Labour Party spokesman, before he began to speak in a House of Commons debate immediately preceding the declaration of war, 2 Sept 1939

314 When peace has been broken anywhere, the peace of all countries everywhere is in danger
Franklin D. Roosevelt (1882–1945) US Democratic president.
Radio broadcast, 3 Sept 1939

315 Winston's back.
Referring to Churchill's reappointment as First Lord of the Admiralty; he had previously held the office from 1911 to 1915
Radio message from the Admiralty to all ships of the Royal Navy, 3 Sept 1939

316 I cannot forecast to you the action of Russia. It is a riddle wrapped in a mystery inside an enigma.
Winston Churchill (1874–1965) British statesman.
Radio broadcast, 1 Oct 1939

317 I am reminded of four definitions. A radical is a man with both feet firmly planted – in the air; a conservative is a man with two perfectly good legs who, however, has never learned to walk; a reactionary is a somnambulist walking backwards; a liberal is a man who uses his legs and his hands at the behest of his head.
Franklin D. Roosevelt (1882–1945) US Democratic president.
Radio broadcast, 26 Oct 1939

318 *C'est une drôle de guerre.*
It is a phoney war.
Edouard Daladier (1884–1970) French prime minister.
Speech, Chamber of Deputies, 22 Dec 1939

19 And I said to the man who stood at the gate of
the year: 'Give me a light that I may tread
safely into the unknown'. And he replied: 'Go
out into the darkness and put your hand into
the hand of God. That shall be to you better
than light and safer than a known way.'
Minnie Louise Haskins (1875–1957) US
writer.
Remembered because it was quoted by George
VI in his Christmas broadcast, 1939
The Desert, Introduction

1940
---

20 The Italians will laugh at me; every time Hitler
occupies a country he sends me a message.
Benito Mussolini (1883–1945) Italian
dictator.
Hitler (Alan Bullock), Ch. 8

21 Hitler has missed the bus.
Neville Chamberlain (1869–1940) British
statesman.
Speech, House of Commons, 4 Apr 1940

22 You have sat too long here for any good you
have been doing. Depart, I say, and let us have
done with you. In the name of God, *go!*
Leopold Amery (1873–1955) British
statesman.
Said to Neville Chamberlain using Cromwell's
words
Speech, House of Commons, May 1940

23* He saw foreign policy through the wrong end of
a municipal drainpipe.
David Lloyd George (1863–1945) British
Liberal statesman.
Referring to Neville Chamberlain
The Fine Art of Political Wit (Harris), Ch. 6

24 The language of priorities is the religion of
Socialism.
Aneurin Bevan (1897–1960) British Labour
politician.
Aneurin Bevan (Vincent Brome), Ch. 1

25* I felt as if I were walking with destiny, and that
all my past life had been but a preparation for
this hour and this trial.
Winston Churchill (1874–1965) British
statesman.
The Gathering Storm, Ch. 38

26 I have nothing to offer but blood, toil, tears and
sweat.
Winston Churchill
On becoming prime minister
Speech, House of Commons, 13 May 1940

27 Victory at all costs, victory in spite of all terror,
victory however long and hard the road may
be; for without victory there is no survival.
Winston Churchill
Speech, House of Commons, 13 May 1940

28 We shall not flag or fail. We shall fight in
France, we shall fight on the seas and oceans,
we shall fight with growing confidence and
growing strength in the air, we shall defend
our island, whatever the cost may be, we shall

fight on the beaches, we shall fight on the
landing grounds, we shall fight in the fields
and in the streets, we shall fight in the hills; we
shall never surrender.
Winston Churchill
Speech, House of Commons, 4 June 1940

329 Our great-grandchildren, when they learn how
we began this war by snatching glory out of
defeat . . . may also learn how the little holiday
steamers made an excursion to hell and came
back glorious.
J. B. Priestley (1894–1984) British novelist.
Referring to the British Expeditionary Force's
evacuation from Dunkirk
Radio broadcast, 5 June 1940

330 This was their finest hour.
Winston Churchill (1874–1965) British
statesman.
Referring to the Dunkirk evacuation
Speech, House of Commons, 18 June 1940

331 The little ships, the unforgotten Homeric cata-
logue of *Mary Jane* and *Peggy IV*, of *Folkes-
tone Belle*, *Boy Billy*, and *Ethel Maud*, of *Lady
Haig* and *Skylark* . . . the little ships of Eng-
land brought the Army home.
Philip Guedalla (1889–1944) British writer.
Referring to the evacuation of Dunkirk
Mr. Churchill

332 Wars are not won by evacuations.
Winston Churchill (1874–1965)
Referring to Dunkirk
Their Finest Hour

333 To all Frenchmen: France has lost a battle but
France has not lost the war.
Charles De Gaulle (1890–1970) French gen-
eral and statesman.
Proclamation, June 1940

334 I, General de Gaulle, now in London, call on all
French officers and men who are at present
on British soil, or who may be in the future . . .
to get in touch with me. Whatever happens
the flame of French resistance must not and
shall not be extinguished.
Charles De Gaulle
Broadcast, 18 June 1940

335 In three weeks England will have her neck
wrung like a chicken.
Maxime Weygand (1867–1965) French
general.
Said at the fall of France
Their Finest Hour (Winston S. Churchill)

336 The battle of Britain is about to begin.
Winston Churchill (1874–1965) British
statesman.
Speech, House of Commons, 1 July 1940

337 To make a union with Great Britain would be
fusion with a corpse.
Marshal Pétain (1856–1951) French marshal.
On hearing Churchill's suggestion for an Anglo-
French union, 1940
Their Finest Hour (Winston S. Churchill), Ch. 10

338 Never in the field of human conflict was so
     much owed by so many to so few.
     Winston Churchill (1874–1965) British
     statesman.
     Referring to the Battle of Britain pilots
     Speech, House of Commons, 20 Aug 1940

339 The universe is so vast and so ageless that the
     life of one man can only be justified by the
     measure of his sacrifice.
     V. A. Rosewarne (1916–1940) British pilot.
     Inscribed on the portrait of the 'Young Airman' in
     the RAF Museum
     Letter to his mother, 1940

340 It is not the walls that make the city, but the
     people who live within them. The walls of
     London may be battered, but the spirit of the
     Londoner stands resolute and undismayed.
     George VI (1895–1952) King of the United
     Kingdom.
     Radio broadcast to the Empire, 23 Sept 1940

341 Now we can look the East End in the face.
     Elizabeth the Queen Mother (1900–)
     The wife of King George VI.
     Surveying the damage caused to Buckingham
     Palace by a bomb during the Blitz in World War II
     Attrib.

342 We are waiting for the long-promised invasion.
     So are the fishes.
     Winston Churchill (1874–1965) British
     statesman.
     Radio broadcast to the French people, 21 Oct
     1940

343 The best immediate defence of the United
     States is the success of Great Britain defending
     itself.
     Franklin D. Roosevelt (1882–1945) US
     Democratic president.
     At press conference, 17 Dec 1940
     Their Finest Hour (Winston S. Churchill), Ch. 28

344 We must be the great arsenal of democracy.
     Franklin D. Roosevelt (1882–1945) US
     Democratic president.
     Broadcast address to Forum on Current Prob-
     lems, 29 Dec 1940

345* The Americans cannot build aeroplanes. They
     are very good at refrigerators and razor blades.
     Hermann Goering (1893–1946) German
     leader.
     Assurance to Hitler
     America (Alistair Cooke)

346 There are not enough prisons and concentra-
     tion camps in Palestine to hold all the Jews
     who are ready to defend their lives and
     property.
     Golda Meir (1898–1978) Russian-born Israeli
     stateswoman.
     Speech, 2 May 1940

     ————
     1941

347 We look forward to a world founded upon four
     essential human freedoms. The first is free-
     dom of speech and expression – everywhere
     in the world. The second is freedom of ev-
     ery person to worship God in his own way –
     everywhere in the world. The third is freedom
     from want . . . everywhere in the world. The
     fourth is freedom from fear . . . anywhere in the
     world.
     Franklin D. Roosevelt (1882–1945) US
     Democratic president.
     Speech to Congress, 6 Jan 1941

348 The tasks of the party are . . . to be cautious
     and not allow our country to be drawn into con-
     flicts by warmongers who are accustomed to
     have others pull the chestnuts out of the fire
     for them.
     Joseph Stalin (J. Dzhugashvili; 1879–1953)
     Soviet statesman.
     Speech, 8th Congress of the Communist Party,
     6 Jan 1941

349 The crafty, cold-blooded, black-hearted Italian.
     Winston Churchill (1874–1965) British
     statesman.
     Referring to Benito Mussolini
     Radio broadcast, 9 Feb 1941

350 Give us the tools, and we will finish the job.
     Winston Churchill
     Referring to Lend-lease, which was being legis-
     lated in the USA
     Radio broadcast, 9 Feb 1941

351 We have finished the job, what shall we do with
     the tools?
     Haile Selassie (1892–1975) Emperor of
     Ethiopia.
     Telegram sent to Winston Churchill, mimicking
     his 'Give us the tools, and we will finish the job'
     Ambrosia and Small Beer, Ch. 4 (Edward
     Marsh)

352 This whipped jackal . . . is frisking up by the
     side of the German tiger.
     Winston Churchill (1874–1965) British
     statesman.
     Referring to Mussolini
     Speech, House of Commons, Apr 1941

353 Like German opera, too long and too loud.
     Evelyn Waugh (1903–66) British novelist.
     Giving his opinions of warfare after the Battle of
     Crete, 1941
     Attrib.

354 When Barbarossa commences, the world will
     hold its breath and make no comment.
     Adolf Hitler (1889–1945) German dictator.
     Referring to the planned invasion of the USSR,
     Operation Barbarossa, which began on 22
     June 1941
     Attrib.

355 If we see that Germany is winning the war we
     ought to help Russia, and if Russia is winning
     we ought to help Germany, and in that way
     let them kill as many as possible.
     Harry S. Truman (1884–1972) US
     statesman.
     New York Times, 24 July 1941, when Russia
     was invaded by Germany

56 You do your worst, and we will do our best.
Winston Churchill (1874–1965) British statesman.
Addressed to Hitler
Speech, 14 July 1941

57 Do not despair
For Johnny head-in-air;
He sleeps as sound
As Johnny underground.
John Sleigh Pudney (1909–77) British poet and writer.
For Johnny

58 Do not let us speak of darker days; let us rather speak of sterner days. These are not dark days: these are great days — the greatest days our country has ever lived.
Winston Churchill (1874–1965) British statesman.
Address, Harrow School, 29 Oct 1941

59 Probably the Battle of Waterloo *was* won on the playing-fields of Eton, but the opening battles of all subsequent wars have been lost there.
George Orwell (Eric Blair; 1903–50) British novelist.
The Lion and the Unicorn, 'England, Your England'

60 Praise the Lord and pass the ammunition!
Howell Maurice Forgy (1908–   ) US naval lieutenant.
Remark made during the Japanese attack on Pearl Harbor, 7 Dec 1941
Attrib. in The Los Angeles Times

61 A date that shall live in infamy.
Franklin D. Roosevelt (1882–1945) US Democratic president.
Referring to 7 Dec 1941, when Japan attacked Pearl Harbor
Message to Congress, 8 Dec 1941

62 I fear we have only awakened a sleeping giant, and his reaction will be terrible.
Isoroku Yamamoto (1884–1943) Japanese admiral.
Said after the Japanese attack on Pearl Harbor, 1941

63 When you have to kill a man it costs nothing to be polite.
Winston Churchill (1874–1965) British statesman.
Justifying the fact that the declaration of war against Japan was made in the usual diplomatic language
The Grand Alliance

64 When I warned them that Britain would fight on alone whatever they did, their Generals told their Prime Minister and his divided Cabinet: 'In three weeks England will have her neck wrung like a chicken.'
Some chicken! Some neck!
Winston Churchill
Referring to the French Government
Speech, Canadian Parliament, 30 Dec 1941

65 The high sentiments always win in the end, the leaders who offer blood, toil, tears and sweat

always get more out of their followers than those who offer safety and a good time. When it comes to the pinch, human beings are heroic.
George Orwell (Eric Blair; 1903–50) British novelist.
The Art of Donald McGill

1942

366 War is not an adventure. It is a disease. It is like typhus.
Antoine de Saint-Exupéry (1900–44) French novelist and aviator.
Flight to Arras

367 The soldier's body becomes a stock of accessories that are not his property.
Antoine de Saint-Exupéry
Flight To Arras

368 I shall return.
Douglas MacArthur (1880–1964) US general.
Message (11 Mar 1942) on leaving for Australia from Corregidor Island (Philippines), which he had been defending against the Japanese

369 Defeat of Germany means the defeat of Japan, probably without firing a shot or losing a life.
Franklin D. Roosevelt (1882–1945) US Democratic president.
The Hinge of Fate (Winston S. Churchill), Ch. 25

370* I have only one purpose, the destruction of Hitler, and my life is much simplified thereby. If Hitler invaded Hell I would make at least a favourable reference to the Devil in the House of Commons.
Winston Churchill (1874–1965) British statesman.
The Grand Alliance

371 A revolutionary France would always rather win a war with General Hoche than lose it with Marshal Soubise.
Charles De Gaulle (1890–1970) French general and statesman.
Speech, London, 1 Apr 1942

372* I herewith commission you to carry out all preparations with regard to . . . a *total solution* of the Jewish question, in those territories of Europe which are under German influence.
Hermann Goering (1893–1946) German leader.
The Rise and Fall of the Third Reich (William Shirer)

373 I think if the people of this country can be reached with the truth, their judgment will be in favor of the many, as against the privileged few.
Eleanor Roosevelt (1884–1962) US writer and lecturer.
Ladies' Home Journal

374 We all know that books burn — yet we have the greater knowledge that books cannot be killed by fire. People die, but books never die. No

man and no force can abolish memory ... In
this war, we know, books are weapons.
Franklin D. Roosevelt (1882–1945) US
Democratic president.
Message to American Booksellers Association,
23 Apr 1942

375   Never before have we had so little time in
which to do so much.
Franklin D. Roosevelt
Radio broadcast, 23 Feb 1942

376   Stalin hates the guts of all your top people. He
thinks he likes me better, and I hope he will
continue to do so.
Franklin D. Roosevelt
The Hinge of Fate (Winston S. Churchill), Ch. 11

377   The century on which we are entering – the
century which will come out of this war – can
be and must be the century of the common
man.
Henry Wallace (1888–1965) US economist
and politician.
Speech, 'The Price of Free World Victory', 8
May 1942

378   I have not become the King's First Minister in
order to preside over the liquidation of the
British Empire.
Winston Churchill (1874–1965) British
statesman.
Speech, Mansion House, 10 Nov 1942

379   Before Alamein we never had a victory. After
Alamein we never had a defeat.
Winston Churchill
The Hinge of Fate, Ch. 33

380   This is not the end. It is not even the beginning
of the end. But it is, perhaps, the end of the
beginning.
Winston Churchill
Referring to the Battle of Egypt
Speech, Mansion House, 10 Nov 1942

381   The Almighty in His infinite wisdom did not see
fit to create Frenchmen in the image of
Englishmen.
Winston Churchill
Speech, House of Commons, 10 Dec 1942

382   The object of government in peace and in war
is not the glory of rulers or of races, but the
happiness of the common man.
Lord Beveridge (1879–1963) British
economist.
Social Insurance

383   In place of the conception of the Power-State
we are led to that of the Welfare-State.
William Temple (1881–1944)
British churchman.
Citizen and Churchman, Ch. 11

1943

384* In defeat unbeatable; in victory unbearable.
Winston Churchill (1874–1965) British
statesman.
Referring to Viscount Montgomery
Ambrosia and Small Beer (E. Marsh), Ch. 5

385   You may take the most gallant sailor, the mo
intrepid airman, or the most audacious soldier
put them at a table together – what do you
get? *The sum of their fears.*
Winston Churchill
Talking about the Chiefs of Staffs system, 16
Nov 1943
The Blast of War (H. Macmillan), Ch. 16

386   Politics is the art of preventing people from ta
ing part in affairs which properly concern
them.
Paul Valéry (1871–1945) French poet and
writer.
Tel quel

387   Freedom is an indivisible word. If we want t
enjoy it, and fight for it, we must be prepared
extend it to everyone, whether they are rich
or poor, whether they agree with us or not, r
matter what their race or the colour of their
skin.
Wendell Lewis Willkie (1892–1944) US la
yer and businessman.
One World, Ch. 13

1944

388   It was very successful, but it fell on the wro
planet.
Wernher von Braun (1912–77) German
rocket engineer.
Referring to the first V2 rocket to hit London d
ing World War II
Attrib.

389   Liberty is so much latitude as the powerful
choose to accord to the weak.
Judge Learned Hand (1872–1961) US
judge.
Speech, University of Pennsylvania Law Scho
21 May 1944

390   The eyes of the world are upon you. The hop
and prayers of liberty-loving people everywhere march with you.
Dwight D. Eisenhower (1890–1969) US
general and statesman.
Order to his troops, 6 June 1944 (D-Day)

391   Older men declare war. But it is youth that
must fight and die.
Herbert Clark Hoover (1874–1964) US
statesman.
Speech, Republican Convention, Chicago, 27
June 1944

392* They're overpaid, overfed, oversexed and ove
here.
Tommy Trinder (1909–   ) British entertaine
Referring to the G.I.s
Attrib.

393   Our ships have been salvaged and are retirir
at high speed toward the Japanese fleet.
W. C. Halsey (1882–1959) US admiral.
Following Japanese claims that most of the
American Third Fleet had been sunk or were
retiring
Radio message, Oct 1944

394   Dear Ike, Today I spat in the Seine.
General George Patton (1885–1945) US general.
Message sent to Eisenhower reporting his crossing of the Seine in World War II
The American Treasury (C. Fadiman)

395   Is Paris burning?
Adolf Hitler (1889–1945) German dictator.
Referring to the liberation of Paris, 1944

1945

396   This war is not as in the past; whoever occupies a territory also imposes on it his own social system. Everyone imposes his own system as far as his army has power to do so. It cannot be otherwise.
Joseph Stalin (J. Dzhugashvili; 1879–1953) Soviet statesman.
Conversations with Stalin (Milovan Djilas)

397   More than an end to war, we want an end to the beginnings of all wars.
Franklin D. Roosevelt (1882–1945) US Democratic president.
Speech broadcast on the day after his death (13 Apr 1945)

398   He would rather follow public opinion than lead it.
Harry Hopkins (1890–1946) US politician.
Referring to Roosevelt
Attrib.

399   In Franklin Roosevelt there died the greatest American friend we have ever known and the greatest champion of freedom who has ever brought help and comfort from the New World to the Old.
Winston Churchill (1874–1965) British statesman.
The Second World War

400   This was the Angel of History! We felt its wings flutter through the room. Was that not the fortune we awaited so anxiously?
Joseph Goebbels (1897–1945) German politician.
Referring to Roosevelt's death
Diary

401*   They entered the war to prevent us from going into the East, not to have the East come to the Atlantic.
Hermann Goering (1893–1946) German leader.
Referring to the war aims of the British in World War II
Nuremberg Diary (G. M. Gilbert)

402*   Now we are all sons of bitches.
Kenneth Bainbridge (1904–   ) US physicist.
After the first atomic test
The Decision to Drop the Bomb

403   We knew the world would not be the same.
J. Robert Oppenheimer (1904–67) US physicist.
After the first atomic test
The Decision to Drop the Bomb

404   The Bomb brought peace but man alone can keep that peace.
Winston Churchill (1874–1965) British statesman.
Speech, House of Commons, 16 Aug 1945

405   At first it was a giant column that soon took the shape of a supramundane mushroom.
William L. Laurence (1888–1977) US journalist.
Referring to the explosion of the first atomic bomb, over Hiroshima, 6 Aug 1945
The New York Times, 26 Sept 1945

406   We have had our last chance. If we do not devise some greater and more equitable system, Armageddon will be at our door.
Douglas MacArthur (1880–1964) US General.
Broadcast, 2 Sept 1945

407   War is war. The only good human being is a dead one.
George Orwell (Eric Blair; 1903–50) British novelist.
Animal Farm, Ch. 4

408   Peace with Germany and Japan on our terms will not bring much rest. . . . As I observed last time, when the war of the giants is over the wars of the pygmies will begin.
Winston Churchill (1874–1965) British statesman.
Triumph and Tragedy, Ch. 25

409   In war, resolution; in defeat, defiance; in victory, magnanimity; in peace, goodwill.
Winston Churchill
Epigram used by Sir Edward Marsh after World War II; used as 'a moral of the work' in Churchill's book
The Second World War

410   In politics, as in grammar, one should be able to tell the substantives from the adjectives. Hitler was a substantive; Mussolini only an adjective. Hitler was a nuisance. Mussolini was bloody. Together a bloody nuisance.
Salvador de Madariaga y Rogo (1886–1978) Spanish diplomat and writer.
Attrib.

411   In Germany, the Nazis came for the Communists and I didn't speak up because I was not a Communist. Then they came for the Jews and I didn't speak up because I was not a Jew. Then they came for the trade unionists and I didn't speak up because I was not a trade unionist. Then they came for the Catholics and I was a Protestant so I didn't speak up. Then they came for me . . . By that time there was no one to speak up for anyone.
Martin Niemöller (1892–1984) German pastor.
Concise Dictionary of Religious Quotations (W. Neil)

412   To save your world you asked this man to die: Would this man, could he see you now, ask why?
W. H. Auden (1907–73) British poet.
Epitaph for an Unknown Soldier

413* I said that the world must be made safe for at least fifty years. If it was only for fifteen to twenty years then we should have betrayed our soldiers.
Winston Churchill (1874–1965) British statesman.
Closing the Ring, Ch. 20

414* The redress of the grievances of the vanquished should precede the disarmament of the victors.
Winston Churchill
The Gathering Storm, Ch. 3

415 There are few virtues which the Poles do not possess and there are few errors they have ever avoided.
Winston Churchill
Speech, House of Commons, 1945

416* Does that mean that because Americans won't listen to sense, you intend to talk nonsense to them?
John Maynard Keynes (1883–1946) British economist.
Said before a monetary conference, 1944 or 1945

417 The Happy Warrior of Squandermania.
Winston Churchill (1874–1965) British statesman.
Referring to Lloyd George
Attrib.

418 A master of improvised speech and improvised policies.
A. J. P. Taylor (1906–   ) British historian.
Referring to Lloyd George
English History 1914–1945

419 Though the Jazz Age continued, it became less and less an affair of youth. The sequel was like a children's party taken over by the elders.
F. Scott Fitzgerald (1896–1940) US novelist.
The Crack-Up

420 Actually I vote Labour, but my butler's a Tory.
Lord Mountbatten (1900–79) British admiral.
Said to a Tory canvasser during the 1945 election

421 This island is almost made of coal and surrounded by fish. Only an organizing genius could produce a shortage of coal and fish in Great Britain at the same time.
Aneurin Bevan (1897–1960) British Labour politician.
Speech, Blackpool, 18 May 1945

422 Man is the only creature that consumes without producing.
George Orwell (Eric Blair; 1903–50) British novelist.
Animal Farm, Ch. 1

423 All animals are equal but some animals are more equal than others.
George Orwell
Animal Farm, Ch. 10

424 We must plan for freedom, and not only for se-

curity, if for no other reason than that only freedom can make security secure.
Karl Popper (1902–   ) Austrian-born British philosopher.
The Open Society and Its Enemies

425 Man is not a solitary animal, and so long as social life survives, self-realization cannot be the supreme principle of ethics.
Bertrand Russell (1872–1970) British philosopher.
History of Western Philosophy, 'Romanticism'

Attitudes

Art, Literature, and Music

1914

426 It is not good enough to spend time and ink in describing the penultimate sensations and physical movements of people getting into a state of rut, we all know them too well.
John Galsworthy (1867–1933) British novelist.
Referring to D. H. Lawrence's *Sons and Lovers*
Letter to Edward Garnett, 13 Apr 1914

427 I think that I shall never see
A poem lovely as a tree.
Alfred Joyce Kilmer (1886–1918) US poet.
Trees

428 Waldo is one of those people who would be enormously improved by death.
Saki (Hector Hugh Munro; 1870–1916) British writer.
Referring to Ralph Waldo Emerson
The Feast of Nemesis

1916

429 They are great parables, the novels, but false art. They are only parables. All the people are *fallen angels* – even the dirtiest scrubs. This I cannot stomach. People are not fallen angels, they are merely people.
D. H. Lawrence (1885–1930) British novelist
Referring to the novels of Dostoyevsky
Letter to J. Middleton Murry and Katherine Mansfield, 17 Feb 1916

1918

430* His verse exhibits . . . something that is rather like Keats's vulgarity with a Public School accent.
F. R. Leavis (1895–1978) British literary critic
Referring to Rupert Brooke
New Bearings in English Poetry, Ch. 2

431 Music is the arithmetic of sounds as optics is the geometry of light.
Claude Debussy (1862–1918) French composer.
Attrib.

1919

32 I just keep painting till I feel like pinching. Then
I know it's right.
Pierre Auguste Renoir (1841–1919) French
impressionist painter.
Explaining how he achieved such lifelike flesh
tones in his nudes
Attrib.

33 In a few generations you can breed a
racehorse. The recipe for making a man like
Delacroix is less well known.
Pierre Auguste Renoir
Attrib.

34* Poetry is a comforting piece of fiction set to
more or less lascivious music.
H. L. Mencken (1880–1956) US journalist.
Prejudices, 'The Poet and his Art'

35 When one hears of a poet past thirty-five he
seems somehow unnatural and obscene.
H. L. Mencken
Prejudices

1920

36 I am a man, and alive . . . For this reason I am a
novelist. And being a novelist, I consider myself superior to the saint, the scientist, the
philosopher, and the poet, who are all great
masters of different bits of man alive, but never
get the whole hog.
D. H. Lawrence (1885–1930) British novelist.
Phoenix, 'Why the Novel Matters'

37 Immature poets imitate; mature poets steal.
T. S. Eliot (1888–1965) US-born British poet
and dramatist.
Philip Massinger

38* Never compose anything unless the not composing of it becomes a positive nuisance to
you.
Gustav Holst (1874–1934) British composer.
Letter to W. G. Whittaker

39 Jazz will endure just as long as people hear it
through their feet instead of their brains.
John Philip Sousa (1854–1932) US composer, conductor, and writer.
Attrib.

1922

40 A true poet does not bother to be poetical. Nor
does a nursery gardener scent his roses.
Jean Cocteau (1889–1963) French poet and
artist.
Professional Secrets

41 Literature flourishes best when it is half a trade
and half an art.
Dean Inge (1860–1954) British churchman.
The Victorian Age

1923

442 Words are, of course, the most powerful drug
used by mankind.
Rudyard Kipling (1865–1936) Indian-born
British writer.
Speech, 14 Feb 1923

443 The courage of the poet is to keep ajar the door
that leads to madness.
Christopher Morley (1890–1957) US writer
and journalist.
Inward Ho

444 Poetry is the achievement of the synthesis of
hyacinths and biscuits.
Carl Sandburg (1878–1967) US author and
poet.
Atlantic Monthly

445 A house is a machine for living in.
Le Corbusier (Charles-Édouard Jeanneret;
1887–1965) Swiss-born French architect.
Towards an Architecture

1925

446* Art is not a mirror to reflect the world, but a
hammer with which to shape it.
Vladimir Mayakovsky (1893–1930) Soviet
poet.
The Guardian, 11 Dec 1974

447 Another unsettling element in modern art is that
common symptom of immaturity, the dread of
doing what has been done before.
Edith Wharton (1862–1937) US novelist.
The Writing of Fiction, Ch. 1

448 Trivial personalities decomposing in the eternity
of print.
Virginia Woolf (1882–1941) British novelist.
The Common Reader, 'Jane Eyre'

449 *Middlemarch*, the magnificent book which with
all its imperfections is one of the few English
novels for grown up people.
Virginia Woolf (1882–1941) British novelist.
The Common Reader, 'George Eliot'

450 'It's like the question of the authorship of the
Iliad,' said Mr Cardan. 'The author of that
poem is either Homer or, if not Homer, some-
body else of the same name.'
Aldous Huxley (1894–1964) British novelist.
Those Barren Leaves, Pt. V, Ch. 4

451 Music is not written in red, white and blue. It is
written in the heart's blood of the composer.
Nellie Melba (Helen Porter Mitchell; 1861–
1931) Australian soprano.
Melodies and Memories

452 I don't write modern music. I only write good
music.
Igor Stravinsky (1882–1971) Russian-born
US composer.
To journalists on his first visit to America, 1925

1928

453 A bad book is as much a labour to write as a

good one; it comes as sincerely from the author's soul.
Aldous Huxley (1894–1964) British novelist.
Point Counter Point

454 My God, what a clumsy *alla patrida* James Joyce is! Nothing but old fags and cabbage stumps of quotations from the Bible and the rest, stewed in the juice of deliberate, journalistic dirty-mindedness.
D. H. Lawrence (1885–1930) British novelist.
Letter to Aldous Huxley

1929

455 I've never been in there . . . but there are only three things to see, and I've seen colour reproductions of all of them.
Harold W. Ross (1892–1951) US journalist.
Referring to the Louvre
A Farewell to Arms (Ernest Hemingway)

456 Until we learn the use of living words we shall continue to be waxworks inhabited by gramophones.
Walter De La Mare (1873–1956) British poet.
The Observer, 'Sayings of the Week', 12 May 1929

457 Literature is strewn with the wreckage of men who have minded beyond reason the opinions of others.
Virginia Woolf (1882–1941) British novelist.
A Room of One's Own

1930

458 As is the case in all branches of art, success depends in a very large measure upon individual initiative and exertion, and cannot be achieved except by dint of hard work.
Anna Pavlova (1881–1931) Russian ballet dancer.
Pavlova: A Biography (ed. A. H. Franks), 'Pages of My Life'

459 Never mind about my soul, just make sure you get my tie right.
James Joyce (1882–1941) Irish novelist.
Responding to the painter Patrick Tuohy's assertion that he wished to capture Joyce's soul in his portrait of him
James Joyce (R. Ellmann)

460 A work of art is part of nature seen through a temperament.
André Gide (1869–1951) French novelist.
Protests

461 No poet, no artist of any sort, has his complete meaning alone. His significance, his appreciation is the appreciation of his relation to the dead poets and artists.
T. S. Eliot (1888–1965) US-born British poet and dramatist.
Tradition and the Individual Talent

462 The whole of art is an appeal to a reality which is not without us but in our minds.
Desmond MacCarthy (1877–1952) British writer and theatre critic.
Theatre, 'Modern Drama'

463 The ability to simplify means to eliminate the unnecessary so that the necessary may speak.
Hans Hofmann (1880–1966) German-born US painter.
Search for the Real

464* I never realized before that Albert married beneath him.
Noël Coward (1899–1973) British dramatist.
After seeing a certain actress in the role of Queen Victoria
Tynan on Theatre (K. Tynan)

465 It is disappointing to report that George Bernard Shaw appearing as George Bernard Shaw is sadly miscast in the part. Satirists should be heard and not seen.
Robert E. Sherwood (1896–1955) US writer and dramatist.
Reviewing a Shaw play

466 This is not a novel to be tossed aside lightly. It should be thrown with great force.
Dorothy Parker (1893–1967) US writer.
Book review
Wit's End (R. E. Dremman)

467 It is the sexless novel that should be distinguished: the sex novel is now normal.
George Bernard Shaw (1856–1950) Irish dramatist and critic.
Table-Talk of G.B.S.

468 All good writing is *swimming under water* and holding your breath.
F. Scott Fitzgerald (1896–1940) US novelist.
Letter

469 Our American professors like their literature clear and cold and pure and very dead.
Sinclair Lewis (1885–1951) US novelist.
Speech, on receiving the Nobel Prize, 1930

470 There are two motives for reading a book: one that you enjoy it, the other that you can boast about it.
Bertrand Russell (1872–1970) British philosopher.
The Conquest of Happiness

471 The poet speaks to all men of that other life of theirs that they have smothered and forgotten.
Edith Sitwell (1887–1964) British poet and writer.
Rhyme and Reason

472 Strange how potent cheap music is.
Noël Coward (1899–1973) British dramatist
Private Lives

473 A good composer does not imitate; he steals
Igor Stravinsky (1882–1971) Russian-born US composer.
Twentieth Century Music (Peter Yates)

474 Rachmaninov's immortalizing totality was his scowl. He was a six-and-a-half-foot-tall scowl.
Igor Stravinsky
Conversations with Igor Stravinsky (Igor Stravinsky and Robert Craft)

475 Wagner is the Puccini of music.
J. B. Morton (1893–1979) British journalist.
Attrib.

476 Madame, there you sit with that magnificent instrument between your legs, and all you can do is *scratch* it!
Arturo Toscanini (1867–1957) Italian conductor.
Rebuking an incompetent woman cellist; also attributed to Sir Thomas Beecham
Attrib.

477 God tells me how he wants this music played — and you get in his way.
Arturo Toscanini
Etude (Howard Tubman)

1931

478 A best-seller is the gilded tomb of a mediocre talent.
Logan Pearsall Smith (1865–1946) US writer.
Afterthoughts, 'Art and Letters'

1933

479 Even when poetry has a meaning, as it usually has, it may be inadvisable to draw it out ... Perfect understanding will sometimes almost extinguish pleasure.
A. E. Housman (1859–1936) British scholar and poet.
The Name and Nature of Poetry

480 People are wrong when they say the opera isn't what it used to be. It is what it used to be. That's what's wrong with it.
Noël Coward (1899–1973) British dramatist.
Design for Living

1934

481 It does not matter that Dickens' world is not life-like; it is alive.
Lord Cecil (1902–86) British writer and critic.
Early Victorian Novelists

482 A combination of Little Nell and Lady Macbeth.
Alexander Woollcott (1887–1943) US journalist.
Referring to Dorothy Parker
While Rome Burns

483 Music begins to atrophy when it departs too far from the dance; ... poetry begins to atrophy when it gets too far from music.
Ezra Pound (1885–1972) US poet.
ABC of Reading, 'Warning'

1935

484* When I hear anyone talk of Culture, I reach for my revolver.
Hermann Goering (1893–1946) German leader.
Attrib. to Goering but probably said by Hanns Johst

485 Writing free verse is like playing tennis with the net down.
Robert Frost (1875–1963) US poet.
Speech, Milton Academy, 17 May 1935

1936

486 He is all blood, dirt and sucked sugar stick.
W. B. Yeats (1865–1939) Irish poet.
Referring to Wilfred Owen
Letters on Poetry to Dorothy Wellesley, Letter, 21 Dec 1936

487 That was the chief difference between literature and life. In books, the proportion of exceptional to commonplace people is high; in reality, very low.
Aldous Huxley (1894–1964) British novelist.
Eyeless in Gaza

488 For Lawrence, existence was one continuous convalescence; it was as though he were newly reborn from a mortal illness every day of his life.
Aldous Huxley
Referring to D. H. Lawrence
The Olive Tree

489 There are passages in *Ulysses* which can be read only in the toilet — if one wants to extract the full flavour of their content.
Henry Miller (1891–1980) US novelist.
Black Spring

490 You must write for children in the same way as you do for adults, only better.
Maxim Gorky (Aleksei Maksimovich Peshkov; 1868–1936) Russian writer.
Attrib.

1937

491 The higher-water mark, so to speak, of Socialist literature is W. H. Auden, a sort of gutless Kipling.
George Orwell (Eric Blair; 1903–50) British novelist.
The Road to Wigan Pier, Ch. 11

1938

492 A great writer creates a world of his own and his readers are proud to live in it. A lesser writer may entice them in for a moment, but soon he will watch them filing out.
Cyril Connolly (1903–74) British journalist.
Enemies of Promise, Ch. 1

493 An author arrives at a good style when his lan-

guage performs what is required of it without shyness.
Cyril Connolly
Enemies of Promise, Ch. 3

494   For to write good prose is an affair of good manners. It is, unlike verse, a civil art.... Poetry is baroque.
W. Somerset Maugham (1874–1965) British novelist.
The Summing Up

495   There is an impression abroad that everyone has it in him to write one book; but if by this is implied a good book the impression is false.
W. Somerset Maugham
The Summing Up

496   It has been said that good prose should resemble the conversation of a well-bred man.
W. Somerset Maugham
The Summing Up

1939

497* At 83 Shaw's mind was perhaps not quite as good as it used to be. It was still better than anyone else's.
Alexander Woollcott (1887–1943) US journalist.
Referring to George Bernard Shaw
While Rome Burns

498   Earth, receive an honoured guest:
William Yeats is laid to rest.
Let the Irish vessel lie
Emptied of its poetry.
W. H. Auden (1907–73) British poet.
In Memory of W. B. Yeats, III

499   No tears in the writer, no tears in the reader.
Robert Frost (1875–1963) US poet.
Collected Poems, Preface

1940

500   Too true, too sincere. The Muse prefers the liars, the gay and warty lads.
W. B. Yeats (1865–1939) Irish poet.
Referring to the poetry of James Reed
The Long Week End (Robert Graves and Alan Hodge)

501   Art is the imposing of a pattern on experience, and our aesthetic enjoyment is recognition of the pattern.
A. N. Whitehead (1861–1947) British philosopher.
Dialogues, 228

502* I enjoyed talking to her, but thought *nothing* of her writing. I considered her 'a beautiful little knitter'.
Edith Sitwell (1887–1964) British poet and writer.
Referring to Virginia Woolf
Letter to G. Singleton

503   It is the logic of our times,
No subject for immortal verse –

That we who lived by honest dreams
Defend the bad against the worse.
C. Day Lewis (1904–72) British poet.
Where are the War Poets?

504   English literature's performing flea.
Sean O'Casey (1884–1964) Irish dramatist.
Referring to P. G. Wodehouse
Attrib.

505   Poetry makes nothing happen, it survives
In the valley of its saying.
W. H. Auden (1907–73) British poet.
In Memory of W. B. Yeats

1941

506   A painter should not paint what he sees, but what will be seen.
Paul Valéry (1871–1945) French poet and writer.
Mauvaises Pensées et Autres

507   What a terrible revenge by the culture of the Negroes on that of the whites.
Ignacy Paderewski (1860–1941) Polish pianist, composer, and statesman.
Referring to jazz
Attrib.

508   Of all the great Victorian writers, he was probably the most antagonistic to the Victorian age itself.
Edmund Wilson (1895–1972) US critic and writer.
Referring to Dickens
The Wound and the Bow, 'The Two Scrooges'

1944

509   The only way for writers to meet is to share a quick pee over a common lamp-post.
Cyril Connolly (1903–74) British journalist.
The Unquiet Grave

1945

510   You can stroke people with words.
F. Scott Fitzgerald (1896–1940) US novelist.
The Crack-up

511   I have only read one book in my life and that is *White Fang*. It's so frightfully good I've never bothered to read another.
Nancy Mitford (1904–73) British writer.
The Pursuit Of Love

512   Music is a beautiful opiate, if you don't take it too seriously.
Henry Miller (1891–1980) US novelist.
The Air Conditioned Nightmare

Daily Life

1917

513   Many a man who thinks to found a home dis-

covers that he has merely opened a tavern for his friends.
Norman Douglas (1868–1952) British novelist.
South Wind, Ch. 24

1920

514* Exercise is bunk. If you are healthy, you don't need it: if you are sick, you shouldn't take it.
Henry Ford (1863–1947) US car manufacturer.
Attrib.

1922

515 Teetotallers lack the sympathy and generosity of men that drink.
W. H. Davies (1871–1940) British poet.
Shorter Lyrics of the 20th Century, Introduction

1925

516 Those comfortably padded lunatic asylums which are known, euphemistically, as the stately homes of England.
Virginia Woolf (1882–1941) British novelist.
The Common Reader, 'Lady Dorothy Nevill'

1930

517 Winter is icummen in,
Lhude sing Goddamm,
Raineth drop and staineth slop
And how the wind doth ramm!
Sing: Goddamm.
Ezra Pound (1885–1972) US poet.
Ancient Music

518* Any time you're Lambeth way,
Any evening, any day,
You'll find us all doin' the Lambeth walk.
Douglas Furber (1885–1961) British songwriter.
Doin' the Lambeth Walk

519* Smokers, male and female, inject and excuse idleness in their lives every time they light a cigarette.
Colette (1873–1954) French novelist.
Earthly Paradise, 'Freedom'

1932

520 The quality of Mersey is not strained.
Anonymous
Referring to the polluted condition of the River Mersey
Sunday Graphic, 14 Aug 1932

1934

521 The feeling of Sunday is the same everywhere,

heavy, melancholy, standing still. Like when they say, 'As it was in the beginning, is now, and ever shall be, world without end.'
Jean Rhys (1894–1979) Dominican-born British novelist.
Voyage in the Dark, Ch. 4

1935

522 The Stately Homes of England
How beautiful they stand,
To prove the upper classes
Have still the upper hand.
Noël Coward (1899–1973) British dramatist.
Operette, 'The Stately Homes of England'

1938

523 A hundred and fifty accurate reproductions of Anne Hathaway's cottage, each complete with central heating and garage.
Osbert Lancaster (1908–86) British cartoonist.
Pillar to Post, 'Stockbrokers Tudor'

Death

1924

524 What we call mourning for our dead is perhaps not so much grief at not being able to call them back as it is grief at not being able to want to do so.
Thomas Mann (1875–1955) German novelist.
The Magic Mountain

1936

525 Death . . . It's the only thing we haven't succeeded in completely vulgarizing.
Aldous Huxley (1894–1964) British novelist.
Eyeless in Gaza, Ch. 31

1941

526 It is the only disease you don't look forward to being cured of.
Herman J. Mankiewicz (1897–1953) US journalist and screenwriter.
Referring to death
Citizen Kane

1944

527 Ignore death until the last moment; then when it can't be ignored any longer have yourself squirted full of morphia and shuffle off in a corner.
Aldous Huxley (1894–1964) British novelist.
Time Must Have A Stop

Education, Knowledge, and Learning

1918

528* An idea isn't responsible for the people who believe in it.
Don Marquis (1878–1937) US journalist.
New York Sun

1920

529* Intelligence is quickness to apprehend as distinct from ability, which is capacity to act wisely on the thing apprehended.
A. N. Whitehead (1861–1947) British philosopher.
Dialogues, 135

530 They go forth into it with well-developed bodies, fairly developed minds, and undeveloped hearts.
E. M. Forster (1879–1970) British novelist.
Referring to public schoolboys going into the world
Abinger Harvest, 'Notes on the English Character'

1921

531 The proper study of mankind is books.
Aldous Huxley (1894–1964) British novelist.
Chrome Yellow

532 In order to draw a limit to thinking, we should have to be able to think both sides of this limit.
Ludwig Wittgenstein (1889–1951) Austrian philosopher.
Tractatus Logico-Philosophicus, Preface

533 Philosophy is not a theory but an activity.
Ludwig Wittgenstein
Tractatus Logico-Philosophicus, Ch. 4

534 Whereof one cannot speak, thereon one must remain silent.
Ludwig Wittgenstein
Tractatus Logico-Philosophicus, Ch. 7

1922

535 The refined punishments of the spiritual mode are usually much more indecent and dangerous than a good smack.
D. H. Lawrence (1885–1930) British novelist.
Fantasia of the Unconscious, Ch. 4

536 The tendency of the casual mind is to pick out or stumble upon a sample which supports or defines its prejudices, and then to make it representative of a whole class.
Walter Lippmann (1889–1974) US editor and writer.
Public Opinion

1923

537 Knowledge can be communicated but not wisdom.
Hermann Hesse (1877–1962) German novelist and poet.
Siddhartha

1924

538 Education is simply the soul of a society as it passes from one generation to another.
G. K. Chesterton (1874–1936) British writer.
The Observer, 'Sayings of the Week', 6 July 1924

1926

539 One does not discover new lands without consenting to lose sight of the shore for a very long time.
André Gide (1869–1951) French novelist.
The Counterfeiters

1927

540 The voice of the intellect is a soft one, but it does not rest till it has gained a hearing.
Sigmund Freud (1856–1939) Austrian psychoanalyst.
The Future of an Illusion

541 If you make people think they're thinking, they'll love you: but if you really make them think, they'll hate you.
Don Marquis (1878–1937) US journalist.
Archy and Mehitabel

1928

542 Silence is as full of potential wisdom and wit as the unhewn marble of great sculpture.
Aldous Huxley (1894–1964) British novelist.
Point Counter Point

543 It is undesirable to believe a proposition when there is no ground whatever for supposing it true.
Bertrand Russell (1872–1970) British philosopher.
Sceptical Essays

1929

544 Thought must be divided against itself before it can come to any knowledge of itself.
Aldous Huxley (1894–1964) British novelist.
Do What You Will

545 The safest general characterization of the European philosophical tradition is that it consists of a series of footnotes to Plato.
A. N. Whitehead (1861–1947) British philosopher.
Process and Reality

1930

546* It is a great advantage for a system of philosophy to be substantially true.
George Santayana (1863–1952) US philosopher.
The Unknowable

547 Philosophy is the product of wonder.
A. N. Whitehead (1861–1947) British philosopher.
Nature and Life, Ch. 1

548 Philosophy, as we use the word, is a fight against the fascination which forms of expression exert upon us.
Ludwig Wittgenstein (1889–1951) Austrian philosopher.
The Blue Book

549* Stupidity does not consist in being without ideas. Such stupidity would be the sweet, blissful stupidity of animals, molluscs and the gods. Human Stupidity consists in having lots of ideas, but stupid ones.
Henry de Montherlant (1896–1972) French novelist.
Notebooks

550* The point of philosophy is to start with something so simple as to seem not worth stating, and to end with something so paradoxical that no one will believe it.
Bertrand Russell (1872–1970) British philospher.
Logic and Knowledge

551 Do not on any account attempt to write on both sides of the paper at once.
W. C. Sellar (1898–1951) British humorous writer.
1066 And All That, Test Paper 5

1931

552 What is a highbrow? It is a man who has found something more interesting than women.
Edgar Wallace (1875–1932) British thriller writer.
Interview

1935

553* An intellectual is someone whose mind watches itself.
Albert Camus (1913–60) French existentialist writer.
Notebooks, 1935–42

1936

554 The principles of logic and metaphysics are true simply because we never allow them to be anything else.
A. J. Ayer (1910–) British philosopher.
Language, Truth and Logic

1938

555 The ape-like virtues without which no one can enjoy a public school.
Cyril Connolly (1903–74) British journalist.
Enemies of Promise, Ch. 1

556 My thought is *me*: that is why I can't stop. I exist by what I think . . . and I can't prevent myself from thinking.
Jean-Paul Sartre (1905–80) French writer.
Nausea

1942

557 Disinterested intellectual curiosity is the life blood of real civilisation.
George Macaulay Trevelyan (1876–1962) British historian
English Social History, Preface

558 Education . . . has produced a vast population able to read but unable to distinguish what is worth reading.
George Macaulay Trevelyan
English Social History, Ch. 18

1944

559 Facts are ventriloquists' dummies. Sitting on a wise man's knee they may be made to utter words of wisdom; elsewhere they say nothing or talk nonsense.
Aldous Huxley (1894–1964) British novelist.
Time Must Have A Stop

1945

560 If one is too lazy to think, too vain to do a thing badly, too cowardly to admit it, one will never attain wisdom.
Cyril Connolly (1903–74) British journalist.
The Unquiet Grave

History

1916

561 History is more or less bunk. It's tradition. We don't want tradition. We want to live in the present and the only history that is worth a tinker's damn is the history we make today.
Henry Ford (1863–1947) US car manufacturer.
Chicago Tribune, 25 May 1916

1920

562* What we know of the past is mostly not worth knowing. What is worth knowing is mostly uncertain. Events in the past may roughly be divided into those which probably never happened and those which do not matter.
Dean Inge (1860–1954) British churchman.
Assessments and Anticipations, 'Prognostications'

563 The historian must have . . . some conception of

how men who are not historians behave. Otherwise he will move in a world of the dead.
E. M. Forster (1879–1970) British novelist.
Abinger Harvest, 'Captain Edward Gibbon'

1922

564 'History', Stephen said, 'is a nightmare from which I am trying to awake'.
James Joyce (1882–1941) Irish novelist.
Ulysses

1925

565 Why doesn't the past decently bury itself, instead of sitting and waiting to be admitted by the present?
D. H. Lawrence (1885–1930) British novelist.
St. Mawr

1926

566 I do not know which makes a man more conservative – to know nothing but the present, or nothing but the past.
John Maynard Keynes (1883–1946) British economist.
The End of Laisser-Faire, I

1933

567 It is not the neutrals or the lukewarm who make history.
Adolf Hitler (1889–1945) German dictator.
Speech, Berlin, 23 Apr 1933

1935

568 The Common Law of England has been laboriously built about a mythical figure – the figure of 'The Reasonable Man'.
A. P. Herbert (1890–1971) British writer and politician.
Uncommon Law

1936

569 The greater part of what passes for diplomatic history is little more than the record of what one clerk said to another clerk.
G. M. Young (1882–1959) British historian.
Victorian England: Portrait of an Age

1938

570 The attitude of the English . . . toward English history reminds one a good deal of the attitude of a Hollywood director toward love.
Margaret Halsey (1910–) US writer.
With Malice Toward Some

1942

571 To a surprising extent the war-lords in shining armour, the apostles of the martial virtues,

tend not to die fighting when the time comes. History is full of ignominious getaways by the great and famous.
George Orwell (Eric Blair; 1903–50) British novelist.
Who Are the War Criminals?

1945

572 There is no history of mankind, there are only many histories of all kinds of aspects of human life. And one of these is the history of political power. This is elevated into the history of the world.
Karl Popper (1902–   ) Austrian-born British philosopher.
The Open Society and Its Enemies

Human Nature

1914

573 The secret of being miserable is to have leisure to bother about whether you are happy or not.
George Bernard Shaw (1856–1950) Irish dramatist and critic.
Misalliance, Preface

574 One's religion is whatever he is most interested in, and yours is Success.
J. M. Barrie (1860–1937) British novelist and dramatist.
The Twelve-Pound Look

1915

575 Mediocrity knows nothing higher than itself, but talent instantly recognizes genius.
Arthur Conan Doyle (1856–1930) British writer.
The Valley of Fear

576 Like all weak men he laid an exaggerated stress on not changing one's mind.
W. Somerset Maugham (1874–1965) British novelist.
Of Human Bondage, Ch. 37

1917

577 Happiness is not best achieved by those who seek it directly.
Bertrand Russell (1872–1970) British philosopher.
Mysticism and Logic

1918

578 The human face is indeed, like the face of the God of some Oriental theogony, a whole cluster of faces, crowded together but on different surfaces so that one does not see them all at once.
Marcel Proust (1871–1922) French novelist.
À la recherche du temps perdu: À l'ombre des jeunes filles en fleurs

579* Happiness is beneficial for the body, but it is grief that develops the powers of the mind.
Marcel Proust
À la recherche du temps perdu: Le Temps retrouvé

1919

580 It takes in reality only one to make a quarrel. It is useless for the sheep to pass resolutions in favour of vegetarianism while the wolf remains of a different opinion.
Dean Inge (1860–1954) British churchman.
Outspoken Essays

581 It is hard to believe that a man is telling the truth when you know that you would lie if you were in his place.
H. L. Mencken (1880–1956) US journalist.
Prejudices

582 I don't owe a penny to a single soul – not counting tradesmen, of course.
P. G. Wodehouse (1881–1975) British humorous novelist.
My Man Jeeves, 'Jeeves and the Hard-Boiled Egg'

1920

583 If I ever felt inclined to be timid as I was going into a room full of people, I would say to myself, 'You're the cleverest member of one of the cleverest families in the cleverest class of the cleverest nation in the world, why should you be frightened?'
Beatrice Webb (1858–1943) British economist and writer.
Portraits from Memory (Bertrand Russell), 'Sidney and Beatrice Webb'

584 Although there exist many thousand subjects for elegant conversation, there are persons who cannot meet a cripple without talking about feet.
Ernest Bramah (1869–1942) British writer.
The Wallet of Kai Lung

585 I can sympathize with people's pains, but not with their pleasures. There is something curiously boring about somebody else's happiness.
Aldous Huxley (1894–1964) British novelist.
Limbo, 'Cynthia'

586 It is the unbroken testimony of all history that alcoholic liquors have been used by the strongest, wisest, handsomest, and in every way best races of all times.
George Edward Bateman Saintsbury (1845–1933) British writer and critic.
Notes on a Cellar-Book

587 My candle burns at both ends;
It will not last the night;
But ah, my foes, and oh my friends –
It gives a lovely light!
Edna St Vincent Millay (1892–1950) US poet.
A Few Figs from Thistles, 'First Fig'

1922

588 War hath no fury like a non-combatant.
C. E. Montague (1867–1928) British editor and writer.
Disenchantment, Ch. 15

589 Never ascribe to an opponent motives meaner than your own.
J. M. Barrie (1860–1937) British novelist and dramatist.
Speech, St Andrews, 3 May 1922

590 Sadness is almost never anything but a form of fatigue.
André Gide (1869–1951) French novelist.
Journals, 1922

1923

591 I have the true feeling of myself only when I am unbearably unhappy.
Franz Kafka (1883–1924) Czech novelist.
Diaries

592 That which you love most in him (a friend) may be clearer in his absence.
Kahil Gibran (1883–1931) Lebanese mystic poet and novelist.
The Prophet

593 Because it is there.
George Mallory (1886–1924) British mountaineer.
Answer to the question 'Why do you want to climb Mt. Everest?'
George Mallory (D. Robertson)

1924

594 A platitude is simply a truth repeated till people get tired of hearing it.
Stanley Baldwin (1867–1947) British statesman.
Attrib.

595 Curious things, habits. People themselves never knew they had them.
Agatha Christie (1891–1976) British detective-story writer.
Witness for the Prosecution

596 It is seldom indeed that one parts on good terms, because if one were on good terms one would not part.
Marcel Proust (1871–1922) French novelist.
À la recherche du temps perdu: La Prisonnière

1925

597* What men value in this world is not rights but privileges.
H. L. Mencken (1880–1956) US journalist.
Minority Report

598 There is no surer way of calling the worst out of anyone than that of taking their worst as being their true selves; no surer way of bringing out the best than by only accepting that as being true of them.
E. F. Benson (1867–1940) British novelist.
Rex

599 The latest definition of an optimist is one who fills up his crossword puzzle in ink.
Clement King Shorter (1857–1926) British journalist and critic.
The Observer, 'Sayings of the Week', 22 Feb 1925

1926

600 The optimist proclaims we live in the best of all possible worlds; and the pessimist fears this is true.
James Cabell (1879–1958) US novelist and journalist.
The Silver Stallion

601 All men dream: but not equally. Those who dream by night in the dusty recesses of their minds wake in the day to find that it was vanity: but the dreamers of the day are dangerous men, for they may act their dream with open eyes, to make it possible.
T. E. Lawrence (1888–1935) British soldier and writer.
Seven Pillars of Wisdom, Ch. 1

1927

602 Faith may be defined briefly as an illogical belief in the occurrence of the improbable.
H. L. Mencken (1880–1956) US journalist.
Prejudices, 'Types of Men'

603* It is easier to fight for one's principles than to live up to them.
Alfred Adler (1870–1937) Austrian psychiatrist.
Alfred Adler (P. Bottome)

1928

604 Watch how a man takes praise and there you have the measure of him.
Thomas Burke (1886–1945) British writer.
T. P.'s Weekly, 8 June 1928

605 Happiness is like coke - something you get as a by-product in the process of making something else.
Aldous Huxley (1894–1964) British novelist.
Point Counter Point

606 It takes two to make a murder. There are born victims, born to have their throats cut.
Aldous Huxley
Point Counter Point

607 I can't quite explain it, but I don't believe one can ever be unhappy for long provided one does just exactly what one wants to and when one wants to.
Evelyn Waugh (1903–66) British novelist.
Decline and Fall, Pt. I, Ch. 5

1929

608 Consistency is contrary to nature, contrary to life. The only completely consistent people are the dead.
Aldous Huxley (1894–1964) British novelist.
Do What you Will

609 Most of the time we think we're sick, it's all in the mind.
Thomas Wolfe (1900–38) US novelist.
Look Homeward, Angel, Pt. I, Ch. 1

1930

610 Being Southerners, it was a source of shame to some members of the family that we had no recorded ancestors on either side of the Battle of Hastings.
Harper Lee (1926–) US writer.
To Kill a Mockingbird, Pt. I, Ch. 1

611 One of the things that makes a Negro unpleasant to white folk is the fact that he suffers from their injustice. He is thus a standing rebuke to them.
H. L. Mencken (1880–1956) US journalist.
Notebooks, 'Minority Report'

612 War will never cease until babies begin to come into the world with larger cerebrums and smaller adrenal glands.
H. L. Mencken
Notebooks, 'Minority Report'

613* Of course I don't believe in it. But I understand that it brings you luck whether you believe in it or not.
Niels Bohr (1885–1962) Danish physicist.
When asked why he had a horseshoe on his wall
Attrib.

614 It is no good casting out devils. They belong to us, we must accept them and be at peace with them.
D. H. Lawrence (1885–1930) British novelist.
Phoenix, 'The Reality of Peace'

615 It is not the ape, nor the tiger in man that I fear, it is the donkey.
William Temple (1881–1944) British churchman.
Attrib.

616 The aristocratic pleasure of displeasing is not the only delight that bad taste can yield. One can love a certain kind of vulgarity for its own sake.
Aldous Huxley (1894–1964) British novelist.
Vulgarity in Literature, Ch. 4

617 Those who believe that they are exclusively in the right are generally those who achieve something.
Aldous Huxley
Proper Studies

618 The megalomaniac differs from the narcissist by the fact that he wishes to be powerful rather than charming, and seeks to be feared rather than loved. To this type belong many lunatics and most of the great men of history.
Bertrand Russell (1872–1970) British philosopher.
The Conquest of Happiness

9 Ambition is the grand enemy of all peace.
John Cowper Powys (1872–1963) British
novelist.
The Meaning of Culture

1931

0 Only solitary men know the full joys of friendship. Others have their family – but to a solitary and an exile his friends are everything.
Willa Cather (1873–1947) US writer and poet.
Shadows On the Rock

1932

1 To the Puritan all things are impure, as some-
body says.
D. H. Lawrence (1885–1930) British novelist.
Etruscan Places, 'Cerveteri'

1935

2 Nobody speaks the truth when there's some-
thing they must have.
Elizabeth Bowen (1899–1973) Irish novelist.
The House in Paris, Ch. 5

3 It is a kind of spiritual snobbery that makes
people think that they can be happy without
money.
Albert Camus (1913–60) French existentialist
writer.
Notebooks, 1935–1942

4* Human kind
Cannot bear very much reality.
T. S. Eliot (1888–1965) US-born British poet
and dramatist.
Four Quartets, 'Burnt Norton'

1936

5 Fighting is like champagne. It goes to the heads
of cowards as quickly as of heroes. Any fool
can be brave on a battle field when it's be
brave or else be killed.
Margaret Mitchell (1909–49) US novelist.
Gone with the Wind

1937

6 The more you are in the right the more natural
that everyone else should be bullied into
thinking likewise.
George Orwell (Eric Blair; 1903–50) British
novelist.
The Road to Wigan Pier

7 No one can make you feel inferior without your
consent.
Eleanor Roosevelt (1884–1962) US writer
and lecturer.
This is My Story

1938

8 Had I been a man I might have explored the
Poles or climbed Mount Everest, but as it was
my spirit found outlet in the air.
Amy Johnson (1903–41) British flyer.
Myself When Young (ed. Margot Asquith)

629 I'll give you my opinion of the human race . . .
Their heart's in the right place, but their head
is a thoroughly inefficient organ.
W. Somerset Maugham (1874–1965) British
novelist.
The Summing Up

630 You get the impression that their normal condition is silence and that speech is a slight fever
which attacks them now and then.
Jean-Paul Sartre (1905–80) French writer.
Nausea

1939

631 It's easy to make a man confess the lies he
tells to himself; it's far harder to make him confess the truth.
Geoffrey Household (1900–   ) British
writer.
Rogue Male

632 Man, unlike any other thing organic or inor-
ganic in the universe, grows beyond his work,
walks up the stairs of his concepts, emerges
ahead of his accomplishments.
John Steinbeck (1902–68) US novelist.
The Grapes of Wrath, Ch. 14

1940

633 I hate that aesthetic game of the eye and the
mind, played by these connoisseurs, these
mandarins who 'appreciate' beauty. What *is*
beauty, anyway? There's no such thing. I never
'appreciate', any more than I 'like'. I love or I
hate.
Pablo Picasso (1881–1973) Spanish painter.
Life with Picasso (Françoise Gilot and Carlton
Lake), Ch. 2

634 The moment a man talks to his fellows he begins to lie.
Hilaire Belloc (1870–1953) French-born British poet.
The Silence of the Sea

1941

635 I don't trust him. We're friends.
Bertolt Brecht (1898–1956) German
dramatist.
Mother Courage, III

636 The finest plans have always been spoiled by
the littleness of those that should carry them
out. Even emperors can't do it all by
themselves.
Bertolt Brecht
Mother Courage, VI

637 Sentimentality is only sentiment that rubs you
up the wrong way.
W. Somerset Maugham (1874–1965) British
novelist.
A Writer's Notebook

1942

638   One of the mysteries of human conduct is why
       adult men and women all over England are
       ready to sign documents which they do not
       read, at the behest of canvassers whom they
       do not know, binding them to pay for articles
       which they do not want, with money which
       they have not got.
       Gerald Hurst (1877–1957) British writer and
       judge.
       Closed Chapters

1943

639   Wherever an inferiority complex exists, there is
       a good reason for it. There is always some-
       thing inferior there, although not just where we
       persuade ourselves that it is.
       Carl Gustav Jung (1875–1961) Swiss
       psychoanalyst.
       Interview, 1943

640   It is such a secret place, the land of tears.
       Antoine de Saint-Exupéry (1900–44)
       French novelist and aviator.
       The Little Prince, Ch. 7

1944

641   Imprisoned in every fat man a thin one is wildly
       signalling to be let out.
       Cyril Connolly (1903–74) British journalist.
       The Unquiet Grave

1945

642   There are many who dare not kill themselves
       for fear of what the neighbours might say.
       Cyril Connolly
       The Unquiet Grave

643   One can present people with opportunities.
       One cannot make them equal to them.
       Rosamond Lehmann (1901–   ) British
       novelist.
       The Ballad and the Source

644   Each generation imagines itself to be more in-
       telligent than the one that went before it, and
       wiser than the one that comes after it.
       George Orwell (Eric Blair; 1903–50) British
       novelist.
       Book Review

645   Serious sport has nothing to do with fair play. It
       is bound up with hatred, jealousy, boastful-
       ness, disregard of all rules and sadistic pleas-
       ure in witnessing violence; in other words it
       is war minus the shooting.
       George Orwell
       The Sporting Spirit

Humour

1919

646   Impropriety is the soul of wit.
       W. Somerset Maugham (1874–1965) Briti
       novelist.
       The Moon and Sixpence, Ch. 4

1926

647   Comedy, we may say, is society protecting i
       self – with a smile.
       J. B. Priestley (1894–1984) British novelis
       George Meredith

1930

648*   I must get out of these wet clothes and into
       dry Martini.
       Alexander Woollcott (1887–1943) US
       journalist.
       Reader's Digest

1931

649   A comedian can only last till he either takes
       himself serious or his audience takes him
       serious.
       Will Rogers (1879–1935) US actor and
       humorist.
       Newspaper article, 1931

650*   I've been accused of every death except the
       casualty list of the World War.
       Al Capone (1899–1947) Italian-born US
       gangster.
       The Bootleggers (Kenneth Allsop), Ch. 11

1938

651   Early to rise and early to bed makes a male
       healthy and wealthy and dead.
       James Thurber (1894–1961) US humorist.
       Fables for Our Time, 'The Shrike and the
       Chipmunks'

1940

652*   There, but for the Grace of God, goes God.
       Herman J. Mankiewicz (1897–1953) US
       journalist and screenwriter.
       Said of Orson Welles in the making of *Citizer
       Kane*. Also attributed to others
       The Citizen Kane Book

Life

1915

653   How reconcile this world of fact with the brig
       world of my imagining? My darkness has bee
       filled with the light of intelligence, and be-

hold, the outer day-light world was stumbling
and groping in social blindness.
Helen Keller (1880–1968) US writer and
lecturer.
The Cry for Justice (ed. Upton Sinclair)

1916

4 A man travels the world over in search of what
he needs and returns home to find it.
George Moore (1852–1933) Irish writer and
art critic.
The Brook Kerith, Ch. 11

1917

5 The degree of a nation's civilization is marked
by its disregard for the necessities of
existence.
W. Somerset Maugham (1874–1965) British
novelist.
Our Betters, I

6 The right people are rude. They can afford to
be.
W. Somerset Maugham
Our Betters, II

7 There are three ingredients in the good life:
learning, earning and yearning.
Christopher Darlington Morley (1890–
1957) US writer.
Parnassus on Wheels, Ch. 10

1919

8 The whole of nature is a conjugation of the verb
to eat, in the active and the passive.
Dean Inge (1860–1954) British churchman.
Outspoken Essays

9 So many gods, so many creeds,
So many paths that wind and wind,
While just the art of being kind
Is all the sad world needs.
Ella Wheeler Wilcox (1850–1919) US poet.
The World's Need

0 Laugh, and the world laughs with you;
Weep, and you weep alone,
For the sad old earth must borrow its mirth,
But has trouble enough of its own.
Ella Wheeler Wilcox
Solitude

1 The outcome of any serious research can only
be to make two questions grow where only
one grew before.
Thorstein Bunde Veblen (1857–1929) US
social scientist.
The Place of Science in Modern Civilization

1920

2 When a dog bites a man that is not news, but
when a man bites a dog that is news.
John B. Bogart (1845–1920) US journalist.
Sometimes attributed to Charles Dana and Amos
Cummings
Attrib.

663* People do not live nowadays – they get about
ten percent out of life.
Isadora Duncan (1878–1927) US dancer.
This Quarter Autumn, 'Memoirs'

664 Ideal mankind would abolish death, multiply itself million upon million, rear up city upon
city, save every parasite alive, until the accu-
mulation of mere existence is swollen to a
horror.
D. H. Lawrence (1885–1930) British novelist.
St Mawr

665 Away with all ideals. Let each individual act
spontaneously from the for ever incalculable
prompting of the creative wellhead within him.
There is no universal law.
D. H. Lawrence
Phoenix, Preface to 'All Things are Possible' by
Leo Shostov

666 The young man who has not wept is a savage,
and the old man who will not laugh is a fool.
George Santayana (1863–1952) US
philosopher.
Dialogues in Limbo, Ch. 3

667 Old men are dangerous; it doesn't matter to
them what is going to happen to the world.
George Bernard Shaw (1856–1950) Irish
dramatist and critic.
Heartbreak House

668 It isn't mere convention. Everyone can see that
the people who hunt are the right people and
the people who don't are the wrong ones.
George Bernard Shaw
Heartbreak House

669 What is this life if, full of care,
We have no time to stand and stare?
W. H. Davies (1871–1940) British poet.
Leisure

670 But I, being poor, have only my dreams;
I have spread my dreams under your feet;
Tread softly because you tread on my dreams.
W. B. Yeats (1865–1939) Irish poet.
He Wishes for the Cloths of Heaven

671 'I know myself,' he cried, 'but that is all.'
F. Scott Fitzgerald (1896–1940) US novelist.
This Side of Paradise, Bk. II, Ch. 5

672* Be nice to people on your way up because
you'll meet 'em on your way down.
Wilson Mizner (1876–1933) US writer and
wit.
Also attributed to Jimmy Durante
A Dictionary of Catch Phrases (Eric Partridge)

673 You can measure the social caste of a person
by the distance between the husband's and
wife's apartments.
Alfonso XIII (1886–1941) Spanish monarch.
Attrib.

1921

674 Oh to be seventy again.
Georges Clemenceau (1841–1929) French
statesman.
Remark on his eightieth birthday, noticing a
pretty girl in the Champs Elysées
Ego 3 (James Agate)

675 You can do anything in this world if you are
prepared to take the consequences.
W. Somerset Maugham (1874–1965) British
novelist.
The Circle

676 As soon as he ceased to be mad he became
merely stupid. There are maladies we must not
seek to cure because they alone protect us
from others that are more serious.
Marcel Proust (1871–1922) French novelist.
*À la recherche du temps perdu: Le Côté de
Guermantes*

677 The world is everything that is the case.
Ludwig Wittgenstein (1889–1951) Austrian
philosopher.
Tractatus Logico-Philosophicus, Ch. 1

1922

678 They say my verse is sad: no wonder;
Its narrow measure spans
Tears of eternity, and sorrow,
Not mine, but man's.
A. E. Housman (1859–1936) British scholar
and poet.
Last Poems, 'Fancy's Knell'

679 Most of one's life . . . is one prolonged effort to
prevent oneself thinking.
Aldous Huxley (1894–1964) British novelist.
Mortal Coils, 'Green Tunnels'

680 The now, the here, through which all future
plunges to the past.
James Joyce (1882–1941) Irish novelist.
Ulysses

681 There is no cure for birth and death save to enjoy the interval.
George Santayana (1863–1952) US
philosopher.
Soliloquies in England, 'War Shrines'

682 Life is a disease, and the only difference between one man and another is the stage of the
disease at which he lives.
George Bernard Shaw (1856–1950) Irish
dramatist and critic.
Back to Methuselah

683 Each has his past shut in him like the leaves of
a book known to him by heart and his friends
can only read the title.
Virginia Woolf (1882–1941) British novelist.
Jacob's Room

1923

684 The place where optimism most flourishes is
the lunatic asylum.
Havelock Ellis (1859–1939) British
sexologist.
The Dance of Life

685 The world continues to offer glittering prizes
those who have stout hearts and sharp
swords.
F. E. Smith (1872–1930) British lawyer and
politician.
Speech, Glasgow University, 7 Nov 1923

1924

686 What price Glory?
Maxwell Anderson (1888–1959) US
playwright.
Play title

687 It isn't important to come out on top; what ma
ters is to come out alive.
Bertolt Brecht (1898–1956) German
dramatist.
Jungle of Cities

1925

688 We are the hollow men
We are the stuffed men
Leaning together
Headpiece filled with straw.
T. S. Eliot (1888–1965) US-born British poe
The Hollow Men

689 This is the way the world ends
Not with a bang but a whimper.
T. S. Eliot
The Hollow Men

690 One of those men who reach such an acute
limited excellence at twenty-one that everythir
afterward savours of anti-climax.
F. Scott Fitzgerald (1896–1940) US novelis
The Great Gatsby, Ch. 1

691 Between
Our birth and death we may touch
understanding
As a moth brushes a window with its wing.
Christopher Fry (1907–   ) British dramatis
The Boy with a Cart

692 I'm afraid of losing my obscurity. Genuinene
only thrives in the dark. Like celery.
Aldous Huxley (1894–1964) British novelis
Those Barren Leaves, Pt. I, Ch. 1

693 The first rule in opera is the first rule in life: se
to everything yourself.
Nellie Melba (Helen Porter Mitchell; 1861–
1931) Australian soprano.
Melodies and Memories

1926

694 I have learned to live each day as it comes, a
not to borrow trouble by dreading tomorrow.

is the dark menace of the future that makes cowards of us.
Dorothy Dix (Elizabeth Meriwether Gilmer; 1861–1951) US journalist and writer.
Dorothy Dix, Her Book, Introduction

95* Birth, and copulation, and death.
That's all the facts when you come to brass tacks.
T. S. Eliot (1888–1965) US-born British poet and dramatist.
Sweeney Agonistes, 'Fragment of an Agon'

96 An optimist is a guy that never had much experience.
Don Marquis (1878–1937) US journalist.
Archy and Mehitabel

97 We begin to live when we have conceived life as a tragedy.
W. B. Yeats (1865–1939) Irish poet.
Autobiography

1927
----

98 My own suspicion is that the universe is not only queerer than we suppose, but queerer than we *can* suppose.
J. B. S. Haldane (1892–1964) British geneticist.
Possible Worlds, 'On Being the Right Size'

99 Life is for each man a solitary cell whose walls are mirrors.
Eugene O'Neill (1888–1953) US dramatist.
Lazarus Laughed

1928
----

00 There is no substitute for talent. Industry and all the virtues are of no avail.
Aldous Huxley (1894–1964) British novelist.
Point Counter Point

01 Life is perhaps best regarded as a bad dream between two awakenings.
Eugene O'Neill (1888–1953) US dramatist.
Marco Millions

1930

02* Underneath the arches
We dream our dreams away.
Bud Flanagan (Robert Winthrop; 1896–1968) British comedian.
Underneath the Arches

03 The meek do not inherit the earth unless they are prepared to fight for their meekness.
H. J. Laski (1893–1950) British political theorist.
Attrib.

04 No absolute is going to make the lion lie down with the lamb unless the lamb is inside.
D. H. Lawrence (1885–1930) British novelist.
The Later D. H. Lawrence

05 Most of the change we think we see in life
Is due to truths being in and out of favour.
Robert Frost (1875–1963) US poet.
The Black Cottage

706 A single death is a tragedy; a million is a statistic.
Joseph Stalin (J. Dzhugashvili; 1879–1953) Soviet statesman.
Attrib.

707 It is good to know what a man is, and also what the world takes him for. But you do not understand him until you have learnt how he understands himself.
F. H. Bradley (1846–1924) British philosopher.
Aphorisms

708 I never think of the future. It comes soon enough.
Albert Einstein (1879–1955) German-born US physicist.
Interview, 1930

709 The universe begins to look more like a great thought than like a great machine.
James Jeans (1877–1946) British scientist.
The Mysterious Universe

710 From the earliest times the old have rubbed it into the young that they are wiser than they, and before the young had discovered what nonsense this was they were old too, and it profited them to carry on the imposture.
W. Somerset Maugham (1874–1965) British novelist.
Cakes and Ale, Ch. 9

1933
----

711 Civilization is a method of living, an attitude of equal respect for all men.
Jane Addams (1860–1935) US social worker.
Speech, Honolulu, 1933

712 The modern world . . . has no notion except that of simplifying something by destroying nearly everything.
G. K. Chesterton (1874–1936) British writer.
All I Survey

713 The universe is not hostile, nor yet is it friendly. It is simply indifferent.
John Haynes Holmes (1879–1964) US clergyman.
A Sensible Man's View of Religion

714 The least of things with a meaning is worth more in life than the greatest of things without it.
Carl Gustav Jung (1875–1961) Swiss psychoanalyst.
Modern Man in Search of a Soul

715 Youth is a malady of which one becomes cured a little every day.
Benito Mussolini (1883–1945) Italian dictator.
Said on his 50th birthday

1934
----

716 Fortunately, in her kindness and patience, Nature has never put the fatal question as to the meaning of their lives into the mouths of

most people. And where no one asks, no one needs to answer.
Carl Gustav Jung (1875–1961) Swiss psychoanalyst.
The Development of Personality

717 Philosophy is the product of wonder.
A. N. Whitehead (1861–1947) British philosopher.
Nature and Life, Ch. 1

1935

718 We live in stirring times – tea-stirring times.
Christopher Isherwood (1904–86) British novelist.
Mr Norris Changes Trains

719 Society goes on and on and on. It is the same with ideas.
Ramsey MacDonald (1866–1937) British statesman and prime minister.
Speech, 1935

1936

720 Time present and time past
Are both perhaps present in time future
And time future contained in time past.
T. S. Eliot (1888–1965) US-born British poet and dramatist.
Four Quartets

721 Optimism is the content of small men in high places.
F. Scott Fitzgerald (1896–1940) US novelist.
The Crack-Up

722 Worldly wisdom teaches that it is better for the reputation to fail conventionally than to succeed unconventionally.
John Maynard Keynes (1883–1946) British economist.
The General Theory of Employment, Interest and Money, Bk. IV, Ch. 12

723 Until you've lost your reputation, you never realize what a burden it was or what freedom really is.
Margaret Mitchell (1909–49) US novelist.
Gone with the Wind

724 Now: heaven knows, anything goes.
Cole Porter (1893–1964) US songwriter.
Anything Goes, title song

1938

725 If there are obstacles, the shortest line between two points may be the crooked one.
Bertolt Brecht (1898–1956) German dramatist.
Galileo

726 Whom the gods wish to destroy they first call promising.
Cyril Connolly (1903–74) British journalist.
Enemies of Promise, Ch. 3

727 I have always disliked myself at any given m ment; the total of such moments is my life.
Cyril Connolly
Enemies of Promise, Ch. 18

728 Boys do not grow up gradually. They move fo ward in spurts like the hands of clocks in rail way stations.
Cyril Connolly
Enemies of Promise, Ch. 18

729 The future will one day be the present and w seem as unimportant as the present does now.
W. Somerset Maugham (1874–1965) Britis novelist.
The Summing Up

730 I know perfectly well that I don't want to do anything; to do something is to create existence – and there's quite enough existence a it is.
Jean-Paul Sartre (1905–80) French writer.

731 When I think of all the books I have read, an of the wise words I have heard spoken, and ol the anxiety I have given to parents and grandparents, and of the hopes that I have had all life weighed in the scales of my own life seems to me preparation for something that never happens.
W. B. Yeats (1865–1939) Irish poet.
Autobiography

1939

732 ANDREA. Unhappy the land that has no heroes.
GALILEO. No, unhappy the land that needs heroes.
Bertolt Brecht (1898–1956) German dramatist.
Galileo, 13

733 Success is relative. It is what we can make the mess we have made of things.
T. S. Eliot (1888–1965) US-born British poe and dramatist.
The Family Reunion

1940

734* The world is becoming like a lunatic asylum ru by lunatics.
David Lloyd George (1863–1945) British Liberal statesman.
The Observer, 'Sayings of Our Times', 31 Ma 1953

735 Sorrow is tranquillity remembered in emotion
Dorothy Parker (1893–1967) US writer.
Sentiment

736 One may not regard the world as a sort of metaphysical brothel for emotions.
Arthur Koestler (1905–83) Hungarian-born British writer.
Darkness at Noon, 'The Second Hearing'

737* The future is made of the same stuff as the present.
Simone Weil (1909–43) French philosopher
On Science, Necessity, and the Love of God

(ed. Richard Rees). 'Some Thoughts on the Love of God'

38* **What we must decide is perhaps how we are valuable, rather than how valuable we are.**
F. Scott Fitzgerald (1896–1940) US novelist.
The Crack-Up

1942

39 **There is but one truly serious philosophical problem, and that is suicide. Judging whether life is, or is not worth living amounts to answering the fundamental question of philosophy.**
Albert Camus (1913–60) French existentialist writer.
The Myth of Sisyphus

40 **The Future is something which everyone reaches at the rate of sixty minutes an hour, whatever he does, whoever he is.**
C. S. Lewis (1898–1963) British academic and writer.
The Screwtape Letters

41 **God made everything out of nothing. But the nothingness shows through.**
Paul Valéry (1871–1945) French poet and writer.
Mauvaises Pensées et autres

1943

42 **One should try everything once, except incest and folk-dancing.**
Arnold Bax (1883–1953) British composer.
Farewell to My Youth

43 **Scratch a pessimist, and you find often a defender of privilege.**
Lord Beveridge (1879–1963) British economist.
The Observer, 'Sayings of the Week', 17 Dec 1943

1944

44 **Alone, alone, about the dreadful wood
Of conscious evil runs a lost mankind,
Dreading to find its Father.**
W. H. Auden (1907–73) British poet.
For the Time Being, 'Chorus'

45 **Life is a maze in which we take the wrong turning before we have learnt to walk.**
Cyril Connolly (1903–74) British journalist.
The Unquiet Grave

1945

46 **The visible universe was an illusion or, more precisely, a sophism. Mirrors and fatherhood are abominable because they multiply it and extend it.**
Jorge Luis Borges (1899–1986) Argentinian writer.
Ficciones, 'Tlön, Uqbar, Orbis Tertius'

Love and Sex

1919

747 **...I don't want to live – I want to love first, and live incidentally...**
Zelda Fitzgerald (1900–48) US writer.
Letter to F. Scott Fitzgerald, 1919

1920

748* **You must always be a-waggle with LOVE.**
D. H. Lawrence (1885–1930) British novelist.
Bibbles

749 **Pornography is the attempt to insult sex, to do dirt on it.**
D. H. Lawrence
Phoenix, 'Pornography and Obscenity'

1926

750 **Love is also like a coconut which is good while it is fresh, but you have to spit it out when the juice is gone, what's left tastes bitter.**
Bertolt Brecht (1898–1956) German dramatist.
Baal

751 **We have long passed the Victorian Era when asterisks were followed after a certain interval by a baby.**
W. Somerset Maugham (1874–1965) British novelist.
The Constant Wife

1927

752 **I'm not sure if a mental relation with a woman doesn't make it impossible to love her. To know the *mind* of a woman is to end in hating her. Love means the pre-cognitive flow...it is the honest state before the apple.**
D. H. Lawrence (1885–1930) British novelist.
Letter to Dr Trigant Burrow, 3 Aug 1927

1928

753 **You mustn't think I advocate perpetual sex. Far from it. Nothing nauseates me more than promiscuous sex in and out of season.**
D. H. Lawrence
Referring to *Lady Chatterley's Lover*
Letter to Lady Ottoline Morrell, 22 Dec 1928

1929

754 **To fear love is to fear life, and those who fear life are already three parts dead.**
Bertrand Russell (1872–1970) British philosopher.
Marriage and Morals

755 **Of all forms of caution, caution in love is perhaps the most fatal to true happiness.**
Bertrand Russell
Marriage and Morals

1934

756 If all the young ladies who attended the Yale promenade dance were laid end to end, no one would be the least surprised.
Dorothy Parker (1893–1967) US writer.
While Rome Burns (Alexander Woollcott)

1936

757 People will insist . . . on treating the *mons Veneris* as though it were Mount Everest.
Aldous Huxley (1894–1964) British novelist.
Eyeless in Gaza, Ch. 30

758 By the time you say you're his,
Shivering and sighing
And he vows his passion is
Infinite, undying –
Lady, make a note of this
One of you is lying.
Dorothy Parker (1893–1967) US writer.
Not So Deep as a Well

759* Love and marriage, love and marriage,
Go together like a horse and carriage.
Sammy Cahn (Samuel Cohen; 1913–   ) US songwriter.
Our Town, 'Love and Marriage'

1940

760 But did thee feel the earth move?
Ernest Hemingway (1899–1961) US novelist.
For Whom the Bell Tolls, Ch. 13

1942

761 You must remember this;
A kiss is just a kiss,
A sigh is just a sigh –
The fundamental things apply
As time goes by.
Herman Hupfeld (20th century) US songwriter.
From the film *Casablanca*
As Time Goes By

1943

762 I know nothing about platonic love except that it is not to be found in the works of Plato.
Edgar Jepson (1863–1938) British novelist.
EGO 5 (James Agate)

Marriage and the Family

1914

763* My father was frightened of his mother. I was frightened of my father, and I'm damned well going to make sure that my children are frightened of me.
George V (1865–1936) King of the United Kingdom (1910–36).
Attrib.

1915

764 Never trust a husband too far, nor a bachelo too near.
Helen Rowland (1876–1950) US writer.
The Rubaiyat of a Bachelor

1920

765* Being a husband is a whole-time job. That is why so many husbands fail. They cannot giv their entire attention to it.
Arnold Bennett (1867–1931) British novelis
The Title, I

766* To marry a man out of pity is folly; and, if yo think you are going to influence the kind of fellow who has 'never had a chance, poor devil,' you are profoundly mistaken. One can only influence the strong characters in life, n the weak; and it is the height of vanity to suppose that you can make an honest man o anyone.
Margot Asquith (1865–1945) The second wife of Herbert Asquith.
The Autobiography of Margot Asquith, Ch. 6

1922

767 Always see a fellow's weak point in his wife.
James Joyce (1882–1941) Irish novelist.
Ulysses

768 In fact there was but one thing wrong with th Babbitt house; it was not a home.
Sinclair Lewis (1885–1951) US novelist.
Babbitt, Ch. 2

1925

769* What a marvellous place to drop one's mothe in-law!
Marshal Foch (1851–1929) French soldier.
Remark on being shown the Grand Canyon
Attrib.

1926

770 Now one of the great reasons why so many husbands and wives make shipwreck of their lives together is because a man is always see ing for happiness, while a woman is on a per petual still hunt for trouble.
Dorothy Dix (Elizabeth Meriwether Gilmer; 1861–1951) US journalist and writer.
Dorothy Dix, Her Book, Ch. 1

1928

771 There are no illegitimate children – only illegit mate parents.
Léon R. Yankwich US lawyer.
Decision, State District Court, Southern Distri of California, Jun 1928, quoting columnist O. O. McIntyre

1929

772 Marriage is for women the commonest mode of livelihood, and the total amount of undesired sex endured by women is probably greater in marriage than in prostitution.
Bertrand Russell (1872–1970) British philosopher.
Marriage and Morals

1930

773* All the unhappy marriages come from the husbands having brains. What good are brains to a man? They only unsettle him.
P. G. Wodehouse (1881–1975) British humorous novelist.
The Adventures of Sally

774 Who has not watched a mother stroke her child's cheek or kiss her child *in a certain way* and felt a nervous shudder at the possessive outrage done to a free solitary human soul?
John Cowper Powys (1872–1963) British novelist.
The Meaning of Culture

1931

775 Married women are kept women, and they are beginning to find it out.
Logan Pearsall Smith (1865–1946) US writer.
Afterthoughts, 'Other people'

1935

776* Unlike the male codfish which, suddenly finding itself the parent of three million five hundred thousand little codfish, cheerfully resolves to love them all, the British aristocracy is apt to look with a somewhat jaundiced eye on its younger sons.
P. G. Wodehouse (1881–1975) British humorous novelist.
Wodehouse at Work to the End (Richard Usborne), Ch. 5

1938

777 That dear octopus from whose tentacles we never quite escape, nor in our innermost hearts never quite wish to.
Dodie Smith (1896–) British dramatist and novelist.
Dear Octopus

1939

778 A loving wife will do anything for her husband except stop criticising and trying to improve him.
J. B. Priestley (1894–1984) British novelist.
Rain on Godshill

1940

779 The concept of two people living together for

25 years without having a cross word suggests a lack of spirit only to be admired in sheep.
A. P. Herbert (1890–1971) British writer and politician.
News Chronicle, 1940

1943

780 There is no finer investment for any community than putting milk into babies.
Winston Churchill (1874–1965) British statesman.
Radio Broadcast, 21 Mar 1943

Men and Women

1918

781 Mother is far too clever to understand anything she does not like.
Arnold Bennett (1867–1931) British novelist.
The Title

1919

782 Because women can do nothing except love, they've given it a ridiculous importance.
W. Somerset Maugham (1874–1965) British novelist.
The Moon and Sixpence, Ch. 41

783 Thousands of American women know far more about the subconscious than they do about sewing.
H. L. Mencken (1880–1956) US journalist.
Prejudices

1920

784* The 'homo' is the legitimate child of the 'suffragette'.
Wyndham Lewis (1882–1957) British novelist.
The Art of Being Ruled, Pt. VIII, Ch. 4

785 The great question . . . which I have not been able to answer, despite my thirty years of research into the feminine soul, is 'What does a woman want'?
Sigmund Freud (1856–1939) Austrian psychoanalyst.
Psychiatry in American Life (Charles Rolo)

786 Women have served all these centuries as looking-glasses possessing the magic and delicious power of reflecting the figure of man at twice its natural size.
Virginia Woolf (1882–1941) British novelist.
A Room of One's Own

1921

787 One realizes with horror, that the race of men is almost extinct in Europe. Only Christ-like heroes and woman-worshipping Don Juans, and rabid equality-mongrels.
D. H. Lawrence (1885–1930) British novelist.
Sea and Sardinia, Ch. 3

788 A woman will always sacrifice herself if you
     give her the opportunity. It is her favourite form
     of self-indulgence.
     W. Somerset Maugham (1874–1965) British
     novelist.
     The Circle, III

1922

789 To the old saying that man built the house but
     woman made of it a 'home' might be added
     the modern supplement that woman accepted
     cooking as a chore but man has made of it
     a recreation.
     Emily Post (1873–1960) US writer.
     Etiquette, Ch. 34

1925

790* How beastly the bourgeois is
     especially the male of the species.
     D. H. Lawrence (1885–1930) British novelist.
     How beastly the bourgeois is

1926

791 It is only the women whose eyes have been
     washed clear with tears who get the broad vi-
     sion that makes them little sisters to all the
     world.
     Dorothy Dix (Elizabeth Meriwether Gilmer;
     1861–1951) US journalist and writer.
     Dorothy Dix, Her Book, Introduction

1928

792 Any girl who was a lady would not even think of
     having such a good time that she did not re-
     member to hang on to her jewelry.
     Anita Loos (1891–1981) US novelist.
     Gentlemen Prefer Blondes, Ch. 4

793 Instead of this absurd division into sexes they
     ought to class people as static and dynamic.
     Evelyn Waugh (1903–66) British novelist.
     Decline and Fall, Pt. III, Ch. 7

1929

794 Why are women . . . so much more interesting
     to men than men are to women?
     Virginia Woolf (1882–1941) British novelist.
     A Room of One's Own

795 I would venture to guess that Anon, who wrote
     so many poems without signing them, was of-
     ten a woman.
     Virginia Woolf
     A Room of One's Own

1930

796* There are two kinds of women — goddesses
     and doormats.
     Pablo Picasso (1881–1973) Spanish painter.
     Attrib.

797 Certain women should be struck regularly, like
     gongs.
     Noël Coward (1899–1973) British dramatist.
     Private Lives

1938

798 Intimacies between women often go back-
     wards, beginning in revelations and ending in
     small talk without loss of esteem.
     Elizabeth Bowen (1899–1973) Irish novelist.
     The Death of the Heart

1939

799 I often want to cry. That is the only advantage
     women have over men — at least they can
     cry.
     Jean Rhys (1894–1979) Dominican-born Brit-
     ish novelist.
     Good Morning, Midnight, Pt. II

1940

800* Women do not find it difficult nowadays to be-
     have like men; but they often find it extremely
     difficult to behave like gentlemen.
     Compton Mackenzie (1883–1972) British
     writer.
     On Moral Courage

801 Woman's virtue is man's greatest invention.
     Cornelia Otis Skinner (1901–79) US stage
     actress.
     Attrib.

1944

802 In the sex-war thoughtlessness is the weapon
     of the male, vindictiveness of the female.
     Cyril Connolly (1903–74) British journalist.
     The Unquiet Grave

Morality, Vices, and Virtues

1915

803* Right is more precious than peace.
     Woodrow Wilson (1856–1925) US
     statesman.
     Radio Times, 10 Sept 1964

1918

804 As soon as one is unhappy one becomes moral
     Marcel Proust (1871–1922) French novelist.
     *À la recherche du temps perdu: À l'ombre des
     jeunes filles en fleurs*

1920

805 Justice should not only be done, but should

manifestly and undoubtedly be seen to be done.
Gordon Hewart (1870–1943) British lawyer and politician.
The Chief (R. Jackson)

806* If you do not tell the truth about yourself you cannot tell it about other people.
Virginia Woolf (1882–1941) British novelist.
The Moment and Other Essays

807 An intellectual hatred is the worst.
W. B. Yeats (1865–1939) Irish poet.
A Prayer for My Daughter

1921

808 You can't learn too soon that the most useful thing about a principle is that it can always be sacrificed to expediency.
W. Somerset Maugham (1874–1965) British novelist.
The Circle, III

809 Silence is the most perfect expression of scorn.
George Bernard Shaw (1856–1950) Irish dramatist and critic.
Back to Methuselah

810 The older one grows the more one likes indecency.
Virginia Woolf (1882–1941) British novelist.
Monday or Tuesday

1922

811 Morality which is based on ideas, or on an ideal, is an unmitigated evil.
D. H. Lawrence (1885–1930) British novelist.
Fantasia of the Unconscious, Ch. 7

1923

812 Mr Mercaptan went on to preach a brilliant sermon on that melancholy sexual perversion known as continence.
Aldous Huxley (1894–1964) British novelist.
Antic Hay, Ch. 18

1925

813 There's nothing so artificial as sinning nowadays. I suppose it once was real.
D. H. Lawrence (1885–1930) British novelist.
St Mawr

814 It is just when opinions universally prevail and we have added lip service to their authority that we become sometimes most keenly conscious that we do not believe a word that we are saying.
Virginia Woolf (1882–1941) British novelist.
The Common Reader

1928

815 Puritanism – The haunting fear that someone, somewhere, may be happy.
H. L. Mencken (1880–1956) US journalist.
A Book of Burlesques

816 The wickedness of the world is so great you have to run your legs off to avoid having them stolen from under you.
Bertolt Brecht (1898–1956) German dramatist.
The Threepenny Opera, I:3

817 Only reason can convince us of those three fundamental truths without a recognition of which there can be no effective liberty: that what we believe is not necessarily true; that what we like is not necessarily good; and that all questions are open.
Clive Bell (1881–1964) British art critic.
Civilization, Ch. 5

818 We have, in fact, two kinds of morality side by side; one which we preach but do not practise, and another which we practise but seldom preach.
Bertrand Russell (1872–1970) British philosopher.
Sceptical Essays

1930

819 The propriety of some persons seems to consist in having improper thoughts about their neighbours.
F. H. Bradley (1846–1924) British philosopher.
Aphorisms

820 Tact consists in knowing how far we may go too far.
Jean Cocteau (1889–1963) French poet and artist.
In *Treasury of Humorous Quotations*

821 Hypocrisy is the most difficult and nerve-racking vice that any man can pursue; it needs an unceasing vigilance and a rare detachment of spirit. It cannot, like adultery or gluttony, be practised at spare moments; it is a whole-time job.
W. Somerset Maugham (1874–1965) British novelist.
Cakes and Ale, Ch. 1

822 Suspicion of one's own motives is especially necessary for the philanthropist.
Bertrand Russell (1872–1970) British philosopher.
The Conquest of Happiness

823* There are no whole truths; all truths are half-truths. It is trying to treat them as whole truths that plays the devil.
A. N. Whitehead (1861–1947) British philosopher.
Dialogues, 16

1932

824 Never forget that two blacks do not make a white.
George Bernard Shaw (1856–1950) Irish dramatist and critic.
The Adventures of the Black Girl in her Search for God

825   What is moral is what you feel good after, and
       what is immoral is what you feel bad after.
       Ernest Hemingway (1899–1961) US
       novelist.
       Death in the Afternoon

1935

826   Jealousy is no more than feeling alone among
       smiling enemies.
       Elizabeth Bowen (1899–1973) Irish novelist.
       The House in Paris

1938

827   Perfection has one grave defect; it is apt to be
       dull.
       W. Somerset Maugham (1874–1965) British
       novelist.
       The Summing Up

1939

828   Whenever there are tremendous virtues it's a
       sure sign something's wrong.
       Bertolt Brecht (1898–1956) German
       dramatist.
       Mother Courage

1941

829   The quality of moral behaviour varies in inverse
       ratio to the number of human beings involved.
       Aldous Huxley (1894–1964) British novelist.
       Grey Eminence, Ch. 10

1942

830   The truth that makes men free is for the most
       part the truth which men prefer not to hear.
       Herbert Sebastian Agar (1897–1980) US
       writer.
       A Time for Greatness

831   The only truths which are universal are those
       gross enough to be thought so.
       Paul Valéry (1871–1945) French poet and
       writer.
       Mauvaises Pensées et autres

832   Real nobility is based on scorn, courage, and
       profound indifference.
       Albert Camus (1913–60) French existentialist
       writer.
       Notebooks

Other People

1919

833   Sometimes people call me an idealist. Well,
       that is the way I know I am an American.
       America is the only idealistic nation in the
       world.
       Woodrow Wilson (1856–1925) US
       statesman.
       Speech, Sioux Falls, 8 Sept 1919

1920

834*   Frenchmen drink wine just like we used to drink
       water before Prohibition.
       Ring Lardner Jnr (1885–1933) American
       humorist.
       Wit's End (R. E. Drennan)

835   The English people on the whole are surely the
       nicest people in the world, and everyone
       makes everything so easy for everybody else,
       that there is almost nothing to resist at all.
       D. H. Lawrence (1885–1930) British novelist.
       Dull London

1922

836   In other countries, art and literature are left to
       lot of shabby bums living in attics and feeding
       on booze and spaghetti, but in America the
       successful writer or picture-painter is indistin-
       guishable from any other decent business
       man.
       Sinclair Lewis (1885–1951) US novelist.
       Babbitt, Ch. 14

837   Trust the man who hesitates in his speech and
       is quick and steady in action, but beware of
       long arguments and long beards.
       George Santayana (1863–1952) US
       philosopher.
       Soliloquies in England, 'The British Character'

838   England is the paradise of individuality, eccen-
       tricity, heresy, anomalies, hobbies, and
       humours.
       George Santayana
       Soliloquies in England, 'The British Character'

1923

839   The very best that is in the Jewish blood: a
       faculty for pure disinterestedness, and warm,
       physically warm love, that seems to make the
       corpuscles of the blood glow.
       D. H. Lawrence (1885–1930) British novelist.
       Kangaroo, Ch. 6

1928

840   The American system of rugged individualism.
       Herbert Clark Hoover (1874–1964) US
       statesman.
       Speech, New York, 22 Oct 1928

841   The sound of the English county families baying
       for broken glass.
       Evelyn Waugh (1903–66) British novelist.
       Decline and Fall, Prelude

842   For generations the British bourgeoisie have
       spoken of themselves as gentlemen, and by
       that they have meant, among other things, a
       self-respecting scorn of irregular perquisites. I
       is the quality that distinguishes the gentle-
       man from both the artist and the aristocrat.
       Evelyn Waugh
       Decline and Fall, Pt. I, Ch. 6

843 We can trace almost all the disasters of English
history to the influence of Wales.
Evelyn Waugh
Decline and Fall, Pt. I, Ch. 8

844 'The Welsh,' said the Doctor, 'are the only nation in the world that has produced no graphic
or plastic art, no architecture, no drama.
They just sing,' he said with disgust, 'sing and
blow down wind instruments of plated silver.'
Evelyn Waugh
Decline and Fall, Pt. I, Ch. 8

1929

845 America is the only nation in history which mi-
raculously has gone directly from barbarism to
degeneration without the usual interval of
civilization.
Georges Clemenceau (1841–1929) French
statesman.
Attrib.

846 Long Island represents the American's idea of
what God would have done with Nature if
he'd had the money.
Peter Fleming (1907–71) British writer.
Letter to his brother Rupert, 29 Sept 1929

847 America . . . where law and customs alike
are based on the dreams of spinsters.
Bertrand Russell (1872–1970) British
philosopher.
Marriage and Morals

1930

848* The English may not like music – but they absolutely love the noise it makes.
Thomas Beecham (1879–1961) British
conductor.
The Wit of Music (L. Ayre)

849 That typically English characteristic for which
there is no English name – *esprit de corps.*
Frank Ezra Adcock (1886–1968) British
classicist.
Presidential address

850 The United States is like a gigantic boiler. Once
the fire is lighted under it there is no limit to
the power it can generate.
Lord Grey (1862–1933) British statesman.
Their Finest Hour (Winston S. Churchill), Ch. 32

851 Like so many substantial Americans, he had
married young and kept on marrying, springing
from blonde to blonde like the chamois of the
Alps leaping from crag to crag.
P. G. Wodehouse (1881–1975) British humorous novelist.
Wodehouse at Work to the End (Richard Usborne), Ch. 2

852 How appallingly thorough these Germans always managed to be, how emphatic! In sex no
less than in war – in scholarship, in science.

Diving deeper than anyone else and coming
up muddier.
Aldous Huxley (1894–1964) British novelist.

853 I think it would be a good idea.
Mahatma Gandhi (Mohandas Karamchand
Gandhi; 1869–1948) Indian national leader.
On being asked for his view on Western
civilization
Attrib.

1931

854 Now Spring, sweet laxative of Georgian strains,
Quickens the ink in literary veins,
The Stately Homes of England ope their doors
To piping Nancy-boys and Crashing Bores.
Roy Campbell (1901–57) South African poet.
The Georgiad

855 There is nothing the matter with Americans except their ideals. The real American is all
right; it is the ideal American who is all wrong.
G. K. Chesterton (1874–1936) British writer.
New York Times, 1 Feb 1931

856 There won't be any revolution in America . . .
The people are too clean. They spend all their
time changing their shirts and washing themselves. You can't feel fierce and revolutionary
in a bathroom.
Eric Linklater (1889–1974) Scottish novelist.
Juan in America, Pt. V. Ch. 3 .

857 That strange blend of the commercial traveller,
the missionary, and the barbarian conqueror,
which was the American abroad.
Olaf Stapledon (1886–1950) British philosopher and science-fiction writer.
Last and First Men, Ch. 3

1935

858 The Englishman never enjoys himself except for
a noble purpose.
A. P. Herbert (1890–1971) British writer and
politician.
Uncommon Law

1936

859 An Englishman has to have a Party, just as he
has to have trousers.
Bertrand Russell (1872–1970) British
philosopher.
Letter to Maurice Amos MP, 16 June 1936

860 In the United States there is more space where
nobody is than anybody is. That is what
makes America what it is.
Gertrude Stein (1874–1946) US writer.
The Geographical History of America

1937

861 There can hardly be a town in the South of Eng-

land where you could throw a brick without hitting the niece of a bishop.
George Orwell (Eric Blair; 1903–50) British novelist.
The Road to Wigan Pier, Ch. 7

1938

862   ...the English think of an opinion as something which a decent person, if he has the misfortune to have one, does all he can to hide.
Margaret Halsey (1910–   ) US writer.
With Malice Toward Some

863   Living in England, provincial England, must be like being married to a stupid but exquisitely beautiful wife.
Margaret Halsey
With Malice Toward Some

864   ...it takes a great deal to produce ennui in an Englishman and if you do, he only takes it as convincing proof that you are well-bred.
Margaret Halsey
With Malice Toward Some

865   Never judge a country by its politics. After all, we English are quite honest by nature, aren't we?
Alfred Hitchcock (1889–1980) British film director.
The Lady Vanishes

1940

866* There's something Vichy about the French.
Ivor Novello (David Ivor Davies; 1893–1951) British actor, composer, and dramatist.
Ambrosia and Small Beer (Edward Marsh), Ch. 4

867   Long experience has taught me that in England nobody goes to the theatre unless he or she has bronchitis.
James Agate (1877–1947) British theatre critic.
Ego, 6

1941

868   A family with the wrong members in control – that, perhaps, is as near as one can come to describing England in a phrase.
George Orwell (Eric Blair; 1903–50) British novelist.
The Lion and the Unicorn, 'The Ruling Class'

1943

869   There exists in the world today a gigantic reservoir of good will toward us, the American people.
Wendell Lewis Willkie (1892–1944) US lawyer and businessman.
One World, Ch. 10

1945

870   Everything about the behaviour of American society reveals that it is half judaised and half

negrified. How can one expect a state like that to hold together?
Adolf Hitler (1889–1945) German dictator.
Attrib.

Religion

1914

871   Even God has been defended with nonsense.
Walter Lippmann (1889–1974) US editor and author.
A Preface to Politics

872   Heaven, as conventionally conceived, is a place so inane, so dull, so useless, so miserable, that nobody has ever ventured to describe a whole day in heaven, though plenty of people have described a day at the seaside.
George Bernard Shaw (1856–1950) Irish dramatist and critic.
Misalliance, Preface

873   God heard the embattled nations shout
Gott strafe England and God save the King.
Good God, said God,
I've got my work cut out.
John Collings Squire (1884–1958) British journalist.
1914

1920

874* It is a mistake to assume that God is interested only, or even chiefly, in religion.
William Temple (1881–1944) British archbishop.
Attrib.

875   Fools! For I also had my hour;
One far fierce hour and sweet;
There was a shout about my ears,
And palms before my feet.
G. K. Chesterton (1874–1936) British writer.
The Donkey

876   Many people believe that they are attracted by God, or by Nature, when they are only repelled by man.
Dean Inge (1860–1954) British churchman.
More Lay Thoughts of a Dean

877   To become a popular religion, it is only necessary for a superstition to enslave a philosophy.
Dean Inge
Outspoken Essays

1921

878   The whole religious complexion of the modern world is due to the absence from Jerusalem of a lunatic asylum.
Havelock Ellis (1859–1939) British sexologist.
Impressions and Comments

879   It has been said that the highest praise of God consists in the denial of Him by the atheist,

who finds creation so perfect that he can dispense with a creator.
Marcel Proust (1871–1922) French novelist.
À la recherche du temps perdu: Le Côté de Guermantes

1925

80 I do not consider it an insult but rather a compliment to be called an agnostic. I do not pretend to know where many ignorant men are sure.
Clarence Seward Darrow (1857–1938) US lawyer.
Remark during the trial (1925) of John Scopes for teaching the theory of evolution in school

1926

81 There's no reason to bring religion into it. I think we ought to have as great a regard for religion as we can, so as to keep it out of as many things as possible.
Sean O'Casey (1884–1964) Irish dramatist.
The Plough and the Stars, I

82 Religion is love; in no case is it logic.
Beatrice Webb (1858–1943) British economist and writer.
My Apprenticeship, Ch. 2

1928

83 There is a species of person called a 'Modern Churchman' who draws the full salary of a beneficed clergyman and need not commit himself to any religious belief.
Evelyn Waugh (1903–66) British novelist.
Decline and Fall, Pt. II, Ch. 4

1930

84* I was fired from there, finally, for a lot of things, among them my insistence that the Immaculate Conception was spontaneous combustion.
Dorothy Parker (1893–1967) US writer.
Writers at Work, First Series (Malcolm Cowley)

85 For when the One Great Scorer comes
To write against your name,
He marks – not that you won or lost –
But how you played the game.
Grantland Rice (1880–1954) US sportswriter.
Alumnus Football

86 There once was a man who said 'God
Must think it exceedingly odd
If he finds that this tree
Continues to be
When there's no one about in the Quad.'
Ronald Knox (1888–1957) British Roman Catholic priest.
Attrib.

87 Dear Sir, Your astonishment's odd:
I am always about in the Quad.
And that's why the tree
Will continue to be,

Since observed by Yours faithfully, God.
Anonymous

1933

888 He said he was against it.
Calvin Coolidge (1872–1933) US president.
Reply when asked what a clergyman had said regarding sin in his sermon
Attrib.

889 Religion is an illusion and it derives its strength from the fact that it falls in with our instinctual desires.
Sigmund Freud (1856–1939) Austrian psychoanalyst.
New Introductory Lectures on Psychoanalysis, 'A Philosophy of Life'

890 Among all my patients in the second half of life ... there has not been one whose problem in the last resort was not that of finding a religious outlook on life.
Carl Gustav Jung (1875–1961) Swiss psychoanalyst.
Modern Man in Search of a Soul

1935

891 Imagine the Lord talking French! Aside from a few odd words in Hebrew, I took it completely for granted that God had never spoken anything but the most dignified English.
Clarence Shepard Day (1874–1935) US writer.
Life With Father, 'Father interferes'

1936

892* A God who let us prove his existence would be an idol.
Dietrich Bonhoeffer (1906–45) German theologian.
No Rusty Swords

1938

893 Religions, which condemn the pleasures of sense, drive men to seek the pleasures of power. Throughout history power has been the vice of the ascetic.
Bertrand Russell (1872–1970) British philosopher.
New York Herald-Tribune Magazine, 6 May 1938

1939

894 I feel no need for any other faith than my faith in human beings.
Pearl Buck (1892–1973) US novelist.
I Believe

895 Christianity is the most materialistic of all great religions.
William Temple (1881–1944) British churchman.
Reading in St John's Gospel, Vol. I, Introduction

1941

896 We have no reliable guarantee that the afterlife will be any less exasperating than this one, have we?
Noël Coward (1899–1973) British dramatist.
Blithe Spirit, I

897 Christianity accepted as given a metaphysical system derived from several already existing and mutually incompatible systems.
Aldous Huxley (1894–1964) British novelist.
Grey Eminence, Ch. 3

1944

898 I believe in the Church, One Holy, Catholic and Apostolic, and I regret that it nowhere exists.
William Temple (1881–1944) British churchman.
Attrib.

899 The Church exists for the sake of those outside it.
William Temple
Attrib.

900 Man has learned to cope with all questions of importance without recourse to God as a working hypothesis.
Dietrich Bonhoeffer (1906–45) German theologian.
Letters and Papers from Prison, 8 June 1944

901 Hell is other people.
Jean-Paul Sartre (1905–80) French philosopher and writer.
Huis clos

Science, Medicine, and Technology

1917

902 The true spirit of delight, the exaltation, the sense of being more than Man, which is the touchstone of the highest excellence is to be found in mathematics as surely as in poetry.
Bertrand Russell (1872–1970) British philosopher.
Mysticism and Logic

903 Mathematics, rightly viewed, possesses not only truth by supreme beauty – a beauty cold and austere like that of sculpture.
Bertrand Russell
Mysticism and Logic

904 Pure mathematics consists entirely of assertions to the effect that, if such and such a proposition is true of *anything*, then such and such another proposition is true of that thing. It is essential not to discuss whether the first proposition is really true, and not to mention what the anything is, of which it is supposed to be true.
Bertrand Russell
Mysticism and Logic

1920

905* We have no right to assume that any physical laws exist, or if they have existed up to now, that they will continue to exist in a similar manner in the future.
Max Planck (1858–1947) German physicist.
The Universe in the Light of Modern Physics

906 We haven't the money, so we've got to think.
Ernest Rutherford (1871–1937) British physicist.
Attrib.

1923

907 The machine threatens all achievement.
Rainer Maria Rilke (1875–1926) Austrian poet.
Die Sonette an Orpheus, II, 10

1924

908 Shelley and Keats were the last English poets who were at all up to date in their chemical knowledge.
J. B. S. Haldane (1892–1964) British geneticist.
Daedalus or Science and the Future

909 Einstein – the greatest Jew since Jesus. I have no doubt that Einstein's name will still be remembered and revered when Lloyd George, Foch and William Hohenzollern share with Charlie Chaplin that ineluctable oblivion which awaits the uncreative mind.
J. B. S. Haldane
'William Hohenzollern' was Emperor Wilhelm II of Germany
Daedalus or Science and the Future

1925

910 Mathematics is thought moving in the sphere of complete abstraction from any particular instance of what it is talking about.
A. N. Whitehead (1861–1947) British philosopher.
Science and the Modern World

911 It requires a very unusual mind to undertake the analysis of the obvious.
A. N. Whitehead
Science and the Modern World

1926

912 After all, science is essentially international, and it is only through lack of the historical sense that national qualities have been attributed to it.
Marie Curie (1867–1934) Polish chemist.
Memorandum, 'Intellectual Co-operation'

913 Mystics always hope that science will some day overtake them.
Booth Tarkington (1869–1946) US novelist.
Looking Forward to the Great Adventure

1927

914 Man is slightly nearer to the atom than the stars. From his central position he can survey the grandest works of Nature with the astronomer, or the minutest works with the physicist.
Arthur Eddington (1882–1944) British astronomer.
Stars and Atoms

1928

915 Electrical force is defined as something which causes motion of electrical charge; an electrical charge is something which exerts electric force.
Arthur Eddington
The Nature of the Physical World

916 If all the arts aspire to the condition of music, all the sciences aspire to the condition of mathematics.
George Santayana (1863–1952) US philosopher.
The Observer, 'Sayings of the Week', 4 Mar 1928

1930

917* God is subtle but he is not malicious.
Albert Einstein (1879–1955) German-born US physicist.
Inscribed over the fireplace in the Mathematical Institute, Princeton; it refers to Einstein's objection to the quantum theory
Albert Einstein (Carl Seelig), Ch. 8

918 God does not play dice.
Albert Einstein
Einstein's objection to the quantum theory, in which physical events can only be known in terms of probabilities. It is sometimes quoted as 'God does not play dice with the Universe'
Albert Einstein, Creator and Rebel (B. Hoffman), Ch. 10

919 As far as the laws of mathematics refer to reality, they are not certain, and as far as they are certain, they do not refer to reality.
Albert Einstein
The Tao of Physics (F. Capra), Ch. 2

920* It did not last: the Devil howling 'Ho! Let Einstein be!' restored the status quo.
John Collings Squire (1884–1958) British journalist.
Answer to Pope's Epitaph for Newton
Epigrams, 'The Dilemma'

921 A science which hesitates to forget its founders is lost.
A. N. Whitehead (1861–1947) British philosopher.
Attrib.

922 The evolution of the human race will not be accomplished in the ten thousand years of tame animals, but in the million years of wild animals, because man is and will always be a wild animal.
Charles Darwin (1887–1962) British life scientist.
The Next Ten Million Years, Ch. 4

923 Life exists in the universe only because the carbon atom possesses certain exceptional properties.
James Jeans (1877–1946) British scientist.
The Mysterious Universe, Ch. 1

924 Science should leave off making pronouncements: the river of knowledge has too often turned back on itself.
James Jeans
The Mysterious Universe, Ch. 5

1932

925 The time of our Ford.
Aldous Huxley (1894–1964) British novelist.
Brave New World, Ch. 3

926 That is how the atom is split. But what does it mean? To us who think in terms of practical use it means – Nothing!
Ritchie Calder (1898–   ) US engineer and sculptor.
The Daily Herald, 27 June 1932

927 When we have found how the nucleus of atoms are built-up we shall have found the greatest secret of all – except life. We shall have found the basis of everything – of the earth we walk on, of the air we breathe, of the sunshine, of our physical body itself, of everything in the world, however great or however small – except life.
Ernest Rutherford (1871–1937) British physicist.
Passing Show 24

928 The term Science should not be given to anything but the aggregate of the recipes that are always successful. All the rest is literature.
Paul Valéry (1871–1945) French poet and writer.
Moralités

1933

929 Her own mother lived the latter years of her life in the horrible suspicion that electricity was dripping invisibly all over the house.
James Thurber (1894–1961) US humorist.
My Life and Hard Times, Ch. 2

930 Numbers constitute the only universal language.
Nathaniel West (1903–40) US novelist and scriptwriter.
Miss Lonelyhearts

1936

931 Is ditchwater dull? Naturalists with microscopes have told me that it teems with quiet fun.
G. K. Chesterton (1874–1936) British writer.
The Spice of Life

1938

932 I believe my theory of relativity to be true. But it will only be proved for certain in 1981, when I am dead.
Albert Einstein (1879–1955) German-born US physicist.
Einstein: A Study in Simplicity

1940

933* Modern Physics is an instrument of Jewry for the destruction of Nordic science . . . True physics is the creation of the German spirit.
Rudolphe Tomaschek (20th century) German scientist.
The Rise and Fall of the Third Reich (W. L. Shirer), Ch. 8

1944

934* Medicine is a noble profession but a damn bad business.
Humphrey Rolleston (1862–1944) British physician.
Attrib.

Wealth and Poverty

1915

935 Money is like a sixth sense without which you cannot make a complete use of the other five.
W. Somerset Maugham (1874–1965) British novelist.
Of Human Bondage, Ch. 51

1920

936 The surest way to ruin a man who doesn't know how to handle money is to give him some.
George Bernard Shaw (1856–1950) Irish dramatist and critic.
Heartbreak House

1921

937 As long as men are men, a poor society cannot be too poor to find a right order of life, nor a rich society too rich to have need to seek it.
R. H. Tawney (1880–1962) British economist and historian.
The Acquisitive Society

1923

938 "To make money", said Mr. Porteous, "one must be really interested in money."
Aldous Huxley (1894–1964) British novelist.
Antic Hay

1925

939 It is only the poor who pay cash, and that not

from virtue, but because they are refused credit.
Anatole France (Jacques Anatole François Thibault; 1844–1924) French writer.
A Cynic's Breviary (J. R. Solly)

1930

940* The rich man has his motor car,
His country and his town estate.
He smokes a fifty-cent cigar
And jeers at Fate.
F. P. Adams (1881–1960) US journalist.
The Rich Man

941 Yet though my lamp burns low and dim,
Though I must slave for livelihood –
Think you that I would change with him?
You bet I would!
F. P. Adams
The Rich Man

942 For one person who dreams of making fifty thousand pounds, a hundred people dream of being left fifty thousand pounds.
A. A. Milne (1882–1956) British writer.
If I May, 'The Future'

1932

943 God shows his contempt for wealth by the kind of person he selects to receive it.
Austin O'Malley (1858–1932) US writer.
Attrib.

1934

944 People don't resent having nothing nearly as much as too little.
Ivy Compton-Burnett (1892–1969) British novelist.
A Family and a Fortune

1937

945 I believe the power to make money is a gift of God.
J. D. Rockefeller (1839–1937) US oil magnate.
Attrib.

1940

946* If you can actually count your money you are not really a rich man.
J. Paul Getty (1892–1976) US oil magnate.
Gossip (A. Barrow)

947 One can never be too thin or too rich.
Duchess of Windsor (Wallis Warfield Simpson; 1896–1986) The wife of the Duke of Windsor (formerly Edward VIII).
Attrib.

Work and Occupations

1919

948 The mystic sees the ineffable, and the psychopathologist the unspeakable.
W. Somerset Maugham (1874–1965) British novelist.
The Moon and Sixpence, Ch. 1

949* He is the only man who is for ever apologizing for his occupation.
H. L. Mencken (1880–1956) US journalist.
Referring to the businessman
Prejudices, 'Types of Men'

1920

950* Journalists say a thing that they know isn't true, in the hope that if they keep on saying it long enough it will be true.
Arnold Bennett (1867–1931) British novelist.
The Title, II

951 You cannot hope
to bribe or twist,
thank God! the
British journalist.

But, seeing what
the man will do
unbribed, there's
no occasion to.
Humbert Wolfe (1886–1940) British poet.
The Uncelestial City, Bk. I, 'Over the Fire'

952 The army ages men sooner than the law and philosophy; it exposes them more freely to germs, which undermine and destroy, and it shelters them more completely from thought, which stimulates and preserves.
H. G. Wells (1866–1946) British writer.
Bealby, Pt. VIII, Ch. 1

953 Philosophers are as jealous as women. Each wants a monopoly of praise.
George Santayana (1863–1952) US philosopher.
Dialogues In Limbo

1921

954 It is very unfair to expect a politician to live in private up to the statements he makes in public.
W. Somerset Maugham (1874–1965) British novelist.
The Circle

955 A doctor who doesn't say too many foolish things is a patient half-cured, just as a critic is a poet who has stopped writing verse and a policeman a burglar who has retired from practice.
Marcel Proust (1871–1922) French novelist.
À la recherche du temps perdu: Le Côté de Guermantes

956 My doctor said to me afterwards, "When you were ill you behaved like a true philosopher.

Every time you came to yourself you made a joke." I never had a compliment that pleased me more.
Bertrand Russell (1872–1970) British philosopher.
Letter to Jean Nichol, 2 Oct 1921

1923

957 You sought the last resort of feeble minds with classical educations. You became a schoolmaster.
Aldous Huxley (1894–1964) British novelist and essayist.
Antic Hay

1926

958 Its primary office is the gathering of news. At the peril of its soul it must see that the supply is not tainted. Neither in what it gives, nor in what it does not give, nor in the mode of presentation, must the unclouded face of truth suffer wrong. Comment is free but facts are sacred.
C. P. Scott (1846–1932) British journalist.
Manchester Guardian, 6 May 1926

1927

959 The work of a Prime Minister is the loneliest job in the world.
Stanley Baldwin (1867–1947) British statesman.
Speech, 9 Jan 1927

1930

960* A musicologist is a man who can read music but can't hear it.
Thomas Beecham (1879–1961) British conductor.
Beecham Remembered (H. Procter-Gregg)

961 Soldiers are citizens of death's grey land, Drawing no dividend from time's tomorrows.
Siegfried Sassoon (1886–1967) British poet.
Dreamers

962 If Max gets to Heaven he won't last long. He will be chucked out for trying to pull off a merger between Heaven and Hell . . . after having secured a controlling interest in key subsidiary companies in both places, of course.
H. G. Wells (1866–1946) British writer.
Referring to Lord Beaverbrook
Beaverbrook (A. J. P. Taylor)

963 By working faithfully eight hours a day you may eventually get to be a boss and work twelve hours a day.
Robert Frost (1875–1963) US poet.
Attrib.

1931

964 A reporter is a man who has renounced every-

thing in life but the world, the flesh, and the devil.
David Murray (1888–1962) British journalist.
The Observer, 'Sayings of the Week', 5 July 1931

1935
---

965 There's no better way of exercising the imagination than the study of law. No poet ever interpreted nature as freely as a lawyer interprets truth.
Jean Giraudoux (1882–1944) French dramatist.
Tiger at the Gates, I

966* There is dignity in work only when it is work freely accepted.
Albert Camus (1913–60) French existentialist writer.
Notebooks, 1935–42

1938
---

967 Literature is the art of writing something that will be read twice; journalism what will be grasped at once.
Cyril Connolly (1903–74) British journalist.
Enemies of Promise, Ch. 3

968 As repressed sadists are supposed to become policemen or butchers so those with irrational fear of life become publishers.
Cyril Connolly
Enemies of Promise, Ch. 3

969 Life is too short to do anything for oneself that one can pay others to do for one.
W. Somerset Maugham (1874–1965) British novelist.
The Summing Up

970 I don't think the profession of historian fits a man for psychological analysis. In our work we have to deal only with simple feelings to which we give generic names such as Ambition and Interest.
Jean-Paul Sartre (1905–80) French writer.
Nausea

1939
---

971 So, perhaps, I may escape otherwise than by death the last humiliation of an aged scholar, when his juniors conspire to print a volume of essays and offer it to him as a sign that they now consider him senile.
Robin George Collingwood (1889–1943) British philosopher and archaeologist.
Autobiography

1940

972* What do you want to be a sailor for? There are greater storms in politics than you'll ever find

at sea. Piracy, broadsides, blood on the deck – you'll find them all in politics.
David Lloyd George (1863–1945) British Liberal statesman.
Remark to Julian Amery
The Observer, 2 Jan 1966

Sayings of the Time

1914
---

973 *L'acte gratuite.*
The unmotivated action.
André Gide (1869–1951) French novelist.
Les Caves du Vatican

1920

974* Any colour, so long as it's black.
Henry Ford (1863–1947) US car manufacturer.
Referring to the colour options offered for the Model-T Ford car
Attrib.

1924
---

975 They're changing guard at Buckingham Palace
Christopher Robin went down with Alice.
Alice is marrying one of the guard.
'A soldier's life is terrible hard,'
Says Alice.
A. A. Milne (1882–1956) British writer.
When We Were Very Young, 'Buckingham Palace'

1926
---

976 I am a Bear of Very Little Brain, and long words Bother me.
A. A. Milne (1882–1956) British writer.
Winnie-the-Pooh, Ch. 4

1927
---

977 You ain't heard nothin' yet, folks.
Al Jolson (Asa Yoelson; 1886–1950) US actor and singer.
In the film *The Jazz Singer*, July 1927
The Jazz Singer

1929
---

978 I'm singing in the rain, just singing in the rain
What a wonderful feeling, I'm happy again.
Arthur Freed (1894–1973) US film producer and songwriter.
From the musical, *Hollywood Revue of 1929*
Singing in the Rain

979 All Quiet on the Western Front.
Erich Maria Remarque (1898–1970) German novelist.
Title of novel

1930

980　Very flat, Norfolk.
Noël Coward (1899–1973) British dramatist.
Private Lives

981*　Poor Little Rich Girl.
Noël Coward
Title of song

1932

982　I want to be alone.
Greta Garbo (1905–　) Swedish-born US film star.
Words spoken by Garbo in the film *Grand Hotel*, and associated with her for the rest of her career.

1935

983　However, one cannot put a quart in a pint cup.
Charlotte Perkins Gilman (1860–1935) US writer.
The Living of Charlotte Perkins Gilman

1936

984*　I murdered my grandmother this morning.
Franklin D. Roosevelt (1882–1945) US Democratic president.
His habitual greeting to any guest at the White House he suspected of paying no attention to what he said
Ear on Washington (D. McClellan)

1937

985　How to Win Friends and Influence People.
Dale Carnegie (1888–1955) US lecturer and writer.
Book title

1938

986　Last night I dreamt I went to Manderley again.
Daphne Du Maurier (1907–　) British novelist.
Rebecca, Ch. 1

987*　Music, Maestro, Please.
Herb Magidson (20th century) US songwriter.
Song title

988　You can fool too many of the people too much of the time.
James Thurber (1894–1961) US humorist.
Fables for Our Time, 'The Owl Who Was God'

1941

989　What they could do with round here is a good war.
Bertolt Brecht (1898–1956) German dramatist.
Mother Courage, I

1942

990　Play it, Sam. Play 'As Time Goes By.'
Humphrey Bogart (1899–1957) US film star.
Often misquoted as 'Play it again, Sam'
Casablanca

1944

991　Don't eat too many almonds; they add weight to the breasts.
Colette (1873–1954) French novelist.
Gigi

With Hindsight

992　He did not care in which direction the car was travelling, so long as he remained in the driver's seat.
Lord Beaverbrook (1879–1964) Canadian-born British newspaper proprietor.
Referring to Lloyd George
New Statesman, 14 June 1963

993　Marxian Socialism must always remain a portent to the historians of Opinion – how a doctrine so illogical and so dull can have exercised so powerful and enduring an influence over the minds of men, and, through them, the events of history.
John Maynard Keynes (1883–1946) British economist.
The End of Laisser-Faire, III

994　Communism continued to haunt Europe as a spectre – a name men gave to their own fears and blunders. But the crusade against Communism was even more imaginary than the spectre of Communism.
A. J. P. Taylor (1906–　) British historian.
The Origins of the Second World War, Ch. 2

995　Lenin was the first to discover that capitalism 'inevitably' caused war; and he discovered this only when the First World War was already being fought. Of course he was right. Since every great state was capitalist in 1914, capitalism obviously 'caused' the First World War; but just as obviously it had 'caused' the previous generation of Peace.
A. J. P. Taylor
The Origins of the Second World War, Ch. 6

996　A racing tipster who only reached Hitler's level of accuracy would not do well for his clients.
A. J. P. Taylor
The Origins of the Second World War, Ch. 7

997　When I look back on all these worries I remember the story of the old man who said on his deathbed that he had had a lot of trouble in his life, most of which had never happened.
Winston Churchill (1874–1965) British statesman.
Their Finest Hour

998 The nation had the lion's heart. I had the luck to give the roar.
Winston Churchill
Said on his 80th birthday

999 Hitler showed surprising loyalty to Mussolini, but it never extended to trusting him.
Alan Bullock (1914–   ) British academic and historian.
Hitler, A Study in Tyranny, Ch. 11

1000 The people Hitler never understood, and whose actions continued to exasperate him to the end of his life, were the British.
Alan Bullock
Hitler, A Study in Tyranny, Ch. 8

13

The Post-War World

As World War II ended, the conflicting ideologies and interests of the communist and non-communist powers, which had been suppressed during the war, re-emerged. Europe was divided along the line where the Soviet and Western armies met when Germany was defeated. In 1949 the USSR acquired its own atomic bomb to match that of the Americans, and the next 30 years were dominated by the threat of nuclear war. During the Cuban missile crisis (1962) nuclear war seemed unnervingly close, but usually the USA and USSR have exercised their rivalry indirectly, by supporting and influencing smaller states or rival groups within states, especially in the Third World. Where they have intervened directly, neither has dared to use its full strength lest it provoke the other. The Korean War (1950–53) ended in stalemate; America was forced to withdraw from Vietnam, allowing a communist victory (1975); and in 1988 the USSR's eight-year attempt to subdue Afghanistan ended in failure. By the mid-1980s a more hopeful mood prevailed, and an agreement to reduce nuclear weapons was signed in 1987.

World War II also marked the final eclipse of the West European states as world powers. Economically exhausted, they had to be supported in the immediate post-war years by the USA. Their overseas empires were dissolved, particularly in the 1950s and 1960s and they began to look towards some form of European unity for prosperity and security. The European Economic Community, founded 1957, now includes most of non-communist Europe.

The proliferation of new states outside Europe has caused its own problems. Israel, founded in 1948 as a homeland for the Jews, has never been accepted by its Arab neighbours. In Africa, the arbitrary frontiers inherited from the colonial period have left many states with internal conflicts between different tribes. The economic problems of most Third World countries have contributed to their political fragility, and in the 1980s many were facing problems servicing their overseas debts.

Technological change since 1945 has proceeded at a pace hitherto unknown. The first computer was built during World War II; today, computers are part of everyday life, with uses ranging from warfare to popular music. However, increased technology has led to increased energy demands as the traditional source—fossil fuels—are becoming exhausted. In the immediate post-war years, nuclear energy was thought to be the answer to all energy problems. Today there is widespread concern about the effects of its by-products—and all other pollutants associated with technological advance—on the environment.

Politics, Government, and World Events

1946

1   **An iron curtain has descended across the Continent.**
Winston Churchill (1874–1965) British statesman.
The phrase 'iron curtain' was originally coined by Joseph Goebbels
Address, Westminster College, Fulton, USA, 5 Mar 1946

2   **We are the masters at the moment — and not only for the moment, but for a very long time to come.**
Lord Shawcross (1902–   ) British Labour politician and lawyer.
Sometimes misquoted as, 'We are the masters now!'
House of Commons, 2 Apr 1946

3   **Our hospital organization has grown up with no plan, with no system; it is unevenly distributed over the country . . . I would rather be kept alive in the efficient if cold altruism of a large hospital than expire in a gush of warm sympathy in a small one.**
Aneurin Bevan (1897–1960) British Labour politician.
Introducing the National Health Service Bill
Speech, House of Commons, 30 Apr 1946

4   **I stuffed their mouths with gold!**
Aneurin Bevan
Explaining how he persuaded doctors not to oppose the introduction of the National Health Service
Attrib.

5   **We must build a kind of United States of Europe.**
Winston Churchill (1874–1965) British statesman.
Speech, Zurich, 19 Sept 1946

6   **Our agenda is now exhausted. The secretary general is exhausted. All of you are exhausted. I find it comforting that, beginning with our very first day, we find ourselves in such complete unanimity.**
Paul Henri Spaak (1899–1972) Belgian statesman.
Concluding the first General Assembly meeting of the United Nations

7   **Since wars begin in the minds of men, it is in the minds of men that the defences of peace must be constructed.**
Anonymous
Constitution of UNESCO

8   **The atom bomb is a paper tiger which the United States reactionaries use to scare people.**
Mao Tse-Tung (1893–1976) Chinese communist leader.
Interview, Aug 1946

9   **I am against government by crony.**
Harold L. Ickes (1874–1952) US Republican politician.
Comment on his resignation as Secretary of the Interior (1946) after a dispute with President Truman

1947

10   **Let us not be deceived — we are today in the midst of a cold war.**
Bernard Baruch (1870–1965) US financier and presidential adviser.
Speech, South Carolina Legislature, 16 Apr 1947

11   **The tragedy of the Police State is that it always regards all opposition as a crime, and there are no degrees.**
Lord Vansittart (1881–1957) British politician.
Speech, House of Lords, June 1947

12   **No annihilation without representation.**
Arnold Toynbee (1889–1975) British historian.
Urging the need for a greater British influence in the UN

13   **Wars, conflict, it's all business. One murder makes a villain. Millions a hero. Numbers sanctify.**
Charlie Chaplin (Sir Charles Spencer C.; 1889–1977) British film actor.
Monsieur Verdoux

14   **There are three groups that no British Prime Minister should provoke: the Vatican, the Treasury and the miners.**
Stanley Baldwin (1867–1947) British statesman.
A similar remark is often attributed to Harold Macmillan in 1960
Attrib.

15   **I would rather be an opportunist and float than go to the bottom with my principles round my neck.**
Stanley Baldwin
Attrib.

1948

16   **There is only a certain sized cake to be divided up, and if a lot of people want a larger slice they can only take it from others who would, in terms of real income, have a smaller one.**
Sir Stafford Cripps (1889–1952) British Labour politician.
Speech, Trade Union Congress, 7 Sept 1948

17   **I like old Joe Stalin. He's a good fellow but he's a prisoner of the Politburo. He would make certain agreements but they won't let him keep them.**
Harry S. Truman (1884–1972) US statesman.
News Review, 24 June 1948

18 All human beings are born free and equal in dignity and rights.
Anonymous
Universal Declaration of Human Rights (1948), Article 1

19 The House of Lords must be the only institution in the world which is kept efficient by the persistent absenteeism of most of its members.
Herbert Samuel (1870–1963) British Liberal statesman.
News Review, 5 Feb 1948

20 I will shake my little finger – and there will be no more Tito. He will fall.
Joseph Stalin (J. Dzhugashvili; 1879–1953) Soviet statesman.
Said to Khrushchev
Attrib.

21 I have never seen a human being who more perfectly represented the modern conception of a robot.
Winston Churchill (1874–1965) British statesman.
Referring to the Soviet statesman Molotov
The Second World War

22 Wars come because not enough people are sufficiently afraid.
Hugh Schonfield (1901–) British writer and editor.
The News Review, 26 Feb 1948

1949

23 No attempt at ethical or social seduction can eradicate from my heart a deep burning hatred for the Tory Party . . . So far as I am concerned they are lower than vermin.
Aneurin Bevan (1897–1960) British Labour politician.
Speech, Manchester, 4 July 1949

24 If ever he went to school without any boots it was because he was too big for them.
Ivor Bulmer-Thomas (1905–) British writer and politician.
Referring to Harold Wilson
Remark, Conservative Party Conference, 1949

25 Now we are in a period which I can characterize as a period of cold peace.
Trygve Lie (1896–1968) Norwegian lawyer.
The Observer, 'Sayings of the Week', 21 Aug 1949

26 Hansard is history's ear, already listening.
Herbert Samuel (1870–1963) British Liberal statesman.
Speech, Dec 1949

27 Those who have had no share in the good fortunes of the mighty often have a share in their misfortunes.
Bertolt Brecht (1898–1956) German dramatist.
The Caucasian Chalk Circle

28 No one can guarantee success in war, but only deserve it.
Winston Churchill (1874–1965) British statesman.
Their Finest Hour

29 Big Brother is watching you.
George Orwell (Eric Blair; 1903–50) British novelist.
Nineteen Eighty-Four

30 War is Peace, Freedom is Slavery, Ignorance is Strength.
George Orwell
Nineteen Eighty-Four

31 Doublethink means the power of holding two contradictory beliefs in one's mind simultaneously, and accepting both of them.
George Orwell
Nineteen Eighty-Four

32 Who controls the past controls the future. Who controls the present controls the past.
George Orwell
Nineteen Eighty-Four

1950s

33 He is not only a bore but he bores for England.
Malcolm Muggeridge (1903–) British writer.
Referring to Sir Anthony Eden
In *Newstatesmanship* (E. Hyams), 'Boring for England'

34 He is a man suffering from petrified adolescence.
Aneurin Bevan (1897–1960) British Labour politician.
Referring to Winston Churchill
Aneurin Bevan (Vincent Brome), Ch. 11

35 A desiccated calculating machine.
Aneurin Bevan
Referring to Hugh Gaitskell
Hugh Gaitskell (W. T. Rodgers)

36 Its relationship to democratic institutions is that of the death watch beetle – it is not a Party, it is a conspiracy.
Aneurin Bevan
Referring to the Communist Party
Tribune

37 I'm not interested in classes . . . Far be it from me to foster inferiority complexes among the workers by trying to make them think they belong to some special class. That has happened in Europe but it hasn't happened here yet.
John Llewellyn Lewis (1880–1969) US labour leader.
The Coming of the New Deal (A. M. Schlesinger, Jnr), Pt. 7, Ch. 25

38 In a civil war, a general must know – and I'm afraid it's a thing rather of instinct than of

practice – he must know exactly when to move over to the other side.
Henry Reed (1914–) British poet and dramatist.
Not a Drum was Heard: The War Memoirs of General Gland

39 Who live under the shadow of a war,
What can I do that matters?
Stephen Spender (1909–) British poet.
Who live under the Shadow

40 'War is the continuation of politics'. In this sense war is politics and war itself is a political action.
Mao Tse-Tung (1893–1976) Chinese communist leader.
Quotations from Chairman Mao Tse-Tung, Ch. 5

41 We are advocates of the abolition of war, we do not want war; but war can only be abolished through war, and in order to get rid of the gun it is necessary to take up the gun.
Mao Tse-Tung
Quotations from Chairman Mao Tse-Tung, Ch. 5

42 Politics is a blood sport.
Aneurin Bevan (1897–1960) British Labour politician.
My Life with Nye (Jennie Lee)

43 We're not a family; we're a firm.
George VI (1895–1952) King of the United Kingdom.
Our Future King (Peter Lane)

44 The worst government is the most moral. One composed of cynics is often very tolerant and human. But when fanatics are on top there is no limit to oppression.
H. L. Mencken (1880–1956) US journalist.
Notebooks, 'Minority Report'

1950

45 Perhaps it is better to be irresponsible and right than to be responsible and wrong.
Winston Churchill (1874–1965) British statesman.
Party Political Broadcast, London, 26 Aug 1950

46* The buck stops here.
Harry S. Truman (1884–1972) US statesman.
Sign kept on his desk during his term as president (1945–53)
Presidential Anecdotes (P. Boller)

47 When old settlers say 'One has to understand the country', what they mean is, 'You have to get used to our ideas about the native.' They are saying, in effect, 'Learn our ideas, or otherwise get out; we don't want you.'
Doris Lessing (1919–) British novelist.
Referring specifically to South Africa
The Grass is Singing, Ch. 1

48 When a white man in Africa by accident looks into the eyes of a native and sees the human being (which it is his chief preoccupation to avoid), his sense of guilt, which he denies,

fumes up in resentment and he brings down the whip.
Doris Lessing
The Grass is Singing, Ch. 8

49 In our time, political speech and writing are largely the defence of the indefensible.
George Orwell (Eric Blair; 1903–50) British novelist.
Politics and the English Language

1951

50 My policy is to be able to take a ticket at Victoria Station and go anywhere I damn well please.
Ernest Bevin (1881–1951) British trade-union leader and politician.
The Spectator, 20 Apr 1951

51 The wrong war, at the wrong place, at the wrong time, and with the wrong enemy.
Omar Nelson Bradley (1893–1981) US general.
Said in evidence to a Senate inquiry, May 1951, over a proposal by MacArthur that the Korean war should be extended into China

52 I didn't fire him because he was a dumb son of a bitch, although he was, but that's not against the law for generals. If it was, half to three-quarters of them would be in gaol.
Harry S. Truman (1884–1972) US statesman.
Referring to General MacArthur
Plain Speaking (Merle Miller)

53 Whose Finger do you want on the Trigger When the World Situation Is So Delicate?
Anonymous
Headline from the *Daily Mirror* on the day before the General Election, Oct 1951
Publish and Be Damned (Hugh Cudlipp), 1953

54 Our great democracies still tend to think that a stupid man is more likely to be honest than a clever man, and our politicians take advantage of this prejudice by pretending to be even more stupid than nature has made them.
Bertrand Russell (1872–1970) British philosopher.
New Hopes for a Changing World

55 When the rich wage war it is the poor who die.
Jean-Paul Sartre (1905–80) French writer.
The Devil and the Good Lord

56 Communism is the corruption of a dream of justice.
Adlai Stevenson (1900–65) US statesman.
Speech, 1951

57 What is a rebel? A man who says no.
Albert Camus (1913–60) French existentialist writer.
The Rebel

58 I am not made for politics because I am incapable of wishing for, or accepting the death of my adversary.
Albert Camus
The Rebel

59 All modern revolutions have ended in a rein-
forcement of the power of the State.
Albert Camus
The Rebel

60 The future is the only kind of property that the
masters willingly concede to slaves.
Albert Camus
The Rebel

61 The slave begins by demanding justice and
ends by wanting to wear a crown. He must
dominate in his turn.
Albert Camus
The Rebel

62 There will soon be only five kings left – the
Kings of England, Diamonds, Hearts, Spades
and Clubs.
Farouk I (1920–65) The last king of Egypt.
Remark made to Lord Boyd-Orr

63 I hate the idea of causes, and if I had to choose
between betraying my country and betraying
my friend, I hope I should have the guts to betray my country.
E. M. Forster (1879–1970) British novelist.
Two Cheers for Democracy, 'What I Believe'.

64 The French will only be united under the threat
of danger. Nobody can simply bring together a
country that has 265 kinds of cheese.
Charles De Gaulle (1890–1970) French general and statesman.
Speech, 1951

1952

65 The way to win an atomic war is to make certain it never starts.
Omar Nelson Bradley (1893–1981) US
general.
The Observer, 'Sayings of the Week', 20 Apr
1952

66 McCarthyism is Americanism with its sleeves
rolled.
Joseph R. McCarthy (1908–57) US senator.
Speech, 1952

67 I cannot and will not cut my conscience to fit
this year's fashions, even though I long ago
came to the conclusion that I was not a political
person and could have no comfortable place
in any political group.
Lillian Hellman (1905–84) US dramatist.
Letter to the US House of Representatives Committee on Un-American Activities, *The Nation*,
31 May 1952

68 Let's talk sense to the American people. Let's
tell them the truth, that there are no gains
without pains.
Adlai Stevenson (1900–65) US statesman.
Speech, Chicago, 26 July 1952

69 Man has wrested from nature the power to
make the world a desert or to make the deserts
bloom. There is no evil in the atom, only in
men's souls.
Adlai Stevenson
Speech, 18 Sept 1952

70 I will undoubtedly have to seek what is happily

known as gainful employment, which I am
glad to say does not describe holding public
office.
Dean Acheson (1893–1971) US lawyer and
statesman.
Remark made on leaving his post as secretary c
state, 1952; he subsequently returned to private legal practice

71 My definition of a free society is a society
where it is safe to be unpopular.
Adlai Stevenson (1900–65) US statesman.
Speech, Detroit, Oct. 1952

72 Nothing is news until it has appeared in *The
Times*.
Ralph Deakin (1888–1952) Foreign News Ed
tor of *The Times*.
Attrib.

1953

73 We know what happens to people who stay i
the middle of the road. They get run over.
Aneurin Bevan (1897–1960) British Labour
politician.
The Observer, 'Sayings of the Week', 9 Dec
1953

74 Whatever America hopes to bring to pass in
this world must first come to pass in the hea•
of America.
Dwight D. Eisenhower (1890–1969) US
general and statesman.
Inaugural address, 1953

75 There is one thing about being President – no
body can tell you when to sit down.
Dwight D. Eisenhower
The Observer, 'Sayings of the Week', 9 Aug
1953

76 The countries of western Europe are no longe•
in a position to protect themselves
individually.
Konrad Adenauer (1876–1967) West German chancellor.
Speech, May 1953

77 As far as I knew, he had never taken a photograph before, and the summit of Everest was
hardly the place to show him how.
Edmund Hillary (1919–   ) New Zealand
mountaineer.
Referring to Tenzing Norgay, his companion on
the conquest of Mt Everest
High Adventure

78 The party is the rallying-point for the best ele
ments rf the working class.
Joseph Stalin (J. Dzhugashvili; 1879–1953)
Soviet statesman.
Attrib.

79 REPORTER. If Mr Stalin dies, what will be the effect on international affairs?
EDEN. That is a good question for you to ask,
not a wise question for me to answer.
Anthony Eden (1897–1977) British
statesman.
Interview on board the *Queen Elizabeth*, 4 Mar
1953

80 ... that great lover of peace, a man of giant stature who moulded, as few other men have done, the destinies of his age.
Jawaharlal Nehru (1889–1964) First Indian Prime Minister.
Referring to Stalin
Obituary tribute, Indian Parliament, 9 Mar 1953

81 For many years I thought what was good for our country was good for General Motors, and vice versa.
Charles Erwin Wilson (1890–1961) US engineer.
Said in testimony to the Senate Armed Services Committee, Jan 1953
Attrib.

82 It will be said of this generation that it found England a land of beauty and left it a land of beauty spots.
Cyril Joad (1891–1953) British writer and broadcaster.
The Observer, 'Sayings of Our Times', 31 May 1953

1954

83 You have a row of dominoes set up; you knock over the first one, and what will happen to the last one is that it will go over very quickly.
Dwight D. Eisenhower (1890–1969) US general and statesman.
The so-called 'domino effect'; said during the Battle of Dien Bien Phu, in which the French were defeated by the communist Viet-Minh
Press conference, 7 Apr 1954

84 To jaw-jaw is better than to war-war.
Winston Churchill (1874–1965) British statesman.
Speech, Washington, 26 June 1954

85* An appeaser is one who feeds a crocodile – hoping that it will eat him last.
Winston Churchill
Attrib.

86 All diplomacy is a continuation of war by other means.
Chou En Lai (1898–1976) Chinese statesman.

1955

87 Mr Macmillan is the best prime minister we have.
R. A. Butler (1902–82) British Conservative politician.
Often quoted in the form above. In fact, Butler simply answered 'Yes' to the question 'Would you say that this is the best prime minister we have?'
Interview, London Airport, Dec 1955

88 Not a gentleman; dresses too well.
Bertrand Russell (1872–1970) British philosopher.
Referring to Anthony Eden
Six Men (A. Cooke)

89 The word 'revolution' is a word for which you kill, for which you die, for which you send the

labouring masses to their death, but which does not possess any content.
Simone Weil (1909–43) French philosopher.
Oppression and Liberty, 'Reflections Concerning the Causes of Liberty and Social Oppression'

1956

90 Everybody is always in favour of general economy and particular expenditure.
Anthony Eden (1897–1977) British statesman.
Speech, June 1956

91 We must face the fact that the United Nations is not yet the international equivalent of our own legal system and the rule of law.
Anthony Eden
Speech, House of Commons, 1 Nov 1956

92 We are not at war with Egypt. We are in an armed conflict.
Anthony Eden
Referring to the Suez crisis
Speech, House of Commons, 4 Nov 1956

93 During the last few weeks I have felt that the Suez Canal was flowing through my drawing room.
Clarissa Eden (1920–85) Wife of Anthony Eden.
Attrib.

94 Russian communism is the illegitimate child of Karl Marx and Catherine the Great.
Clement Attlee (1883–1967) British statesman and Labour prime minister.
Speech, 11 Apr 1956

95 Every year humanity takes a step towards Communism. Maybe not you, but at all events your grandson will surely be a Communist.
Nikita Khrushchev (1894–1971) Soviet statesman.
Said to Sir William Hayter

96 We will bury you.
Nikita Khrushchev
Said at a reception at the Kremlin, 26 Nov 1956

97 With the publication of his Private Papers in 1952, he committed suicide 25 years after his death.
Lord Beaverbrook (1879–1964) British newspaper owner and politician.
Referring to Earl Haig, British commander in chief in World War I
Men and Power

98 An aristocracy in a republic is like a chicken whose head has been cut off: it may run about in a lively way, but in fact it is dead.
Nancy Mitford (1904–73) British writer.
Noblesse Oblige

99 The official world, the corridors of power, the dilemmas of conscience and egotism – she disliked them all.
C. P. Snow (1905–80) British novelist.
Homecomings, Ch. 22

100 Jam today, and men aren't at their most excit-

ing: Jam tomorrow, and one often sees them at their noblest.
C. P. Snow
The Two Cultures and the Scientific Revolution, 4

1957

101 Surely the right course is to test the Russians, not the bombs.
Hugh Gaitskell (1906–63) British Labour politician.
Observer, 'Sayings of the Week', 23 June 1957

102 Most of our people have never had it so good.
Harold Macmillan (1894–1986) British politician and prime minister.
Speech, Bedford Football Ground, 20 July 1957

103 If you carry this resolution and follow out all its implications and do not run away from it you will send a Foreign Minister, whoever he may be, naked into the conference chamber.
Aneurin Bevan (1897–1960) British Labour politician.
Opposing a motion advocating unilateral nuclear disarmament
Speech, Labour Party Conference, 3 Oct 1957

104 The only inequalities that matter begin in the mind. It is not income levels but differences in mental equipment that keep people apart, breed feelings of inferiority.
Jacquetta Hawkes (1910–) British archeologist.
New Statesman, Jan 1957

1958

105 *Algérie Française.*
Algeria is French.
Slogan of the opponents of Algerian independence

106 When you're abroad you're a statesman: when you're at home you're just a politician.
Harold Macmillan (1894–1986) British statesman.
Speech, 1958

107 Introducing Super-Mac.
Vicky (Victor Weisz; 1913–66) German-born British cartoonist.
Cartoon caption depicting Harold Macmillan as Superman
Evening Standard, 6 Nov 1958

108 It's a recession when your neighbour loses his job; it's a depression when you lose your own.
Harry S. Truman (1884–1972) US statesman.
The Observer, 'Sayings of the Week', 6 Apr 1958

109 A politician is a man who understands government, and it takes a politician to run a government. And a statesman is a politician who's been dead ten or fifteen years.
Harry S. Truman
New York World Telegram and Sun, 12 Apr 1958

110 The British, being brought up on team games, enter their House of Commons in the spirit of those who would rather be doing something else. If they cannot be playing golf or tennis, they can at least pretend that politics is a game with very similar rules.
Cyril Northcote Parkinson (1919–) British historian and writer.
Parkinson's Law, Ch. 2

111 No one can go on being a rebel too long without turning into an autocrat.
Lawrence Durrell (1912–) British novelist.
Balthazar, II

112 More die in the United States of too much food than of too little.
The Affluent Society, Ch. 9
John Kenneth Galbraith (1908–) US economist.

113 Few things are as immutable as the addiction of political groups to the ideas by which they have once won office.
John Kenneth Galbraith
The Affluent Society, Ch. 13

114 The Rise of the Meritocracy.
Michael Young (1915–) British political writer.
Book title

1959

115 Churchill on top of the wave has in him the stuff of which tyrants are made.
Lord Beaverbrook (1879–1964) Canadian-born British newspaper proprietor.
Politicians and the War

1960s

116 All wars are popular for the first thirty days.
Arthur Schlesinger Jnr (1917–) US historian, educator, and author.
Attrib.

117 The military don't start wars. The politicians start wars.
William Westmorland (1914–) US army officer.
Attrib.

118 It is worse than immoral, it's a mistake.
Dean Acheson (1893–1971) US lawyer and statesman.
Describing the Vietnam war
Quoted by Alistair Cooke in his radio programme *Letter from America*

119 People don't seem to realize that it takes time and effort and preparation to think. Statesmen are far too busy making speeches to think.
Bertrand Russell (1872–1970) British philosopher.
Kenneth Harris Talking To: 'Bertrand Russell' (Kenneth Harris)

120 You may reasonably expect a man to walk a tightrope safely for ten minutes; it would be un-

reasonable to do so without accident for two hundred years.
Bertrand Russell
On the subject of nuclear war between the USA and the Soviets
The Tightrope Men (D. Bagley)

121   **What a genius the Labour Party has for cutting itself in half and letting the two parts writhe in public.**
Cassandra (William Neil Cannon; 1910–67) Irish journalist.
The Daily Mirror

122   **Men of power have not time to read; yet men who do not read are unfit for power.**
Michael Foot (1913–   ) British Labour politician and journalist.
Debts Of Honour

123   **Equality of opportunity means equal opportunity to be unequal.**
Iain Macleod (1913–70) British politician.
Way Of Life (John Boyd Carpenter)

124   **An independent is a guy who wants to take the politics out of politics.**
Adlai Stevenson (1900–65) US statesman.
The Art Of Politics.

125   **No Jewish blood runs among my blood, but I am as bitterly and hardly hated by every anti-semite as if I were a Jew. By this I am a Russian.**
Yevgeny Yevtushenko (1933–   ) Soviet poet.
Babi Yar

1960

126*   **Classical physics has been superseded by quantum theory: quantum theory is verified by experiments. Experiments must be described in terms of classical physics.**
C. F. von Weizsäcker (1912–   ) German physicist and philosopher.
Attrib.

127   **One does not arrest Voltaire.**
Charles De Gaulle (1890–1970) French general and statesman.
Explaining why he had not arrested Jean-Paul Sartre for urging French soldiers in Algeria to desert
Attrib.

128   **We stand today on the edge of a new frontier.**
John Fitzgerald Kennedy (1917–63) US statesman.
Said on his nomination as Presidential candidate
Speech, Democratic Party Convention, 15 July 1960

129   **Do you realize the responsibility I carry? I'm the only person standing between Nixon and the White House.**
John Fitzgerald Kennedy
Said to Arthur Schlesinger, 13 Oct 1960; Richard Nixon was the Republican candidate in the 1960 US Presidential election
A Thousand Days (Arthur M. Schlesinger, Jnr)

130   **There are some of us . . . who will fight, fight, fight, and fight again to save the party we love.**
Hugh Gaitskell (1906–63) British Labour politician.
After his policy for a nuclear deterrent had been defeated.
Speech, Labour Party conference, Scarborough, 3 Oct 1960

131   **The wind of change is blowing through the continent. Whether we like it or not, this growth of national consciousness is a political fact.**
Harold Macmillan (1894–1986) British politician and prime minister.
Speech, South African Parliament, 3 Feb 1960

132*   **There is no reason to attack the monkey when the organ-grinder is present.**
Aneurin Bevan (1897–1960) British Labour politician.
The 'monkey' was Selwyn Lloyd; the 'organ-grinder' was Harold Macmillan
Remark, House of Commons

133   **Macmillan seemed, in his very person, to embody the national decay he supposed himself to be confuting. He exuded a flavour of mothballs.**
Malcolm Muggeridge (1903–   ) British writer.
Tread Softly For You Tread on My Jokes, 'England, whose England'

134   **Politicians are the same everywhere. They promise to build bridges even where there are no rivers.**
Nikita Khrushchev (1894–1971) Soviet statesman.
Attrib., Oct 1960

135   **The statesmen of the world who boast and threaten that they have Doomsday weapons are far more dangerous, and far more estranged from 'reality', than many of the people on whom the label 'psychotic' is affixed.**
R. D. Laing (1927–   ) British psychiatrist.
The Divided Self, Preface

136   **The expression 'positive neutrality' is a contradiction in terms. There can be no more positive neutrality than there can be a vegetarian tiger.**
V. K. Krishna Menon (1897–   ) Indian barrister and writer.
The New York Times, 18 Oct 1960

137*   **Democracy means government by discussion but it is only effective if you can stop people talking.**
Clement Attlee (1883–1967) British statesman and Labour prime minister.
Anatomy of Britain (Anthony Sampson)

138   **The one class you *do* not belong to and are not proud of at all is the lower-middle class. No one ever describes himself as belonging to the lower-middle class.**
George Mikes (1912–87) Hungarian-born British writer.
How to be Inimitable

139 The nobility of England, my lord, would have snored through the Sermon on the Mount.
Robert Bolt (1924–   ) British playwright.
A Man for All Seasons

140 You don't set a fox to watching the chickens just because he has a lot of experience in the hen house.
Harry S. Truman (1884–1972) US statesman.
Referring to Vice-President Nixon's nomination for President
Speech, 30 Oct 1960

141* A coloured man can tell, in five seconds dead, whether a white man likes him or not. If the white man *says* he does, he is instantly – and usually quite rightly – mistrusted.
Colin MacInnes (1914–76) British novelist.
England, Half English, 'A Short Guide for Jumbles'

1961

142 A revolution is not a bed of roses. A revolution is a struggle to the death between the future and the past.
Fidel Castro (1926–   ) Cuban statesman.
Speech, Havana, Jan 1961 (2nd anniversary of Revolution)

143 The Irish don't know what they want and are prepared to fight to the death to get it.
Sidney Littlewood (1895–1967) President of The Law Society.
Speech, 13 Apr 1961

144 I think it is about time we pulled our fingers out ... The rest of the world most certainly does not owe us a living.
Prince Philip (1921–   ) The consort of Queen Elizabeth II.
Speech, London, 17 Oct 1961

145 And so, my fellow Americans: ask not what your country can do for you – ask what you can do for your country. My fellow citizens of the world: ask not what America will do for you, but what together we can do for the freedom of man.
John Fitzgerald Kennedy (1917–63) US statesman.
Inaugural address, 20 Jan 1961

146 I believe that this nation should commit itself to achieving the goal, before this decade is out, of landing a man on the Moon and returning him safely to earth.
John Fitzgerald Kennedy
Supplementary State of the Union Message, 25 May 1961

147 We must use time as a tool, not as a couch.
John Fitzgerald Kennedy
The Observer, 'Sayings of the Week', 10 Dec 1961

148 The worse I do, the more popular I get.
John Fitzgerald Kennedy
Referring to his popularity following the 'Bay of Pigs' fiasco – an abortive US-supported invasion of Cuba by Cuban exiles
The People's Almanac (D. Wallechinsky)

149 I can't see that it's wrong to give him a little legal experience before he goes out to practice law.
John Fitzgerald Kennedy
On being criticized for making his brother Robert attorney general
Nobody Said It Better (M. Ringo)

150 When you are skinning your customers you should leave some skin on to grow, so that you can skin them again.
Nikita Khrushchev (1894–1971) Soviet statesman.
Speech to British industrialists, May 1961

151 A politician rises on the backs of his friends ... but it is through his enemies he will have to govern afterwards.
Richard Hughes (1900–76) British writer.
The Fox in the Attic

152 I'd like to see the government get out of war altogether and leave the whole feud to private industry.
Joseph Heller (1923–   ) US novelist.
Catch 22

153 But bombs *are* unbelievable until they actually fall.
Patrick White (1912–   ) British-born Australian novelist.
Riders in the Chariot, I:4

1962

154 The House of Lords is the British Outer Mongolia for retired politicians.
Tony Benn (1925–   ) British politician.
Speech, 11 Feb 1962

155 Great Britain has lost an Empire and has not yet found a role.
Dean Acheson (1893–1971) US lawyer and statesman.
Speech, Military Academy, West Point, 5 Dec 1962

156 You won't have Nixon to kick around any more, gentlemen. This is my last Press Conference.
Richard Milhous Nixon (1913–   ) US president.
Press conference, after losing the election for the governorship of California, 2 Nov 1962

157 I guess this is the week I earn my salary.
John Fitzgerald Kennedy (1917–63) US statesman.
Comment made during the Cuban missile crisis
Nobody Said It Better (M. Ringo)

158 Arms alone are not enough to keep the peace – it must be kept by men.
John Fitzgerald Kennedy
The Observer, 'Sayings of the Decade', 1962

159 She would rather light candles than curse the darkness, and her glow has warmed the world.
Adlai Stevenson (1900–65) US statesman.
Referring to Eleanor Roosevelt, who had recently died. She was the wife of President Franklin D.

Roosevelt and chairman (1946–51) of the UN commission on human rights.
Address, United Nations General Assembly, 9 Nov 1962

10 They talk about who won and who lost. Human reason won. Mankind won.
Nikita Khrushchev (1894–1971) Soviet statesman.
Referring to the Cuban missiles crisis
Speech, Nov 1962

11 I want to be the white man's brother, not his brother-in-law.
Martin Luther King (1929–68) US Black civil-rights leader.
New York Journal-American, 10 Sept 1962

12 Since a politician never believes what he says, he is surprised when others believe him.
Charles De Gaulle (1890–1970) French general and statesman.
Attrib.

13 They really are bad shots.
Charles De Gaulle
Remark after narrowly escaping death in an assassination attempt
Ten First Ladies of the World (Pauline Frederick)

14 A small acquaintance with history shows that all Governments are selfish and the French Governments more selfish than most.
David Eccles (1904–) British politician.
The Observer, 'Sayings of the Year', 29 Dec 1962

15 The collection of prejudices which is called political philosophy is useful provided that it is not called philosophy.
Bertrand Russell (1872–1970) British philosopher.
Remark, 1962

16 Greater love hath no man than this, that he lay down his friends for his life.
Jeremy Thorpe (1929–) British politician.
After Macmillan's 1962 Cabinet reshuffle
The Pendulum Years (Bernard Levin), Ch. 12

17 Democracy means government by discussion but it is only effective if you can stop people talking.
Clement Attlee (1883–1967) British statesman and Labour prime minister.
Anatomy of Britain

18 It is better for aged diplomats to be bored than for young men to die.
Warren Austin (1877–1962) US politician and diplomat.
When asked if he got tired during long debates at the UN
Attrib.

19 I wish I could bring Stonehenge to Nyasaland to show there was a time when Britain had a savage culture.
Hastings Banda (1906–) Malawi statesman.
The Observer, 'Sayings of the Week', 10 Mar 1963

170 If we cannot now end our differences, at least we can help make the world safe for diversity.
John Fitzgerald Kennedy (1917–63) US statesman.
Speech, American University (Washington, DC), 10 June 1963

171 All free men, wherever they may live, are citizens of Berlin. And therefore, as a free man, I take pride in the words *Ich bin ein Berliner*.
John Fitzgerald Kennedy
Speech, City Hall, West Berlin, 26 June 1963

172 Human salvation lies in the hands of the creatively maladjusted.
Martin Luther King (1929–68) US Black civil-rights leader.
Strength to Love

173 If a man hasn't discovered something that he would die for, he isn't fit to live.
Martin Luther King
Speech, Detroit, 23 June 1963

174 I have a dream that one day this nation will rise up, live out the true meaning of its creed: we hold these truths to be self-evident, that all men are created equal.
Martin Luther King
He used the words 'I have a dream' in a number of speeches
Speech, Washington, 27 Aug 1963

175 A constant effort to keep his party together, without sacrificing either principle or the essentials of basic strategy, is the very stuff of political leadership. Macmillan was canonised for it.
Harold Wilson (1916–) British politician and prime minister.
Final Term: The Labour Government 1974–76

176 A great party is not to be brought down because of a scandal by a woman of easy virtue and a proved liar.
Lord Hailsham (1907–) British Conservative politician.
Referring to the Profumo affair, in BBC interview, 13 June 1963
The Pendulum Years, Ch. 3 (Bernard Levin)

177 There is something utterly nauseating about a system of society which pays a harlot 25 times as much as it pays its Prime Minister, 250 times as much as it pays its Members of Parliament, and 500 times as much as it pays some of its ministers of religion.
Harold Wilson (1916–) British politician and prime minister.
Referring to the case of Christine Keeler
Speech, House of Commons, June 1963

178 He would, wouldn't he?
Mandy Rice-Davies (1944–) British call girl.
Of Lord Astor, when told that he had repudiated her evidence at the trial of Stephen Ward, 29 June 1963

179 The members of our secret service have apparently spent so much time looking under the

beds for Communists, they haven't had time to look in the bed.
Michael Foot (1913–   ) British Labour politician and journalist.
Referring to the Profumo affair
Attrib.

180   The United States has to move very fast to even stand still.
John Fitzgerald Kennedy (1917–63) US statesman.
The Observer, 'Sayings of the Week', 21 July 1963

181   We are redefining and we are restating our socialism in terms of the scientific revolution . . . the Britain that is going to be forged in the white heat of this revolution will be no place for restrictive practices or out-dated methods on either side of industry.
Harold Wilson (1916–   ) British politician and prime minister.

182   After half a century of democratic advance, the whole process has ground to a halt with a 14th Earl.
Harold Wilson
Speech, Manchester, 19 Oct 1963
Referring to the 4th Earl of Home who, after the retirement of Harold Macmillan, was chosen to be the new prime minister by 'a process of consultation'. The Labour Party criticized him for his aristocratic background. Lord Home was foreign secretary at the time; he renounced his peerage and became Sir Alec Douglas-Home.
Speech, Labour Party Conference, 1 Oct 1963

183   As far as the 14th Earl is concerned, I suppose Mr Wilson, when you come to think of it, is the 14th Mr Wilson.
Alec Douglas-Home (1903–   ) British statesman.
TV interview, 21 Oct 1963

184   He is used to dealing with estate workers. I cannot see how anyone can say he is out of touch.
Lady Caroline Douglas-Home (1937–   )
Daughter of Alec Douglas-Home.
When asked about her father's suitability for his new role as prime minister
Daily Herald, 21 Oct 1963

185   A piece of each of us died at that moment.
Michael J. Mansfield (1903–   ) US senator.
Referring to the assassination (22 Nov 1963) of President Kennedy
Speech, Senate, 24 Nov 1963

186   Christ in this country would quite likely have been arrested under the Suppression of Communism Act.
Joost de Blank (1908–68) Dutch-born British churchman.
Referring to South Africa
The Observer, 'Sayings of the Week', 27 Oct 1963

187   I myself have become a Gaullist only little by little.
Charles De Gaulle (1890–1970) French general and statesman.
The Observer, 'Sayings of the Year', 29 Dec 1963

188   Treaties are like roses and young girls – they last while they last.
Charles De Gaulle
Attrib.

189   The great nations have always acted like gangsters, and the small nations like prostitutes.
Stanley Kubrick (1928–   ) US film director
The Guardian, 5 June 1963

190   In Western Europe there are now only small countries – those that know it and those that don't know it yet.
Théo Lefèvre (1914–73) Belgian prime minister.
Speech

191   Every communist has a fascist frown, every fascist a communist smile.
Muriel Spark (1918–   ) British novelist.
The Girls of Slender Means, Ch. 4

192   Power corrupts, but lack of power corrupts absolutely.
Adlai Stevenson (1900–65) US statesman.
Speech, Jan 1963

193   Everybody should have an equal chance – bu[they shouldn't have a flying start.
Harold Wilson (1916–   ) British politician an[prime minister.
The Observer, 'Sayings of the Year', 1963

194   All terrorists, at the invitation of the Government, end up with drinks at the Dorchester.
Hugh Gaitskell (1906–63) British Labour politician.
Letter to *The Guardian*, 23 Aug 1977 (Dora Gaitskell)

1964

195   There are two problems in my life. The politica[ones are insoluble and the economic ones are incomprehensible.
Alec Douglas-Home (1903–   ) British statesman.
Speech, Jan 1964

196   This Administration here and now declares un[conditional war on poverty in America.
Lyndon B. Johnson (1908–73) US statesman.
State of the Union message, 8 Jan 1964

197   For Hon. Members opposite the deterrent is a phallic symbol. It convinces them that they are men.
George Wigg (1900–76) British politician.
The Observer, 'Sayings of the Week', 8 Mar 1964

198   One fifth of the people are against everything all the time.
Robert Kennedy (1925–68) US politician.
Speech, May 1964

9　The great society is a place where men are more concerned with the quality of their goods than the quantity of their goods.
Lyndon B. Johnson (1908–73) US statesman.
Speech, 22 May 1964

0　I would remind you that extremism in the defence of liberty is no vice. And let me remind you also that moderation in the pursuit of justice is no virtue!
Barry Goldwater (1904–) US politician.
Speech, San Francisco, 17 July 1964

1　If the British public falls for this, I say it will be stark, staring bonkers.
Lord Hailsham (1907–) British Conservative politician.
Referring to Labour policy in the 1964 general-election campaign
Press conference, Conservative Central Office, 12 Oct 1964

2　I am going to build the kind of nation that President Roosevelt hoped for, President Truman worked for and President Kennedy died for.
Lyndon B. Johnson (1908–73) US statesman.
The Sunday Times, 27 Dec 1964

3　A Royal Commission is a broody hen sitting on a china egg.
Michael Foot (1913–) British Labour politician and journalist.
Speech, House of Commons, 1964

4　My government will protect all liberties but one – the liberty to do away with other liberties.
Gustavo Diaz Ordaz (1911–) President of Mexico (1964–1970).
Inaugural speech

5　I can honestly say that I was never affected by the question of the success of an undertaking. If I felt it was the right thing to do, I was for it regardless of the possible outcome.
Golda Meir (1898–1978) Russian-born Israeli stateswoman.
Golda Meir: Woman with a Cause (Marie Syrkin)

1965

6　The vote is the most powerful instrument ever devised by man for breaking down injustice and destroying the terrible walls which imprison men because they are different from other men.
Lyndon B. Johnson (1908–73) US statesman.
Address on signing Voting Rights Bill, Washington D.C., 6 Aug 1965

7　It is a great shock at the age of five or six to find that in a world of Gary Coopers you are the Indian.
James Baldwin (1924–87) US writer.
Speech, Cambridge Union, 17 Feb 1965

208　If only I had known, I should have become a watchmaker.
Albert Einstein (1879–1955) German-born US physicist.
Reflecting on his role in the development of the atom bomb
New Statesman, 16 Apr 1965

209　If someone puts his hand on you, send him to the cemetery.
Malcolm X (1925–65) US Black leader.
Malcolm X Speaks

210　A week is a long time in politics.
Harold Wilson (1916–) British politician and prime minister.
First said in 1965 or 1966, and repeated on several occasions
Attrib.

211　To be absolutely honest, what I feel really bad about is that I don't feel worse. There's the ineffectual liberal's problem in a nutshell.
Michael Frayn (1933–) British journalist and writer.
The Observer, 8 Aug 1965

212　I believe in the armed struggle as the only solution for those people who fight to free themselves, and I am consistent with my beliefs. Many will call me an adventurer – and that I am, only one of a different sort: one of those who risks his skin to prove his platitudes.
Che Guevara (Ernesto G.; 1928–67) Argentine revolutionary.
On leaving Cuba to join guerrillas in the Bolivian jungle
Last letter to his parents (1965)

213　Simply a radio personality who outlived his prime.
Evelyn Waugh (1903–66) British novelist.
Referring to Winston Churchill
Evelyn Waugh (Christopher Sykes)

1966

214　I respect only those who resist me; but I cannot tolerate them.
Charles De Gaulle (1890–1970) French general and statesman.
New York Times magazine, 12 May 1966

215　The House of Lords, an illusion to which I have never been able to subscribe – responsibility without power, the prerogative of the eunuch throughout the ages.
Tom Stoppard (1937–) Czech-born British dramatist.
Lord Malquist and Mr Moon, Pt. VI, Ch. 1

216　Catholics and Communists have committed great crimes, but at least they have not stood aside, like an established society, and been indifferent. I would rather have blood on my hands than water like Pilate.
Graham Greene (1904–) British novelist.
The Comedians, Pt. III, Ch. 4

1967

217　You've got to forget about this civilian. When-

ever you drop bombs, you're going to hit civilians.
Barry Goldwater (1904–) US politician.
Speech, New York, 23 Jan 1967

218 ...if there was one word I would use to identify modern socialism, it was 'Science'.
Harold Wilson (1916–) British politician and prime minister.
Speech, 17 June 1967

219 From now, the pound is worth 14 per cent or so less in terms of other currencies. It does not mean, of course, that the pound here in Britain, in your pocket or purse or in your bank, has been devalued.
Harold Wilson
Speech after devaluation of the pound, 20 Nov 1967

220 The House of Lords is like a glass of champagne that has stood for five days.
Clement Attlee (1883–1967) British statesman and Labour prime minister.
Attrib.

221 A riot is at bottom the language of the unheard.
Martin Luther King (1929–68) US Black civil-rights leader.
Chaos or Community, Ch. 4

222 Patriots always talk of dying for their country and never of killing for their country.
Bertrand Russell (1872–1970) British philosopher.
The Autobiography of Bertrand Russell

223 I was obviously destined to go down and down when in 1958 my father and brother died within ten days of each other and I became an Earl...Life is much easier, being an Earl. It has changed me a lot. I'm much nastier now.
Earl of Arran (1938–) British publisher.
The Sunday Times, 15 Jan 1967

1968

224 There are times in politics when you must be on the right side and lose.
John Kenneth Galbraith (1908–) US economist.
The Observer, 'Sayings of the Week', 11 Feb 1968

225 Communism with a human face.
Alexander Dubček (1921–) Czech statesman.
A resolution by the party group in the Ministry of Foreign Affairs, on 14 March 1968, referred to Czechoslovak foreign policy acquiring 'its own defined face'.
Attrib.

226 ...when internal and external forces that are hostile to socialism try to turn the development of some socialist country towards the restoration of a capitalist regime, when socialism in that country and the socialist community as a whole is threatened...
Leonid Brezhnev (1906–82) Soviet statesman.
The 'Brezhnev doctrine', used to justify Russia's

intervention in Czechoslovakia, stated the circumstances when Russia had a right to intervene

227 The monarchy is part of the fabric of the country. And, as the fabric alters, so the monarchy and its people's relations to it alters.
Prince Philip (1921–) The consort of Queen Elizabeth II.
Television interview, 20 Mar 1968

228 Let us begin by committing ourselves to the truth, to see it like it is and to tell it like it is, find the truth, to speak the truth and live with the truth. That's what we'll do.
Richard Milhous Nixon (1913–) US president.
Nomination acceptance speech, Miami, 8 Aug 1968

229 One of those ideas was that man was not born to go down on his belly before the state.
Alan Paton (1903–88) South African novelist.
Speech at the last meeting of the South African Liberal party, 1968; referring to the party's principles

230 I suffer from an incurable disease – colour blindness.
Joost de Blank (1908–68) Dutch-born British churchman.
Attrib.

231 As I look ahead, I am filled with foreboding. Like the Roman, I seem to see 'the River Tiber foaming with much blood'.
Enoch Powell (1912–) British politician.
Talking about the effects of immigration; Powell was quoting the Roman poet Virgil (*Aeneid*, Bk. VI)
Speech in Birmingham, 20 Apr 1968

232 Remember this, Griffin. The revolution eats its own. Capitalism re-creates itself.
Mordecai Richler (1931–) Canadian novelist.
Cocksure, Ch. 22

1969

233 That's one small step for man, one giant leap for mankind.
Neil Armstrong (1930–) US astronaut.
Said on stepping onto the moon. Often quoted as, 'small step for a man...' (which is probably what he intended)
Remark, 21 July 1969

234 This is the greatest week in the history of the world since the creation.
Richard Milhous Nixon (1913–) US president.
Said when men first landed on the moon
Attrib., 24 July 1969

235 As far as criticism is concerned, we don't resent that unless it is absolutely biased, as it is in most cases.
John Vorster (Balthazar Johannes Vorster; 1915–83) South African politician.
The Observer, 'Sayings of the Week', 9 Nov 1969

36* The coach has turned into a pumpkin and the mice have all run away.
Lady Bird Johnson (1912–) Wife of Lyndon B. Johnson.
Said after Lyndon Johnson gave up the presidency
The Vantage Point (Lyndon B. Johnson)

37 By yesterday morning British troops were patrolling the streets of Belfast. I fear that once Catholics and Protestants get used to our presence they will hate us more than they hate each other.
Richard Crossman (1907–74) British politician.
British troops were sent to Northern Ireland in 1969, originally to protect the Catholic minority
Diaries, 17 Aug 1969

38 The conventional army loses if it does not win. The guerrilla wins if he does not lose.
Henry Kissinger (1923–) German-born US politician and diplomat.
Foreign Affairs, XIII (Jan 1969), 'The Vietnam Negotiations'

39 You took my freedom away a long time ago and you can't give it back because you haven't got it yourself.
Alexander Solzhenitsyn (1918–) Soviet novelist.
The First Circle, Ch. 17

40 You only have power over people so long as you don't take *everything* away from them. But when you've robbed a man of everything he's no longer in your power – he's free again.
Alexander Solzhenitsyn
The First Circle, Ch. 17

1970s
---

41 The U.S. has broken the second rule of war. That is, don't go fighting with your land army on the mainland of Asia. Rule One is don't march on Moscow. I developed these two rules myself.
Lord Montgomery (1887–1976) British field marshal.
Referring to the Vietnam war
Montgomery of Alamein (Chalfont)

42 To win in Vietnam, we will have to exterminate a nation.
Dr Benjamin Spock (1903–) US paediatrician and psychiatrist.
Dr Spock on Vietnam, Ch.7

43 This universal, obligatory force-feeding with lies is now the most agonizing aspect of existence in our country – worse than all our material miseries, worse than any lack of civil liberties.
Alexander Solzhenitsyn (1918–) Soviet novelist.
Letter to Soviet Leaders, 6

44 If people behaved in the way nations do they would all be put in straitjackets.
Tennessee Williams (1911–83) US dramatist.
BBC interview

1970
---

245 One man's wage rise is another man's price increase.
Harold Wilson (1916–) British politician and prime minister.
The Observer, 'Sayings of the Week', 11 Jan 1970

246 The House of Lords is a perfect eventide home.
Mary Stocks (1891–1975) British politician and writer.
Remark, Oct 1970

247 It is time for the great silent majority of Americans to stand up and be counted.
Richard Milhous Nixon (1913–) US president.
Election speech, Oct 1970

248 We had no use for the policy of the Gospels: if someone slaps you, just turn the other cheek. We had shown that anyone who slapped us on our cheek would get his head kicked off.
Nikita Khrushchev (1894–1971) Soviet statesman.
Khrushchev Remembers, Vol. II

249 I have come to the conclusion that politics are too serious a matter to be left to the politicians.
Charles De Gaulle (1890–1970) French general and statesman.
Attrib.

250 In order to become the master, the politician poses as the servant.
Charles De Gaulle
Attrib.

1971
---

251 You cannot shake hands with a clenched fist.
Indira Gandhi (1917–84) Indian stateswoman.
Remark at a press conference, New Delhi, 19 Oct 1971

252 I'd much rather have that fellow inside my tent pissing out, than outside my tent pissing in.
Lyndon B. Johnson (1908–73) US statesman.
When asked why he retained J. Edgar Hoover at the FBI
Guardian Weekly, 18 Dec 1971

253 I would rather be British than just.
Ian Paisley (1926–) Northern Irish politician.
The Sunday Times, 12 Dec 1971

254 Inflation in the Sixties was a nuisance to be endured, like varicose veins or French foreign policy.
Bernard Levin (1928–) British journalist.
The Pendulum Years, 'Epilogue'

255 We intend to remain alive. Our neighbors want to see us dead. This is not a question that leaves much room for compromise.
Golda Meir (1898–1978) Russian-born Israeli stateswoman.
Reader's Digest (July 1971), 'The Indestructible Golda Meir'

256 Politics is the art of the possible.
R. A. Butler (1902–82) British Conservative
politician.
Often attrib. to Butler but used earlier by others,
including Bismarck
The Art of the Possible, Epigraph

257 I was a man who was lucky enough to have discovered a political theory, a man who was
caught up in the whirlpool of Cuba's political
crisis long before becoming a fully fledged
Communist... discovering Marxism... was
like finding a map in the forest.
Fidel Castro (1926–) Cuban statesman.
Speech, Chile, 18 Nov 1971

258 If you feed people just with revolutionary slogans they will listen today, they will listen tomorrow, they will listen the day after tomorrow,
but on the fourth day they will say 'To hell
with you!'
Nikita Khrushchev (1894–1971) Soviet
statesman.
Attrib.

1972

259 I think that everyone will conceed that – today
of all days – I should begin by saying, 'My
husband and I'.
Elizabeth II (1926–) Queen of the United
Kingdom.
On her silver wedding
Speech, Guildhall, 1972

260 Censorship is more depraving and corrupting
than anything pornography can produce.
Tony Smythe (1938–) Chairman of the National Council for Civil Liberties, Great Britain.
The Observer, 'Sayings of the Week', 18 Sept
1972

261 Nothing and no one can destroy the Chinese
people. They are relentless survivors. They are
the oldest civilized people on earth. Their civilization passes through phases but its basic
characteristics remain the same. They yield,
they bend to the wind, but they never break.
Pearl Buck (1892–1973) US novelist.
China, Past and Present, Ch. 1

262 I'm not hard – I'm frightfully soft. But I will not
be hounded.
Margaret Thatcher (1925–) British politician and prime minister.
Daily Mail, 1972

263 It's not the voting that's democracy; it's the
counting.
Tom Stoppard (1937–) Czech-born British
dramatist.
Jumpers

264 The defiance of established authority, religious
and secular, social and political, as a world-
wide phenomenon may well one day be ac-
counted the outstanding event of the last
decade.
Hannah Arendt (1906–75) German-born US
philosopher and historian.
Crises of the Republic, 'Civil Disobedience'

1973

265 No wonder Harold is back in form – every Labour politician feels more at home attacking
his own party's politics.
Referring to Harold Wilson
Cartoon caption, *Punch*, 31 Jan 1973

266 It is the unpleasant and unacceptable face of
capitalism but one should not suggest that th
whole of British industry consists of practices
of this kind.
Edward Heath (1916–) British politician ar
prime minister.
Referring to the Lonrho Affair – a scandal invol
ing financial dealings in the City
Speech, House of Commons, 15 May 1973

267 This is a very fine country to be acutely ill or
injured in, but take my advice and do not be o
and frail or mentally ill here – at least not for
a few years. This is definitely not a good coun
try to be deaf or blind in either.
Keith Joseph (1918–) British politician.
The Observer, 'Sayings of the Week', 1 July
1973

268 There will be no whitewash in the White Hous
Richard Milhous Nixon (1913–) US
president.
Referring to the Watergate scandal
Statement, 17 Apr 1973

269 I am not a crook.
Richard Milhous Nixon
Attrib., 17 Nov 1973

270* Would you buy a second-hand car from this
man?
Mort Sahl (1926–) US political comedian.
Referring to President Nixon
Attrib.

271 If sunbeams were weapons of war, we would
have had solar energy long ago.
George Porter (1920–) British chemist.
Remark, Aug 1973

272 I am MacWonder one moment and MacBlund
the next.
Harold Macmillan (1894–1986) British poli
cian and prime minister.
Daily Telegraph, 15 Nov 1973

273 A statesman is a politician who places himse
at the service of the nation. A politician is a
statesman who places the nation at his
service.
Georges Pompidou (1911–74) French
statesman.
The Observer, 'Sayings of the Year', 30 Dec
1973

274 I do not intend to prejudge the past.
William Whitelaw (1918–) British politicia
Said on arriving in Ulster as Minister for Northe
Ireland
The Times, 3 Dec 1973

275 If I had to give a definition of capitalism I wou

say: the process whereby American girls turn into American women.
Christopher Hampton (1946–) British writer and dramatist.
Savages, Sc. 16

76 A just society would be one in which liberty for one person is constrained only by the demands created by equal liberty for another.
Ivan Illich (1926–) Austrian sociologist.
Tools for Conviviality

1974

77 If you want to see the acceptable face of capitalism, go out to an oil rig in the North Sea.
Edward Heath (1916–) British politician.
Speech, Edinburgh, 18 Feb 1974

78 We are all the President's men.
Henry Kissinger (1923–) German-born US politician and diplomat.
Said regarding the invasion of Cambodia, 1970
The Sunday Times Magazine, 4 May 1975

79 I do not mind the Liberals, still less do I mind the Country Party, calling me a bastard. In some circumstances I am only doing my job if they do. But I hope you will not publicly call me a bastard, as some bastards in the Caucus have.
Gough Whitlam (1916–) Australian statesman.
Speech to the Australian Labor Party, 9 June 1974

80 President Nixon's motto was, if two wrongs don't make a right, try three.
Norman Cousins (1915–) US editor and author.
Daily Telegraph, 17 July 1979

81 Our long national nightmare is over. Our constitution works.
Gerald Ford (1913–) US president.
On being sworn in as President after the resignation of Richard Nixon
Speech, 9 Aug 1974

82 It will be years – and not in my time – before a woman will lead the party or become Prime Minister.
Margaret Thatcher (1925–) British politician and prime minister.
Said when she was minister for health
Speech, 1974

83 The charm of Britain has always been the ease with which one can move into the middle class.
Margaret Thatcher
Speech, Oct 1974

84 In our country the lie has become not just a moral category but a pillar of the State.
Alexander Solzhenitsyn (1918–) Soviet novelist.
The Observer, 'Sayings of the Year', 29 Dec 1974

85 A committee is an animal with four back legs.
John Le Carré (1931–) British writer.
Tinker, Tailor, Soldier, Spy

1975

286 This going into Europe will not turn out to be the thrilling mutual exchange supposed. It is more like nine middle-aged couples with failing marriages meeting in a darkened bedroom in a Brussels hotel for a Group Grope.
E. P. Thompson (1924–) British historian.
On the Europe debate, *Sunday Times*, 27 Apr 1975

287 Television brought the brutality of war into the comfort of the living room. Vietnam was lost in the living rooms of America – not on the battlefields of Vietnam.
Marshall McLuhan (1911–81) Canadian sociologist.
Montreal *Gazette*, 16 May 1975

288 There exists no politician in India daring enough to attempt to explain to the masses that cows can be eaten.
Indira Gandhi (1917–84) Indian stateswoman.
New York Review of Books, 'Indira's Coup' (Oriana Fallaci)

289 To bear many children is considered not only a religious blessing but also an investment. The greater their number, some Indians reason, the more alms they can beg.
Indira Gandhi
New York Review of Books, 'Indira's Coup' (Oriana Fallaci)

290 I believe the greatest asset a head of state can have is the ability to get a good night's sleep.
Harold Wilson (1916–) British politician and prime minister.
The World Tonight, BBC Radio, 16 Apr 1975

291 We are not just here to manage capitalism but to change society and to define its finer values.
Tony Benn (1925–) British politician.
Speech, Labour Party Conference, 1 Oct 1975

292 It might be said that it is the ideal of the employer to have production without employees and the ideal of the employee is to have income without work.
E. F. Schumacher (1911–77) German-born economist.
The Observer, 'Sayings of the Week', 4 May 1975

293 War is capitalism with the gloves off.
Tom Stoppard (1937–) Czech-born British dramatist.
Travesties

294 Let our children grow tall, and some taller than others if they have it in them to do so.
Margaret Thatcher (1925–) British politician and prime minister.
Speech, US tour, 1975

295 We cannot remove the evils of capitalism without taking its source of power: ownership.
Neil Kinnock (1942–) British politician.
Tribune, 1975

296 The ship follows Soviet custom: it is riddled

with class distinctions so subtle, it takes a
trained Marxist to appreciate them.
Paul Theroux (1941–) US-born writer.
The Great Railway Bazaar, Ch. 30

297   Britain is not a country that is easily rocked by
revolution . . . In Britain our institutions evolve.
We are a Fabian Society writ large.
William Hamilton (1917–) Scottish MP.
My Queen and I, Ch. 9

1976

298   This is a rotten argument, but it should be good
enough for their lordships on a hot summer
afternoon.
Anonymous
A note on a ministerial brief read out by mistake
in the House of Lords
The Way the Wind Blows (Lord Home)

299   I don't believe in black majority rule ever in
Rhodesia . . . not in a thousand years.
Ian Smith (1919–) Rhodesian (Zimbabwe)
politician.
Speech, Mar 1976

300   Britain has lived for too long on borrowed time,
borrowed money and even borrowed ideas.
James Callaghan (1912–) British politician
and prime minister.
The Observer, 'Sayings of the Week', 3 Oct
1976

301   A lie can be half-way round the world before
the truth has got its boots on.
James Callaghan
Speech, 1 Nov 1976

302   Power is the ultimate aphrodisiac.
Henry Kissinger (1923–) German-born US
politician and diplomat.
The Guardian, 28 Nov 1976

303   In so far as socialism means anything, it must
be about the wider distribution of smoked
salmon and caviar.
Richard Marsh (1928–) British
businessman.
Remark, Oct 1976

304   There comes a time in every man's life when he
must make way for an older man.
Reginald Maudling (1917–77) British
politician.
Remark made on being replaced in the shadow
cabinet by John Davies, his elder by four years
The Guardian, 20 Nov 1976

305   You cannot control a free society by force.
Robert Mark (1917–) British police
commissioner.
The Observer, 'Sayings of the Week', 25 July
1976

306   We thus denounce the false and dangerous
programme of the arms race, of the secret rivalry between peoples for military
superiority.
John Paul II (Karol Wojtyla; 1920–) Polish
pope (1978–).
Speech, Dec 1976

307   The Iron Lady of British politics is seeking to
revive the cold war.
Commenting on a speech by Margaret Thatcher
Red Star, 23 Jan 1976

308   Margaret Thatcher's great strength seems to be
the better people know her, the better they
like her. But, of course, she has one great disadvantage – she is a daughter of the people
and looks trim, as the daughters of the people
desire to be. Shirley Williams has such an
advantage over her because she's a member of
the upper-middle class and can achieve that
kitchen-sink-revolutionary look that one cannot
get unless one has been to a really good
school.
Rebecca West (Cicely Isabel Fairfield; 1892–
1983) British novelist and journalist.
Said in an interview with Jilly Cooper
The Sunday Times, 25 July 1976

309   Once, when a British Prime Minister sneezed,
men half a world away would blow their
noses. Now when a British Prime Minister
sneezes nobody else will even say 'Bless You'.
Bernard Levin (1928–) British journalist.
The Times, 1976

1977

310   I let down my friends, I let down my country. I
let down our system of government.
Richard Milhous Nixon (1913–) US
president.
The Observer, 'Sayings of the Week', 8 May
1977

311   I have come to regard the law courts not as a
cathedral but rather as a casino.
Richard Ingrams (1937–) British editor.
The Guardian, 30 July 1977

312   Whenever you accept our views we shall be in
full agreement with you.
Moshe Dayan (1915–81) Israeli general.
Said to Cyrus Vance during Arab-Israeli
negotiations
The Observer, 'Sayings of the Week', 14 Aug
1977

313   As the Prime Minister put it to me . . . he saw
his role as being that of Moses.
Peter Jay (1937–) British economist and
broadcaster.
Referring to a conversation with James
Callaghan
Guardian Weekly, 18 Sept 1977

314   Parliament is the longest running farce in the
West End.
Cyril Smith (1928–) British Liberal politician.
The Times, 23 Sept 1977

315   Either back us or sack us.
James Callaghan (1912–) British politician
and prime minister.
Speech, Labour Party Conference, Brighton, 5
Oct 1977

316   All political lives, unless they are cut off in mid
stream at a happy juncture, end in failure.
Enoch Powell (1912–) British politician.
Sunday Times, 6 Nov 1977

17 Britain is no longer in the politics of the pendulum, but of the ratchet.
Margaret Thatcher (1925–) British politician and prime minister.
Speech, Institute of Public Relations, 1977

18 Much of the world's work, it has been said, is
done by men who do not feel quite well. Marx
is a case in point.
John Kenneth Galbraith (1908–) US
economist.
The Age of Uncertainty, Ch. 3

1978

19 Like being savaged by a dead sheep.
Denis Healey (1917–) British Labour
politician.
Referring to the attack launched by Geoffrey
Howe upon his Budget proposals
The Listener, 21 Dec 1978

20 Of course they have, or I wouldn't be sitting
here talking to someone like you.
Barbara Cartland (1902–) British romantic
novelist.
When asked in a radio interview whether she
thought that British class barriers had broken
down
Class (J. Cooper)

21 Not every problem someone has with his girl-
friend is necessarily due to the capitalist
mode of production.
Herbert Marcuse (1898–1979) German-born
US philosopher.
The Listener

1979

22 I don't think that other people in the world
would share the view that there is mounting
chaos.
James Callaghan (1912–) British politician
and prime minister.
Referring to increasing industrial unrest in Britain;
generally misquoted as 'Crisis? What crisis?'
Remark, 10 Jan 1979

23 British management doesn't seem to understand the importance of the human factor.
Charles, Prince of Wales (1948–) Eldest
son of Elizabeth II.
*Speech, Parliamentary and Scientific Committee
lunch, 21 Feb 1979*

24 As a military man who has given half a century
of active service, I say in all sincerity that the
nuclear arms race has no military purpose.
Wars cannot be fought with nuclear weapons;
their existence only adds to our perils because of the illusions which they have
generated.
Earl Mountbatten of Burma (1900–79) British admiral and statesman.
Speech, Strasbourg, 11 May 1979

25 We are unable to influence events in the way

we want because we do not have the power
or will to do so.
Nicholas Henderson (1919–) British
diplomat.
Referring to Britain; written on ceasing to be ambassador to France
*Letter to the foreign secretary, David Owen,
1979*

326 And I don't feel the attraction of the Kennedys
at all . . . I don't think they are Christians; they
may be Catholics but they are not Christians,
in my belief anyway.
Mary McCarthy (1912–) US novelist.
The Observer, 14 Oct 1979

327 I am a socialist – and I only wish the Labour
Party was.
Donald Soper (1903–) British Methodist
Minister and writer.
Any Questions (radio programme), 11 May 1979

328 For us in Russia communism is a dead dog,
while, for many people in the West, it is still a
living lion.
Alexander Solzhenitsyn (1918–) Soviet
novelist.
The Listener, 15 Feb 1979

329 Any woman who understands the problems of
running a home will be nearer to understanding the problems of running a country.
Margaret Thatcher (1925–) British politician and prime minister.
The Observer, 8 May 1979

330 She is trying to wear the trousers of Winston
Churchill.
Leonid Brezhnev (1906–82) Soviet
statesman.
Referring to Margaret Thatcher
Speech, 1979

331 Margaret Thatcher is David Owen in drag.
The Rhodesia Herald, 8 Aug 1979

1980

332 It is difficult to go on strike if there is no work
in the first place.
Lord George-Brown (1914–85) British
statesman.
The Observer, 24 Feb 1980

333 The British civil service . . . is a beautifully
designed and effective braking mechanism.
Shirley Williams (1930–) British politician.
*Speech, Royal Institute of Public Administration,
11 Feb 1980*

334 She is the Enid Blyton of economics. Nothing
must be allowed to spoil her simple plots.
Richard Holme (1936–) British campaigner
for electoral reform.
Referring to Margaret Thatcher
Speech, Liberal Party Conference, 10 Sept 1980

335 I love argument, I love debate. I don't expect
anyone just to sit there and agree with me,
that's not their job.
Margaret Thatcher (1925–) British politician and prime minister.
The Times, 1980

336   If a woman like Eva Peron with no ideals can
      get that far, think how far I can go with all the
      ideals that I have.
      Margaret Thatcher
      The Sunday Times, 1980

337   U-turn if you want to. The lady's not for turning.
      Margaret Thatcher
      Speech, Conservative Conference, 1980

338   She is clearly the best man among them.
      Barbara Castle (1910–   ) British politician.
      Referring to Margaret Thatcher
      The Castle Diaries

339   You can tell a British workman by his hands.
      They are always in his pockets.
      Anonymous
      Quote Unquote (radio programme), 26 June
      1980

340   Voodoo economics.
      George Bush (1924–   ) US statesman.
      Referring to Ronald Reagan's economic policies
      Remark during the 1980 presidential election
      campaign

341   Like the sorry tapping of Neville Chamberlain's
      umbrella on the cobblestones of Munich.
      Ronald Reagan (1911–   ) US politician and
      president.
      Referring to President Carter's foreign policy

342* The monarchy is the oldest profession in the
      world.
      Charles, Prince of Wales (1948–   ) Eldest
      son of Elizabeth II.
      Attrib.

1981

343   Marxism is like a classical building that fol-
      lowed the Renaissance; beautiful in its way, but
      incapable of growth.
      Harold Macmillan (1894–1986) British politi-
      cian and prime minister.
      Speech to the Primrose League, 29 Apr 1981

344   The House of Lords is a model of how to care
      for the elderly.
      Frank Field (1942–   ) British politician.
      The Observer, 24 May 1981

345   My advice was delicately poised between the
      cliché and the indiscretion.
      Robert Runcie (1921–   ) British churchman
      (Archbishop of Canterbury).
      Comment to the press concerning his advice to
      the Prince of Wales and Lady Diana Spencer
      on their approaching wedding, 13 July 1981

346   I know all about these problems. I grew up in
      the thirties with an unemployed father. He
      didn't riot. He got on his bike and looked for
      work. And he found it!
      Norman Tebbitt (1931–   ) British Conserva-
      tive politician.
      Speech, Conservative Party conference, 1981

347   I have never understood why one's affections

must be confined, as once with women, to a
single country.
John Kenneth Galbraith (1908–   ) US
economist.
A Life in our Times

348   I have always said about Tony that he imma-
      tures with age.
      Harold Wilson (1916–   ) British politician and
      prime minister.
      Referring to Anthony Wedgwood Benn
      The Chariot of Israel

349   A triumph of the embalmer's art.
      Gore Vidal (1925–   ) US novelist.
      Referring to Ronald Reagan
      The Observer, 26 Apr 1981

1982

350   Giz a job.
      Alan Bleasdale
      Said by his character Yosser Hughes
      Boys From the Blackstuff

351   The British won't fight.
      Leopoldo Galtieri (1924–   ) President of
      Argentina.
      Referring to the Falklands crisis
      Remark to Alexander Haig, US Secretary of
      State, 10 Apr 1982

352   We have suffered the inevitable consequence
      of a combination of unpreparedness and fee-
      ble counsel.
      Julian Amery (1919–   ) British Conservative
      politician.
      Referring to Argentina's seizure of the Falkland
      Islands
      Speech, House of Commons, 3 Apr 1982

353   The *Daily Mirror* does not believe that patriot-
      ism had to be proved in blood. Especially
      someone else's blood.
      Referring to the Falklands War
      The Daily Mirror, Apr 1982

354   For the past few months she has been charging
      about like some bargain-basement Boadicea.
      Denis Healey (1917–   ) British Labour
      politician.
      Referring to Margaret Thatcher
      Observer, 'Sayings of the Week', 7 Nov 1982

355   War should belong to the tragic past, to his-
      tory: it should find no place on humanity's
      agenda for the future.
      John Paul II (Karol Wojtyla; 1920–   ) Polish
      pope (1978–   ).
      Speech, Coventry, 30 May 1982

356   Members rise from CMG (known sometimes in
      Whitehall as 'Call me God') to the KCMG
      ('Kindly Call me God') to ... The GCMG ('God
      Calls me God').
      Anthony Sampson (1926–   ) British writer
      and journalist.
      Anatomy of Britain, Ch. 18

57 **Let no one expect us to disarm unilaterally. We are not a naive people.**
Yuri Andropov (1914–83) Soviet statesman and president.
Speech, Central Committee of the Soviet Communist Party, 22 Nov 1982

58 **In politics, if you want anything said, ask a man; if you want anything done, ask a woman.**
Margaret Thatcher (1925–) British politician and prime minister.
The Changing Anatomy of Britain (Anthony Sampson)

59 **Victorian values . . . were the values when our country became great.**
Margaret Thatcher
Television interview, 1982

60 **We have to believe in free will. We've got no choice.**
Isaac Bashevis Singer (1904–) Polish-born US writer.
The Times, 21 June 1982

1983

61 **Those who prate about Blimpish patriotism in the mode of Margaret Thatcher are also the ones who will take millions off the caring services of this country.**
Neil Kinnock (1942–) British politician.
Speech, Labour Party Conference, Brighton, 1983

62 **Proportional Representation, I think, is fundamentally counter-democratic.**
Neil Kinnock
Marxism Today, 1983

63 **It is inconceivable that we could transform this society without a major extension of public ownership.**
Neil Kinnock
Marxism Today, 1983

64* **She has no imagination and that means no compassion.**
Michael Foot (1913–) British Labour politician and journalist.
Referring to Margaret Thatcher
Attrib.

65 **I am painted as the greatest little dictator, which is ridiculous – you always take some consultations.**
Margaret Thatcher (1925–) British politician and prime minister.
The Times, 1983

66 **Oh. I have got lots of human weaknesses, who hasn't?**
Margaret Thatcher
The Times, 1983

67 **And what a prize we have to fight for: no less than the chance to banish from our land the dark divisive clouds of Marxist socialism.**
Margaret Thatcher
Speech, Scottish Conservative Conference, 1983

368 **We are the true peace movement.**
Margaret Thatcher
The Times, 1983

369 **State socialism is totally alien to the British character.**
Margaret Thatcher
The Times, 1983

370 **Down South where I come from you don't go around hitting too many white keys.**
Eubie Blake (1883–1983) US pianist and ragtime composer.
When asked why his compositions contained so many sharps and flats
Attrib.

1984

371 **Young people ought not to be idle. It is very bad for them.**
Margaret Thatcher (1925–) British politician and prime minister.
The Times, 1984

1985

372 **Politics come from man. Mercy, compassion and justice come from God.**
Terry Waite (1939–) British churchman.
The Observer, 'Sayings of the Week', 13 Jan 1985

373 **I cannot and will not give any undertaking at a time when I, and you, the people, are not free. Your freedom and mine cannot be separated.**
Nelson Mandela (1918–) South African lawyer and politician.
Message read by his daughter to a rally in Soweto, 10 Feb 1985

374 **We don't want apartheid liberalized. We want it dismantled. You can't improve something that is intrinsically evil.**
Desmond Tutu (1931–) South African clergyman.
Speech, Mar 1985

375 **Go back to your constituencies and prepare for government!**
David Steel (1938–) British politician.
Speech to party conference, 1985

376 **The grotesque chaos of a Labour council – a *Labour* council – hiring taxis to scuttle around a city handing out redundancy notices to its own workers.**
Neil Kinnock (1942–) British politician.
Referring to Liverpool City Council
Speech, Labour Party Conference, Bournemouth, 1985

377 **I'm not interested in the bloody system! Why has he no food? Why is he starving to death?**
Bob Geldof (1952–) Irish rock musician.
Interview, Oct 1985

378 **Without class differences, England would cease to be the living theatre it is.**
Anthony Burgess (John Burgess Wilson; 1917–) British novelist.
Remark, May 1985

1986

379   Democracy is the wholesome and pure air without which a socialist public organisation cannot live a full-blooded life.
Mikhail Gorbachov (1931–   ) Soviet statesman.
Report to 27th Party Congress Speech, 25 Feb, 1986

380   No one can kill Americans and brag about it. No one.
Ronald Reagan (1911–   ) US politician and president.
Remark, Apr 1986

381   It seems that the British Government sees black people as expendable.
Desmond Tutu (1931–   ) South African clergyman.
Speech, June 1986

382   Irish Americans are about as Irish as Black Americans are African.
Bob Geldof (1952–   ) Irish rock musician.
The Observer, 'Sayings of the Week', 22 Jun 1986

383   Preparing for suicide is not a very intelligent means of defence.
Bruce Kent (1929–   ) British campaigner for nuclear disarmament.
Speech, Aug 1986

384   The thing I value about Wales and Welsh background is that it has always been a genuinely more classless society than many people present England as being.
Geoffrey Howe (1926–   ) British politician.
Remark, Nov 1986

385   There are three groups that no prime minister should provoke: the Treasury, the Vatican, and the National Union of Mineworkers.
Harold Macmillan (1894–1986) British politician and prime minister.
First used by Stanley Baldwin
Attrib.

386   It was on this issue, the nuclear defence of Britain, on which I left the Labour Party, and on this issue I am prepared to stake my entire political career.
David Owen (1938–   ) British politician.
Speech, Nov 1986

387   The idea that there is a model Labour voter, a blue-collar council house tenant who belongs to a union and has 2.4 children, a five-year-old car and a holiday in Blackpool, is patronizing and politically immature.
Neil Kinnock (1942–   ) British politician.
Speech, 1986

388   Selling the family silver.
Harold Macmillan (1894–1986) British politician and prime minister.
Referring to privatization of profitable nationalized industries
Speech, House of Lords, 1986

1987

389   I would die for my country . . . but I would no let my country die for me.
Neil Kinnock (1942–   ) British politician.
Speech on nuclear disarmament, 1987

390   She only went to Venice because somebody told her she could walk down the middle of th street.
Neil Kinnock
Referring to Margaret Thatcher, who attended meeting in Venice just before the 1987 election
Speech, Leeds, 9 June 1987

391   Above any other position of eminence, that of Prime Minister is filled by fluke.
Enoch Powell (1912–   ) British politician.
Remark, Mar 1987

392   I don't mind how much my ministers talk – a long as they do what I say.
Margaret Thatcher (1925–   ) British politician and prime minister.
The Times, 1987

393   I am certain that we will win the election with good majority. Not that I am ever overconfident.
Margaret Thatcher
Evening Standard, 1987

394   I bear no ill-will against those responsible for this. That sort of talk will not bring her back t life. I know there has to be a plan even though we might not understand it. God is good and we shall meet again.
Gordon Wilson Retired businessman.
Speaking of the murder of his daughter, Marie Wilson, in an IRA bombing at the Enniskillen Re membrance Day service, 8 Nov 1987

395   Some comrades apparently find it hard to un derstand that democracy is just a slogan.
Mikhail Gorbachov (1931–   ) Soviet statesman.
The Observer, 'Sayings of the Week', 1 Feb 1987

396   Only socialism would put up with it for so lon Capitalism would have gone bankrupt years ago.
Mikhail Gorbachov
Talking of sub-standard workmanship in the So viet Union
TV documentary, 23 March 1987

397   The essence of perestroika lies in the fact tha it unites socialism with democracy and revives the feminist concept of socialist construction both in theory and in practice.
Mikhail Gorbachov
Perestroika

398   Our rockets can find Halley's comet and fly t Venus with amazing accuracy, but side by side with these scientific and technical triumphs is an obvious lack of efficiency in usin scientific achievements for economic needs, and many Soviet household appliances are of poor quality.
Mikhail Gorbachov
Perestroika

399 And if the Russian word 'perestroika' has easily entered the international lexicon, this is due to more than just interest in what is going on in the Soviet Union. Now the whole world needs restructuring i.e. progressive development, a fundamental change.
Mikhail Gorbachov
Perestroika

1988

400 The spread of personal ownership is in harmony with the deepest instincts of the British people. Few changes have done more to create one nation.
Nigel Lawson (1932–) British politician.
Speech, Jan 1988

401 Everything that is most beautiful in Britain has always been in private hands.
Malcolm Rifkind (1946–) British politician.
The Observer, 'Sayings of the Week', 17 Jan 1988

402 It seems that the historic inability in Britain to comprehend Irish feelings and sensitivities still remains.
Charles Haughey (1925–) Irish statesman.
Speech, Feb 1988

403 The United States is the best and fairest and most decent nation on the face of the earth.
George Bush (1924–) US statesman.
Speech, May 1988

404 The worst fault of the working classes is telling their children they're not going to succeed, saying: "There is a life, but it's not for you".
John Mortimer (1923–) British lawyer and dramatist.
The Observer, 'Sayings of the Week', 5 June 1988

405 You don't have power if you surrender all your principles – you have office.
Ron Todd Trade union leader.
Remark, June 1988

406 The Soviet people want full-blooded and unconditional democracy.
Mikhail Gorbachov (1931–) Soviet statesman.
Speech, July 1988

407 Sanctions are now the only feasible, non-violent way of ending apartheid. The other road to change is covered with blood.
Neil Kinnock (1942–) British politician.
Speech, July 1988

Attitudes

Art, Literature, and Music

1946

408 To be a poet is a condition rather than a profession.
Robert Graves (1895–1985) British poet and novelist.
Horizon

1947

409 A work of art has an author and yet, when it is perfect, it has something which is anonymous about it.
Simone Weil (1909–43) French philosopher.
Gravity and Grace

410 Imagination and fiction make up more than three quarters of our real life.
Simone Weil
Gravity and Grace

1948

411 The idea that it is necessary to go to a university in order to become a successful writer, or even a man or woman of letters (which is by no means the same thing), is one of those phantasies that surround authorship.
Vera Brittain (1893–1970) British writer and feminist.
On Being an Author, Ch. 2

412 The metaphor is probably the most fertile power possessed by man.
José Ortega y Gasset (1883–1955) Spanish philosopher.
The Dehumanization of Art

1949

413 Art is the only thing that can go on mattering once it has stopped hurting.
Elizabeth Bowen (1899–1973) Irish novelist.
The Heat of the Day, Ch. 16

414 Authors are easy to get on with – if you're fond of children.
Michael Joseph (1897–1958) British publisher.
The Observer, 1949

1950s

415 It's either easy or impossible.
Salvador Dali (1904–) Spanish painter.
Reply when asked if he found it hard to paint a picture
Attrib.

1950

416 Poetry is the language in which man explores his own amazement.
Christopher Fry (1907–) British dramatist.
Time, 3 Apr 1950

417 The poet gives us his essence, but prose takes the mould of the body and mind entire.
Virginia Woolf (1882–1941) British novelist.
The Captain's Death Bed, 'Reading'

1951

418 Photography can never grow up if it imitates some other medium. It has to walk alone; it has to be itself.
Berenice Abbott (1898–) US photographer.
Infinity, 'It Has to Walk Alone'

419 A writer's ambition should be to trade a hundred contemporary readers for ten readers in ten years' time and for one reader in a hundred years' time.
Arthur Koestler (1905–83) Hungarian-born British writer.
New York Times Book Review, 1 Apr 1951

1952

420 We participate in a tragedy; at a comedy we only look.
Aldous Huxley (1894–1964) British novelist.
The Devils of Loudon, Ch. 11

421 If people dug up the remains of this civilization a thousand years hence, and found Epstein's statues and that man Ellis, they would think we were just savages.
Doris Lessing (1919–) British novelist.
Martha Quest, Pt. I, Ch. 1

422 In recommending a book to a friend the less said the better. The moment you praise a book too highly you awaken resistance in your listener.
Henry Miller (1891–1980) US novelist.
The Books In My Life

1953

423 Literature is the orchestration of platitudes.
Thornton Wilder (1897–1975) US novelist and dramatist.
Time magazine

1954

424* These poems, with all their crudities, doubts, and confusions, are written for the love of Man and in praise of God, and I'd be a damn' fool if they weren't.
Dylan Thomas (1914–53) Welsh poet.
Collected Poems, Note

425 My poems are hymns of praise to the glory of life.
Edith Sitwell (1887–1964) British poet and writer.
Collected Poems, 'Some Notes on My Poetry'

1955

426* I do not know whether he draws a line himself. But I assume that his is the direction . . . It makes Disney the most significant figure in graphic art since Leonardo.
David Low (1871–1963) New-Zealand-born newspaper cartoonist.
Walt Disney (R. Schickel), Ch. 20

427 The public doesn't want new music: the main thing it demands of a composer is that he be dead.
Arthur Honegger (1892–1955) French composer.
Attrib.

428 I do not mind what language an opera is sung in so long as it is a language I don't understand.
Edward Appleton (1892–1965) British physicist.
The Observer, 'Sayings of the Week,' 28 Aug 1955

1956

429 Why should people go out and pay money to see bad films when they can stay at home and see bad television for nothing?
Samuel Goldwyn (Samuel Goldfish; 1882–1974) Polish-born US film producer.
The Observer, 'Sayings of the Week', 9 Sept 1956

430 Thanks to words, we have been able to rise above the brutes; and thanks to words, we have often sunk to the level of the demons.
Aldous Huxley (1894–1964) British novelist.
Adonis and the Alphabet

1957

431 Farce is the essential theatre. Farce refined becomes high comedy: farce brutalized becomes tragedy.
Gordon Craig (1872–1966) British actor.
The Story of my Days

432 A good many inconveniences attend play-going in any large city, but the greatest of them is usually the play itself.
Kenneth Tynan (1927–80) British theatre critic.
New York Herald Tribune

433 The poet is the priest of the invisible.
Wallace Stevens (1879–1955) US poet.
Opus Posthumous, 'Adagio'

434 . . . any authentic work of art must start an argument between the artist and his audience.
Rebecca West (Cicely Isabel Fairfield; 1892–1983) British novelist and journalist.
The Court and the Castle, Pt. I, Ch. 1

1958

5 The notes I handle no better than many pianists. But the pauses between the notes – ah, that is where the art resides.
Artur Schnabel (1882–1951) Austrian concert pianist.
Chicago Daily News, 11 June 1958

1960s

6 In England, pop art and fine art stand resolutely back to back.
Colin MacInnes (1914–76) British novelist.
England, Half English, 'Pop Songs and Teenagers'

7 Shakespeare – the nearest thing in incarnation to the eye of God.
Laurence Olivier (1907–) British actor.
Kenneth Harris Talking To, 'Sir Laurence Olivier'

8 Better to write for yourself and have no public, than write for the public and have no self.
Cyril Connolly (1903–74) British journalist.
Turnstile One (ed. V. S. Pritchett)

9 Since Mozart's day composers have learned the art of making music throatily and palpitatingly sexual.
Aldous Huxley (1894–1964) British novelist.
Along the Road, 'Popular music'

0 Get stewed:
Books are a load of crap.
Philip Larkin (1922–85) British poet.
A Study of Reading Habits

1960

1 Music was invented to confirm human loneliness.
Lawrence Durrell (1912–) British novelist.
Clea

2 Would you allow your wife or your servant to read this book?
Mervyn Griffith-Jones (1909–78) British lawyer.
As counsel for the prosecution in the *Lady Chatterley's Lover* trial

1961

3 More to the point, would you allow your gamekeeper to read it?
Anonymous
Referring to Mervyn Griffiths-Jones' remark during the *Lady Chatterley's Lover* trial

4 *Lady Chatterley's Lover* is a book that all Christians might read with profit.
John Robinson (1919–83) Bishop of Woolwich.
Said in the court case against Penguin Books
Attrib.

5 A novel is a static thing that one moves through; a play is a dynamic thing that moves past one.
Kenneth Tynan (1927–80) British theatre critic.
Curtains

446 William Congreve is the only sophisticated playwright England has produced; and like Shaw, Sheridan, and Wilde, his nearest rivals, he was brought up in Ireland.
Kenneth Tynan
Curtains, 'The Way of the World'

447 No good opera plot can be sensible, for people do not sing when they are feeling sensible.
W. H. Auden (1907–73) British poet.
Time, 29 Dec 1961

448 My music is best understood by children and animals.
Igor Stravinsky (1882–1971) Russian-born US composer.
The Observer, 'Sayings of the Week', 8 Oct 1961

1962

449 You know, I go to the theatre to be entertained ... I don't want to see plays about rape, sodomy and drug addiction ... I can get all that at home.
Peter Cook (1937–) British writer and entertainer.
The Observer, caption to cartoon, 8 July 1962

450 If Botticelli were alive today he'd be working for *Vogue*.
Peter Ustinov (1921–) British actor.
Remark, Oct 1962

1963

451 In free society art is not a weapon ... Artists are not engineers of the soul.
John Fitzgerald Kennedy (1917–63) US statesman.
Address at Dedication of the Robert Frost Library, 26 Oct 1963

452 When power narrows the areas of man's concern, poetry reminds him of the richness and diversity of his existence.
John Fitzgerald Kennedy
Address at Dedication of the Robert Frost Library, 26 Oct 1963

453 The reason why Absurdist plays take place in No Man's Land with only two characters is primarily financial.
Arthur Adamov (1908–70) Russian-born French dramatist.
Said at the Edinburgh International Drama Conference, 13 Sept 1963

454 I wanted a play that would paint the full face of sensuality, rebellion and revivalism. In South Wales these three phenomena have played second fiddle only to the Rugby Union which is a distillation of all three.
Gwyn Thomas (1913–1981) British writer.
Jackie the Jumper (Introduction), 'Plays and Players'

1964

455 The British love permanence more than they
love beauty.
Hugh Casson (1910–   ) British architect.
The Observer, 'Sayings of the Week', 14 June
1964

456 The remarkable thing about Shakespeare is that
he is really very good – in spite of all the people who say he is very good.
Robert Graves (1895–1985) British poet and
novelist.
Remark, Dec 1964

1965

457 Literature is mostly about having sex and not
much about having children; life is the other
way round.
David Lodge (1935–   ) British author.
The British Museum is Falling Down, Ch. 4

1966

458 Poetry is as much a part of the universe as
mathematics and physics. It is not a cleverer
device or recreation, unless the Eternal is
clever.
Edmund Blunden (1896–1974) British poet.
Speech on his election as Professor of Poetry at
Oxford University, 1966

459 I put the words down and push them a bit.
Evelyn Waugh (1903–66) British novelist.
Obituary, *New York Times*, 11 Apr 1966

460* We're more popular than Jesus Christ now. I
don't know which will go first. Rock and roll or
Christianity.
John Lennon (1940–80) British rock musician.
The Beatles Illustrated Lyrics

1968

461 Musicians don't retire; they stop when there's
no more music in them.
Louis Armstrong (1900–71) US jazz
trumpeter.
The Observer, 'Sayings of the Week', 21 Apr
1968

462 The novel being dead, there is no point to writing made-up stories. Look at the French who
will not and the Americans who cannot.
Gore Vidal (1925–   ) US novelist.
Myra Breckinridge, Ch. 2

1969

463 One cannot assess in terms of cash or exports
and imports an imponderable thing like the
turn of a lane or an inn or a church tower or a
familiar skyline.
John Betjeman (1906–84) British poet.
On siting a new London airport at Wing.
Remark, July 1969

464 We all write poems; it is simply that poets are
the ones who write in words.
John Fowles (1926–   ) British novelist.
The French Lieutenant's Woman, Ch. 19

465 A novelist who writes nothing for 10 years finds
his reputation rising. Because I keep on producing books they say there must be something wrong with this fellow.
J. B. Priestley (1894–1984) British novelist.
Remark, Sept 1969

466 No regime has ever loved great writers, only
minor ones.
Alexander Solzhenitsyn (1918–   ) Soviet
novelist.
The First Circle, Ch. 57

467 Their teacher had advised them not to read Tolstoy novels, because they were very long and
would easily confuse the clear ideas which
they had learned from reading critical studies
of him.
Alexander Solzhenitsyn
The First Circle, Ch. 40

1970s

468 The basic difference between classical music
and jazz is that in the former the music is always greater than its performance – whereas
the way jazz is performed is always more
important than what is being played.
André Previn (1929–   ) German-born
conductor.
An Encyclopedia of Quotations about Music
(Nat Shapiro)

1970

469 I'd say award winning plays are written only for
the critics.
Lew Grade (Lewis Winogradsky; 1906–   )
British film and TV producer.
The Observer, 'Sayings of the Week', 18 Oct
1970

1972

470 I have nothing to say, I am saying it, and that is
poetry.
John Cage (1912–   ) US composer.
In *The Sunday Times* (quoted by Cyril Connolly,
10 Sept 1972

471 No one really understood music unless he was
a scientist, her father had declared, and not
just a scientist, either, oh, no, only the real
ones, the theoreticians, whose language
was mathematics.
Pearl Buck (1892–1973) US novelist.
The Goddess Abides, Pt. I

472 Skill without imagination is craftsmanship and
gives us many useful objects such as wicker-
work picnic baskets. Imagination without skill
gives us modern art.
Tom Stoppard (1937–   ) Czech-born British
dramatist.
Artist Descending a Staircase

1973

473 I paint objects as I think them, not as I see them.
Pablo Picasso (1881–1973) Spanish painter.
Attrib.

474* Painting is a blind man's profession. He paints not what he sees, but what he feels, what he tells himself about what he has seen.
Pablo Picasso
Journals (Jean Cocteau), 'Childhood'

475 The object of art is to give life a shape.
Jean Anouilh (1910–87) French dramatist.
The Rehearsal

476 Rehearsing a play is making the word flesh. Publishing a play is reversing the process.
Peter Shaffer (1926–) British dramatist.
Equus, Note

477 People sometimes divide others into those you laugh at and those you laugh with. The young Auden was someone you could laugh-at-with.
Stephen Spender (1909–) British poet.
Address, W. H. Auden's memorial service, Oxford, 27 Oct 1973

1974

478 All art deals with the absurd and aims at the simple. Good art speaks truth, indeed *is* truth, perhaps the only truth.
Iris Murdoch (1919–) Irish-born British novelist.
The Black Prince, 'Bradley Pearson's Foreword'

479 This music won't do. There's not enough sarcasm in it.
Samuel Goldwyn (Samuel Goldfish; 1882–1974) Polish-born US film producer.
Attrib.

480 Please write music like Wagner, only louder.
Samuel Goldwyn
Instructions to composer for movie score
Attrib.

481 Writing is like getting married. One should never commit oneself until one is amazed at one's luck.
Iris Murdoch (1919–) Irish-born British novelist.
The Black Prince, 'Bradley Pearson's Foreword'

482 Depending upon shock tactics is easy, whereas writing a good play is difficult. Pubic hair is no substitute for wit.
J. B. Priestley (1894–1984) British novelist.
Outcries and Asides

483 The greater part of critics are parasites, who, if nothing had been written, would find nothing to write.
J. B. Priestley
Outcries and Asides

1975

484 Walt Whitman who laid end to end words never

seen in each other's company before outside of a dictionary.
David Lodge (1935–) British author.
Changing Places, Ch. 5

485 I never deliberately set out to shock, but when people don't walk out of my plays I think there is something wrong.
John Osborne (1929–) British dramatist.
Remark, Jan 1975

486 People think that because a novel's invented, it isn't true. Exactly the reverse is the case. Biography and memoirs can never be wholly true, since they cannot include every conceivable circumstance of what happened. The novel can do that.
Anthony Powell (1905–) British novelist.
A Dance to the Music of Time: Hearing Secret Harmonies, Ch. 3

1976

487 Music creates order out of chaos; for rhythm imposes unanimity upon the divergent, melody imposes continuity upon the disjointed, and harmony imposes compatibility upon the incongruous.
Yehudi Menuhin (1916–) US-born British violinist.
The Sunday Times, 10 Oct 1976

488 Poetry is to prose as dancing is to walking.
John Wain (1925–) British novelist and poet.
Talk, BBC radio, 13 Jan 1976

1977

489 We were put to Dickens as children but it never quite took. That unremitting humanity soon had me cheesed off.
Alan Bennett (1934–) British playwright.
The Old Country, II

490 There are many reasons why novelists write, but they all have one thing in common – a need to create an alternative world.
John Fowles (1926–) British novelist.
The Sunday Times Magazine, 2 Oct 1977

491 Asking a working writer what he thinks about critics is like asking a lamp-post how it feels about dogs.
Christopher Hampton (1946–) British writer and dramatist.
The Sunday Times Magazine, 16 Oct 1977

492 It's not a writer's business to hold opinions.
W. B. Yeats (1865–1939) Irish poet.
Speaking to playwright, Denis Johnston
The Guardian, 5 May 1977

493 A photograph is not only an image (as a painting is an image), an interpretation of the real; it is also a trace, something directly stencilled off the real, like a footprint or a death mask.
Susan Sontag (1933–) US novelist and essayist.
On Photography

494   I doubt that art needed Ruskin any more than a moving train needs one of its passengers to shove it.
Tom Stoppard (1937–   ) Czech-born British dramatist.
Times Literary Supplement, 3 June 1977

1978

495   It is not possible for a poet to be a professional. Poetry is essentially an amateur activity.
Lord Barrington (1908–   ) British barrister and peer.
Speech, House of Lords, 23 Nov 1978

496   The cliché is dead poetry. English, being the language of an imaginative race, abounds in clichés, so that English literature is always in danger of being poisoned by its own secretions.
Gerald Brenan (Edward Fitzgerald Brenan; 1894–1987) British writer.
Thoughts in a Dry Season, 'Literature'

497   Miller is not really a writer but a non-stop talker to whom someone has given a typewriter.
Gerald Brenan
Referring to Henry Miller
Thoughts in a Dry Season, 'Literature'

498   Far too many relied on the classic formula of a beginning, a muddle, and an end.
Philip Larkin (1922–85) British poet.
Referring to modern novels
New Fiction, 15 (Jan 1978)

499   Tragedy is if I cut my finger. Comedy is if I walk into an open sewer and die.
Mel Brooks (Melvyn Kaminsky; 1926–   ) US film director.
New Yorker, 30 Oct 1978

1980

500   You see, our fingers are circumcised, which gives it a very good dexterity, you know, particularly in the pinky.
Itzhak Perlman (1945–   ) Israeli violinist.
Responding to an observation that many great violinists are Jewish
Close Encounters (M. Wallace)

1983

501   What has happened to architecture since the second world war that the only passers-by who can contemplate it without pain are those equipped with a white stick and a dog?
Bernard Levin (1928–   ) British journalist.
The Times, 1983

1985

502   Everybody writes a book too many.
Mordecai Richler (1931–   ) Canadian novelist.
The Observer, 'Sayings of the Week', 9 Jan 1985

1986

503   Like a carbuncle on the face of an old and val‐ ued friend.
Charles, Prince of Wales (1948–   ) Eldes‐ son of Elizabeth II.
Referring to a proposed modern extension to the National Gallery
Speech, 1986

1987

504   . . . a jostling scrum of office buildings so medi‐ ocre that the only way you ever remember them is by the frustration they induce – like a basketball team standing shoulder to shoul‐ der between you and the Mona Lisa.
Charles, Prince of Wales
Referring to the buildings surrounding St Paul's Cathedral
Speech, London, 1 Dec 1987

505   You have to give this much to the Luftwaffe – when it knocked down our buildings it did not replace them with anything more offensive than rubble. We did that.
Charles, Prince of Wales
The Observer, 'Sayings of the Week', 6 Dec 1987

Daily Life

1950s

506   Come, friendly bombs, and fall on Slough
It isn't fit for humans now.
There isn't grass to graze a cow
Swarm over, Death!
. . .
Come, friendly bombs, and fall on Slough
To get it ready for the plough.
The cabbages are coming now:
The earth exhales.
John Betjeman (1906–84) British poet.
Slough

1959

507   Fings Ain't Wot They Used T'Be.
Frank Norman (1931–   ) British dramatist and broadcaster.
Title of musical

1960s

508   The car has become the carapace, the protec‐ tive and aggressive shell, of urban and subur‐ ban man.
Marshall McLuhan (1911–81) Canadian sociologist.
Understanding Media, Ch. 22

1960

09 I read the newspaper avidly. It is my one form of continuous fiction.
Aneurin Bevan (1897–1960) British Labour politician.
Remark, Apr 1960

1961

10 A good newspaper, I suppose, is a nation talking to itself.
Arthur Miller (1915–) US dramatist.
Remark, Nov 1961

1962

11 Over increasingly large areas of the United States, spring now comes unheralded by the return of the birds, and the early mornings are strangely silent where once they were filled with the beauty of bird song.
Rachel Carson (1907–64) US biologist.
The Silent Spring

12 It must be generations since anyone but highbrows lived in this cottage . . . I imagine most of the agricultural labourers round here commute from London.
Anthony Powell (1905–) British novelist.
A Dance to the Music of Time: The Kindly Ones, Ch. 2

1963

13 On the whole I would not say that our Press is obscene. I would say that it trembles on the brink of obscenity.
Lord Longford (1905–) British politician and social reformer.
The Observer, 'Sayings of the Year', 1963

14* They're all made out of ticky-tacky, and they all look just the same.
Malvina Reynolds (1900–78) US folksinger and songwriter.
Little Boxes, song describing a housing scheme built in the hills south of San Francisco
Little Boxes

1969

15 Clearly, then, the city is not a concrete jungle, it is a human zoo.
Desmond Morris (1928–) British biologist and writer.
The Human Zoo, Introduction

1971

16 Television is an invention that permits you to be entertained in your living room by people you wouldn't have in your home.
David Frost (1939–) British television personality.
Attrib., CBS television, 1971

1975

517 The British, he thought, must be gluttons for satire: even the weather forecast seemed to be some kind of spoof, predicting every possible combination of weather for the next twenty-four hours without actually committing itself to anything specific.
David Lodge (1935–) British author.
Changing Places, Ch. 2

1976

518 It's just like having a licence to print your own money.
Lord Thomson of Fleet (1894–1976) Canadian-born British newspaper proprietor.
Speaking about commercial television
Attrib.

1981

519 Football isn't a matter of life and death – it's much more important than that.
Bill Shankly (1914–81) British football manager.
Attrib.

520 *Punch* – the official journal of dentists' waiting rooms.
The Times, 7 Oct 1981

1986

521 I answer 20 000 letters a year and so many couples are having problems because they are not getting the right proteins and vitamins.
Barbara Cartland (1902–) British romantic novelist.
The Observer, 'Sayings of the Week', 31 Aug 1986

522 Blood sport is brought to its ultimate refinement in the gossip columns.
Bernard Ingham (1932–) British journalist.
Remark, Dec 1986

Death

1952

523 When you're between any sort of devil and the deep blue sea, the deep blue sea sometimes looks very inviting.
Terence Rattigan (1911–77) British dramatist.
The Deep Blue Sea

524 Do not go gentle into that good night,
Old age should burn and rave at close of day;
Rage, rage, against the dying of the light.
Dylan Thomas (1914–53) Welsh poet.
Do not go gentle into that good night

1964

525 I am sick of this way of life. The weariness and sadness of old age make it intolerable. I have

walked with death in hand, and death's own
hand is warmer than my own. I don't wish to
live any longer.
W. Somerset Maugham (1874–1965) British
novelist.
Said on his ninetieth birthday
Familiar Medical Quotations (M. B. Strauss)

1969

526 I do really think that death will be marvellous
. . . If there wasn't death, I think you couldn't go
on.
Stevie Smith (Florence Margaret Smith;
1902–71) British poet.
The Observer, 9 Nov 1969

1972

527 Few men of action have been able to make a
graceful exit at the appropriate time.
Malcolm Muggeridge (1903–) British
writer.
Chronicles Of Wasted Time

1976

528 It's not that I'm afraid to die. I just don't want to
be there when it happens.
Woody Allen (Allen Stewart Konigsberg;
1935–) US film actor.
Without Feathers, 'Death (A Play)'

1978

529 It is important what a man still plans at the end.
It shows the measure of injustice in his death.
Elias Canetti (1905–) Bulgarian-born
novelist.
The Human Province

Education, Knowledge, and Learning

1949

530 Most people are such fools that it is really no
great compliment to say that a man is above
the average.
W. Somerset Maugham (1874–1965) British
novelist.
A Writer's Notebook

531 We teachers can only help the work going on,
as servants wait upon a master.
Maria Montessori (1870–1952) Italian doctor
and educationalist.
The Absorbent Mind

532 And if education is always to be conceived
along the same antiquated lines of a mere
transmission of knowledge, there is little to be
hoped from it in the bettering of man's future.
For what is the use of transmitting knowledge if the individual's total development lags
behind?
Maria Montessori
The Absorbent Mind

1951

533 Spoon feeding in the long run teaches us noth-
ing but the shape of the spoon.
E. M. Forster (1879–1970) British novelist.
Remark, Oct 1951

534 There was never an age in which useless
knowledge was more important than in our
own.
Cyril Joad (1891–1953) British philosopher
and broadcaster.
Remark, Sept 1951

1952

535 Culture is an instrument wielded by professor
to manufacture professors, who when their
turn comes will manufacture professors.
Simone Weil (1909–43) French philosopher.
The Need for Roots

1953

536 Our principal writers have nearly all been fortu-
nate in escaping regular education.
Hugh MacDiarmid (Christopher Murray
Grieve; 1892–1978) Scottish poet.
The Observer, 'Sayings of the Week', 29 Mar
1953

537 A philosopher of imposing stature doesn't think
in a vacuum. Even his most abstract ideas are,
to some extent, conditioned by what is or
what is not known in the time when he lives.
A. N. Whitehead (1861–1947) British
philosopher.
Dialogues

1958

538 It is the tragedy of the world that no one know
what he doesn't know – and the less a man
knows, the more sure he is that he knows
everything.
Joyce Cary (1888–1957) British novelist.
Art and Reality

1959

539* Letting a hundred flowers blossom and a hundred schools of thought contend is the policy
for promoting the progress of the arts and
the sciences.
Mao Tse-Tung (1893–1976) Chinese communist leader.
Quotations from Chairman Mao Tse-Tung, Ch
32

540 The intellectuals' chief cause of anguish are
one another's works.
Jacques Barzun (1907–) US writer.
The House of Intellect

1960s

541 Our knowledge can only be finite, while our ignorance must necessarily be infinite.
Karl Popper (1902–) Austrian-born British philosopher.
Conjectures and Refutations

1960

542 What was once thought can never be unthought.
Friedrich Dürrenmatt (1921–) Swiss writer.
The Physicists

1961

543 To me education is a leading out of what is already there in the pupil's soul. To Miss Mackay it is a putting in of something that is not there, and that is not what I call education, I call it intrusion....
Muriel Spark (1918–) British novelist.
The Prime of Miss Jean Brodie, Ch. 2

544 Art and religion first; then philosophy; lastly science. That is the order of the great subjects of life, that's their order of importance.
Muriel Spark
The Prime of Miss Jean Brodie, Ch. 2

1962

545 The greater our knowledge increases the more our ignorance unfolds.
John Fitzgerald Kennedy (1917–63) US statesman.
Speech, Rice University, 12 Sept 1962

546 There are no new truths, but only truths that have not been recognized by those who have perceived them without noticing.
Mary McCarthy (1912–) US novelist.
On the Contrary

1963

547 Nothing in the world is more dangerous than sincere ignorance and conscientious stupidity.
Martin Luther King (1929–68) US Black civil-rights leader.
Strength To Love

548 It is a good morning exercise for a research scientist to discard a pet hypothesis every day before breakfast. It keeps him young.
Konrad Lorenz (1903–) Austrian zoologist.
On Aggression, Ch. 2

1964

549 Education is what survives when what has been learnt has been forgotten.
B. F. Skinner (1904–) US psychologist.
New Scientist, 21 May 1964, 'Education in 1984'

1966

550 The possession of a book becomes a substitute for reading it.
Anthony Burgess (John Burgess Wilson; 1917–) British novelist.
New York Times Book Review

1967

551 The average man's opinions are much less foolish than they would be if he thought for himself.
Bertrand Russell (1872–1970) British philosopher.
Autobiography

1969

552 I have yet to see any problem, however complicated, which, when looked at in the right way, did not become still more complicated.
Poul Anderson
New Scientist, 1969

553 ...that is what learning is. You suddenly understand something you've understood all your life, but in a new way.
Doris Lessing (1919–) British novelist.
The Four-Gated City

1970

554 You know very well that unless you're a scientist, it's much more important for a theory to be shapely, than for it to be true.
Christopher Hampton (1946–) British writer and dramatist.
The Philanthropist, Sc. 1

1974

555 Every intellectual attitude is latently political.
Thomas Mann (1875–1955) German novelist.
The Observer, 11 Aug 1974

556 For hundreds of pages the closely-reasoned arguments unroll, axioms and theorems interlock. And what remains with us in the end? A general sense that the world can be expressed in closely-reasoned arguments, in interlocking axioms and theorems.
Michael Frayn (1933–) British journalist and writer.
Constructions

557 That's the classical mind at work, runs fine inside but looks dingy on the surface.
Robert T. Pirsig (1928–) US writer.
Zen and the Art of Motorcycle Maintenance, Pt. III, Ch. 25

1975

558 Four times, under our educational rules, the human pack is shuffled and cut – at elevenplus, sixteen-plus, eighteen-plus and twentyplus – and happy is he who comes top of the deck on each occasion, but especially the last.

This is called Finals, the very name of which implies that nothing of importance can happen after it. The British postgraduate student is a lonely forlorn soul . . . for whom nothing has been real since the Big Push.
David Lodge (1935–) British author.
Changing Places, Ch. 1

559 It is never wise to try to appear to be more clever than you are. It is sometimes wise to appear slightly less so.
William Whitelaw (1918–) British politician.
The Observer, 'Sayings of the Year', 1975

1976

560 A theory can be proved by experiment; but no path leads from experiment to the birth of a theory.
Albert Einstein (1879–1955) German-born US physicist.
The Sunday Times, 18 July 1976

561 Common sense is the collection of prejudices acquired by age eighteen.
Albert Einstein
Scientific American, Feb 1976

1977

562 To read too many books is harmful.
Mao Tse-Tung (1893–1976) Chinese communist leader.
The New Yorker, 7 Mar 1977

1978

563 Intellectuals are people who believe that ideas are of more importance than values. That is to say, their own ideas and other people's values.
Gerald Brenan (Edward Fitzgerald Brenan; 1894–1987) British writer.
Thoughts in a Dry Season, 'Life'

564 The great writers of aphorisms read as if they had all known each other well.
Elias Canetti (1905–) Bulgarian-born novelist.
The Human Province

1979

565 The ratio of literacy to illiteracy is constant, but nowadays the illiterates can read and write.
Alberto Moravia (Alberto Pincherle; 1907–) Italian novelist.
The Observer, 14 Oct 1979

1982

566 My father still reads the dictionary every day. He says your life depends on your power to master words.
Arthur Scargill (1941–) British trades union leader.
Sunday Times, 10 Jan 1982

History

1950s

567 The anthropologist respects history, but he does not accord it a special value. He conceives it as a study complementary to his own: one of them unfurls the range of human societies in time, the other in space.
Claude Lévi-Strauss (1908–) French anthropologist.
The Savage Mind

1953

568 The past is a foreign country: they do things differently there.
L. P. Hartley (1895–1972) British novelist.
The Go-Between

1960

569 The most persistent sound which reverberates through men's history is the beating of war drums.
Arthur Koestler (1905–83) Hungarian-born British writer.
Janus: A Summing Up, Prologue

1961

570 History is too serious to be left to historians.
Iain Macleod (1913–70) British politician.
The Observer, 'Sayings of the Week', 16 July 1961

571 Human blunders usually do more to shape history than human wickedness.
A. J. P. Taylor (1906–) British historian.
The Origins of the Second World War, Ch. 10

1962

572 Man is a history-making creature who can neither repeat his past nor leave it behind.
W. H. Auden (1907–73) British poet.
The Dyer's Hand, 'D. H. Lawrence'

1965

573 History gets thicker as it approaches recent times.
A. J. P. Taylor (1906–) British historian.
English History, 1914–1945, Bibliography

1968

574 History never looks like history when you are living through it. It always looks confusing and messy, and it always feels uncomfortable.
John W. Gardner (1912–) US writer.
No Easy Victories

1971

575 Political history is far too criminal and pathological to be a fit subject of study for the young

Children should acquire their heroes and villains from fiction.
W. H. Auden (1907–73) British poet.
A Certain World

576   There are moments in history when brooding tragedy and its dark shadows can be lightened by recalling great moments of the past.
Indira Gandhi (1917–84) Indian stateswoman.
Letter to Richard Nixon, 16 Dec 1971

1972

577   A study of history shows that civilizations that abandon the quest for knowledge are doomed to disintegration.
Bernard Lovell (1913–) British astronomer and writer.
The Observer, 'Sayings of the Week', 14 May 1972

Human Nature

1945

578   I have known uncertainty: a state unknown to the Greeks.
Jorge Luis Borges (1899–1986) Argentinian writer.
Ficciones, 'The Babylonian Lottery'

1946

579   No, it is not only our fate but our business to lose innocence, and once we have lost that, it is futile to attempt a picnic in Eden.
Elizabeth Bowen (1899–1973) Irish novelist.
In *Orion III*, 'Out of a Book'

1947

580   Gamesmanship or The Art of Winning Games Without Actually Cheating.
Stephen Potter (1900–69) British writer.
Book title

1950

581   Friendship is unnecessary, like philosophy, like art . . . . It has no survival value; rather it is one of those things that give value to survival.
C. S. Lewis (1898–1963) British academic and writer.
The Four Loves, Friendship

582*   The man who is master of his passions is Reason's slave.
Cyril Connolly (1903–74) British journalist.
Turnstile One (ed. V. S. Pritchett)

583   *How to be one up* – how to make the other man feel that something has gone wrong, however slightly.
Stephen Potter (1900–69) British writer.
Lifemanship, Introduction

584   Most human beings have an almost infinite capacity for taking things for granted.
Aldous Huxley (1894–1964) British novelist.
Themes and Variations

585   It is an important general rule always to refer to your friend's country establishment as a 'cottage'.
Stephen Potter (1900–69) British writer.
Lifemanship, Ch. 2

1951

586   Pray that your loneliness may spur you into finding something to live for, great enough to die for.
Dag Hammarskjöld (1905–61) Swedish diplomat.
Diaries, 1951

1952

587   Habit is a great deadener.
Samuel Beckett (1906–) Irish novelist and dramatist.
Waiting for Godot, III

588   We all are born mad. Some remain so.
Samuel Beckett
Waiting for Godot, II

1953

589   Sentimentality is a superstructure covering brutality.
Carl Gustav Jung (1875–1961) Swiss psychoanalyst.
Reflections

1954

590   Men have never been good, they are not good, they never will be good.
Karl Barth (1886–1968) Swiss Protestant theologian.
Time, 12 Apr 1954

591   When people are free to do as they please, they usually imitate each other.
Eric Hoffer (1902–) US writer.
The Passionate State of Mind

592   Many things – such as loving, going to sleep or behaving unaffectedly – are done worst when we try hardest to do them.
C. S. Lewis (1898–1963) British academic and writer.
Studies in Medieval and Renaissance Literature

1955

593*   We need more understanding of human nature, because the only real danger that exists is man himself . . . We know nothing of man, far too little. His psyche should be studied because we are the origin of all coming evil.
Carl Gustav Jung (1875–1961) Swiss psychoanalyst.
BBC television interview

1956

594 A single sentence will suffice for modern man: he fornicated and read the papers.
Albert Camus (1913–60) French existentialist writer.
The Fall

595 Style, like sheer silk, too often hides eczema.
Albert Camus
The Fall

596 When a small child . . . I thought that success spelled happiness. I was wrong. Happiness is like a butterfly which appears and delights us for one brief moment, but soon flits away.
Anna Pavlova (1881–1931) Russian ballet dancer.
Pavlova: A Biography (ed. A. H. Franks), 'Pages of My Life'

1959

597 My problem lies in reconciling my gross habits with my net income.
Errol Flynn (1909–59) Australian actor.
Attrib.

1960s

598 Cocaine isn't habit-forming. I should know — I've been using it for years.
Tallulah Bankhead (1903–68) US actress.
Pentimento (Lillian Hellman), 'Theatre'

599 Experience teaches you that the man who looks you straight in the eye, particularly if he adds a firm handshake, is hiding something.
Clifton Fadiman (1904–) US writer.
Enter, Conversing

1960

600 Schizophrenia cannot be understood without understanding despair.
R. D. Laing (1927–) British psychiatrist.
The Divided Self, Ch. 2

1961

601 There was only one catch and that was Catch-22, which specified that a concern for one's own safety in the face of dangers that were real and immediate was the process of a rational mind.
Joseph Heller (1923–) US novelist.
Catch-22, Ch. 5

1962

602 Solitude is the playfield of Satan.
Vladimir Nabokov (1899–1977) Russian-born US novelist.
Pale Fire

1965

603 Being a star has made it possible for me to get insulted in places where the average Negro could never hope to get insulted.
Sammy Davis Jnr (1925–) Black US singer.
Yes I Can

604 He's a real Nowhere Man,
Sitting in his Nowhere Land,
Making all his nowhere plans for nobody.
Doesn't have a point of view,
Knows not where he's going to,
Isn't he a bit like you and me?
John Lennon (1940–80) British rock musician.
Nowhere Man (with Paul McCartney)

1966

605 Waits at the window, wearing the face that she keeps in a jar by the door
Who is it for? All the lonely people, where do they all come from?
All the lonely people, where do they all belong?
John Lennon (1940–80) British rock musician.
Eleanor Rigby (with Paul McCartney)

1967

606 Madness need not be all breakdown. It may also be break-through. It is potential liberation and renewal as well as enslavement and existential death.
R. D. Laing (1927–) British psychiatrist.
The Politics of Experience, Ch. 16

607 Schizophrenic behaviour is a special strategy that a person invents in order to live in an unlivable situation.
R. D. Laing
The Politics of Experience

608 Three passions, simple but overwhelmingly strong, have governed my life: the longing for love, the search for knowledge, and unbearable pity for the suffering of mankind.
Bertrand Russell (1872–1970) British philosopher.
The Autobiography of Bertrand Russell, Prologue

609 I discovered to my amazement that average men and women were delighted at the prospect of war. I had fondly imagined what most pacifists contended, that wars were forced upon a reluctant population by despotic and Machiavellian governments.
Bertrand Russell
The Autobiography of Bertrand Russell

1968

610 A man is happy so long as he chooses to be happy and nothing can stop him.
Alexander Solzhenitsyn (1918–) Soviet novelist.
Cancer Ward

1970s

611 There are only two kinds of people in the world

Those who are nice to their servants and those who aren't.
Duke of Argyll (1937–)
Attrib.

1970

12 You see, I always divide people into two groups. Those who live by what they know to be a lie, and those who live by what they believe, falsely, to be the truth.
Christopher Hampton (1946–) British writer and dramatist.
The Philanthropist, Sc. 6

13 Of course not. After all, I may be wrong.
Bertrand Russell (1872–1970) British philosopher.
On being asked whether he would be prepared to die for his beliefs
Attrib.

1971

14 A memorandum is written not to inform the reader but to protect the writer.
Dean Acheson (1893–1971) US lawyer and statesman.
Attrib.

1973

15 Man is the only animal that learns by being hypocritical. He pretends to be polite and then, eventually, he *becomes* polite.
Jean Kerr (1923–) US dramatist.
Finishing Touches

1974

16 Happiness is an imaginary condition, formerly often attributed by the living to the dead, now usually attributed by adults to children, and by children to adults.
Thomas Szasz (1920–) US psychiatrist.
The Second Sin

17 The stupid neither forgive nor forget; the naive forgive and forget; the wise forgive but do not forget.
Thomas Szasz
The Second Sin

18 Men are rewarded and punished not for what they do, but rather for how their acts are defined. This is why men are more interested in better justifying themselves than in better behaving themselves.
Thomas Szasz
The Second Sin

1975

19 If you haven't been happy very young, you can

still be happy later on, but it's much harder. You need more luck.
Simone de Beauvoir (1908–86) French writer.
The Observer, 'Sayings of the Week', 19 May 1975

620 I've noticed your hostility towards him . . . I ought to have guessed you were friends.
Malcolm Bradbury (1932–) British academic and novelist.
The History Man, Ch. 7

1976

621 It's possible to disagree with someone about the ethics of non-violence without wanting to kick his face in.
Christopher Hampton (1946–) British writer and dramatist.
Treats, Sc. 4

1977

622 Only the man who finds everything wrong and expects it to get worse is thought to have a clear brain.
John Kenneth Galbraith (1908–) US economist.
The Age of Uncertainty

1979

623 We confess our bad qualities to others out of fear of appearing naive or ridiculous by not being aware of them.
Gerald Brenan (Edward Fitzgerald Brenan; 1894–1987) British writer.
Thoughts in a Dry Season

624 Worrying is the most natural and spontaneous of all human functions. It is time to acknowledge this, perhaps even to learn to do it better.
Lewis Thomas (1913–) US pathologist.
More Notes of a Biology Watcher, 'The Medusa and the Snail'

1980

625 People will not readily bear pain unless there is hope.
Michael Edwards (1930–) South African businessman.
Speech, 2 July 1980

1988

626 Shyness is just egotism out of its depth.
Penelope Keith British actress.
Remark, July 1988

Humour

1947

627 It has been discovered experimentally that you

can draw laughter from an audience anywhere in the world, of any class or race, simply by walking on to a stage and uttering the words "I am a married man".
Ted Kavanagh (1892–1958) British radio scriptwriter.
News Review, 10 July 1947

1950

628* The coarse joke proclaims that we have here an animal which finds its own animality either objectionable or funny.
C. S. Lewis (1898–1963) British academic and writer.
Miracles

629 As for the Freudian, it is a very low, Central European sort of humour.
Robert Graves (1895–1985) British poet and novelist.
Occupation: Writer

1951

630 A lie is an abomination unto the Lord and a very present help in trouble.
Adlai Stevenson (1900–65) US statesman.
Speech, Jan 1951

1953

631 Check enclosed.
Dorothy Parker (1893–1967) US writer.
Giving her version of the two most beautiful words in the English language
Attrib.

1956

632 Being published by the O.U.P. is rather like being married to a duchess; the honour is almost greater than the pleasure.
G. M. Young
Letter to Rupert Hart-Davis, 20 Nov 1956

1960

633 All English shop assistants are Miltonists. All Miltonists firmly believe that 'they also serve who only stand and wait.'
George Mikes (1912–87) Hungarian-born British writer.
How to be Inimitable

1964

634 All I need to make a comedy is a park, a policeman and a pretty girl.
Charlie Chaplin (Sir Charles Spencer C.; 1889–1977) British film actor.
My Autobiography

635 Thank you, sister. May you be the mother of a bishop!
Brendan Behan (1923–64) Irish playwright.
Said to a nun nursing him on his deathbed
Attrib.

636 She believed in nothing; only her scepticism kept her from being an atheist.
Jean-Paul Sartre (1905–80) French writer.
Words

1965

637 The trouble with Freud is that he never played the Glasgow Empire Saturday night.
Ken Dodd (1931–   ) British comedian.
TV interview, 1965

1966

638 It is not for nothing that, in the English language alone, to accuse someone of trying to be funny is highly abusive.
Malcolm Muggeridge (1903–   ) British writer.
Tread Softly For You Tread on My Jokes

1969

639 Comedy, like sodomy, is an unnatural act.
Marty Feldman (1933–83) British comedian.
The Times, 9 June 1969

1980

640 John Wayne is dead
The hell I am
Anonymous
Inscription on a wall in Bermondsey Antique Market, together with a ghostly denial
Evening Standard, 1980

Life

1946

641 I have recently been all round the world and have formed a very poor opinion of it.
Thomas Beecham (1879–1961) British conductor.
Speech at the Savoy
The News Review, 22 Aug 1946

642 Anything that is worth doing has been done frequently. Things hitherto undone should be given, I suspect, a wide berth.
Max Beerbohm (1872–1956) British writer.
Mainly on the Air

1947

643 Man is condemned to be free.
Jean-Paul Sartre (1905–80) French writer.
Existentialism is a Humanism

644 What a strange thing is memory, and hope; one looks backward, the other forward. The one is of today, the other is the Tomorrow. Memory is history recorded in our brain, memory is a

painter, it paints pictures of the past and of the day.
Grandma Moses (Anna Mary Robertson Moses; 1860–1961) US primitive painter.
Grandma Moses, My Life's History (ed. Aotto Kallir), Ch. 1

1948

645 Without measureless and perpetual uncertainty the drama of human life would be destroyed.
Winston Churchill (1874–1965) British statesman.
The Gathering Storm

646 Man's 'progress' is but a gradual discovery that his questions have no meaning.
Antoine de Saint-Exupéry (1900–44) French novelist and aviator.
The Wisdom of the Sands

1949

647 Hell is oneself;
Hell is alone, the other figures in it
Merely projections. There is nothing to escape from
And nothing to escape to. One is always alone.
T. S. Eliot (1888–1965) US-born British poet and dramatist.
The Cocktail Party, I:3

648 At fifty everyone has the face he deserves.
George Orwell (Eric Blair; 1903–50) British novelist.
Final entry in his notebook

1950

649 The world is made of people who never quite get into the first team and who just miss the prizes at the flower show.
Jacob Bronowski (1908–74) British scientist and writer.
The Face of Violence, Ch. 6

650 Most people get a fair amount of fun out of their lives, but on balance life is suffering and only the very young or the very foolish imagine otherwise.
George Orwell (Eric Blair; 1903–50) British novelist.
Shooting an Elephant

651 Contemporary man has rationalised the myths, but he has not been able to destroy them.
Octavio Paz (1914–) Mexican author and poet.
The Labyrinth of Solitude

652 The most savage controversies are those about matters as to which there is no good evidence either way.
Bertrand Russell (1872–1970) British philosopher.
Unpopular Essays

653 Facts speak louder than statistics.
Geoffrey Streatfield (1897–1978) British lawyer.
Remark, Mar 1950

1951

654 He who despairs over an event is a coward, but he who holds hopes for the human condition is a fool.
Albert Camus (1913–60) French existentialist writer.
The Rebel

655 Everybody has a right to pronounce foreign names as he chooses.
Winston Churchill (1874–1965) British statesman.
The Observer, 'Sayings of the Week', 5 Aug 1951

1952

656 There are no gains without pains.
Adlai Stevenson (1900–65) US statesman.
Speech, Chicago, 26 July 1952

1954

657 Now all the world she knew is dead
In this small room she lives her days.
The wash-hand stand and single bed
Screened from the public gaze.
John Betjeman (1906–84) British poet.
A Few Late Chrysanthemums, 'House of Rest'

658 Oh, isn't life a terrible thing, thank God?
Dylan Thomas (1914–53) Welsh poet.
Under Milk Wood

659 But there comes a moment in everybody's life when he must decide whether he'll live among human beings or not – a fool among fools or a fool alone.
Thornton Wilder (1897–1975) US novelist and dramatist.
The Matchmaker, IV

1955

660 I will never be an old man. To me, old age is always fifteen years older than I am.
Bernard Baruch (1870–1965) US financier and presidential adviser.
The Observer, 'Sayings of the Week', 21 Aug 1955

661 Many men would take the death-sentence without a whimper to escape the life-sentence which fate carries in her other hand.
T. E. Lawrence (1888–1935) British soldier and writer.
The Mint, Pt. I, Ch. 4

662 A vacuum is a hell of a lot better than some of the stuff that nature replaces it with.
Tennessee Williams (1911–83) US dramatist.
Cat On A Hot Tin Roof

1956

663 The penalty of success is to be bored by people who used to snub you.
Nancy Astor (1879–1964) American-born British politician.
Sunday Express, 12 Jan 1956

664 A society made up of individuals who were all capable of original thought would probably be unendurable. The pressure of ideas would simply drive it frantic.
H. L. Mencken (1880–1956) US journalist.
Notebooks, 'Minority Report'

665 Poor old Daddy – just one of those sturdy old plants left over from the Edwardian Wilderness, that can't understand why the sun isn't shining any more.
John Osborne (1929–   ) British dramatist.
Look Back in Anger, II.2

666 I never give them hell. I just tell the truth and they think it is hell.
Harry S. Truman (1884–1972) US statesman.
Look magazine, 3 Apr 1956

1957

667 Sweet Smell of Success.
Ernest Lehman (1920–   ) US screenwriter.
Novel and film title

1959

668 People are inexterminable – like flies and bed-bugs. There will always be some that survive in cracks and crevices – that's us.
Robert Frost (1875–1963) US poet.
The Observer, 29 Mar 1959

669 Being over seventy is like being engaged in a war. All our friends are going or gone and we survive amongst the dead and the dying as on a battlefield.
Muriel Spark (1918–   ) British novelist.
Memento Mori, Ch. 4

1960

670 Not a future. At least not in Europe. America's different, of course, but America's really only a kind of Russia. You've no idea how pleasant it is not to have any future. It's like having a totally efficient contraceptive.
Anthony Burgess (John Burgess Wilson; 1917–   ) British novelist.
Honey for the Bears, Pt. II, Ch. 6

671 Nobody hears old people complain because people think that's all old people do. And that's because old people are gnarled and sagged and twisted into the shape of a complaint.
Edward Albee (1928–   ) US dramatist.
The American Dream

672 All evil comes from the old. They grow fat on ideas and young men die of them.
Jean Anouilh (1910–87) French dramatist.
Catch as Catch Can

673 Children have never been very good at listening to their elders, but they have never failed to imitate them.
James Baldwin (1924–87) US writer.
Esquire, 1960

674 There is precious little in civilization to appeal to a Yeti.
Edmund Hillary (1919–   ) New Zealand mountaineer.
The Observer, 'Sayings of the Week', 3 June 1960

1961

675 Nature is as wasteful of promising young men as she is of fish spawn.
Richard Hughes (1900–   ) British novelist and playwright.
The Fox in the Attic

676 Stop the World, I Want to Get Off.
Anthony Newley (1931–   ) British actor, composer, singer, and comedian.
With Leslie Bricusse
Title of musical

1962

677 The weak have one weapon: the errors of those who think they are strong.
Georges Bidault (1899–1983) French statesman.
The Observer, 1962

678 In this unbelievable universe in which we live there are no absolutes. Even parallel lines, reaching into infinity, meet somewhere yonder.
Pearl Buck (1892–1973) US novelist.
A Bridge for Passing

679 He who confronts the paradoxical exposes himself to reality.
Friedrich Dürrenmatt (1921–   ) Swiss writer.
The Physicists

680 How many roads must a man walk down
Before you call him a man?
Bob Dylan (Robert Allen Zimmerman; 1941–   ) US popular singer.
Blowin' in the Wind

681 As far as we can discern, the sole purpose of human existence is to kindle a light in the darkness of mere being.
Carl Gustav Jung (1875–1961) Swiss psychoanalyst.
Memories, Dreams, Reflections, Ch. 11

682 There is always inequality in life. Some men are killed in a war and some men are wounded and some men never leave the country – Life is unfair.
John Fitzgerald Kennedy (1917–63) US statesman.
Speech, 21 Mar 1962

683   The new electronic interdependence recreates the world in the image of a global village.
Marshall McLuhan (1911–81) Canadian sociologist.
The Gutenberg Galaxy

684   One of the worst things about life is not how nasty the nasty people are. You know that already. It is how nasty the nice people can be.
Anthony Powell (1905–) British novelist.
A Dance to the Music of Time: The Kindly Ones, Ch. 4

1963

685   Yes, 'n' how many years can some people exist
Before they're allowed to be free?
Yes, 'n' how many times can a man turn his head,
Pretending he just doesn't see?
The answer, my friend, is blowin' in the wind.
Bob Dylan (Robert Allen Zimmerman; 1941–) US popular singer.
Blowin' in the Wind

686   The war against hunger is truly mankind's war of liberation.
John Fitzgerald Kennedy (1917–63) US statesman.
Speech, World Food Congress, 4 June 1963

687   The supreme reality of our time is . . . the vulnerability of this planet.
John Fitzgerald Kennedy
Speech, Dublin, 28 June 1963

688   Victory has a thousand fathers but defeat is an orphan.
John Fitzgerald Kennedy
Attrib.

689   One starts to get young at the age of sixty and then it is too late.
Pablo Picasso (1881–1973) Spanish painter.
Sunday Times, 20 Oct 1963

1964

690   There is no security in this life. There is only opportunity.
Douglas MacArthur (1880–1964) US general.
MacArthur, His Rendezvous with History (Courtney Whitney)

1965

691   I've looked at life from both sides now
From win and lose and still somehow
It's life's illusions I recall
I really don't know life at all.
Joni Mitchell (1945–) Singer and songwriter.
Both Sides Now

692*   Youth is something very new: twenty years ago no one mentioned it.
Coco Chanel (1883–1971) French dress designer.
Coco Chanel, Her Life, Her Secrets (Marcel Haedrich)

693   How does it feel
To be without a home
Like a complete unknown
Like a rolling stone?
Bob Dylan (Robert Allen Zimmerman; 1941–) US popular singer.
Like a Rolling Stone

694   Every luxury was lavished on you — atheism, breast-feeding, circumcision. I had to make my own way.
Joe Orton (1933–67) British dramatist.
Loot, I

695   In other words, apart from the known and the unknown, what else is there?
Harold Pinter (1930–) British dramatist.
The Homecoming, II

696   A lady asked me why, on most occasions, I wore black. 'Are you in mourning?'
'Yes.'
'For whom are you in mourning?'
'For the world.'
Edith Sitwell (1887–1964) British poet and writer.
Taken Care Of, Ch. 1

697   The only way to succeed is to make people hate you. That way, they remember you.
Joseph von Sternberg (1894–1969) US film director.
Autobiography (Fun in a Chinese Laundry)

698   One of the most obvious facts about grown-ups to a child is that they have forgotten what it is like to be a child.
Randall Jarrell (1914–65) US author.
Third Book of Criticism

1966

699   Longevity is the revenge of talent upon genius.
Cyril Connolly (1903–74) British journalist.
Sunday Times, 19 June 1966

1967

700   What is an adult? A child blown up by age.
Simone de Beauvoir (1908–86) French writer.
La Femme rompue

701   One doesn't recognize in one's life the really important moments — not until it's too late.
Agatha Christie (1891–1976) British detective-story writer.
Endless Night, Bk. II, Ch. 14

702   Two half-truths do not make a truth, and two half-cultures do not make a culture.
Arthur Koestler (1905–83) Hungarian-born British writer.
The Ghost in the Machine, Preface

703   We are effectively destroying ourselves by violence masquerading as love.
R. D. Laing (1927–) British psychiatrist.
The Politics of Experience, Ch. 13

1968

704   Life was a funny thing that occurred on the way
to the grave.
Quentin Crisp (c. 1910–   ) British model,
publicist, and writer.
The Naked Civil Servant

705   The young always have the same problem —
how to rebel and conform at the same time.
They have now solved this by defying their par-
ents and copying one another.
Quentin Crisp
The Naked Civil Servant

706   Years ago a person, he was unhappy, didn't
know what to do with himself — he'd go to
church, start a revolution — *something*. Today
you're unhappy? Can't figure it out? What is
the salvation? Go shopping.
Arthur Miller (1915–   ) US dramatist.
The Price, I

1969

707   People talking without speaking,
People listening without hearing,
People writing songs that voices never
shared.
Paul Simon (1941–   ) US singer.
Sound of Silence

708   I am a passenger on the spaceship, Earth.
Richard Buckminster Fuller (1895–1983)
US architect and inventor.
Operating Manual for Spaceship Earth

709   The trouble with the world is that the stupid are
cocksure and the intelligent full of doubt.
Bertrand Russell (1872–1970) British
philosopher.
Autobiography

1970

710   In my youth I regarded the universe as an open
book, printed in the language of physical
equations, whereas now it appears to me as a
text written in invisible ink, of which in our
rare moments of grace we are able to decipher
a small fragment.
Arthur Koestler (1905–83) Hungarian-born
British writer.
Bricks to Babel, Epilogue

711   The salvation of mankind lies only in making
everything the concern of all.
Alexander Solzhenitsyn (1918–   ) Soviet
novelist.
Nobel Lecture, 1970

712   Winning isn't everything, but wanting to win is.
Vince Lombardi (1913–70) US football
coach.
Attrib.

1971

713   We must rediscover the distinction between
hope and expectation.
Ivan Illich (1926–   ) Austrian sociologist.
Deschooling Society, Ch. 7

714   Being seventy is not a sin.
Golda Meir (1898–1978) Russian-born Israeli
stateswoman.
Reader's Digest (July 1971), 'The Indestructible
Golda Meir'

1972

715   The only way of finding the limits of the possible is by going beyond them into the
impossible.
Arthur C. Clarke (1917–   ) British science-
fiction writer.
The Lost Worlds of 2001

1973

716   Every animal leaves traces of what it was; man
alone leaves traces of what he created.
Jacob Bronowski (1908–74) British scientist
and writer.
The Ascent of Man, Ch. 1

717   In a consumer society there are inevitably two
kinds of slaves: the prisoners of addiction and
the prisoners of envy.
Ivan Illich (1926–   ) Austrian sociologist.
Tools for Conviviality

718   Growing old is like being increasingly penalized
for a crime you haven't committed.
Anthony Powell (1905–   ) British novelist.
*A Dance to the Music of Time: Temporary
Kings*, Ch. 1

1974

719   At sixteen I was stupid, confused, insecure and
indecisive. At twenty-five I was wise, self-con-
fident, prepossessing and assertive. At forty-
five I am stupid, confused, insecure and indecisive. Who would have supposed that maturity
is only a short break in adolescence?
Jules Feiffer (1929–   ) US writer, cartoonist,
and humorist.
The Observer, 3 Feb 1974

720   It is the true nature of mankind to learn from
mistakes, not from example.
Fred Hoyle (1915–   ) British astronomer.
Into Deepest Space

721   We are living beyond our means. As a people
we have developed a life-style that is draining
the earth of its priceless and irreplaceable resources without regard for the future of our
children and people all around the world.
Margaret Mead (1901–78) US
anthropologist.
Redbook, 'The Energy Crisis — Why Our World
Will Never Again Be the Same.'

722   It isn't evil that is ruining the earth, but medioc

rity. The crime is not that Nero played while Rome burned, but that he played badly.
Ned Rorem (1923–) US composer and writer.
The Final Diary

723 A child becomes an adult when he realizes that he has a right not only to be right but also to be wrong.
Thomas Szasz (1920–) US psychiatrist.
The Second Sin

1975

724 We may become the makers of our fate when we have ceased to pose as its prophets.
Karl Popper (1902–) Austrian-born British philosopher.
The Observer, 28 Dec 1975

725 Loneliness and the feeling of being unwanted is the most terrible poverty.
Mother Teresa (Agnes Gonxha Bojaxhui; 1910–) Yugoslavian missionary in Calcutta.
Time, 'Saints Among Us', 29 Dec 1975

1976

726 It is not enough to succeed. Others must fail.
Gore Vidal (1925–) US novelist.
Antipanegyric for Tom Driberg (G. Irvine)

1977

727 Life is a tragedy when seen in close-up, but a comedy in long-shot.
Charlie Chaplin (Sir Charles Spencer C.; 1889–1977) British film actor.
In *The Guardian*, Obituary, 28 Dec 1977

728 If we see light at the end of the tunnel it is the light of an oncoming train.
Robert Lowell (1917–77) US poet.
Day by Day

729 I do not keep a diary. Never have. To write a diary every day is like returning to one's own vomit.
Enoch Powell (1912–) British politician.
Sunday Times, 6 Nov 1977

1978

730 Old age takes away from us what we have inherited and gives us what we have earned.
Gerald Brenan (Edward Fitzgerald Brenan; 1894–1987) British writer.
Thoughts in a Dry Season, 'Life'

1979

731 To be old is to be part of a huge and ordinary multitude . . . the reason why old age was venerated in the past was because it was extraordinary.
Ronald Blythe (1922–) British author.
The View in Winter

732 Life is something to do when you can't get to sleep.
Fran Lebowitz (1950–) US writer.
The Observer, 21 Jan 1979

733 Life is what happens to you while you're busy making other plans.
John Lennon (1940–80) British rock musician.
Beautiful Boy

1980s

734 There is no reason to assume that the universe has the slightest interest in intelligence – or even in life. Both may be random accidental by-products of its operations like the beautiful patterns on a butterfly's wings. The insect would fly just as well without them.
Arthur C. Clarke (1917–) British science-fiction writer.
The Lost Worlds of 2001

1980

735 Better to enjoy and suffer than sit around with folded arms. You know the only true prayer? Please God, lead me into temptation.
Jennie Lee (1904–) British politician and writer.
My Life with Nye

1982

736 When the white man came we had the land and they had the Bibles; now they have the land and we have the Bibles.
Dan George (1899–1982) Canadian Indian chief.
Attrib.

737 We have to believe in free-will. We've got no choice.
Isaac Bashevis Singer (1904–) Polish-born US novelist.
The Times, 21 June 1982

738 Pennies do not come from heaven. They have to be earned here on earth.
Margaret Thatcher (1925–) British politician and prime minister.
Sunday Telegraph, 1982

1987

739 The issues are the same. We wanted peace on earth, love, and understanding between everyone around the world. We have learned that change comes slowly.
Paul McCartney (1943–) British rock musician.
Comparing 1967 and 1987
Remark, June 1987

1988

740 We do not necessarily improve with age: for

better or worse we become more like
ourselves.
Peter Hall (1930–) British theatre director.
The Observer, 'Sayings of the Week', 24 Jan
1988

741   The British loathe the middle-aged and I await
rediscovery at 65, when one is too old to be
in anyone's way.
Roy Strong (1935–) British art critic.
Remark, Jan 1988

Love and Sex

1948

742   Oh, love is real enough, you will find it some
day, but it has one arch-enemy – and that is
life.
Jean Anouilh (1910–87) French dramatist.
Ardèle

1949

743   The moon is nothing
But a circumambulating aphrodisiac
Divinely subsidized to provoke the world
Into a rising birth-rate.
Christopher Fry (1907–) British dramatist.
The Lady's Not for Burning

1950s

744   Now the peak of summer's past, the sky is
overcast
And the love we swore would last for an age
seems deceit.
C. Day Lewis (1904–72) British poet.
Hornpipe

1951

745   Sex is something I really don't understand too
hot. You never know *where* the hell you are. I
keep making up these sex rules for myself,
and then I break them right away.
J. D. Salinger (1919–) US novelist.
The Catcher in the Rye, Ch. 9

1955

746   Self-love seems so often unrequited.
Anthony Powell (1905–) British novelist.
The Acceptance World

1956

747   'Bed,' as the Italian proverb succinctly puts it,
'is the poor man's opera.'
Aldous Huxley (1894–1964) British novelist.
Heaven and Hell

1960s

748   The orgasm has replaced the Cross as the fo-
cus of longing and the image of fulfilment.
Malcolm Muggeridge (1903–) British
writer.
The Most of Malcolm Muggeridge, 'Down with
Sex'

1961

749   The Christian view of sex is that it is, indeed, a
form of holy communion.
John Robinson (1919–83) Bishop of
Woolwich.
Giving evidence in the prosecution of Penguin
Books for publishing *Lady Chatterly's Lover*

1964

750   It has to be admitted that we English have sex
on the brain, which is a very unsatisfactory
place to have it.
Malcolm Muggeridge (1903–) British
writer.
The Observer, 'Sayings of the Decade', 1964

1965

751   This sort of thing may be tolerated by the
French, but we are British – thank God.
Lord Montgomery (1887–1976) British field
marshal.
Comment on a bill to relax the laws against
homosexuals
Daily Mail, 27 May 1965

1968

752   It is better to be unfaithful than faithful without
wanting to be.
Brigitte Bardot (1934–) French film
actress.
Remark, Feb 1968

753   No more about sex, it's too boring.
Lawrence Durrell (1912–) British novelist.
Tunc

1970

754   Love, love, love – all the wretched cant of it,
masking egotism, lust, masochism, fantasy
under a mythology of sentimental postures, a
welter of self-induced miseries and joys,
blinding and masking the essential personalities in the frozen gestures of courtship, in the
kissing and the dating and the desire, the
compliments and the quarrels which vivify its
barrenness.
Germaine Greer (1939–) Australian-born
British writer and feminist.
The Female Eunuch

1972

55 I don't think pornography is very harmful, but it is terribly, terribly boring.
Noël Coward (1899–1973) British dramatist. Remark, Sept 1972

1974

56 Masturbation: the primary sexual activity of mankind. In the nineteenth century it was a disease; in the twentieth, it's a cure.
Thomas Szasz (1920–   ) US psychiatrist.
The Second Sin

57 Traditionally, sex has been a very private, secretive activity. Herein perhaps lies its powerful force for uniting people in a strong bond. As we make sex less secretive, we may rob it of its power to hold men and women together.
Thomas Szasz
The Second Sin

1976

58 I'll wager you that in 10 years it will be fashionable again to be a virgin.
Barbara Cartland (1902–   ) British romantic novelist.
The Observer, 'Sayings of the Week', 20 June 1976

1987

59 I said 10 years ago that in 10 years time it would be smart to be a virgin. Now everyone is back to virgins again.
Barbara Cartland
The Observer, 'Sayings of the Week', 12 July 1987

60 You think intercourse is a private act; it's not, it's a social act. Men are sexually predatory in life; and women are sexually manipulative. When two individuals come together and leave their gender outside the bedroom door, then they make love. If they take it inside with them, they do something else, because society is in the room with them.
Andrea Dworkin US feminist.
Intercourse

61 I know it does make people happy but to me it is just like having a cup of tea.
Cynthia Payne (1934–   ) London housewife
After her acquittal on a charge of controlling prostitutes in a famous 'sex-for-luncheon-vouchers' case, 8 Nov 1987

Marriage and the Family

1949

62 Few misfortunes can befall a boy which bring

worse consequences than to have a really affectionate mother.
W. Somerset Maugham (1874–1965) British novelist.
A Writer's Notebook

1950

763 They fuck you up, your mum and dad.
They may not mean to, but they do.
They fill you with the faults they had
And add some extra, just for you.
Philip Larkin (1922–85) British poet.
This be the Verse

764 A group of closely related persons living under one roof; it is a convenience, often a necessity, sometimes a pleasure, sometimes the reverse; but who first exalted it as admirable, an almost religious ideal?
Rose Macaulay (1889–1958) British writer.
The World My Wilderness, Ch. 20

1954

765 There are times when parenthood seems nothing but feeding the mouth that bites you.
Peter De Vries (1910–   ) US novelist.
Tunnel of Love

766 Marriage isn't a process of prolonging the life of love, but of mummifying the corpse.
P. G. Wodehouse (1881–1975) British humorous novelist.
Bring on the Girls (with Guy Bolton)

1955

767 This man, she reasons, as she looks at her husband, is a poor fish. But he is the nearest I can get to the big one that got away.
Nigel Dennis (1912–   ) British writer.
Cards of Identity

1956

768 Most marriages don't add two people together. They subtract one from the other.
Ian Fleming (1908–64) British journalist and author.
Diamonds are Forever

1957

769 "Parents are strange," said Amy, "for their age."
Amanda Vail (Warren Miller; 1921–66) US writer.
Love Me Little

1958

770 It is now known . . . that men enter local politics solely as a result of being unhappily married.
Cyril Northcote Parkinson (1919–   ) British historian and writer.
Parkinson's Law, Ch. 10

771 A man in love is incomplete until he has married. Then he's finished.
Zsa Zsa Gabor (1919–) Hungarian-born US
film star.
Newsweek, 28 Mar 1960

772 Come mothers and fathers
Throughout the land
And don't criticize
What you can't understand.
Bob Dylan (Robert Allen Zimmerman;
1941–) US popular singer.
The Times They Are A-Changin'

773 I'd the upbringing a nun would envy and that's
the truth. Until I was fifteen I was more familiar with Africa than my own body.
Joe Orton (1933–67) British dramatist.
Entertaining Mr Sloane, I

774 Happy is the man with a wife to tell him what to
do and a secretary to do it.
Lord Mancroft (1917–) British businessman and writer.
Remark, Dec 1966

775 Possessive parents rarely live long enough to
see the fruits of their selfishness.
Alan Garner (1934–) British writer.
The Owl Service

776 Far from being the basis of the good society,
the family, with its narrow privacy and tawdry
secrets, is the source of all our discontents.
Edmund Leach (1910–) British social
anthropologist.
In the BBC Reith Lectures for 1967. Lecture re-
printed in *The Listener*

777 Most married couples in the end arrive at tolerable arrangements for living – arrangements
that may strike others as odd, but which suit
them very well.
John Braine (1922–86) British author.
Remark, June 1970

778 Mother is the dead heart of the family, spending father's earnings on consumer goods to
enhance the environment in which he eats,
sleeps and watches the television.
Germaine Greer (1939–) Australian-born
British writer and feminist.
The Female Eunuch

779 Of course, I do have a slight advantage over
the rest of you. It helps in a pinch to be able to

remind your bride that you gave up a throne
for her.
Duke of Windsor (1894–1972) King of the
United Kingdom; abdicated 1936.
Discussing the maintenance of happy marital
relations
Attrib.

780 'We stay together, but we distrust one another.'
'Ah, yes . . . but isn't that a definition of
marriage?'
Malcolm Bradbury (1932–) British aca-
demic and novelist.
The History Man, Ch. 3

781 Parents are the bones on which children
sharpen their teeth.
Peter Ustinov (1921–) British actor.
Dear Me

782 Children . . . have no use for psychology. They
detest sociology. They still believe in God,
the family, angels, devils, witches, goblins,
logic, clarity, punctuation, and other such obso-
lete stuff . . . When a book is boring, they
yawn openly. They don't expect their writer to
redeem humanity, but leave to adults such
childish illusions.
Isaac Bashevis Singer (1904–) Polish-
born US writer.
Speech on receiving the Nobel Prize for
Literature
The Observer, 17 Dec 1978

783 If men had to have babies they would only eve
have one each.
Diana, Princess of Wales (1961–) Wife
of Prince Charles.
Remark, July 1984

784 Being married six times shows a degree of optimism over wisdom, but I am incorrigibly
optimistic.
Norman Mailer (1923–) US writer.
The Observer, 'Sayings of the Week', 17 Jan
1988

Men and Women

785 One is not born a woman, one becomes one.
Simone de Beauvoir (1908–86) French
writer.
Le Deuxième Sexe (trans. The Second Sex)

786 The Professor of Gynaecology began his cours

of lectures as follows: Gentlemen, woman is an animal that micturates once a day, defecates once a week, menstruates once a month, parturates once a year and copulates whenever she has the opportunity.
W. Somerset Maugham (1874–1965) British novelist.
A Writer's Notebook

1950s

7 Women have always been the guardians of wisdom and humanity which makes them natural, but usually secret, rulers. The time has come for them to rule openly, but together with and not against men.
Charlotte Wolff (1904–) German-born British writer.
Bisexuality: A Study, Ch. 2

1954

88 The average man is more interested in a woman who is interested in him than he is in a woman – any woman – with beautiful legs.
Marlene Dietrich (Maria Magdalene von Losch; 1904–) German-born film star.
News item, 13 Dec 1954

1955

89 There is more difference within the sexes than between them.
Ivy Compton-Burnett (1892–1969) British novelist.
Mother and Son

90 Women are most fascinating between the ages of thirty-five and forty, after they have won a few races and know how to pace themselves. Since few women ever pass forty, maximum fascination can continue indefinitely.
Christian Dior (1905–57)
Colliers Magazine, 10 June 1955

1956

91 Women are equal because they are not different any more.
Erich Fromm (1910–80) US writer.
The Art of Loving

92 Why can't a woman be more like a man?
Men are so honest, so thoroughly square;
Eternally noble, historically fair.
Alan Jay Lerner (1918–86) US songwriter.
My Fair Lady, II:4

1957

93 There are only three things to be done with a woman. You can love her, you can suffer for her, or you can turn her into literature.
Lawrence Durrell (1912–) British novelist.
Justine

794 Every little girl knows about love. It is only her capacity to suffer because of it that increases.
Françoise Sagan (1935–) French writer.
Daily Express

795 Sometimes I think if there was a third sex men wouldn't get so much as a glance from me.
Amanda Vail (Warren Miller; 1921–66) US writer.
Love Me Little, Ch. 6

1958

796 Women want mediocre men, and men are working to be as mediocre as possible.
Margaret Mead (1901–78) US anthropologist.
Quote Magazine, 15 May 1958

797 Women never have young minds. They are born three thousand years old.
Shelagh Delaney (1939–) British dramatist.
A Taste of Honey, I:1

1960s

798 People call me a feminist whenever I express sentiments that differentiate me from a doormat or a prostitute.
Rebecca West (1892–) British novelist.
Attrib.

1964

799 A woman should be an illusion.
Ian Fleming (1908–64) British journalist and author.
Life of Ian Fleming (John Pearson)

1966

800 She takes just like a woman, yes, she does
She makes love just like a woman, yes, she does
And she aches just like a woman
But she breaks just like a little girl.
Bob Dylan (Robert Allen Zimmerman; 1941–) US popular singer.
Just Like a Woman

801 A woman should open everything to a man except her mouth.
Derek Marlowe
A Dandy in Aspic

1970s

802 A woman needs a man like a fish needs a bicycle.
Graffiti

1970

803 Probably the only place where a man can feel really secure is in a maximum security prison, except for the imminent threat of release.
Germaine Greer (1939–) Australian-born British writer and feminist.
The Female Eunuch

804 Women fail to understand how much men hate them.
Germaine Greer
The Female Eunuch

1972
---

805 All Berkshire women are very silly. I don't know why women in Berkshire are more silly than anywhere else.
Claude Duveen (1903–) British judge.
Said in Reading County Court, July 1972

1973
---

806 I'm furious about the Women's Liberationists. They keep getting up on soapboxes and proclaiming that women are brighter than men. That's true, but it should be kept very quiet or it ruins the whole racket.
Anita Loos (1891–1981) US novelist.
The Observer, 'Sayings of the Year', 30 Dec 1973

1974
---

807 No woman so naked as one you can see to be naked underneath her clothes.
Michael Frayn (1933–) British journalist and writer.
Constructions

1975
---

808 If women didn't exist, all the money in the world would have no meaning.
Aristotle Onassis (1906–75) Greek businessman.
Attrib.

809 Our motto: Life is too short to stuff a mushroom.
Shirley Conran (1932–) Designer and journalist.
Superwoman, Epigraph

1977
---

810 It makes me feel masculine to tell you that I do not answer questions like this without being paid for answering them.
Lillian Hellman (1905–84) US dramatist.
When asked by *Harper's* magazine when she felt most masculine; this question had already been asked of several famous men
Reader's Digest, July 1977

1978
---

811 Women's Liberation is just a lot of foolishness. It's the men who are discriminated against. They can't bear children. And no one's likely to do anything about that.
Golda Meir (1898–1978) Israeli stateswoman.
Attrib.

1981
---

812 I do, and I also wash and iron them.
Denis Thatcher (1915–) British business man, husband of Margaret Thatcher.
Replying to the question "Who wears the pan in this house?"
Times (Los Angeles), 21 Apr 1981

1982
---

813 The battle for women's rights has been large won.
Margaret Thatcher (1925–) British politician.
The Guardian, 1982

1988
---

814 I shrug my shoulders in despair at women wh moan at the lack of opportunities and then take two weeks off as a result of falling out with their boyfriends.
Sophie Mirman British business woman.
On receiving the *Business Woman of the Yea Award*

Morality, Vices, and Virtues

1947
---

815 Without doubt the greatest injury . . . was don by basing morals on myth, for sooner or later myth is recognized for what it is, and disappears. Then morality loses the foundation o which it has been built.
Herbert Samuel (1870–1963) British Libera statesman.
Romanes Lecture, 1947

1948
---

816 It is better to be violent, if there is violence i our hearts, than to put on the cloak of non-violence to cover impotence.
Mahatma Gandhi (Mohandas Karamchand Gandhi; 1869–1948) Indian national leader.
Non-Violence in Peace and War

817 They had been corrupted by money, and he ha been corrupted by sentiment. Sentiment was the more dangerous, because you couldn't name its price. A man open to bribes was to b relied upon below a certain figure, but sentiment might uncoil in the heart at a name, a photograph, even a smell remembered.
Graham Greene (1904–) British novelist.
The Heart of the Matter

1949
---

818 No action is in itself good or bad, but only suc according to convention.
W. Somerset Maugham (1874–1965) Britis novelist.
A Writer's Notebook

1950

19 Euthanasia is a long, smooth-sounding word, and it conceals its danger as long, smooth words do, but the danger is there, nevertheless.
Pearl Buck (1892–1973) US novelist.
The Child Who Never Grew, Ch. 2

20 Ethical axioms are found and tested not very differently from the axioms of science. Truth is what stands the test of experience.
Albert Einstein (1879–1955) German-born US physicist.
Out of My Later Years

1952

21 It is often easier to fight for principles than to live up to them.
Adlai Stevenson (1900–65) US statesman.
Speech, New York, 27 Aug 1952

1953

22 What is morality in any given time or place? It is what the majority then and there happen to like and immorality is what they dislike.
A. N. Whitehead (1861–1947) British philospher.
Dialogues (Lucien Price)

1954

23 Obscenity is what happens to shock some elderly and ignorant magistrate.
Bertrand Russell (1872–1970) British philosopher.
Look magazine

1955

24 Kill a man, and you are a murderer. Kill millions of men, and you are a conqueror. Kill everyone, and you are a god.
Jean Rostand (1894–1977) French biologist and writer.
Pensées d'un biologiste

1956

25 Gluttony is an emotional escape, a sign something is eating us.
Peter De Vries (1910–) US novelist.
Comfort me with Apples, Ch. 7

1958

26 He who passively accepts evil is as much involved in it as he who helps to perpetrate it.
Martin Luther King (1929–68) US Black civil-rights leader.
Stride Towards Freedom

1959

27 Saintliness is also a temptation.
Jean Anouilh (1910–87) French dramatist.
Becket

1960

828 Propaganda is that branch of the art of lying which consists in nearly deceiving your friends without quite deceiving your enemies.
F. M. Cornford (1886–1960) British poet.
New Statesman, 15 Sept 1978

829 Morality's not practical. Morality's a gesture. A complicated gesture learnt from books.
Robert Bolt (1924–) British playwright.
A Man for All Seasons

830 War is, after all, the universal perversion. We are all tainted: if we cannot experience our perversion at first hand we spend our time reading war stories, the pornography of war; or seeing war films, the blue films of war; or tititlating our senses with the imagination of great deeds, the masturbation of war.
John Rae (1931–) British schoolmaster and writer.
The Custard Boys, Ch. 6

1961

831 Moral indignation is in most cases 2 percent moral, 48 percent indignation and 50 percent envy.
Vittorio De Sica (1901–74) Italian film director.
The Observer, 1961

832 Only lies and evil come from letting people off.
Iris Murdoch (1919–) Irish-born British novelist.
A Severed Head

1962

833 Righteous people terrify me ... Virtue is its own punishment.
Aneurin Bevan (1897–1960) British Labour politician.
Aneurin Bevan (Michael Foot), Vol I

834 Every form of addiction is bad, no matter whether the narcotic be alcohol or morphine or idealism.
Carl Gustav Jung (1875–1961) Swiss psychoanalyst.
Memories, Dreams, Reflections, Ch. 12

835 Punctuality is the virtue of the bored.
Evelyn Waugh (1903–66) British novelist.
Diaries, 'Irregular Notes', 26 Mar 1962

1963

836 The so-called new morality is too often the old immorality condoned.
Lord Shawcross (1902–) British Labour politician and lawyer.
The Observer, 17 Nov 1963

1967

837 A leader who doesn't hesitate before he sends his nation into battle is not fit to be a leader.
Golda Meir (1898–1978) Russian-born Israeli stateswoman.
As Good as Golda (ed. Israel and Mary Shenker)

1968

838 Vice is its own reward.
Quentin Crisp (c. 1910–   ) Model, publicist, and writer.
The Naked Civil Servant

839 Some of the worst men in the world are sincere and the more sincere they are the worse they are.
Lord Hailsham (1907–   ) British Conservative politician.
Speech, Jan 1968

1969

840 I made a remark a long time ago. I said I was very pleased that television was now showing murder stories, because it's bringing murder back into its rightful setting – in the home.
Alfred Hitchcock (1889–1980) British film director.
The Observer, 'Sayings of the Week', 17 Aug 1969

1970

841 Good can imagine Evil; but Evil cannot imagine Good.
W. H. Auden (1907–73) British poet.
A Certain World: A Commonplace Book

842 Few people can be happy unless they hate some other person, nation or creed.
Bertrand Russell (1872–1970) British philosopher.
Attrib.

1971

843 All sin tends to be addictive, and the terminal point of addiction is what is called damnation.
W. H. Auden (1907–73) British poet.
A Certain World

1973

844 Abortion leads to an appalling trivialisation of the act of procreation.
Donald Coggan (1909–   ) Archbishop of York.
Speech to the Shaftesbury Society, 2 Oct 1973

845 . . . there's no difference between one's killing and making decisions that will send others to

kill. It's exactly the same thing, or even worse.
Golda Meir (1898–1978) Russian-born Israeli stateswoman.
L'Europeo (Oriana Fallaci)

846 It's better to be quotable than to be honest.
Tom Stoppard (1937–   ) Czech-born British dramatist.
The Guardian

1974

847 It is difficult to be humble. Even if you aim at humility, there is no guarantee that when you have attained the state you will not be proud of the feat.
Bonamy Dobrée (1891–   ) British scholar and writer.
John Wesley

848 He led a double life. Did that make him a liar? He did not feel a liar. He was a man of two truths.
Iris Murdoch (1919–   ) Irish-born British novelist.
The Sacred and Profane Love Machine

1975

849 To keep a lamp burning we have to keep putting oil in it.
Mother Teresa (Agnes Gonxha Bojaxhui; 1910–   ) Yugoslavian missionary in Calcutta.
Time, 'Saints Among Us', 29 Dec 1975

1976

850 I have looked on a lot of women with lust. I've committed adultery in my heart many times. God recognises I will do this and forgives me.
Jimmy Carter (1924–   ) US statesman and president.
Remark

1979

851 It is heartless and it is mindless and it is a lie.
John McGahern (1934–   ) British writer.
The Pornographer

852 The greatest destroyer of peace is abortion because if a mother can kill her own child what is left for me to kill you and you to kill me? There is nothing between.
Mother Teresa (1910–   ) Yugoslavian missionary in Calcutta.
Nobel Peace Prize Lecture

1982

853 Moderation is a virtue only in those who are thought to have an alternative.
Henry Kissinger (1923–   ) German-born US politician and diplomat.
The Observer, 24 Jan 1982

Other People

1946

854 An Englishman, even if he is alone, forms an orderly queue of one.
George Mikes (1912–87) Hungarian-born British writer and humorist.
How to be an Alien

855 Continental people have sex life; the English have hot-water bottles.
George Mikes
How to be an Alien

1947

856 The English instinctively admire any man who has no talent and is modest about it.
James Agate (1877–1947) British theatre critic.
Attrib.

1948

857 You must not miss Whitehall. At one end you will find a statue of one of our kings who was beheaded; at the other the monument to the man who did it. This is just an example of our attempts to be fair to everybody.
Edward Appleton (1892–1965) British physicist.
Referring to Charles I and Cromwell
Speech, Stockholm, 1 Jan 1948

858 You never find an Englishman among the underdogs – except in England of course.
Evelyn Waugh (1903–66) British novelist.
The Loved One

1949

859 In Italy for thirty years under the Borgias they had warfare, terror, murder, bloodshed – they produced Michelangelo, Leonardo da Vinci and the Renaissance. In Switzerland they had brotherly love, five hundred years of democracy and peace, and what did they produce . . . ? The cuckoo clock.
Orson Welles (1915–85) US film actor.
The Third Man

1950s

860 God bless the USA, so large,
So friendly, and so rich.
W. H. Auden (1907–73) British poet.
On the Circuit

861 First the sweetheart of the nation, then the aunt, woman governs America because America is a land of boys who refuse to grow up.
Salvador de Madariaga y Rogo (1886–1978) Spanish diplomat and writer.
The Perpetual Pessimist (Sagitarius and George)

862 The land of my fathers. My fathers can have it.
Dylan Thomas (1914–53) Welsh poet.
Referring to Wales
Dylan Thomas (John Ackerman)

863 . . . an impotent people,
Sick with inbreeding,
Worrying the carcase of an old song.
R. S. Thomas (1913–   ) Welsh poet.
Welsh Landscape

864 This Englishwoman is so refined
She has no bosom and no behind.
Stevie Smith (Florence Margaret Smith; 1902–71) British poet.
This Englishwoman

1950

865 In America everybody is of the opinion that he has no social superiors, since all men are equal, but he does not admit that he has no social inferiors.
Bertrand Russell (1872–1970) British philosopher.
Unpopular Essays

866 To be an Englishman is to belong to the most exclusive club there is.
Ogden Nash (1902–71) US poet.
England Expects

1953

867 Courtesy is not dead – it has merely taken refuge in Great Britain.
Georges Duhamel (1884–1966) French writer.
The Observer, 'Sayings of Our Times', 31 May 1953

1954

868 To Americans English manners are far more frightening than none at all.
Randall Jarrell (1914–65) US author.
Pictures from an Institution, Pt. I, Ch. 5

869 I like the English. They have the most rigid code of immorality in the world.
Malcolm Bradbury (1932–   ) British academic and novelist.
Eating People is Wrong, Ch. 5

870 America is a large, friendly dog in a very small room. Every time it wags its tail it knocks over a chair.
Arnold Toynbee (1889–1975) British historian.
Broadcast news summary, 14 July 1954

1955

871* On the Continent people have good food; in England people have good table manners.
George Mikes (1912–87) Hungarian-born British writer.
How to be an Alien

1956

872 An Englishman's way of speaking absolutely classifies him
The moment he talks he makes some other Englishman despise him.
Alan Jay Lerner (1918–86) US songwriter.
My Fair Lady, I:1

1957

873 The thing that impresses me most about America is the way parents obey their children.
Duke of Windsor (1894–1972) King of the United Kingdom; abdicated 1936.
Look Magazine, 5 Mar 1957

1958

874 There are still parts of Wales where the only concession to gaiety is a striped shroud.
Gwyn Thomas (1913–81) British writer.
Punch, 18 June 1958

1959

875 Latins are tenderly enthusiastic. In Brazil they throw flowers at you. In Argentina they throw themselves.
Marlene Dietrich (Maria Magdalene von Losch; 1904–) German-born film star.
Newsweek, 24 Aug 1959

1960s

876 Other people have a nationality. The Irish and the Jews have a psychosis.
Brendan Behan (1923–64) Irish playwright.
Richard's Cork Leg, I

877 The English and Americans dislike only *some* Irish – the same Irish that the Irish themselves detest, Irish writers – the ones that *think*.
Brendan Behan
Richard's Cork Leg, I

878 The United States, I believe, are under the impression that they are twenty years in advance of this country; whilst, as a matter of actual verifiable fact, of course, they are just about six hours behind it.
Harold Hobson (1904–) British theatre critic and writer.
The Devil in Woodford Wells, Ch. 8

879 England is . . . a country infested with people who love to tell us what to do, but who very rarely seem to know what's going on.
Colin MacInnes (1914–76) British novelist.
England, Half English, 'Pop Songs and Teenagers'

1960

880 An American is either a Jew, or an anti-Semite, unless he is both at the same time.
Jean-Paul Sartre (1905–80) French writer.
Altona

1961

881 Venice is like eating an entire box of chocolate liqueurs at one go.
Truman Capote (1924–84) US novelist.
Remark, Nov 1961

882 The difference between our decadence and the Russians' is that while theirs is brutal, ours is apathetic.
James Thurber (1894–1961) US humorist.
Remark, Feb 1961

883 We are all American at puberty; we die French
Evelyn Waugh (1903–66) British novelist.
Diaries, 'Irregular Notes', 18 July 1961

1962

884 The immense popularity of American movies abroad demonstrates that Europe is the unfinished negative of which America is the proof.
Mary McCarthy (1912–) US novelist.
On the Contrary

885 When an American heiress wants to buy a man she at once crosses the Atlantic. The only really materialistic people I have ever met have been Europeans.
Mary McCarthy
On the Contrary 1962

1965

886 The English are polite by telling lies. The Americans are polite by telling the truth.
Malcolm Bradbury (1932–) British academic and novelist.
Stepping Westward, Bk. II, Ch. 5

887 To eat well in England you should have breakfast three times a day.
W. Somerset Maugham (1874–1965) British novelist.
Attrib.

1968

888 The most dangerous thing in the world is to make a friend of an Englishman, because he'll come sleep in your closet rather than spend 10s on a hotel.
Truman Capote (1924–84) US novelist.
Remark, Mar 1968

889 There are many things in life more worthwhile than money. One is to be brought up in this our England which is still the envy of less happy lands.
Lord Denning (1899–) British judge.
The Observer, 'Sayings of the Week', 4 Aug 1968

1969

90 Scratch an American and you get a Seventh Day Adventist every time.
Lord Hailsham (1907–) British Conservative politician.
Remark, June 1969

91 A Jewish man with parents alive is a fifteen-year-old boy, and will remain a fifteen-year-old boy till they die.
Philip Roth (1933–) US novelist.
Portnoy's Complaint

1970

92 We may be a small island, but we are not a small people.
Edward Heath (1916–) British politician.
Speech, June 1970

1972

93 Pass a law to give every single wingeing bloody Pommie his fare home to England. Back to the smoke and the sun shining ten days a year and shit in the streets. Yer can have it.
Thomas Keneally (1935–) Australian novelist.
The Chant of Jimmy Blacksmith

1974

94 Pessimism is a luxury that a Jew never can allow himself.
Golda Meir (1898–1978) Russian-born Israeli stateswoman.
The Observer, 'Sayings of the Year', 29 Dec 1974

95 A lot of men who have accepted – or had imposed upon them in boyhood – the old English public school styles of careful modesty in speech, with much understatement, have behind their masks an appalling and impregnable conceit of themselves. If they do not blow their own trumpets it is because they feel you are not fit to listen to the performance.
J. B. Priestley (1894–1984) British novelist.
Outcries and Asides

1975

96 Americans have been conditioned to respect newness, whatever it costs them.
John Updike (1932–) US novelist.
A Month of Sundays, Ch. 18

97 The Japanese have perfected good manners and made them indistinguishable from rudeness.
Paul Theroux (1941–) US-born writer.
The Great Railway Bazaar, Ch. 2

1977

98 All races have produced notable economists, with the exception of the Irish who doubtless can protest their devotion to higher arts.
John Kenneth Galbraith (1908–) US economist.
The Age of Uncertainty, Ch. 1

899 The problem with Ireland is that it's a country full of genius, but with absolutely no talent.
Hugh Leonard (1926–) Irish dramatist.
Said during an interview
The Times, Aug 1977

900 The national dish of America is menus.
Robert Robinson (1927–) British writer and broadcaster.
BBC TV programme, *Robinson's Travels*, Aug 1977

901 I believe that the Jews have made a contribution to the human condition out of all proportion to their numbers: I believe them to be an immense people. Not only have they supplied the world with two leaders of the stature of Jesus Christ and Karl Marx, but they have even indulged in the luxury of following neither one nor the other.
Peter Ustinov (1921–) British actor.
Dear Me, Ch. 19

1978

902 I find it hard to say, because when I was there it seemed to be shut.
Clement Freud (1924–) British Liberal politician and broadcaster.
On being asked for his opinion of New Zealand. Similar remarks have been attributed to others
BBC radio, 12 Apr 1978

Religion

1948

903 Religion
Has made an honest woman of the supernatural,
And we won't have it kicking over the traces again.
Christopher Fry (1907–) British dramatist.
The Lady's Not for Burning, II

904 If a Jew is fascinated by Christians it is not because of their virtues, which he values little, but because they represent anonymity, humanity without race.
Jean-Paul Sartre (1905–80) French writer.
Anti-Semite and Jew

1949

905 The dogma of the Ghost in the Machine.
Gilbert Ryle (1900–76) British philosopher.
The Concept of Mind, Ch. 1

906 'God knows how you Protestants can be expected to have any sense of direction,' she said. 'It's different with us. I haven't been to mass for years, I've got every mortal sin on my

conscience, but I know when I'm doing wrong.
I'm still a Catholic.
Angus Wilson (1913–) British novelist.
The Wrong Set, 'Significant Experience'

1950s

907 Becoming an Anglo-Catholic must surely be a
sad business – rather like becoming an amateur conjurer.
John St Loe Strachey (1901–63) British
politician.
The Coming Struggle for Power, Pt. III, Ch. 11

908 Operationally, God is beginning to resemble
not a ruler but the last fading smile of a cosmic
Cheshire cat.
Julian Huxley (1887–1975) British biologist.
Religion without Revelation

909 It is now quite lawful for a Catholic woman to
avoid pregnancy by a resort to mathematics,
though she is still forbidden to resort to
physics and chemistry.
H. L. Mencken (1880–1956) US journalist.
Notebooks, 'Minority Report'

1950

910 One cannot really be a Catholic and grown-up.
George Orwell (Eric Blair; 1903–50) British
novelist.
Collected Essays

1953

911 There are many who stay away from church
these days because you hardly ever mention
God any more.
Arthur Miller (1915–) US dramatist.
The Crucible, I

1954

912 There seems to be a terrible misunderstanding
on the part of a great many people to the effect that when you cease to believe you may
cease to behave.
Louis Kronenberger (1904–80) US writer
and literary critic.
Company Manners

913 To perceive Christmas through its wrapping becomes more difficult with every year.
Elwyn Brooks White (1899–1985) US journalist and humorist.
The Second Tree from the Corner

1956

914 God is the immemorial refuge of the incompetent, the helpless, the miserable. They find
not only sanctuary in His arms, but also a kind
of superiority, soothing to their macerated
egos; He will set them above their betters.
H. L. Mencken (1880–1956) US journalist.
Notebooks, 'Minority Report'

1958

915 It is the final proof of God's omnipotence tha
he need not exist in order to save us.
Peter De Vries (1910–) US novelist.
The Mackerel Plaza, Ch. 2

1961

916 Those who marry God . . . can become domest
cated too – it's just as humdrum a marriage
as all the others.
Graham Greene (1904–) British novelist.
A Burnt-Out Case, Ch. 1

917 Your cravings as a human animal do not become a prayer just because it is God whom yo
must ask to attend to them.
Dag Hammarskjöld (1905–61) Swedish
diplomat.
Markings

1962

918 To die for a religion is easier than to live it
absolutely.
Jorge Luis Borges (1899–1986) Argentinia
writer.
Labyrinthes

919 Forgive, O Lord, my little jokes on Thee
And I'll forgive Thy great big one on me.
Robert Frost (1875–1963) US poet.
In the clearing, 'Cluster of Faith'

1963

920 If the concept of God has any validity or use,
can only be to make us larger, freer, and more
loving. If God cannot do this, then it is time
we got rid of Him.
James Baldwin (1924–1987) US writer.
The Fire next Time

1965

921 The most odious of concealed narcissisms –
prayer.
John Fowles (1926–) British novelist.
The Aristos

922 God can stand being told by Professor Ayer
and Marghanita Laski that He doesn't exist.
J. B. Priestley (1894–1984) British novelist.
The Listener, 1 July 1965, 'The BBC's Duty to
Society'

1970

923 Meditation is not a means to an end. It is bot
the means and the end.
Jiddu Krishnamurti (1895–) Indian Hindu
philosopher.
The Penguin Krishnamurti Reader

24 There's a Bible on that shelf there. But I keep it next to Voltaire — poison and antidote.
Bertrand Russell (1872–1970) British philosopher.
Kenneth Harris Talking To: 'Bertrand Russell' (Kenneth Harris)

1974

25 If you talk to God, you are praying; if God talks to you, you have schizophrenia. If the dead talk to you, you are a spiritualist; if God talks to you, you are a schizophrenic.
Thomas Szasz (1920–) US psychiatrist.
The Second Sin

1975

26 In general the churches, visited by me too often on weekdays . . . bore for me the same relation to God that billboards did to Coca-Cola: they promoted thirst without quenching it.
John Updike (1932–) US novelist.
A Month of Sundays, Ch. 2

1977

27 The idea that He would take his attention away from the universe in order to give me a bicycle with three speeds is just so unlikely I can't go along with it.
Quentin Crisp (?1910–) British model, publicist, and writer.
The Sunday Times, 18 Dec 1977

28 It is no accident that the symbol of a bishop is a crook, and the sign of an archbishop is a double-cross.
Dom Gregory Dix (1901–52) British monk.
Letter to *The Times*, 3 Dec 1977 (Francis Bown)

1981

29 If this is God's world there are no unimportant people.
George Thomas (1909–) British politician.
Remark, in a television interview

1983

30 The purpose of population is not ultimately peopling earth. It is to fill heaven.
Graham Leonard (1921–) British churchman (Bishop of London).
Said during a debate on the Church and the Bomb
Speech, General Synod of the Church of England, 10 Feb 1983

1986

31 Organized religion is making Christianity political rather than making politics Christian.
Laurens Van der Post (1906–) South African novelist.
The Observer, 'Sayings of the Week', 9 Nov 1986

1987

932 Beware when you take on the Church of God. Others have tried and have bitten the dust.
Desmond Tutu (1931–) South African clergyman.
Speech, Apr 1987

1988

933 We must reject a privatization of religion which results in its reduction to being simply a matter of personal salvation.
Robert Runcie (1921–) British churchman (Archbishop of Canterbury).
The Observer, 'Sayings of the Week', 17 Apr 1988

Science, Medicine, and Technology

1946

934 MASTER. They split the atom by firing particles at it, at 5,500 miles a second.
BOY. Good heavens. And they only split it?
Will Hay (1888–1949) British comedian.
The Fourth Form at St Michael's

1949

935 When you are courting a nice girl an hour seems like a second. When you sit on a red-hot cinder a second seems like an hour. That's relativity.
Albert Einstein (1879–1955) German-born US physicist.
News Chronicle, 14 Mar 1949

1950s

936 Show me a sane man and I will cure him for you.
Carl Gustav Jung (1875–1961) Swiss psychoanalyst.
The Observer, 19 July 1975

937 Science must begin with myths, and with the criticism of myths.
Karl Popper (1902–) Austrian-born British philosopher.
British Philosophy in the Mid-Century (ed. C. A. Mace)

1950

938 Science without religion is lame, religion without science is blind.
Albert Einstein (1879–1955) German-born US physicist.
Out of My Later Years

939 The whole of science is nothing more than a refinement of everyday thinking.
Albert Einstein
Out of My Later Years

1951

940 By his very success in inventing labour-saving devices modern man has manufactured an abyss of boredom that only the privileged classes in earlier civilisations have ever fathomed.
Lewis Mumford (1895–) US social philosopher.
The Conduct of Life

1952

941 There is no evil in the atom; only in men's souls.
Adlai Stevenson (1900–65) US statesman.
Speech, Hartford, Connecticut, 18 Sept 1952

1953

942 Factual evidence can never 'prove' a hypothesis; it can only fail to disprove it, which is what we generally mean when we say, somewhat inexactly, that the hypothesis is 'confirmed' by experience.
Milton Friedman (1912–) US economist.
Essays in Positive Economics

1955

943 From an evolutionary point of view, man has stopped moving, if he ever did move.
Pierre Teilhard de Chardin (1881–1955) French Jesuit and palaeontologist.
The Phenomenon of Man, Postscript

1958

944 Don't tell me that man doesn't belong out there. Man belongs wherever he wants to go; and he'll do plenty well when he gets there.
Wernher von Braun (1912–77) German rocket engineer.
Referring to space flights

1962

945 When I find myself in the company of scientists, I feel like a shabby curate who has strayed by mistake into a drawing-room full of dukes.
W. H. Auden (1907–73) British poet.
The Dyer's Hand

946 As cruel a weapon as the cave man's club, the chemical barrage has been hurled against the fabric of life.
Rachel Carson (1907–64) US biologist.
The Silent Spring

947 The true men of action in our time, those who transform the world, are not the politicians and statesmen, but the scientists. Unfortunately, poetry cannot celebrate them, because their deeds are concerned with things, not persons and are, therefore, speechless.
W. H. Auden (1907–73) British poet.
The Dyer's Hand

948 The content of physics is the concern of physicists, its effect the concern of all men.
Friedrich Dürrenmatt (1921–) Swiss writer.
The Physicists

1963

949 Our scientific power has outrun our spiritual power. We have guided missiles and misguided men.
Martin Luther King (1929–68) US Black civil-rights leader.
Strength to Love

950 We have genuflected before the god of science only to find that it has given us the atomic bomb, producing fears and anxieties that science can never mitigate.
Martin Luther King
Strength through Love, Ch. 13

1964

951* Science has 'explained' nothing; the more we know the more fantastic the world becomes and the profounder the surrounding darkness.
Aldous Huxley (1894–1964) British novelist.
Views Of Holland

1967

952 There are one hundred and ninety-three living species of monkeys and apes. One hundred and ninety-two of them are covered with hair. The exception is a naked ape self-named *Homo sapiens*.
Desmond Morris (1928–) British biologist and writer.
The Naked Ape, Introduction

1968

953 Already for thirty-five years he had not stopped talking and almost nothing of fundamental value had emerged.
James Dewey Watson (1928–) US geneticist.
Referring to Francis Crick, with whom Watson had discovered the structure of DNA
The Double Helix, Ch. 8

1969

954 Machines from the Maxim gun to the computer are for the most part means by which a minority can keep free men in subjection.
Kenneth Clark (1903–83) British art historian
Civilisation

1970

955* The emergence of intelligence, I am convinced, tends to unbalance the ecology. In other words, intelligence is the great polluter. It is

not until a creature begins to manage its environment that nature is thrown into disorder.
Clifford D. Simak (1904–) US journalist.
Shakespeare's Planet

956 Freud is the father of psychoanalysis. It has no mother.
Germaine Greer (1939–) Australian-born British writer and feminist.
The Female Eunuch

1972

957 Any sufficiently advanced technology is indistinguishable from magic.
Arthur C. Clarke (1917–) British science-fiction writer.
The Lost Worlds of 2001

1973

958 That is the essence of science: ask an impertinent question, and you are on the way to the pertinent answer.
Jacob Bronowski (1908–74) British scientist and writer.
The Ascent of Man, Ch. 4

959 When a distinguished but elderly scientist states that something is possible, he is almost certainly right. When he states that something is impossible, he is very probably wrong.
Arthur C. Clarke (1917–) British science-fiction writer.
Profiles of the Future

1974

960 Traditional scientific method has always been at the very *best*, 20-20 hindsight. It's good for seeing where you've been.
Robert T. Pirsig (1928–) US writer.
Zen and the Art of Motorcycle Maintenance, Pt. III, Ch. 24

961 Formerly, when religion was strong and science weak, men mistook magic for medicine, now, when science is strong and religion weak, men mistake medicine for magic.
Thomas Szasz (1920–) US psychiatrist.
The Second Sin

1978

962 Out of all possible universes, the only one which can exist, in the sense that it can be known, is simply the one which satisfies the narrow conditions necessary for the development of intelligent life.
Bernard Lovell (1913–) British astronomer and writer.
In the Centre of Immensities

1979

963 Space isn't remote at all. It's only an hour's

drive away if your car could go straight upwards.
Fred Hoyle (1915–) British astronomer.
The Observer, 9 Sept 1979

1982

964 Science may be described as the art of systematic over-simplification.
Karl Popper (1902–) Austrian-born British philosopher.
Remark, Aug 1982

1983

965 It is, of course, a bit of a drawback that science was invented after I left school.
Lord Carrington (1919–) British statesman.
The Observer, 23 Jan 1983

1986

966 Should we force science down the throats of those that have no taste for it? Is it our duty to drag them kicking and screaming into the twenty-first century? I am afraid that it is.
George Porter (1920–) British chemist.
Speech, Sept 1986

1987

967 My message to the businessmen of this country when they go abroad on business is that there is one thing above all they can take with them to stop them catching Aids, and that is the wife.
Edwina Currie (1946–) British politician.
Speech, Feb 1987

1988

968 It could be said that the Aids pandemic is a classic own-goal scored by the human race against itself.
Princess Anne (1950–) The Princess Royal, only daughter of Elizabeth II.
Remark, Jan 1988

969 The strongest possible piece of advice I would give to any young woman is: Don't screw around, and don't smoke.
Edwina Currie (1946–) British politician.
The Observer, 'Sayings of the Week', 3 Apr 1988

Wealth and Poverty

1946

970 A rich man is one who isn't afraid to ask the salesman to show him something cheaper.
Anonymous
Ladies Home Journal, Jan 1946

1948

971 Increase of material comforts, it may be generally laid down, does not in any way whatsoever conduce to moral growth.
Mahatma Gandhi (Mohandas Karamchand Gandhi; 1869–1948) Indian national leader.
Obituary, *News Chronicle*

1956

972 Who Wants to Be a Millionaire? I don't.
Cole Porter (1893–1964) US songwriter.
Who Wants to be a Millionaire?, title song

1958

973 In the affluent society no useful distinction can be made between luxuries and necessaries.
John Kenneth Galbraith (1908–) US economist.
The Affluent Society, Ch. 21

974 Wealth has never been a sufficient source of honour in itself. It must be advertised, and the normal medium is obtrusively expensive goods.
John Kenneth Galbraith
The Affluent Society, Ch. 7

975 Wealth is not without its advantages, and the case to the contrary, although it has often been made, has never proved widely persuasive.
John Kenneth Galbraith
The Affluent Society, Ch. 1

1960

976* The heart of the matter, as I see it, is the stark fact that world poverty is primarily a problem of two million villages, and thus a problem of two thousand million villagers.
E. F. Schumacher (1911–77) German-born economist.
Small is Beautiful, A Study of Economics as if People Mattered, Ch. 13

1961

977 Money, it turned out, was exactly like sex, you thought of nothing else if you didn't have it and thought of other things if you did.
James Baldwin (1924–87) US writer.
Nobody Knows My Name

978 For every talent that poverty has stimulated, it has blighted a hundred.
John W. Gardner (1912–) US writer.
Excellence

979 If a free society cannot help the many who are poor it cannot save the few who are rich.
John Fitzgerald Kennedy (1917–63) US statesman.
Speech, 20 Jan 1961

1962

980 People who are much too sensitive to demand

of cripples that they run races ask of the poor that they get up and act just like everyone else in society.
Michael Harrington (1928–) US socialist and writer.
The Other America

1967

981 I don't know how much money I've got . . . I did ask the accountant how much it came to. I wrote it down on a bit of paper. But I've lost the bit of paper.
John Lennon (1940–80) British rock musician.
The Beatles (Hunter Davies)

1968

982 To some extent, if you've seen one city slum you've seen them all.
Spiro Agnew (1918–) US politician.
Election speech, Detroit, 18 Oct 1968

1975

983 . . . the poor are our brothers and sisters. . . . people in the world who need love, who need care, who have to be wanted.
Mother Teresa (Agnes Gonxha Bojaxhui; 1910–) Yugoslavian missionary in Calcutta.
Time, 'Saints Among Us', 29 Dec 1975

1980

984 The rich hate signing cheques. Hence the success of credit cards.
Graham Greene (1904–) British novelist.
Dr. Fischer of Geneva

985 No one would have remembered the Good Samaritan if he'd only had good intentions. He had money as well.
Margaret Thatcher (1925–) British politician and prime minister.
Television interview, 1980

1981

986 They gave me star treatment because I was making a lot of money. But I was just as good when I was poor.
Bob Marley (1945–81) Jamaican reggae singer.
The Radio Times, 18 Sept 1981

Work and Occupations

1946

987 Today we have naming of parts. Yesterday,
We had daily cleaning. And tomorrow morning
We shall have what to do after firing. But today,

Today we have naming of parts.
Henry Reed (1914–) British poet and dramatist.
Naming of Parts

1950s

988 A politician is an arse upon which everyone has sat except a man.
e. e. cummings (1894–1962) US poet.
A Politician

1951

989 I was born at the age of twelve on a Metro-Goldwyn-Mayer lot.
Judy Garland (Frances Gumm; 1922–69) US film star.
The Observer, 'Sayings of the Week', 18 Feb 1951

1953

990 The physician can bury his mistakes, but the architect can only advise his client to plant vines.
Frank Lloyd Wright (1869–1959) US architect.
New York Times Magazine, 4 Oct 1953

1958

991 The rise in the total of those employed is governed by Parkinson's Law and would be much the same whether the volume of work were to increase, diminish or even disappear.
Cyril Northcote Parkinson (1919–) British historian and writer.
Parkinson's Law, Ch. 1

992 Work expands so as to fill the time available for its completion.
Cyril Northcote Parkinson
Parkinson's Law, Ch. 1

1960

993 You ask me what it is I do. Well actually, you know,
I'm partly a liaison man and partly P.R.O.
Essentially I integrate the current export drive
And basically I'm viable from ten o'clock till five.
John Betjeman (1906–84) British poet.
Executive

994 An artist is someone who produces things that people don't need to have but that he – for *some reason* – thinks it would be a good idea to give them.
Andy Warhol (Andrew Warhola; 1926–87) US pop artist.
From A to B and Back Again, 'Atmosphere'

1961

995 A psychiatrist is a man who goes to the Folies-Bergère and looks at the audience.
Mervyn Stockwood (1913–) British churchman.
Remark, Oct 1961

996 A judge is not supposed to know anything about the facts of life until they have been presented in evidence and explained to him at least three times.
Hubert Lister Parker (1900–72) Lord Chief Justice of England.
The Observer, 'Sayings of the Week', 12 Mar 1961

1963

997 Work is much more fun than fun.
Noël Coward (1899–1973) British dramatist.
Remark, June 1963

1964

998 Once a newspaper touches a story, the facts are lost forever, even to the protagonists.
Norman Mailer (1923–) US writer.
The Presidential Papers

999 I have nothing against undertakers personally. It's just that I wouldn't want one to bury my sister.
Jessica Mitford (1917–) British writer.
Attrib. in *Saturday Review*, 1 Feb 1964

1967

1000 Journalism is the only job that requires no degrees, no diplomas and no specialised knowledge of any kind.
Patrick Campbell (1913–80) British humorous writer and editor.
My Life and Easy Times

1970s

1001 The only place where success comes before work is a dictionary.
Vidal Sassoon (1928–) British hair stylist.
Quoting one of his teachers in a BBC radio broadcast

1970

1002 No brilliance is needed in the law. Nothing but common sense, and relatively clean finger nails.
John Mortimer (1923–) British lawyer and dramatist.
A Voyage Round My Father, I

1974

1003 Publication is the male equivalent of childbirth.
Richard Acland (1906–) British politician and writer.
The Observer, 'Sayings of the Week', 19 May 1974

1004 Some breakfast food manufacturer hit upon the simple notion of emptying out the leavings of carthorse nosebags, adding a few other things like unconsumed portions of chicken layer's mash, and the sweepings of racing stables, packing the mixture in little bags and selling them in health food shops.
Frank Muir (1920–) British writer and broadcaster.
Upon My Word!

1005 Psychiatrists classify a person as neurotic if he suffers from his problems in living, and a psychotic if he makes others suffer.
Thomas Szasz (1920–) US psychiatrist.
The Second Sin

1975

1006 The best careers advice to give to the young is 'Find out what you like doing best and get someone to pay you for doing it.'
Katherine Whitehorn (1926–) British journalist.
The Observer, 1975

1978

1007 Poets and painters are outside the class system, or rather they constitute a special class of their own, like the circus people and the gipsies.
Gerald Brenan (Edward Fitzgerald Brenan; 1894–1987) British writer.
Thoughts in a Dry Season, 'Writing'

1979

1008 We are closer to the ants than to the butterflies. Very few people can endure much leisure.
Gerald Brenan
Thoughts in a Dry Season

1009 I used to say that politics was the second lowest profession and I have come to know that it bears a great similarity to the first.
Ronald Reagan (1911–) US politician and president.
The Observer, 13 May 1979

1010 I should have worked just long enough to discover that I didn't like it.
Paul Theroux (1941–) US-born writer.
The Observer Magazine, 1 Apr 1979

1981

1011 The affluent society has made everyone dislike work, and come to think of idleness as the happiest life.
Geoffrey Keynes (1887–) British surgeon and literary scholar.
The Observer, 25 Oct 1981

1012 Politicians can forgive almost anything in the way of abuse; they can forgive subversion, revolution, being contradicted, exposed as liars, even ridiculed, but they can never forgive being ignored.
Auberon Waugh (1939–) British novelist and critic.
The Observer, 11 Oct 1981

1982

1013 Nowadays there are no serious philosophers who are not looking forward to the pension to which their involvement with the subject entitles them.
Anthony Quinton (1925–) British philosopher.
Thoughts and Thinkers

1985

1014 The schoolteacher is certainly underpaid as a childminder, but ludicrously overpaid as an educator.
John Osborne (1929–) British dramatist.
The Observer, 'Sayings of the Week', 21 July 1985

1015 All politicians have vanity. Some wear it more gently than others.
David Steel (1938–) British politician.
Remark, July 1985

1986

1016 To finish is both a relief and a release from an extraordinarily pleasant prison.
Dr. Robert Burchfield (1923–) New Zealand editor.
On completing the supplements to the Oxford English Dictionary, Sept 1986

Sayings of the Time

1945

1017 Four legs good, two legs bad.
George Orwell (Eric Blair; 1903–50) British novelist.
Animal Farm, Ch. 3

1950s

1018 SIXTY HORSES WEDGED IN A CHIMNEY
The story to fit this sensational headline has not turned up yet.
J. B. Morton (1893–1979) British journalist.
The Best of Beachcomber, 'Mr Justice Cocklecarrot: Home Life'

1019 **Call me madame.**
Francis Perkins (1882–1965) US social worker and politician.
Deciding the term of address she would prefer when made the first woman to hold a cabinet office in the USA
Familiar Quotations (J. Bartlett)

1951

1020 **Angry Young Man.**
Leslie Paul (1905–) British writer.
Book title

1955

1021 **I never said, 'I want to be alone.' I only said, 'I want to be *left* alone.' There is all the difference.**
Greta Garbo (1905–) Swedish-born US. film star.
Garbo (John Bainbridge)

1960

1022 **Shoot all the bluejays you want, if you can hit 'em, but remember it's a sin to kill a mockingbird.**
Harper Lee (1926–) US writer.
To Kill a Mockingbird, Pt. II, Ch. 10

1962

1023 **Who's Afraid of Virginia Woolf?**
Edward Albee (1928–) US dramatist.
Play title

1024 **It is hard to tell where MCC ends and the Church of England begins.**
J. B. Priestley (1894–1984) British novelist.
New Statesman, 20 July 1962, 'Topside Schools'

1973

1025 **All the faces here this evening seem to be bloody Poms.**
Charles, Prince of Wales (1948–) Eldest son of Elizabeth II.
Remark at Australia Day dinner, 1973

1977

1026 **May the Force be with you.**
George Lucas (1945–) US film director.
Star Wars

With Foresight

1027 **Boast not thyself of tomorrow; for thou knowest not what a day may bring forth.**
Bible: Proverbs
27:1

1028 **If you want a picture of the future, imagine a boot stamping on a human face — for ever.**
George Orwell (Eric Blair; 1903–50) British novelist.
Nineteen Eighty-Four

1029 **I have seen the future and it works.**
Lincoln Steffens (1879–1955)
Said after visiting the Soviet Union
Autobiography, Ch. 18

1030 **I have a vision of the future, chum.
The workers' flats in fields of soya beans
Tower up like silver pencils.**
John Betjeman (1906–84) British poet.

1031 **The future is made of the same stuff as the present.**
Simone Weil (1909–43) French philosopher.
On Science, Necessity, and the Love of God (ed. Richard Rees), 'Some Thoughts on the Love of God'

1032 **This is the way the world ends
Not with a bang but a whimper**
T. S. Eliot (1888–1965) US born British poet and dramatist.
The Hollow Men

Keyword Index

when Mozart was my a. 8:670
Years hence, perhaps, may dawn an a. 10:567
aged a. diplomats . . . bored than for young men to die 13:168
agenda Our a. is now exhausted 13:6
agent prime a. of all human perception 10:359
ages His acts being seven a. 7:274
aggregate the a. of the recipes 12:928
aggressor whole world should be ranged against an a. 12:255
agnostic rather a compliment to be called an a. 12:880
agony a lonely spasm of helpless a. 11:244
agreeable I do not want people to be very a. 9:146
agreement My people and I have come to an a. 8:178
Whenever you accept our views we shall be in full a. 13:312
agricultural A. . . . classic own-goal scored by the human race 13:968
the a. labourers . . . commute from London 13:512
Aids to stop them catching A. 13:967
air my spirit found outlet in the a. 12:628
to the Germans that of the a. 9:39
airplane The a. stays up because it doesn't have the time to fall 11:492
Alamein Before A. we never had a victory 12:379
alarm The tocsin you hear today is not an a. but an alert 9:17
Albert ask me to take a message to A. 11:26
A. was merely a young foreigner 10:657
that A. married beneath him 12:464
alcohol A. . . . enables Parliament to do things at eleven 11:132
alcoholic a. liquors have been used by the . . . best races 12:586
ale no more cakes and a. 7:362
ale-house jangled in every a. and tavern 7:32
alert The tocsin you hear today is not an alarm but an a. 9:17
Alexander If I were not A. 2:12
Algérie A. Française 13:105
alien State socialism is totally a. 13:369
alive Bliss was it in that dawn to be a. 9:208
needst not strive . . . to keep a. 10:568
not one will still be a. in a hundred years' time 2:49
We intend to remain a. 13:255
what matters is to come out a. 12:687
all A. for one, and one for all 10:642
a. our yesterdays 7:287
Damn you, Jack – I'm a. right 11:542
allegiance Not bound to swear a. to any master 4:15
allies former a. had blundered 12:251
ally An a. has to be watched 12:190
almonds Don't eat too many a. 12:991
alone All we ask is to be let a. 10:192
And we are left, or shall be left, a. 9:64
I want to be a. 12:982
'I want to be a.' 13:1021
No poet . . . has . . . meaning a. 12:461
To be a. is the fate of all great minds 10:468
woe to him that is a. when he falleth 1:69
Alpha A. and Omega 3:120
altars struggled in poverty to build these a. 11:468
alternative a need to create an a. world 13:490
am I a. that I a. 1:35
in the infinite I A. 10:359
I think therefore I a. 7:304
amateur America . . . is the prize a. nation 12:56
amateurs a disease that afflicts a. 11:209
nation of a. 11:94
ambition A. is the grand enemy of all peace 12:619
A. should be made of sterner stuff 7:358
A writer's a. should be 13:419
Every man has . . . an a. to be a wag 8:442
Let not A. mock 8:627
What argufies pride and a. 8:322
America A. . . . based on the dreams of spinsters 12:847
A. cannot be an ostrich 12:36
A.! . . . God shed His grace on thee 11:70

A. . . . has gone directly from barbarism to degeneration 12:845
A. is a country of young men 11:455
A. is a large, friendly dog 13:870
A. is just ourselves 10:250
A. is . . . the great Melting-Pot 11:135
A. is the only idealistic nation 12:833
A. . . . is the prize amateur nation 12:56
ask not what A. will do for you 13:145
A.'s really only a kind of Russia 13:670
declares unconditional war on poverty in A. 13:196
elected a vestryman by the people of any parish in A. 8:261
first come to pass in the heart of A. 13:74
most memorable epoch in the history of A. 8:205
The business of A. is business 12:159
the greatest that we owe to the discovery of A. 10:340
The national dish of A. 13:900
to be willing to grant A. independence 8:235
Vietnam was lost in the living rooms of A. 13:287
what makes A. what it is 12:860
when we think of thee, O A. 8:202
Why will A. not reach out . . . to Russia 12:126
woman governs A. 13:861
You cannot conquer A. 8:221
American A. continents, . . . not to be considered as subjects for future colonization 10:20
A. heiress wants to buy a man 13:885
An A. is either a Jew, or an anti-Semite 13:880
A. society . . . half judaised and half negrified 12:870
A. system of rugged individualism 12:840
I am not a Virginian, but an A. 8:191
I am willing to love all mankind, except an A. 8:228
If I were an A., as I am an Englishman 8:223
Let's talk sense to the A. people 13:68
Long Island represents the A.'s idea 12:846
Scratch an A. 13:890
the A. abroad 12:857
the A. flag will float over . . . the British North A. possessions 11:154
the greatest A. friend we have ever known 12:399
Thirteen States . . . , concur in erecting one great A. system 8:257
We are all A. at puberty 13:883
whereby A. girls turn into A. women 13:275
Americanism hyphenated A. 12:29
McCarthyism is A. 13:66
Americans A. have a perfect right to exist 11:271
A. have been conditioned to respect newness 13:896
A. . . . very good at refrigerators 12:345
because A. won't listen to sense 12:416
No one can kill A. and brag 13:380
the matter with A. 12:855
when good A. die they go to Paris 11:457
ammunition Praise the Lord and pass the a. 12:360
am'rous dire offence from a. causes springs 8:489
analysed Everything has been discussed and a. 8:346
analysis historian fits a man for psychological a. 12:970
anarchy grieved under a democracy, call it a. 7:152
ancestor I am my own a. 9:99
ancestors a. on either side of the Battle of Hastings 12:610
when his half-civilized a. were hunting the wild boar 10:436
ancient with the a. is wisdom 1:61
anecdotage man fell into his a. 11:324
angel A. of Death has been abroad 10:153
A. of the Lord came down 8:593
in action, how like an a. 7:240
In heaven an a. is nobody in particular 11:352
This was the A. of History 12:400
angels a little lower than the a. 6:18
fools rush in where a. fear to tread 8:337
I . . . am on the side of the a. 10:620
Not Angles, but a. 5:3
People are not fallen a. 12:429
the tongues of men and of a. 3:95
anger A. is one of the sinews of the soul 7:259
Grief and disappointment give rise to a. 8:550
he that is slow to a. is better than the mighty 1:83

Angles Not A.. but angels 5:3
Angli the *Saxones, A.,* and *lutae* 5:1
Anglo-Catholic Becoming an A. must . . . be a sad business 13:907
angry A. Young Man 13:1020
   The man who gets a. . . . in the right way . . . is commended 2:65
animal Man is a gaming a. 10:403
   man is and will always be a wild a. 12:922
   Man is an intellectual a. 10:363
   man is . . . a religious a. 9:196
   Man is a social a. 8:387
   Man is by nature a political a. 2:14
   Man is the only a. . . . on friendly terms with the victims . . . he eats 11:313
animality its own a. either objectionable or funny 13:628
animals a. . . . know nothing . . . of what people say about them 8:413
   All a. are equal 12:423
   all a. were created . . . for the use of man 10:442
   all there is to distinguish us from other a. 8:425
   My music . . . understood by children and a. 13:448
   paragon of a. 7:240
   some a. are more equal than others 12:423
   There are two things for which a. are . . . envied 8:413
   Wild a. never kill for sport 11:286
annals short and simple a. of the poor 8:627
Anne Move Queen A.? Most certainly not 11:80
annihilation No a. 13:12
anomaly Poverty is an a. to rich people 11:497
anon I would . . . guess that A. . . . was often a woman 12:795
another A. year! – another deadly blow 9:64
   He who would do good to a. 9:189
   Life is just one damned thing after a. 11:371
   No man can . . . condemn a. 7:380
answer give a. as need requireth 1:64
   I do not a. questions like this without being paid 13:810
   The a. . . . is blowin' in the wind 13:685
   where no one asks, no one needs to a. 12:716
antagonistic the most a. to the Victorian age 12:508
anticipation the intelligent a. of facts 11:518
anti-climax everything afterward savours of a. 12:690
antipathy dislike the French from . . . vulgar a. 8:580
antiquated war . . . will be considered as a. as a duel 11:153
anti-semite An American is either a Jew, or an a. 13:880
   hated by every a. as if I were a Jew 13:125
anywhere go a. I damn well please 13:50
apartheid Sanctions are now the only . . . way of ending a. 13:407
   We don't want a. liberalized 13:374
ape Is man an a. or an angel 10:620
   It is not the a., nor the tiger 12:615
   the a. from which he is descended 10:618
   The exception is a naked a. 13:952
ape-like The a. virtues without which 12:555
aphorisms The great writers of a. 13:564
aphrodisiac Power is the ultimate a. 13:302
   The moon is nothing But a circumambulating a. 13:743
apology Never make a defence or a. 7:113
Apostasy is A. too hard a word to describe the temper of the nation 10:50
apostle the a. of class-hatred 12:179
apparel a. oft proclaims the man 7:238
appeal The whole of art is an a. to a reality 12:462
appealed hast thou a. unto Caesar 3:49
appearances shallow people . . . do not judge by a. 11:290
appeaser An a. is one who feeds a crocodile 13:85
appetite a. may sicken and so die 7:172
   the desire of satisfying a voracious a. 8:491
apple want the a. for the a.'s sake 11:295
applications only a. of science 11:485
applied no such things as a. sciences 11:485
appointment a. by the corrupt few 11:115
appreciate I never 'a.' 12:633
apprehend Intelligence is quickness to a. 12:529
approve They that a. . . . call it opinion 7:148

approved I never a. either the errors of his book, or the trivial truths 8:349
April gloomy in England are March and A. 10:345
arbitrator the a. of the affairs of Christendom 7:4
archbishop the sign of an a. is a double-cross 13:928
arch-enemy love . . . has one a. – and that is life 13:742
arches Underneath the a. 12:702
architect Each man the a. of his own fate 4:56
   not a great sculptor or painter can be an a. 10:308
   the a. can only advise 13:990
architecture A. has its political use 8:280
   What has happened to a. . . . that the only passers-by who can contemplate it 13:501
ardua Per a. ad astra 12:73
argument All a. is against it 8:477
   I love a, I love debate 13:335
   work of art must start an a. 13:434
arguments beware of long a. and long beards 12:837
   the world can be expressed in . . . a. 13:556
arise A., O Lord, plead Thine own cause 7:6
aristocracy a. . . . government by the badly educated 12:205
   an absentee a. 10:96
   An a. in a republic is like a chicken 13:98
   displeased with a., call it *oligarchy* 7:152
   If human beings could be propagated . . . a. would be . . . sound 12:220
   Unlike the male codfish . . . the British a. is 12:776
aristocrat the gentleman from both the artist and the a. 12:842
aristocratic to distinguish . . . the a. class from the Philistines 10:252
arithmetic Music is the a. of sounds 12:431
ark an a. of bulrushes 1:31
   into the a., two and two 1:19
Armageddon A. will be at our door 12:406
Armenteers A mademoiselle from A. 12:77
armistice a short a. with truth 13:127
   dream of . . . another wild A. day 12:95
arms I never would lay down my a. 8:223
army An a. is a nation within a nation 10:65
   An a. marches on its stomach 9:105
   contemptible little A. 12:9
   her a. has had a glorious victory 8:77
   If you don't want to use the a., I should like to borrow it 10:204
   little ships of England brought the A. home 12:331
   no longer have an a. 12:93
   The a. ages men sooner than the law 12:952
   The a. is the true nobility of our country 10:154
   The conventional a. loses if it does not win 13:238
arrest One does not a. Voltaire 13:127
arrested Christ . . . would quite likely have been a. 13:186
arrive To travel hopefully is . . . better . . . than to a. 11:425
arrow Every a. . . . feels the attraction of earth 10:564
   I, said the Sparrow, With my bow and a. 6:3
Ars A. 2:72
arse A politician is an a. 13:988
arsenal a. of democracy 12:344
art A. and religion first; then philosophy 13:544
   A. . . . can go on mattering 13:413
   A. for art's sake 10:264
   A. is not a mirror . . . but a hammer 12:446
   a. is not a weapon 13:451
   A. is ruled . . . by the imagination 11:205
   A. is the imposing of a pattern 12:501
   A. is the most intense mode 11:189
   A. is . . . the transmission of feeling 11:194
   a. is to give life a shape 13:475
   All a. deals with the absurd 13:478
   All A. is quite useless 11:188
   A. never expresses anything 11:190
   a. of pleasing consists 9:153
   aspires . . . to the condition of a. 11:193
   A work of a. . . . has something which is anonymous 13:409
   A work of a. . . . seen through a temperament 12:460
   excellence of every a. is its intensity 10:259
   Fine a. is that in which the hand 10:314
   great parables . . . but false a. 12:429

half a trade and half an a.　12:441
Insurrection is an a.　12:210
nature is the a. of God　7:307
princes learn no a. truly, but . . . horsemanship　7:114
Rules and models destroy genius and a.　10:290
the a. of the possible　13:256
The whole of a. is an appeal to a reality　12:462
True ease in writing comes from a.　8:279
work of a. must start an argument　13:434
article　It all depends upon that a. there　9:108
articles　to pay for a. . . . they do not want　12:638
artificial　All things are a.　7:307
　nothing so a. as sinning nowadays　12:813
artist　the gentleman from both the a. and the aristocrat
　12:842
artistic　a. temperament . . . afflicts amateurs　11:209
　There never was an a. period　11:179
artists　A. are not engineers of the soul　13:451
　Great a. have no country　10:302
　The a. retired. The British remained　11:185
art-loving　an A. nation　11:179
arts　If all the a. aspire to the condition of music　12:916
　rustics . . . bringing up their . . . offspring to the liberal a.
　6:17
　secret of the a. is to correct nature　8:276
ashamed　not a. of having been in love　8:482
　to see them not a.　8:400
　We are not a. of what we have done　11:137
Asia　There is too much A.　11:456
　the Sultan were driven, bag and baggage, into the heart
　of A.　10:14
ask　a., and it shall be given　3:129
　To labour and not a. for any reward　7:349
asks　where no one a., no one needs to answer　12:716
aspires　a. . . . to the condition of art　11:193
ass　An unlettered king is a crowned a.　6:133
　every a. thinks he may kick at him　8:307
assassination　Absolutism tempered by a.　10:42
　A. has never changed　10:232
　A. . . . the extreme form of censorship　11:145
assemblance　Care I for the . . . a. of a man　7:232
assertions　Pure mathematics consists entirely of a.　12:904
asset　the greatest a. a head of state can have　13:290
associate　good must a.　8:177
assure　a. him that he'd live tomorrow　7:392
astonished　a. at my own moderation　8:187
asunder　let not man put a.　3:73
asylum　the absence from Jerusalem of a lunatic a.　12:878
　world is . . . like a lunatic a.　12:734
asylums　lunatic a. . . . the stately homes　12:516
atheism　a., breast-feeding, circumcision　13:694
　miracle to convince a.　7:400
atheist　an a. if the king were　8:590
　he was no a.　8:42
　scepticism kept her from being an a.　13:636
Athens　A. arose　10:16
　a new A. might be created in the land of the Franks　5:7
　men of A. . . . ye are too superstitious　3:47
Atlantic　The Admiral of the A.　11:92
　to have the East come to the A.　12:401
atom　carbon a. possesses certain exceptional properties
　12:923
　how the a. is split　12:926
　nearer to the a. than the stars　12:914
　The a. bomb is a paper tiger　13:8
　There is no evil in the a.　13:941
　They split the a. by firing particles at　13:934
atomic　The way to win an a. war　13:65
atoms　fortuitous concurrence of a.　10:166
atone　a. for the sins of your fathers　4:14
atrophy　Music begins to a.　12:483
attack　love until after the first a.　11:377
　situation excellent. I shall a.　12:80
attainments　rare a. . . . but . . . can she spin　7:346
attention　a. to the inside . . . contempt for the outside
　8:344
　take his a. away from the universe　13:927
attorney　the gentleman is an a.　8:643
attraction　Every arrow . . . feels the a. of earth　10:564

audacity　a. of elected persons　10:164
Auden　A. was someone you could laugh-at-with　13:477
　W. H. A., a sort of gutless Kipling　12:491
audience　the a. was a disaster　11:201
Augustus　said of A. that he found Rome brick　10:160
Austen　Jane A.　10:278
Austerlitz　There rises the sun of A.　9:89
Australia　guess . . . he was born in A.　11:460
author　bad novel tells us . . . about its a.　11:208
authority　a. be a stubborn bear　7:102
　A. forgets a dying king　10:183
　Nothing destroyeth a. so much　7:99
　purge the land of . . . false a.　6:36
　The defiance of established a.　13:264
authors　A. are easy to get on with　13:414
　much exposed to a.　10:291
　The faults of great a.　9:126
　The reciprocal civility of a.　8:288
autocracy　maintain the principle of a.　11:75
autocrat　be an a.: that's my trade　8:143
avarice　rich beyond the dreams of a.　8:628
ave　a. atque vale　4:96
avenged　the satisfaction of knowing that we are a.　10:570
average　no great compliment to say that a man is above
　the a.　13:530
　Take the saving lie away from the a. man　11:332
avoiding　Reading . . . ingenious device for a. thought
　10:377
Avon　Sweet Swan of A.　7:175
a-waggle　You must always be a.　12:748
awake　At last a.　10:470
　I dream when I am a.　7:303
　Onaway! A., beloved　10:508
away　the big one that got a.　13:767
awfulness　by its very a.　11:383
awoke　I a. one morning　9:128
axe　his keener eye The a.'s edge did try　7:137
　Lizzie Borden took an a.　11:67
axioms　the world can be expressed in . . . arguments, . . . a.
　and theorems　13:556
axis　This Berlin–Rome connection is . . . an a.　12:273
aye　A., and what then　10:584

B

baa　B., b., black sheep　6:56
Babbitt　one thing wrong with the B. house　12:768
Babel　B.; because the Lord did there confound the lan-
　guage　1:23
　the tower of B. should have got language all mixed up
　8:165
babies　If men had to have b.　13:783
　putting milk into b.　12:780
　War will never cease until b.　12:612
baby　my b. at my breast　4:10
　no new b. in the womb of our society　12:68
Babylon　B. the great　3:100
　By the waters of B. we sit down and weep　8:202
Bach　J. S. B.　8:669
bachelor　Never trust . . . a b. too near　12:764
bachelors　reasons for b. to go out　10:535
back　Either b. us or sack us　13:315
　Will ye no come b. again　8:662
backs　With our b. to the wall . . . each . . . must fight on to
　the end　12:78
backward　In a country economically b., the proletariat can
　take power earlier　12:175
bad　a b. man must have brains　11:303
　a b. novel tells us the truth about its author　11:208
　a brave b. man　7:163
　A truth that's told with b. intent　9:188
　Defend the b. against the worse　12:503
　never was a b. peace　8:249
　nothing either good or b.　7:359
　the name of . . . obstinacy in a b. one　8:556
　two legs b.　13:1017
　what I feel really b. about　13:211
　When b. men combine　8:177
bag　b. and baggage　11:6

bell B., book, and candle 7:351
for whom the b. tolls 7:214
I'll b. the cat 6:78
Bellamy I could eat one of B.'s veal pies 9:60
bells The b. of hell go ting-a-ling-a-ling 12:43
belly to banish hunger by rubbing the b. 2:80
upon thy b. shalt thou go 1:13
victory under the b. of a Cossack's horse 12:213
beloved Onaway! Awake, b. 10:508
below Capten, art tha sleepin' there b. 7:63
benefits It is the nature of men to be bound by the b. they confer 6:110
Berlin when staring at our soldiers drilling in B. 8:579
Berliner Ich bin ein B. 13:171
berth Things hitherto undone should be given . . . a wide b. 13:642
best as in the b. it is 7:361
b. of life is but intoxication 10:329
For home is b. 7:189
His worst is better than any other person's b. 10:267
It was the b. of times 9:210
Men of few words are the b. 7:234
The b. is the enemy of the good 8:559
the b. of possible worlds 8:470
There died a myriad, And of the b. 12:117
we live in the b. of all possible worlds 12:600
we will do our b. 12:356
bestial what remains is b. 7:285
best-seller A b. is the gilded tomb of a mediocre talent 12:478
Bethlehem O come ye to B. 10:592
betray All a man can b. is his conscience 11:454
betrayed woe unto that man by whom the Son of man is b. 3:26
betraying if I had to choose between b. my country and b. my friend 13:63
better always . . . trying to get the b. 10:403
B. than a play 8:14
b. to have no opinion of God 7:403
b. to marry than to burn 3:74
for b. for worse 7:339
I am getting b. and b. 11:537
no b. than you should be 7:249
When you meet someone b. . . . turn your thoughts to becoming his equal 2:42
You're a b. man than I am, Gunga Din 11:530
bewailing the sum of life's b. 10:456
Bible have used the B. as if it was a constable's handbook 10:110
the B. tells me so 10:600
There's a B. on that shelf there 13:924
Bibles they have the land and we have the B. 13:736
bicycle a b. made for two 11:372
big B. Brother is watching you 13:29
he was too b. for them 13:24
the b. one that got away 13:767
bike He got on his b. and looked for work 13:346
billabong Once a jolly swagman camped by a b. 11:535
billboards same relation to God that b. did to Coca-Cola 13:926
billiards to play b. well 11:305
biographies History is the essence of . . . b. 10:390
biography a man is nobody unless his b. 10:486
history . . . the b. of great men 10:392
bird keep such a b. in a cage 7:101
She's only a b. in a gilded cage 11:534
birds b. . . . caught in the snare 1:76
I see all the b. are flown 7:120
spring now comes unheralded by the return of the b. 13:511
that make fine b. 2:34
Birmingham One has no great hopes from B. 10:326
birth B., and copulation, and death 12:695
no credentials . . . not even . . . a certificate of b. 11:143
no cure for b. and death 12:681
birthplace accent of one's b. lingers 8:376
bishop a b. . . . must be blameless 3:127
May you be the mother of a b. 13:635
No B., no King 7:86

the symbol of a b. is a crook 13:928
bisier he semed b. than he was 6:131
bitch an old b. gone in the teeth 12:117
bitches Now we are all sons of b. 12:402
bite would b. some other of my generals 8:133
bites dead woman b. not 7:56
when a man b. a dog that is news 12:662
bivouac an armed camp of Blackshirts, a b. for corpses 12:131
black A lady asked me why . . . , I wore b. 13:696
Any colour, so long as it's b. 12:974
I don't believe in b. majority rule 13:299
looking for a b. hat 11:257
sees b. people as expendable 13:381
The Ethiopians say that their gods are . . . b. 2:70
blacks two b. do not make a white 12:824
Blackshirt Before the organization of the B. movement 12:275
Blackshirts an armed camp of B., a bivouac for corpses 12:131
blame Everyone threw the b. on me 12:202
blast The First B. of the Trumpet 7:41
bleed If you prick us, do we not b. 7:231
blemish Christianity . . . the one immortal b. of mankind 11:473
blessed all generations shall call me b. 3:2
B. are the meek 3:80
b. are the poor in spirit 3:79
b. are they that have not seen, and yet have believed 3:42
b. is he that cometh in the name of the Lord 3:25
b. is the man that endureth temptation 1:89
blessings all which we behold Is full of b. 9:163
a world of b. by good Queen Elizabeth 7:40
blind A b. man in a dark room 11:257
Booth died b. 11:166
Country of the B. 11:367
love is b. 7:316
old, mad, b., despised and dying king 10:4
Painting is a b. man's profession 13:474
wing'd Cupid painted b. 7:315
blindness the . . . world was stumbling . . . in social b. 12:653
bliss B. was it in that dawn to be alive 9:208
block a chip of the old b. 8:247
blockhead No man but a b. ever wrote 8:300
blonde springing from b. to b. like the chamois of the Alps 12:851
blood b. and iron 10:207
be his b. on your own conscience 8:30
B. sport is brought to its ultimate refinement 13:522
b., toil, tears and sweat 12:326
He is all b., dirt and sucked sugar stick 12:486
his b. be on us 3:33
my b. of the new testament 3:27
rather have b. on my hands 13:216
shed his b. for the country 11:112
The b. of the martyrs is the seed of the Church 4:89
the River Tiber foaming with much b. 13:231
thy brother's b. crieth unto me 1:16
trading on the b. of my men 10:256
without shedding of b. is no remission 3:51
your b. of your lives will I require 1:21
bloody All the faces . . . seem to be b. Poms 13:1025
not half b. enough 8:45
bloom It's a sort of b. on a woman 11:415
blow A b. in cold blood 11:386
Another year! − another deadly b. 9:64
B., b., thou winter wind 7:357
b. the Scots back again into Scotland 7:89
themselves must strike the b. 9:94
bludgeoning the b. of the people 11:65
blue The b. ribbon of the turf 10:343
bluffed Winston Churchill has b. them all 12:165
blunder poverty . . . is a b. 11:500
worse than a crime, it is a b. 9:49
blunders b. usually do more to shape history than . . . wickedness 13:571
blushes Man is the only animal that b. 11:299
Boadicea some bargain-basement B. 13:354

oar the b. out of the wood doth waste it 7:6
when his half-civilized ancestors were hunting the wild b. 10:436

oat a beautiful pea-green b. 10:655
in the same b. . . . not a chance of recording the vote 11:141

oating Jolly b. weather 10:348

odies many b. of the saints which slept arose 3:39
our dead b. must tell the tale 11:159
well-developed b., fairly developed minds 12:530

ody a sound mind in a sound b. 4:67
b. of a weak and feeble woman 7:65
Happiness is beneficial for the b. 12:579
Man has no B. distinct from his Soul 9:197
mind that makes the b. rich 7:350
more familiar with Africa than my own b. 13:773
Our b. is a machine for living 10:622
take, eat; this is my b. 3:27
your b. is the temple of the Holy Ghost 3:66

3ognor Bugger B. 12:262

oiler The United States is like a gigantic b. 12:850

omb god of science . . . has given us the atomic b. 13:950

ombed no power on earth that can protect him from being b. 12:221

ombs b. are unbelievable until they . . . fall 13:153
Come, friendly b., and fall on Slough 13:506
drop b. . . . hit civilians 13:217
test the Russians, not the b. 13:101

3onaparte three-o'-clock in the morning courage, which B. thought 9:209

3onar Law all the politicians . . . least significant was B. 12:140

ones Bleach the b. of comrades slain 11:78
O ye dry b. 1:107
The healthy b. of a single Pomeranian grenadier 11:7

bonkers If the British public falls for this . . . it will be . . . b. 13:201

bonny Is b. and blithe, and good and gay 10:640

book a b. . . . sealed with seven seals 3:121
A b. that furnishes no quotations is, . . . a plaything 10:281
A good b. is the best of friends 10:288
A good b. is the precious life-blood 7:183
Another damned, thick, square b. 8:309
any b. should be banned 12:172
Bell, b., and candle 7:351
Everybody writes a b. too many 13:502
he who destroys a good b., kills reason 7:182
I have only read one b. 12:511
little woman who wrote the b. 10:198
moral or an immoral b. 11:187
that everyone has it in him to write one b. 12:495
The possession of a b. 13:550
There are two motives for reading a b. 12:470
There must be a man behind the b. 10:315
When a b. is boring, they yawn openly 13:782
Would you allow your wife . . . to read this b. 13:442

books All b. are divisible into two classes 10:319
B. are a load of crap 13:440
B. are . . . a mighty bloodless substitute for life 11:174
B. are well written, or badly written 11:187
b. by which the printers have lost 7:222
b. cannot be killed by fire 12:374
be not swallowed up in b. 8:336
between a man of sense and his b. 8:344
B. must follow sciences 7:405
B. . . . propose to *instruct* or to *amuse* 10:310
but b. never die 12:374
b. . . . written by people who don't understand them 8:292
Give me b., fruit, French wine and fine weather 10:330
Morality's a gesture. . . . learnt from b. 13:829
proper study of mankind is b. 12:531
the b. of the hour 10:319
the disease of writing b. 8:287
The reading of all good b. 7:181
To read too many b. 13:562
We all know that b. burn 12:374
Whenever b. are burned 10:15
When I think of all the b. I have read 12:731

booksellers b. are generous liberal-minded men 8:640

---

nor even b. have put up with poets' being second-rate 4:30

boorish the opinionated, the ignorant, and the b. 2:44

boot imagine a b. stamping on a human face 13:1028

Booth B. died blind 11:166

boots before the truth has got its b. on 13:301
If ever he went to school without any b. 13:24

bore a b., a bounder and a prig 12:253

bored aged diplomats to be b. 13:168
Punctuality is the virtue of the b. 13:835

boredom three great evils, b., vice, and poverty 8:641

bores he b. for England 13:33

Bores the B. and Bored 10:444

boring curiously b. about . . . happiness 12:585

born a time to be b., and a time to die 1:75
better if neither of us had been b. 9:80
he is not conscious of being b. 8:450
I was b. at the age of twelve 13:989
joy that a man is b. into the world 3:76
Man was b. free 8:144
natural to die as to be b. 7:206
One is not b. a woman 13:785
Some are b. great 7:282
sucker b. every minute 11:289
to have been b. 7:302
We are all b. mad 13:588

borrow If you don't want to use the army, I should like to b. it 10:204

borrowed Britain has lived . . . on b. time 13:300

borrower Neither a b. nor a lender be 7:360

borrowing b. dulls the edge of husbandry 7:360
be not made a beggar by banqueting upon b. 1:86

boss working . . . eight hours a day . . . get to be a b. 12:963

Boston this is good old B. 11:150

bother long words B. me 12:976

Botticelli If B. were alive today 13:450

bottinney b. means a knowledge of plants 10:372

bottles the English have hot-water b. 13:855

bottom b. of the economic pyramid 12:217

boundary right to fix the b. 11:46

bountiful Lady B. 8:651

bourgeois How beastly the b. is 12:790

bourgeoisie the British b. have spoken of themselves as gentlemen 12:842

bourn from whose b. No traveller returns 7:208

bow B. b., ye lower middle classes 11:32
I, said the Sparrow, With my b. and arrow 6:3

bowels in the b. of Christ 7:145

boy And said, What a good b. am I 7:25
every b. and every gal 11:34
He was a b. to the last 10:367
Let the b. win his spurs 6:44
Love is a b. 8:498
rarely . . . one can see in a little b. the promise of a man 10:538
Shades of the prison-house begin to close Upon the growing b. 9:199
the b. will ruin himself 12:258
the little b. Who lives down the lane 6:56

boys As flies to wanton b. 7:210
B. and girls come out to play 8:652
B. are capital fellows in their own way 10:513
B. do not grow up gradually 12:728
Where are the b. of the Old Brigade 11:536
Where . . . b. plan for what . . . young girls plan for whom 11:411
Written by office b. for office b. 11:79

brain a Bear of Very Little B. 12:976
Let schoolmasters puzzle their b. 8:351

brains b. enough to make a fool of himself 11:249
our b. as fruitful as our bodies 8:510
What good are b. to a man 12:773

brainsick folly of one b. Pole 7:27

braking British civil service . . . effective b. mechanism 13:333

brandy I am not well; pray get me . . . b. 9:29

brass Men's evil manners live in b. 7:375
sounding b. 3:95

brave Any fool can be b. on a battle field 12:625

land of the free, and the home of the b. 9:103
Many b. men . . . before Agamemnon's time 2:82
we could never learn to be b. . . . if there were only joy 11:338
bravery man of the greatest honour and b. 6:22
breach Once more unto the b. 6:61
breaches lay the b. at their door 8:15
bread b. and circuses 4:24
I am the b. of life 3:109
Jesus took b., and blessed it 3:27
man shall not live by b. alone 3:78
Peace, B. and Land 12:60
that b. should be so dear 10:95
the living b. 3:14
breakfast-table ready for the national b. 10:486
breast charms to soothe a savage b. 8:275
my baby at my b. 4:10
breast-feeding atheism, b., circumcision 13:694
breasts they add weight to the b. 12:991
breath Can storied urn . . . Back to its mansion call the fleeting b. 8:319
He reaps the bearded grain at a b. 10:354
world will hold its b. 12:354
breathed God . . . b. into his nostrils 1:7
breed happy b. of men 7:69
more careful of the b. of their horses and dogs than of their children 8:501
breezes spicy b. Blow soft o'er Ceylon's isle 10:405
bribe You cannot hope to b. or twist 12:951
bride as a b. adorned for her husband 3:124
It helps . . . to remind your b. that you gave up a throne for her 13:779
bridge London B. is broken down 8:654
brief Out, out, b. candle 7:287
brigade Forward the Light B. 10:149
Where are the boys of the Old B. 11:536
bright b. with hope 12:178
brightness To pass away ere life hath lost its b. 10:353
brilliance No b. is needed in the law 13:1002
brilliant a far less b. pen than mine 11:549
b. men . . . will come to a bad end 11:366
The dullard's envy of b. men 11:366
Britain a time when B. had a savage culture 13:169
battle of B. is about to begin 12:336
B. . . . Fabian Society writ large 13:297
B. fit country for heroes to live in 12:98
B. is no longer in the politics of the pendulum 13:317
B. is not . . . easily rocked by revolution 13:297
When B. first, at heaven's command 8:115
Britannia Rule, B., rule the waves 8:115
British B. loathe the middle-aged 13:741
but we are B. – thank God 13:751
I would rather be B. than just 13:253
less known by the B. than these selfsame B. Islands 10:341
socialism . . . alien to the B. character 13:369
the American flag will float over . . . the B. North American possessions 11:154
The artists retired. The B. remained 11:185
The B., being brought up on team games 13:110
The B. love permanence 13:455
The B. won't fight 13:351
the magnificent fair play of the B. criminal law 11:124
the most vulgar, . . . is the B. tourist 11:223
when a B. Prime Minister sneezed 13:309
British Empire 'Can't' will be the epitaph of the B. 12:292
liquidation of the B. 12:378
Briton as only a free-born B. can do 10:108
I glory in the name of B. 8:139
Britons B. never will be slaves 8:115
B. were only natives 4:102
broils never to entangle ourselves in the b. of Europe 10:19
broken A b. head in Cold Bath Fields 10:53
baying for b. glass 12:841
broker An honest b. 11:13
bronchitis nobody goes to the theatre unless he . . . has b. 12:867

brothel a sort of metaphysical b. for emotions 12:736
brothels b. with bricks of Religion 9:25
brother Big B. is watching you 13:29
I want to be the white man's b. 13:161
brotherhood Freedom! Equality! B. 9:2
brother-in-law not his b. 13:161
brotherly let b. love continue 3:98
brother's am I my b. keeper 1:16
brothers the poor are our b. and sisters 13:983
brought b. nothing into this world 3:71
bruise it shall b. thy head 1:13
sweetest fragrance from the herb . . . tread on it and b. it 10:539
Brummel patronized . . . by B. and the Prince Regent 9:132
Brussels meeting in a darkened bedroom in a B. hotel 13:286
brutality Sentimentality is a superstructure covering b. 13:589
brutes Thanks to words, we have been able to rise above the b. 13:430
Brutus Caesar had his B. – Charles the First, his Cromwell 8:154
bubble Life is mostly froth and b. 10:494
buck The b. stops here 11:43
Buckingham changing guard at B. Palace 12:975
bugger B. Bognor 12:262
build let us think that we b. for ever 10:298
The *end* is to b. well 7:178
builder he can only be a b. 10:308
building Well b. hath three Conditions 7:178
buildings jostling scrum of office b. 13:504
Luftwaffe – . . . knocked down our b. 13:505
piles of b. now rise up and down 8:313
built till we have b. Jerusalem 9:73
bull Down at the old 'B. and Bush' 11:237
bullet Each b. has got its commission 8:322
The b. that is to kill me 9:101
bulrushes an ark of b. 1:31
bums art and literature are left to a lot of shabby b. 12:836
bunk History is more or less b. 12:561
burden Take up the White Man's b. – 11:95
The dreadful b. 8:543
burial Knight of the Crimean B. Grounds 10:159
burn better to marry than to b. 3:74
burned Whenever books are b. 10:15
burning To keep a lamp b. 13:849
burnings B. of people 7:419
bury I come to b. Caesar, not to praise him 4:7
We will b. you 13:96
bus Hitler has missed the b. 12:321
bush the b. burned with fire 1:33
business a woman's b. to get married 11:387
B. as usual 12:11
B. . . . may bring money, . . . friendship hardly ever does 10:623
B. underlies everything in our national life 11:369
future Englishmen must take b. as seriously 11:110
If everybody minded their own b. 10:498
it is . . . our b. to lose innocence 13:579
That's the true b. precept 10:415
The b. of America is b. 12:159
businessmen My message to the b. of this country 13:967
busy How doth the little b. bee 8:637
It is a stupidity . . . to b. oneself with the correction of the world 8:446
thou knowest how b. I must be this day 7:122
butchers Governments needs to have both shepherds and b. 8:232
butchery Had any Christian bishop visited that scene of b. 10:165
butler I vote Labour, but my b.'s a Tory 12:420
butter b. will only make us fat 12:274
fine words b. no parsnips 10:448
buttered I had never had a piece of toast . . . But fell . . . on the b. side 11:333
butterfly a man dreaming I was a b. 2:53
Happiness is like a b. 13:596
buttress a b. of the church 10:79

cemetery send him to the c. 13:209
censor Deleted by French c. 12:53
censorship Assassination . . . the extreme form of c. 11:145
C. . . . depraving and corrupting 13:260
censure All c. of a man's self 8:426
century The c. on which we are entering . . . must be the c. of the common man 12:377
the twentieth c. will be . . . the c. of Fascism 12:229
cerebrums larger c. and smaller adrenal glands 12:612
certain I am c. that we will win the election with a good majority 13:393
certainties begin with c. 7:217
certainty C. is the Mother of Repose 8:70
cesspool London, that great c. 11:227
Ceylon spicy breezes Blow soft o'er C.'s isle 10:405
chains It's often safer to be in c. 12:17
Man . . . everywhere he is in c. 8:144
nothing to lose but their c. 10:118
chalices In old time we had treen c. and golden priests 7:45
Cham That great C. of literature, Samuel Johnson 8:289
Chamberlain C.'s umbrella on the cobblestones of Munich 13:341
chamois springing from blonde to blonde like the c. of the Alps 12:851
champagne Fighting is like c. 12:625
like a glass of c. that has stood 13:220
water flowed like c. 11:29
chance c. favours only the prepared mind 10:614
time and c. happeneth to them all 1:76
We have had our last c. 12:406
Chancellor C. of the Exchequer 11:1
change C. is not made without inconvenience 7:263
If you leave a thing alone you leave it to a torrent of c. 11:363
Most of the c. we think we see 12:705
Plus ça c. 10:465
Popularity? . . . glory's small c. 10:459
The more things c. 10:465
The wind of c. 13:131
changing Woman is always fickle and c. 4:77
Channel let the last man . . . brush the C. with his sleeve 12:6
chaos The grotesque c. of a Labour council 13:376
the view that there is mounting c. 13:322
chapel Devil always builds a c. there 8:594
characteristic typically English c. 12:849
characters Most women have no c. 8:517
charge Electrical force . . . causes motion of electrical c. 12:915
Charing-Cross the full tide of human existence is at C. 8:194
chariot a c. . . . of fire 1:52
charity C. is the power of defending that which we know to be indefensible 11:442
c. never faileth 3:95
c. suffereth long, and is kind 3:95
knowledge puffeth up, but c. edifieth 3:56
now abideth faith, hope, c. 3:95
the greatest of these is c. 3:95
Charles Caesar had his Brutus – C. the First, his Cromwell 8:154
cast out C. our Norman oppressor 7:141
Charlie C. is my darling 8:663
charter This c. . . . constitutes an insult to the Holy See 6:32
chaste godly poet must be c. himself 2:25
chastity Give me c. and continence 5:29
cheap flesh and blood so c. 10:95
check C. enclosed 13:631
cheek whosoever shall smite thee on thy right c. 3:83
cheer Don't c., boys; the poor devils are dying 11:85
cheese 265 kinds of c. 13:64
chemical c. barrage has been hurled against the fabric of life 13:946
Shelley and Keats were . . . up to date in . . . c. knowledge 12:908
cheques The rich hate signing c. 13:984

cherish to love and to c. 7:339
cherry Loveliest of trees, the c. 11:232
chess-board c. is the world; the pieces . . . the phenomena of the universe 10:495
chestnuts warmongers who . . . have others pull the c. out of the fire 12:348
chicken a c. in his pot every Sunday 7:78
England will have her neck wrung like a c. 12:335
Some c. 12:364
chickens children are more troublesome and costly than c. 11:390
Don't count your c. 2:32
You don't set a fox to watching the c. 13:140
child A c. becomes an adult when 13:723
getting wenches with c. 7:196
give her the living c. 1:49
If you strike a c. 11:386
spoil the c. 8:498
sweetest Shakespeare, Fancy's c. 7:180
Think no more of it, John; you are only a c. 6:24
unto us a c. is born 1:99
when I was a c., I spake as a c. 3:95
wise father that knows his own c. 7:332
childbirth the male equivalent of c. 13:1003
childish I put away c. things 3:95
childishness second c. 7:275
children as c. fear to go in the dark 7:205
c. are more troublesome and costly than chickens 11:390
C. have never been very good at listening 13:673
C. . . . have no use for psychology. They detest sociology 13:782
c., obey your parents 3:75
C. should acquire . . . heroes and villains from fiction 13:575
C. sweeten labours 7:335
desire not a multitude of unprofitable c. 1:80
except ye . . . become as little c. 3:104
He that loves not his wife and c. 7:338
in sorrow thou shalt bring forth c. 1:13
Let our c. grow tall 13:294
like a c.'s party taken over by the elders 12:419
make your c. capable of honesty is the beginning of education 10:386
Men are but c. of a larger growth 8:388
more careful of the breed of their horses and dogs than of their c. 8:501
My music . . . understood by c. and animals 13:448
the early marriages of silly c. 10:516
the Revolution may . . . devour each of her c. 9:24
To bear many c. is considered . . . an investment 13:289
To employ women and c. unduly 10:540
to seyn, to syngen and to rede, as smale c. doon 6:105
write for c. . . . as you do for adults 12:490
chimney sixty horses wedged in a c. 13:1018
chimney-sweepers As c., come to dust 7:212
Chinese Nothing . . . can destroy the C. people 13:261
chip c. of the old block 8:247
chirche-dore Housbondes at c. 6:118
chivalry age of c. is gone 9:10
The age of c. is never past 10:467
chocolate Venice is like eating . . . c. liqueurs 13:881
choose We can believe what we c. 10:596
chose plus c'est la même c. 10:465
Christ C. . . . would quite likely have been arrested 13:186
I beseech you, in the bowels of C. 7:145
We're more popular than Jesus C. 13:460
Christendom Of the two lights of C. 6:70
wisest fool in C. 7:100
Christian A C. . . . feels Repentance on a Sunday 11:479
Better sleep with a sober cannibal than a drunken C. 10:562
C. glories in the death of a pagan 6:6
C. Science explains all cause and effect as mental 11:465
I die a C. 7:136
I was born of C. race 8:458
No Jew was ever fool enough to turn C. 11:470
The C. religion . . . cannot be believed by any reasonable person 8:598
The C. religion not only was at first attended with miracles 8:598

Christianity C. accepted as given a metaphysical system 12:897
C. is part of the Common Law of England 7:162
C. is the most materialistic of all great religions 12:895
C. . . . says that they are all fools 11:477
C. the one great curse 11:473
C. . . . the one immortal blemish of mankind 11:473
local cult called C. 11:476
loving C. better than Truth 10:586
Rock and roll or C. 13:460
single friar who goes counter to all C. 7:8
Christians these C. love one another 4:88
they may be Catholics but they are not C. 13:326
Christ-like C. heroes and woman-worshipping Don Juans 12:787
Christmas Eating a C. pie 7:25
For C. comes but once a year 7:188
perceive C. through its wrapping 13:913
'Twas the night before C. 10:333
Christopher C. Robin went down with Alice 12:975
church an alien C. 10:96
Beware when you take on the C. of God 13:932
custom of the Roman C. 5:33
he'd go to c., start a revolution 13:706
I believe in the C. 12:898
I should never have entered the c. on that day 5:8
The blood of the martyrs is the seed of the C. 4:89
The C. exists 12:899
The farther you go from the c. of Rome 7:402
There are many who stay away from c. 13:911
There is no salvation outside the c. 4:90
We Italians then owe to the C. of Rome 6:91
where MCC ends and the C. of England begins 13:1024
churches c. have kill'd their Christ 10:606
the c. . . . bore for me the same relation to God 13:926
Churchill C. on top of the wave 13:115
Winston C. has bluffed them all 12:165
churchman a species of person called a 'Modern C.' 12:883
chymists good understanding between the c. and the mechanical philosophers 8:613
Cinderella poetry, 'The C. of the Arts.' 11:198
circle All things from eternity . . . come round in a c. 4:42
circumcised our fingers are c. 13:500
When they c. Herbert Samuel 12:204
circumcision atheism, breast-feeding, c. 13:694
circumstance Pride, pomp, and c. 7:95
To a philosopher no c., . . . is too minute 8:642
circumstances to face straitened c. at home 4:94
circumstantial Some c. evidence is very strong 10:648
circuses bread and c. 4:24
cities The government burns down whole c. 12:244
citizen a c. of the world 2:51
first requisite of a good c. 11:106
citizens All free men, . . . are c. of Berlin 13:171
A nation is the universality of c. 10:49
city great c. . . . has the greatest men and women 10:482
hiring taxis to scuttle around a c. 13:376
most pleasant sight to see the C. . . . with a glory about it 7:164
the c. is not a concrete jungle, it is a human zoo 13:515
the holy c., new Jerusalem 3:124
civil In a c. war, a general must know 13:38
civilian forget about this c. 13:217
civilians drop bombs . . . hit c. 13:217
civilisation Disinterested intellectual curiosity . . . life blood of . . . c. 12:557
civility The reciprocal of authors 8:288
civilization As c. advances, poetry . . . declines 10:275
C. is a method of living 12:711
C. is . . . equal respect for all men 12:711
little in the c. to appeal to a Yeti 13:674
Madam, I am the c. they are fighting to defend 12:88
Our c. is founded on the shambles 11:244
The degree of a nation's c. 12:655
the Renaissance was . . . the green end of one of c.'s hardest winters 6:138
without the usual interval of c. 12:845
civilized it proved that I was in a c. society 9:170

Woman will be the last thing c. by Man 10:534
civil service British c. . . . effective braking mechanism 13:333
Civis C. *Romanus sum* 10:123
clapped c. the glass to his sightless eye 9:41
class an . . . young Englishman of our upper c. 10:251
a special machine for the suppression of one c. by another 12:146
Every c. is unfit to govern 11:25
For this c. we have . . . the designation of Philistines 10:324
No one ever describes himself as . . . lower-middle c. 13:138
Poets and painters . . . constitute a special c. 13:1007
The history of all . . . society is the history of c. struggles 10:117
The interest of the landlord is always opposed to . . . every other c. 10:2
the proletariat will . . . wage a c. struggle for Socialism 12:147
The state is an instrument . . . of the ruling c. 12:149
Without c. differences, . . . living theatre 13:378
classes back the masses against the c. 11:50
I'm not interested in c. 13:37
responsible and the irresponsible c. 12:142
classical C. quotation is the *parole* of literary men 8:304
That's the c. mind at work 13:557
The basic difference between c. music and jazz 13:468
Classicism C., . . . the literature that gave . . . pleasure to their great-grandfathers 10:277
clean c. your plate 11:99
We draw the sword . . . with c. hands 12:4
clearing-house the C. of the World 11:119
clenched You cannot shake hands with a c. fist 13:251
Cleopatra Had C.'s nose been shorter 4:97
clergy c. are men 8:639
I never saw . . . the c. were beloved in any nation. 8:605
clergyman good enough to be a c. 8:644
clerk C. ther was of Oxenford also 6:104
diplomatic history is . . . what one c. said to another c. 12:569
the smartness of an attorney's c. 10:185
clever c. man . . . came of . . . stupid people 11:250
never wise to try to appear . . . more c. 13:559
To be c. enough to get . . . money, one must be stupid 11:509
cleverest You're the c. member of . . . the c. nation in the world 12:583
cliché The c. is dead poetry 13:496
cliffs the chalk c. of Dover 12:241
climbed c. to the top of the greasy pole 10:245
clock c. in the steeple strikes one 11:222
clocks hands of c. in railway stations 12:728
close a breathless hush in the C. tonight 11:541
closet sleep in your c. rather than 13:888
close-up Life is a tragedy . . . in c. 13:727
clothes bought her wedding c. 8:515
enterprises that require new c. 10:649
No woman so naked as . . . underneath her c. 13:807
walked away with their c. 10:99
wrapped him in swaddling c. 3:4
cloud a c. received him out of their sight 3:43
a pillar of a c. 1:37
clouds But trailing c. of glory 9:199
club Mankind is a c. 11:358
the best c. in London 10:228
the most exclusive c. there is 13:866
cluster The human face is . . . a whole c. of faces 12:578
CMG Members rise from C. 13:356
coach c. and six horses through the Act of Settlement 8:16
coal best sun . . . made of Newcastle c. 8:166
having a live c. in his hand 1:96
though the whole world turn to c. 7:379
coarse barefoot and wearing c. wool, he stood pitifully 5:13
coaster Dirty British c. 11:238
coat a c. of many colours 1:28
cobwebs Laws are like c. 8:83
laws were like c. 7:110

Coca-Cola that billboards did to C. 13:926
cocaine C. isn't habit-forming 13:598
cock before the c. crow, thou shalt deny me 3:28
we owe a c. to Aesculapius 2:6
cod The home of the bean and the c. 11:150
codfish Unlike the male c.... the British aristocracy is 12:776
coffee-house It is folly... to mistake the echo of a... c. for the ... kingdom 8:86
coffin the silver plate on a c. 10:64
cogito C., ergo sum 7:304
coil shuffled off this mortal c. 7:209
coin realm cannot be rich whose c. 7:74
coinage one c. throughout the king's dominions 5:20
coke Happiness is like c. 12:605
Colbert I can pay some of my debt with this gift – C. 8:1
cold a period of c. peace 13:25
Europe catches c. 10:40
she should catch a c. on overexposure 11:435
The Irish,... are needed in this c. age 10:92
we are... in the midst of a c. war 13:10
collapse Russia is a c., not a revolution 12:68
collapses Force... c. through its own mass 4:11
collective the greatest c. work of science 11:548
colleges a liberal education at the C. of Unreason 11:246
colonel The gatling's jammed and the c. dead 11:541
Colonies C. in the Indies,... are yet babes 7:161
these United C. are,... free and independent states 8:204
colonization American continents,... not to be considered as subjects for future c. 10:20
colour an incurable disease – c. blindness 13:230
Any c., so long as it's black 12:974
colours a coat of many c. 1:28
column The Fifth C. 12:291
combine When bad men c. 8:177
combustion the Immaculate Conception was spontaneous c. 12:884
come C. what come may 7:290
I do not say the French cannot c. 9:46
Mr Watson, c. here; I want you 11:487
O c. all ye faithful 10:592
Will ye no c. back again 8:662
comedian A c. can only last 12:649
comedy All I need to make a c. 13:634
at a c. we only look 13:420
C. is if I walk into an open sewer and die 13:499
C., like sodomy, is an unnatural act 13:639
C., we may say, is society 12:647
Farce refined becomes high c. 13:431
Life is... a c. in long-shot 13:727
What a fine c. this world would be 8:471
world is a c. to those who think 8:475
cometh he c. with clouds 3:120
comfort carrion c., Despair, not feast on thee 11:334
c. ye, c. ye my people 1:54
From ignorance our c. flows 8:330
thought of suicide is a great... c. 11:242
comforters miserable c. are ye all 1:102
comforts Increase of material c.... moral growth 13:971
coming he... c. after me is preferred before me 3:11
who may abide the day of his c. 1:59
command mortals to c. success 8:457
commandments fear God, and keep his c. 1:95
commend into thy hands I c. my spirit 3:40
commended The man who gets angry... in the right way... is c. 2:65
comment C. is free but facts are sacred 12:958
commerce Friendship is a disinterested c. between equals 8:492
honour sinks where c. long prevails 8:150
commission A Royal C. is a broody hen 13:203
Each bullet has got its c. 8:322
commit woman alone, can... c. them 10:523
committee A c. is an animal 13:285
commodity C., Firmness, and Delight 7:178
common C. Law adapts itself by a perpetual process of growth 10:249
C. Law of England 12:568
C. sense is the collection of prejudices 13:561

good thing, to make it too c. 7:383
He nothing c. did or mean 7:137
lose the c. touch 11:531
the happiness of the c. man 12:382
The trivial round, the c. task 10:335
'Tis education forms the c. mind 8:339
trained and organized c. sense 11:490
commonplaces c. are the great poetic truths 11:345
Commons The C., faithful to their system 9:13
Commonwealth a C. of Nations 11:42
communism arrested under the Suppression of C. Act 13:186
A spectre is haunting Europe – the spectre of c. 10:116
C. continued to haunt Europe as a spectre 12:994
C. is in fact the completion of Socialism 11:69
C. is like prohibition 12:169
C. is Soviet power plus the electrification 12:111
C. is the corruption of a dream of justice 13:56
c. is Tsarist autocracy turned upside down 10:143
C. with a human face 13:225
For us in Russia c. is a dead dog 13:328
Russian c. is the illegitimate child 13:94
communist Every c. has a fascist frown 13:191
your grandson will... be a C. 13:95
communists Catholics and C. have committed great crimes 13:216
In Germany, the Nazis came for the C. 12:411
looking under the beds for C. 13:179
community journalism... keeps us in touch with the ignorance of the c. 11:516
the c. of Europe 11:55
commute the agricultural labourers... c. from London 13:512
compact the damned, c., liberal majority 11:36
companionable so c. as solitude 10:424
companions c. for middle age 7:334
comparative progress is simply a c. 11:356
compared The war we have just been through,... is not to be c. 12:96
complex Wherever an inferiority c. exists, there is... reason 12:639
compliance by a timely c. 8:490
compliment returned the c. 8:610
compose Never c.... unless... not composing... becomes a positive nuisance 12:438
composer A good c.... steals 12:473
demands of a c. is that he be dead 13:427
composition difference between... prose and metrical c. 9:120
compromise All government... is founded on c. and barter 8:197
C. used to mean that half a loaf 11:147
not a question that leaves much room for c. 13:255
comrades Bleach the bones of c. slain 11:78
Dear c., soldiers, sailors and workers 12:61
concealed Much truth is spoken,... more... c. 11:427
conceit public school... an appalling and impregnable c. 13:895
conceited what man will do any good who is not c. 10:569
concept If the c. of God has 13:920
Conception the Immaculate C. was spontaneous combustion 12:884
concepts walks up the stairs of his c. 12:632
concessions The c. of the weak are the c. of fear 8:199
conclusions Life is the art of drawing... c. 11:349
concord toleration produced... religious c. 4:99
concurrence fortuitous c. of atoms 10:166
condemn No man can justly censure or c. another 7:380
condemned If God were suddenly c. to live the life 10:493
I have... taken his side when absurd men have c. him 8:349
Man is c. to be free 13:643
condemning One should examine oneself... before... c. others 8:531
condition fools decoyed into our c. 8:496
hopes for the human c. 13:654
The c. of man... is a c. of war 7:147
the Jews have made a contribution to the human c. 13:901

To be a poet is a c.   13:408

conditioned   Americans have been c. to respect newness   13:896

conditions   my people live in such awful c.   12:157

condolence   visit of c. to the Queen of England   7:139

confess   It's easy to make a man c. . . . lies   12:631
Men will c.   11:320
We c. our bad qualities . . . out of fear   13:623

confessing   women . . . ill-using them and then c. it   10:539

conflict   We are in an armed c.   13:92

conform   how to rebel and c. at the same time   13:705

conformable   Nature is very consonant and c.   8:615

Congrès   Le C. ne marche pas, il danse   9:102

Congress   The C. is getting nowhere, it dances   9:102

Congreve   C. is the only sophisticated playwright   13:446

conquer   easier to c. it   8:183
in the end the truth will c.   6:52
not the man to c. a country   6:23
They will c., but . . . not convince   12:269
We'll fight and we'll c.   8:132
when we c. without danger   7:255

conquered   I came, I saw, God c.   7:34, 8:37
I came, I saw, I c.   4:4
the English seem . . . to have c. and peopled half the world   11:38

conquering   not c. but fighting well   11:361
See, the c. hero comes   8:124

conquest   The Roman C. was, however, a *Good Thing*   4:102
the United States will never again seek . . . territory by c.   11:163

conscience   C. is the internal perception of the rejection of a particular wish   11:315
dilemmas of c. and egotism   13:99
freedom of speech, freedom of c.   11:82
I cannot . . . cut my c. to fit this year's fashions   13:67
Now war has a bad c.   12:48
We draw the sword with a clear c.   12:4

consent   deep c. of all great men   10:313
No one can make you feel inferior without your c.   12:627

consequences   do anything . . . if you are prepared to take the c.   12:675
men never violate the laws of God without suffering the c.   10:571

conservatism   c. . . . adherence to the old and tried   10:190
c. is based upon the idea   11:363

Conservative   Or else a little C.   11:34
the C. Party at prayer   12:55
to what is called the Tory . . . called the C.. party   10:34

conservative   most c. man . . . is the British Trade Unionist   12:166
The radical invents the views. . . . the c. them   11:96
which makes a man more c.   12:566

consistency   C. is contrary to nature   12:608

consonant   Nature is very c. and conformable   8:615

conspiracy   not a Party, it is a c.   13:36
People of the same trade . . . conversation ends in a c.   8:214

conspirators   All the c.   4:9

constant   Friendship is c. in all other things   7:233

constitution   c. is extremely well   8:179
I invoke the genius of the C.   8:222
Our c. works   13:281
the pale of the c.   10:221
The principles of a free c.   8:219

constitutional   c. right   10:193
definition of a c. statesman   10:122
I have no eyes but c. eyes   10:222

construction   Our object in the c. of the state   2:7

consultations   dictator . . . always take some c.   13:365

consulted   the right to be c.. . . . to encourage. . . . to warn   10:237

consume   I have often seen the King c.   8:311
statistics, born to c. resources   4:61

consumer   In a c. society there are . . . two kinds of slaves   13:717

consumes   Man . . . c. without producing   12:422

consummation   a c. Devoutly to be wish'd   7:209

consummatum   c. est   3:41

consumption   Conspicuous c.. . . is a means of reputability   11:91

contemplate   the only passers-by who can c. it . . . are those . . . with a white stick and a dog   13:501

contemplates   Beauty in things exists in the mind which c. them   8:414

contemplation   right mindfulness, right c.   2:62

contemporary   C. man has rationalised the myths   13:651
to trade a hundred c. readers for   13:419

contempt   attention to the inside . . . c. for the outside   8:344
To show pity is felt as a sign of c.   11:282

contemptible   c. little Army   12:9

contentment   Where wealth and freedom reign, c. fails   8:150

contests   mighty c. rise from trivial things   8:489
that melancholy sexual perversion known as c.   12:812

Continent   On the C. people have good food   13:871

Continental   C. people have sex life   13:855

continual   c. state of inelegance   9:129

continuation   All diplomacy is a c. of war   13:86
War is the c. of politics   10:47

contraceptive   It's like having a totally efficient c.   13:670

contract   Every law is a c.   8:61
Marriage is . . . but a civil c.   8:499

contradictory   Doublethink . . . holding two c. beliefs   13:31

contraries   Without C. is no progression   9:158

control   we ought to c. our thoughts   11:421

controlled   events have c. me   10:214

controversies   savage c.. . . . no good evidence either way   13:652

controversy   that c. is either superfluous or hopeless   10:410

conventional   The c. army loses if it does not win   13:238

conventionally   to fail c.   12:722

conversation   a c. with the finest men   7:181
a proper subject of c.   8:600
Writing . . . is but a different name for c.   8:290

convince   They will conquer, but . . . not c.   12:269

cooking   woman accepted c. . . . but man . . . made of it a recreation   12:789

copier   c. of nature can never produce anything great   8:296

copulation   Birth, and c., and death   12:695

copying   by defying their parents and c. one another   13:705

cordial   gold in phisik is a c.   6:132

cordiale   La c. entente   10:94

corn   make two ears of c.. . . . grow . . . where only one grew before   8:98

corner   some c. of a foreign field   12:31

corpse   He'd make a lovely c.   10:355

corpses   an armed camp of Blackshirts, a bivouac for c.   12:131

corpuscles   make the c. of the blood glow   12:839

correction   It is a stupidity . . . to busy oneself with the c. of the world   8:446

corridors   c. of power   13:99

corrupt   Among a people generally c.   8:225
appointment by the c. few   11:115
I have exercised the powers committed to me from no c. or interested motives   10:103
power is apt to c.   8:172
Power tends to c.   11:54

corrupted   They had been c. by money   13:817

corruption   C.. the most infallible symptom of constitutional liberty   8:562
purge the land of all C.   6:36
the foul dregs of his power, the tools of despotism and c.   8:145

corrupts   lack of power c. absolutely   13:192

corse   As his c. to the rampart   9:76

cost   To give and not to count the c.   7:349

cottage   poorest man may in his c. bid defiance to . . . the Crown   8:148
to refer to your friend's country establishment as a 'c.'   13:585

cottages Pale Death kicks his way equally into the c. of the poor 4:37

couch time as a tool not as a c. 13:147

council The grotesque chaos of a Labour c. 13:376

counsel C. of her country's gods 4:98
consequences of . . . unpreparedness and feeble c. 13:352
give me that c. that you think best 7:42

count Don't c. your chickens 2:32
If you can . . . c. your money you are not . . . rich man 12:946
To give and not to c. the cost 7:349

counter-democratic Proportional Representation . . . is fundamentally c. 13:362

counterpoint Too much c.; what is worse, Protestant c. 8:669

country A c. governed by a despot 8:229
a c. of young men 11:455
affections must be confined . . . to a single c. 13:347
A man should know something of his own c. 8:469
an honest man sent to lie abroad for . . . his c. 7:414
Anyone who loves his c., follow me 10:112
c. from whose bourn no traveller returns 7:208
Counsel of her c.'s gods 4:98
God made the c. 8:478
Great artists have no c. 10:302
How I leave my c. 9:61
I have but one life to lose for my c. 8:211
I know that I can save this c. 8:128
I would die for my c. 13:389
My c., right or wrong 11:100
nothing good . . . in the c. 9:133
Our c. is the world 10:70
she is my c. still 8:149
The past is a foreign c. 13:568
The undiscover'd c. 7:208
This c. . . . belongs to the people who inhabit it 10:193
to leave his c. as good as he had found it 10:48
understanding the problems of running a c. 13:329
we can die but once to serve our c. 8:89
what was good for our c. 13:81
Your c. needs YOU 12:13

countryside a more dreadful record of sin than . . . c. 11:228

county The sound of the English c. families 12:841

courage be strong and of a good c. 1:45
prince of royal c. 7:18
tale . . . of . . . c. of my companions 11:159
three o'clock in the morning c. 9:209

couragious Of hearte c., politique in counsaile 6:80

course c. of true love never did run smooth 7:314

court The history of the World is the World's c. 9:142

courtesy C. is not dead 13:867

courtiers c. . . . forgotten nothing and learnt nothing 9:31

courting When you are c. a nice girl 13:935

courts I have come to regard . . . c. . . . as a casino 13:311

covenant a c. with death 10:93

Covenants C. without the sword are but words 7:151

Coventry putting him into a moral C. 11:22

covet thou shalt not c. 1:40

cow A c. is a very good animal in the field 8:138
The c. jumped over the moon 7:52
Truth, Sir, is a c. 8:603

coward better to be the widow of a hero than the wife of a c. 12:270

cowardly took a grip on c. Marxism 12:231

cowards the future . . . makes c. of us 12:694

cows daring . . . to explain . . . that c. can be eaten 13:288

coxcomb to hear a c. ask two hundred guineas 11:170

cradle Between the c. and the grave 8:459

craft c. so long to lerne 6:128
The life so short, the c. so long to learn 2:72

craftsmanship Skill without imagination is c. 13:472

crap Books are a load of c. 13:440

created God c. . . the earth 1:1
man alone leaves traces of what he c. 13:716
Man, . . . had been c. to jab the life out of Germans 12:83
we cannot be c. for this sort of suffering 10:450

creates he c. Gods by the dozen 7:396

creation greatest week . . . since the c. 13:234

Had I been present at the C. 1:108

creator Man . . . hasn't been a c., only a destroyer 11:347

creature Who kills a man kills a reasonable c. 7:182

credentials no c. . . . not even . . . a certificate of birth 11:143

credulity C. is . . . the child's strength 10:402

creed got the better of his c. 8:601
wrought . . . the c. of creeds 10:603

creeds So many gods, so many c. 11:474

Cretians the C. are alway liars 1:92

cricket I do love c. – it's so very English 11:319
If the French noblesse had been capable of playing c. with their peasants 9:213
when at leisure from c. 8:121

crieth thy brother's blood c. unto me 1:16

crime C., like virtue, has its degrees 8:537
Count not his broken pledges as a c. 12:128
Do you call poverty a c. 11:505
If poverty is the mother of c., stupidity is its father 8:451
man's greatest c. 7:302
no . . . c. so shameful as poverty 8:625
The atrocious c. of being a young man 8:461
Treason was no C. 8:35
worse than a c., it is a blunder 9:49

Crimean Knight of the C. Burial Grounds 10:159

crimes Catholics and Communists have committed great c. 13:216
history . . . a tableau of c. and misfortunes 8:363
Oh liberty! . . . What c. are committed in thy name 9:23

cripple persons who cannot meet a c. without talking about feet 12:584

crisis C.? What c. 13:322

criticism As far as c. is concerned 13:235

criticize don't c. What you can't understand 13:772

critics Asking a working writer . . . about c. 13:491
award winning plays are written only for the c. 13:469
The greater part of c. are parasites 13:483

crocodile An appeaser is one who feeds a c. 13:85

crocodiles wisdom of the c. 7:250

Cromwell Caesar had his Brutus – Charles the First, his C. 8:154
restless C. could not cease 7:146

crony government by c. 13:9

crook I am not a c. 13:269
the symbol of a bishop is a c. 13:928

crooked the c. timber of humanity 8:434
the shortest line . . . may be the c. one 12:725

cross make the gallows glorious like the c. 10:173
sign of the c. . . . an indulgence for all the sins 6:7
The orgasm has replaced the C. 13:748

crossed a girl likes to be c. in love a little now and then 9:186

crossword an optimist . . . fills up his c. puzzle in ink 12:599

crow before the cock c., thou shalt deny me 3:28

crowd Far from the madding c. 8:657

crowds It brings men together in c. and mobs in bar-rooms 10:563

crown poorest man . . . bid defiance to . . . the C. 8:148
risk my C. than do what I think personally disgraceful 8:227
the c. of life 1:89
The influence of the C. has increased 8:236
Uneasy lies the head that wears a c. 7:72
we received from that See our C. 7:10
within the hollow c. 6:55

crowned An unlettered king is a c. ass 6:133
He was my c. King 6:85
not a single c. head in Europe 8:261

Crucible America is God's C. 11:135

cry I often want to c. 12:799
make 'em c. 11:178
mother, do not c. 10:644
She hears stories that make her c. 11:287
the c. of him that ruleth among fools 1:65
the only advantage women have over men – . . . they can c. 12:799

crying An infant c. in the night 10:473

crystal as clear as a c., the synthesis – German National Socialism 12:231

uckoo This is the weather the c. likes 11:233

ucumbers they are but c. after all 8:303

ult local c. called Christianity 11:476

ulture C. is an instrument wielded by professors 13:535
C. is the passion for sweetness and light 11:168
two half-cultures do not make a c. 13:702
When I hear anyone talk of C. 12:484

up Ah, fill the C. 10:489

upid wing'd C. painted blind 7:315

ur the c. dog of Britain and spaniel of Spain 8:101

ure C. the disease 7:406
no c. for birth and death 12:681
Show me a sane man and I will c. him for you 13:936
the c. for admiring the House of Lords 10:236
There are maladies we must not seek to c. 12:676

ured the only disease you don't look forward to being c.
of 12:526

uriosity Disinterested intellectual c. . . . life blood of . . .
civilisation 12:557

urse Christianity the one great c. 11:473
She would rather light candles than c. the darkness 13:159
Work is the c. of the drinking classes 11:520

ursed thou art c. above all cattle 1:13

urtain An iron c. 13:1

ustodiet Quis c. ipsos custodes 4:23

ustom A c. loathsome to the eye, hateful to the nose
7:194
C., then, is the great guide of human life 8:466

ustomer The c. is always right 12:153

ustomers When you are skinning your c. 13:150

ut the human pack is shuffled and c. 13:558

utlasses lads, sharpen your c., and the day is your own
10:144

uts he that c. off twenty years of life 7:207

ymbal a tinkling c. 3:95

ynicism no literature can outdo the c. of real life 11:180

D

lad They fuck you up, your mum and d. 13:763

affodils I never saw d. so beautiful 9:123

laisy D., give me your answer, do 11:372

lalliance primrose path of d. 7:398

lamage nothing which might d. his career 11:459

lame one for the d. 6:56

lamn D. with faint praise 8:656
not worth a d. 9:109

lamnation there would be no d. 7:345
the terminal point of addiction is . . . d. 13:843

lamned a covenant with d. 9:112
d. good-natured friend 8:427
d. if you do — And . . . damned if you don't 10:588
Life is just one d. thing after another 11:371
Publish and be d. 10:637
The public be d., I am working for my stockholders 11:47

lances The Congress is getting nowhere, it d. 9:102

lancing d. on a volcano 10:39

landy the d. of sixty 10:9

langer A nation is not in d. 12:235
d. . . . lies in acting well 8:557
the only real d. that exists is man himself 13:593
when we conquer without d. 7:255

langerous more d. the abuse 8:181

langers D. by being despised 9:15

laniel brought D. and cast him into the den 1:56

lanse Le Congrès ne marche pas, il d. 9:102

lare and d. for ever; and thus will France be saved 9:17
I cannot pardon him because I d. not 8:30

larien Silent, upon a peak in D. 10:257

laring d. to excel 8:557

lark A blind man in a d. room 11:257
children fear . . . the d. 7:205
Genuineness only thrives in the d. 12:692
The d. night of the soul 7:227
What in me is d. Illumine 8:585

larkling D. I listen 10:350

larkly through a glass, d. 3:95

larkness d. was upon the face of the deep 1:1
men loved d. . . . because their deeds were evil 3:108

She would rather light candles than curse the d. 13:159
the people that walked in d. 1:98

darling Charlie is my d. 8:663

date A d. that shall live in infamy 12:361

daughter I always remember that I am Caesar's d. 4:17
the earth is free for every son and d. of mankind 7:142

daughters Words are men's d. 8:284

David D. his ten thousands 1:47
Once in royal D.'s city 10:595

dawn Bliss was it in that d. to be alive 9:208

dawned each day that has d. is your last 4:60

day count as profit every d. that Fate allows you 4:62
each d. is like a year 11:88
each d. that has dawned is your last 4:60
from this d. forward 7:339
God called the light D. 1:1
I look upon every d. to be lost 8:432
Seize the d. 4:63
when the d. of Pentecost was fully come 3:44

days d. of wine and roses 11:343
Do not let us speak of darker d. 12:358
Ten D. that Shook the World 12:67

dead all the world she knew is d. 13:657
A master is d. 11:175
A statesman is a politician who's been d. 13:109
d., but in the Elysian fields 11:8
England mourns for her d. across the sea 12:91
God is d. 11:469
If the d. talk to you, you are a spiritualist 13:925
most of 'em d. 12:81
Mother is the d. heart of the family 13:778
move in a world of the d. 12:563
the d. shall be raised incorruptible 3:53
The novel being d. 13:462
The only completely consistent people are the d. 12:608
The only good Indians I ever saw were d. 10:255
The past is the only d. thing 11:278
To one d. deathless hour 11:173
to the d. we owe only truth 8:365
we survive amongst the d. and the dying as on a battlefield
13:669

deadener Habit is a great d. 13:587

deadly the female of the species is more d. than the male
11:417

deaf Historians are like d. people 11:279

deal a new d. for the American people 12:218
Shed his blood . . . given a square d. 11:112

dear that bread should be so d. 10:95

dearer d. still is truth 2:66

death a covenant with d. 10:93
Any man's d. diminishes me 7:214
a Reaper whose name is D. 10:354
a remedy for everything except d. 7:213
A single d. is a tragedy 12:706
A useless life is an early d. 8:480
Birth, and copulation, and d. 12:695
d. after life does greatly please 7:201
D. destroys a man 11:245
D. is the veil 10:351
dread of something after d. 7:208
d.'s own hand is warmer than my own 13:525
d. . . . the least of all evils 7:203
D. . . . we haven't succeeded in . . . vulgarizing 12:525
D. will disprove you 10:357
enormously improved by d. 12:428
Football isn't a matter of life and d. 13:519
give me liberty or give me d. 8:200
Go and try to disprove d. 10:357
half in love with easeful D. 10:350
I am signing my d. warrant 12:124
Ideal mankind would abolish d. 12:664
I do really think that d. will be marvellous 13:526
Ignore d. until the last moment 12:527
Into the jaws of D. 10:148
Into the valley of D. 10:149
it is not d., but dying, which is terrible 8:318
I've been accused of every d. 12:650
I will defend to the d. your right to say it 8:349

man and wife with their children . . . traversed . . . the road of
d. 6:45
man fears . . . only the stroke of d. 7:204
Many men would take the d.-sentence 13:661
Men fear d. 7:205
no cure for birth and d. 12:681
O d., where is thy sting 3:53
O D., where is thy sting-a-ling-a-ling 12:43
Pale D. kicks his way equally into the cottages of the poor
and the castles of kings 4:37
sad stories of the d. of kings 6:55
Sickness, sin and d. . . . do not originate in God 11:466
Sin brought d. 11:241
Soldiers are citizens of d.'s grey land 12:961
Swarm over, D. 13:506
the d. of Little Nell without laughing 11:202
the land of the shadow of d. 1:98
there's always d. 9:114
till d. us do part 7:339
Time flies, d. urges 8:462
way to dusty d. 7:287
we owe God a d. 7:202
what a man still plans . . . shows the . . . injustice in his d.
13:529
who fears dishonour more than d. 4:50
debate daughter of d. 7:57
I love argument, I love d. 13:335
debt I can pay some of my d. with this gift – Colbert 8:1
not quite forget . . . Baldwin till we're out of d. 12:288
to run into d. with Nature 10:540
decadence The difference between our d. and the Russians' 13:882
decay Macmillan seemed . . . to embody the national d.
13:133
deceit love we swore . . . seems d. 13:744
philosophy and vain d. 3:62
Where rumour of oppression and d. 8:479
deceive if we say that we have no sin, we d. 3:63
deceived take heed . . . that your heart be not d. 1:44
deceiving without quite d. your enemies 13:828
decent d. means poor 10:625
decision if usage so choose, with whom resides the d.
4:31
decisive Marriage is a step so grave and d. 11:383
declare they should d. the causes which impel them to . . .
separation 8:206
decomposing d. in the eternity of print 12:448
decorated proverb . . . much matter d. 8:323
decorum Dulce et d. est 4:13
deed good d. in a naughty world 7:352
death D. is an ende of every worldly sore 6:112
defeat a d. without a war 12:305
d. is an orphan 13:688
D. of Germany means 12:369
God's will to lead . . . South Africa through d. and humiliation
11:103
In d. unbeatable 12:384
we are not interested in the possibilities of d. 11:89
defence England's chief d. depends upon the navy 7:36
Never make a d. or apology 7:113
Preparing for suicide . . . means of d. 13:383
The best immediate d. of the United States 12:343
the d. of England 12:241
The only d. is in offence 12:225
Truth telling is not compatible with the d. of the realm
12:121
defend I will. d. to the death your right to say it 8:231,
8:349
defiance in defeat, d. 12:409
poorest man may in his cottage bid d. to . . . the Crown
8:148
The d. of established authority 13:264
defiled Hell itself is d. by . . . King John 6:33
definition This d. . . . would not do for a policeman 10:635
defying by d. their parents and copying another one
13:705
degenerates everything d. in the hands of man 8:611
degree d. of delight 8:418
degrees Crime, like virtue, has its d. 8:537

deities the d. so kindly 7:392
Deity to distinguish between the D. and the Drains 10:658
Delacroix The recipe for making a man like D. 12:433
deleted D. by French censor 12:53
delight a degree of d. 8:418
Commodity, Firmness, and D. 7:178
delights Man d. not me 7:240
deliverer their d. from Popish tyranny 8:53
deluge After us the d. 8:130
delved When Adam d. 6:49
demagogues the vilest specimens of human nature are . . .
found among d. 10:120
demands the populace cannot exact their d. 10:60
demented shrill d. choirs of wailing shells 12:90
democracies d. . . . think that a stupid man is more likely
to be honest 13:54
democracy arsenal of d. 12:344
D. . . . government by the uneducated 12:205
D. is only an experiment in government 12:181
D. is the wholesome and pure air 13:379
D. means government by discussion 13:167
D. passes into despotism 2:10
d. . . . recognises the subjecting of the minority 12:108
D. substitutes election by the incompetent many 11:115
extreme d. or absolute oligarchy . . . will come 2:15
grieved under a d., call it anarchy 7:152
In Switzerland . . . five hundred years of d. and peace
13:859
not the voting that's d. 13:263
unites socialism with d. 13:397
world . . . made safe for d. 12:51
democratic thoroughly d. and patronise everybody 11:355
demons We have often sunk to the level of the d. 13:430
den a d. of thieves 3:116
denial the highest praise of God consists in the d. of Him
12:879
denounce We thus d. . . . the arms race 13:306
deny before the cock crow, thou shalt d. me thrice 3:28
let him d. himself 3:24
depart D., . . . and let us have done with you 12:322
lettest thou thy servant d. in peace 3:8
when the great and good d. 9:67
depends It all d. upon that article there 9:108
desert The sand of the d. is sodden red 11:541
deserves the government it d. 9:86
desiccated A d. calculating machine 13:35
desire a universal innate d. 11:351
D. is the very essence of man 8:386
d. to be praised twice over 8:528
desist to d. from the experiment in despair 10:579
desolated from the province they have d. and profaned
11:6
despair carrion comfort, D., not feast on thee 11:334
some divine d. 10:417
to desist from the experiment in d. 10:579
without understanding d. 13:600
despairs He who d. over an event is a coward 13:654
despicable this formidable Kingdom is . . . a province of a
d. Electorate 8:117
despise I d. Shakespeare 11:213
some other Englishman d. him 11:462
despised A poor man is d. the whole world over 11:500
I doubt if the philosopher lives . . . who could know himself
. . . d. by a street boy 11:517
old, mad, blind, d. and dying king 10:4
despises A woman d. a man for loving her 11:402
despot A country governed by a d. 8:229
despotism Democracy passes into d. 2:10
d. tempered by casualness 11:60
extreme democracy or absolute oligarchy or d. will come
2:15
France was a long d. 9:206
the foul dregs of his power, the tools of d. and corruption
8:145
destination I do not think this poem will reach its d. 8:302
destinies in determining the future d. of mankind 12:97
destiny we were walking with d. 12:325
destroy whom God wishes to d. 2:71
Whom the gods wish to d. 12:726

estroy'd a bold peasantry . . . When once d. 8:180
estroyer Man . . . hasn't been a creator, only a d. 11:347
estroying simplifying something by d. nearly everything 12:712
estroys he who d. a good book, kills reason 7:182
estruction broad is the way, that leadeth to d. 3:130
one purpose . . . d. of Hitler 12:370
eterrent the d. is a phallic symbol 13:197
etest they d. at leisure 10:501
eutschland D., D. über alles 10:89
evice A banner with the strange d., Excelsior 10:653
evil between any sort of d. and the deep blue sea 13:523
D. always builds a chapel there 8:594
d. can cite Scripture 7:230
preserve me from the D. 10:54
Renounce the d. 8:584
resist the d., and he will flee 3:99
sacrifice . . . of the d.'s leavings 8:453
Sarcasm . . . the language of the d. 10:438
the d. did not play in tempting of me 8:268
the world, the flesh, and the d. 12:964
evils It is no good casting out d. 12:614
many d. would set on me in Worms 7:9
evoted definition of . . . a nurse . . . 'd. and obedient.' 10:635
evotion The almighty dollar . . . object of universal d. 10:158
evour shed tears when they would d. 7:250
the Revolution may . . . d. each of her children 9:24
exterity Your d. seems a happy compound 10:185
ialect D. words – those terrible marks of the beast 11:53
iamond D.! D. 8:617
more of rough than polished d. 8:122
iamonds the Kings of England, D., Hearts, Spades and Clubs 13:62
iana great is D. of the Ephesians 3:48
iary To write a d. . . . returning to one's own vomit 13:729
ickens D. . . . never quite took 13:489
D.' world is not life-like 12:481
ictation God wrote it. I merely did his d. 10:139
ictator and finally a single d. substitutes himself 11:128
I am painted as the greatest little d. 13:365
ictators D. ride to and fro upon tigers 12:306
ictatorship The d. of the proletariat 10:128
ictionary words never seen . . . before outside of a d. 13:484
iddle Hey d. d., The cat and the fiddle 7:52
ie but to do and d. 10:149
d. on your feet than to live on your knees 12:271
D. when I may . . . I have always plucked a thistle 10:189
How often are we to d. 8:317
I am ready to d. for my Lord 6:12
I d. a Christian 7:136
I d. because I do not d. 7:395
If a man hasn't discovered something that he would d. for 13:173
If I should d. 12:31
I have been learning how to d. 6:114
It is natural to d. 7:206
it is youth that must fight and d. 12:391
I will d. in peace 8:135
I would d. for my country 13:389
let me d. drinking in an inn 6:95
Let us determine to d. here 10:195
man can d. but once 7:202
More d. in the United States 13:112
No young man believes he shall ever d. 9:166
one may d. without ever laughing 8:395
place . . . to d. in 7:309
Rather suffer than d. 8:316
save your world you asked this man to d. 12:412
The d. is cast 4:3
those who are about to d. salute you 4:18
we can d. but once to serve our country 8:89
We d. – does it matter when 11:330
we must live as though . . . never going to d. 8:463
when good Americans d. they go to Paris 11:457
ied A piece of each of us d. at that moment 13:185

Men have d. from time to time 7:319
there were people who d. of dropsies 8:188
diem Carpe d. 4:63
dies a young person, who . . . marries or d., is sure to be kindly spoken of 10:394
he d. in pain 8:450
It matters not how a man d. 8:321
king never d. 8:156
Dieu D. et mon droit 6:27
difference Because there is no d. 2:47
d. between . . . prose and metrical composition 9:120
made the d. of forty thousand men 9:115
more d. within the sexes than between them 13:789
differences If we cannot now end our d. 13:170
differently I would have done it d. 11:207
difficult It is d. to be humble 13:847
digestion Things sweet to taste prove in d. sour 7:269
Diggers You noble D. all 7:140
dignity human beings are born free . . . d. and rights 13:18
dilemmas d. of conscience and egotism 13:99
diligently Had I . . . served God as d. as I have served the king 7:17
dim my lamp burns low and d. 12:941
dimensions sickness enlarges the d. of a man's self 10:404
diminished ought to be d. 8:236
diminution to subsist . . . without either increase or d. 10:3
dine wretches hang that jury-men may d. 8:88
dinky Hinky, d., par-lee-voo 12:77
dinner A man is . . . better pleased when he has a good d. upon his table 8:522
people . . . would ask him to d. 10:597
diplomacy All d. is a continuation of war 13:86
diplomatic d. history is . . . what one clerk said to another clerk 12:569
diplomats aged d. to be bored 13:168
direction God knows how you Protestants . . . have any sense of d. 13:906
disadvantage d. of merely counting votes 12:181
disappointment Grief and d. give rise to anger 8:550
disapprove I d. of what you say 8:231, 8:349
disarm Let no one expect us to d. unilaterally 13:357
disarmament precede the d. of the victors 12:414
disaster the audience was a d. 11:201
disasters trace . . . the d. of English history to . . . Wales 12:843
disciple a d. . . . of the fiend, called the Pucelle 6:64
discontent To be discontented with the divine d. 11:423
winter of our d. 6:81
discontents the family . . . source of all our d. 13:776
discover not d. new lands 12:539
discretion better part of valour is d. 7:354
discussed Everything has been d. and analysed 8:346
discussion more time for d. . . . more mistakes 12:189
disease amusing the patient while Nature cures the d. 8:622
an incurable d. – colour blindness 13:230
Cure the d. 7:406
desperate d. requires a dangerous remedy 7:88
Life is an incurable d. 8:444
strange d. of modern life 10:477
the d. of writing books 8:287
the incurable d. of writing 4:34
the only d. you don't look forward to being cured of 12:526
diseases Extreme remedies . . . for extreme d. 2:73
disguise virtues are . . . vices in d. 8:530
dish And the d. ran away with the spoon 7:52
The national d. of America 13:900
dished We have d. the Whigs 10:235
dishonour who fears d. more than death 4:50
disillusionments d. in the lives of the medieval saints 6:136
disinterested D. intellectual curiosity . . . life blood of . . . civilisation 12:557
dislike that my statue should be moved, which I should much d. 11:80
The law of d. for the unlike 11:461
disliked I have always d. myself 12:727

Disney D. the most significant figure . . . since Leonardo 13:426

disobedience Of Man's first d. 1:110

disposes God d. 6:125

dispute Many a long d. among divines 8:599

dis-satisfaction balanced state of well-modulated d. 11:28

dissimulate how to d. is the knowledge of kings 7:115

distance The d. doesn't matter 8:658

distinguish all there is to d. us from other animals 8:425

distinguished When a d. but elderly scientist states 13:959

distress the mean man is always full of d. 2:40

distribution the wider d. of smoked salmon 13:303

distrust shameful to d. one's friends 8:372
stay together, but we d. one another 13:780

distrusts him who d. himself 8:373

ditchwater Is d. dull 12:931

diversion Most sorts of d. . . . are an imitation of fighting 8:402

diversity make the world safe for d. 13:170

divided Obstinate people can be d. into 2:44
Thought must be d. against itself 12:544

divine The right of kings to govern wrong 8:99
To be discontented with the d. discontent 11:423
To err is human, to forgive, d. 8:401, 8:547

divines Many a long dispute among d. 8:599

divinity a d. that shapes our ends 7:399
a piece of d. in us 7:308
There's such d. doth hedge a king 7:82

divisions How many d. has he got 12:260

do D. as you would be done by 8:553
D. other men 10:415
for they know not what they d. 3:35
I am to d. what I please 8:178
Nature . . . hath done her part; D. thou but thine 8:378
they would d. you 10:415

Dobest Dowel, Dobet and D. 6:119

doctor A d. . . . is a patient half-cured 12:955

doctrine a d. so illogical and so dull 12:993

documents sign d. which they do not read 12:638

dog America is a large, friendly d. 13:870
A woman's preaching is like a d.'s walking on his hinder legs 8:521
The little d. laughed To see such sport 7:52
the only passers-by who can contemplate it . . . are those . . . with a white stick and a d. 13:501

dogs how much more d. are animated when they hunt in a pack 8:412
let slip the d. of war 7:77
like asking a lamp-post . . . about d. 13:491
more careful of the breed of their horses and d. than of their children 8:501
woman who is . . . kind to d. 11:420

doing Anything that is worth d. 13:642
Find out what you like d. best and get someone to pay you for d. it 13:1006
let us not be weary in well d. 3:70
we learn by d. 2:28
Whatever is worth d. 8:552

dollar The almighty d. . . . object of universal devotion 10:158

dominion establish . . . sure English d. in India for all time to come 8:49

dominions The sun does not set in my d. 7:73

dominoes a row of d. set up; you knock over the first 13:83

done Do as you would be d. by 8:553
d. those things we ought not 8:368
Justice should . . . be seen to be d. 12:805
Let justice be d. 7:44
the dread of doing what has been d. before 12:447
thy worldly task hast d. 7:212
What you do not want d. to yourself 2:61

Don Juans Christ-like heroes and woman-worshipping D. 12:787

donkeys lions led by d. 12:27

Dons If the D. sight Devon 7:64

Doodle Yankee D. came to town 8:212

door I am the d. 3:111

the judge standeth before the d. 3:64
world will make a beaten path to his d. 10:432

Dorchester All terrorists . . . end up with drinks at the D. 13:194

doublethink D. . . . holding two contradictory beliefs 13:31

doubt new Philosophy calls all in d. 7:407
O thou of little faith, wherefore didst thou d. 3:132
When a man is in d. about . . . his writing 11:218

doubts end in d. 7:217

Dove No visit to D. Cottage, Grasmere, is complete 9:215

dove and the d. came in to him 1:20
the wings of a d. 8:429

Dover It is burning a farthing candle at D. 8:291
the chalk cliffs of D. 12:241

Dowel D., Dobet and Dobest 6:119

dower forfeited their ancient English d. 9:71

down for coming d. let me shift for myself 7:21
He that is d. 8:448
Yes, and they went d. very well too 9:113

drainpipe wrong end of a municipal d. 12:323

drains to distinguish between the Deity and the D. 10:658

Drake D. he's in his hammock 7:63

dramatist Sherard Blaw, the d. who had discovered himse[11:219

Drang Sturm und D. 8:301

drawing the Suez Canal was flowing through my d. room 13:93

dread the d. of doing what has been done before 12:447

dreadful Other people are quite d. 11:296

Dreadnoughts A . . . Duke costs as much . . . as two D. 11:144

dream All men d.: but not equally 12:601
awakened from the d. of life 10:451
For life is but a d. 11:328
Happiness is no vague d. 10:429
hope is . . . the d. of those that wake 8:404
I d. when I am awake 7:303
I have a d. 13:174
The young men's vision, and the old men's d. 8:32
To sleep, perchance to d. 7:209
warned of God in a d. 3:10
Where is it now, the glory and the d. 9:199

dreamer this d. cometh 1:29

dreamers the d. of the day are dangerous men 12:601

dreamin' d. . . . o' Plymouth Hoe 7:63

dreaming a man d. I was a butterfly 2:53
City with her d. spires 10:349

dreams D. and predictions 7:294
dream our d. away 12:702
For one person who d. of making fifty thousand pounds 12:942
I, being poor, have only my d. 12:670
show life . . . as we see it in our d. 11:192
Than this world d. of 10:608
We are nothing; less than nothing, and d. 10:452
We are such stuff As d. are made on 7:174
what d. may come 7:209

dreamt d. of in your philosophy 7:280
I d. that I was making a speech 11:73

dreary d. intercourse of daily life 9:163
If your morals make you d. 11:430

dregs the foul d. of his power, the tools of despotism and corruption 8:145

dress The Englishman's d. is like a traitor's body 7:384

dressed All d. up, with nowhere to go 12:35

drink A population sodden with d. 11:226
D. to me only with thine eyes 7:329
I commended mirth . . . to eat . . . to d., and to be merry 1:71
let us eat and d.; for tomorrow we . . . die 1:78
woe unto them that . . . follow strong d. 1:87

drinkers no verse can give pleasure . . . that is written by d. of water 4:28

drinking D. . . . and making love 8:425
let me die d. in an inn 6:95
the increase in d. is to be laid mainly to the account of the female sex 11:414
'Tis not the d. . . . but the excess 8:312
Work is the curse of the d. classes 11:520

the defence of E.   12:241
the earth of E. is in my two hands   5:12
the Kings of E., Diamonds, Hearts, Spades and Clubs
13:62
this generation . . . found E. a land of beauty   13:82
this realm, this E.   7:69
we are the people of E.   12:33
English   Dr Johnson's morality was as E. . . . as a beefsteak
8:666
E. people . . . are surely the *nicest* people in the world
12:835
E. soldiers fight like lions   12:27
E. . . . the language of an imaginative race   13:496
Every man who comes to England is entitled to the protection of the E. law   8:184
exterminate . . . the treacherous E.   12:9
forfeited their ancient E. dower   9:71
give him seven feet of E. ground   5:11
I do love cricket – it's so very E.   11:319
If you get the E. people into the way of making kings   10:81
my own heart to be entirely E.   8:76
one of the few E. novels for grown up people   12:449
our E. nation, if they have a good thing, to make it too
common   7:383
stones kissed by the E. dead   12:22
The attitude of the E. . . . toward E. history   12:570
The E. . . . are rather a foul-mouthed nation   10:576
the E. are . . . the least a nation of pure philosophers
10:240
the E. have hot-water bottles   13:855
The E. have no respect for their language   11:462
The E. instinctively admire   13:856
The E. may not like music   12:848
The E. nation . . . has successfully regulated the power of its
kings   8:570
the E. seem . . . to have conquered and peopled half the
world   11:38
The E. take their pleasures   7:387
The E. want *inferiors*   10:580
ther is so greet diversitee in E.   6:93
To Americans E. manners are . . . frightening   13:868
to the E. that of the sea   9:39
typically E. characteristic   12:849
Englishman   An E. . . . forms an orderly queue of one
13:854
an E.'s heaven-born privilege of doing as he likes   10:253
An E.'s way of speaking   13:872
an . . . young E. of our upper class   10:251
E. never enjoys himself except for a noble purpose   12:858
E. . . . weighs up the birth, the rank, . . . the wealth of the
people he meets   8:571
how a carter, a common sailor, a beggar is still . . . an E.
8:579
If I were an American, as I am an E.   8:223
it takes a great deal to produce ennui in an E.   12:864
never find an E. among the underdogs   13:858
Remember that you are an E.   11:107
some other E. despise him   11:462
tale . . . which would have stirred . . . E.   11:159
there are fifty thousand men slain . . . , and not one E.
8:104
To be an E.   13:866
You may be the most liberal Liberal E.   12:142
Englishmen   E. to be subject to Frenchmen   5:18
Our fathers were E.   7:107
the future E. must take business as seriously as their grandfathers had done   11:110
to create Frenchmen in the image of E.   12:381
to see the absurd nature of E.   8:568
When two E. meet, their first talk is of the weather   8:572
Englishwoman   This E. is so refined   13:864
enigma   a riddle wrapped in a mystery inside an e.   12:316
enjoy   Better to e. and suffer   13:735
Since God has given us the papacy . . . e. it   6:90
ennui   it takes a great deal to produce e. in an Englishman
12:864
enough   It comes soon e.   12:708
It is e.   10:107
patriotism is not e.   12:32

entangle   never to e. ourselves in the broils of Europe
10:19
entente   *La cordiale* e.   10:94
enter   but the King of England cannot e.   8:148
entered   I should never have e. the church on that day   5:8
enterprises   e. that require new clothes   10:649
entertained   Television . . . permits you to be e. in your living room   13:516
enthusiasm   Nothing great was ever achieved without e.
10:460
enthusiastic   Latins are tenderly e.   13:875
entities   E. should not be multiplied   6:102
entitled   bill of rights is what the people are e. to   8:260
entuned   E. in hir nose   6:124
envied   There are two things for which animals are . . . e.
8:413
envy   2 percent moral, 48 percent indignation and 50 percent e.   13:831
prisoners of addiction and . . . prisoners of e.   13:717
The dullard's e. of brilliant men   11:366
the upbringing a nun would e.   13:773
Ephesians   great is Diana of the E.   3:48
epigrams   long despotism tempered by e.   9:206
epitaph   'Can't' will be the e. of the British Empire   12:292
epoch   From today . . . there begins a new e. in the history
of the world   9:18
Epstein's   If people . . . a thousand years hence . . . found E.
statues   13:421
equal   All animals are e.   12:423
all men are created e.   8:207, 13:174
all were created e. by nature   6:50
Everybody should have an e. chance   13:193
Inferiors revolt . . . that they may be e.   2:16
That all men are e. is a proposition   12:196
When you meet someone better . . . turn your thoughts to
becoming his e.   2:42
equality   E. may perhaps be a right, but no . . . fact   10:61
E. must yield   8:243
Freedom! E.! Brotherhood   9:2
never be e. in the servants' hall   11:234
equally   Pale Death kicks his way e. into the cottages of
the poor   4:37
Pale Death kicks his way e.   4:37
That all who are happy, are e. happy   8:422
equals   the Republic of E.   9:33
equitable   some greater and more e. system   12:406
ergo   *Cogito, e. sum*   7:304
err   The Most may e. as grosly   8:33
To e. is human, to forgive, divine   8:401, 8:547
erred   We have e., and strayed from thy ways   8:367
error   show a man that he is in an e.   8:329
errors   E., like Straws, upon the surface flow   8:538
few e. they have ever avoided   12:415
I never approved either the e. of his book, or the trivial
truths   8:349
the e. of those who think they are strong   13:677
Esau   E. . . . a hairy man   1:27
escape   Gluttony is an emotional e.   13:825
escaped   e. from a mad and savage master   2:54
escaping   fortunate in e. regular education   13:536
esprit   English characteristic . . . e. de corps   12:849
essence   Desire is the very e. of man   8:386
The poet gives us his e.   13:417
essential   liberty as an e. condition of excellence   11:256
establishment   to refer to your friend's country e. as a
'cottage'   13:585
estate   a fourth e. of the realm   10:28
at no time stand so highly in our e. royal   7:31
the Third E. contains . . . a nation   9:4
État   *L'É. c'est moi*   8:90
eternal   content to die for God's e. truth   10:172
service rendered to the temporal king to the prejudice of
the e. king   6:30
The e. *not ourselves* that makes for righteousness   11:422
We feel . . . we are e.   8:589
eternity   All things from e. . . . come round in a circle   4:42
E. in an hour   9:168
from e. spinning the thread of your being   4:73
Tears of e. and sorrow   12:678

Ethiopians The E. say that their gods are . . . black 2:70
Eton the Battle of Waterloo *was* won on the playing-fields of E. 12:359
the playing fields of E. 9:141
Eureka *E.* 2:78
Euripides E. portrays them as they are 2:23
Europe another war in E. 11:83
A spectre is haunting E. – the spectre of communism 10:116
Communism continued to haunt E. as a spectre 12:994
countries of western E. . . . no longer . . . protect themselves 13:76
E. catches cold 10:40
E. is the unfinished negative 13:884
glory of E. is extinguished 9:10
In Western E. there are now only small countries 13:190
lamps are going out all over E. 12:3
never to entangle ourselves in the broils of E. 10:19
sick man of E. 10:140
the community of E. 11:55
the last territorial claim which I have to make in E. 12:302
the race of men is almost extinct in E. 12:787
This going into E. 13:286
United States of E. 13:5
European In the wars of the E. powers . . . we have never taken any part 10:20
Europeans only really materialistic people . . . E. 13:885
Eva If a woman like E. Peron with no ideals 13:336
evacuations Wars are not won by e. 12:332
Eve E. . . . the mother of all living 1:14
event greatest e. . . . that ever happened 9:6
one far-off divine e. 10:472
events all great e. and personalities in . . . history reappear 10:137
E. which . . . never happened 12:562
There are only three e. in a man's life 8:450
When in the course of human e., it becomes necessary 8:206
Everest the summit of E. was hardly the place 13:77
treating the *mons Veneris* as . . . Mount E. 12:757
every E. day in every way 11:537
everybody E. is always in favour of general economy 13:90
everyone e. against e. 7:147
everything A place for e. 11:329
destroying nearly e. 12:712
E. has been discussed and analysed 8:346
e. that lives is holy 9:159
God made e. out of nothing 12:741
making e. the concern of all 13:711
men we like are good for e. 8:392
One fifth of the people are against e. 13:198
evidence Most men . . . give e. against their own understanding 8:326
Some circumstantial e. is very strong 10:648
evil about the dreadful wood Of conscious e. 12:744
as gods, knowing good and e. 1:12
a thing may look e. in theory 8:262
belief in a supernatural source of e. 11:453
deliver us from e. 3:102
E. be to him who e. thinks 6:43
Good can imagine E. 13:841
Government, . . . is but a necessary e. 8:215
He who passively accepts e. 13:826
know all the e. he does 8:375
love of money is the root of all e. 3:97
men loved darkness . . . because their deeds were e. 3:108
Men's e. manners live in brass 7:375
Only lies and e. come from letting people off 13:832
party is a political e. 8:108
The e. that men do lives after them 4:7
the fear of one e. 8:536
the love of money is the root of all e. 11:496
There is no e. in the atom 13:941
Vice itself lost half its e. 9:11
we are the origin of all coming e. 13:593
evils death . . . the least of all e. 7:203
He . . . must expect new e. 7:293
To great e. we submit; we resent little provocations 10:400

We cannot remove the e. of capitalism 13:295
Work banishes those three great e. 8:641
evolution e. of the human race 12:922
sex . . . must itself be subject . . . to e. 11:486
exact Politics is not an e. science 10:213
examine One should e. oneself . . . before . . . condemning others 8:531
example E. is the school of mankind 9:161
George the Third . . . *may profit by their* e. 8:154
exasperating that the afterlife will be any less e. 12:896
excel daring to e. 8:557
excellence acute limited e. at twenty-one 12:690
liberty as an essential condition of e. 11:256
excellences e. carried to an excess 9:126
Excelsior A banner with the strange device, E. 10:653
excess excellences carried to an e. 9:126
Give me e. of it 7:172
'Tis not the drinking . . . but the e. 8:312
Exchequer Chancellor of the E. 11:1
exciting Jam today, and men aren't at their most e. 13:100
exclude we cannot e. the intellect from . . . any of our functions 11:259
excluded when you have e. the impossible 11:528
exclusive the most e. club there is 13:866
execution some are daily led to e. 7:283
exercise E. is bunk 12:514
exertion success depends . . . upon individual initiative and e. 12:458
exhausted Our agenda is now e. 13:6
exist I e. by what I think 12:556
If God did not e. 8:612
liberty cannot long e. 8:225
No more things should be presumed to e. 6:102
existence A God who let us prove his e. 12:892
disregard for the necessities of e. 12:655
experimental reasoning, concerning matter of fact and e. 8:342
individual e. goes out in a lonely spasm of helpless agony 11:244
mere e. is swollen to a horror 12:664
the sole purpose of human e. is to kindle a light 13:681
the struggle for e. 10:615
to deny the e. of an unseen kingdom is bad 11:463
to do something is to create e. 12:730
exit Few men of action have been able to make a graceful e. 13:527
exits They have their e. and their entrances 7:274
expect you e. other people to be . . . to your liking 6:109
expectation the distinction between hope and e. 13:713
expects England e. every man will do his duty 9:53
expediency the most useful thing about a principle . . . sacrificed to e. 12:808
expenditure annual e. nineteen nineteen six 10:626
in favour of . . . particular e. 13:90
experience I can't see that it's wrong to give him a little legal e. 13:149
moment's insight . . . worth a life's e. 10:384
the light which e. gives 10:387
The triumph of hope over e. 8:506
experiences the child should be allowed to meet the real e. of life 11:389
experiment a great social and economic e. 12:174
A theory can be proved by e. 13:560
existence remains a . . . lamentable e. 11:307
no path leads from e. to . . . theory 13:560
to desist from the e. in despair 11:259
experimental *Does it contain any e. reasoning* 8:342
experts administration must be entrusted to e. 12:155
export I integrate the current e. drive 13:993
to e. revolution is nonsense 12:265
ex-president No candidate . . . elected e. by such a large majority 11:157
expression Italy is a geographical e. 10:581
supreme e. of the mediocrity 12:150
expropriators The e. are expropriated 10:244
exquisite the e. touch . . . is denied to me 10:278
exterminate e. . . . the treacherous English 12:9
extinguished glory of Europe is e. 9:10

the flame of French resistance must not . . . be e. 12:334
extraordinary this is an e. man 8:252
extravagance Our love of what is beautiful does not lead to e. 2:5
extreme E. remedies . . . for extreme diseases 2:73
extremism e. in the defence of liberty is no vice 13:200
exuberance e. of his own verbosity 11:15
eye A custom loathsome to the e., hateful to the nose 7:194
clapped the glass to his sightless e. 9:41
e. for e. 1:41
Every tear from every e. 9:149
his keener e. The axe's edge did try 7:137
I have only one e. 9:40
man who looks you . . . in the e. . . . hiding something 13:599
neither e. to see, nor tongue to speak 7:121
with an e. made quiet . . . We see into the life of things 9:134
eyes Drink to me only with thine e. 7:329
Look at that man's e. 12:138
Love looks not with the e. 7:315
Mine e. have seen the glory of the coming of the Lord 10:206
the e. of the blind shall be opened 1:106
the whites of their e. 8:203

F

Fabian Britain . . . F. Society writ large 13:297
Fabians A good man fallen among F. 11:177
fabric chemical barrage has been hurled against the f. of life 13:946
the baseless f. of this vision 7:174
face At fifty everyone has the f. he deserves 13:648
Communism with a human f. 13:225
everybody's f. but their own 8:436
from whose f. the earth and the heaven fled 3:55
My f. is my fortune, sir, she said 9:177
The human f. is . . . a whole cluster of faces 12:578
to order a new stamp . . . with my f. on it 12:39
facetious You must not think me . . . foolish because I am f. 10:413
fact the slaying of a beautiful hypothesis by an ugly f. 11:491
faction f. is the worst of all parties 8:108
impossible that the whisper of a f. 10:44
To die for f. 8:36
facts Comment is free but f. are sacred 12:958
F. alone are wanted in life 10:474
F. are ventriloquists' dummies 12:559
F. speak louder than statistics 13:653
Once a newspaper touches a story, the f. are lost 13:998
fail Others must f. 13:726
to f. conventionally 12:722
failed Here lies Joseph, who f. in everything he undertook 8:264 .
faileth charity never f. 3:95
failure All political lives . . . end in f. 13:316
faint Damn with f. praise 8:656
fair F. stood the wind for France 6:62
Monday's child is f. of face 10:640
Serious sport has nothing to do with f. play 12:645
the name of Vanity F. 8:539
Whitehall . . . our attempts to be f. to everybody 13:857
faith an absolute f. that all things are possible to God 11:464
F. . . . an illogical belief in . . . the improbable 12:602
F. consists in believing when it is beyond the power of reason to believe 8:609
f. is the substance of things hoped for 3:119
no need for any other f. than . . . f. in human beings 12:894
now abideth f., hope, charity 3:95
O thou of little f., wherefore didst thou doubt 3:132
O ye of little f. 3:20
Reason is itself a matter of f. 11:362
the f. and morals hold Which Milton held 9:44
we walk by f., not by sight 3:69
whoever is moved by f. to assent to it 8:598

faithful If this man is not f. to his God 5:30
O come all ye f. 10:592
fall and an haughty spirit before a f. 1:82
The airplane stays up because it doesn't have the time to f. 11:492
fallen A good man f. among Fabians 11:177
falleth woe to him that is alone when he f. 1:69
false f. to his friends . . . true to the public 8:125
She wore f. hair and that red 7:71
The religions we call f. were once true 10:593
Thou canst not then be f. 7:360
thou shalt not bear f. witness 1:40
Vain wisdom all, and f. philosophy 8:325
falsehood Let her and F. grapple 7:381
fame F. is sometimes like unto a . . . mushroom 7:310
F. is the spur 7:306
Love of f. is the last thing . . . to be parted from 4:51
families There are only two f. in the world 7:103
family A f. with the wrong members in control 12:868
Mother is the dead heart of the f. 13:778
my f. begins with me 2:11
the f. . . . source of all our discontents 13:776
famous I awoke . . . found myself f. 9:128
let us now praise f. men 1:104
famylyarytie He used towardes every men . . . f. 6:79
fanatics when f. are on top there is no limit to oppression 13:44
fancies All universal moral principles are idle f. 8:567
fancy sweetest Shakespeare, F.'s child 7:180
far how f. we may go too f. 12:820
The night is dark, and I am f. from home 10:587
Thursday's child has f. to go 10:640
Faraday remain plain Michael F. to the last 10:422
farce F. is the essential theatre 13:431
Parliament is the longest running f. 13:314
farewell F., a long farewell, to all my greatness 7:296
hail and f. 4:96
farmyard nothing to distinguish human society from the f. 11:390
the f. world of sex 11:381
far-reaching Life's short span forbids us to enter on f. hopes 4:64
farthing It is burning a f. candle at Dover 8:291
fascination Philosophy, . . . is a fight against . . . f. 12:548
war . . . will always have its f. 11:428
Fascism F. is a religion 12:229
F. is not an article for export 12:224
F. means war 12:193
For F. the State is absolute 12:248
the twentieth century will be . . . the century of F. 12:229
fascist Every communist has a f. frown 13:191
fashion after the f. of their country 7:387
Nothing else holds f. 7:323
the f. of this world passeth away 3:67
the unreasoning laws of markets and f. 10:131
fashionable an idea . . . to be f. is ominous 11:483
fashions I cannot . . . cut my conscience to fit this year's f. 13:67
fast they stumble that run f. 7:216
US has to move very f. 13:180
faster the world would go round a deal f. 10:498
fat butter will only make us f. 12:274
in every f. man a thin one 12:641
Who's your f. friend 9:83
fatal Nature has never put the f. question as to the meaning of their lives 12:716
fate count as profit every day that F. allows you 4:62
Each man the architect of his own f. 4:56
hostages given to f. 4:76
How wayward the decrees of F. 10:457
It is not only our f. but our business to lose innocence 13:579
jeers at F. 12:940
master of his f. 10:491
the life-sentence which f. carries 13:661
the master of my f. 11:335
the severity of f. 7:301
We may become the makers of our f. 13:724
father a wise f. that knows his own child 7:332

brood of Folly without f. 7:254
Dreading to find its F. 12:744
F..... come home with me now 11:222
God is ... an exalted f. 11:482
he loved the stags as ... though he had been their f. 5:14
If poverty is the mother of crime, stupidity is its f. 8:451
in my F.'s house are many mansions 3:114
left me by my F. 7:136
My f. ... deals in nice polonies 10:82
our F. 3:102
fatherhood Mirrors and f. are abominable 12:746
fathers atone for the sins of your f. 4:14
Come mothers and f. Throughout the land 13:772
land of my f. 13:862
Our f. were Englishmen 7:107
Victory has a thousand f. 13:688
fatuity the English seem ... to act with ... the f. of idiots 9:68
fault f., do not fear to abandon them 2:39
Shakespeare never had six lines together without a f. 8:295
The fundamental f. of the female character 10:529
worst f. of the working classes 13:404
faults If we had no f. of our own 8:526
When you have f. 2:39
favour accepts a smaller as a f. 10:156
every man feel that he is enjoying his special f. 7:1
Many terms ... out of f., will be revived 4:31
truths being in and out of f. 12:705
favoured thou that art highly f. 3:1
favours On whom their f. fall 10:524
Whether a pretty woman grants or withholds her f. 4:79
fear concessions of f. 8:199
do I f. thy nature 7:244
f. God, and keep his commandments 1:95
F. no more the heat o' th' sun 7:212
fools rush in where angels f. to tread 8:337
freedom from f. 12:347
Men f. death 7:205
one has ... ceased to be an object of f. as soon as one is pitied 11:282
only thing we have to f. is f. 12:219
Perhaps your f. in passing judgement 7:76
the f. of one evil 8:536
fears A man who f. suffering 7:226
man f. ... only the stroke of death 7:204
The sum of their f. 12:385
feathers not only fine f. 2:34
February dreadful pictures of January and F. 10:345
Excepting F. alone And that has twenty-eight days clear 7:415
feed You cannot f. the hungry on statistics 11:121
feeding Spoon f. ... teaches us nothing but the shape of the spoon 13:533
feel what I f. really bad about 13:211
feels A really intelligent man f. what other men ... know 8:410
feet An emperor ought at least to die on his f. 4:20
die on your f. than to live on your knees 12:271
those f. in ancient time 9:73
feigning truest poetry is the most f. 7:170
fell f. among thieves 3:16
· men f. out 8:369
fellows Boys are capital f. in their own way 10:513
fellowship such a f. of good knights shall never be together 6:76
female male and f. created he them 1:5
the f. of the species is more deadly than the male 11:417
The fundamental fault of the f. character 10:529
the increase in drinking is to be laid mainly to the account of the f. sex 11:414
feminine Taste is the f. of genius 11:395
Février Generals Janvier and F. 10:141
few err as grossly as the F. 8:33
owed by so many to so f. 12:338
fickle Woman is always f. and changing 4:77
fiction ancient history, ... is no more than accepted f. 8:362
Children should acquire ... heroes and villains from f. 13:575

one form of continuous f. 13:509
Poetry is a comforting piece of f. 12:434
fiddle Hey diddle diddle. The cat and the f. 7:52
field A cow is a very good animal in the f. 8:138
Man for the f. and woman for the hearth 10:528
shepherds abiding in the f. 3:5
some corner of a foreign f. 12:31
fields East and west on f. forgotten 11:78
Now there are f. where Troy once was 2:83
fiend forgive the f. for becoming a torrent 9:100
fierce f. and bald and short of breath 12:82
fifteen we might more reasonably expect f. years of peace 9:14
fifth One f. of the people are against everything 13:198
The F. Column 12:291
fifty At f. everyone has the face he deserves 13:648
F.-four forty or fight 10:98
For one person who dreams of making f. thousand pounds 12:942
there are f. thousand men slain .... and not one Englishman 8:104
fight a great cause to f. for 11:137
easier to f. for one's principles 12:603
f., f., f., and f. again 13:130
F. the good f. with all thy might 10:599
I have not yet begun to f. 8:233
I purpose to f. it out on this line 10:215
I will not cease from mental f. 9:73
Our cock won't f. 12:283
The British won't f. 13:351
To f. and not to heed the wounds 7:349
too proud to f. 12:26
Ulster will f. 11:49
We don't want to f., but, by jingo if we do 11:16
We'll f. and we'll conquer 8:132
we shall f. on the beaches 12:328
With our backs to the wall ... each ... must f. on to the end 12:78
You cannot f. against the future 10:233
fighting F. is like champagne 12:625
Most sorts of diversion ... are an imitation of f. 8:402
not conquering but f. well 11:361
This is against f. ever hereafter 7:128
What are we f. for 12:195
fights I can't spare this man; he f. 10:217
fig leaves they sewed f. together 1:12
films Why ... pay money to see bad f. 13:429
fine f. feathers that make f. birds 2:34
In England, pop art and f. art 13:436
finest their f. hour 12:330
finger I will shake my little f. – and there will be no more Tito 13:20
fingers about time we pulled our f. out 13:144
our f. are circumcised 13:500
Fings F. Ain't Wot They Used T'Be 13:507
finished it is f. 3:38
finite Our knowledge can only be f. 13:541
fire a chariot ... of f. 1:52
All things, oh priests, are on f. 2:68
a pillar of f. 1:37
cloven tongues like as of f. 3:44
French Guard, f. first 8:120
F. – without hatred 12:272
Ideas that enter the mind under f. 12:188
It is with our passions as it is with f. and water 8:487
that deplorable f. near Fish Street in London 8:8
the bush burned with f. 1:33
The f. ... walks in a broader gross 8:9
The f. which in the heart resides 10:566
two irons in the f. 7:373
firebell a f. in the night 10:12
fireside A man may surely be allowed to take a glass of wine by his own f. 9:125
firm not a family; we're a f. 13:43
firmness *Commodity, F., and Delight* 7:178
first many that are f. shall be last 3:65
The F. Blast of the Trumpet 7:41
there is no last or f. 10:591
Who ever loved, that loved not at f. sight 7:317

firstborn I . . . will smite all the f. 1:36
first-rate the powers of a f. man and the creed of a second-rate man 10:122
fish a great f. to swallow up Jonah 1:58
No human being, . . . was ever so free as a f. 10:490
This man . . . is a poor f. 13:767
fishers f. of men 3:19
fishes five barley loaves, and two small f. 3:13
f. live in the sea 7:245
So are the f. 12:342
fishing Time is but the stream I go a-f. in 10:479
fist You cannot shake hands with a clenched f. 13:251
fit It is not f. that you should sit here 7:157
fitly no one in the realm . . . f. to come to me 6:71
fits periodical f. of morality 10:274
five If you don't find a God by f. o'clock this afternoon 11:472
practise f. things 2:60
The formula 'Two and two make f.' 10:654
flabbiness The moral f. born of . . . Success 11:360
flag But spare your country's f. 10:199
futile exhibition, this singing of the Red F. 12:2
keep the red f. flying here 11:61
Tonight the American f. floats from yonder hill 8:220
flame like a moth, the simple maid Still plays about the f. 8:516
flames commit it then to the f. 8:342
Superstition sets the whole world in f. 8:348
Flanders In F. fields 12:28
You have sent me a F. mare 7:28
flat Very f., Norfolk 12:980
flatter not f. me 7:160
flatterer the brave beast is no f. 7:114
flattering It is f. some men to endure them 8:393
flattery Imitation is the sincerest form of f. 10:636
ne'er Was f. lost 9:124
woman . . . to be gained by . . . f. 8:520
flea English literature's performing f. 12:504
fleas F. . . . upon the body of a giant 10:454
fled I f. Him, down the nights 11:471
flesh f. and blood so cheap 10:95
Rehearsing a play is making the word f. 13:476
the f. is weak 3:59
the world, the f., and the devil 12:964
fleshly The F. School of Poetry 11:167
flies As f. to wanton boys 7:210
Time f., death urges 8:462
float rather be an opportunist and f. 13:15
flock keeping watch over their f. by night 3:5
flog f. the rank and file 10:29
flood the f. was forty days upon the earth 1:19
Which, taken at the f. 7:277
flowed water f. like champagne 11:29
flower just miss the prizes at the f. show 13:649
flowers Letting a hundred f. blossom 13:539
Their f. the tenderness of patient minds 12:21
flown I see all the birds are f. 7:120
flows Everything f. and nothing stays 2:48
fly Who saw him die? I, said the F. 6:3
foes judge of a man by his f. 11:301
fog a London particular . . . A f. 10:342
Folies-Bergère A psychiatrist is a man who goes to the F. 13:995
folk-dancing except incest and f. 12:742
follies f. as the special evidences of our wisdom 10:583
lovers cannot see the pretty f. 7:316
The f. which a man regrets 11:354
follow He would rather f. public opinion 12:398
I have to f. them, I am their leader 10:113
take up his cross, and f. me 3:24
folly brood of F. without father 7:254
the slightest f. That ever love did make thee run into 7:318
food f. in music 8:282
f. to one man is bitter poison to others 4:45
On the Continent people have good f. 13:871
The perpetual struggle for room and f. 9:36
fool f. among fools or a f. alone 13:659
A f. sees not the same tree 9:137
brains enough to make a f. of himself 11:249

f. his whole life long 7:184
He who holds hopes . . . is a f. 13:654
more of the f. than of the wise 7:246
the old man who will not laugh is a f. 12:666
The wisest f. in Christendom 7:100
Wise Man or a F. 9:139
You can f. too many of the people 12:988
foolish A f. consistency 10:375
anything very f. 10:399
You must not think me . . . f. because I am facetious 10:413
fools Christianity . . . says that they are all f. 11:477
F. are in a terrible, overwhelming majority 11:331
f. decoyed into our condition 8:496
f. rush in where angels fear to tread 8:337
Is Pride, the never-failing vice of f. 8:546
Many have been the wise speeches of f. 7:223
suffer f. gladly 3:61
Thirty millions, mostly f. 10:582
this great stage of f. 7:288
football F. isn't a matter of life and death 13:519
footbail F. . . . causeth fighting 7:190
footsteps home his f. he hath turn'd 9:169
foppery excellent f. of the world 7:243
forbearance f. ceases to be a virtue 8:561
forbidden he wanted it only because it was f. 11:295
we're f. to know — what end the gods have in store 4:86
force control a free society by f. 13:305
f. alone is but temporary 8:198
F., if unassisted by judgement, collapses 4:11
F. is not a remedy 11:21
May the F. be with you 13:1026
Other nations use 'f.': we Britons . . . use 'Might' 12:307
Who overcomes By f. 8:10
force-feeding This universal, obligatory f. with lies 13:243
Ford The time of our F. 12:925
forefathers Think of your f. 9:43
foreign pronounce f. names as he chooses 13:655
wandering on a f. strand 9:169
foreigner f. should . . . be wiser than ourselves 10:583
foreigners the time had passed . . . merely to teach f. 11:110
forest His f. fleece the Wrekin heaves 11:231
Wandering in a vast f. at night 8:602
forever That is f. England 12:31
forget Oh Lord! . . . if I f. thee, do not thou f. me 7:122
When I f. my sovereign 8:230
forgetting You are f. the postchaise 10:32
forgive do not have to f. my enemies 10:248
Father, f. them 3:35
how oft shall . . . I f. him 3:90
To err is human, to f., divine 8:401, 8:547
forgotten I have f. more law than you ever knew 8:27
The f. man 12:217
what has been learnt has been f. 13:549
forlorn The British postgraduate student is a lonely f. soul 13:558
formed not f. by nature to bear 4:72
fornicated f. and read the papers 13:594
forsaken my God, why hast thou f. me 3:37
fortress f. built by Nature 7:69
fortuitous f. concurrence of atoms 10:166
fortune greater virtues to sustain good f. 8:525
hostages to f. 7:336
people of f. . . . a few delinquencies 10:427
slings and arrows of outrageous f. 7:209
to make your f. . . . let people see . . . it is in their interests to promote yours 8:624
What is your f., my pretty maid 9:177
fortunes f. sharp adversitee 6:130
share in the good f. of the mighty 13:27
forty f. days and f. nights 3:78
made the difference of f. thousand men 9:115
fought better to have f. and lost 10:471
foul Murder most f. 7:361
found I have f. it 2:78
Pleasure is . . . seldom f. where it is sought 8:419
foundation the final stone . . . in the f. of St Petersburg 8:82
fountains their f. piped an answer 2:85

four f. essential human freedoms 12:347
F. legs good 13:1017
Great God grant that twice two be not f. 10:609
fourth a f. estate of the realm 10:28
on the f. day they will say 'To hell with you!' 13:258
Fox Charles James F. 9:67
fox The f. knows many things 2:81
You don't set a f. to watching the chickens 13:140
fraction Only a residual f. is thought 12:185
frailty F., thy name is woman 7:344
Française Algérie F. 13:105
France all roads lead to F. 12:54
and dare for ever; and thus will F. be saved 9:17
A revolutionary F. . . . rather win a war 12:371
but F. has not lost the war 12:333
Fair stood the wind for F. 6:62
F. before everything 9:78
F. has more need of me 9:97
F. regenerated by the Revolution 10:130
F. was a long despotism 9:206
king of F. . . . would assent to no peace or treaty 6:42
The best thing I know between F. and England 10:175
Thus we have defeated the king of F. 6:26
Francis My cousin F. and I are in perfect accord 7:5
frankincense gold, and f., and myrrh 3:10
Franks a new Athens might be created in the land of the F. 5:7
fraternité Liberté! Égalité! F. 9:2
frauds pious f. of friendship 8:416
free a f. society . . . where it is safe to be unpopular 13:71
All f. men, . . . are citizens of Berlin 13:171
All human beings are born f. 13:18
F. Will and Predestination 12:201
Greece might still be f. 10:6
In a f. society the state . . . administers justice among men 12:184
land of the f., and the home of the brave 9:103
Man is condemned to be f. 13:643
Man was born f. 8:144
No human being, . . . was ever so f. as a fish 10:490
none the less f. than you were 4:25
order you to hold a f. election 6:14
safer to be in chains than to be f. 12:17
truth that makes men f. 12:830
We have to believe in f. will 13:360
We must be f. or die 9:44
Who would be f. 9:94
wish that all men everywhere could be f. 10:201
freedom enemies of F. 12:115
F.! Equality! Brotherhood 9:2
F. is an indivisible word 12:387
F. is Slavery 13:30
F. is the right to tell . . . do not want to hear 12:296
fit to use their f. 10:22
f. of speech, f. of conscience, and the prudence never to practise . . . them 11:82
f. to print . . . proprietor's prejudices 12:171
giving f. to the slave 10:203
In solitude alone can he know true f. 7:265
Me this unchartered f. tires 9:70
Necessity is the plea for every infringement of human f. 8:250
None can love f. heartily, but good men 7:143
only f. can make security secure 12:424
So greatly did she care for f. that she died for it 11:165
So long as the state exists there is no f. 12:70
The worst enemy of truth and f. 11:36
Those who deny f. to others 10:162
Until you've lost your reputation, you never realize . . . what f. really is 12:723
what is F. 10:55
Your f. and mine cannot be separated 13:373
You took my f. away a long time ago 13:239
freedoms four essential human f. 12:347
free-labour entirely a slave-holding nation, or entirely a f. nation 10:171
free-will believe in f.. We've got no choice 13:737
French dislike the F. from . . . vulgar antipathy 8:580
everyone would always have spoken F. 8:165

fear that the F. would invade 8:62
F. governments more selfish than most 13:164
F. Guard, fire first 8:120
Give me books, fruit, F. wine and fine weather 10:330
I do not say the F. cannot come 9:46
I hate the F. 8:576
Imagine the Lord talking F. 12:891
I speak . . . Italian to women, F. to men 7:16
The F. are wiser than they seem 7:385
the flame of F. resistance must not . . . be extinguished 12:334
The F. want no-one to be their superior 10:580
The F. will only be united under the threat of danger 13:64
There's something Vichy about the F. 12:866
too early to form a final judgement on the F. Revolution 9:214
to the F. the empire of the land 9:39
Frenchman F. must be always talking 8:578
You must hate a F. 9:38
Frenchmen Englishmen to be subject to F. 5:18
F. drink wine just like 12:834
to create F. in the image of Englishmen 12:381
freshen a mighty storm . . . to f. us up 11:101
Freud The trouble with F. 13:637
Freudian the F., it is a very low, Central European sort of humour 13:629
Friday F.'s child is loving and giving 10:640
I takes my man F. 8:653
friend A f. should bear his f.'s infirmities 7:236
a new f. is as new wine 1:70
A woman can become a man's f. 11:410
damned good-natured f. 8:427
forsake not an old f. 1:70
f., wherefore art thou come 3:29
In every f. we lose a part of ourselves 8:317
no f. like a sister 10:519
friendly Man is the only animal . . . on f. terms with the victims . . . he eats 11:313
so large, So f., and so rich 13:860
friends false to his f. . . . true to the public 8:125
F., Romans, countrymen 4:7
Good thoughts his only f. 7:376
guessed you were f. 13:620
Have no f. not equal 2:37
How to Win F. 12:985
I don't trust him. We're f. 12:635
I let down my f. 13:310
In the misfortune of our best f. 8:374
Job endured everything — until his f. came 10:419
lay down his f. for his life 13:166
not so much our f. help that helps us 2:45
Once more unto the breach, dear f. 6:61
shameful to distrust one's f. 8:372
that a man lay down his life for his f. 3:60
friendship A man, Sir, should keep his f. in constant repair 8:417
Business . . . may bring money, . . . f. hardly ever does 10:623
F. is a disinterested commerce between equals 8:492
F. is constant in all other things 7:233
F. is unnecessary 13:581
love . . . looks more like hatred than like f. 8:483
Most f. is feigning 7:237
Society, f., and love 8:429
To like . . . the same things, that is . . . true f. 4:46
frighten by God, they f. me 9:81
f. the horses 11:380
frightened My father was f. of his mother 12:763
frittered life is f. away by detail 10:478
frivolity gay without f. 10:567
frog A f. he would a-wooing go 7:416
your f. lives in hope 7:51
frogs F. and snails And puppy-dogs' tails 10:526
frontier We stand today on the edge of a new f. 13:128
froth Life is mostly f. and bubble 10:494
fruit she took of the f. thereof 1:12
the f. Of that forbidden tree 1:110
fruitful be f. and multiply 1:5
fuck They f. you up, your mum and dad 13:763

ugitive a f. and a vagabond 1:17
ührer *Ein Reich, Ein Volk, Ein F.* 12:242
ull Reading maketh a f. man 7:221
ulness the earth is the Lord's, and the f. 3:68
un Most people get a fair amount of f. out of their lives 13:650
the people have f. 8:112
Work is much more f. than f. 13:997
   its own animality either objectionable or f. 13:628
to accuse someone of trying to be f. is highly abusive 13:638
ury full of sound and f. 7:287
hell a f. like a woman scorned 8:514
nothing but beastly f. and extreme violence 7:185
strength and f. 8:381
the F. of a Patient Man 8:391
ustest I got there f. with the mostest 10:211
utility the f. of human endeavour 9:104
uture how pleasant . . . not to have any f. 13:670
If you want a picture of the f. 13:1028
if you would divine the f. 2:29
I have seen the f. 12:109
I never think of the f. 12:708
The f. is made of the same stuff 12:737
The f. is the only kind of property 13:60
the f. . . . makes cowards of us 12:694
The past was nothing . . . The f. was a mystery 11:336
Who controls the past controls the f. 13:32

G

gaiety the only concession to g. 13:874
gained learning hath g. most 7:222
gainful I will undoubtedly have to seek . . . g. employment 13:70
gains no g. without pains 13:68, 13:656
Galileo If G. had said in verse that the world moved 7:420
gallant a loyal, a g., a generous, an ingenious, and good-temper'd people 8:574
gallows make the g. glorious like the cross 10:173
game how you played the g. 12:885
It's more than a g. It's an institution 10:344
Play up! play up! and play the g. 11:541
win this g. and thrash the Spaniards 7:62
gamekeeper would you allow your g. to read it 13:443
games The most important thing in the Olympic G. 11:361
gamesmanship G. or The Art of Winning Games 13:580
gaming Man is a g. animal 10:403
gangsters The great nations have always acted like g. 13:189
garden Come into the g., Maud 10:650
the g. of Eden 1:8
gardener Nor does a . . . g. scent his roses 12:440
gas-masks digging trenches and trying on g. 12:303
gate I am here at the g. 10:650
I said to the man who stood at the g. of the year 12:319
matters not how strait the g. 11:335
gather G. ye rosebuds while ye may 7:330
gatling The g.'s jammed and the colonel dead 11:541
Gaul G. is divided into three 2:22
Gaulle I, General de G., now in London 12:334
Gaullist I . . . have become a G. . . . little by little 13:187
gave God . . . g. his only begotten Son 3:107
gay g. without frivolity 10:567
I love the g. Eastertide 6:96
general caviare to the g. 7:171
In a civil war, a g. must know 13:38
was good for G. Motors 13:81
generalizations All g. are dangerous 10:652
generals Dead battles, like dead g. 12:23
It is not the business of g. to shoot one another 9:110
that's not against the law for g. 13:52
wish he would *bite* . . . my g. 8:133
generation Each g. imagines itself . . . more intelligent 12:644
You are a lost g. 12:162
generations all g. shall call me blessed 3:2
g. . . . have struggled in poverty to build these altars 11:468
g. . . . pass in a short time 4:58

generous a loyal, a gallant, a g., an ingenious, and good-temper'd people 8:574
genius a country full of g., but with absolutely no talent 13:899
a German and a g. 8:283
G. does what it must 8:283
I invoke the g. of the Constitution 8:222
Only an organizing g. 12:421
Rules and models destroy g. and art 10:290
Since when was g. . . . respectable 10:481
talent instantly recognizes g. 12:575
Taste is the feminine of g. 11:395
the difference between talent and g. 10:499
true g. is a mind of large general powers 8:355
True g. walks along a line 8:468
When a true g. appears 8:454
gentil parfit, g. knyght 6:120
Gentiles a light to lighten the G. 3:8
gentleman a g. . . . never inflicts pain 10:423
g. of leisure 11:91
g. . . . . robbing the poor 11:117
Not a g.; dresses too well 13:88
the g. is an *attorney* 8:643
Who was then the g. 6:49
gentlemanly secondly, g. conduct 10:368
gentlemen by g. for g. 10:297
extremely difficult to behave like g. 12:800
g., let us do something today 9:51
religion for g. 8:13
the British bourgeoisie have spoken of themselves as g. 12:842
gentlewoman a g. made ready 7:341
genuineness G. only thrives in the dark 12:692
geographical India is a g. term 12:208
Italy is a g. expression 10:581
geometricians we are g. only by chance 8:621
geometry Poetry is as exact a science as g. 10:307
There is no 'royal road' to g. 2:76
George Death of King G. V 12:263
G. III was a kind of 'consecrated obstruction' 8:667
G., be a King 8:142
G. the First knew nothing 8:661
G. the Third . . . . . . *may profit by their example* 8:154
King G. will be able to read that 8:209
Georgia marching through G. 10:219
German a G. and a genius 8:283
I speak . . . G. to my horse 7:16
The G. army was stabbed in the back 12:94
The G. Empire has become a world empire 11:76
Germans Don't let's be beastly to the G. 12:198
How . . . thorough these G. always managed to be 12:852
Man, . . . had been created to jab the life out of G. 12:83
The G. . . . . are going to be squeezed, as a lemon 12:99
to the G. that of the air 9:39
Germany Defeat of G. means 12:369
G., G. before all else 10:89
G. will be . . . a world power 12:137
G. is winning 12:355
In G., the Nazis came for the Communists 12:411
Nazi G. had become a menace to all mankind 12:251
Prussia merges into G. 10:114
getting G. and spending 9:172
ghost the G. in the Machine 13:905
The Papacy is not other than the G. of the deceased Roman Empire 7:153
yielded up the g. 3:39
giant Fleas . . . upon the body of a g. 10:454
we have only awakened a sleeping g. 12:362
giants A battle of g. 9:116
it is by standing on the shoulders of g. 8:614
war of the g. is over 12:408
gibes a great master of g. 11:5
gift the timeliness of the g. 8:542
worth more than the g. 8:523
gifts deserves the name of happy who knows how to use the gods' g. wisely 4:50
gilded A best-seller is the g. tomb of a mediocre talent 12:478
She's only a bird in a g. cage 11:534

girl　Every little g. knows about love　13:794
one can . . . see in a little g. the threat of a woman　10:538
park, a policeman and a pretty g.　13:634
girlfriend　Not every problem someone has with his g. is
. . . due to . . . capitalist . . . production　13:321
girls　Boys and g. come out to play　8:652
g. are so queer　10:543
My life with g. has ended　4:75
the . . . rift between the sexes is . . . widened by . . . teaching
. . . to the g.　11:398
Treaties are like roses and young g.　13:188
Where . . . boys plan for what . . . young g. plan for whom
11:411
give　g. me liberty or g. me death　8:200
G. me your tired, . . . Your huddled masses　11:52
To g. and not to count the cost　7:349
gives　He g. twice who g. promptly　4:80
giving　The manner of g.　8:523
Gladstone　G.　10:184
G., like Richelieu, can't write　11:10
Mr G. read Homer for fun　11:545
Glasgow　never played the G. Empire　13:637
glass　baying for broken g.　12:841
Satire is a sort of g.　8:436
through a g., darkly　3:95
you won't intoxicate with one g.　11:180
glisters　Nor all that g. gold　8:465
glittering　The world continues to offer g. prizes　12:685
global　the world in the image of a g. village　13:683
globe　the great g. itself　7:174
gloire　Le jour de g. est arrivé　9:16
gloria　Sic transit g. mundi　6:113
glorious　Happy and g.　8:114
her army has had a g. victory　8:77
make the gallows g. like the cross　10:173
glory　An enchanted pile . . . raised for the g. of England
10:132
But trailing clouds of g.　9:199
g. to God in the highest　3:6
I g. in the name of Briton　8:139
It is a great g. in a woman　2:55
Land of Hope and G.　11:149
Mine eyes have seen the g. of the coming of the Lord
10:206
paths of g. lead but to the grave　8:320
Popularity? . . . g.'s small change　10:459
So passes the g. of the world　6:28
the g. of Europe is extinguished for ever　9:10
the g. of the Lord shall be revealed　1:54
we left him alone with his g.　9:77
What price G.　12:686
Where is it now, the g. and the dream　9:199
glow　make the corpuscles of the blood g.　12:839
glum　speed g. heroes . . . to death　12:82
gluttony　G. is an emotional escape　13:825
go　In the name of God, g.!　12:322
I will neither g. nor hang　6:37
goat-footed　This g. bard　12:237
God　A G. who let us prove his existence　12:892
A man with G.　7:393
America is G.'s Crucible　11:135
an absolute faith that all things are possible to G.　11:464
An honest G.　11:467
as though you were G. on earth　8:67
better to have no opinion of G.　7:403
concept of G. has any validity　13:920
even by G. himself they are called Gods　7:96
Even G. cannot change the past　2:30
final proof of G.'s omnipotence　13:915
G. and my right　6:27
G. as a working hypothesis　12:900
'G. bless us every one!'　10:641
G. blew and they were scattered　7:66
G. can stand being told　13:922
G. did send me　6:66
G. disposes　6:125
G. does not play dice　12:918
G. erects a house of prayer　8:594
G. is always on the side of the big battalions　8:17

G. is beginning to resemble . . . the last fading smile of a
cosmic Cheshire cat　13:908
G. is dead　11:469
G. is nothing more than an exalted father　11:482
G. is on the side . . . of the best shots　8:441
G. is subtle but he is not malicious　12:917
G. is the immemorial refuge of the incompetent　13:914
G. made everything out of nothing　12:741
G. made the country　8:478
Good G., said G.　12:873
Great G. grant that twice two be not four　10:609
G. said, *Let Newton be*　8:618
G. save our gracious King　8:114
G. will pardon me. It is His trade　10:607
Had I . . . served G. as diligently as I have served the king
7:17
her conception of G. was certainly not orthodox　10:658
How could G. do this to me　8:78
If G. did not exist　8:612
if G. had wanted to create slaves　6:50
If G. made us in His image　8:610
If G. were suddenly condemned to live the life　10:493
If this man is not faithful to his G.　5:30
If you don't find a G. by five o'clock this afternoon　11:472
If you talk to G., you are praying　13:925
justify the ways of G. to men　8:585
Know then thyself, presume not G. to scan　8:407
Live among men as if G. beheld you　4:83
Many people believe that they are attracted by G.　12:876
May G. deny you peace　11:370
nature is the art of G.　7:307
none deny there is a G.　7:401
One G., one law, one element　10:472
poems . . . for the love of Man and in praise of G.　13:424
put your hand into the hand of G.　12:319
Sickness, sin and death . . . do not originate in G.　11:466
Since G. has given us the papacy . . . enjoy it　6:90
speak to G. as if men were listening　4:83
that G. is interested only . . . in religion　12:874
that great Leviathan, or rather . . . that *Mortal* G.　7:150
the highest praise of G. consists in the denial of Him
12:879
the nearer you are to G.　7:402
There, but for the Grace of G., goes G.　12:652
The true G., . . . G. of ideas　10:385
Those who marry G. . . . can become domesticated too
13:916
we come From G., who is our home　9:199
we owe G. a death　7:202
whom G. wishes to destroy　2:71
you hardly ever mention G. any more　13:911
god　Either a beast or a g.　2:43
I believe I am becoming a g.　4:20
if triangles invented a g., they would make him three-
sided　8:596
Kill everyone, and you are a g.　13:824
to the unknown g.　3:47
Goddamm　Lhude sing G.　12:517
godlike　patient endurance is g.　10:557
gods　Against stupidity the g. . . . struggle in vain　9:138
deserves the name of happy who knows how to use the g.
gifts wisely　4:50
G. help them　2:46
Kings are earth's g.　7:97
no other g. before me　1:40
So many g., so many creeds　11:474
The Ethiopians say that their g. are . . . black　2:70
we're forbidden to know — what end the g. have in store
4:86
Whom the g. love　2:26
Whom the g. wish to destroy　12:726
goe　to morowe longe I to g. to God　7:20
going　I am just g. outside　11:160
gold　all the g. that the goose could give　2:57
cursed craving for g.　4:81
For g. in phisik is a cordial　6:132
I stuffed their mouths with g.　13:4
Nor all that glisters g.　8:465
To a shower of g.　10:553

greater g. love hath no man 3:60
The g. the power 8:181
greatest great city . . . has the g. men and women 10:482
the g. deeds require a certain insensitiveness 8:472
The g. happiness of the g. number 10:8
the g. of these is charity 3:95
great-grandfathers Classicism, . . . the literature that gave
. . . pleasure to their g. 10:277
greatness long farewell to all my g. 7:296
Men who have g. . . . don't go in for politics 12:257
some have g. thrust upon 'em 7:282
Greek never was such a humbug as the G. affair 10:27
Nobody can say a word against G. 11:268
the intrigue of a G. of the lower empire 10:185
We were taught . . . Latin and G. 11:270
Greeks The Romans and G. found everything human 2:85
To the G. the Muse gave native wit 2:67
uncertainty: a state unknown to the G. 13:578
where the G. had modesty, we have cant 10:280
green I was g. in judgment 7:291
tree of life is g. 9:140, 9:173
green-ey'd jealousy . . . g. monster 7:366
greetings g. where no kindness is 9:163
grenadier The healthy bones of a single Pomeranian g.
11:7
grey theory is all g. 9:140
theory is all g. 9:173
grief calms one's g. by recounting it 7:257
G. and disappointment give rise to anger 8:550
in much wisdom is much g. 1:63
grievances redress of the g. of the vanquished 12:414
grieve G. not that I die young 10:353
Men are we, and must g. 9:154
grind mills of God g. slowly 8:583
yet they g. exceeding small 8:583
grinders Writers, like teeth, are divided into incisors and g.
10:312
grip took a g. on cowardly Marxism 12:231
gross reconciling my g. habits with my net income 13:597
group A g. of closely related persons 13:764
grovelled Whenever he met a great man he g. 10:108
groves And seek for truth in the g. of Academe 4:40
grow make two ears of corn . . . g. . . . where only one grew
before 8:98
make two questions g. where only one 12:661
They shall g. not old 12:92
groweth no grass there g., Only their engines' dung
11:225
growing G. old is like being increasingly penalized 13:718
grown one of the few English novels for g. up people
12:449
grown-ups g. . . . have forgotten what it is like to be a child
13:698
grub it is poor g., poor pay, and easy work 11:111
guarantee No one can g. success in war 13:28
guard That g. our native seas 9:42
guards Up, G., and at 'em 9:111
Who is to guard the g. themselves 4:23
guerre ce n'est pas la g. 10:150
une drôle de g. 12:318
guerrilla The g. wins if he does not lose 13:238
guest Earth, receive an honoured g. 12:498
guide Custom, then, is the great g. of human life 8:466
I have only a faint light to g. me 8:602
guilty I declare myself g. 6:15
ten g. persons escape than one innocent suffer 8:160
guinea I would not give half a g. to live under one form of
government 8:185
guineas I have only five g. in my pocket 8:84
gun it is necessary to take up the g. 13:41
we have got The Maxim G. 11:84
Gunga Din You're a better man than I am, G. 11:530
gunpowder G., Printing, and the Protestant Religion
10:458
guns But it's 'Saviour of 'is country' when the g. 11:515
G. will make us powerful 12:274
gutless W. H. Auden, a sort of g. Kipling 12:491
gutter We are all in the g. 11:342

H

habit H. is a great deadener 13:587
honour peereth in the meanest h. 7:350
habits Curious things, h. 12:595
h. that carry them far apart 2:38
hack Do not h. me 8:44
hail h. and farewell 4:96
hairy Esau . . . a h. man 1:27
half And when they were only h. way up 9:8
h. a loaf is better than a whole 11:147
longest h. of your life 9:174
half-developed the working-class which, raw and h.
10:253
hall one of the sparrows . . . flew . . . through the h. 5:24
halt the whole process has ground to a h. with a 14th Earl
13:182
hammer Art is not a mirror . . . but a h. 12:446
hand educate with the head instead of with the h. 11:269
one of those parties which got out of h. 3:136
put your h. into the h. of God 12:319
touch his weaknesses with a delicate h. 8:560
handbook have used the Bible as if it was a constable's h
10:110
handicraft Art is not a h. 11:194
hands into thy h. I commend my spirit 3:40
Pilate . . . washed his h. 3:33
temples made with h. 3:47
the earth of England is in my two h. 5:12
To be played with both h. in the pocket 11:196
We draw the sword . . . with clean h. 12:4
You cannot shake h. with a clenched fist 13:251
hang I will find something . . . to h. him 7:258
I will neither go nor h. 6:37
We must indeed all h. together 8:208
wretches h. that jury-men may dine 8:88
hanged h. privily by night 6:29
if the King beat us once we shall all be h. 7:127
if they were going to see me h. 7:158
Men are not h. for stealing 8:48
resolved to be h. with the Bible 7:130
to be h. for nonsense 8:36
hangman if I were a grave-digger, or . . . a h. 10:634
Hansard H. is history's ear 13:26
happened most of which had never h. 12:997
happens Everything that h. happens as it should 4:70
I just don't want to be there when it h. 13:528
life . . . seems to me preparation for something that never h
12:731
happiest Poetry is the record of the best and h. moments
10:268
happiness A lifetime of h. . . . hell on earth 11:304
a man is always seeking for h. 12:770
curiously boring about . . . h. 12:585
h. fails, existence remains . . . experiment 11:307
H. in marriage 9:180
H. is a mystery like religion 11:306
H. is an imaginary condition 13:616
H. is beneficial for the body 12:579
H. is like a butterfly 13:596
H. is like coke 12:605
H. is no laughing matter 10:411
H. is not an ideal of reason 8:435
H. is not best achieved 12:577
H. is no vague dream 10:429
H. is the only sanction of life 11:307
h. makes them good 10:551
In solitude What h. 8:379
I thought that success spelled h. 13:596
It is of no moment to the h. of an individual 8:185
life, liberty, and the pursuit of h. 8:207
nothing . . . by which so much h. is produced as by a good
tavern 8:315
Poverty is a great enemy to human h. 8:632
recall a time of h. when in misery 6:108
result h. 10:626
the greatest h. for the greatest numbers 8:549
the greatest h. of the whole 2:7
the h. of the common man 12:382

you take away his h. 11:332

appy Ask . . . whether you are h. 11:281
be h. later on, but it's much harder 13:619
Few people can be h. unless they hate 13:842
Goodness does not . . . make men h. 10:551
H. Days 12:216
laugh before one is h. 8:395
Let us all be h., and live within our means 10:565
man is h. so long as he chooses to be h. 13:610
Mankind are always h. for having been h. 9:150
Not the owner of many possessions will you be right to call
h. 4:50
One is h. as a result of one's own efforts 10:429
Puritanism – The haunting fear that someone . . . may be h.
12:815
That all who are h., are equally h. 8:422
the duty of being h. 11:283
. . . the one and only thing . . . that can make a man h. . . .
4:48
We are never so h. nor so unhappy as we imagine 8:371
what it is that makes a Scotchman h. 8:575

ard I'm not h. – I'm frightfully soft 13:262
Saturday's child works h. for his living 10:640

ard-faced A lot of h. men 12:100

ardly the summit of Everest was h. the place 13:77

ardness without h. will be sage 10:567

ardships we shall be glad to remember even these h.
4:16

lardy Kiss me, H. 9:54

arlot society . . . pays a h. 25 times as much as it pays its
Prime Minister 13:177
the prerogative of the h. through the ages 12:207

arm No people do so much h. 11:434

armony h. imposes compatibility upon the incongruous
13:487

arp The h. that once 9:69

arvest His Royal Highness . . . prides himself upon . . . the
excellent h. 9:82

lastings ancestors on either side of the Battle of H.
12:610

at a h. that lets the rain in 8:113
looking for a black h. 11:257
the h., the headgear worn by the whole civilized world
12:168

atched chickens before they are h. 2:32

ate feel no h. for him 8:485
Few . . . can be happy unless they h. 13:842
I h. the whole race . . . your professional poets 10:284
I love or I h. 12:633
Let them h. 2:19
men h. one another so damnably 10:63
not to weep at them, nor to h. them 8:385
scarcely h. any one that we know 9:191
to h. the man you have hurt 4:52
You must h. a Frenchman 9:38

ated h. by every anti-semite as if I were a Jew 13:125

ates Everybody h. house-agents 11:523
It does not matter . . . what a man h. 11:437

lathaway accurate reproductions of Anne H.'s cottage
12:523

atred a deep burning h. for the Tory Party 13:23
An intellectual h. 12:807
Fire – without h. 12:272
love . . . looks more like h. than like friendship 8:483

ave To h. and to hold 7:339

aves H. and the Have-nots 7:103

laydn certain H., who has some peculiar ideas 8:297

ead anyone who slapped us . . . would get his h. kicked off
13:248
educate with the h. instead of with the hand 11:269
If you can keep your h. 11:531
I'll hold my h. so high it'll strike the stars 4:27
in politics there is no heart, only h. 9:75
it shall bruise thy h. 1:13
John Baptist's h. in a charger 3:21
no matter which way the h. lies 7:105
show my h. to the people 9:26
the greatest asset a h. of state can have 13:290
Uneasy lies the h. that wears a crown 7:72

you are like a pin, but without . . . h. or . . . point 10:440

head-in-air Johnny h. 12:357

health in sickness and in h. 7:339
Only do always in h. what you have often promised to do
when you are sick 6:107
selling them in h. food shops 13:1004

healthy h. and wealthy and dead 12:651
Nobody is h. in London 10:325

hear ears to h., let him h. 3:131
one is always sure to h. of it 8:427
truth which men prefer not to h. 12:830

heard I have already h. it 11:195

heart Because my h. is pure 10:556
first come to pass in the h. of America 13:74
h. and stomach of a King 7:65
in politics there is no h., only head 9:75
Mary . . . pondered them in her h. 3:7
Mother is the dead h. of the family 13:778
Once a woman has given you her h. 8:513
So the h. be right 7:105
take heed . . . that your h. be not deceived 1:44
The fire which in the h. resides 10:566
The h. has its reasons 8:384
The intellect is always fooled by the h. 8:324
Their h.'s in the right place 12:629
The way to a man's h. is through his stomach 10:510

hearth Man for the field and woman for the h. 10:528

heartless It is h. and it is mindless 13:851

hearts the Kings of England, Diamonds, H., Spades and
Clubs 13:62
the song that is sung in our h. 11:169
those who have stout h. and sharp swords 12:685
well-developed bodies, fairly developed minds, and undeveloped h. 12:530

heat Britain . . . is going to be forged in the white h. of this
revolution 13:181

Heathen I was born of Christian race, And not a H., or a
Jew 8:458

heaven All place shall be hell that is not h. 7:266
a new h. and a new earth 3:124
ascend to h. 9:22
from whose face the earth and the h. fled 3:55
God created the h. 1:1
h. and earth shall pass away 3:105
H. in a wild flower 9:168
H. . . . is a place so inane, so dull 12:872
house as nigh h. as my own 7:19
If Max gets to H. 12:962
If this belief from h. be sent 9:147
In h. an angel is nobody in particular 11:352
man is as H. made him 7:252
more things in h. and earth 7:280
no invention came more easily to man than H. 8:604
Now: h. knows 12:724
Order is h.'s first law 8:102
Pennies do not come from h. 13:738
steep and thorny way to h. 7:398
the Hell I suffer seems a H. 8:587
the starry h. above me 8:481
to be young and was very h. 9:208
We are as near to h. by sea as by land 7:228
what's a h. for 10:480
What they do in h. 8:503

heavenward A homely face . . . aided many women h.
11:413

heed To fight and not to h. the wounds 7:349

heights If suffer we must, let's suffer on the h. 10:651

heiress American h. wants to buy a man 13:885

hell A lifetime of happiness . . . h. on earth 11:304
All place shall be h. that is not heaven 7:266
Better to reign in H. 8:11
h. a fury like a woman scorned 8:514
H. is other people 12:901
H. itself is defiled by . . . King John 6:33
h. upon earth . . . in a melancholy man's heart 7:298
Italy . . . h. for women 7:386
on the fourth day they will say 'To h. with you!' 13:258
out of h. leads up to light 8:586
The h. I am 13:640

the H. I suffer seems a Heaven 8:587
the h. of horses 7:382
the little holiday steamers made an excursion to h. 12:329
War is h. 11:20
Which way I fly is H.; myself am H. 8:587
help gods h. them that h. themselves 2:46
going in without the h. of Russia 12:310
not so much our friends' h. that helps us 2:45
People must h. one another 8:389
the h. of too many physicians 2:75
helps not so much our friends' help that h. us 2:45
hen a broody h. sitting on a china egg 13:203
Henry Junker H. means to be God 7:30
pig of a H. VIII 7:112
Prince H.,...something of royalty in his demeanour 6:86
herb sweetest fragrance from the h....tread on it and
bruise it 10:539
herbs nature runs either to h., or to weeds 7:247
herd-morality Morality...is h. 11:426
heresies new truths...begin as h. 11:248
heresy h. signifies no more than private opinion 7:148
heretic I shall never be a h. 7:2
hero better to be the widow of a hero than the wife of a coward 12:270
heroes Children should acquire...h. and villains from fiction 13:575
fit country for h. to live in 12:98
speed glum h....to death 12:82
Unhappy the land that has no h. 12:732
heroic human beings are h. 12:365
hert Myn h. ys set 6:68
hesitate A leader who doesn't h....is not fit to be a
leader 13:837
hesitates A science which h. to forget 12:921
heterodoxy H. or Thy-doxy 10:371
hidden Nature is often h. 7:248
hiding man who looks you...in the eye...h. something
13:599
high civil fury first grew h. 8:369
highbrow What is a h. 12:552
highly at no time stand so h. in our estate royal 7:31
Highness His Royal H....prides himself upon...the excellent harvest 9:82
will not fail to attend your H. upon your landing 8:54
hill If the h. will not come to Mahomet 7:98
Tonight the American flag floats from yonder h. 8:220
hills a fine thing to be out on the h. alone 11:224
him he could not avoid making H. set the world in motion
8:588
himself He would kill H. 10:493
hinky H., dinky, par-lee-voo 12:77
historian A good h. is timeless 8:359
A h. is a prophet in reverse 9:143
Great abilities are not requisite for an H. 8:361
h. fits a man for psychological analysis 12:970
The h. must have...some conception of how men...be-
have 12:563
historians H. are like deaf people 11:279
H. tell the story of the past 10:323
history ancient h.,...is no more than accepted fiction
8:362
blunders usually do more to shape h. than...wickedness
13:571
deal of h. to produce...literature 11:171
diplomatic h. is...what one clerk said to another clerk
12:569
From today...there begins a new epoch in the h. of the
world 9:18
h....a tableau of crimes and misfortunes 8:363
He was...– a student of h. 10:659
H. gets thicker 13:573
H. is more or less bunk 12:561
H. is past politics 11:273
H. is philosophy teaching by examples 4:41
H. is the essence of...biographies 10:390
H. is too serious 13:570
h. must be false 8:360
h. of England is...the h. of progress 10:393
h....the biography of great men 10:392

h....the register of the...misfortunes of mankind 8:364
If men could learn from h. 10:387
It is impossible to write ancient h. 11:277
Man is a h.-making creature 13:572
never looks like h. 13:574
no h.; only biography 10:391
one of these is the h. of political power 12:572
poetry is...more philosophical...than h. 2:31
Political h. is far too criminal...to be...fit...for the
young 13:575
The attitude of the English...toward English h. 12:570
the greatest week in the h. of the world 13:234
The h. of all...society is the h. of class struggles 10:117
The h. of the World is the World's court 9:142
the lukewarm who make h. 12:567
The most persistent sound...through men's h. 13:569
This was the Angel of H. 12:440
trace...the disasters of English h. to...Wales 12:843
War makes...good h. 11:274
hit If you would h. the mark 10:564
never h. softly 11:164
Hitler every time H. occupies a country 12:320
Herr H. and Signor Mussolini had been at Oxford 12:290
H. has carried out a revolution on our lines 12:249
H. has missed the bus 12:321
H. showed surprising loyalty to Mussolini 12:999
H. was a nuisance. Mussolini was bloody 12:410
one purpose, the destruction of H. 12:370
The people H. never understood 12:1000
tipster who...reached H.'s level of accuracy 12:996
hobgoblin the h. of little minds 10:375
hog he rides like a h. in armour 8:58
Rule all England under a h. 6:82
hoi the multitude, the h. polloi 8:56
hold To have and to h. 7:339
holder office sanctifies the h. 11:54
holiday the little h. steamers made an excursion to hell
12:329
holiness put off H. 9:139
the h. of the heart's affections 10:546
hollow We are the h. men 12:688
within the h. crown 6:55
Hollywood the attitude of a H. director toward love
12:570
holy everything that lives is h. 9:159
h., h., h., is the Lord of hosts 1:96
the Holy Roman Empire was neither h., nor Roman, nor an
empire 8:169
unite in some h. confederacy 7:26
Holy See This charter...constitutes an insult to the H.
6:32
home Father,...come h. with me now 11:222
For h. is best 7:189
h. his footsteps he hath turn'd 9:169
H. is the sailor, h. from sea 11:243
H. of lost causes 10:230
I can get all that at h. 13:449
Irish H. Rule is conceded 11:71
Many a man who thinks to found a h. 12:513
permits you to be entertained...by people you wouldn't
have in your h. 13:516
there's no place like h. 10:514
We are all H. Rulers today 12:103
we come From God, who is our h. 9:199
homely A h. face...aided many women heavenward
11:413
Homer even excellent H. nods 4:29
Mr Gladstone read H. for fun 11:545
The author of that poem is either H. 12:450
homo The 'h.' is the legitimate child 12:784
honest An h. broker 11:13
An h. God 11:467
an h. man sent to lie abroad for...his country 7:414
give me six lines...by the most h. man 7:258
It's better to be quotable than...h. 13:846
not an h. man 10:561
Though I am not naturally h. 7:374
honestly If possible h., if not, somehow, make money
4:91

honesty H. is the best policy 10:561
make your children *capable of h.* is the beginning of education 10:386

honey a land flowing with milk and h. 1:34
gather h. all the day 8:637
They took some h., and plenty of money 10:655

honi H. *soit qui mal y pense* 6:43

honour All is lost save h. 7:12
could not love thee . . . Loved I not H. 7:123
h. all men 3:50
H. pricks me on 7:353
h. sinks where commerce long prevails 8:150
h. thy father and thy mother 1:40
if I accepted the h. . . . I would not answer 10:422
man of the greatest h. and bravery 6:22
only h. and life have been spared 7:12
peace I hope with h. 11:14
So h. peereth in the meanest habit 7:350
To h. we call you 8:132
Wealth has never been a sufficient source of h. 13:974

honourable His designs were strictly h. 8:504
the most h. thing that man . . . has ever produced 10:311

hook canst thou draw out leviathan with an h. 1:103

hope Abandon h., all ye who enter here 6:123
a faint h. that he will die 10:430
bright with h. 12:178
green the colour of h. 9:3
H. is . . . the dream of those that wake 8:404
H. is the power of being cheerful 11:442
H. may vanish, but can die not 10:503
Land of H. and Glory 11:149
no other medicine but only h. 7:242
now abideth faith, h., charity 3:95
the distinction between h. and expectation 13:713
The triumph of h. over experience 8:506
What a strange thing is memory, and h. 13:644

hopeless that controversy is either superfluous or h. 10:410

hopes Life's short span forbids us to enter on far-reaching h. 4:64
My h. no more must change their name 9:70
The h. and prayers of liberty-loving people 12:390

Horner Little Jack H. Sat in the corner 7:25

horny-handed H. sons of toil 11:19

horror mere existence is swollen to a h. 12:664

horse a pale h. 3:54
Go together like a h. and carriage 12:759
my kingdom for a h. 6:84
victory under the belly of a Cossack's h. 12:213

horsemanship princes learn no art truly, but . . . h. 7:114

horses England . . . hell for h. 7:386
England . . . hell of h. 7:382
frighten the h. 11:380
Men are . . . more careful of the breed of their h. and dogs 8:501
sixty h. wedged in a chimney 13:1018

hosanna h. in the highest 3:25

hospital Our h. organization has grown up with no plan 13:3
the world, I count it not an inn, but an h. 7:309

host of all this h. of men not one will still be alive in a hundred years' time 2:49

hostages h. given to fate 4:76
h. to fortune 7:336

hostile The universe is not h. 12:713

hostility your h. towards him 13:620

hot-water the English have h. bottles 13:855

hounded I will not be h. 13:262

hour at the rate of sixty minutes an h. 12:740
I also had my h. 12:875
Milton! thou shouldst be living at this h. 9:71
nothing can bring back the h. 9:171
their finest h. 12:330
Time and the h. runs through 7:290
To one dead deathless h. 11:173
wage war until the last quarter of an h. 12:76

hours h. will take care of themselves 8:464
Three h. a day 11:176

housbondes H. at chirche-dore 6:118

house A h. is a machine for living in 12:445
Every man has a H. of Lords in his own head 12:164
get thee out . . . from thy father's h. 1:24
h. as nigh heaven as my own 7:19
in my Father's h. are many mansions 3:114
leader of the H. of Commons 10:80
my h. shall be called the h. of prayer 3:116
that D—d H. 8:127
The h. of every one is to him as his castle 7:199
The H. of Lords, an illusion 13:215
The H. of Lords . . . how to care for the elderly 13:344
The H. of Lords is a perfect eventide home 13:246
The H. of Lords is the British Outer Mongolia 13:154
The H. of Lords . . . kept efficient by . . . persistent absenteeism 13:19

house-agents Everybody hates h. 11:523

housekeeping H. ain't no joke 10:542

House of Peers The H. . . . Did nothing 11:33

houses H. are built to live in 7:195

Hugo H. – hélas 11:197

human Adam was but h. 11:295
All that is h. must retrograde 8:424
evolution of the h. race 12:922
h. beings are heroic 12:365
h. beings have an . . . infinite capacity for taking things for granted 13:584
H. kind cannot bear 12:624
h. nature . . . more of the fool 7:246
If h. beings could be propagated . . . aristocracy would be . . . sound 12:220
I have got lots of h. weaknesses 13:366
imagine a boot stamping on a h. face 13:1028
my opinion of the h. race 12:629
No h. being, . . . was ever so free as a fish 10:490
no need for any other faith than . . . faith in h. beings 12:894
nothing h. foreign to me 4:43
nothing to distinguish h. society from the farm-yard 11:390
not linen you're wearing out, But h. creatures' lives 10:525
the full tide of h. existence is at Charing-Cross 8:194
The h. face is . . . a whole cluster of faces 12:578
the importance of the h. factor 13:323
The Romans and Greeks found everything h. 2:85
the vilest specimens of h. nature are . . . found among demagogues 10:120
To err is h., to forgive, divine 8:401, 8:547
To kill a h. being 10:574
When in the course of h. events, it becomes necessary 8:206

humanity Every year h. takes a step towards Communism 13:95
That unremitting h. 13:489
the crooked timber of h. 8:434
The still, sad music of h. 9:162

humble It is difficult to be h. 13:847

humbug never was such a h. as the Greek affair 10:27

humiliating Corporal punishment is . . . h. for him who gives it 11:452

humiliation the last h. of an aged scholar 12:971
the moment of greatest h. is . . . when the spirit is proudest 11:137

humour deficient in a sense of h. 10:437
Freudian . . . low . . . sort of h. 13:629
own up to a lack of h. 11:320

hump A woman . . . without a positive h., may marry whom she likes 10:517

Humpty H. Dumpty sat on a wall 7:124

hundred a h. schools of thought contend 13:539
it would be all the same a h. years hence 10:462
Letting a h. flowers blossom 13:539
of all this host of men not one will still be alive in a h. years' time 2:49
to trade a h. contemporary readers for 13:419

hunger The war against h. 13:686
to banish h. by rubbing the belly 2:80

hungry h. as a hunter 9:204
You cannot feed the h. on statistics 11:121

hunt how much more dogs are animated when they h. in a pack 8:412

people who h. are the right people 12:668
hunter hungry as a h. 9:204
  Nimrod the mighty h. 1:22
hunting when his half-civilized ancestors were h. the wild boar 10:436
hurrah h.! we bring the Jubilee 10:219
hurry An old man in a h. 11:51
hurt Those have most power to h. 7:327
hurting Art . . . can go on mattering once it has stopped h. 13:413
husband Being a h. is a whole-time job 12:765
  My h. and I 13:259
  Never trust a h. too far 12:764
husbandry borrowing dulls the edge of h. 7:360
husbands h. and wives make shipwreck of their lives 12:770
  h. to stay at home 10:535
hush a breathless h. in the Close tonight 11:541
hymns My poems are h. of praise 13:425
hyphenated h. Americanism 12:29
hypocrisy an organized h. 10:100
  H. . . . is a whole-time job 12:821
  H. is the homage paid by vice to virtue 8:529
  H. is the most . . . nerve-racking vice 12:821
  neither man nor angel can discern H. 8:532
hypocrite No man is a h. in his pleasures 8:433
hypocritical Man . . . learns by being h. 13:615
hypothesis Factual evidence can never 'prove' a h. 13:942
  I have no need of that h. 9:201
  the slaying of a beautiful h. by an ugly fact 11:491
  to discard a pet h. every day 13:548

I

I I also had my hour 12:875
  in the infinite I AM 10:359
  I would have done it differently 11:207
ice A Shape of I. 11:162
iceberg as the smart ship grew . . . grew the I. too 11:162
idea An i. does not pass from one language 11:272
  An i. isn't responsible for the people 12:528
  constant repetition . . . in imprinting an i. 12:135
  I think it would be a good i. 12:853
  no stand can be made against invasion by an i. 10:379
  they will end by ruining our i. 12:249
ideal the i. American 12:855
idealist people call me an i. 12:833
ideals Away with all i. 12:665
  think how far I can go with all the i. that I have 13:336
ideas Human Stupidity consists in having lots of i. 12:549
  i. are of more importance than values 13:563
  I. that enter the mind under fire 12:188
  Learn our i., or otherwise get out 13:47
  Morality which is based on i. 12:811
  the addiction of political groups to the i. 13:113
  The true God, . . . God of i. 10:385
ides Beware the i. of March 4:5
idiot tale told by an i. 7:287
idiots the English seem . . . to act with . . . the fatuity of i. 9:68
idle Satan finds . . . mischief . . . For i. hands 8:548
  thousands of i. persons are within this realm 7:191
  We would all be i. 8:646
  Young people ought not to be i. 13:371
idleness i. and indifference 11:101
  I. . . . the refuge of weak minds 8:554
  Research! A mere excuse for i. 11:255
idling It is impossible to enjoy i. 11:288
idol one-eyed yellow i. to the north of Khatmandu 11:544
idolatry There is no i. in the Mass 8:607
if I. you can keep your head 11:531
ignominious History is full of i. getaways by the great 12:571
Ignoramus I., . . . person unacquainted with . . . knowledge familiar to yourself 11:267
ignorance From i. our comfort flows 8:330
  I. is Strength 13:30
  I. of the law excuses 8:60

journalism. . . . keeps us in touch with the i. of the community 11:516
  knowledge increases . . . i. unfolds 13:545
  no sin but i. 7:397
ignorant Let no one i. of mathematics enter here 2:74
  The i. man always adores 11:310
  the opinionated, the i., and the boorish 2:44
  what may follow it, or what preceded it, we are absolutely i. 5:24
ill If . . . someone is speaking i. of you 4:53
  the Prince . . . is restrained from doing i. 8:570
  very fine country to be acutely i. 13:267
illegal collect legal taxes from i. money 12:187
illegitimate There are no i. children 12:771
ill-housed one-third of a nation i. 12:287
illiteracy The ratio of literacy to i. 13:565
illogical Faith . . . an i. belief in . . . the improbable 12:602
ills sharp remedy . . . for all i. 7:106
ill-spent sign of an i. youth 11:305
illuminate i. our whole country with the bright light of their preaching 6:34
illumine What in me is dark I. 8:585
ill-usage complaints of i. contemptible 10:59
illusion it can contain nothing but sophistry and i. 8:342
  Religion is an i. 12:889
  The House of Lords, an i. 13:215
  visible universe was an i. 12:746
illusions It's life's i. I recall 13:691
ill-will I bear no i. against those responsible for this 13:39
image any graven i. 1:40
  A photograph is not only an i. 13:493
  If God made us in His i. 8:610
  make man in our own i. 1:5
  Why should I consent to the perpetuation of the i. of this i. 4:35
imaginary Happiness is an i. condition 13:616
imagination Art is ruled . . . by the i. 11:205
  I. and fiction . . . three quarters of our real life 13:410
  I. without skill gives us modern art 13:472
  no i. and . . . no compassion 13:364
  not an ideal of reason but of i. 8:435
  The primary i. 10:359
imagine never so happy . . . as we i. 8:371
imagined What is now proved was . . . i. 9:136
imagining How reconcile this world . . . with . . . my i. 12:653
imitate An original writer is . . . one whom nobody can i. 9:122
  never failed to i. 13:673
  obliged to i. himself, and to repeat 8:352
  people . . . usually i. each other 13:591
imitates Photography can never grow up if it i. 13:418
Immaculate the I. Conception was spontaneous combustion 12:884
Immanuel call his name I. 1:97
immaturity common symptom of i. 12:447
immoral moral or an i. book 11:187
  worse than i. 13:118
immorality the most rigid code of i. 13:869
immortal I have lost the i. part 7:285
  Why are you weeping? Did you imagine that I was i. 8:93
immutable Few things are as i. 13:113
impediment cause. or just i. 8:495
imperative This i. is Categorical 8:566
imperial be yourself, i., plain and true 10:425
imperialism i. is the monopoly stage of capitalism 12:65
impersonal In the philosopher there is nothing whatever i. 11:514
impertinent ask an i. question 13:958
important One doesn't recognize . . . the really i. moments . . . until it's too late 13:701
impossibility a physical and metaphysical i. 10:286
impossible I believe because it is i. 4:87
  It's either easy or i. 13:415
  something is i., he is . . . wrong 13:959
  when you have excluded the i. 11:528
impotent an i. people. Sick with inbreeding 13:863
impression knowledge and wonder . . . is an i. of pleasure 7:218

impressions i. . . . lasting as . . . an oar upon the water 11:337

improbable Faith . . . an illogical belief in . . . the i. 12:602
whatever remains, however i., must be the truth 11:528

impropriety I. is the soul of wit 12:646

improved enormously i. by death 12:428

improvement most schemes of political i. are very laughable 8:170

improvised A master of i. speech and i. policies 12:418

impure To the Puritan all things are i. 12:621

inactivity wise and masterly i. 9:13

inartistic He was unperfect, unfinished, i. 11:172

inbreeding an impotent people, Sick with i. 13:863

incapacitated every man who is not presumably i. 10:221

incest except i. and folk-dancing 12:742

incisors Writers, like teeth, are divided into i. and grinders 10:312

income Annual i. twenty pounds 10:626
hardest thing . . . to understand is i. tax 12:186
live beyond its i. 11:351

incompetent Democracy substitutes election by the i. many 11:115
God is the immemorial refuge of the i. 13:914
i. swine 12:81

incomplete A man in love is i. until . . . married 13:771

incomprehensible an old, wild, and i. man 11:66

inconvenience Change is not made without i. 7:263

inconveniences A good many i. attend play-going 13:432

incorruptible seagreen I. 9:207
the dead shall be raised i. 3:53

increase to subsist . . . without either i. or diminution 10:3

increased influence of the Crown has i. 8:236

incurable the i. disease of writing 4:34

indecency prejudicial . . . as a public i. 7:377
The older one grows the more one likes i. 12:810

indecent much more i. . . . than a good smack 12:535

indefensible political speech and writing are largely the defence of the i. 13:49

Independence principles of the Declaration of I. bear no relation 10:536

independent An i. . . . wants to take the politics out of politics 13:124
these United Colonies are, . . . free and i. states 8:204

India establish . . . sure English dominion in I. for all time to come 8:49
I. is a geographical term 12:208
I. . . . the strength and the greatness of England 11:68

Indian in a world of Gary Coopers you are the I. 13:207
I. wars have had their origin in broken promises 11:11
lay out ten to see a dead I. 7:251

Indians The only good I. I ever saw were dead 10:255

indictment an i. against an whole people 8:196

indifference idleness and i. 11:101
Nothing is so fatal to religion as i. 9:198

indignation Moral i. is in most cases 2 percent moral 13:831
Wrongdoing can only be avoided if those who are not wronged feel the same i. 2:58

indistinguishable in America the successful writer or picture-painter is i. from any other decent business man 12:836

individual It is of no moment to the happiness of an i. 8:185
The liberty of the i. must be thus far limited 10:180

individualism American system of rugged i. 12:840
Art is the most intense mode of i. 11:189

individuality England is the paradise of i. 12:838

indulgence sign of the cross . . . an i. for all the sins 6:7

industry i. will supply their deficiency 8:474

inebriated i. with . . . his own verbosity 11:15

inelegance a continual state of i. 9:129

inequalities only i. that matter begin in the mind 13:104

inequality saddest sight that fortune's i. exhibits 10:630
There is always i. . . . Life is unfair 13:682

inevitability The i. of gradualness 12:143

inexactitude terminological i. 11:126

infallible The only i. criterion of wisdom 9:202

infamous I have got an i. army 9:106

infamy A date that shall live in i. 12:361

infancy Heaven lies about us in our i. 9:199

infant An i. crying in the night 10:473

infanticide as indefensible as i. 12:172

inferior No one can make you feel i. without your consent 12:627
Switzerland . . . an i. sort of Scotland 9:195

inferiority Wherever an i. complex exists, there is . . . reason 12:639

inferiors I. revolt in order that they may be equal 2:16
The English want i. 10:580

infinite The sight . . . gave me i. pleasure 9:170

infinity I. in the palm of your hand 9:168

infirmities friend should bear his friend's i. 7:236

infirmity last i. of noble mind 7:306

inflation I. in the Sixties was a nuisance 13:254

influence How to . . . I. People 12:985
i. of the Crown has increased 8:236
unable to i. events . . . do not have the power 13:325

inform not to i. the reader 13:614

infortune The worst kinde of i. is this 6:130

infringement Necessity is the plea for every i. of human freedom 8:250

ingenious a loyal, a gallant, a generous, an i., and good-temper'd people 8:574

inglorious the i. arts of peace 7:146

ingratitude I hate i. more in a man 7:363
I., thou marble-hearted fiend 7:333
man's i. 7:357

ingress Our i. . . . Was naked and bare 11:326

inherit Russia will certainly i. the future 12:110

initiative success depends . . . upon individual i. and exertion 12:458

injury Recompense i. with justice 2:2

injustice A lawyer has no business with . . . justice or i. 8:645
fear of suffering i. 8:7
strong arm of England will protect him against i. 10:123
threatened with a great i. 10:156
what a man still plans . . . shows the . . . i. in his death 13:59

ink an optimist . . . fills up his crossword puzzle in i. 12:599

inn no room for them in the i. 3:4

innocence it is . . . our business to lose i. 13:579

innocent ten guilty persons escape than one i. suffer 8:160

innocently i. employed than in getting money 8:629

innovator time is the greatest i. 7:293

inquiry The world is but a school of i. 7:264

insane Man is quite i. 7:396

insect the Egyptians worshipped an i. 10:80

insensitiveness the greatest deeds require a certain i. 8:472

inseparably Taxation and representation are i. united 8:161

inside attention to the i. . . . contempt for the outside 8:344

insight moment's i. . . . worth a life's experience 10:384

insignificance A man of . . . the utmost i. 12:141

insignificant as i. men as any in England 8:118

insolence the i. of wealth 8:631

insolent their i. and unfounded airs of superiority 8:580

institution Any i. which does not suppose the people good 9:21

institutions working of great i. 12:185

instructed the worst i. 8:94

instrument there you sit with that magnificent i. between your legs 12:476
The state is an i. . . . of the ruling class 12:149

insurrection I. is an art 12:210

integrate I i. the current export drive 13:993

integrity if I accepted the honour . . . I would not answer for the i. of my intellect 10:422
I. without knowledge is weak 8:347
I. without knowledge is weak 8:555

intellect I. is . . . fooled by the heart 8:324
I. is invisible 10:366
put on I. 9:139
the soul of a martyr with the i. of an advocate 10:184
The voice of the i. is a soft one 12:540

we cannot exclude the i. from . . . any of our functions 11:259

intellects highest i., like the tops of mountains 10:369
There is a wicked inclination . . . to suppose an old man decayed in his i. 8:431

intellectual an i. . . . mind watches itself 12:553
Every i. attitude is latently political 13:555
Man is an i. animal 10:363
thirdly, i. ability 10:368

intellectuals i.' chief cause of anguish 13:540

intelligence I. is quickness to apprehend 12:529
i. is the great polluter 13:955
The more i. . . . the more . . . one finds original 8:383

intelligent A really i. man feels what other men . . . know 8:410
Each generation imagines itself . . . more i. 12:644
stupid are cocksure . . . i. full of doubt 13:709

intent A truth that's told with bad i. 9:188

intercourse dreary i. of daily life 9:163
i. is . . . a social act 13:760

interest The i. of the landlord is always opposed to . . . every other class 10:2

interested I have exercised the powers committed to me from no corrupt or i. motives 10:103
The average man is . . . i. in a woman who is i. in him 13:788

interests all these great i. entrusted to the shaking hand 11:66

intérieur 'Vive l'i'. 9:212

intermarriage By i. and by every means in his power 6:2

intermission Pleasure is . . . i. of pain 8:397

international I. Woman's Day 12:71
science is essentially i. 12:912

intoxicate you won't i. with one glass someone who has . . . drunk . . . a . . . barrel 11:180

intrigue the i. of a Greek of the lower empire 10:185

invasion no stand can be made against i. by an idea 10:379
the long-promised i. 12:342

invent it would be necessary to i. Him 8:612

invention Woman's virtue is man's greatest i. 12:801

inventions All one's i. are true 10:307

investment There is no finer i. 12:780
To bear many children is considered . . . an i. 13:289

invisible the only evil that walks I. 8:532

invisibly electricity was dripping i. 12:929

Ireland I. is the old sow 12:41
I never met anyone in I. who understood the Irish question 12:104
The moment . . . I. is mentioned 9:68
The problem with I. 13:899

Irish All races have . . . economists, with the exception of the I. 13:898
as I. as Black Americans 13:382
historic inability in Britain to comprehend I. feelings 13:402
I. . . . devotion to higher arts 13:898
I. might do very good Service 7:388
That is the I. Question 10:96
The English and Americans dislike only *some* I. 13:877
The I. and the Jews have a psychosis 13:876
The I. are a fair people 8:577
The I. . . . are needed in this cold age 10:92
The I. don't know what they want 13:143

iron also wash and i. them 13:812
An i. curtain 13:1
blood and i. 10:207
The I. Lady of British politics 13:307

irons two i. in the fire 7:373

irrelevant the most i. thing in nature 10:512

irresponsible better to be i. and right 13:45

Islam I. unashamedly came with a sword 5:35

island No man is an I. 7:299
wealth of our i. may be diminished 9:65

islands less known by the British than these selfsame British I. 10:341

isle this sceptred i. 7:69

isolating by i. him . . . as if he were a leper 11:22

isolation our splendid i. 11:77

Italia I. *farà da se* 10:111

Italian imitation of the most fam'd I. masters 8:272
I speak . . . I. to women, French to men 7:16
The crafty, cold-blooded, black-hearted I. 12:349

Italians The I. will laugh at me 12:320

Italy A man who has not been in I. 8:217
I. a paradise for horses 7:386
I. is a geographical expression 10:581
without Rome I. cannot be constituted 10:197

itch the i. of literature 10:294

lutae the *Saxones, Angli*, and *I.* 5:1

J

jab Man, . . . had been created to j. the life out of Germans 12:83

J'accuse 11:86

Jack Damn you, J. – I'm all right 11:542
J. the Ripper's dead 11:59
Little J. Horner Sat in the corner 7:25
Two little whores . . . J.'s knife flashes 11:57
Yours truly, J. the Ripper 11:58

jackal This whipped j. 12:352

Jackson J. standing like a stone wall 10:195

jam J. today, and men aren't at their most exciting 13:100

James King J. is good and honest 8:65

James Joyce J. . . . Nothing but old fags and cabbage stumps of quotations 12:454

jangled j. in every ale-house and tavern 7:32

January dreadful pictures of J. and February 10:345

Janvier Generals J. and Février 10:141

Japanese The J. have perfected good manners 13:897

jaw-jaw To j. is better than to war-war 13:84

jazz J. . . . people hear it through their feet 12:439
The basic difference between classical music and j. 13:468
the J. Age . . . became less and less an affair of youth 12:419

jealous a j. God 1:40

jealousy J. . . . feeling alone among smiling enemies 12:826
J.'s rife in heroes' hall 12:165
of j.; It is the green-ey'd monster 7:366
the ear of j. heareth all things 1:91

jeering laughing and j. at everything . . . strange 8:568

jeers j. at Fate 12:940

Jerusalem J. 9:73
the holy city, new J. 3:124
Till we have built J. 9:73

jest A j.'s prosperity lies in the ear 7:260
Life is a j. 8:460

Jesus If J. Christ were to come to-day 10:597
J. loves me – this I know 10:600
J. was . . . a first-rate political economist 11:481
when J. was born in Bethlehem of Judaea 3:9

Jew An American is either a J., or an anti-Semite 13:880
Einstein – the greatest J. since Jesus 12:909
hated by every anti-semite as if I were a J. 13:125
Hath not a J. eyes 7:231
I was born of Christian race, And not a Heathen, or a J. 8:458
No J. was ever fool enough to turn Christian 11:470
Pessimism is a luxury that a J. never can allow himself 13:894

jewel that most precious j., the Word of God 7:32

jewelry she did not remember . . . her j. 12:792

Jewish A J. man with parents alive 13:891
a *total solution* of the J. question 12:372
best that is in the J. blood 12:839

Jewry Modern Physics is an instrument of J. 12:933

Jews King of the J. 3:9
not enough prisons . . . in Palestine to hold all the J. 12:346
The Irish and the J. have a psychosis 13:876
the J. bring the unlike into the heart of *every milieu* 11:461
the J. have made a contribution to the human condition 13:901

jingo We don't want to fight, but, by j. if we do 11:16

Job J. endured everything – until his friends came 10:419

job Being a husband is a whole-time j. 12:765
Giz a j. 13:350
We have finished the j. 12:351
we will finish the j. 12:350

John Hell itself is defiled by . . . King J. 6:33
  J., King and Priest, who dwells in the extreme Orient 6:111
  Think no more of it, J.; you are only a child 6:24
Johnny J. head-in-air 12:357
Johnson Dr J.'s morality was as English . . . as a beefsteak 8:666
  That great Cham of literature, Samuel J. 8:289
  There is no arguing with J. 8:294
oin He's gone to j. the majority 4:38
oined what . . . God hath j. together 3:73
oke
  A j.'s a very serious thing 8:440
  Housekeeping ain't no j. 10:542
  The coarse j. proclaims 13:628
okes different taste in j. is a . . . strain on the affections 11:316
  Forgive . . . my little j. on Thee 13:919
oking My way of j. is to tell the truth 11:321
Jonah a great fish to swallow up J. 1:58
Joseph Here lies J., who failed in everything he undertook 8:264
ournal *Punch* – the official j. 13:520
ournalism J. is the only job that requires no degrees 13:1000
  j. . . . . keeps us in touch with the ignorance of the community 11:516
  j. what will be grasped at once 12:967
ournalist the functions of the modern j. 11:518
  to bribe or twist . . . the British j. 12:951
ournalists J. say a thing that they know isn't true 12:950
oy Strength through j. 12:246
  we could never learn to be brave . . . if there were only j. 11:338
oys For present j. 8:394
  Hence, vain deluding J. 7:254
Jubilee hurrah! we bring the J. 10:219
udge A j. is not supposed to know 13:996
  j. not, that ye be not judged 3:57
  j. of a man by his foes 11:301
  shallow people . . . do not j. by appearances 11:290
  the j. standeth before the door 3:64
udged they were j. every man according to their works 3:55
udgement Force, if unassisted by j., collapses 4:11
  let my will replace reasoned j. 4:22
  Perhaps your fear in passing j. 7:76
  too early to form a final j. on the French Revolution 9:214
  your j. will probably be right 8:171
  Your representative owes you . . . his j. 8:189
udgment I expect a j. 10:309
ury Trial by j. itself . . . will be a delusion 10:97
ury-men wretches hang that j. may dine 8:88
ust rain on the j. and on the unjust 3:84
ustice A lawyer has no business with . . . j. or injustice 8:645
  In a free society the state . . . administers j. among men 12:184
  J. . . . allowed to do whatever I like 11:302
  J. is open to all 11:134
  J. is such a fine thing 8:81
  J. is the means by which established injustices are sanctioned 11:102
  J. is the . . . perpetual wish 5:2
  J. should not only be done 12:805
  law implies a common foundation of j. 9:19
  Let j. be done 7:44
  moderation in the pursuit of j. is no virtue 13:200
  Recompense injury with j. 2:2
  Revenge is a kind of wild j. 7:371
  The love of j. in most men 8:7
ustification carry its j. in every line 11:193
ustified life of one man can only be j. 12:339
ustifying men are more interested in . . . j. themselves 13:618

K

Kaiser she took down the signed photograph of the K. 12:7

Keats K.'s vulgarity with a Public School accent 12:430
  Shelley and K. were . . . up to date in . . . chemical knowledge 12:908
keen Satire should, like a polished razor k. 8:438
keep if they k. on saying it . . . it will be true 12:950
  they should k. who can 9:165
keeper am I my brother's k. 1:16
  a poacher a k. turned inside out 10:434
Kennedy the kind of nation . . . President K. died for 13:202
Kennedys I don't feel the attraction of the K. at all 13:326
kept He k. us out of war 12:38
  Married women are k. women 12:775
kettle *this* is a pretty k. of fish 12:282
key lawyers . . . have taken away the k. of knowledge 3:125
keys all the k. should hang from the belt of one woman 6:47
  don't go around hitting too many white k. 13:370
  the k. of the kingdom of heaven 3:23
Khatmandu one-eyed yellow idol to the north of K. 11:544
kick every ass thinks he may k. at him 8:307
  to k. against the pricks 3:45
kicked anyone who slapped us . . . would get his head k. off 13:248
kill churchmen fain would k. their church 10:606
  good to k. an admiral 8:136
  He would k. Himself 10:493
  it's a sin to k. a mockingbird 13:1022
  It was not . . . our intention to k. the king 6:58
  K. a man, and you are a murderer 13:824
  K. everyone, and you are a god 13:824
  k. the patient 7:406
  k. us for their sport 7:210
  The bullet that is to k. me 9:101
  The word 'revolution' is a word for which you k. 13:89
  thou shalt not k. 1:40
  To k. a human being 10:574
  When you have to k. a man 12:363
killed He must have k. a lot of men 8:623
  I don't mind your being k. 12:12
  it is better that all of these peasants should be k. 7:14
killing no difference between . . . k. and making decisions that . . . 13:845
  To save a man's life against his will is . . . k. him 4:82
kills Time is a great teacher, but . . . k. all its pupils 10:466
  time quietly k. them 10:461
  Who k. a man k. a reasonable creature 7:182
kind being k. Is all the sad world needs 11:474
  charity suffereth long, and is k. 3:95
kindle the sole purpose of human existence is to k. a light 13:681
kindly a young person, who . . . marries or dies, is sure to be k. spoken of 10:394
  the deities so k. 7:392
kindness full o' th' milk of human k. 7:244
  greetings where no k. is 9:163
  recompense k. with k. 2:2
  set a high value on spontaneous k. 8:428
  unremembered acts Of k. and of love 9:187
kindred Like k. drops, been mingled 8:255
king a k. may make a nobleman 9:28
  All the k.'s horses, And all the k.'s men 7:124
  an atheist if he were 8:590
  and Northcliffe has sent for the K. 11:148
  An unlettered k. is a crowned ass 6:133
  Authority forgets a dying k. 10:183
  A worse k. never left a realm undone 10:10
  better have one K. than five hundred 8:29
  but the K. of England cannot enter 8:148
  Every subject's duty is the K.'s 7:75
  George, be a K. 8:142
  God save our Gracious K. 8:114
  great k., ... fell all at once 8:51
  harm that cometh of a k.'s poverty 6:74
  heart and stomach of a K. 7:65
  He played the K. as though 11:317
  I'm the k. of the castle 10:656
  I think the K. is but a man 7:272
  I will that a k. succeed me 7:84

king is always a k. 9:183
k. is incompetent to govern 6:41
K. of England changes his ministers 8:251
K. of Scots was named to succeed her 7:85
k. reigns, but does not govern 7:93
k.'s council . . . chosen of the great princes 6:75
No Bishop, no K. 7:86
service rendered to the temporal k. to the prejudice of the eternal k. 6:30
such divinity doth hedge a k. 7:82
That whatsoever K. shall reign, I'll be the Vicar of Bray, Sir 8:69
the k. can do no wrong 8:159
the K. . . . could see things if he would 8:50
The k. has been very good to me 7:24
The k. never dies 8:156
The K. over the Water 8:71
The k. reigns, and the people govern themselves 10:38
The present life of men on earth, O k. 5:24
this house will in no circumstances fight for its K. and country 12:230
wash the balm from an anointed k. 7:70
When a K. has Dethron'd himself 8:63
kingdom glory of your k. 5:6
It is folly . . . to mistake the echo of a . . . coffee-house for the . . . k. 8:86
k. and the priesthood, are brought together by divine mystery 5:10
my k. for a horse 6:84
No k. has . . . had as many . . . wars as the k. of Christ 8:595
Our k. . . . we place at your disposal 6:8
repent: for the k. of heaven is at hand 3:18
the k. of God is not in word, but in power 3:118
this formidable K. is . . . a province of a despicable Electorate 8:117
kings Conquering k. their titles take 10:125
how to dissimulate is the knowledge of k. 7:115
If you get the English people into the way of making k. 10:81
K. are earth's gods 7:97
K. are naturally lovers of low company 8:238
K. are not born 11:118
k. enough in England 8:127
K. will be tyrants from policy 9:12
Or walk with K. 11:531
Pale Death kicks his way . . . into . . . the castles of k. 4:37
sad stories of the death of k. 6:55
Such grace had k. 10:91
teeming womb of royal k. 7:69
The English nation . . . has successfully regulated the power of its k. 8:570
the K. of England, Diamonds, Hearts, Spades and Clubs 13:62
The power of k. and magistrates 7:144
This royal throne of k. 7:69
till philosophers become k. 2:8
'Twixt k. and tyrants there's this difference 7:133
kingship k. approaches tyranny it is near its end 6:39
Kipling W. H. Auden, a sort of gutless K. 12:491
kiss K. me, Hardy 9:54
Then come k. me, sweet and twenty 7:320
You must remember this; A k. is just a k. 12:761
kissed hail, master; and k. him 3:29
kit-bag pack up your troubles in your old k. 12:44
Kitchener If K. was not a great man, he was . . . a great poster 12:14
knees die on your feet than to live on your k. 12:271
knell The k. of private property sounds 10:244
the k. of the Union 10:12
knight K. of the Crimean Burial Grounds 10:159
mounted k. is irresistible 8:71
knights gives me great joy to see . . . k. and horses in battle array 6:96
sorrier for my good k.' loss than for . . . my fair queen 6:76
knitter a beautiful little k. 12:502
knock k., and it shall be opened unto you 3:129
know all Ye k. on earth 10:446
A really intelligent man feels what other men . . . k. 8:410

for they k. not what they do 3:35
I do not k. myself 10:406
I k. myself 12:671
I k. that my redeemer liveth 1:94
K. then thyself, presume not God to scan 8:407
Mad, bad, and dangerous to k. 9:127
scarcely hate any one that we k. 9:191
To k. how to say what others only . . . think 10:497
tragedy of the world that no one knows what he doesn't k. 13:538
What we k. of the past 12:562
knowed The clever men at Oxford Know all that there is to be k. 11:540
knowing A woman, especially if she have the misfortune of k. anything 10:522
knowledge All k. is of itself of some value 8:353
an age in which useless k. 13:534
civilizations . . . abandon the quest for k. 13:577
how to dissimulate is the k. of kings 7:115
if education is . . . a mere transmission of k. 13:532
Integrity without k. is weak 8:347, 8:555
K. advances by steps 10:365
k. and wonder . . . is an impression of pleasure 7:218
K. can be communicated but not wisdom 12:537
K. dwells In heads replete 8:357
K. itself is power 7:220
k. puffeth up 3:56
lawyers . . . have taken away the key of k. 3:125
Our k. can only be finite 13:541
province of k. to speak 11:247
the river of k. has too often turned back on itself 12:924
the search for k. 13:608
the tree of the k. of good and evil 1:7
worth a pound of k. 8:336
known apart from the k. and the unknown 13:695
knows he thinks he k. everything 11:133
knuckle-end k. of England 10:155
knyght parfit, gentil k. 6:120

L

laboring rights and interests of the l. man 11:105
Labour disastrous element in the L. party 12:182
genius the L. Party has for cutting itself in half 13:121
L. is not fit to govern 12:112
model L. voter 13:387
The grotesque chaos of a L. council – a L. council 13:376
labour Man . . . can only find relaxation from one . . . l. by taking up another 11:512
The natural price of l. 10:3
To l. and not ask for any reward 7:349
labours Children sweeten l. 7:335
labour-saving inventing l. devices . . . manufactured an abyss of boredom 13:940
labyrinthine I fled Him, down the l. ways 11:471
lack l. of power corrupts absolutely 13:192
own up to a l. of humour 11:320
ladder We make ourselves a l. out of our vices 4:85
ladies How sweet are looks that l. bend 10:524
lady A combination of Little Nell and L. Macbeth 12:482
L. Bountiful 8:651
L. Chatterley's Lover . . . all Christians might read with prof 13:444
l. of Christ's College 8:274
My fair l. 8:654
The Iron L. of British politics 13:307
The l.'s not for turning 13:337
Lafayette L. we are here 12:52
lag a comfortable time l. . . . between the perception 12:226
laid all the young ladies who attended the Yale promenade dance were l. end to end 12:756
laissez L. faire, laissez passer 8:131
lamb a l. as it had been slain 3:122
the L. of God 3:12
to make the lion lie down with the l. 12:704
Lambeth doin' the L. walk 12:518
lament reason to l. What man has made of man 9:147
lamp my l. burns low and dim 12:941
To keep a l. burning 13:849

The principles of l. and metaphysics are true 12:554
logik un-to l. hadde longe y-go 6:104
London Dublin, though . . . much worse than L. 8:240
great city of L. 5:19
l, General de Gaulle, now in L. 12:334
I would sell L. 6:19
L. . . . Clearing-house of the World 11:119
L., that great cesspool 11:227
L., that great sea 10:331
L., thou art the flour of Cities all 6:99
the agricultural labourers . . . commute from L. 13:512
the best club in L. 10:228
the lowest and vilest alleys of L. 11:228
When a man is tired of L. 8:226
You will hear more good things on . . . a stagecoach from L.
to Oxford 10:362
Londoner spirit of the L. stands resolute 12:340
loneliest the l. job in the world 12:959
loneliness L . . . . is the most terrible poverty 13:725
l. may spur you into finding something 13:586
lonely All the l. people 13:605
I wandered l. as a cloud 9:151
long a l., l. way to Tipperary 12:16
Like German opera, too l. and too loud 12:353
L. Island represents the American's idea 12:846
L. is the way And hard 8:586
longer I have made this letter l. 8:366
Was there ever yet anything written . . . that was wished l.
by its readers 8:285
longest l. half of your life 9:174
one unclouded l. day 10:134
longevity L. is the revenge of talent 13:699
longing the l. for love 13:608
looker-on sit thou a patient l. 7:179
looks man who l. you . . . in the eye . . . hiding something
13:599
Lord Mine eyes have seen the glory of the coming of the
L. 10:206
Praise the L. and pass the ammunition 12:360
the L. is a man of war 1:93
the L. . . . shall suddenly come to his temple 1:59
lords Great l. have their pleasures 8:112
he was a king's son and one of the greatest l. in the kingdom 6:48
None ought to be l. or landlords over another 7:142
Lords the cure for admiring the House of L. 10:236
The House of L., an illusion 13:215
The House of L. . . . how to care for the elderly 13:344
The House of L. is a perfect eventide home 13:246
The House of L. is the British Outer Mongolia 13:154
lordships good enough for their l. on a hot summer afternoon 13:298
lose A man who does not l. his reason 8:423
In every friend we l. a part of ourselves 8:317
l. the substance 2:56
nothing to l. but their chains 10:118
We Don't Want To L. You 12:15
losers In war . . . all are l. 12:301
loses The conventional army l. if it does not win 13:238
lost All is l. save honour 7:12
better to have fought and l. 10:471
I look upon every day to be l. 8:432
never to have l. at all 11:376
You are a l. generation 12:162
lots they parted his raiment, and cast l. 3:35
loud Like German opera, too long and too l. 12:353
Louis Son of Saint L. 9:22
love a girl likes to be crossed in l. a little now and then
9:186
a man in l. with a dimple 11:391
An ounce of l. 8:336
ashamed of having been in l. 8:482
Because women can do nothing except l. 12:782
brief is life but l. is long 10:507
But L. has pitched his mansion 11:378
could not l. thee . . . Loved I not Honour 7:123
Drinking . . . and making l. 8:425
England! . . . What l. I bore to thee 9:72
Every little girl knows about l. 13:794

folly . . . l. did make thee run into 7:318
God is l. 3:72
greater l. hath no man 3:60
help . . . of the woman I l. 12:284
If music be the food of l. 7:172
I know nothing about platonic l. 12:762
I l. or I hate 12:633
In Switzerland they had brotherly l. 13:859
I understand only because I l. 10:511
I want to l. first, and live incidentally 12:747
l. — all the wretched cant of it 13:754
l. and marriage 12:759
l. and murder will out 8:544
l., an . . . intercourse between tyrants and slaves 8:492
l. a place the less for having suffered 9:176
L. built on beauty 7:312
L. conquers all things 4:74
let brotherly l. continue 3:98
let us too give in to L. 4:74
l. . . . has one arch-enemy — and that is life 13:742
lightly turns to thoughts of l. 10:505
L. is a boy 8:498
L. is a sickness 7:328
l. is blind 7:316
L. is . . . like a coconut 12:750
L. is moral even without . . . marriage 11:393
L. is my religion 10:502
L. is not love Which alters 7:324
l. . . . looks more like hatred than like friendship 8:483
L. looks not with the eyes 7:315
L. means the pre-cognitive flow 12:752
L. of honour 6:117
l. of justice in most men 8:7
l. of liberty is the l. of others 10:549
l. of money is the root of all evil 3:97
longing for l. 13:608
L.'s like the measles 10:509
L. sought is good 7:321
L.'s pleasure lasts but a moment 8:494
l. the Lord thy God with all thy heart 3:103
l. thy neighbour as thyself 3:103
l. until after the first attack 11:377
l. . . . was not as l. is nowadays 6:116
l. we swore . . . seems deceit 13:744
l. your enemies 3:84
Men l. in haste 10:501
no man dies for l., but on the stage 8:486
Nuptial l. maketh mankind 7:326
office and affairs of l. 7:233
O Lord, to what a state . . . those who l. Thee 7:394
One can l. . . . vulgarity 12:616
Our l. of what is beautiful does not lead to extravagance
2:5
poet without l. 10:286
Religion is l. 12:882
She makes l. just like a woman 13:800
Society, friendship, and l. 8:429
these Christians l. one another 4:88
Those have most power to hurt us that we l. 7:327
To be wise and l. 7:322
To fear l. is to fear life 12:754
to l. and to cherish 7:339
vanity and l. . . . universal characteristics 8:519
violence masquerading as l. 13:703
what a mischievous devil L. is 11:382
What is commonly called l. 8:491
What is l.? 'Tis not hereafter 7:320
When a man is in l. he endures more 11:375
where the course of true l. may be expected to run smooth
10:504
worms have eaten them, but not for l. 7:319
loved better to be left than never to have been l. 8:488
better to have l. and lost 11:376
I have l. him too much 8:485
It seems to me that he has never l. 11:373
Who ever l., that l. not at first sight 7:317
loveliest L. of trees, the cherry 11:232
lovers l. cannot see The pretty follies 7:316
loves Anyone who l. his country, follow me 10:112

He that l. not his wife and children 7:338
I have reigned with your l. 7:80
loving A woman despises a man for l. her 11:402
Friday's child is l. and giving 10:640
l. himself better than all 10:586
most l. mere folly 7:237
low He that is l. 8:448
Kings are naturally lovers of l. company 8:238
my lamp burns l. and dim 12:941
when your powder's runnin' l. 7:64
lower if the l. orders don't set us a good example 11:230
lowly In l. pomp ride on to die 10:598
loyal a l. . . . and good-temper'd people 8:574
loyalty Hitler showed surprising l. to Mussolini 12:999
Party l. lowers the greatest of men 8:55
When l. no harm meant 8:69
luck it brings you l. whether you believe . . . or not 12:613
l. to give the roar 12:998
lunatic l. asylums . . . the stately homes 12:516
lust l. in action 7:325
Nonconformity and l. stalking hand in hand 12:173
Lutheran I have a Catholic soul, but a L. stomach 7:390
luxury Every l. . . . – atheism, breast-feeding, circumcision 13:694
lyf That l. so short 6:128
lying you say you're his . . . his passion is Infinite, . . . One of you is l. 12:758
lyre on this wall hang my weapons and my l. 4:75
lyric if you include me among the l. poets, I'll hold my head . . . high . . . 4:27

M

macaroni He stuck a feather in his cap And called it m. 8:212
MacDonald Ramsay M. 12:256
mace that fool's bauble, the m. 7:156
machine a taxing m. 11:1
cannot endow . . . m. with initiative 11:495
Our body is a m. for living 10:622
the Ghost in the M. 13:905
The m. is running away with *him* 12:312
The m. threatens 12:907
machinery liberty . . . is to be measured not by the governmental m. 11:44
machines M. are the produce of the mind of man 10:610
M. . . . keep free men in subjection 13:954
no reason . . . these m. will ever force themselves into general use 10:612
Macmillan M. is the best prime minister 13:87
M. seemed . . . to embody the national decay 13:133
MacWonder M. one moment and MacBlunder the next 13:272
mad escaped from a m. and savage master 2:54
half of the nation is m. 8:140
he ceased to be m. he became merely stupid 12:676
he first makes m. 2:71
M., bad, and dangerous to know 9:127
Men will always be m. 8:619
We all are born m. 13:588
madame Call me m. 13:1019
maddest those who think they can cure them are the m. 8:619
made My father m. . . . you . . . out of nothing 7:35
mademoiselle A m. from Armenteers 12:77
The m. . . . has lost everything except his reason 11:309
madman The m. is not the man who has lost his reason 11:309
madness devil's m – War 12:195
Great Wits . . . to M. near alli'd 8:447
M. need not be all breakdown 13:606
maestro Music, M., Please 12:987
maggot how to create a m. 7:396
magic men mistook m. for medicine 13:961
magicians if the way had not been prepared by m. 11:488
magistrate Obscenity . . . happens to shock some elderly . . . m. 13:823
suppose . . . the m. corruptible 9:21

magistrates rather than that the sovereigns and m. should be destroyed 7:14
The power of kings and m. 7:144
Magna Charta M. is such a fellow 7:111
magnanimity in victory, m. 12:409
magnificent some m. myth 2:9
there you sit with that m. instrument between your legs 12:476
magnify my soul doth m. the Lord 3:2
Mahomet If the hill will not come to M. 7:98
maid like a moth, the simple m. 8:516
majesty A sight so touching in its m. 9:130
Ride on! ride on in m. 10:598
This earth of m. 7:69
When I invented the phrase 'His M.'s Opposition' 10:229
majority A m. is always the best repartee 10:106
Fools are in a terrible . . . m. 11:331
He's gone to join the m. 4:38
I am certain that we will win the election with a good m. 13:393
No candidate . . . elected ex-president by such a large m. 11:157
the damned, compact, liberal m. 11:36
the great silent m. 13:247
The m. has the might 11:35
Majors scarlet M. 12:82
make a Scotsman on the m. 11:458
The white man knows how to m. everything 11:63
maker he adores his m. 10:104
making If you get the English people into the way of m. kings 10:81
mal *Honi soit qui m.* y pense 6:43
maladies Medical men . . . call all sorts of m. . . . by one name 10:629
There are m. we must not seek to cure 12:676
male especially the m. of the species 12:790
In the sex-war thoughtlessness is the weapon of the m. 12:802
m. and female created he them 1:5
more deadly than the m. 11:417
malicious God is subtle but he is not m. 12:917
malt M. does more than Milton 11:297
malvesye drowned in a barrel of m. 6:77
man a cold, hard, silent, practical 10:300
all animals were created . . . for the use of m. 10:442
a m. can die but once 7:202
a m. has no reason to be ashamed of having an ape for his grandfather 10:619
a m. is always seeking for happiness 12:770
A m. should . . . own he has been in the wrong 8:399
A m. with God 7:393
apparel oft proclaims the m. 7:238
behold the m. 3:31
condition of m. is a condition of war 7:147
England expects every m. will do his duty 9:53
Every m. is as Heaven made him 7:252
Every m. meets his Waterloo 11:385
figure of 'The Reasonable M.' 12:568
Go West, young m. 10:225
hate ingratitude more in a m. 7:363
I care not whether a m. is Good 9:139
I myself also am a m. 3:46
I said to the m. who stood at the gate of the year 12:319
It is good to know what a m. is 12:707
It takes . . . twenty years to make a m. 11:385
King is but a m. 7:272
make m. in our own image 1:5
m. alone leaves traces of what he created 13:716
M., being reasonable, must get drunk 10:329
M. belongs wherever he wants to go 13:944
M. . . . can neither repeat his past nor leave it behind 13:572
M. . . . can only find relaxation from one . . . labour by taking up another 11:512
M. . . . consumes without producing 12:422
M. delights not me 7:240
mean m. is always full of distress 2:40
m. fell into his anecdotage 11:324
M. for the field and woman for the hearth 10:528

M. . . . . grows beyond his work 12:632
m. has stopped moving 13:943
M. is a history-making creature 13:572
M. is an intellectual animal 10:363
M. is . . . a political animal 2:14
m. is . . . a religious animal 9:196
M. is a social animal 8:387
M. is a tool-making animal 8:620
m. is . . . a wild animal 12:922
M. is not a solitary animal 12:425
M. is something that is to be surpassed 11:285
M. is the hunter 10:527
M. is the only animal that can remain on friendly terms 11:313
m. made the town 8:478
M. proposes 6:125
m.'s greatest crime 7:302
M.'s love is of man's life a thing apart 10:500
m. that hath no music in himself 7:167
m. that is born of a woman 1:73
m. that is young in years 7:297
M. to command and woman to obey 10:528
M. wants but little 8:473
M. was born free 8:144
m. who . . . had the largest . . . soul 8:270
m. with all his noble qualities 11:484
M. with the head and woman with the heart 10:528
No m. is an Island 7:299
Nothing happens to any m. 4:72
No young m. believes he shall ever die 9:166
Of M.'s first disobedience 1:110
On earth there is nothing great but m. 10:382
One cannot be always laughing at a m. 9:185
one m. pick'd out of ten thousand 7:239
One m. shall have one vote 8:239
one small step for m. 13:233
only m. is vile 10:405
only place where a m. can feel . . . secure 13:803
rarely . . . one can see in a little boy the promise of a m. 10:538
reason to lament What m. has made of m. 9:147
She is clearly the best m. among them 13:338
single sentence . . . for modern m. 13:594
some meannesses . . . too mean even for m. 10:523
superior m. is distressed by his want of ability 2:41
superior m. is satisfied 2:40
Tears of eternity, and sorrow, Not mine, but m.'s 12:678
that grand old m. 11:31
The atrocious crime of being a young m. 8:461
the century of the common m. 12:377
the m. whose second thoughts are good 11:308
the only real danger that exists is m. himself 13:593
The proper study of Mankind is M. 8:407
The really original woman . . . imitates a m. 11:399
There must be a m. behind the book 10:315
the state . . . M. is in 11:469
This is the state of m. 7:296
this is the whole duty of m. 1:95
'Tis strange what a m. may do 10:531
We have on our hands a sick m. 10:140
We know nothing of m., far too little 13:593
What a piece of work is a m. 7:240
What's a m.'s first duty 10:573
When a m. is in love he endures more 11:375
whether he is a Wise M. or a Fool 9:139
Why can't a woman be more like a m. 13:792
you asked this m. to die 12:412
You cannot make a m. by standing a sheep 11:312
you'll be a M. my son 11:531
young m. not yet 7:337
Manderley I dreamt I went to M. again 12:986
manger In a m. for His bed 10:595
laid him in a m. 3:4
mankind about the dreadful wood . . . runs a lost m. 12:744
a decent respect to the opinions of m. 8:206
As I know more of m. 8:430
giant leap for m. 13:233
Human reason won. M. won 13:160

I am willing to love all m., *except an American* 8:228
Ideal m. would abolish death 12:664
If all m. minus one, were of one opinion 10:178
in determining the future destinies of m. 12:97
M. is a club 11:358
M. is not a tribe of animals 11:358
Nazi Germany had become a menace to all m. 12:251
proper study of m. is books 12:531
Spectator of m. 8:455
the earth is free for every son and daughter of m. 7:142
The proper study of M. is Man 8:407
truly m.'s war of liberation 13:686
manna it is m. 1:39
your fathers did eat m. . . . and are dead 3:14
manners in England people have good table m. 13:871
M. maketh man 6:106
The Japanese have perfected good m. 13:897
To Americans English m. are . . . frightening 13:868
to write good prose is an affair of good m. 12:494
mansion Back to its m. call the fleeting breath 8:319
Can storied urn . . . Back to its m. call the fleeting breath 8:319
mansions in my Father's house are many m. 3:114
manure The tree of liberty must be refreshed . . . It is its natural m. 8:259
many so much owed by so m. 12:338
what are they among so m. 3:13
map Roll up that m. 9:57
Marathon mountains look on M. 10:6
marble Not m., nor the gilded monuments 7:173
March Beware the ides of M. 4:5
gloomy in England are M. and April 10:345
M., whan God first maked man 1:109
march Napoleon's armies used to m. on their stomachs 9:212
Truth is on the m. 11:87
marche Le Congrès ne m. pas, il danse 9:102
marched He m. them up to the top of the hill 9:8
marching m. through Georgia 10:219
mare Though patience be a tired m. 7:356
You have sent me a Flanders m. 7:28
Margaret Thatcher M. . . . David Owen in drag 13:331
Mariners Ye M. of England 9:42
mark an ever-fixed m. 7:324
If you would hit the m. 10:564
the Lord set a m. upon Cain 1:18
the m. . . . of the beast 3:135
markets the unreasoning laws of m. and fashion 10:131
marriage Happiness in m. 9:180
In no country . . . are the m. laws so iniquitous as in England 10:69
love and m. 12:759
Love is moral even without . . . m. 11:393
M. has many pains 8:505
M. is a step so grave and decisive 11:383
M. is . . . but a civil contract 8:499
M. is for women the commonest mode of livelihood 12:772
M. is like a cage 7:331
M. isn't a process of prolonging the life of love 13:766
m. of true minds 7:324
rob a lady of her fortune by way of m. 8:504
they neither marry, nor are given in m. 8:503
Women . . . care fifty times more for a m. than a ministry 10:541
marriages m. don't add two people together 13:768
the early m. of silly children 10:516
married A man in love is incomplete until . . . m. 13:771
a woman's business to get m. 11:387
I m. beneath me 11:384
Living in England . . . like being m. to a stupid wife 12:863
Most m. couples . . . arrive at tolerable arrangements for living 13:777
m. six times shows a degree of optimism 13:784
M. women are kept women 12:775
that Albert m. beneath him 12:464
what delight we m. people have to see 8:496
Writing is like getting m. 13:481
marries a young person, who . . . m. or dies, is sure to be kindly spoken of 10:394

doesn't much signify whom one m. 9:178

marry better to m. than to burn 3:74
Every woman should m. 10:520
M. those who are single 5:25
Then I can't m. you, my pretty maid 9:177
Those who m. God . . . can become domesticated too 13:916
To m. a man out of pity is folly 12:766
when a man should m. 7:337
marry'd M. in haste 8:500
Mars seat of M. 7:69
marshal We may pick up a m. or two 9:109
Martini out of these wet clothes and into a dry M. 12:648
martyr Now he will raise me to be a m. 7:24
the soul of a m. with the intellect of an advocate 10:184
martyrdom M. is the test 8:241
martyrs The blood of the m. is the seed of the Church 4:89
marvel To m. at nothing is just about the one and only thing 4:48
Marx M. is a case in point 13:318
not even M. is more precious . . . than the truth 12:239
Marxian M. Socialism must always remain a portent 12:993
Marxism M. is like a classical building that followed the Renaissance 13:343
took a grip on cowardly M. 12:231
Marxist I am not a M. 11:40
to banish . . . M. socialism 13:367
Mary Hail M., full of grace 5:32
masculine It makes me feel m. to tell you 13:810
mass I am a Catholic. . . . I go to M. every day 11:125
Paris is worth a m. 7:68
There is no idolatry in the M. 8:607
masses Give me your tired, . . . Your huddled m. 11:52
I will back the m. against the classes 11:50
master A m. is dead 11:175
commerce between m. and slave is . . . exercise of . . . boisterous passions 8:244
m., is it I 3:26
m. of himself 7:253
Not bound to swear allegiance to any m. 4:15
One for the m. 6:56
the m. of my fate 11:335
masterpiece the m. of Nature 10:412
masters good servants, but bad m. 8:487
imitation of the most fam'd Italian m. 8:272
people are the m. 8:237
that the m. willingly concede to slaves 13:60
We are the m. at the moment 13:2
masturbation m. of war 13:830
M.: the primary sexual activity 13:756
material Increase of m. comforts . . . moral growth 13:971
materialistic Christianity is the most m. of all great religions 12:895
only really m. people . . . Europeans 13:885
materialists all the books with which m. have pestered the world 8:606
mathematics All science requires m. 6:127
As far as the laws of m. refer to reality 12:919
I like m. because it is *not* human 11:493
Let no one ignorant of m. enter here 2:74
M. . . . possesses . . . supreme beauty 12:903
M. . . . sphere of complete abstraction 12:910
Pure m. consists entirely of assertions 12:904
quite lawful for a Catholic woman to avoid pregnancy by . . . m. 13:909
spirit of delight . . . in m. 12:902
Matilda You'll come a-waltzing, M. 11:535
matter It is not much m. which we say 10:78
proverb is much m. decorated 8:323
We die – does it m. when 11:330
Women represent . . . m. over mind 11:406
mattering Art . . . can go on m. once it has stopped hurting 13:413
maturity m. is only a short break in adolescence 13:719
maunder m. and mumble 10:62
Max If M. gets to Heaven 12:962
Maxim we have got The M. Gun 11:84

May got through the perils of winter till at least the seventh of M. 10:345
maze Life is a m. 12:745
MCC where M. ends and the Church of England begins 13:1024
McCarthyism M. is Americanism 13:66
me between m. and the sun 2:13
My thought is m. 12:556
mean He nothing common did or m. 7:137
He who meanly admires m. things is a Snob 10:418
meaner motives m. than your own 12:589
meanest the m. . . . deeds require spirit and talent 8:472
the m. of his creatures Boasts two soul-sides 10:533
meaning Even when poetry has a m. 12:479
Nature has never put the fatal question as to the m. of their lives 12:716
The least of things with a m. is worth more . . . than the greatest 12:714
meannesses some m. . . . too mean even for man 10:523
means Errors look so very ugly in persons of small m. 10:427
Let us all be happy, and live within our m. 10:565
We are living beyond our m. 13:721
measles Love's like the m. 10:509
meddle 'm.' and 'muddle' 10:220
medicine men mistook magic for m. 13:961
M. is a noble profession 12:934
miserable have no other m. 7:242
medieval disillusionments in the lives of the m. saints 6:136
mediocre A best-seller is the gilded tomb of a m. talent 12:478
Titles distinguish the m. 11:114
Women want m. men 13:796
mediocrity It isn't evil . . . but m. 13:722
M. knows nothing higher 12:575
supreme expression of the m. 12:150
meditation M. is . . . both the means and the end 13:923
meek Blessed are the m. 3:80
The m. do not inherit the earth 12:703
meet never the twain shall m. 11:543
The only way for writers to m. 12:509
Two may talk . . . yet never really m. 11:300
meeting as if I was a public m. 11:23
megalomaniac m. . . . seeks to be feared 12:618
melancholy hell upon earth . . . in a m. man's heart 7:298
melodies caressing, chiming and intertwining m. 6:92
melody m. imposes continuity upon the disjointed 13:487
the m. of our sweet isle 7:169
melting America is . . . the great M.-Pot 11:135
the races of Europe are m. 11:135
même *plus c'est la m. chose* 10:465
memorandum A m. is written 13:614
memory For my name and m., I leave it to . . . the next ages 7:300
His m. is going 8:431
m. is a painter 13:644
Time whereof the m. of man 8:158
Unless a man feels he has a good enough m. 7:225
What a strange thing is m., and hope 13:644
men all m. are created equal 8:207
all m. would be tyrants 8:398
depict m. as they ought to be 2:23
England . . . purgatory of m. 7:382
fishers of m. 3:19
give place to better m. 7:157
great city . . . has the greatest m. and women 10:482
Great m. are almost always bad m. . . . 11:54
great m. have not commonly been great scholars 10:483
happy breed of m. 7:69
honour all m. 3:50
It brings m. together in crowds and mobs in bar-rooms 10:563
Many m. would take the death-sentence 13:661
M. are but children of a larger growth 8:388
M. are . . . more careful of the breed of their horses and dogs 8:501
M. are not hanged for stealing horses 8:48
M. are we, and must grieve 9:154

m. . . . capable of every wickedness 11:453
M. fear death 7:205
M. have never been good 13:590
M. of few words are the best men 7:234
Most m. admire Virtue 8:535
m. represent . . . mind over morals 11:406
M.'s natures are alike 2:38
M. will always be mad 8:619
M. will confess 11:320
O! m. with sisters dear 10:525
rich m. rule the law 8:151
So many m., so many opinions 4:44
That all m. are equal 12:196
the m. who borrow, and the m. who lend 10:401
the only advantage women have over m. – . . . they can cry 12:799
the race of m. is almost extinct in Europe 12:787
the tongues of m. and of angels 3:95
those m. have their price 8:110
tide in the affairs of m. 7:277
To famous m. all the earth is a sepulchre 2:50
We are the hollow m. 12:688
Why are women . . . so much more interesting to m. 12:794
Women . . . are either better or worse than m. 8:512

menace Nazi Germany had become a m. to all mankind 12:251
mental Christian Science explains all cause and effect as m. 11:465
meritocracy The Rise of the M. 13:114
merry A m. monarch 8:18
I commended mirth . . . to eat . . . to drink, and to be m. 1:71
Mersey quality of M. 12:520
Messiah He was the M. of the new age 12:106
metaphor m. . . . most fertile power possessed by man 13:412
metaphysical a physical and m. impossibility 10:286
a sort of m. brothel for emotions 12:736
metaphysics M. is the finding of bad reasons 11:254
method Traditional scientific m. has always been 13:960
You know my m. 11:527
methods m. of barbarism 11:104
metre Poetry is opposed to science, . . . prose to m. 10:260
without . . . understanding what m. 10:283
metrical difference between . . . prose and m. composition 9:120
mice Three blind m., see how they run 7:37
Michael Angelo last words . . . name of – M. 9:117
middle a whole is that which has a beginning, a m., and an end 2:24
Bow, bow, ye lower m. classes 11:32
no m. course between the throne and the scaffold 10:32
people who stay in the m. of the road 13:73
the ease . . . move into the m. class 13:283
midnight To cease upon the m. with no pain 10:350
mid-stream best to swap horses in m. 10:216
might Fight the good fight with all thy m. 10:599
The majority has the m. 11:35
we Britons . . . use 'M.' 12:307
We m. have been 10:456
mighty Another m. empire overthrown 9:64
put down the m. 3:106
share in the good fortunes of the m. 13:27
Milan he wants M., and so do I 7:5
militarism m. . . . is one of the chief bulwarks of capitalism 11:109
milk a land flowing with m. and honey 1:34
as when you find a trout in the m. 10:648
putting m. into babies 12:780
too full o' th' m. of human kindness 7:244
million I have had no real gratification . . . more than my neighbor . . . who is worth only half a m. 11:499
millionaire He must be a m. 11:498
I am a m.. That is my religion 11:504
Who Wants to Be a M. 13:972
millions take m. off the caring services 13:361
mills m. of God grind slowly 8:583
Milton Malt does more than M. can 11:297

M.! thou shouldst be living at this hour 9:71
the faith and morals hold Which M. held 9:44
the making up of a Shakespeare or a M. 9:200
mind an exaggerated stress on not changing one's m. 12:576
an unseemly exposure of the m. 10:373
a sound m. in a sound body 4:67
Beauty in things exists in the m. which contemplates them 8:414
clear your m. of cant . . . 8:356
it's all in the m. 12:609
men represent . . . m. over morals 11:406
m. that makes the body rich 7:350
never to ransack any m. but his own 8:352
No m. is thoroughly well organized 10:437
only inequalities that matter begin in the m. 13:104
our love . . . of the m. does not make us soft 2:5
Reading is to the m. 8:332
someone whose m. watches itself 12:553
That's the classical m. at work 13:557
The tendency of the casual m. 12:536
'Tis education forms the common m. 8:339
to change your m. 4:25
To know the m. of a woman 12:752
true genius is a m. of large general powers 8:355
Women represent . . . matter over m. 11:406
minds marriage of true m. 7:324
Superstition is the religion of feeble m. 9:157
the hobgoblin of little m. 10:375
To be alone is the fate of all great m. 10:468
well-developed bodies, fairly developed m. 12:530
miners it is only because m. sweat their guts out 12:297
the Vatican, the Treasury and the m. 13:14
mingled Like kindred drops, been m. 8:255
minister safety of a m. lies in his having the approbation of this House 8:109
three groups that no prime m. should provoke 13:385
ministers I don't mind how much my m. talk 13:392
King of England changes his m. 8:251
my actions are my m. 8:23
ministry Women . . . care fifty times more for a marriage than a m. 10:541
minority The m. is always right 11:35
minute M. Particulars 9:189
not a m. on the day 12:161
sucker born every m. 11:289
To a philosopher no circumstance, . . . is too m. 8:642
minutes at the rate of sixty m. an hour 12:740
take care of the m. 8:464
Yes, about ten m. 10:604
miracle man prays . . . for a m. 10:609
miracles The Christian religion not only was at first attended with m. 8:598
There are as many m. 6:103
mirror A novel is a m. 10:279
Art is not a m. . . . but a hammer 12:446
mirrors M. and fatherhood are abominable 12:746
mirth I commended m. . . . to eat . . . to drink, and to be merry 1:71
miscast George Bernard Shaw is sadly m. 12:465
mischief Satan finds . . . m. . . . For idle hands 8:548
thou little knowest the m. done 8:617
To mourn a m. that is past 7:286
mischievous what a m. devil Love is 11:382
miserable m. have no other medicine 7:242
The secret of being m. is to have leisure 12:573
misery certain amount of m. . . . to distribute as fairly as he can 11:1
greatest m. is a battle gained 10:46
he Who finds himself, loses his m. 10:435
M. acquaints a man with strange bedfellows 7:295
M. generates hate 10:119
misfortune In the m. of our best friends 8:374
the most unhappy kind of m. 5:23
worst m. was his birth 12:151
misfortunes history . . . a tableau of crimes and m. 8:363
history . . . the register of the . . . m. of mankind 8:364
The m. of poverty 4:93
the real m. and pains of others 8:418

misguided We have guided missiles and m. men 13:949
mislead One to m. the public, another to m. the Cabinet 12:113
missiles We have guided m. and misguided men 13:949
missionary he would begin fattening a m. on the White House backyard 12:277
mistake Live all you can; it's a m. not to 11:353
Woman was God's *second* m. 11:407
mistaken think it possible you may be m. 7:145
mistakes Young men make great m. in life 11:374
a m., and only then a friend 11:410
A m. should be like a . . . retreat 8:497
mistresses No, I shall have m. 8:107
one wife and hardly any m. 11:392
mistress Wives are young men's m. 7:334
mistrusted If the white man *says* he does, he is instantly . . . m. 13:141
misunderstood no worse lie than a truth m. 11:436
To be great is to be m. 10:414
mob Our supreme governors, the m. 8:119
mobs It brings men together in crowds and m. in bar-rooms 10:563
mock Let not Ambition m. 8:627
mockingbird it's a sin to kill a m. 13:1022
model The idea that there is a m. Labour voter, . . . is patronizing 13:387
models Rules and m. destroy genius and art 10:290
moderation astonished at my own m. 8:187
m. in the pursuit of justice is no virtue 13:200
M. is a virtue only in those 13:853
still for m. and will govern by it 8:85
modern Imagination without skill gives us m. art 13:472
modest and is m. about it 13:856
modester People ought to be m. 10:469
modesty a woman . . . ought to lay aside . . . m. with her skirt 7:311
His m. amounts to a deformity 12:280
lay aside . . . m. . . . and put it on again with her petticoat 7:311
There is false m., but there is no false pride 11:451
where the Greeks had m., we have cant 10:280
Mohammed If the mountain will not come to M.' 7:98
Mohicans The Last of the M. 10:638
moi *L'État c'est* m. 8:90
Molly Tonight the American flag floats from yonder hill or M. Stark sleeps a widow 8:220
moment A m. of time may make us unhappy for ever 8:405
A piece of each of us died at that m. 13:185
in a m. of time 3:15
monarch in 1802 every hereditary m. was insane 9:211
monarchy decide the fate of the m. 9:1
Helm of this Imperial M. 7:49
M. is a strong government 10:241
m. is part of the fabric of the country 13:227
The m. . . . oldest profession in the world 13:342
The Sovereign has, under a constitutional m. . . . three rights 10:237
The state of m. is the supremest thing upon earth 7:96
They that are discontented under m., call it *tyranny* 7:152
Monday is going to do on M. 11:479
M.'s child is fair of face 10:640
money a licence to print your own m. 13:518
a man who doesn't know how to handle m. 12:936
art . . . of draining m. 8:213
Business . . . may bring m., . . . friendship hardly ever does 10:623
collect legal taxes from illegal m. 12:187
Good Samaritan . . . had m. as well 13:985
hired the m. 12:158
I don't know how much m. I've got 13:981
If possible honestly, if not, somehow, make m. 4:91
If women didn't exist, . . . m. . . . no meaning 13:808
If you can . . . count your m. you are not . . . rich man 12:946
I hate m. but it's the lack of it I hate most 11:507
innocently employed than in getting m. 8:629
killed a lot of men to have made so much m. 8:623
Lack of m. 11:502

love of m. is the root of all evil 3:97
m. answereth all things 1:101
M. is like a sixth sense 12:935
M. is like muck 7:413
M. is the most important thing in the world 11:503
M., it turned out, was exactly like sex 13:977
M., n. A blessing . . . of no advantage to us 11:506
Neither is m. the sinews of war 8:79
power to make m. is a gift 12:945
spiritual snobbery . . . happy without m. 12:623
the love of m. is the root of all evil 11:496
The profession . . . in which one can make no m. without being ridiculous 11:211
They had been corrupted by m. 13:817
time is m. 8:647
To be clever enough to get . . . m., one must be stupid 11:509
''To make m.'', said Mr. Porteous 12:938
We haven't the m., so we've got to think 12:906
We've got the ships, we've got the men, we've got the m. too 11:16
with m. . . . they have not got 12:638
monkey no reason to attack the m. when the organ-grinder is present 13:132
the faith of a m. 7:51
monkish that old m. place 10:346
monopoly imperialism is the m. stage of capitalism 12:65
Monroe adherence . . . to the M. Doctrine may force the United States 11:122
mons treating the *m. Veneris* as . . . Mount Everest 12:757
monster jealousy . . . green-ey'd m. 7:366
monstrous the M. Regiment of Women 7:41
Monte Carlo the man who broke the Bank at M. 11:498
months two m. of every year 10:328
monument sonnet is a moment's m. 11:173
monuments Not marble, nor the gilded m. 7:173
moon If they had said the sun and the m. was gone 10:271
landing a man on the M. 13:146
The m. doth shine as bright as day 8:652
The m. is nothing But a circumambulating aphrodisiac 13:743
moral All universal m. principles are idle fancies 8:567
Everything's got a m. 10:572
Love is m. even without . . . marriage 11:393
m. attribute of a Scotsman 11:459
M. indignation is in most cases 2 percent moral 13:831
m. is what you feel good after 12:825
m. or an immoral book 11:187
one is unhappy one becomes m. 12:804
putting him into a m. Coventry 11:22
The highest possible stage in m. culture 11:421
the m. law 8:481
The worst government is the most m. 13:44
moralist no sterner m. than Pleasure 10:547
morality Dr Johnson's m. was as English . . . as a beefsteak 8:666
live for others . . . middle class m. 11:240
M. . . . is herd-morality 11:426
M.'s a gesture. . . . learnt from books 13:829
M.'s not practical 13:829
m. . . . what the majority . . . happen to like 13:822
M. which is based on ideas 12:811
new m. . . . the old immorality condoned 13:836
periodical fits of m. 10:274
This imperative may be called that of M. 8:566
two kinds of m. 12:818
morals basing m. on myth 13:815
If your m. make you dreary 11:430
M. are an acquirement 11:449
men represent . . . mind over m. 11:406
the faith and m. hold Which Milton held 9:44
mordre M. wol out 6:121
more As I know m. of mankind 8:430
Oliver Twist has asked for m. 10:72
mores *O tempora! O m.* 2:20
morning I awoke one m. 9:128
the m. cometh, and also the night 1:105
morrow take . . . no thought for the m. 3:87

entirely a slave-holding n., or entirely a free-labour n. 10:171

is Apostasy too hard a word to describe the temper of the n. 10:50

I will make of thee a great n. 1:24

n. . . . fall victim to a big lie 12:134

n. had the lion's heart 12:998

No n. is fit to sit in judgement 12:24

n. shall not lift up sword against n. 1:53

N. shall speak peace 12:163

the English are . . . the least a n. of pure philosophers 10:240

the kind of n. . . . President Kennedy died for 13:202

the kind of n. that President Roosevelt hoped for 13:202

the Third Estate contains . . . a n. 9:4

ventured my life in defence of this n. 8:43

ational as clear as a crystal, the synthesis – German N. Socialism 12:231

Our long n. nightmare is over 13:281

ationality Other people have a n. 13:876

ations Commonwealth of N. 11:42

If people behaved in the way n. do 13:244

The day of small n. has long passed away 11:120

The great n. have always acted like gangsters 13:189

three very powerful n. of the Germans 5:1

Two n. 10:102

ative my own, my n. land 9:169

white man . . . looks into the eyes of a n. 13:48

atives Britons were only n. 4:102

The fault of our younger politicians . . . is a contempt for the n. 10:5

atural It is n. to die 7:206

Nothing prevents us from being n. 8:377

The n. price of labour 10:3

aturally Though I am not n. honest 7:374

ature Accuse not N., she hath done her part 8:378

Consistency is contrary to n. 12:608

drive out n. with a pitchfork 4:49

fortress built by N. 7:69

Human n. is so well disposed 10:394

I have learned To look on n. 9:162

Little we see in N. that is ours 9:172

Man has wrested from n. 13:69

N. abhors a vacuum 7:261

N. has left this tincture 8:398

N. has never put the fatal question as to the meaning of their lives 12:716

N. has no cure for this sort of madness 12:170

n. is a conjugation of the verb to eat 12:658

N. is often hidden 7:248

n. is the art of God 7:307

N. is usually wrong 11:339

N. is very consonant and conformable 8:615

N. made him, and then broke the mould 6:115

not formed by n. to bear 4:72

n.'s law 8:389

N.'s laws lay hid in night 8:618

N. . . . wasteful of promising young men 13:675

rules of the game are what we call the laws of N. 10:495

secret of the arts is to correct n. 8:276

The Duke of Wellington had exhausted n. 10:134

the most irrelevant thing in n. 10:512

to run into debt with N. 10:540

to see the absurd n. of Englishmen 8:568

True wit is n. to advantage dress'd 8:437

vacuum . . . better . . . stuff that n. replaces 13:662

We need more understanding of human n. 13:593

atures Men's n. are alike 2:38

avy England's chief defence depends upon the n. 7:36

The Royal N. of England . . . its greatest defence 8:157

upon the n. . . . safety, honour, and welfare . . . chiefly attend 7:154

Nazi N. Germany had become a menace to all mankind 12:251

Nazis In Germany, the N. came for the Communists 12:411

earer the n. you are to God 7:402

earest the n. run thing you ever saw 9:112

ecessary Government, . . . is but a n. evil 8:215

necessities disregard for the n. of existence 12:655

necessity N. hath no law 7:159

N. is the plea for every infringement of human freedom 8:250

N. knows no law 4:2

no virtue like n. 7:270

neck England will have her n. wrung like a chicken 12:335

go to the bottom with my principles round my n. 13:15

my n. is very short 7:22

Some n. 12:364

the Roman people had but one n. 4:19

need An artist . . . produces things that people don't n. 13:994

needle easier for a camel to go through the eye of a n. 3:91

needs to each according to his n. 10:127

Your country n. YOU 12:13

negation Capitalist production begets . . . its own n. 10:243

the n. of God erected into a system of Government 10:129

negative Europe is the unfinished n. 13:884

negligent Celerity . . . admired . . . by the n. 7:367

Negro One of the things that makes a N. unpleasant to white folk 12:611

Negroes revenge by the culture of the N. 12:507

neighbor I have had no real gratification . . . more than my n. 11:499

neighbour It's a recession when your n. 13:108

love thy n. as thyself 3:103

neighbours fear of what the n. might say 12:642

improper thoughts about n. 12:819

make sport for our n. 9:155

neither better if n. of us had been born 9:80

Nell Pretty witty N. 8:3

the death of Little N. without laughing 11:202

Nelly let not poor N. starve 8:41

Nelson death of N. was felt in England 9:55

The N. touch 9:50

nest broods a n. of sorrows 7:338

Netherlands a pretty fly out of the King of the N. 10:45

nets Laws are generally found to be n. 8:153

neurotic Psychiatrists classify a person as n. 13:1005

neurotics Everything great in the world is done by n. 11:365

neutral United States must be n. 12:8

neutrality people of this country are overwhelmingly for a policy of n. 12:264

'positive n.' is a contradiction in terms 13:136

never I n. would lay down my arms 8:223

our people have n. had it so good 13:102

new a n. heaven and a n. earth 3:124

He that will not apply n. remedies 7:293

He was dull in a n. way 8:299

He was the Messiah of the n. age 12:106

I make all things n. 3:124

n. deal for the American people 12:218

n. wine into old bottles 3:58

Revolution is . . . the setting-up of a n. order 12:192

something n. out of Africa 4:66

There are no n. truths 13:546

there is no n. thing under the sun 1:74

We stand today on the edge of a n. frontier 13:128

You suddenly understand something . . . in a n. way 13:553

Youth is something very n. 13:692

newness Americans have been conditioned to respect n. 13:896

news Nothing is n. until it has appeared in *The Times*. 13:72

when a man bites a dog that is n. 12:662

newspaper good n., . . . is a nation talking to itself 13:510

I read the n. avidly 13:509

Once a n. touches a story, the facts are lost 13:998

newspapers N. always excite curiosity 10:332

Newton God said, Let N. be 8:618

Newtons the souls of five hundred . . . N. 9:200

New York 'tis now called N. 8:2

nice Be n. to people on your way up 12:672

how nasty n. people can be 13:684

Sugar and spice And all that's n. 10:526

nicest English people . . . are surely the n. people in the world 12:835
Nicholas St N. soon would be there 10:333
nigger Catch a n. by his toe 11:41
nigh draw n. to God 3:99
night a firebell in the n. 10:12
An infant crying in the n. 10:473
calm passage . . . across many a bad n. 11:242
Do not go gentle into that good n. 13:524
hanged privily by n. 6:29
Nature's laws lay hid in n. 8:618
Ships that pass in the n. 11:327
the black bat, n., has flown 10:650
the darkness he called N. 1:1
The dark n. of the soul 7:227
the morning cometh, and also the n. 1:105
The n. is dark, and I am far from home 10:587
nightmare 'History', Stephen said, is a 'n.' 12:564
Our long national n. is over 13:281
Nimrod N. the mighty hunter 1:22
Nixon standing between N. and the White House 13:129
You won't have N. to kick around 13:156
no become accustomed to n. one governing 12:72
rebel . . . man who says n. 13:57
why Absurdist plays take place in N. Man's Land 13:453
nobility leave us still our old n. 10:90
N. has its own obligations 9:74
Real n. is based on scorn 12:832
The army is the true n. of our country 10:154
The n. . . . snored through the Sermon 13:139
noble Englishman never enjoys himself except for a n. purpose 12:858
n. grounds for the n. emotions 11:183
scarcely a man learned in the laws . . . who is not n. 6:73
nobleman a king may make a n. 9:28
noblesse If the French n. had been capable of playing cricket with their peasants 9:213
noblest n. Roman of them all 4:9
nobody a man is n. unless his biography 10:486
N. asked you, sir, she said 9:177
Nod the land of N. 1:18
nods even excellent Homer n. 4:29
noise they . . . love the n. it makes 12:848
noisy The people would be just as n. 7:158
nominated I will not accept if n. 11:64
non-combatant War hath no fury like a n. 12:588
nonconformity N. and lust stalking hand in hand 12:173
nonsense Even God has been defended with n. 12:871
you intend to talk n. 12:416
non-violence to disagree . . . about . . . n. without wanting to kick 13:621
Norfolk bear him up the N. sky 12:263
Very flat, N. 12:980
Norgay Tenzing N. 13:77
nose A custom loathsome to the eye, hateful to the n. 7:194
Entuned in hir n. ful semely 6:124
Had Cleopatra's n. been shorter 4:97
led by the n. with gold 7:102
nostrils God . . . breathed into his n. 1:7
not How n. to do it 10:167
note The world will little n., nor long remember 10:209
notes the pauses between the n. 13:435
nothin' You ain't heard n. yet 12:977
nothing certain we can carry n. out 3:71
George the First knew n. 8:661
God made everything out of n. 12:741
n. can bring back the hour 9:171
n. either good or bad 7:359
n. is law that is not reason 8:73
opened it only to find − n. 2:57
People don't resent having n. 12:944
Signifying n. 7:287
The House of Peers . . . Did n. 11:33
The temerity to believe in n. 10:496
To marvel at n. is just about the one and only thing 4:48
We are n.; less than n., and dreams 10:452
When you have n. to say, say n. 10:449

Where some people are very wealthy and others have n. 2:15
nothingness the n. shows through 12:741
notice The State, in choosing men . . . takes no n. of their opinions 7:126
novel A n. is a mirror 10:279
A n. is a static thing 13:445
because a n.'s invented, it isn't true 13:486
good n. tells us the truth 11:208
not a n. to be tossed aside lightly 12:466
the last fashionable n. on the tables of young ladies 10:29
The n. being dead 13:462
The only obligation to which . . . we may hold a n. 11:184
the sex n. is now normal 12:467
When I want to read a n. 10:317
novelist n. who writes nothing for 10 years 13:465
novelists n. the story of the present 10:323
There are many reasons why n. write 13:490
novels one of the few English n. for grown up people 12:449
novelty N., n., n. 10:408
November Please to remember the Fifth of N. 7:87
now The n., the here, through which 12:680
We are all Socialists n. 11:123
nowhere All dressed up, with n. to go 12:35
He's a real N. Man 13:604
noxious the most n. is a tourist 11:223
nuclear Wars cannot be fought with n. weapons 13:324
nuisance Inflation in the Sixties was a n. 13:254
Never compose . . . unless . . . not composing . . . becomes a positive n. 12:438
number abstract reasoning concerning quantity or n. 8:342
numbers N. . . . only universal language 12:930
the greatest happiness for the greatest n. 8:549
numble We live in a n. abode 10:647
nun the upbringing a n. would envy 13:773
nurse definition of . . . a n. . . . 'devoted and obedient.' 10:635
nurseries n. of all vice 8:340
nurses old men's n. 7:334

O

oak Heart of o. are our ships 8:132
oar impressions . . . lasting as . . . an o. upon the water 11:337
oat-cakes land of Calvin, o., and sulphur 10:155
obedience The reluctant o. of distant provinces 10:26
obedient definition of . . . a nurse . . . 'devoted and o.' 10:635
obey children, o. your parents 3:75
safer to o. than to rule 6:65
obeyed She-who-must-be-o. 11:400
object o. will be, if possible to form Christian men 10:364
objectionable its own animality either o. or funny 13:628
obligation The only o. to which . . . we may hold a novel 11:184
To the University of Oxford I acknowledge no o. 8:358
oblige One should o. everyone to . . . one's ability 8:380
oblivion that ineluctable o. which awaits the uncreative mind 12:909
obscene would not say that our Press is o. 13:513
obscenity O. . . . happens to shock some elderly . . . magistrate 13:823
observance the o. of trifles 11:527
obstinacy the name of . . . o. in a bad one 8:556
obstinate O. people can be divided into 2:44
obvious the analysis of the o. 12:911
occupation for ever apologizing for his o. 12:949
ocean on the o. of life we pass 11:327
whilst the great o. of truth lay all undiscovered before me 8:616
octopus dear o. from whose tentacles we never quite escape 12:777
odious little o. vermin 8:97
offence dire o. from am'rous causes springs 8:489
greatest o. against virtue 10:554
It is a public scandal that gives o. 8:524

The only defence is in o. 12:225
offend the kind of pride least likely to o. 11:432
Those who o. us are generally punished 10:570
offended This hath not o. the king 7:23
When people do not respect us we are sharply o. 11:311
office not describe holding public o. 13:70
o. sanctifies the holder 11:54
Written by o. boys for o. boys 11:79
officer All evil comes from the o. 13:672
unbecoming the character of an o. 11:511
old an o., wild, and incomprehensible man 11:66
Growing o. is like being increasingly penalized 13:718
inclination . . . to suppose an o. man decayed in his intellects 8:431
I will never be an o. man 13:660
Nobody hears o. people complain 13:671
o. age is . . . older than I am 13:660
O. men are dangerous 12:667
that grand o. man 11:31
that o. monkish place 10:346
the o. have rubbed it into the young that they are wiser 12:710
They shall grow not o. 12:92
To be o. is to be part of a . . . multitude 13:731
too much Asia and she is too o. 11:456
too o. to go again to my travels 8:24
Where are the boys of the O. Brigade 11:536
older make way for an o. man 13:304
O. men declare war 12:391
The o. one grows the more one likes indecency 12:810
oligarchy displeased with *aristocracy*, call it o. 7:152
extreme democracy or absolute o. . . . will come 2:15
olive an o. leaf pluckt off 1:20
Olympic The most important thing in the O. Games 11:361
Omega Alpha and O. 3:120
ominous an idea . . . to be fashionable is o. 11:483
omnipotence final proof of God's o. 13:915
onaway O.! Awake, beloved 10:508
once For Christmas comes but o. a year 7:188
O. more unto the breach, dear friends 6:61
one How to be o. up 13:583
I have only o. eye 9:40
O. Realm 12:242
the United States will never again seek o. additional foot of territory by conquest 11:163
one-eyed o. yellow idol to the north of Khatmandu 11:544
the O. Man is King 11:367
oneself It is a stupidity . . . to busy o. with the correction of the world 8:446
One should examine o. . . . before . . . condemning others 8:531
only possible society is o. 11:296
opened the eyes of the blind shall be o. 1:106
opera Bed . . . is the poor man's o. 11:547
Like German o., too long and too loud 12:353
No good o. plot can be sensible 13:447
o. isn't what it used to be 12:480
The first rule in o. is the first rule in life 12:693
what language an o. is sung in 13:428
operas Our mistake . . . was to write interminable large o. 11:186
opinion better to have no o. of God 7:403
heresy signifies no more than private o. 7:148
He would rather follow public o. 12:398
I agree with no man's o. 10:433
If all mankind minus one, were of one o. 10:178
Nobody holds a good o. of a man who has a low o. of himself 10:569
the English think of an o. as something . . . to hide 12:862
The superiority of one man's o. over another's 11:405
They that approve . . . call it o. 7:148
opinionated the o., the ignorant, and the boorish 2:44
opinions a decent respect to the o. of mankind 8:206
New o. are always suspected 8:328
not a writer's business to hold o. 13:492
So many men, so many o. 4:44
The average man's o. 13:551

The State, in choosing men . . . takes no notice of their o. 7:126
The wish to spread those o. that we hold 11:3
when o. universally prevail 12:814
opium Religion . . . is the o. of the people 10:602
opium-dose an o. for keeping beasts of burden 10:110
opponent Never ascribe to an o. motives meaner than your own 12:589
opportunist rather be an o. and float 13:15
opportunities A wise man will make more o. 7:219
One can present people with o. 12:643
opportunity Equality of o. 13:123
follies . . . he didn't commit when he had the o. 11:354
There is no security . . . only o. 13:690
oppose duty . . . to o. 11:74
o. everything, and propose nothing 10:87
opposition Her Majesty's O. 10:238
The duty of an o. 11:74
When I invented the phrase 'His Majesty's O.' 10:229
oppression when fanatics are on top there is no limit to o. 13:44
Where rumour of o. and deceit 8:479
optimism married six times shows a degree of o. 13:784
O. is the content of small men 12:721
The place where o. most flourishes 12:684
optimist an o. . . . fills up his crossword puzzle in ink 12:599
An o. is a guy that never had much experience 12:696
The o. proclaims 12:600
optimistic O. lies 11:524
orange 'tis an O. 8:59
orangutang an o. trying to play the violin 10:515
oratory object of o. . . . persuasion 10:124
orchestration Literature is the o. of platitudes 13:423
order O. is heaven's first law 8:102
party of o. or stability 10:179
ordering the better o. of the universe 1:108
organ-grinder no reason to attack the monkey when the o. is present 13:132
organization a government o. could do it that quickly 2:86
orgasm The o. has replaced the Cross 13:748
Orientals If . . . O. . . . drank a liquor which . . . made them vomit 8:569
origin the indelible stamp of his lowly o. 11:484
original An o. writer is . . . one whom nobody can imitate 9:122
The more intelligence . . . the more . . . one finds o. 8:383
originality All good things . . . are the fruits of o. 10:383
without o. or moral courage 4:101
orphan defeat is an o. 13:688
orthodoxy 'o.' . . . no longer means being right 11:263
O. or My-doxy 10:371
ostrich America cannot be an o. 12:36
other O. people are quite dreadful 11:96
you expect o. people to be . . . to your liking 6:109
others By persuading o. we convince ourselves 8:168
delight in . . . misfortunes . . . of o. 8:418
to encourage the o. 8:136
otherwise Some folk . . . are o. 8:343
ounce An o. of a man's own wit 12:392
ours We have met the enemy, and they are o. 9:98
ourselves By persuading others we convince o. 8:168
In every friend we lose a part of o. 8:317
remedies oft in o. do lie 7:241
we but praise o. in other men 8:545
out Mordre wol o. 6:121
outlive o. this powerful rhyme 7:173
outlook religious o. on life 12:890
outside I am just going o. 11:160
I support it from the o. 10:79
overcomes Who o. By force 8:10
over-confident Not that I am ever o. 13:393
overexposure she should catch a cold on o. 11:435
overpaid They're o., overfed, oversexed and over here 12:392
overthrown Another mighty empire o. 9:64
owe I don't o. a penny to a single soul 12:582
owed so much o. by so many to so few 12:338

owes A nation is not in danger . . . because it o. itself money 12:235

owl The O. and the Pussy-Cat went to sea 10:655

ownership its source of power: o. 13:295
personal o. is in harmony with . . . British people 13:400
transform this society without . . . extension of public o. 13:363

ox This dumb o. will fill the whole world 6:100

Oxenford Clerk . . . of O. 6:104

Oxford Herr Hitler and Signor Mussolini had been at O. 12:290
The clever men at O. Know all that there is to be knowed 11:540
The King to O. sent a troop of horse 8:335
To O. sent a troop of horse 8:334
To the University of O. I acknowledge no obligation 8:358
You will hear more good things on . . . a stagecoach from London to O. 10:362

oyster world's mine o. 7:279

P

pace this petty p. from day to day 7:287

Pacific salutes the Admiral of the P. 11:92

pacifism My p. is not based on . . . intellectual theory 12:19

pack how much more dogs are animated when they hunt in a p. 8:412
the human p. is shuffled and cut 13:558

pagan Christian glories in the death of a p. 6:6

pageant insubstantial p. faded 7:174

paid I do not answer questions like this without being p. 13:810

palementz Daily many warantis come to me of p. 6:67

pain a gentleman . . . never inflicts p. 10:423
I have no p., dear mother, now 10:644
Neither shame nor physical p. have any . . . effect 11:452
People will not . . . bear p. unless there is hope 13:625
Pleasure is . . . intermission of p. 8:397

pains He therefore was at strenuous p. 12:183
no gains without p. 13:68

paint flinging a pot of p. in the public's face 11:170
I p. objects as I think them 13:473
My business is to p. . . . what I see 10:296

painted I am p. as the greatest little dictator 13:365

painter A p. should not paint what he sees 12:506
memory is a p. 13:644
not a great sculptor or p. can be an architect 10:308

painters Good p. imitate nature 7:168
P. and poets . . . licence to dare anything 4:33
p., poets and builders have very high flights 8:281
Poets and p. are outside the class system 13:1007

painting If people only knew . . . about p. 10:301
I just keep p. till I feel like pinching 12:432
P. is a blind man's profession 13:474

palaces Mid pleasures and p. though we may roam 10:514

pale a p. horse 3:54
the p. of the constitution 10:221

Palestine not enough prisons . . . in P. to hold all the Jews 12:346

pall The pallor of girls' brows shall be their p. 12:21

palladium Liberty of the press is the P. of . . . rights 8:167

pallor The p. of girls' brows shall be their pall 12:21

palms p. before my feet 12:875

papacy Since God has given us the p. . . . enjoy it 6:90
The P. is not other than the Ghost of the deceased Roman Empire 7:153
The P. is . . . the ghost of the deceased Roman empire 8:581

paper The atom bomb is a p. tiger 13:8

papers a great heap of p. 8:64
fornicated and read the p. 13:594

papists revenged to the utmost upon all P. 8:21

parables great p. . . . but false art 12:429

parade solemnized with pomp and p. 8:205
the chief employment of riches consists in the p. of riches 8:630

paradise England is a p. for women 7:386
England is the p. of individuality 12:838

England is the p. of women 7:382
If a man could pass through P. 10:584

paradoxes P. are useful 11:261

paradoxical He who confronts the p. 13:679

paragon the p. of animals 7:240

parallel We never remark any passion . . . in others, of which, . . . we may not find a p. 8:411

paralyse p. it by encumbering it with remedies 10:622

pardon God may p. you, but I never can 7:58
God will p. me. It is His trade 10:607
the government that should ask me for a p. 12:125

parenthood p. . . . feeding the mouth that bites you 13:765

parents A Jewish man with p. alive 13:891
by defying their p. and copying one another 13:705
children, obey your p. 3:75
P. are strange 13:769
P. . . . bones on which children sharpen their teeth 13:781
Possessive p. rarely live long enough to see 13:775
the way p. obey their children 13:873

Paris found P. stinking and left it sweet 10:160
Is P. burning 12:395
P. is worth a mass 7:68
when good Americans die they go to P. 11:457
When P. sneezes 10:40

parish all the world as my p. 8:597
man who left a wife and six children on the p. 8:106

Parkinson The rise in the . . . employed is governed by P.'s Law 13:991

par-lee-voo Hinky, dinky, p. 12:77

parliament a regular income from his p. 8:25
build your House of P. upon the river 10:60
more fit for a grammar school than a Court of P. 7:79
nailed up the doors of P. 12:131
P. is the longest running farce 13:314
The rights of p. should be preserved 8:68

parliaments P. are the great lie of our time 8:152

parochial worse than provincial — he was p. 11:172

parole Classical quotation is the p. of literary men 8:304

parsnips fine words butter no p. 10:448

part In every friend we lose a p. of ourselves 8:317
it is a little flesh and breath, and the ruling p. 4:54
till death us do p. 7:339

particular a London p. . . . A fog 10:342
did nothing in p. 11:33

particulars Minute P. 9:189

parties one of those p. which got out of hand 3:136
things must be done by p. 10:105

partridge well-shot woodcock, p., snipe 12:263

parts It is seldom . . . one p. on good terms 12:596
one man in his time plays many p. 7:274
Today we have naming of p. 13:987

party A great p. is not to be brought down 13:176
Englishman has to have a P. 12:859
I always voted at my p.'s call 11:18
p. is a political evil 8:108
the Conservative P. at prayer 12:55
The p. is the rallying-point for the . . . working class 13:78

pass Praise the Lord and p. the ammunition 12:360
They shall not p. 12:46
To p. away ere life hath lost its brightness 10:353

passage calm p. . . . across many a bad night 11:242
Patience and p. of time 8:381

passed p. by on the other side 3:16

passeront Ils ne p. pas 12:46

passeth the fashion of this world p. away 3:67

passion Culture is the p. for sweetness and light 11:168
one master-p. . . . swallows up the rest 8:406
p. and party blind our eyes 10:387
p. in the human soul 8:282
The ruling p. conquers reason still 8:408
We never remark any p. . . . in others, of which, . . . we may not find a parallel 8:411
you say you're his . . . his p. is Infinite, . . . One of you is lying 12:758

passions It is with our p. as it is with fire and water 8:487
not his reason, but his p. 8:601
The man who is master of his p. 13:582
Three p. simple but overwhelmingly strong, have governed my life 13:608

passover it is the Lord's p. 1:36
past Even God cannot change the p. 2:30
his p. shut in him like the leaves 12:683
Historians tell the story of the p. 10:323
I do not . . . prejudge the p. 13:274
something . . . absurd about the p. 11:280
Study the p. 2:29
The p., at least, is secure 10:389
The p. is a foreign country 13:568
The p. is the only dead thing 11:278
The p. was nothing . . . The future was a mystery 11:336
Those who cannot remember the p. 11:276
to know nothing but the present, or nothing but the p. 12:566
What we know of the p. is 12:562
Who controls the p. controls the future 13:32
Why doesn't the p. decently bury itself 12:565
pastoral investiture by the gift of the p. staff 5:16
path the primrose p. of dalliance 7:398
patience P. and passage of time 8:381
Though p. be a tired mare 7:356
patient A doctor . . . is a p. half-cured 12:955
amusing the p. while Nature cures the disease 8:622
Fury of a P. Man 8:391
kill the p. 7:406
p. endurance is godlike 10:557
p. patrie Allons, enfants, de la p. 9:16
patriot A good historian . . . is a p. 8:359
The summer soldier and the sunshine p. 8:253
patriotism attractions of p. – it fulfils our worst wishes 12:278
Blimpish p. in the mode of Margaret Thatcher 13:361
p. had to be proved in blood 13:353
P. . . . is a revolutionary duty 12:69
p. is not enough 12:32
P. is the last refuge 8:195
P. . . . looking out for yourself while 12:227
True p. is of no party 8:141
patriots P. always talk of dying for their country 13:222
patronizing The idea that there is a model Labour voter,
. . . is p. 13:387
paucity the p. of restraints it imposes 11:44
pauses the p. between the notes 13:435
pay get someone to p. you for doing it 13:1006
it is poor grub, poor p., and easy work 11:111
Life is too short to do anything . . . one can p. others to do 12:969
Not a penny off the p. 12:161
we cannot p. too dearly for it 8:81
peace achieve and cherish a just and lasting p. among ourselves 10:226
a period of cold p. 13:25
Arms alone are not enough to keep the p. 13:158
depart in p. 3:8
If p. cannot be maintained with honour 10:142
In Switzerland they had brotherly love . . . and p. 13:859
it is in the minds of men that the defences of p. must be
constructed 13:7
I will die in p. 8:135
king of France . . . would assent to no p. or treaty 6:42
Let him who desires p., prepare for war 4:26
Let us have p. 10:247
make a wilderness and call it p. 4:21
makes a good war makes a good p. 7:109
May God deny you p. 11:370
Nation shall speak p. 12:163
never was a good war or a bad p. 8:249
no p. . . . unto the wicked 1:55, 1:88
on earth p., good will toward men 3:6
p. at that price would be a humiliation 11:151
P., Bread and Land 12:60
p. for our time 12:304
P. hath her victories 7:155
P. I hope with honour 11:14
P. is indivisible 12:266
P. is not only better than war 12:120
P. is poor reading 11:274
p. with honour 12:304
The Bomb brought p. but man alone 12:404

The Empire means P. 10:136
the inglorious arts of p. 7:146
the Prince of P. 1:99
those who could make a good p. 12:200
War is P. 13:30
We are the true p. movement 13:368
we might more reasonably expect fifteen years of p. 9:14
We wanted p. on earth 13:739
When p. has been broken anywhere 12:314
peak One sees . . . only small things from the p. 11:364
pearls He who would search for P. 8:538
p. before swine 3:89
peasantry a bold p. . . . When once destroy'd 8:180
peasants If the French noblesse had been capable of playing cricket with their p. 9:213
it is better that all of these p. should be killed 7:14
Peccavi 10:439
pee share a quick p. over a common lamp-post 12:509
Peel P.'s smile 10:64
Sir Robert P. 10:122
That prig P. 10:25
peers Fears, prejudices, misconceptions – those are the p. 12:164
pen how much more cruel the p. 7:177
less brilliant p. than mine 11:549
nothing can cure it but the scratching of a p. 10:294
pence Take care of the p. 8:626
pendulum politics of the p., but of the ratchet 13:317
penetrable most things are p. 10:553
pennies P. do not come from heaven 13:738
penny I don't owe a p. to a single soul 12:582
Not a p. off the pay 12:161
pense Honi soit qui mal y p. 6:43
Pentecost when the day of P. was fully come 3:44
people a loyal, a gallant, a generous, an ingenious, and
good-temper'd p. 8:574
Be nice to p. on your way up 12:672
bill of rights is what the p. are entitled to 8:260
good of the p. 4:1
government . . . must be built upon the rights of the p. 12:155
government of the p., by the p., and for the p. 10:209
Hell is other p. 12:901
If p. behaved in the way nations do 13:244
if the p. . . . can be reached with the truth 12:373
indictment against an whole p. 8:196
in trust from the p. to the common good of them all 7:144
my p. live in such awful conditions 12:157
Once the p. begin to reason 8:163
p. . . . are attracted by God 12:876
P. are not fallen angels 12:429
p. are the masters 8:237
p. may be made to follow a course of action 2:3
P. must help one another 8:389
p.'s government 10:41
p. . . . usually imitate each other 13:591
p. who stay in the middle of the road 13:73
Religion . . . is the opium of the p. 10:602
show my head to the p. 9:26
the bludgeoning of the p. 11:65
the p. are forbidden to light lamps 12:244
The p.'s flag is deepest red 11:61
The p. would be just as noisy 7:158
there are no unimportant p. 13:929
The right p. are rude 12:656
This country . . . belongs to the p. who inhabit it 10:193
two kinds of p. in the world 13:611
we are not a small p. 13:892
When . . . it becomes necessary for one p. to dissolve political bonds 8:206
When the P. contend for their Liberty 8:46
You can fool too many of the p. 12:988
perception prime agent of all human p. 10:359
perestroika essence of p. 13:397
Russian word 'p.' has easily entered the international lexicon 13:399
perfection P. has one grave defect 12:827
The pursuit of p. 10:575
performing English literature's p. flea 12:504

perfumes No p., but very fine linen 9:131
peril an imperative principle which statesmen . . . ignore at
their p. 12:75
perish they that take the sword shall p. with the sword
3:133
though the world p. 7:44
permanence love p. more than . . . beauty 13:455
pernicious the most p. race 8:97
Peron If a woman like Eva P. with no ideals 13:336
perpetual Literary men are . . . a p. priesthood 10:287
perpetuation Why should I consent to the p. of the image
of this image 4:35
persecutest Saul, why p. thou me 3:45
persecution P. produced its natural effect 7:418
perseverance the name of p. in a good cause 8:556
persistent The most p. sound . . . through men's history
13:569
person the only thing that can exist is an uninterested p.
11:262
personalities all great events and p. in . . . history reappear
10:137
personality Simply a radio p. 13:213
perversion that melancholy sexual p. known as continence
12:812
War is, after all, the universal p. 13:830
pessimism P. is a luxury that a Jew never can allow himself 13:894
pessimist Scratch a p. 12:743
the p. fears this is true 12:600
Peter thou art P. 3:23
Petersburg the final stone . . . in the foundation of St P.
8:82
petrified a man suffering from p. adolescence 13:34
petticoat lay aside . . . modesty . . . and put it on again with
her p. 7:311
phallic the deterrent is a p. symbol 13:197
Pharisees the scribes and P. 3:101
phenomena chess-board is the world; the pieces . . . the p.
of the universe 10:495
philanthropist Suspicion . . . necessary for the p. 12:822
Philistines For this class we have . . . the designation of P.
10:324
society distributes itself into Barbarians, P., and Populace
10:250
to distinguish . . . the aristocratic class from the P. 10:252
philosopher I doubt if the p. lives . . . who could know himself . . . despised by a street boy 11:517
In the p. there is nothing whatever impersonal 11:514
p. . . . doesn't think in a vacuum 13:537
some p. has said it 4:95
The p. is Nature's pilot 11:264
To a p. no circumstance . . . is too minute 8:642
When you were ill you behaved like a true p. 12:956
philosophers good understanding between the chymists
and the mechanical p. 8:613
now-a-days professors of philosophy but not p. 10:632
P. are as jealous as women 12:953
p. have only interpreted the world 11:39
serious p. . . . looking forward to the pension 13:1013
the English are . . . the least a nation of pure p. 10:240
till p. become kings 2:8
philosophical European p. tradition . . . consists of a series
of footnotes to Plato 12:545
philosophy a great advantage for . . . p. to be . . . true
12:546
Art and religion first; then p. 13:544
Axioms in p. are not axioms 10:360
collection of prejudices which is called political p. 13:165
dreamt of in your p. 7:280
History is p. . . . by examples 4:41
necessary for a superstition to enslave a p. 12:877
new P. calls all in doubt 7:407
Not to care for p. 8:635
now-a-days professors of p. but not philosophers 10:632
p. and vain deceit 3:62
P., . . . is a fight against . . . fascination 12:548
P. is not a theory 12:533
P. is the product of wonder 12:547, 12:717
point of p. is to start with something so simple 12:550

Vain wisdom all, and false p. 8:325
phoney a p. war 12:318
photograph A p. is not only an image 13:493
she took down the signed p. of the Kaiser 12:7
photography P. can never grow up if it imitates 13:418
phrase Self-determination is not a mere p. 12:75
physical a p. and metaphysical impossibility 10:286
no right to assume that any p. laws exist 12:905
physician The p. can bury his mistakes 13:990
physicians the help of too many p. 2:75
physics Classical p. . . . superseded by quantum theory
13:126
Modern P. is an instrument of Jewry 12:933
The content of p. is the concern 13:948
Piccadilly Good-bye P., Farewell Leicester Square 12:16
pickle weaned on a p. 12:243
picnic futile to attempt a p. in Eden 13:579
picture If you want a p. of the future 13:1028
pictures would never buy my p. 10:301
piece A p. of each of us died at that moment 13:185
p. of divinity in us 7:308
What a p. of work is a man 7:240
pies I could eat one of Bellamy's veal p. 9:60
pig p. of a Henry VIII 7:112
pigs What men call social virtues, . . . is . . . but the virtue of
p. in a litter 10:563
Pilate P. . . . washed his hands 3:33
rather have blood on my hands . . . P. 13:216
pillar a p. of a cloud 1:37
a p. of salt 1:25
the lie has become . . . a p. of the State 13:284
pilot Dropping the p. 11:62
Pimpernel That damned elusive P. 11:539
pin you are like a p., but without . . . head or . . . point
10:440
pinching I just keep painting till I feel like p. 12:432
pinko-gray white races are . . . p. 12:154
pint one cannot put a quart in a p. cup 12:983
pious A p. man . . . would be an atheist 8:590
p. frauds of friendship 8:416
piped their fountains p. an answer 2:85
pipers Wi' a hundred p. an' a', an' a' 8:664
pips squeezed – until the p. squeak 12:99
pissing inside my tent p. out 13:252
pitchfork drive out nature with a p. . . . she'll be constantly
running back 8:86
pitied one has . . . ceased to be an object of *fear* as soon
as one is p. 11:282
pitifully barefoot and wearing coarse wool, he stood p.
5:13
Pitt P. . . . given by the people to the King 8:182
P. is to Addington 9:45
pity A p. beyond all telling 11:379
My subject is War, and the p. of War 12:20
p. for the suffering of mankind 13:608
The Poetry is in the p. 12:20
To marry a man out of p. is folly 12:766
To show p. is felt as a sign of contempt 11:282
place A p. for everything 11:329
everything in its p. 11:329
firm p. to stand 2:79
give p. to better men 7:157
I go to prepare a p. for you 3:114
That is the right p. 10:107
there's no p. like home 10:514
the summit of Everest was hardly the p. 13:77
this is an awful p. 11:158
plagues of all p. with which mankind are curst 8:75
plain be p. and simple 8:268
be yourself, imperial, p. and true 10:425
plaisir P. d'amour 8:494
planet it fell on the wrong p. 12:388
When a new p. swims into his ken 10:257
plans Life . . . happens . . . while you're busy making other p[?]
13:733
The finest p. have always been spoiled 12:636
what a man still p. . . . shows the . . . injustice in his death
13:529

Plantagenet   the winding ivy of a P. should kill the . . . tree   6:134
plants   bottinney means a knowledge of p.   10:372
p. left over from the Edwardian Wilderness   13:665
plate   clean your p.   11:99
the silver p. on a coffin   10:64
platitude   A p. is simply a truth repeated   12:594
platitudes   Literature is the orchestration of p.   13:423
Plato   P. is dear to me   2:66
platonic   I know nothing about p. love   12:762
play   a p. is a dynamic thing   13:445
Better than a p.   8:14
Judge not the p.   7:179
p., I remember, pleas'd not the million   7:171
P. up! p. up! and p. the game   11:541
Rehearsing a p. is making the word flesh   13:476
writing a good p. is difficult   13:482
player   poor p., That struts and frets his hour   7:287
players   men and women merely p.   7:274
play-going   A good many inconveniences attend p.   13:432
plays   p. about rape, sodomy and drug addiction   13:449
plaything   A book that furnishes no quotations is, . . . a p.   10:281
plead   Arise, O Lord, p. Thine own cause   7:6
please   go anywhere I damn well p.   13:50
I . . . do what I p.   8:178
Music, Maestro, P.   12:987
Nothing can permanently p.   10:545
They . . . say what they p.   8:178
pleasing   The art of p. consists in   9:153
the surest method . . . of p.   8:553
pleasure   breathe the p. of natural freedom   6:94
Everyone is dragged on by their favourite p.   4:47
gave p. to the spectators   8:591
hatred is by far the longest p.   10:501
He that takes p. to hear sermons   8:396
knowledge and wonder . . . is an impression of p.   7:218
no sterner moralist than P.   10:547
P. after all is a safer guide   11:439
P. is . . . intermission of pain   8:397
P. is . . . seldom found where it is sought   8:419
p. requires an aristocratic setting   11:357
Romanticism is . . . presenting people with the literary works . . . affording . . . the greatest . . . p.   10:277
The only sensual p. without vice   8:305
The sight . . . gave me infinite p.   9:170
The ugliest of trades have their moments of p.   10:634
understanding will . . . extinguish p.   12:479
what p. . . . they have in taking their roguish tobacco   7:192
Youth is full of p.   7:273
pleasures   Mid p. and palaces though we may roam   10:514
No man is a hypocrite in his p.   8:433
P. are all alike   8:396
P. newly found are sweet   9:148
The English take their p.   7:387
pledges   Count not his broken p. as a crime   12:128
plenty   that p. should attain the poor   10:18
plot   p. hath many changes   7:179
p. was to have blown up the King   7:90
plough   To get it ready for the p.   13:506
plowshares   beat their swords into p.   1:53
pluck   if thy right eye offend thee, p. it out   3:82
plunder   What a place to p.   9:194
plus   P. ça change   10:465
Plymouth   dreamin' . . . o' P. Hoe   7:63
poacher   a p. a keeper turned inside out   10:434
pocket   To be played with both hands in the p.   11:196
pockets   the p. of the people   8:213
poem   A p. lovely as a tree   12:427
I do not think this p. will reach its destination   8:302
My p. are hymns of praise   13:425
poems   p. . . . for the love of Man and in praise of God   13:424
that Anon, who wrote so many p.   12:795
We all write p.   13:464
poet   a p. past thirty-five . . . seems . . . unnatural and obscene   12:435
A true p. does not bother to be poetical   12:440

godly p. must be chaste himself   2:25
no person can be a p. . . . without . . . unsoundness of mind   10:276
No p., no artist of any sort, has his complete meaning alone   12:461
p. without love   10:286
The p. gives us his essence   13:417
The p. is the priest   13:433
the p. . . . keep ajar the door that leads to madness   12:443
The p. speaks . . . of that other life   12:471
To be a p. is a condition   13:408
unmourned and unknown . . . because they lack their sacred p.   2:82
poetic   the laws of p. truth and p. beauty   11:181
poetical   A true poet does not bother to be p.   12:440
poetry   As civilization advances, p. . . . declines   10:275
Even when p. has a meaning   12:479
If p. comes not . . . as leaves to a tree   10:262
Mr Shaw . . . has never written any p.   11:214
no man ever talked p.   10:285
P. is a comforting piece of fiction   12:434
P. is as exact a science as geometry   10:307
P. is as much a part of the universe   13:458
P. is baroque   12:494
P. is essentially an amateur activity   13:495
p. is . . . more philosophical . . . than history   2:31
P. is opposed to science, . . . prose to metre   10:260
P. is the record of the best and happiest moments   10:268
P. is the spontaneous overflow of powerful feelings   9:119
P. is to prose   13:488
P. makes nothing happen   12:505
P. . . . man explores his own amazement   13:416
p. reminds him of the richness   13:452
P. . . . set to more or less lascivious music   12:434
P. should be great and unobtrusive   10:261
p. sinks and swoons under . . . prose   10:272
p. = the best words in the best order   10:282
p., 'The Cinderella of the Arts.'   11:198
P. . . . the synthesis of hyacinths and biscuits   12:444
Superstition is the p. of life   10:445
that is p.   13:470
The difference between genuine p.   11:182
The P. is in the pity   12:20
truest p. is the most feigning   7:170
What is p.   11:183
poets   among the English P. after my death   10:263
excellent p. that have never versified   7:166
if you include me among the lyric p., I'll hold my head . . . high . . .   4:27
I hate the whole race . . . your professional p.   10:284
Immature p. imitate   12:437
nor even booksellers have put up with p.' being second-rate   4:30
Painters and p. . . . licence to dare anything   4:33
P. and painters are outside the class system   13:1007
p. are the ones who write in words   13:464
Popular p. are the parish priests   11:212
point   you are like a pin, but without . . . head or . . . p.   10:440
poison   food to one man is bitter p. to others   4:45
strongest p. ever known   9:47
pokers   Wreathe iron p. into true-love knots   10:266
pole   climbed to the top of the greasy p.   10:245
Pole   folly of one brainsick P.   7:27
Poles   few virtues . . . the P. do not possess   12:415
police   improvement of the situation of a common p. constable   10:33
P. State . . . always regards all opposition as a crime   13:11
the exercise of an international p. power   11:122
policeman   park, a p. and a pretty girl   13:634
This definition . . . would not do for a p.   10:635
policemen   repressed sadists . . . become p. or butchers   12:968
policy   My home p.? I wage war   12:76
polished   Satire should, like a p. razor keen   8:438
polite   it costs nothing to be p.   12:363
p. by telling lies   13:886
political   addiction of p. groups to ideas   13:113
After all, we are not p. whores   12:250

a man who was lucky enough to have discovered a p. theory 13:257
Every intellectual attitude is latently p. 13:555
Jesus was ... a first-rate p. economist 11:481
most schemes of p. improvement are very laughable 8:170
necessary elements ... of p. life 10:179
one of these is the history of p. power 12:572
p. speech and writing are largely the defence of the indefensible 13:49
retired into ... his p. Cave of Adullam 10:234
That points clearly to a p. career 11:133
the formation of the p. will of the nation 12:222
When in the course of human events, it becomes necessary for one people to dissolve ... p. bonds 8:206
politician A p. is an arse 13:988
A p. rises on the backs 13:151
A statesman is a p. who 13:273
A statesman is a p. who's been dead 13:109
at home you're just a p. 13:106
every Labour p. feels more at home attacking his own 13:265
p. never believes what he says 13:162
the p. poses as the servant 13:250
The proper memory for a p. 12:59
unfair to expect a p. to live ... up to the statements he makes in public 12:954
politicians All p. have vanity 13:1015
all the p. ... least significant was Bonar Law 12:140
P. ... can never forgive being ignored 13:1012
P. neither love nor hate 8:636
politics are too serious ... to be left to the p. 13:249
P. ... promise to build bridges 13:134
There is just one rule for p. 12:206
politics An independent ... wants to take the p. out of p. 13:124
A week is a long time in p: 13:210
Britain is no longer in the p. of the pendulum 13:317
can't adopt p. ... and remain honest 12:234
his amusements, like his p., are essentially destructive 11:43
History is past p. 11:273
I am not made for p. 13:58
In p., ... ask a woman 13:358
in p. there is no heart, only head 9:75
making p. Christian 13:931
Men who have greatness ... don't go in for p. 12:257
Never judge a country by its p. 12:865
P. are now nothing more than 8:193
p. are too serious ... to be left to the politicians 13:249
P. come from man. Mercy 13:372
P. is a blood sport 13:42
P. is not an exact science 10:213
P. is the art of preventing people from taking part 12:386
P. is ... the only profession 11:513
p. was the second lowest profession 13:1009
that men enter local p. 13:770
There are times in p. 13:224
the science of p. deals with the government of men 10:88
they can at least pretend that p. is a game 13:110
War is the continuation of p. 10:47, 13:40
polloi the multitude, the hoi p. 8:56
polluter intelligence is the great p. 13:955
polonies My father ... deals in nice p. 10:82
polygamy P. was made a Sin 8:34
Pomeranian The healthy bones of a single P. grenadier 11:7
pomp In lowly p. ride on to die 10:598
Pride, p., and circumstance 7:95
solemnized with p. and parade 8:205
Poms All the faces ... seem to be bloody P. 13:1025
pondered Mary ... p. them in her heart 3:7
pontifical royal power takes all its reputation ... from the p. power 6:25
poodle Mr Balfour's P. 11:130
poor A p. man is despised the whole world over 11:500
a p. society cannot be too p. 12:937
as difficult to elevate the p. ... depress the rich 10:56
ask of the p. that they get up and act 13:980
cynical gestures of the p. 12:176

decent means p. 10:625
Hard to train to accept being p. 4:92
I, being p., have only my dreams 12:670
If a free society cannot help the ... p. 13:979
it is p. grub, p. pay, and easy work 11:111
Laws grind the p. 8:151
many a p. man ... has been relieved and helped by him 6:83
only the p. who pay cash 12:939
p. have no right to the property of the rich 10:208
P. Little Rich Girl 12:981
p. relation 10:512
Resolve not to be p. 8:632
short and simple annals of the p. 8:627
that plenty should attain the p. 10:18
the p. are our brothers and sisters 13:983
the p. ... need love, ... need care, ... have to be wanted 13:983
To be p. and independent 10:624
very p. are unthinkable 11:508
poorer for richer for p. 7:339
poorest p. ... hath a life to live as the greatest 7:132
p. man may in his cottage bid defiance to ... the Crown 8:148
pop In England, p. art and fine art 13:436
popery No P., No Slavery 8:28
popish their deliverer from P. tyranny 8:53
poppies the p. blow 12:28
populace society distributes itself into Barbarians, Philistines, and P. 10:250
the p. cannot exact their demands 10:60
this vast residuum we may ... give the name of P. 10:253
popular Nothing can render them p. 8:605
The worse I do, the more p. I get 13:148
We're more p. than Jesus Christ 13:460
popularity P.? ... glory's small change 10:459
P. is a crime 8:540
population a starving p. 10:96
The purpose of p. ... is to fill heaven 13:930
populi vox p., vox dei 5:5
pornography P. is the attempt to insult sex 12:749
p. ... it is terribly, terribly boring 13:755
p. of war 13:830
portion best p. of a good man's life 9:187
portrait Every man's work ... is always a p. of himself 11:206
possess poor men and rich may p. what they rightly acquire 5:9
possessior, The p. of a book 13:550
possessions Not the owner of many p. will you be right to call happy 4:50
possibility too much of a sceptic to deny the p. of anything 11:251
possible something is p., he is ... right 13:959
the art of the p. 13:256
The only way of finding the limits of the p. 13:715
postchaise You are forgetting the p. 10:32
posterity doing something for p. 8:456
Think of your p. 9:43
postgraduate The British p. student is a lonely forlorn soul 13:558
potent how p. cheap music is 12:472
pound the p. ... in your pocket 13:219
pounds the p. will take care of themselves 8:626
poverty crime so shameful as p. 8:625
declares unconditional war on p. in America 13:196
Do you call p. a crime 11:505
For every talent that p. has stimulated 13:978
generations ... have struggled in p. to build these altars 11:468
If p. is the mother of crime, stupidity is its father 8:451
It is easy enough to say that p. is no crime 11:500
Loneliness ... is the most terrible p. 13:725
p. ... is a blunder 11:500
P. is a great enemy to human happiness 8:632
P. is an anomaly to rich people 11:497
The misfortunes of p. 4:93
three great evils, boredom, vice, and p. 8:641
world p. is primarily a problem of two million villages 13:976

powder when your p.'s runnin' low 7:64

power All P. to the Soviets 12:62

All that is literature seeks to communicate p. 10:310

As we make sex less secretive, we may rob it of its p. 13:757

corridors of p. 13:99

don't have p. if you surrender all your principles 13:405

Germany will be . . . a world p. 12:137

greater the p. 8:181

In a country economically backward, the proletariat can take p. earlier 12:175

its source of p.: ownership 13:295

Knowledge itself is p. 7:220

life depends on your p. to master words 13:566

love of p. is the love of ourselves 10:549

Men of p. have not time to read 13:122

one of these is the history of political p. 12:572

P. . . . and Liberty . . . are seldom upon good Terms 8:47

P. corrupts 13:192

p. has been the vice of the ascetic 12:893

p. is apt to corrupt 8:172

P. is the ultimate aphrodisiac 13:302

p. should always be distrusted 8:248

P. tends to corrupt 11:54

p. without responsibility 12:207

royal p. takes all its reputation . . . from the pontifical p. 6:25

The balance of p. 8:116

The English nation . . . has successfully regulated the p. of its kings 8:570

the exercise of an international police p. 11:122

the foul dregs of his p., the tools of despotism and corruption 8:145

the kingdom of God is not in word, but in p. 3:118

The p. of kings and magistrates 7:144

they . . . take, who have the p. 9:165

unable to influence events . . . do not have the p. 13:325

War knows no p. 12:30

When p. narrows the areas of man's concern 13:452

You only have p. over people 13:240

powerful a more p. or a more violent empire 12:97

Guns will make us p. 12:274

powers a taste for *hidden* and *forbidden* 11:488

England is one of the greatest p. of the world 10:177

I have exercised the p. committed to me from no corrupt or interested motives 10:103

the p. of a first-rate man and the creed of a second-rate man 10:122

practical meddling with any p. part of life 8:455

P. men, . . . are usually the slaves of some defunct economist 12:276

practice a thing may look evil in theory, . . . in p. excellent 8:262

practise two kinds of morality . . . one which we preach but do not p. 12:818

praise bury Caesar, not to p. him 4:7

Damn with faint p. 8:656

how a man takes p. 12:604

if we p. ourselves fearlessly, something will always stick 7:364

My poems are hymns of p. 13:425

P. the Lord and pass the ammunition 12:360

The moment you p. a book 13:422

To refuse p. 8:528

we but p. ourselves in other men 8:545

praises He who p. everybody 8:563

praising advantage of . . . p. . . . oneself 11:440

pray Common people do not p. 11:236

watch and p. 3:59

when ye p., use not vain repetitions 3:102

praye Fare well . . . and p. for me 7:20

prayer cravings . . . do not become a p. 13:917

More things are wrought by p. 10:608

most odious of . . . narcissisms – p. 13:921

the Conservative Party at p. 12:55

The people's p. 8:32

The p. that . . . heals the sick 11:464

prayers The hopes and p. of liberty-loving people 12:390

prays man p. . . . for a miracle 10:609

preach two kinds of morality . . . one which we p. but do not practise 12:818

preaching A woman's p. is like a dog's walking on his hinder legs 8:521

illuminate our whole country with the bright light of their p. 6:34

precious Right is more p. 12:803

so p. that it must be rationed 12:148

that most p. jewel, the Word of God 7:32

pre-cognitive Love means the p. flow 12:752

predestination Free Will and P. 12:201

predictions Dreams and p. 7:294

preferred he . . . coming after me is p. before me 3:11

pregnancy quite lawful for a Catholic woman to avoid p. by . . . mathematics 13:909

prejudge I do not . . . p. the past 13:274

prejudice skilled appeals to religious p. 10:619

prejudices collection of p. which is called political philosophy 13:165

Common sense is the collection of p. 13:561

freedom to print . . . proprietor's p. 12:171

premise fundamental p. of a revolution 12:212

pre-natal the greatness of Russia is only her p. struggling 12:110

preparation life . . . seems to me p. for something that never happens 12:731

no p. is thought necessary 11:513

prepare I go to p. a place for you 3:114

presbyter P. is but old Priest writ large 7:129

present novelists the story of the p. 10:323

P. mirth hath present laughter 7:320

The future will one day be the p. 12:729

to know nothing but the p., or nothing but the past 12:566

preservation Government has no other end but the p. of property 8:31

preserve meeting together to p. ourselves 10:51

president not choose to run for P. in 1928 12:167

one thing about being P. 13:75

the P. is dead, but the Government lives 10:231

We are all the P.'s men 13:278

press would not say that our P. is obscene 13:513

presume Dr Livingstone, I p. 11:525

Know then thyself, p. not God to scan 8:407

pretty P. witty Nell 8:3

preventing Politics is the art of p. people from taking part 12:386

prevents Nothing p. us from being natural 8:377

price her p. is far above rubies 1:81

The natural p. of labour 10:3

the p. of everything and the value of nothing 11:291

those men have their p. 8:110

prick If you p. us, do we not bleed 7:231

pricks to kick against the p. 3:45

pride Is P., the never-failing vice of fools 8:546

it is p., but understood in a different way 10:580

p. goeth before destruction 1:82

So sleeps the p. of former days 9:49

the kind of p. least likely to offend 11:432

There is false modesty, but there is no false p. 11:451

prides His Royal Highness . . . p. himself upon . . . the excellent harvest 9:82

priest For a p. to turn a man when he lies a-dying 8:592

Presbyter is but old P. writ large 7:129

rid me of this turbulent p. 6:11

Priest-craft e'r P. did begin 8:34

priesthood kingdom and the p., are brought together by divine mystery 5:10

Literary men are . . . a perpetual p. 10:287

priests All things, oh p., are on fire 2:68

In old time we had treen chalices and golden p. 7:45

prime minister It will be years . . . before a woman will . . . become P. 13:282

society . . . pays a harlot 25 times as much as it pays its P. 13:177

that of P. is filled by fluke 13:391

when a British P. sneezed 13:309

prime ministers rogue elephant among British p. 12:127

prince p. of royal courage 7:18

P. was . . . a libertine over head and ears in debt 9:95

the P. . . . is restrained from doing ill 8:570

Prince Regent patronized . . . by Brummel and the P.
9:132

princes mine were p. of the earth 10:436
p. learn no art truly, but . . . horsemanship 7:114

principle an imperative p. which statesmen . . . ignore at
their peril 12:75
except from some strong p. 10:399
the most useful thing about a p. . . . sacrificed to expediency
12:808

principles All universal moral p. are idle fancies 8:567
easier to fight for one's p. 12:603
It is often easier to fight for p. 13:821
The p. of a free constitution 8:219
The p. of logic and metaphysics are true 12:554
whoever is moved . . . is conscious of a continued miracle
. . . which subverts all the p. of his understanding 8:598

print decomposing in the eternity of p. 12:448

printers those books by which the p. have lost 7:222

priorities The language of p. is 12:324

prison an extraordinarily pleasant p. 13:1016
Stone walls do not a p. make 7:119
The p. inspector . . . would never look at a p. 10:13
the true place for a just man is also a p. 10:121
The world . . . is but a large p. 7:283

prisoner I object to your being taken p. 12:12

prisoners p. of addiction and . . . p. of envy 12:685

prisons not enough p. . . . in Palestine to hold all the Jews
12:346
P. are built with stones of Law 9:25

private most beautiful in Britain . . . in p. hands 13:401
sex has been a very p . . . secretive activity 13:757
The knell of p. property sounds 10:244

privilege a defender of p. 12:743
an Englishman's heaven-born p. of doing as he likes 10:253

privileges men value . . . not rights but p. 12:597

privily hanged p. by night 6:29

prize Not all that tempts your wand'ring eyes . . . is lawful p.
8:465

prizes just miss the p. at the flower show 13:649
The world continues to offer glittering p. 12:685

P.R.O. partly a liaison man and partly P. 13:993

problem ineffectual liberal's p. 13:211
Not every p. someone has with his girlfriend is . . . due to
. . . capitalist . . . production 13:321

problems There are two p. in my life 13:195

procreation Abortion . . . an appalling trivialisation of . . . p.
13:844

producing Man . . . consumes without p. 12:422

production Capitalist p. begets . . . its own negation
10:243

profaned from the province they have desolated and p.
11:6

profession Politics is . . . the only p. 11:513

professors American p. like their literature clear and cold
and pure and very dead 12:469
As to religion, . . . duty of government to protect all . . . p.
thereof 8:216
Culture is an instrument wielded by p. 13:535
now-a-days p. of philosophy but not philosophers 10:632

profit Drop . . . what tomorrow may bring . . . count as p. every day that Fate allows you 4:62

profound turbid look the most p. 10:273

progress All p. is based 11:351
history of England is . . . the history of p. 10:393
Man's 'p.' is but a gradual discovery 13:646
Our p. . . . Is trouble and care 11:326
P. . . . depends on retentiveness 11:276
'p.' is simply a comparative 11:356
What p. . . . In the Middle Ages 12:232

progression Without Contraries is no p. 9:158

prohibition Communism is like p. 12:169

proletarian substitution of the p. for the bourgeois state
12:63

proletariat In a country economically backward, the p. can
take power earlier 12:175
The dictatorship of the p. 10:128
the p. will . . . wage a class struggle for Socialism 12:147

prolonged the War is being deliberately p. 12:86

promise rarely . . . one can see in a little boy the p. of a
man 10:538

promised Only do always in health what you have often p.
to do when you are sick 6:107

promises Indian wars have had their origin in broken p.
11:11
young man of p. 11:90

promptly He gives twice who gives p. 4:80

pronounce p. foreign names as he chooses 13:655

pronounced not only suspected but p. for a witch 7:131

pronouncements Science should leave off making p.
12:924

propaganda P. . . . consists in nearly deceiving your friends
13:828

propagandist The p.'s purpose 12:295

propagated If human beings could be p. . . . aristocracy
would be . . . sound 12:220

propagation we were meerly intended for the world's p.
8:510

proper The p. study of Mankind is Man 8:407

property Government has no other end but the preserva-
tion of p. 8:31
P. has its duties 10:75
P. is organised robbery 11:131
P. is theft 10:86
poor have no right to the p. of the rich 10:208
The future is the only kind of p. 13:60
The knell of private p. sounds 10:244
the right of governing was not p. but a trust 8:254

prophet A historian is a p. in reverse 9:143

Prophet single look at the P.'s face 5:4

proportion strangeness in the p. 7:292

proportional representation P. . . . fundamentally
counter-democratic 13:362

propose oppose everything, and p. nothing 10:87

proposes Man p. 6:125

proposition undesirable to believe a p. 12:543

propriety The p. of . . . having improper thoughts about . . .
neighbours 12:819

prose difference between . . . p. and metrical composition
9:120
good p. should resemble the conversation 12:496
P. . . . can bear a great deal of poetry 10:272
Poetry is opposed to science, . . . p. to metre 10:260
Poetry is to p. 13:488
poetry sinks and swoons under . . . p. 10:272
p. = words in their best order 10:282
the cradle of English p. 6:137
to write good p. is an affair of good manners 12:494

prosper Treason doth never p. 7:104

prosperitee A man to have ben in p. 6:130

prostitutes the small nations like p. 13:189

protect countries of western Europe . . . no longer . . . p.
themselves 13:76
p. the writer 13:614

protection Every man who comes to England is entitled to
the p. of the English law 8:184

protestant Gunpowder, Printing, and the P. Religion
10:458
I am the P. whore 8:20
Too much counterpoint; what is worse, P. counterpoint
8:669

protestants God knows how you P. . . . have any sense of
direction 13:906

proud He who does not need to lie is p. 11:284
no guarantee . . . you will not be p. of the feat 13:847
scattered the p. 3:106
too p. to fight 12:26

proudest the moment of greatest humiliation is . . . when
the spirit is p. 11:137

proved p. upon our pulses 10:360
What is now p. was . . . imagined 9:136
Which was to be p. 2:77

proverb A p. is much matter 8:323
no p. to you till your life has illustrated it 10:447

proverbs p. provide them with wisdom 11:253

providence that P. dictates with the assurance of a sleepwalker 12:268

Q

R

rapidly Lord Raglan wishes the cavalry to advance r. 10:146

rarity Their r. prompts them to be the first nation 10:85

rascal Get down you dirty r. 10:656

rascals R., would you live for ever 8:129

ratchet politics of the pendulum, but of the r. 13:317

rationalized Happiness . . . should never be r. 11:306

rats I see some r. have got in 11:142

ravages What do the r. of time not injure 4:12

ravished He . . . r. this fair creature 8:490

raw the working-class which, r. and half-developed 10:253

razor Satire should, like a polished r. keen 8:438

reach a man's r. should exceed his grasp 10:480

read books. . . . criticized and r. by people who don't understand them 8:292
Education . . . has produced a vast population able to r. 12:558
everybody wants to have r. 11:200
King George will be able to r. that 8:209
Men of power have not time to r. 13:122
will bear to be r. twice, . . . was thought twice 10:295

reader A r. seldom peruses a book with pleasure 8:277
not to inform the r. 13:614

readers his r. are proud to live in it 12:492
to trade a hundred contemporary r. for 13:419
Was there ever yet anything written . . . that was wished longer by its r. 8:285

reading a substitute for r. it 13:550
a tragedy and therefore not worth r. 9:118
Peace is poor r. 11:274
R. . . . ingenious device for avoiding thought 10:377
R. is to the mind 8:332
R. maketh a full man 7:221
There are two motives for r. a book 12:470
The r. of all good books 7:181

ready necessity of being r. increases 10:194

real art . . . r. which is . . . in our minds 12:462
Nothing ever becomes r. till it is experienced 10:447

reality As far as the laws of mathematics refer to r. 12:919
Cannot bear very much r. 12:624
statesmen of the world . . . are far more dangerous, and far more estranged from . . . r. 13:135
The whole of art is an appeal to a r. 12:462

realm A worse king never left a r. undone 10:10
no one in the r. . . . fitly to come to me 6:71
One R. 12:242

reap sown the wind . . . r. the whirlwind 1:57
whatsoever a man soweth, that shall he also r. 3:70

reaper a R. whose name is Death 10:354

reappear all great events and personalities in . . . history r. 10:137

reason always with right r. dwells 8:12
A man who does not lose his r. 8:423
Faith consists in believing when it is beyond the power of r. to believe 8:609
Happiness is not an ideal of r. 8:435
he who destroys a good book, kills r. 7:182
Human r. won. Mankind won 13:160
man . . . is R.'s slave 13:582
nothing is law that is not r. 8:73
not to r. why 10:149
Once the people begin to r. 8:163
Only r. can convince us 12:817
R. is itself a matter of faith 11:362
The madman . . . has lost everything except his r. 11:309
the r. of the case 8:3
The ruling passion conquers r. still 8:408
woman's r. 7:342

reasonable figure of 'The R. Man' 12:568
Who kills a man kills a r. creature 7:182

reasoners most plausible r. 10:409

reasoning abstract r. concerning quantity or number 8:342

reasons Metaphysics is the finding of bad r. 11:254
never give your r. 8:171
The heart has its r. 8:384

rebel how to r. and conform at the same time 13:705
What is a r. 13:57

rebellion A little r. now and then 8:258
a standard of r. 8:52

received a cloud r. him out of their sight 3:43

recession r. when . . . neighbour loses his job 13:108

recognized The true system of the World has been r. 8:346

recoils Revenge . . . back on itself r. 8:533

recompense R. injury with justice 2:2

reconcile How r. this world . . . with . . . my imagining 12:653

recounting calms one's grief by r. it 7:257

recreation woman accepted cooking . . . but man . . . made of it a r. 12:789

red Red lips are not so r. 12:22
She wore false hair and that r. 7:71
The people's flag is deepest r. 11:61
The sand of the desert is sodden r. 11:541
thin r. line tipped with steel 10:151

redeemer I know that my r. liveth 1:94

redundancy hiring taxis . . . handing out r. notices to its own workers 13:376

reform All r. . . . will prove unavailing 10:71
Beginning r. is beginning revolution 10:36

refreshed The tree of liberty must be r. 8:259

refuge God is the immemorial r. of the incompetent 13:914
Idleness . . . the r. of weak minds 8:554
Patriotism is the last r. 8:195

refuse To r. praise 8:528

regenerated France r. by the Revolution 10:130

regime No r. has ever loved great writers 13:466

regiment the Monstrous R. of Women 7:41

register history . . . the r. of the . . . misfortunes of mankind 8:364

regrets the Cup that clears TO-DAY of past R. 10:488
The follies which a man r. 11:354

regulated The English nation . . . has successfully r. the power of its kings 8:570

rehearsing R. a play is making the word flesh 13:476

Reich *Ein R., Ein Volk, Ein Führer* 12:242

reign Better to r. in Hell 8:11

reigned I have r. with your loves 7:80

reigns king r., but does not govern 7:93

reject If you r. me on account of my religion 11:125

rejoiced my spirit hath r. in God my Saviour 3:2

related A group of closely r. persons 13:764

relations great men have their poor r. 10:518

relativity I believe my theory of r. 12:932

relaxation Man . . . can only find r. from one . . . labour by taking up another 11:512

relief thou wilt give thyself r. 4:68

religion Art and r. first; then philosophy 13:544
As to r. . . . . duty of government to protect all . . . professors thereof 8:216
brothels with bricks of R. 9:25
Fascism is a r. 12:229
I am of the same r. as all those who are brave and true 7:50
If you reject me on account of my r. 11:125
Men will wrangle for r. 10:585
none of you suffer for your opinions or r. 7:165
no reason to bring r. into it 12:881
Not a r. for gentlemen 8:13
Nothing is so fatal to r. as indifference 9:198
One r. is as true as another 7:404
One's r. . . . . yours is Success 12:574
R. Has made an honest woman of the supernatural 13:903
R. is an illusion 12:889
R. is by no means a proper subject 8:600
R. is love 12:882
R. . . . is the opium of the people 10:602
r. of feeble minds 9:157
r. of Socialism 12:324
r. without a prelate 10:589
Science without r. is lame 13:938
talks loudly against r. 8:601
that God is interested only . . . in r. 12:874
To become a popular r. 12:877
To die for a r. is easier than to live it absolutely 13:918

when r. was strong . . . men mistook magic for medicine 13:961

eligions a country with thirty-two r. and only one sauce 10:577

The r. we call false were once true 10:593

eligious a r. animal 9:196
first, r. and moral principles 10:368
r. outlook on life 12:890
skilled appeals to r. prejudice 10:619
To be at all is to be r. 11:475

elished the taste by which he is . . . r. 9:121

eluctant The r. obedience of distant provinces 10:26

emedies Extreme r. . . . for extreme diseases 2:73
He that will not apply new r. 7:293
Our r. oft in ourselves do lie 7:241
paralyse it by encumbering it with r. 10:622

emedy a r. for everything except death 7:213
Force is not a r. 11:21
Tis a sharp r., but a sure one 7:106

emember she did not r. . . . her jewelry 12:792
The world will little note, nor long r. 10:209
we shall be glad to r. even these hardships 4:16
We will r. them 12:92
Who will r., . . . The unheroic dead 12:84

emove all faith, so that I could r. mountains 3:95

Renaissance R. is a mere ripple on the surface of literature 6:139
the R. was . . . the green end of one of civilization's hardest winters 6:138

ender r. . . . unto Caesar 3:117

endezvous a r. with Death 12:45

epartee A majority is always the best r. 10:106

epeal the r. of bad or obnoxious laws 10:254

epeat obliged to imitate himself, and to r. 8:352

epeated A platitude is simply a truth r. 12:594

epent r. at leisure 8:500
r.: for the kingdom of heaven is at hand 3:18

epentance A Christian . . . feels R. on a Sunday 11:479
with the morning cool r. 10:395

epetition constant r. will finally succeed in imprinting an idea 12:135

eporter A r. is a man who has renounced everything 12:964

epresentation In Scotland there is no shadow even of r. 9:34
Proportional R. . . . is fundamentally counter-democratic 13:362
Taxation and r. are inseparably united 8:161
Taxation without r. 8:137

eproductions accurate r. of Anne Hathaway's cottage 12:523
I've seen colour r. 12:455

epublic An aristocracy in a r. is like a chicken 13:98

epublics Revolts, r., revolutions 10:464

epugnant Woman to bear rule . . . is r. to Nature 7:340

epulsive Roundheads (Right but R.) 7:421

eputability Conspicuous consumption . . . is a means of r. 11:91

eputation it is better for the r. 12:722
O, I have lost my r. 7:285
spotless r. 7:267
Until you've lost your r., you never realize . . . what freedom really is 12:723

esearch R.! A mere excuse for idleness 11:255
The outcome of any serious r. 12:661

esent To great evils we submit; we r. little provocations 10:400

eservoir a gigantic r. of good will 12:869

esiduum this vast r. we may . . . give the name of Populace 10:253

esist I respect only those who r. me 13:214
r. the devil, and he will flee 3:99
there is almost nothing to r. at all 12:835

esistance the flame of French r. must not . . . be extinguished 12:334

esisting fond of r. temptation 8:565

esolution In war, r. 12:409

esources statistics, born to consume r. 4:61

espect Civilization is . . . equal r. for all men 12:711

The English have no r. for their language 11:462
We owe r. to the living 8:365
When people do not r. us we are sharply offended 11:311

respectable R. means rich 10:625

respects no man much r. himself 11:311

responsibility power without r. 12:207

responsible An idea isn't r. for the people 12:528
r. and the irresponsible classes 12:142
r. and wrong 13:45

rest All the r. have thirty-one 7:415
get rid of the r. of her 8:513
Seek home for r. 7:189
To toil and not to seek for r. 7:349

rested God . . . r. on the seventh day 1:6

restore Time may r. us 10:306

restrained the Prince . . . is r. from doing ill 8:570

restraints the paucity of r. it imposes 11:44

resurrection I am the r., and the life 3:113

retain To expect a man to r. everything that he has ever read 10:380

retreat A mistress should be like a . . . r. 8:497

retrograde All that is human must r. 8:424

return I shall r. 12:368

revels Our r. now are ended 7:174

revenge A man that studieth r. 7:369
if you wrong us, shall we not r. 7:231
I will think upon r. 7:47
R., at first though sweet 8:533
R. . . . back on itself recoils 8:533
R. is a . . . wild justice 7:371

revenue name a virtue that brings in as much r. 10:347

revolts R., republics, revolutions 10:464

revolution Beginning reform is beginning r. 10:36
Britain . . . is going to be forged in the white heat of this r. 13:181
Britain is not . . . easily rocked by r. 13:297
France regenerated by the R. 10:130
fundamental premise of a r. 12:212
he'd go to church, start a r. 13:706
Hitler has carried out a r. on our lines 12:249
R. by its very nature 12:259
R. . . . delightful in the preliminary stages 12:267
restating our socialism in terms of the scientific r. 13:181
r. is a struggle to the death 13:142
Russia is a collapse, not a r. 12:68
single carrot . . . will set off a r. 11:210
spirit of r., . . . is . . . radically opposed to liberty 10:43
The r. eats 13:232
the R. may . . . devour each of her children 9:24
The word 'r.' is a word for which you kill 13:89
to export r. is nonsense 12:265

revolutionary fierce and r. in a bathroom 12:856
If you feed people just with r. slogans 13:258
I would be a r. myself 12:157
Patriotism . . . is a r. duty 12:69
r. right 10:193

revolutions All modern r. have ended 13:59
R. are always verbose 12:211
Revolts, republics, r. 10:464
state of mind which creates r. 2:16

revolver I reach for my r. 12:484

reward The r. of a thing well done 10:555
To labour and not ask for any r. 7:349
Vice is its own r. 13:838

rewarded Men are r. and punished not for what they do 13:618

rewards r. . . . disproprotionate to their usefulness to the community 10:631

rhetoric Out of the quarrel . . . we make r. 11:199

Rhine You think of the R. 12:241

rhyme outlive this powerful r. 7:173
R. being no necessary adjunct or true ornament 8:269

rhythm r. imposes unanimity upon the divergent 13:487

rib the r. . . . made he a woman 1:10

ribbon The blue r. of the turf 10:343

rich A r. man is one 13:970
a r. man shall hardly enter into . . . heaven 3:91
as difficult to elevate the poor . . . depress the r. 10:56

If you can... count your money you are not ... r. man 12:946
nor a r. society too r.   12:937
no sin but to be r.   7:411
poor have no right to the property of the r.   10:208
Poor Little R. Girl   12:981
r. beyond the dreams of avarice   8:628
Respectable means r.   10:625
so large, So friendly, and so r.   13:860
The r. are the scum of the earth   11:510
the r. he hath sent empty away   3:106
The r. man has his motor car   12:940
Richelieu R. leaned to the good   7:118
richer for r. for poorer   7:339
riches God commonly gives r. to those gross asses   7:410
R. are for spending   7:412
R. have wings   8:633
the chief employment of r. consists in the parade of r.
8:630
rid gladly ... am I r. of it all   2:54
riddle a r. wrapped in a mystery inside an enigma   12:316
ride R. on! ride on in majesty   10:598
ridiculous a step from the sublime to the r.   9:90
no spectacle so r.   10:274
The profession of letters ... in which one can make no
money without being r.   11:211
The sublime and the r.   9:160
rift the ... r. between the sexes is ... widened by ... teaching ... to the girls   11:398
right better to be irresponsible and r.   13:45
Every man has a r. to utter what he thinks truth   8:241
God and my r.   6:27
have faith that r. makes might   10:191
I am not and never have been, a man of the r.   12:245
I will defend to the death your r. to say it   8:231, 8:349
Liberty is the r. to do everything   8:123
no r. to strike against public safety   12:105
'orthodoxy' ... no longer means being r.   11:263
our country, r. or wrong   10:1
R. is more precious   12:803
r. mindfulness, r. contemplation   2:62
r. of all ... duty of some   9:87
something is possible, he is ... r.   13:959
That is the r. place   10:107
The customer is always r.   12:153
The Duce is always r.   12:130
The man who gets angry ... in the r. way ... is commended
2:65
The minority is always r.   11:35
The more you are in the r.   12:626
The r. divine of kings to govern wrong   8:99
The r. people are rude   12:656
the r. to be consulted, ... to encourage, ... to warn   10:237
the r. to criticize Shakespeare   11:204
Those who believe that they are exclusively in the r.   12:617
Ulster will be r.   11:49
righteous leave r. ways behind   2:69
righteousness The eternal *not ourselves* that makes for r.
11:422
the r. of the scribes and Pharisees   3:101
rights bill of r. is what the people are entitled to   8:260
government ... must be built upon the r. of the people
12:155
human beings are born free ... dignity and r.   13:18
I do not ask for my r.   10:532
r. and interests of the laboring man   11:105
The Sovereign has, under a constitutional monarchy ...
three r.   10:237
We come, our country's r. to save   10:52
women their r. and nothing less   11:403
Women ... were ready to fight for their own human r.
11:140
ring They now r. the bells   8:111
riot A r. is at bottom   13:221
ripe we r. and r.   7:276
Ripper Jack the R.'s dead   11:59
Yours truly, Jack the R.   11:58
rise Early to r. and early to bed   12:651

Thanks to words, we have been able to r. above the brutes
13:430
rising r. hope of those stern and unbending Tories   10:76
Ritz like the R. hotel   11:134
river build your House of Parliament upon the r.   10:60
On the breast of the r. of Time   10:492
the r. of knowledge has too often turned back on itself
12:924
The vanity of human life is like a r.   8:452
road All I seek ... the r. below me   11:346
roads all r. lead to France   12:54
How many r. must a man walk down   13:680
roam Mid pleasures and palaces though we may r.   10:514
roar luck to give the r.   12:998
robbed when you've r. a man of everything   13:240
robber now Barabbas was a r.   3:30
Robin Who killed Cock R.   6:3
robot the modern conception of a r.   13:21
rock R. and roll or Christianity   13:460
upon this r. I will build my church   3:23
rod he that spareth his r. hateth his son   1:79
spare the r.   8:498
rogues we should indeed be very great r.   10:187
role he saw his r. as being that of Moses   13:313
roll R. up that map   9:57
rolling Like a r. stone   13:693
Roma R. locuta est   5:28
Roman noblest R. of them all   4:9
the Holy R. Empire was neither holy, nor R., nor an empire
8:169
The Papacy is not other than the Ghost of the deceased R.
Empire   7:153
the R. people had but one neck   4:19
Romans Friends, R., countrymen, lend me your ears   4:7
The R. and Greeks found everything human   2:85
Romanticism R. is ... presenting people with the literary
works ... affording ... the greatest ... pleasure   10:277
Romanus Civis R. sum   10:123
Rome R. has spoken; the case is concluded   5:28
R.'s gross yoke Drops off   10:601
said of Augustus that he found R. brick   10:160
so much bounden to the See of R.   7:10
The farther you go from the church of R.   -7:402
without R. Italy cannot be constituted   10:197
room no r. for them in the inn   3:4
The perpetual struggle for r. and food   9:36
Roosevelt the kind of nation that President R. hoped for
13:202
root love of money is the r. of all evil   3:97
the r. of all sins   7:193
rose a r. By any other name   7:229
rosebuds Gather ye r. while ye may   7:330
roses days of wine and r.   11:343
Nor does a ... gardener scent his r.   12:440
Ring-a-ring o'r.   8:5
Treaties are like r. and young girls   13:188
rot we r. and r.   7:276
Rouen forcing R. into submission by starvation   6:63
rough-hew R. them how we will   7:399
round The trivial r., the common task   10:335
Roundheads R. (Right but Repulsive)   7:421
Rowley Heigh ho! says R.   7:416
royal A R. Commission is a broody hen   13:203
at no time stand so highly in our estate r.   7:31
Once in r. David's city   10:595
royalty Prince Henry, ... something of r. in his demeanour
6:86
rub there's the r.   7:209
rubies her price is far above r.   1:81
the price of wisdom is above r.   1:62
rubs sentimentality ... r. you up the wrong way   12:637
rude The right people are r.   12:656
rugby R. Union which is a distillation   13:454
ruin the boy will r. himself   12:258
ruined Such another victory and we are r.   2:17
ruining they will end by r. our idea   12:249
rule A little r., a little sway   8:459
he must r. the roast everywhere   10:77
I don't believe in black majority r.   13:299

S

drawback that s.... invented after I left school 13:965
god of s.... has given us the atomic bomb 13:950
great tragedy of S. 11:491
In everything that relates to s. 10:611
Language is only the instrument of s. 8:354
lastly s. 13:544
one word... to identify modern socialism, it was 'S.'
13:218
only applications of s. 11:485
Poetry is opposed to s.,... prose to metre 10:260
Politics is not an exact s. 10:213
s.... a refinement of everyday thinking 13:939
S.... art of systematic over-simplification 13:964
S. has 'explained' nothing 13:951
Should we force s. down the throats 13:966
s. is essentially international 12:912
S. is nothing but trained and organized common sense
11:490
S. must begin with myths 13:937
S. should leave off making pronouncements 12:924
S. without religion is lame 13:938
the essence of s. 13:958
the greatest collective work of s. 11:548
The highest wisdom has but one s. 10:621
The term S. should not be given to anything 12:928
when religion was strong and s. weak, men mistook magic
for medicine 13:961
sciences Books must follow s. 7:405
Do you... believe that the s. would... have... grown if
the way had not been prepared by magicians 11:488
no such things as applied s. 11:485
s. were transmitted into the Arabic language 5:34
scientific lack of efficiency in using s. achievements for economic needs 13:398
restating our socialism in terms of the s. revolution 13:181
Traditional s. method has always been 13:960
scientist I consider myself superior to the saint, the s.
12:436
When a distinguished but elderly s. states 13:959
scientists in the company of s., I feel like a shabby curate
13:945
The true men of action... are... s.' 13:947
scorer when the One Great S. comes 12:885
scorn Silence is the... perfect expression of s. 12:809
scorned fury like a woman s. 8:514
Scotchman Much may be made of a S. 8:186
the noblest prospect which a S. ever sees 8:573
what it is that makes a S. happy 8:575
Scotchmen trying... to like S. 10:579
Scotland blow the Scots back again into S. 7:89
In S. there is no shadow even of representation 9:34
Switzerland... an inferior sort of S. 9:195
Scots blow the S. back again into Scotland 7:89
Scotsman S. on the make 11:458
the grandest moral attribute of a S. 11:459
scourge whore, and the whoremonger, shall ye s. 5:27
scowl Rachmaninov's immortalizing totality was his s.
12:474
scratch S. the Russian and... find the Tartar 9:193
scribble Always s., s., s. 8:309
Scripture devil can cite S. 7:230
Scriptures I believe firmly what I read in the holy S. 6:126
sculptor not a great s. or painter can be an architect
10:308
scum of the s. of the earth 10:628
The rich are the s. of the earth 11:510
sea fishes live in the s. 7:245
Jesus... walking on the s. 3:22
like throwing water into the s. 7:365
precious stone set in the silver s. 7:69
the midst of the s. upon dry ground 1:38
to the English that of the s. 9:39
We are as near to heaven by s. as by land 7:228
seagreen The s. Incorruptible 9:207
sealed My lips are s. 12:252
seals sealed with seven s. 3:121
search s. for knowledge 13:608
seas That guard our native s. 9:42
the waters called he S. 1:2

season to every thing there is a s. 1:75
seasons a man for all s. 7:11
sea-water Wealth is like s. 10:627
second-hand Would you buy a s. car 13:270
second-rate nor even booksellers have put up with poets'
being s. 4:30
secrecy S. is the first essential 7:117
secret it is no sin to sin in s. 8:524
Three may keep a s. 8:409
secretive As we make sex less s., we may rob it of its
power 13:757
sect sedate, sober, silent, serious, sad-coloured s. 10:590
secure only place where a man can feel... s. 13:803
The past, at least, is s. 10:389
security only freedom can make s. secure 12:424
seditious s. person is an outlaw before God 7:13
see change we think we s. 12:705
My business is to paint... what I s. 10:296
See we received from that S. our Crown 7:10
seek I will undoubtedly have to s.... gainful employment
13:70
s., and ye shall find 3:129
To toil and not to s. for rest 7:349
We s. him here, we s. him there 11:539
seen blessed are they that have not s., and yet have believed 3:42
sees fool s. not the same tree 9:137
Seine Today I spat in the S. 12:394
seize S. the day 4:63
selection Natural S. 10:616
self All censure of a man's s. 8:426
sickness enlarges the dimensions of a man's s. 10:404
to thine own s. be true 7:360
self-denial S. is not a virtue 11:443
self-determination S. is not a mere phrase 12:75
self-indulgence her favourite form of s. 12:788
self-interest S. speaks all sorts of tongues 8:527
selfish all Governments are s. 13:164
French governments more s. than most 13:164
I have been a s. being all my life 9:156
self-love S.... unrequited 13:746
self-sacrifice S. enables us to sacrifice 11:445
semed he s. bisier than he was 6:131
senile a sign that they now consider him s. 12:971
sense because Americans won't listen to s. 12:416
between a man of s. and his books 8:344
Common s. is the collection of prejudices 13:561
Let's talk s. to the American people 13:68
Money is like a sixth s. 12:935
The sound must seem an echo to the s. 8:279
trained and organized common s. 11:490
sensual The only s. pleasure without vice 8:305
sent If this belief from heaven be s. 9:147
sentiment Sentimentality is only s. 12:637
sentimentality S. is a superstructure covering brutality
13:589
S. is only sentiment 12:637
s.... rubs you up the wrong way 12:637
sentiments high s. always win in the end 12:365
separation prepare for a s. 9:87
they should declare the causes which impel them to... s.
8:206
September Thirty days hath S., April, June, and November
7:415
sepulchre To famous men all the earth is a s. 2:50
sepulchres whited s. 3:92
seraphims the s.: each one had six wings 1:96
serf No man should be a s. 6:51
serfdom abolish s. from above 10:161
serious a damned s. business 9:112
A joke's a very s. thing 8:440
they are too s. 8:574
seriously Everything must be taken s., nothing tragically
11:325
sermons He that takes pleasure to hear s. 8:396
serpent the s. beguiled me 1:13
the s. was more subtil 1:11
servant the politician poses as the s. 13:250
servants good s., but bad masters 8:487

half of them prefer hiring their s. for life 10:196

We teachers can only help . . . as s. 13:531

serve capacity to permit his ministers to s. him 7:116

They also s. who only stand and wait 8:582

servitude delivered them from s. to other lands 6:46

sets on which the sun never s. 10:30

settlement coach and six horses through the Act of S. 8:16

seven his acts being s. ages 7:274

sealed with s. seals 3:121

seventh God . . . rested on the s. day 1:6

seventy Being over s. is like being engaged in a war 13:669

Being s. is not a sin 13:714

Oh to be s. again 12:674

severity Summer has set in with its usual s. 10:334

sewage piped growing volumes of s. into the sea 11:546

sex As we make s. less secretive, we may rob it of its power 13:757

Christian view of s. 13:749

Continental people have s. life 13:855

farmyard world of s. 11:381

if there was a third s. 13:795

In the s.-war thoughtlessness is the weapon of the male 12:802

Literature is mostly about having s. 13:457

Money, it turned out, was exactly like s. 13:977

no more weakness than is natural to her s. 2:55

Pornography is the attempt to insult s. 12:749

promiscuous s. in and out of season 12:753

s. has been a very private, secretive activity 13:757

S. is something I really don't understand 13:745

s. . . . must itself be subject . . . to evolution 11:486

the s. novel is now normal 12:467

we English have s. on the brain 13:750

sexes more difference within the s. than between them 13:789

the . . . rift between the s. is . . . widened 11:398

sexual music throatily . . . s. 13:439

shade the s. Of that which once was great 9:154

shadow be caves . . . in which his s. will be shown 11:469

lose the substance by grasping at the s. 2:56

Who live under the s. of a war 13:39

shadows brooding tragedy and its dark s. can be lightened 13:576

shake I will s. my little finger — and there will be no more Tito 13:20

Shakespeare I despise S. 11:213

myriad-minded S. 10:258

remarkable thing about S. 13:456

S. is . . . really very good 13:456

S. never had six lines together without a fault 8:295

S. — the nearest thing 13:437

S., undoubtedly wanted taste 8:293

sweetest S., Fancy's child 7:180

the making up of a S. or a Milton 9:200

the right to criticize S. 11:204

tried lately to read S. 10:316

who speak the tongue That S. spake 9:44

Wonderful women! . . . how much we . . . owe to S. 11:216

shaking all these great interests entrusted to the s. hand 11:66

shambles Our civilization is founded on the s. 11:244

shame expense of spirit in a waste of s. 7:325

Neither s. nor physical pain have any . . . effect 11:452

shapely it's . . . more important for a theory to be s., than . . . true 13:554

share s. in the good fortunes of the mighty 13:27

sharp those who have stout hearts and s. swords 12:685

Shaw Bernard S. 11:177

George Bernard S. is sadly miscast 12:465

Mr S. . . . has never written any poetry 11:214

S.'s mind . . . was still better than anyone else's 12:497

she s. is my country still 8:149

S.-who-must-be-obeyed 11:400

sheathe never s. the sword 12:10

Sheba the queen of S. 1:50

shed s. . . . for the remission of sins 3:27

shedding without s. of blood is no remission 3:51

sheep Baa, baa, black s. 6:56

good shepherd giveth his life for the s. 3:112

like lost s. 8:367

make a man by standing a s. 11:312

savaged by a dead s. 13:319

the wolf in the s.'s clothing 2:33

useless for the s. to pass resolutions in favour of vegetarianism 12:580

Shelley S. and Keats were . . . up to date in . . . chemical knowledge 12:908

the right sphere for S.'s genius 10:299

shells shrill demented choirs of wailing s. 12:90

shepherd I am the good s. 3:112

shepherds Governments needs to have both s. and butchers 8:232

s. abiding in the field 3:5

s. watch'd their flocks 8:593

Sherard S. Blaw, the dramatist who had discovered himself 11:219

shift for coming down let me s. for myself 7:21

ship as the smart s. grew . . . grew the Iceberg too 11:162

places his s. alongside that of an enemy 9:52

The s. follows Soviet custom 13:296

They did not, . . . so much as sink . . . one s. 7:67

ships Heart of oak are our s. 8:132

little s. of England brought the Army home 12:331

S. that pass in the night 11:327

We've got the s., we've got the men, we've got the money too 11:16

shipwreck husbands and wives make s. of their lives 12:770

shit the sun shining ten days a year and s. in the streets 13:893

shock deliberately set out to s. 13:485

shocks s. That flesh is heir to 7:209

shoemaker I take my shoes from the s. 8:608

shook Ten Days that S. the World 12:67

shoot It is not the business of generals to s. one another 9:110

S., if you must, this old gray head 10:199

shooting war minus the s. 12:645

shop All English s. assistants are Miltonists 13:633

A man must keep a little back s. 7:265

shopkeepers A nation of s. 8:210

England is a nation of s. 9:63, 9:192

shopping Today you're unhappy? . . . Go s. 13:706

shore waves make towards the pebbled s. 7:211

short it will take a long while to make it s. 10:321

Life is too s. to do anything . . . one can pay others to do 12:969

s. and simple annals of the poor 8:627

the life of man, solitary, poor, nasty, brutish, and s. 7:149

shortage a s. of coal and fish . . . at the same time 12:421

shorter not had the time to make it s. 8:366

shot had them all s. 10:248

shots God is on the side . . . of the best s. 8:441

They really are bad s. 13:163

should no better than you s. be 7:249

shoulders it is by standing on the s. of giants 8:614

shuffled s. off this mortal coil 7:209

the human pack is s. and cut 13:558

shut when I was there it seemed to be s. 13:902

shyness S. is just egotism out of its depth 13:626

sick A person seldom falls s. 10:430

so many poor s. people in the streets full of sores 8:4

The prayer that . . . heals the s. 11:464

We have on our hands s. man 10:140

sickness in s. and in health 7:339

Love is a s. 7:328

s. enlarges the dimensions of a man's self 10:404

S., sin and death . . . do not originate in God 11:466

side passed by on the other s. 3:16

Time in on our s. 10:233

sides Do not . . . write on both s. of the paper 12:551

sighs S. are the natural language of the heart 8:271

sight we walk by faith, not by s. 3:69

Who ever loved, that loved not at first s. 7:317

sightless clapped the glass to his s. eye 9:41

sights few more impressive s. in the world 11:458

sign   s. of an ill-spent youth   11:305
signal   I really do not see the s.   9:40
signifying   S. nothing   7:287
signing   I am s. my death warrant   12:124
silence   S. is as full of potential wisdom   12:542
S. is the best tactic   8:373
S. is the . . . perfect expression of scorn   12:809
Sorrow and s. are strong   10:557
The cruellest lies are . . . told in s.   11:424
the impression that their normal condition is s.   12:630
silent   the great s. majority   13:247
thereon one must remain s.   12:534
silk   s., too often hides eczema   13:595
silly   some damned s. thing in the Balkans   11:83
silver   Selling the family s.   13:388
simple   A s. race   9:124
short and s. annals of the poor   8:627
simplify   ability to s. means   12:463
S., s.   10:478
simplifying   s. something by destroying nearly everything   12:712
sin   A branch of the s. of drunkenness   7:193
All s. tends to be addictive   13:843
a more dreadful record of s. than . . . countryside   11:228
A private s. is not so prejudicial   7:377
Be a sinner and s. strongly   7:391
Being seventy is not a s.   13:714
he that is without s. . . . let him first cast a stone   3:94
if we say that we have no s., we deceive   3:63
it is no s. to s. in secret   8:524
it's a s. to kill a mockingbird   13:1022
no s. but to be rich   7:411
no s. except stupidity   11:252
S. brought death   11:241
Sickness, s. and death . . . do not originate in God   11:466
which taketh away the s. of the world   3:12
sincere   It is dangerous to be s. unless   11:446
Some of the worst men in the world are s.   13:839
sincerity   A little s. is a dangerous thing   11:429
S. is all that counts . . . modern heresy   12:293
style, not s., is the vital thing   11:344
sinecure   a widow . . . is a kind of s.   8:511
sinews   Anger is one of the s. of the soul   7:259
sinful   Popular stage-plays are s., heathenish   7:200
sing   The Welsh . . . just s.   12:844
we s. no more   11:175
singed   s. the Spanish king's beard   7:59
singing   s. in the rain   12:978
single   a s. man in possession of a good fortune must be in want of a wife   9:179
sinning   nothing so artificial as s. nowadays   12:813
sins   atone for the s. of your fathers   4:14
shed . . . for the remission of s.   3:27
sirens   Blest pair of S.   8:267
sister   no friend like a s.   10:519
sisters   little s. to all the world   12:791
O! men with s. dear   10:525
sit   I will s. down now   10:68
nobody can tell you when to s. down   13:75
say what you have to say, and then s. down   10:7
sitting   by s. down round you   10:60
situation   s. excellent. I shall attack   12:80
six   Candidates should not attempt more than s.   11:322
two and two do not make s.   11:480
sixth   Money is like a s. sense   12:935
sixty   at the rate of s. minutes an hour   12:740
S. horses wedged in a chimney   13:1018
skill   S. without imagination is craftsmanship   13:472
skin   never . . . sell the bear's s.   8:382
skinning   When you are s. your customers   13:150
skins   beauty of their s.   10:527
skirt   a woman . . . ought to lay aside . . . modesty with her s.   7:311
slain   a lamb as it had been s.   3:122
Saul hath s. his thousands   1:47
there are fifty thousand men s. . . . , and not one Englishman   8:104
slander   it is always said of s. that something always sticks   7:364

slapped   anyone who s. us . . . would get his head kicked off   13:248
slave   Be not the s. of Words   10:370
commerce between master and s. is . . . exercise of . . . boisterous passions   8:244
giving freedom to the s.   10:203
government cannot endure . . . half s.   10:169
man . . . is Reason's s.   13:582
s. for livelihood   12:941
The s. begins by demanding justice   13:61
slave-holding   entirely a s. nation, or entirely a free-labour nation   10:171
slavery   Freedom is S.   13:30
No Popery, No S.   8:28
s. cannot exist . . . unless   10:170
slaves   forced to continue the employment of his s.   10:157
if God had wanted to create s.   6:50
In a consumer society there are . . . two kinds of s.   13:717
love, an . . . intercourse between tyrants and s.   8:492
Practical men, . . . are usually the s. of some defunct economist   12:276
S. cannot breathe in England   8:256
that the masters willingly concede to s.   13:60
voluntarily to submit to be s.   8:162
slaying   the s. of a beautiful hypothesis by an ugly fact   11:491
sleep   Better s. with a sober cannibal than a drunken Christian   10:562
Our birth is but a s.   9:199
our little life Is rounded with a s.   7:174
To s., perchance to dream   7:209
youth would s. out the rest   7:196
sleepin'   Capten, art tha s. there below   7:63
sleeping   we have only awakened a s. giant   12:362
sleeps   eats, s. and watches the television   13:778
sleepwalker   that Providence dictates with the assurance of a s.   12:268
sleeve   let the last man . . . brush the Channel with his s.   12:6
slept   David s. with his fathers   1:48
slings   s. and arrows of outrageous fortune   7:209
slogan   democracy is just a s.   13:395
slogans   If you feed people just with revolutionary s.   13:258
Slough   Come, friendly bombs, and fall on S.   13:506
slow   too swift arrives as tardy as too s.   7:313
slum   if you've seen one city s.   13:982
smack   much more indecent . . . than a good s.   12:535
small   Errors look so very ugly in persons of s. means   10:427
In Western Europe there are now only s. countries   13:190
Popularity? . . . glory's s. change   10:459
smaller   accepts a s. as a favour   10:156
someone s. than oneself   8:380
smartness   the s. of an attorney's clerk   10:185
smell   rose . . . would s. as sweet   7:229
Sweet S. of Success   13:667
smells   The only dead thing that s. sweet   11:278
smile   S. at us, pay us, pass us   12:33
s., s., s.   12:44
the vain tribute of a s.   9:124
smiled   the soldiers he s. at   12:81
smite   whosoever shall s. thee on thy right cheek   3:83
smoke   Don't screw around, and don't s.   13:969
resembling the horrible Stygian s. of the pit   7:194
s. of their foul dens Broodeth on Thy Earth   11:225
smokers   S., male and female, inject and excuse idleness   12:519
smoking   What a blessing this s. is   10:340
smooth   course of true love never did run s.   7:314
snails   Frogs and s. And puppy-dogs' tails   10:526
sneezed   when a British Prime Minister s.   13:309
sneezes   When Paris s.   10:40
snipe   well-shot woodcock, partridge, s.   12:263
snob   impossible, in our condition of society, not to be sometimes a s.   10:416
so   It is s.. It is not s.   8:599
sober   as s. as a Judge   8:638

Better sleep with a s. cannibal than a drunken Christian 10:562
England should be compulsorily s.   11:4
he that will go to bed s.   7:198
My mother, drunk or s.   11:100
sedate, s., silent, serious, sad-coloured sect   10:590
social   a great s. and economic experiment   12:174
Man is a s. animal   8:387
the . . . world was stumbling . . . in s. blindness   12:653
socialism   as clear as a crystal, the synthesis – German National S.   12:231
Communism is in fact the completion of S.   11:69
Marxian S. must always remain a portent   12:993
one word . . . to identify modern s., it was 'Science'   13:218
Only s. would put up with it   13:396
religion of S.   12:324
restating our s. in terms of the scientific revolution   13:181
s. . . . alien to the British character   13:369
s. . . . as a whole is threatened   13:226
the proletariat will . . . wage a class struggle for S.   12:147
the worst advertisement for S. is its adherents   12:299
to banish . . . the dark divisive clouds of Marxist s.   13:367
To the ordinary working man, . . . S.   12:300
Under s. *all* will govern   12:72
unites s. with democracy   13:397
socialist   construct the s. order   12:66
I am a s. . . . wish the Labour Party was   13:327
socialists   We are all S. now   11:123
what are you s. going to do about me   12:145
societies   range of human s. in time, the other in space   13:567
society   a free s. . . . where it is safe to be unpopular   13:71
a poor s. cannot be too poor   12:937
A s. . . . of individuals . . . capable of original thought would probably be unendurable   13:664
Comedy, we may say, is s.   12:647
impossible, in our condition of s., not to be sometimes a Snob   10:416
In a consumer s. there are . . . two kinds of slaves   13:717
it proved that I was in a civilized s.   9:170
Man was formed for s.   8:155
no new baby in the womb of our s.   12:68
nothing to distinguish human s. from the farm-yard   11:390
only possible s. is oneself   11:296
S., friendship, and love   8:429
S. goes on and on and on   12:719
S. has resembled a pyramid . . . turned upside down   10:135
S. is now one polish'd horde   10:444
s. . . . pays a harlot 25 times as much as it pays its Prime Minister   13:177
The history of all . . . s. is the history of class struggles   10:117
to change s. and to define its finer values   13:291
transform this s. without a major extension of public ownership   13:363
sociology   Children . . . have no use for psychology. They detest s.   13:782
sodomy   Comedy, like s., is an unnatural act   13:639
rum, s., and the lash   12:34
soft   I'm not hard – I'm frightfully s.   13:262
our love . . . of the mind does not make us s.   2:5
soldier   Every French s. carries in his cartridge-pouch   9:79
in the s. is flat blasphemy   7:94
strength and majesty the British s. fights   9:92
The s.'s body . . . a stock of accessories   12:367
The summer s. and the sunshine patriot   8:253
Tinker, Tailor, S., Sailor   10:643
soldiers   Dear comrades, s., sailors and workers   12:61
English s. fight like lions   12:27
S. are citizens of death's grey land   12:961
when staring at our s. drilling in Berlin   8:579
solitary   Life is for each man a s. cell   12:699
Man is not a s. animal   12:425
Only s. men know the full joys of friendship   12:620
solitude   In s. alone can he know true freedom   7:265
In s. What happiness   8:379
S. is the playfield of Satan   13:602
so companionable as s.   10:424
solution   total s. of the Jewish question   12:372

some   I . . . may be s. time   11:160
You can fool s. of the people all the time   10:188
someone   I wouldn't be . . . talking to s. like you   13:320
something   S. must be done   12:228
son   the earth is free for every s. and daughter of mankind   7:142
woman, behold thy s.   3:36
sonatas   The s. of Mozart are unique   8:671
song   the s. that is sung in our hearts   11:169
Who loves not wine, woman and s.   7:184
sonnet   s. is a moment's monument   11:173
sons   I have a wife, I have s.   4:76
my four s. who cease not to persecute me   6:20
Now we are all s. of bitches   12:402
S. of Belial had a Glorious Time   8:35
sophistry   it can contain nothing but s. and illusion   8:342
sorcery   false enchantments and s.   6:64
sorrow   in s. thou shalt bring forth children   1:13
S. and silence are strong   10:557
S. is tranquillity remembered in emotion   12:735
s. makes us wise   10:421
Tears of eternity and s.   12:678
There is no greater s.   6:108
sorrows   When s. come, they come not single spies   7:278
sought   Love s. is good   7:321
Pleasure is . . . seldom found where it is s.   8:419
soul   Anger is one of the sinews of the s.   7:259
Artists are not engineers of the s.   13:451
a . . . s. like season'd timber   7:379
become a living s.   9:134
education is a leading out of what is . . . in the pupil's s.   13:543
Education is . . . the s. of a society   12:538
I am positive I have a s.   8:606
I am the captain of my s.   11:335
Impropriety is the s. of wit   12:646
In mystery our s. abides   10:566
Man has no Body distinct from his S.   9:197
my s. doth magnify the Lord   3:2
Never mind about my s. . . . get my tie right   12:459
passion in the human s.   8:282
possessive outrage done to a free solitary human s.   12:774
The British postgraduate student is a lonely forlorn s.   13:558
The dark night of the s.   7:227
the . . . essence of a human s.   10:292
the largest and most comprehensive s.   8:270
the s. of a martyr with the intellect of an advocate   10:184
The S. that rises with us, our life's Star   9:199
souls   a follower of hounds to become a shepherd of s.   6:10
the s. of five hundred . . . Newtons   9:200
The s. of women are so small   8:507
soul-sides   the meanest of his creatures Boasts two s.   10:533
sound   full of s. and fury   7:287
The most persistent s. . . . through men's history   13:569
The s. must seem an echo to the sense   8:279
The s. of the English county families   12:841
the trumpet shall s.   3:53
sounding   s. brass   3:95
sounds   Music is the arithmetic of s.   12:431
sour   How s. sweet music is   7:268
I am sure the grapes are s.   3:95
south   God's will to lead . . . S. Africa through defeat and humiliation   11:103
hardly be a town in the S. of England   12:861
Three words made peace and union in S. Africa   11:104
sovereign   A Subject and a S. are clean different things   7:135
he will have no s.   7:111
The S. has, under a constitutional monarchy . . . three rights   10:237
The s. is absolute   8:164
When I forget my s.   8:230
sovereigns   rather than that the s. and magistrates should be destroyed   7:14
Soviet   Communism is S. power plus the electrification   12:111

In a free society the s. . . . administers justice among men 12:184

man was not born to go down on his belly before the s. 13:229

O Lord, to what a s. . . . those who love Thee   7:394

Our object in the construction of the s.   2:7

reinforcement of the power of the S.   13:59

So long as the s. exists there is no freedom   12:70

S. socialism is totally alien   13:369

Star for every S.   10:202

the lie has become . . . a pillar of the S.   13:284

The S., in choosing men . . . takes no notice of their opinions   7:126

The s. is an instrument . . . of the ruling class   12:149

The s. is not 'abolished', it withers away   11:17

the s. . . . Man is in   11:469

The worth of a S.   10:181

stately lunatic asylums . . . the s. homes   12:516

S. Homes of England ope their doors   12:854

The S. Homes of England   12:522

states S., like men, have their growth, . . . , their decay   10:21

United S. of Europe   13:5

statesman abroad you're a s.   13:106

A s. is a politician who   13:273

A s. is a politician who's been dead   13:109

definition of a constitutional s.   10:122

if you agree with him he is a s.   12:197

statesmen an imperative principle which s. . . . ignore at their peril   12:75

S. are far too busy making speeches   13:119

s. . . . estranged from reality   13:135

static class change as s. and dynamic   12:793

novel is a s. thing   13:445

stations always know our proper s.   10:101

statistics Facts speak louder than s.   13:653

He uses s. as a drunken man uses lamp-posts   11:323

lies, damned lies and s.   10:559

s., born to consume resources   4:61

You cannot feed the hungry on s.   11:121

statue that *my* s. should be moved, which I should much dislike   11:80

stature man of giant s.   13:80

status restored the s. quo   12:920

steal thou shalt not s.   1:40

stealing hanged for s. horses   8:48

steals A good composer . . . s.   12:473

steel the cold s.   10:210

steeple clock in the s. strikes one   11:222

stem a rod out of the s. of Jesse   1:100

step a s. from the sublime to the ridiculous   9:90

One s. forward, two steps back   11:275

one small s. for man   13:233

only the first s. . . . is difficult   8:658

stern rising hope of those s. and unbending Tories   10:76

stick if we praise ourselves fearlessly, something will always s.   7:364

Speak softly and carry a big s.   11:98

sticks it is always said of slander that something always s.   7:364

still a s. small voice   1:51

sting O death, where is thy s.   3:53

stinking found Paris s. and left it sweet   10:160

stockholders The public be damned. I am working for my s.   11:47

stoic man is . . . either a s. or a satyr   11:293

stomach An army marches on its s.   9:105

No one can worship God . . . on an empty s.   11:369

The way to a man's heart is through his s.   10:510

use a little wine for thy s.'s sake   3:52

stomachs Napoleon's armies used to march on their s.   9:212

stone and youth s. dead   12:85

Constant dripping hollows out a s.   4:57

he that is without sin . . . let him first cast a s.   3:94

Jackson standing like a s. wall   10:195

Like a rolling s.   13:693

precious s. set in the silver sea   7:69

raised not a s.   9:77

tables of s., and a law   1:43

the final s. . . . in the foundation of St Petersburg   8:82

Stonehenge bring S. to Nyasaland   13:169

stones s. kissed by the English dead   12:22

stop S. the World, I Want to Get Off   13:676

stopped man has s. moving   13:943

stops The buck s. here   13:46

stories She likes s. that make her cry   11:287

storm a mighty s. . . . to freshen us up   11:101

storms greater s. in politics than you'll ever find at sea   12:972

story Not that the s. need be long   10:321

stout those who have s. hearts and sharp swords   12:685

strait matters not how s. the gate   11:335

s. is the gate   3:130

straitened to face s. circumstances at home   4:94

strand wandering on a foreign s.   9:169

strange laughing and jeering at everything . . . s.   8:568

strangeness s. in the proportion   7:292

stranger a s. in a strange land   1:32

straw Headpiece filled with s.   12:688

straws Errors, like S.   8:538

strayed s. from thy ways   8:367

stream Time is but the s. I go a-fishing in   10:479

street don't do it in the s.   11:380

I doubt if the philosopher lives . . . who could know himself . . . despised by a s. boy   11:517

strength Credulity is . . . the child's s.   10:402

Ignorance is S.   13:30

My s. is as the s. of ten   10:556

s. and fury   8:381

S. through joy   12:246

strenuous doctrine of the s. life   11:519

strife With phantoms an unprofitable s.   10:451

strike difficult to go on s.   13:332

If you s. a child   11:386

no right to s. against the public safety   12:105

The general s. . . . is the road to anarchy   12:160

themselves must s. the blow   9:94

where ever you meet with a passage . . . s. it out   8:298

strings 'There are s.', said Mr Tappertit, 'in the human heart . . .'   10:506

strive needst not s. . . . to keep alive   10:568

strives s. to touch the stars   7:224

stroke man fears . . . only the s. of death   7:204

strong be s. and of a good courage   1:45

disarm the s. and arm the weak   11:102

how sublime . . . To suffer and be s.   10:560

Sorrow and silence are s.   10:557

the errors of those who think they are s.   13:677

the wall is s.   11:88

woe unto them that . . . follow s. drink   1:87

strongest He who was s. got most   6:4

struck Certain women should be s. regularly   12:797

struggle I believe in the armed s. as the only solution   13:212

The perpetual s. for room and food   9:36

the s. for existence   10:615

struggles The history of all . . . society is the history of class s.   10:117

struggling the greatness of Russia is only her pre-natal s.   12:110

struts player that s. and frets   7:287

stucco aided by the fatal facility of s.   10:318

student a s. to the end of my days   11:260

He was . . . — a s. of history   10:659

study s. at small cost and short wayfaring   6:101

The proper s. of Mankind is Man   8:407

stuff Ambition should be made of sterner s.   7:358

such s. as dreams are made on   7:174

The future is made of the same s.   12:737

the s. of which tyrants are made   13:115

to s. a mushroom   13:809

stuffed We are the s. men   12:688

stumble they s. that run fast   7:216

stumbling the . . . world was s. . . . in social blindness   12:653

stupid clever man . . . came of . . . s. people   11:250

he ceased to be mad he became merely s.   12:676

Living in England. . . must be like being married to a s. . . . wife 12:863

s. are cocksure . . . intelligent full of doubt 13:709

The s. neither forgive 13:617

To be clever enough to get . . . money, one must be s. 11:509

stupidity Against s. the gods . . . struggle in vain 9:138

Human S. consists in having lots of ideas 12:549

If poverty is the mother of crime, s. is its father 8:451

It is a s. . . . to busy oneself with the correction of the world 8:446

no sin except s. 11:252

Nothing . . . more dangerous . . . conscientious s. 13:547

Sturm S. und Drang 8:301

Stygian resembling the horrible S. smoke of the pit 7:194

style s., not sincerity, is the vital thing 11:344

s. . . . often hides eczema 13:595

subconscious American women know far more about the s. 12:783

subject A S. and a Sovereign are clean different things 7:135

Every s.'s duty is the King's 7:75

the individual s. . . . 'has nothing to do with the laws but to obey them.' 9:30

subjects future negotiations with his s. 8:26

sublime a step from the s. to the ridiculous 9:90

how s. . . . To suffer and be strong 10:560

The s. and the ridiculous 9:160

submit To great evils we s.; we resent little provocations 10:400

subsist to s. . . . without either increase or diminution 10:3

substance faith is the s. of things hoped for 3:119

lose the s. by grasping at the shadow 2:56

substantial he that chiefly owes himself . . . is the s. Man 8:403

substantives to tell the s. from the adjectives 12:410

substitute a s. for reading it 13:550

no s. for talent 12:700

Pubic hair is no s. for wit 13:482

substitutes and finally a single dictator s. himself 11:128

subtil the serpent was more s. 1:11

subverts a continued miracle in his own person, which s. all the principles of his understanding 8:598

succeed It is not enough to s. 13:726

to s. unconventionally 12:722

way to s. is to make people hate you 13:697

success I thought that s. spelled happiness 13:596

I was never affected by the question of the s. 13:205

not in mortals to command s. 8:457

only place where s. comes before work 13:1001

religion . . . yours is S. 12:574

s. . . . by dint of hard work 12:458

s. depends . . . upon individual initiative and exertion 12:458

S. is relative 12:733

Sweet Smell of S. 13:667

The moral flabbiness born of . . . S. 11:360

The penalty of s. 13:663

successful It was very s. 12:388

we do everything we can to appear s. 8:445

sucker a s. born every minute 11:289

sucks s. the nurse asleep 4:10

Suez the S. Canal was flowing through my drawing room 13:93

suffer how sublime . . . To s. and be strong 10:560

If s. we must, let's s. on the heights 10:651

Rather s. than die 8:316

s. fools gladly 3:61

suffered love a place the less for having s. 9:176

suffering A man who fears s. 7:226

pity for the s. of mankind 13:608

sympathize with everything, except s. 11:341

we cannot be created for this sort of s. 10:450

sufficient s. unto the day is the evil thereof 3:87

sugar S. and spice And all that's nice 10:526

suicide committed s. 25 years after his death 13:97

Not only is s. a sin 11:450

one truly serious philosophical problem, . . . s. 12:739

thought of s. is a great . . . comfort 11:242

sulphur land of Calvin, oat-cakes, and s. 10:155

Sultan the S. were driven, bag and baggage, into the heart of Asia 10:14

sum Cogito, ergo s. 7:304

Sumer S. is icumen in 6:97

summer Made glorious s. 6:81

Now the peak of s.'s past 13:744

S. has set in with its usual severity 10:334

way to ensure s. in England 8:314

summit the s. of Everest was hardly the place 13:77

sun between me and the s. 2:13

Fear no more the heat o' th' s. 7:212

If they had said the s. and the moon was gone 10:271

let not the s. go down upon your wrath 3:96

on which the s. never sets 10:30

S. remains fixed in the centre 7:408

there is no new thing under the s. 1:74

There rises the s. of Austerlitz 9:89

The s. does not set in my dominions 7:73

the s. shining ten days a year and shit in the streets 13:893

this s. of York 6:81

Sunday A Christian . . . feels Repentance on a S. 11:479

festival must be observed on S. 5:21

The Feeling of S. is the same everywhere 12:521

sunk thanks to words, we have often s. to the level of the demons 13:430

superfluous that controversy is either s. or hopeless 10:410

superior I consider myself s. to the saint, the scientist 12:436

The French want no-one to be their s. 10:580

superiority their insolent and unfounded airs of s. 8:580

The s. of one man's opinion over another's 11:405

superiors In America everybody is of the opinion that he has no social s. 13:865

superlative we have not settled the s. 11:356

Super-Mac Introducing S. 13:107

Superman I teach you the S. 11:285

supernatural Religion Has made an honest woman of the s. 13:903

superstition necessary for a s. to enslave a philosophy 12:877

S. is the poetry of life 10:445

S. is the religion of feeble minds 9:157

S. sets the whole world in flames 8:348

superstitions new truths . . . end as s. 11:248

s. of the human mind 8:493

superstitious men of Athens . . . ye are too s. 3:47

superstructure Sentimentality is a s. covering brutality 13:589

supreme Our s. governors, the mob 8:119

supremest The state of monarchy is the s. thing upon earth 7:96

surmise with a wild s. 10:257

surpassed Man is something that is to be s. 11:285

surrender No terms except . . . s. 10:200

we shall never s. 12:328

survival the S. of the Fittest 10:617

without victory there is no s. 12:327

survive always be some that s. 13:668

survived I s. 9:27

survives Education is what s. 13:549

suspected New opinions are always s. 8:328

not only s. but pronounced for a witch 7:131

suspicion Caesar's wife must be above s. 2:21

suspicions S. amongst thoughts 7:372

swagman Once a jolly s. camped by a billabong 11:535

swallowed death is s. up in victory 3:53

swallows one master-passion . . . s. up the rest 8:406

swan Sweet S. of Avon 7:175

swans his own geese are s. 8:308

sway A little rule, a little s. 8:459

sweat blood, toil, tears and s. 12:326

it is only because miners s. their guts out 12:297

sweet found Paris stinking and left it s. 10:160

How s. are looks that ladies bend 10:524

Pleasures newly found are s. 9:148

Revenge, at first though s. 8:533

S. Smell of Success 13:667

s. will be the flower 8:564
sweetness Culture is the passion for s. and light 11:168
He who works for s. and light 10:575
swift Too s. arrives as tardy as too slow 7:313
swimming s. under water 12:468
swine pearls before s. 3:89
swing S., s. together 10:348
Switzerland S. . . . an inferior sort of Scotland 9:195
swollen mere existence is s. to a horror 12:664
sword Covenants without the s. are but words 7:151
Islam unashamedly came with a s. 5:35
more cruel . . . the pen than the s. 7:177
nation shall not lift up s. against nation 1:53
pen is mightier than the s. 10:289
s. sleep in my hand 9:73
they that take the s. shall perish with the s. 3:133
We draw the s. with a clear conscience 12:4
swords beat their s. into plowshares 1:53
those who have stout hearts and sharp s. 12:685
sympathize s. with everything, except suffering 11:341
sympathy failed to inspire s. in men 11:420
symptom common s. of immaturity 12:447
synthesis as clear as a crystal, the s. – German National
Socialism 12:231
system Christianity accepted . . . a metaphysical s. 12:897
I'm not interested in the bloody s. 13:377
some greater and more equitable s. 12:406
the negation of God erected into a s. of Government
10:129
The true s. of the World has been recognized 8:346

T

table A man is . . . better pleased when he has a good dinner upon his t. 8:522
put them at a t. together 12:385
tableau history . . . a t. of crimes and misfortunes 8:363
tables t. of stone, and a law 1:43
tact T. consists in knowing 12:820
tactic Silence is the best t. 8:373
tailor Tinker, T., Soldier, Sailor 10:643
tainted the supply is not t. 12:958
take they . . . t., who have the power 9:165
taking not winning but t. part 11:361
tale a t. Told by an idiot 7:287
Life is as tedious as a twice-told t. 7:271
thereby hangs a t. 7:276
t. to tell of the hardihood, endurance, and courage of my
companions 11:159
talent A best-seller is the gilded tomb of a mediocre t.
12:478
a country full of genius, but with absolutely no t. 13:899
any man who has no t. 13:856
T. alone cannot make a writer 10:315
T. develops in quiet places 9:145
T. does what it can 11:191
the difference between t. and genius 10:499
the meanest . . . deeds require spirit and t. 8:472
There is no substitute for t. 12:700
t. instantly recognizes genius 12:575
talents If you have great t., industry will improve them
8:474
talk my ministers t. – as long as they do what I say
13:392
Two may t. . . . yet never really meet 11:300
when I hear anyone t. of Culture 12:484
When two Englishmen meet, their first t. is of the weather
8:572
you wished him to t. on for ever 10:265
talked He t. on for ever 10:265
There is only one thing . . . worse than being t. about
11:340
talker a non-stop t. to whom someone has given a typewriter 13:497
talkers fluent t. 10:409
talking for thirty-five years he had not stopped t. 13:953
Frenchman must be always t. 8:578
good newspaper, . . . is a nation t. to itself 13:510
I wouldn't be . . . t. to someone like you 13:320

People t. without speaking 13:707
T. and eloquence are not the same 7:256
tall Let our children grow t. 13:294
tanned getting more t. and more tired 12:285
Tara through T.'s halls 9:69
Tartar Scratch the Russian and . . . find the T. 9:193
task The trivial round, the common t. 10:335
taste different t. in jokes is a . . . strain on the affections
11:316
great common sense and good t. 4:101
Shakespeare, undoubtedly wanted t. 8:293
the t. by which he is . . . relished 9:121
Things sweet to t. prove . . . sour 7:269
T. is the feminine of genius 11:395
tavern he has . . . opened a t. for his friends 12:513
jangled in every ale-house and t. 7:32
nothing . . . by which so much happiness is produced as by
a good t. 8:315
tawney that t. weed tobacco 7:197
tax A hateful t. 8:192
For God's sake, madam, don't say that in England for . . .
they will surely t. it 8:100
hardest thing . . . to understand is income t. 12:186
taxation T. and representation are inseparably united 8:161
T. without representation 8:137
taxed all the world should be t. 3:3
taxes collect legal t. from illegal money 12:187
His t. . . . starve the poor souls 9:37
people overlaid with t. 8:80
taxis hiring t. . . . handing out redundancy notices to its own
workers 13:376
tea it is just like having a cup of t. 13:761
teach the time had passed . . . merely to t. foreigners
11:110
teacher Time is a great t., but . . . kills all its pupils 10:466
teachers We t. can only help . . . as servants 13:531
teaches He who cannot, t. 11:522
team games The British, being brought up on t. 13:110
tear Every t. from every eye 9:149
tears blood, toil, t. and sweat 12:326
He spoke, and loos'd our heart in t. 10:305
No more t. now 7:47
No t. in the writer 12:499
our t. Thaw not the frost 10:269
shed t. when they would devour 7:250
the land of t. 12:640
the women whose eyes have been washed . . . with t.
12:791
T., idle t. 10:417
tea-stirring t. times 12:718
technology t. . . . indistinguishable from magic 13:957
teeth an old bitch gone in the t. 12:117
her lips narrow and her t. black 7:71
They will steal the very t. out of your mouth 10:336
teetotallers T. lack the sympathy 12:515
television eats, sleeps and watches the t. 13:778
stay at home and see bad t. for nothing 13:429
T. brought the brutality of war 13:287
T. . . . permits you to be entertained in your living room
13:516
tell do not t. them so 8:341
How could they t. 12:236
people who love to t. us what to do 13:879
temper is Apostasy too hard a word to describe the t. of
the nation 10:50
temperament artistic t. is a disease 11:209
tempests That looks on t. 7:324
temple the veil of the t. was rent in twain 3:39
your body is the t. of the Holy Ghost 3:66
temples t. made with hands 3:47
tempora O t.! O mores 2:20
temporal service rendered to the t. king to the prejudice of
the eternal king 6:30
temporary force alone is but t. 8:198
temptation blessed is the man that endureth t. 1:89
lead us not into t. 3:102
over-fond of resisting t. 8:565
tempting the devil did not play in t. of me 8:268
ten only t. 11:235

our dykes. . . . are t. feet deep   11:93
T. Days that Shook the World   12:67
Yes. about t. minutes   10:604
tenderness   Their flowers the t. of patient minds   12:21
tennis   playing t. with the net down   12:485
tent   inside my t. pissing out   13:252
tentacles   dear octopus from whose t. we never quite escape   12:777
terminological   t. inexactitude   11:126
terms   No t. except . . . surrender   10:200
terrible   It is well that war is so t.   10:205
territorial   the last t. claim which I have to make in Europe   12:302
territory   the United States will never again seek one additional foot of t. by conquest   11:163
terrorists   All t. . . . end up with drinks at the Dorchester   13:194
test   Martyrdom is the t.   8:241
thanksgiving   With proud t.   12:91
Thatcher   Blimpish patriotism in the mode of Margaret T.   13:361
Margaret T.'s great strength   13:308
theatre   Farce is the essential t.   13:431
nobody goes to the t. unless he . . . has bronchitis   12:867
theft   Property is t.   10:86
theologian   This stranger is a t.   8:602
theorems   the world can be expressed in . . . arguments, . . . axioms and t.   13:556
theory   A t. can be proved by experiment   13:560
a thing may look evil in t.   8:262
it's . . . more important for a t. to be shapely, than . . . true   13:554
no path leads from experiment to . . . t.   13:560
Philosophy is not a t.   12:533
t. is all grey   9:140, 9:173
therapeutic   have such immense t. value   11:524
thieves   a den of t.   3:116
fell among t.   3:16
thin   in every fat man a t. one   12:641
One can never be too t.   12:947
t. red line tipped with steel   10:151
thing   good t., to make it too common   7:383
It is a far, far, better t. that I do   10:356
something between a t. and a thought   10:303
the t. which is good   3:96
thing-in-itself   The t., the will-to-live, exists . . . in every being   10:476
think   I cannot sit and t.   10:270
I exist by what I t.   12:556
If you make people t.   12:541
I never t. of the future   12:708
I t. him so, because I t. him so   7:342
I t. therefore I am   7:304
some . . . speak . . . before they t.   8:327
T. of your posterity   9:43
To know how to say what others only . . . t.   10:497
t. only this of me   12:31
We haven't the money, so we've got to t.   12:906
When I t. of all the books I have read   12:731
thinkers   not always the justest t.   10:409
thinking   In order to draw a limit to t.   12:532
one prolonged effort to prevent oneself t.   12:679
t. makes it so   7:359
We are t. beings   13:8
third   if there was a t. sex   13:795
the T. Estate contains . . . a nation   9:4
thirst   the t. to come   7:186
thirty   T. days hath September, April, June, and November   7:415
T. millions, mostly fools   10:582
thirty-five   for t. years he had not stopped talking   13:953
thorough   How . . . t. these Germans always managed to be   12:852
thought   A society . . . of individuals . . . capable of original t.   13:664
A t. is often original   10:381
Learning without t. is labour lost   2:27
My t. is *me*   12:556
Only a residual fraction is t.   12:185

Reading . . . ingenious device for avoiding t.   10:377
something between a thing and a t.   10:303
T. must be divided against itself   12:544
t. without learning is perilous   2:27
What was once t.   13:542
will bear to be read twice. . . . was t. twice   10:295
thoughtlessness   In the sex-war t. is the weapon of the male   12:802
thoughts   man whose second t. are good   11:308
our life is what our t. make it   4:69
sensations rather than of t.   10:443
Suspicions amongst t.   7:372
we ought to control our t.   11:421
thousand   Victory has a t. fathers   13:688
thread   from eternity spinning the t. of your being   4:73
threat   one can . . . see in a little girl the t. of a woman   10:538
three   t. fundamental truths   12:817
There are only t. events in a man's life   8:450
There are only t. men who have ever understood it   10:212
there are only t. things to see   12:455
t. o'clock in the morning courage   9:209
t. things . . . the public will always clamour for   10:408
three-sided   if triangles invented a god, they would make him t.   8:596
thrice   before the cock crow, thou shalt deny me t.   3:28
throats   cutting each other's t.   10:196
throne   A man may build . . . a t. of bayonets   12:114
he would not now have been sitting on the French t.   10:84
It helps . . . to remind your bride that you gave up a t. for her   13:779
no middle course between the t. and the scaffold   10:32
royal t. of kings   7:69
something behind the t.   8:174
Thurlow   No man . . . so wise as T. looked   8:242
Thursday   T.'s child has far to go   10:640
thyself   Be so true to t.   7:368
Know then t., presume not God to scan   8:407
Resolve to be t.   10:435
Tiber   the River T. foaming with much blood   13:231
ticky-tacky   They're all made out of t.   13:514
tide   a t. in the affairs of men   7:277
the full t. of human existence is at Charing-Cross   8:194
tidings   good t. of great joy   3:5
tie   Never mind about my soul . . . get my t. right   12:459
tiger   It is not the ape, nor the t.   12:615
The atom bomb is a paper t.   13:8
tigers   Dictators ride to and fro upon t.   12:306
tightrope   You may reasonably expect a man to walk a t. safely   13:120
tiller   a t. of the ground   1:15
timber   a . . . soul like season'd t.   7:379
time   a comfortable t. lag . . . between the perception   12:226
advantage of t. and place . . . is half a victory   7:61
As t. goes by   12:761
As T. Goes By   12:990
a t. to be born, and a t. to die   1:75
I haven't got t. to be tired   11:56
I . . . may be some t.   11:160
in a moment of t.   3:15
irretrievable t. is flying   4:59
Men talk of killing t.   10:461
Never before have we had so little t.   12:375
not had the t. to make it shorter   8:366
not of an age, but for all t.   7:176
no t. to stand and stare   12:669
On the breast of the river of T.   10:492
peace for our t.   12:304
range of human societies in t., the other in space   13:567
t. and chance happeneth to them all   1:76
T. and the hour runs through   7:290
t. as a tool not as a couch   13:147
T. flies, death urges   8:462
The supreme reality of our t.   13:687
the t. had passed . . . merely to teach foreigners   11:110
the t. will come when you will hear me   10:68
those feet in ancient t.   9:73
T. is a great teacher, but . . . kills all its pupils   10:466
T. is but the stream I go a-fishing in   10:479

T. is like a river made up of the events which happen   4:71
t. is money   8:647
T. is slipping underneath our Feet   10:489
t. is the greatest innovator   7:293
T. may restore us   10:306
T. present and time past   12:720
t. quietly kills them   10:461
T. whereof the memory of man   8:158
What do the ravages of t. not injure   4:12
Work expands so as to fill the t.   13:992
timeliness   the t. of the gift   8:542
times   It was the best of t.   9:210
logic of our t.   12:503
We live in stirring t.   12:718
Times   The T. has made many ministries   10:242
tinker   T., Tailor, Soldier, Sailor   10:643
tinkling   a t. cymbal   3:95
Tipperary   a long, long way to T.   12:16
tipster   A racing t. who only reached Hitler's level of accuracy   12:996
tired   getting more tanned and more t.   12:285
Give me your t. . . . Your huddled masses   11:52
I haven't got time to be t.   11:56
Life . . . process of getting t.   11:350
Titian   Nobody cares much at heart about T.   10:313
title-page   a t. to a great tragic volume   10:11
titles   T. distinguish the mediocre   11:114
Tito   I will shake my little finger – and there will be no more T.   13:20
toast   I had never had a piece of t. . . . But fell . . . on the buttered side   11:333
tobacco   that tawney weed t.   7:197
what pleasure . . . they have in taking their roguish t.   7:192
who lives without t.   8:370
tocsin   The t. you hear today is not an alarm but an alert   9:17
today   if T. BE SWEET   10:489
the Cup that clears T. of past Regrets   10:488
they will listen t., they will listen tomorrow   13:258
wiser t. than . . . yesterday   8:399
toddle   I'd t. safely home   12:85
together   two people living t. for 25 years without having a cross word   12:779
We must . . . all hang t.   8:208
toil   blood, t., tears and sweat   12:326
Horny-handed sons of t.   11:19
they t. not   3:86
To t. and not to seek for rest   7:349
tolerance   lead this people into war and they'll forget . . . t.   12:25
toleration   t. produced . . . religious concord   4:99
tolls   for whom the bell t.   7:214
Tolstoy   Their teacher had advised them not to read T. novels   13:467
tomb   A best-seller is the gilded t. of a mediocre talent   12:478
tomorrow   assure him that he'd live t.   7:392
Drop . . . what it may bring . . . count as profit every day that Fate allows you   4:62
let us eat and drink; for t. we . . . die   1:78
T., and t., and t.   7:287
tongue   neither eye to see, nor t. to speak   7:121
One t. is sufficient for a woman   8:509
who speak the t. That Shakspeare spake   9:44
tongues   cloven t. like as of fire   3:44
Self-interest speaks all sorts of t.   8:527
Tony   T. . . . he immatures with age   13:348
tool   time as a t., not as a couch   13:147
tools   Give us the t.   12:350
the foul dregs of his power, the t. of despotism and corruption   8:145
tool-using   Man is a t. animal   10:613
tooth   t. for t.   1:41
torch   like runners hand on the t. of life   4:58
Tories   rising hope of those stern and unbending T.   10:76
Tory   a deep burning hatred for the T. Party   13:23
leader of the T. party   10:109
to what is called the T. . . . called the Conservative, party   10:34

total   t. solution of the Jewish question   12:372
touch   Wound with a t.   8:438
tourist   the most vulgar, . . . is the British t.   11:223
towering   the height of his own t. style   11:220
towers   The cloud-capp'd t.   7:174
town   man made the t.   8:478
toy   but a childish t.   7:397
trade   a king that . . . could not endure to have t. sick   6:135
God will pardon me. It is His t.   10:607
half a t. and half an art   12:441
trades   The ugliest of t. have their moments of pleasure   10:634
trades unions   The fault and destruction of all t.   10:58
trading   t. on the blood of my men   10:256
tradition   We don't want t.   12:561
tragedy   a t. and therefore not worth reading   9:118
brooding t. and its dark shadows can be lightened   13:576
farce brutalized becomes t.   13:431
great t. of Science   11:491
That is their t.   11:408
T. is if I cut my finger   13:499
we have conceived life as a t.   12:697
We participate in a t.   13:420
world is a comedy to those who think, a t. to those who feel   8:475
You're a bloody t.   12:256
tragically   Everything must be taken seriously, nothing t.   11:325
trained   t. and organized common sense   11:490
traitor   grieves me that I should be noted as a t.   7:29
traitors   t. rose against him   6:5
trampling   t. out the vintage where the grapes of wrath   10:206
tranquillity   Sorrow is t. remembered in emotion   12:735
transform   t. this society without . . . extension of public ownership   13:363
transformation   The universe is t.   4:69
transit   Sic t. gloria mundi   6:113
travel   he must fly rather than t.   6:16
To t. hopefully is . . . better . . . than to arrive   11:425
wherever the wind takes me I t. as a visitor   4:15
travelled   I t. among unknown men   9:72
traveller   from whose bourn no t. returns   7:208
travelling   The grand object of t.   8:217
T. is . . . like talking with men of other centuries   7:305
travels   A man t. the world over   12:654
too old to go again to my t.   8:24
treachery   Weakness is not t.   11:129
tread   fools rush in where angels fear to t.   8:337
treason   If this be t., make the most of it   8:154
in trust I have found t.   7:55
T. doth never prosper   7:104
T. was no Crime   8:35
treasure   purest t. mortal times afford   7:267
treasures   lay not up . . . t. upon earth   3:85
Treasury   the Vatican, the T. and the miners   13:14
treaties   T. are like roses and young girls   13:188
tree   A poem lovely as a t.   12:427
as the twig is bent, the t.'s inclined   8:339
If poetry comes not . . . as leaves to a t.   10:262
same t. that a wise man sees   9:137
the fruit Of that forbidden t.   1:110
The t. of liberty must be refreshed   8:259
the t. of life   1:7
the t. of the knowledge of good and evil   1:7
t. of life is green   9:140, 9:173
treen   In old time we had t. chalices and golden priests   7:45
trees   Loveliest of t., the cherry   11:232
trenches   boys who were killed in the t.   12:95
digging t. and trying on gas-masks   12:303
triangles   if t. invented a god, they would make him three-sided   8:596
tribe   Mankind is not a t.   11:358
tribute   the vain t. of a smile   9:124
trifles   observance of t.   11:527
trigger   Whose Finger do you want on the T.   13:53
triumph   We t. without glory   7:255

trivial I never approved either the errors of his book, or the t. truths   8:349
  mighty contests rise from t. things   8:489
  The t. round, the common task   10:335
trouble a lot of t. in his life   12:997
  a woman is on a . . . hunt for t.   12:770
  it saves me the t. of liking them   9:146
  man . . . is . . . full of t.   1:73
  Our progress . . . Is t. and care   11:326
troubles pack up your t. in your old kit-bag   12:44
  take arms against a sea of t.   7:209
trousers She is trying to wear the t. of Winston Churchill   13:330
trout as when you find a t. in the milk   10:648
Troy Now there are fields where T. once was   2:83
true a great advantage for . . . philosophy to be . . . t.   12:546
  All one's inventions are t.   10:307
  because a novel's invented, it isn't t.   13:486
  Be so t. to thyself   7:368
  be yourself, imperial, plain and t.   10:425
  false to his friends . . . t. to the public   8:125
  if they keep on saying it . . . it will be t.   12:950
  it's . . . more important for a theory to be shapely, than . . . t.   13:554
  Journalists say a thing that they know isn't t.   12:950
  No man worth having is t. to his wife   8:502
  One religion is as t. as another   7:404
  The religions we call false were once t.   10:593
  The t. system of the World has been recognized   8:346
  to thine own self be t.   7:360
trumpet The First Blast of the T.   7:41
  the t. shall sound   3:53
trust a man could not . . . tell whom he might t. or . . . fear   6:87
  I don't t. him. We're friends   12:635
  in t. from the people to the common good of them all   7:144
  in t. I have found treason   7:55
  Never t. a husband too far   12:764
  the right of governing was not property but a t.   8:254
trusting it never extended to t. him   10:343
truth And seek for t. in the groves of Academe   4:40
  A platitude is simply a t. repeated   12:594
  a short armistice with t.   10:548
  A t. that's told with bad intent   9:188
  a t. universally acknowledged   9:179
  before the t. has got its boots on   13:301
  content to die for God's eternal t.   10:172
  dearer still is t.   2:66
  Every man has a right to utter what he thinks t.   8:241
  hard to believe . . . a man is telling the t.   12:581
  He believes, . . . that there *is* such a thing as t.   10:184
  I am the way, the t., and the life   3:115
  if the people . . . can be reached with the t.   12:373
  If you do not tell the t. about yourself   12:806
  I just tell the t. and they think it is hell   13:666
  in the end the t. will conquer   6:52
  Let us begin by committing ourselves to the t.   13:228
  loving Christianity better than T.   10:586
  Much t. is spoken, . . . more . . . concealed   11:427
  My way of joking is to tell the t.   11:321
  Nobody speaks the t. when   12:622
  No poet ever interpreted nature . . . as a lawyer interprets t.   12:965
  not even Marx is more precious . . . than the t.   12:239
  polite by telling the t.   13:886
  put him in possession of t.   8:329
  Some men love t. so much   11:435
  T. be veiled   10:503
  T. comes out in wine   4:36
  the laws of poetic t. and poetic beauty   11:181
  the t. is not in us   3:63
  the t. of imagination   10:546
  the unclouded face of t. suffer wrong   12:958
  The worst enemy of t. and freedom   11:36
  those who live . . . believe . . . to be the t.   13:612
  T. is on the march   11:87
  T. is . . . the test of experience   13:820
  to the dead we owe only t.   8:365

T., Sir, is a cow   8:603
T. telling is not compatible with the defence of the realm   12:121
t. that makes men free   12:830
Two half-truths do not make a t.   13:702
whatever remains, however improbable, must be the t.   11:528
whilst the great ocean of t. lay all undiscovered before me   8:616
who ever knew T. put to the worse   7:381
truths all t. are half-t.   12:823
  commonplaces are the great poetic t.   11:345
  He was a man of two t.   13:848
  new t. . . . begin as heresies   11:248
  t. being in and out of favour   12:705
  The only t. which are universal   12:831
  There are no new t.   13:546
  those three fundamental t.   12:817
try Many things . . . are done worst when we t. hardest   13:592
  t. everything once   12:742
tu *Et t., Brute*   4:6
Tudor Owen T. . . . was beheaded at the market place   6:72
Tuesday T.'s child is full of grace   10:640
tumbler He who drinks a t. of London water   10:337
tunnel light at the end of the t. . . . of an oncoming train   13:728
turban the royal t. of the Turks   6:69
turbulent rid me of this t. priest   6:11
turf The blue ribbon of the t.   10:343
Turks the royal turban of the T.   6:69
turning Life is a maze in which we take the wrong t.   12:745
  The lady's not for t.   13:337
twain never the t. shall meet   11:543
twelve I was born at the age of t.   13:989
twentieth the t. century will be . . . the century of Fascism   12:229
twenty the first t. years   9:174
  The United States, . . . are t. years in advance of this country   13:878
twice desire to be praised t. over   8:528
  Literature . . . something that will be read t.   12:967
  will bear to be read t., . . . was thought t.   10:295
twig as the t. is bent, the tree's inclined   8:339
twinkle T., t., little star   9:205
twinkling in the t. of an eye   3:53
two Great God grant that twice t. be not four   10:609
  into the ark, t. and t.   1:19
  make t. questions grow where only one   12:661
  Of the t. lights of Christendom   6:70
  One step forward, t. steps back   11:275
  t. and t. do not make six   11:480
  The formula 'T. and t. make five'   10:654
  t. legs bad   13:1017
  T. nations   10:102
typewriter a non-stop talker to whom someone has given a t.   13:497
tyrannies the t. of minorities   11:156
tyranny Ecclesiastic t.'s the worst   8:75
  kingship approaches t. it is near its end   6:39
  the Bolshevik t. is the worst   12:107
  their deliverer from Popish t.   8:53
  They that are discontented under *monarchy*, call it t.   7:152
  Where laws end, t. begins   8:173
tyrant an intolerable t.   6:21
  the makings of a t.   9:9
tyrants all men would be t.   8:398
  Kings will be t. from policy   9:12
  love, an . . . intercourse between t. and slaves   8:492
  the English seem . . . to act with the barbarity of t.   9:68
  the stuff of which t. are made   13:115
  'Twixt kings and t. there's this difference   7:133

U

ugliest The u. of trades have their moments of pleasure   10:634
ugly It's nothing to be born u.   11:418

v. in ambition is violent 7:370
V. is its own punishment 13:833
Woman's v. is man's greatest invention 12:801
virtues ape-like v. without which 12:555
few v. . . . the Poles do not possess 12:415
greater v. to sustain good fortune 8:525
v. and vices couple with one another 8:541
v. are . . . vices in disguise 8:530
v. We write in water 7:375
What men call social v., . . . is . . . but the virtue of pigs in a litter 10:563
Whenever there are tremendous v. 12:828
virtuous more v. man . . . does not exist 9:66
the v. poor 11:501
When men grow v. in their old age 8:453
who can find a v. woman 1:81
visage He was of v. louelye 6:80
vision The young men's v., and the old men's dream 8:32
visionary Whither is fled the v. gleam 9:199
vitai v. lampada 4:58
vitamins the right proteins and v. 13:521
vivify quarrels which v. its barrenness 13:754
voice a still small v. 1:51
The v. of the intellect is a soft one 12:540
v. of the people is the v. of God 5:5
volcano dancing on a v. 10:39
Volk Ein Reich, Ein V., Ein Führer 12:242
Voltaire One does not arrest V. 13:127
vomit If . . . Orientals . . . drank a liquor which . . . made them v. 8:569
To write a diary . . . returning to one's own v. 13:729
voodoo V. economics 13:340
vote in the same boat . . . not a chance of recording the v. 11:141
One man shall have one v. 8:239
v. is the most powerful instrument 13:206
voted I always v. at my party's call 11:18
voter The idea that there is a model Labour v., . . . is patronizing 13:387
votes disadvantage of merely counting v. 12:181
solved by speeches and majority v. 10:207
V. for Women 11:136
vox V. populi, v. dei 5:5
vulgar dislike the French from . . . v. antipathy 8:580
the most v., . . . is the British tourist 11:223
war . . . is looked upon as v. 11:428
vulgarity One can love a certain kind of v. for its own sake 12:616
vulgarizing Death . . . It's the only thing we haven't succeeded in completely v. 12:525

W

wag Every man has . . . an ambition to be a w. 8:442
wage One man's w. rise is another man's price increase 13:245
Wagner W. has lovely moments 10:320
W. is the Puccini of music 12:475
wait I almost had to w. 8:91
They also serve who only stand and w. 8:582
W. and see 11:146
wake hope is . . . the dream of those that w. 8:404
Wales King Edward . . . made Lord Edward . . . Prince of W. 6:40
Shut the door, W. 9:84
trace . . . the disasters of English history to . . . W. 12:843
W. . . . genuinely more classless 13:384
walking I were w. with destiny 12:325
Jesus . . . w. on the sea 3:22
When I am not w., I am reading 10:270
wall Humpty Dumpty sat on a w. 7:124
the w. fell down flat 1:46
With our backs to the w. . . . each . . . must fight on to the end 12:78
walls Stone w. do not a prison make 7:119
Walpole W. . . . given by the King to the people 8:182
waltzing You'll come a-w., Matilda 11:535
wanderer A w. is man from his birth 10:492
wandering W. in a vast forest at night 8:602

want Economy is going without something you do w. 11:294
freedom from w. 12:347
wanton w. and effeminate sound 6:92
war All diplomacy is a continuation of w. 13:86
An empire founded by w. 8:103
a phoney w. 12:318
As long as w. is regarded as wicked 11:428
average men and women were delighted at . . . w. 13:609
Being over seventy is like being engaged in a w. 13:669
but France has not lost the w. 12:333
could lose the w. in an afternoon 12:37
defeat without a w. 12:305
done very well out of the w. 12:100
easier to make w. than 12:102
except the British W. Office 11:81
he came hiccupping to the w. 5:15
He kept us out of w. 12:38
him who desires peace, prepare for w. 4:26
I could have lost the w. in an afternoon 12:47
I'd like to see the government get out of w. altogether 13:152
I don't care for w. 10:176
I have loved w. too much 8:92
I make w. on the living 7:33
In a civil w., a general must know 13:38
In starting and waging w. it is not right that matters, but victory 12:247
In w. . . . there are no winners 12:301
Is it that w. is a luxury 10:145
It is well that w. is so terrible 10:205
I wanted the experience of w. 11:314
lead this people into w. and they'll forget . . . tolerance 12:25
Lenin was the first to discover that capitalism 'inevitably' caused w. 12:995
let slip the dogs of w. 7:77
makes a good w. makes a good peace 7:109
My home policy? I wage w. 12:76
My subject is W., and the pity of W. 12:20
never was a good w. 8:249
No one can guarantee success in w. 13:28
nothing that w. has ever achieved 12:101
Now w. has a bad conscience 12:48
Older men declare w. 12:391
on this wall will hang my weapons and my lyre, discharged from the w. 4:75
Stand your ground . . . if they mean to have a w., let it begin here 8:201
Television brought the brutality of w. 13:287
that devil's madness — W. 12:195
the . . . barbarity of w. . . . forces men . . . to commit acts 12:49
The first casualty when w. comes 12:50
the Lord is a man of w. 1:93
the second rule of w. 13:241
the W. is being deliberately prolonged 12:86
the w. of the giants is over 12:408
The wrong w., at the wrong place 13:51
The w. we have just been through, . . . is not to be compared 12:96
This is how w. is begun 6:13
this massed multitude of silent witnesses to . . . w. 12:129
This w. . . . is a w. to end w. 12:42
This w. is not as in the past 12:396
this w. . . . which did not justify the sacrifice of a single mother's son 12:87
Those who can win a w. well 12:200
To w. and arms I fly 7:123
W. alone brings up to their highest tension all human energies 12:223
w. can only be abolished through w. 13:41
we are . . . in the midst of a cold w. 13:10
We are not at w. with Egypt 13:92
W. hath no fury like a non-combatant 12:588
What they could do with round here is a good w. 12:989
When the rich wage w. 13:55
when they learn how we began this w. 12:329
When was a w. not a w. 11:97

Who live under the shadow of a w.   13:39
W. is, after all, the universal perversion   13:830
W. is capitalism   13:293
W. is hell   11:20
W. is not an adventure   12:366
W. is Peace   13:30
W. is the continuation of politics   10:47, 13:40
W. is w.   12:407
W. knows no power   12:30
W. makes rattling good history   11:274
w. minus the shooting   12:645
W. should belong to the tragic past   13:355
w. . . . will be considered as antiquated as a duel   11:153
W. will never cease until babies   12:612
warantis   Daily many w. come to me of paiementz   6:67
warmongers   w. who . . . have others pull the chestnuts out
of the fire   12:348
warn   the right to be consulted, . . . to encourage, . . . to w.
10:237
warrior   the British w. queen   4:98
wars   All w. are planned by old men   12:194
All w. are popular for the first thirty days   13:116
end to the beginnings of all w.   12:397
In the w. of the European powers . . . we have never taken
any part   10:20
military don't start w.   13:117
No kingdom has . . . had as many . . . w. as the kingdom of
Christ   8:595
Still w. and lechery   7:323
W. are not won by evacuations   12:332
W. cannot be fought with nuclear weapons   13:324
W. come because   13:22
W., conflict, it's all business   13:13
warts   pimples, w., and everything as you see me   7:160
war-war   To jaw-jaw is better than to w.   13:84
washed   Pilate . . . w. his hands   3:33
wasps   w. and hornets break through   8:83
watch   keeping w. over their flock by night   3:5
w. and pray   3:59
watchmaker   I should have become a w.   13:208
water   He who drinks a tumbler of London w.   10:337
impressions . . . lasting as . . . an oar upon the w.   11:337
It is with our passions as it is with fire and w.   8:487
like throwing w. into the sea   7:365
no verse can give pleasure . . . that is written by drinkers of
w.   4:28
virtues we write in w.   7:375
w. flowed like champagne   11:29
Waterloo   Every man meets his W.   10:182
the Battle of W. *was* won on the playing-fields of Eton
12:359
waters   the Spirit of God moved upon . . . the w.   1:1
Watson   Elementary my dear W.   11:533
Mr W., come here; I want you   11:487
wave   Churchill on top of the w.   13:115
waves   the w. make towards the pebbled shore   7:211
waxworks   w. inhabited by gramophones   12:456
way   blow out your candle . . . to find your w.   8:602
catch the nearest w.   7:244
I am the w., the truth, and the life   3:115
The w. to dusty death   7:287
wayfaring   study at small cost and short w.   6:101
Wayne   John W. is dead   13:640
weak   concessions of the w.   8:199
disarm the strong and arm the w.   11:102
Idleness . . . the refuge of w. minds   8:554
Like all w. men . . . an exaggerated stress   12:576
The w. have one weapon   13:677
weaker   the w. vessel   3:77
weakness   no more w. than is natural to her sex   2:55
weaknesses   I have got lots of human w.   13:366
touch his w. with a delicate hand   8:560
weal   I will govern according to the common w.   7:108
wealth   God shows his contempt for w.   12:943
His w. a well-spent age   7:376
the insolence of w.   8:631
W. has never been a sufficient source of honour   13:974
Where w. and freedom reign, contentment fails   8:150
W. I ask not   11:346

W. is, like sea-water   10:627
W. is not without its advantages   13:975
wealthy   Where some people are very w. and others have
nothing   2:15
weaned   w. on a pickle   12:243
weapon   art is not a w.   13:451
In the sex-war thoughtlessness is the w. of the male
12:802
The weak have one w.   13:677
weapons   books are w.   12:374
If sunbeams were w.   13:271
on this wall will hang my w. and my lyre, discharged from
the war   4:75
weary   let us not be w. in well doing   3:70
weather   even the w. forecast seemed to be some kind of
spoof   13:517
Give me books, fruit, French wine and fine w.   10:330
I like the w.   10:328
This is the w. the cuckoo likes   11:233
When two Englishmen meet, their first talk is of the w.
8:572
weather-wise   Some are w.   8:655
web   The w. of our life is of a mingled yarn   7:284
webs   Laws are like spider's w.   2:1
Wednesday   W.'s child is full of woe   10:640
weed   that tawney w. tobacco   7:197
weeds   nature runs either to herbs, or to w.   7:247
Worthless as wither'd w.   10:594
week   A w. is a long time in politics   13:210
the greatest w. in the history of the world   13:234
weep   By the waters of Babylon we sit down and w.   8:202
not to w. at them, nor to hate them, but to understand
them   8:385
weeping   Why are you w.? Did you imagine that I was immortal   8:93
Welfare-State   led to that of the W.   12:383
well   do not speak w. of yourself   8:534
I am not w.; pray get me . . . brandy   9:29
nothing . . . and did it very w.   11:33
the world's work, . . . is done by men who do not feel . . . w.
13:318
worth doing w.   8:552
Wellington   Lord W. was at the ball   9:107
The Duke of W. had exhausted nature   10:134
well-modulated   balanced state of w. dis-satisfaction
11:28
Welsh   The W. . . . just sing   12:844
whole of the W. nation   6:59
wen   the fate of the great w.   10:37
Wenlock Edge   On W. the wood's in trouble . . . the Wrekin
heaves   11:231
wept   young man who has not w.   12:666
West   East is East, and W. is W.   11:543
wet   joly whistle wel y-w.   6:98
out of these w. clothes and into a dry Martini   12:648
what   Aye, and then   10:584
wheels   spoke among your w.   7:417
when   w. a man should marry   7:337
whiff   w. of grapeshot   9:32
whimper   not with a bang but a w.   12:689
whipping   W. and abuse are like laudanum   10:138
whirlwind   Elijah went up by a w. into heaven   1:52
sown the wind . . . reap the w.   1:57
whistle   So was hir joly w. wel y-wet   6:98
white   architecture . . . only passers-by who can contemplate
it . . . are those . . . with a w. stick and a dog   13:501
Britain . . . is going to be forged in the w. heat of this revolution   13:181
If the w. man *says* he does, he is instantly . . . mistrusted
13:141
I want to be the w. man's brother   13:161
so-called w. races   12:154
Take up the W. Man's burden   11:95
The w. man knows how to make everything   11:63
When a w. man in Africa   13:48
When the w. man came we had the land   13:736
Whitehall   She came into W. laughing and jolly   8:57
W. . . . our attempts to be fair to everybody   13:857
White House   Log-cabin to W.   11:30

witnesses this massed multitude of silent w. to . . . war 12:129
wits Great W. . . . to Madness near alli'd 8:447
their poetry is conceived and composed in their w. 11:182
witty Anger makes dull men w. 7:355
Pretty w. Nell 8:3
stumbling on something w. 9:185
wives husbands and w. make shipwreck of their lives 12:770
O! men with mothers and w. 10:525
W. are young men's mistresses 7:334
woe Wednesday's child is full of w. 10:640
w. to him that is alone when he falleth 1:69
W. to the vanquished 4:65
w. unto them that . . . follow strong drink 1:87
wolf The boy cried 'W., w.!' 2:36
the w. in the sheep's clothing 2:33
woman all the keys should hang from the belt of one w. 6:47
Any w. who understands the problems of running a home 13:329
a w. is on a . . . hunt for trouble 12:770
a w. . . . ought to lay aside . . . modesty with her skirt 7:311
A w. should be an illusion 13:799
A w. should open everything 13:801
a w.'s reason 7:342
A w. will always sacrifice herself 12:788
a w. yet think him an angel 10:531
body of a weak and feeble w. 7:65
Christ-like heroes and w.-worshipping Don Juans 12:787
Every old w. with a wrinkled face 7:131
every w. is at heart a rake 8:518
Every w. is infallibly to be gained 8:520
Frailty, thy name is w. 7:344
God made the w. for the man 10:530
hell a fury like a w. scorned 8:514
I am a . . . w. – nothing more 10:537
I am a w.? When I think, I must speak 7:343
If a w. like Eva Peron with no ideals 13:336
International W.'s Day 12:71
It is a great glory in a w. 2:55
It's a sort of bloom on a w. 11:415
I would . . . guess that Anon . . . was often a w. 12:795
Man for the field and w. for the hearth 10:528
No one delights more in vengeance than a w. 4:78
nor w. neither 7:240
No w. so naked as . . . underneath her clothes 13:807
Once a w. has given you her heart 8:513
one can . . . see in a little girl the threat of a w. 10:538
One is not born a w. 13:785
One tongue is sufficient for a w. 8:509
only three things to be done with a w. 13:793
She makes love just like a w. 13:800
the help and support of the w. I love 12:284
The really original w. . . . imitates a man 11:399
the rib . . . made he a w. 1:10
the w. who is really kind to dogs 11:420
To know the *mind* of a w. 12:752
w. alone, can . . . commit them 10:523
w., behold thy son 3:36
w. governs America 13:861
What does a w. want 12:785
who can find a virtuous w. 1:81
Who loves not wine, w. and song 7:184
Why can't a w. be more like a man 13:792
W. is always fickle and changing 4:77
w. is an animal that 13:786
w. is his game 10:527
w. needs a man 13:802
w. seldom asks advice 8:515
W.'s virtue is man's greatest invention 12:801
w.'s whole existence 10:500
W. to bear rule . . . is repugnant to Nature 7:340
W. will be the last thing civilized by Man 10:534
womanhood W. is the great fact in her life 11:397
womb no new baby in the w. of our society 12:68
teeming w. of royal kings 7:69

women A homely face . . . aided many w. heavenward 11:413
All Berkshire w. are very silly 13:805
all w. do 11:384
battle for w.'s rights 13:813
Because w. can do nothing except love 12:782
comely to w. to nourish their hair 7:347
Give w. the vote 11:113
great city . . . has the greatest men and w. 10:482
If men knew how w. pass their time 11:416
If w. didn't exist, . . . money . . . no meaning 13:808
Intimacies between w. 12:798
most important thing w. have to do 10:544
Most w. have no characters 8:517
prolonged slavery of w. 11:404
proper function of w. 10:535
souls of w. are so small 8:507
Suffer the w. whom ye divorce 5:26
the Monstrous Regiment of W. 7:41
the only advantage w. have over men – . . . they can cry 12:799
There are two kinds of w. 12:796
the w. whose eyes have been washed . . . with tears 12:791
To employ w. and children unduly 10:540
Votes for W. 11:136
W. . . . are either better or worse than men 8:512
W. are equal because . . . not different 13:791
W. are most fascinating between the ages of thirty-five and forty 13:790
W. are much more like each other 8:519
w. become like their mothers 11:408
W. . . . care fifty times more for a marriage than a ministry 10:541
Were't not for gold and w. 7:345
W. have served all these centuries 12:786
Why are w. . . . so much more interesting to men 12:794
w. . . . ill-using them and then confessing it 10:539
W. . . . men hate them 13:804
W. . . . natural, but usually secret, rulers 13:787
W. never have young minds 13:797
Wonderful w.! . . . how much we . . . owe to Shakespeare 11:216
W. represent . . . matter over mind 11:406
w. should be struck . . . like gongs 12:797
w. were going to remain in the servant class 11:139
W. . . . were ready to fight for their own human rights 11:140
w. who moan at the lack of opportunities 13:814
womman worthy w. al hir lyve 6:118
won Human reason w. Mankind w. 13:160
wonder knowledge and w. . . . is an impression of pleasure 7:218
Philosophy is the product of w. 12:547, 12:717
wonderful the ancient cathedrals – grand, w., mysterious 11:468
wood about the dreadful w. Of conscious evil 12:744
the boar out of the w. doth waste it 7:6
woodcock well-shot w., partridge, snipe 12:263
woodman W., spare that tree 10:407
word in the captain's but a choleric w. 7:94
Rehearsing a play is making the w. flesh 13:476
that most precious jewel, the W. of God 7:32
the kingdom of God is not in w., but in power 3:118
the W. had breath 10:603
What is honour? A w. 7:353
words Be not the slave of W. 10:370
by skilful arrangement of your w. 4:32
Covenants without the sword are but w. 7:151
Fine w. and an insinuating appearance 2:59
fine w. butter no parsnips 10:448
For w., like Nature, half reveal 10:420
I put the w. down 13:459
learn the use of living w. 12:456
life depends on your power to master w. 13:566
Men of few w. are the best 7:234
my w. are my own 8:23
thanks to w., we have often sunk to the level of the demons 13:430

w. and read comes by nature 7:235
w. for children . . . as you do for adults 12:490
writer A great w. creates a world of his own 12:492
Asking a working w. . . . about critics 13:491
A w.'s ambition should be 13:419
Every great and original w. 9:121
it is necessary to go to a university . . . to become a successful w. 13:411
not a w.'s business to hold opinions 13:492
No tears in the w. 12:499
protect the w. 13:614
successful w. . . . is indistinguishable 12:836
writers Clear w., . . . do not seem so deep as they are 10:273
Irish w. — the ones that *think*. 13:877
No regime has ever loved great w. 13:466
The only way for w. to meet 12:509
W., like teeth, are divided into incisors and grinders 10:312
writing All good w. is swimming under water 12:468
the disease of w. books 8:287
the incurable disease of w. 4:34
True ease in w. comes from art 8:279
w. an exact man 7:221
When a man is in doubt about . . . his w. 11:218
W. . . . is but a different name for conversation 8:290
W. is like getting married 13:481
written Books are well w., or badly w. 11:187
books . . . w. by people who don't understand them 8:292
what I have w. I have w. 3:32
wromantic Cavaliers (wrong but W.) 7:421
wrong A man should . . . own he has been in the w. 8:399
Of course not . . . I may be w. 13:613
Only the man who finds everything w. 13:622
orthodoxy . . . practically means being w. 11:263
responsible and w. 13:45
sentimentality . . . rubs you up the w. way 12:637
something is impossible, he is . . . w. 13:959
The multitude is always in the w. 8:39
The right divine of kings to govern w. 8:99
the unclouded face of truth suffer w. 12:958
The w. war, in the w. place 13:51
wrongdoing W. can only be avoided if those who are not wronged feel the same indignation 2:58
wrongs if two w. don't make a right 13:280

Y

Yale all the young ladies who attended the Y. promenade dance were laid end to end 12:756
Yankee Y. Doodle came to town 8:212
yarn web of our life is of a mingled y. 7:284
yawn When a book is boring, they y. openly 13:782
year Another y.! — another deadly blow 9:64
each day is like a y. 11:88
I said to the man who stood at the gate of the y. 12:319
yearning learning, earning and y. 12:657

years he that cuts off twenty y. of life 7:207
how many y. can some people exist 13:685
world must be made safe for . . . fifty y. 12:413
Y. hence, perhaps, may dawn an age 10:567
yesterday wiser to-day than . . . y. 8:399
yesterdays And all our y. 7:287
yet A young man not y. 7:337
but not y. 4:84
Yeti little in civilization to appeal to a Y. 13:674
yoke Rome's gross y. Drops off 10:601
York Oh! the grand old Duke of Y. 9:8
you For y. but not for me 12:43
Your country needs Y. 12:13
young aged diplomats . . . bored than for y. men to die 13:168
All that the y. can do for the old 11:368
A man that is y. in years 7:297
country of y. men 11:455
Grieve not that I die y. 10:353
One starts to get y. at the age of sixty 13:689
Political history is far too criminal . . . to be . . . fit . . . for the y. 13:575
The atrocious crime of being a y. man 8:461
The best careers advice to give to the y. 13:1006
the old have rubbed it into the y. that they are wiser 12:710
There is . . . an instrument to mould the minds of the y. 12:177
The y. always have the same problem 13:705
to be y. was very heaven 9:208
Y. men make great mistakes in life 11:374
Y. people ought not to be idle 13:371
yourself Better to write for y. 13:438
If you do not tell the truth about y. 12:806
no friends not equal to y. 2:37
What you do not want done to y. 2:61
youth age and y. cannot live together 7:273
everything that is great . . . done by y. 10:463
it is y. that must fight and die 12:391
nothing in thy y. 1:77
sign of an ill-spent y. 11:305
the Jazz Age . . . became less and less an affair of y. 12:419
the world hath lost his y. 1:72
Y. is a malady 12:715
Y. is something very new 13:692
y. now in England . . . be set to learn 5:22
Y.'s a stuff will not endure 7:320
y. would sleep out the rest 7:196
youthe Withouten other companye in y. 6:118

Z

Zaptiehs Their Z. and their Mudirs 11:6
zoo the city is not a concrete jungle, it is a human z. 13:515

Name Index

T